ORACLE® Oracle Press™

Oracle8*i* Advanced PL/SQL Programming

Scott Urman

Osborne/**McGraw-Hill**

Berkeley New York St. Louis San Francisco
Auckland Bogotá Hamburg London Madrid
Mexico City Milan Montreal New Delhi Panama City
Paris São Paulo Singapore Sydney Tokyo Toronto

Osborne/**McGraw-Hill**
2600 Tenth Street
Berkeley, California 94710
U.S.A.

For information on translations or book distributors outside the U.S.A., or to arrange
bulk purchase discounts for sales promotions, premiums, or fund-raisers, please
contact Osborne/**McGraw-Hill** at the above address.

Oracle8*i* Advanced PL/SQL Programming

Oracle is a registered trademark and Oracle8*i* is a trademark or registered trademark
of Oracle Corporation.

234567890 CUS CUS 019876543210

Book P/N 0-07-212144-0   and   CD P/N 0-07-212145-9
parts of
ISBN 0-07-212146-7

Publisher Brandon A. Nordin	**Copy Editor** Claire Splan
Associate Publisher and **Editor-in-Chief** Scott Rogers	**Proofreaders** Linda Medoff Paul Medoff
Acquisitions Editor Jeremy Judson	**Indexer** David Heiret
Project Editor Janet Walden	**Computer Designers** E. A. Pauw Jim Kussow
Acquisitions Coordinator Monika Faltiss	**Illustrators** Michael Mueller Beth Young
Technical Editors Sharon Castledine Bruce Chang Ali Shehadeh Simon Slack	**Series Design** Jani Beckwith

This book was composed with Corel VENTURA ™ Publisher.

This book is dedicated to my wife, Cyndi. Thank you so much for sticking this one out, especially since it took so long. You truly make it all worthwhile, and I love you.

About the Author

Scott Urman is a Senior Member of the Technical Staff in the Diagnostics and Defect Resolution (DDR) team in Oracle's Server Technologies Division. He currently focuses on JDBC, and has worked with both PL/SQL and OCI. Prior to joining DDR, he was a Senior Analyst in the Languages division of Oracle Support Services, focusing on all of Oracle's language tools. He is also the best-selling author of *Oracle8 PL/SQL Programming* and *Oracle PL/SQL Programming*.

Contents at a Glance

v

PART III
Object Features and LOBs

On the CD-ROM

Contents

PART I
Introduction and Development Environments

PART II
Non-Object Features

PART III
Object Features and LOBs

On the CD-ROM

Acknowledgments

A project like this book takes quite a lot of time to do properly. This is even more true for this edition of this book. A year ago, when I began this edition, I did not think that it would take this long to complete. However, I think that the time was very well spent, and the end result is a better book.

There are several groups of people who need to be acknowledged for their help with this project. First of all, thanks to my technical reviewers. Unlike the past editions, four different people from different areas of Oracle helped catch the technical errors in this edition—Sharon Castledine, Bruce W. Chang, Ali Shehadeh, and Simon Slack. I'm pretty sure that we got them all, and any remaining errors are solely my fault. Thanks also to Monika Faltiss, Jeremy Judson, and Janet Walden from Osborne for keeping me (and this project) on track, especially in the last few months. And of course thanks to my family and friends (you know who you are) for their comments, advice, and support throughout the process.

I used a number of resources during the development of this book, including several Oracle manuals. These include the *PL/SQL User's Guide and Reference, Oracle Server Application Developer's Guide, Oracle Server Administrator's Guide, Oracle Server SQL Reference, Oracle Server Concepts Manual,* and the *Programmer's Guide to the Pro*C/C++ Precompiler.*

If you have any comments about this book, I can be reached via e-mail at **Scott.Urman@oracle.com**. One of the best rewards of being an author is the comments and suggestions I have received from you on the first two editions, and I welcome your comments for this book as well.

Introduction

racle is an extremely powerful and flexible relational database system. Along with this power and flexibility, however, comes complexity. In order to design useful applications that are based on Oracle, it is necessary to understand how Oracle manipulates the data stored within the system. PL/SQL is an important tool that is designed for data manipulation, both internally within Oracle and externally in your own applications. PL/SQL is available in a variety of environments, each of which has different advantages.

The first of the PL/SQL books I've written is *Oracle PL/SQL Programming* (1996), which covered up to PL/SQL version 2.3 with Oracle7 Release 7.3—at that time, the most recent version of the database and PL/SQL. The second edition, *Oracle8 PL/SQL Programming* (1997), expanded the material in the first edition and included information up to Oracle8 Release 8.0, the then-current version.

This book, *Oracle8i Advanced PL/SQL Programming*, is therefore the third edition. It incorporates material up to and including Oracle8*i* (which corresponds to release 8.1), now the most current version of the database. Due to the size that it would have been, however, it does not include everything that was in the previous edition. Rather, I have chosen in this book to focus on the advanced usage of PL/SQL. So, if this is your first time with the language you may be better served by the previous edition, at least initially. It is the best way to learn the language. Some of the material in this edition is based on the second edition, but there is substantial new material as well. If you are interested in the new Oracle8*i* features, this is the book for you.

What's New?

So what's new in this edition? The main differences, of course, focus on the features available with Oracle8*i*. The discussions of these new features have been integrated throughout the book, where appropriate. For example, Chapter 8 focuses on dynamic SQL, including both the DBMS_SQL package (available since Oracle 7 Release 7.1) and native dynamic SQL, which is new in Oracle8*i*. The discussion of PL/SQL development and debugging environments has also been significantly enhanced.

Accompanying CD-ROM

The CD-ROM included with this edition contains three different types of information:

- As with the second edition, online versions of all the examples used in the text are included. In several cases, the complete text of the examples are not found in the book itself, but can be found online.

- Trial versions of five different development tools from four different vendors. The second edition contained a trial version of SQL-Station, from Platinum Technologies (now Computer Associates). This edition contains tools from Quest Software, Compuware Corporation, Embarcadero Technologies, and Sylvain Faust International. I will discuss these tools in more detail in Chapters 2 and 3.

- Electronic-only versions of Chapters 15 and 16, and Appendixes A through C. Due to space constraints, these chapters and appendixes could not be included in the bound book. In addition, some of the screenshots referred to in Chapter2 are included.

When you insert the CD-ROM on Microsoft Windows systems, a small application will start automatically that gives you more details about the CD-ROM, along with instructions on how to install each of the development tools. I encourage you to try it out. If you have questions about any of the development tools, please contact the vendors directly, and be sure to mention that you got the trial version from this book. See **readme.html** on the root level of the CD-ROM for more details.

Intended Audience

This book is designed to be both a user's guide and a reference to PL/SQL. It is appropriate primarily for programmers who are already familiar with PL/SQL and who are interested in the advanced features and the new Oracle8*i* material. If you are new to PL/SQL, I encourage you to read both the second edition (*Oracle8 PL/SQL Programming*) and this edition. Although some material is covered in both books, that is the best way to get the complete picture.

How to Use this Book

This book is divided into 16 chapters and 3 appendices. The chapters are organized into three major parts: Introduction and Development Environments, Non-Object Features, and Object Features and LOBs.

Part I: Introduction and Development Environments

The first part of the book introduces PL/SQL and the environments in which it runs. In this section, we will also cover the PL/SQL development environments that are included on the CD-ROM.

CHAPTER 1: INTRODUCTION   This chapter introduces PL/SQL and describes some of the major features of the language. It also discusses the versions of PL/SQL and the database versions to which they correspond. The chapter concludes with a description of the database schema used as an example throughout the book

CHAPTER 2: PL/SQL DEVELOPMENT AND EXECUTION ENVIRONMENTS   PL/SQL can be run in many different types of environments, both on the client and the server. In this chapter, we will discuss different locations for the PL/SQL engine, and see the implications of communication between different engines. We will also examine the development tools included on the CD-ROM, including screen shots.

CHAPTER 3: TRACING AND DEBUGGING   In Chapter 3, we will discuss seven different techniques for debugging your applications, including the graphical debuggers available on the CD-ROM. In the course of the chapter, we will use each technique to solve a common problem in PL/SQL code. We will also cover different methods of tracing existing applications, including the new profiler available with Oracle8*i*.

Part II: Non-Object Features

This section will discuss the relational features of PL/SQL, including procedures, triggers, database jobs and file I/O, dynamic SQL, intersession communication, and external routines. We will also summarize all of the features new to PL/SQL in Oracle8*i*.

CHAPTER 4: CREATING SUBPROGRAMS AND PACKAGES

Subprograms (procedures and functions) provide a powerful means of organizing PL/SQL code into named, callable blocks. They can be stored in the database for later use as well. *Packages* are groups of related subprograms and declarations that can be stored as a unit. In this chapter, we will discuss in detail the syntax of creating subprograms and packages.

CHAPTER 5: USING SUBPROGRAMS AND PACKAGES

Chapter 5 extends the discussion in Chapter 4 to cover additional features of subprograms and packages, including how to call them from SQL statements and the dependencies between them. We will also discuss how packages interact with the shared pool, and cover several new Oracle8*i* features in this chapter, such as invokers-rights procedures.

CHAPTER 6: DATABASE TRIGGERS

Triggers are a special type of PL/SQL block that are executed automatically whenever the triggering event occurs. This can be a DML operation such as an INSERT statement, a DDL statement, or a system event. Triggers can also be executed instead of a given DML statement. We will discuss all of these trigger types in this chapter.

CHAPTER 7: DATABASE JOBS AND FILE I/O

The DBMS_JOB package allows you to schedule PL/SQL jobs (in the form of stored procedures) to run automatically at specified times. The UTL_FILE package allows PL/SQL to read from and write to operating system files. We will discuss both packages in detail in this chapter, along with examples.

CHAPTER 8: DYNAMIC SQL

Dynamic SQL is a very powerful programming technique which allows you to write very flexible programs. In this chapter, we will discuss the DBMS_SQL package and native dynamic SQL, both of which allow you to create and issue SQL statements and PL/SQL blocks at runtime. These methods can be used to overcome the restriction that only DML statements are allowed in PL/SQL.

CHAPTER 9: INTERSESSION COMMUNICATION

There are two built-in packages available for communicating directly between database sessions—database pipes (DBMS_PIPE) and database alerts (DBMS_ALERT). We will see examples of both in this chapter, as well as a comparison between the two packages.

CHAPTER 10: EXTERNAL ROUTINES

External routines allow you to call a function written in C (Oracle8 and higher) or Java (Oracle8*i* and higher) directly from PL/SQL. C routines run in a separate process, while Java routines are loaded into the database and run in the same process as PL/SQL by the Java virtual machine (JServer) included with Oracle8*i*. We will discuss both types of external routines in detail in this chapter.

CHAPTER 11: ADDITIONAL ORACLE8*i* FEATURES   This chapter summarizes all of the new features available for PL/SQL in Oracle8*i*. We will examine in detail those features that have not been discussed elsewhere in the book, along with timing results for the performance enhancements.

Part III: Object Features and LOBs

The third part of this book focuses on the object features of Oracle8 and Oracle8*i*. We will also discuss large objects (LOBs), which enable you to store up to 4G of data in a single database column. Chapters 15 and 16 can be found in electronic form on the CD-ROM.

CHAPTER 12: INTRODUCTION TO OBJECTS   In this chapter, we will discuss the syntax and semantics of declaring Oracle8 object types, including how to initialize object instances and call methods. We will also discuss static methods, available with Oracle8*i*.

CHAPTER 13: OBJECTS IN THE DATABASE   The second of the two objects chapters covers how to store objects in the database, and how to manipulate objects using both SQL and PL/SQL. We will also discuss object references and how they are used.

CHAPTER 14: COLLECTIONS   Collections are groups of PL/SQL objects, and include index-by tables, nested tables, and varrays. These datatypes are all similar to arrays in other languages. We will also discuss how to store nested tables and varrays in the database, along with collection methods.

CHAPTER 15: LARGE OBJECTS (CD-ROM ONLY)   Oracle8 LOBs can store both character (in different character sets) and binary data. In this chapter, we will discuss the different types of LOBs and the interfaces available for accessing them. We will cover the SQL interface to LOBs in detail.

CHAPTER 16: ADVANCED LOB TOPICS AND DBMS_LOB (CD-ROM ONLY)   Our coverage of LOB continues in Chapter 16 with a detailed discussion of the DBMS_LOB package, which is the primary means of manipulating LOB data from PL/SQL. Because it is a PL/SQL package, it can also be used from any environment that can issue a PL/SQL block.

Appendixes

The appendixes supply useful reference information about PL/SQL. They can be found in electronic form on the CD-ROM.

APPENDIX A: GUIDE TO SUPPLIED PACKAGES   This appendix discusses all of the built-in packages available with Oracle. These packages greatly extend the capabilities of the language. Packages not discussed elsewhere in the book are summarized.

APPENDIX B: PL/SQL RESERVED WORDS   This appendix lists all of the reserved words for PL/SQL. You should avoid using these words for variables and other PL/SQL objects.

APPENDIX C: THE DATA DICTIONARY   This appendix summarizes many of the data dictionary views. Those views which are relevant to PL/SQL are discussed in detail, while the others are summarized.

PART

I

Introduction and Development Environments

CHAPTER

1

Introduction

L/SQL is a sophisticated programming language used to access an Oracle database from various environments. It is integrated with the database server, so that the PL/SQL code can be processed quickly and efficiently. It is also available in some client-side Oracle tools.

In this chapter we will discuss the reasons for development of PL/SQL, the major features of the language, and the importance of knowing the PL/SQL and database versions. We will also introduce the advanced concepts that we will study in greater detail throughout the course of the book. The chapter concludes with descriptions of some conventions we will use and the database tables that are used in the examples.

Why PL/SQL?

Oracle is a relational database. The language used to access a relational database is *Structured Query Language* (*SQL*—often pronounced *sequel*). SQL is a flexible, efficient language, with features designed to manipulate and examine relational data. For example, the following SQL statement will delete all students who are majoring in nutrition from the database:

```
DELETE FROM students
   WHERE major = 'Nutrition';
```

(The database tables used in this book, including the **students** table, are described at the end of this chapter in "Example Tables.")

SQL is a *fourth-generation language*. This means that the language describes what should be done, but not how to do it. In the DELETE statement just shown, for example, we don't know how the database will actually determine which students are majoring in nutrition. Presumably, the server will loop through all the students in some order to determine the proper entries to delete. But the details of this are hidden from us.

Third-generation languages, such as C or COBOL, are more procedural in nature. A program in a third-generation language (3GL) implements a step-by-step algorithm to solve the problem. For example, we could accomplish the DELETE operation with something like this:

```
LOOP over each student record
   IF this record has major = 'Nutrition' THEN
     DELETE this record;
   END IF;
END LOOP;
```

Object-oriented languages, such as C++ or Java, are also third-generation. Although they incorporate the principles of object-oriented design, algorithms are still specified step by step.

Each type of language has advantages and disadvantages. Fourth-generation languages such as SQL are generally fairly simple (compared to third-generation languages) and have fewer commands. They also insulate the user from the underlying data structures and algorithms, which are implemented by the runtime system. In some cases, however, the procedural constructs available in 3GLs are useful to express a desired program. This is where PL/SQL comes in—it combines the power and flexibility of SQL (a 4GL) with the procedural constructs of a 3GL.

PL/SQL stands for Procedural Language/SQL. As its name implies, PL/SQL extends SQL by adding constructs found in other procedural languages, such as

- Variables and types (both predefined and user-defined)

- Control structures such as IF-THEN-ELSE statements and loops

- Procedures and functions

- Object types and methods (PL/SQL version 8 and higher)

Procedural constructs are integrated seamlessly with Oracle SQL, resulting in a structured, powerful language. For example, suppose we want to change the major for a student. If the student doesn't exist, then we want to create a new record. We could do this with the following PL/SQL code:

```
-- Available online as 3gl_4gl.sql
DECLARE
  /* Declare variables that will be used in SQL statements */
  v_NewMajor VARCHAR2(10) := 'History';
  v_FirstName VARCHAR2(10) := 'Scott';
  v_LastName VARCHAR2(10) := 'Urman';
BEGIN
  /* Update the students table. */
  UPDATE students
    SET major = v_NewMajor
    WHERE first_name = v_FirstName
    AND last_name = v_LastName;
  /* Check to see if the record was found.  If not, then we need
     to insert this record. */
  IF SQL%NOTFOUND THEN
    INSERT INTO students (ID, first_name, last_name, major)
      VALUES (student_sequence.NEXTVAL, v_FirstName, v_LastName,
              v_NewMajor);
  END IF;
END;
```

This example contains two different SQL statements (UPDATE and INSERT), which are 4GL constructs, along with 3GL constructs (the variable declarations and the conditional IF statement).

NOTE
*In order to run the preceding example, you first need to create the database objects referenced (the **students** table and the **student_sequence** sequence). This can be done with the **relTables.sql** script, provided as part of the CD-ROM included with this book. For more information about creating these objects and the online distribution, see "Included CD-ROM," later in this chapter.*

PL/SQL is unique in that it combines the flexibility of SQL with the power and configurability of a 3GL. Both the necessary procedural constructs and the database access are there, integrated with the language. This results in a robust, powerful language well suited for designing complex applications.

PL/SQL and Network Traffic

Many database applications are built using either a client-server or three-tier model. In the client-server model, the program itself resides on a client machine and sends requests to a database server for information. The requests are done using SQL. Typically, this results in many network trips, one for each SQL statement. This is illustrated by the diagram on the left side of Figure 1-1. Compare this with the situation on the right, however. Several SQL statements can be bundled together into one PL/SQL block and sent to the server as a single unit. This results in less network traffic and a faster application.

Even when the client and the server are both running on the same machine, performance is increased. In this case, there isn't any network, but packaging SQL statements still results in a simpler program that makes fewer calls to the database.

The benefits of packaging PL/SQL apply to a three-tier model as well. In this case, the client (which is often running in an HTML browser) communicates with an application server, which in turn communicates with the database. This latter communication is where the PL/SQL benefits apply. We will examine this type of environment more in Chapter 2.

Standards

Oracle supports the ANSI (American National Standards Institute) standard for the SQL language, as defined in ANSI document X3.135-1992 "Database Language

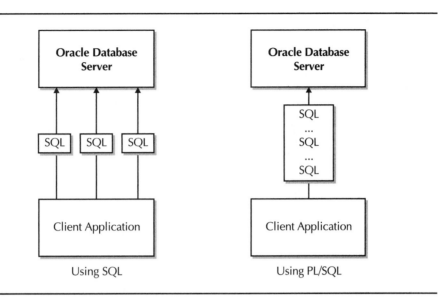

FIGURE 1-1. *PL/SQL in a client-server environment*

SQL." This standard, commonly known as SQL92 (or SQL2), defines the SQL language only. It does not define the 3GL extensions to the language that PL/SQL provides. SQL92 has three compliance levels: Entry, Intermediate, and Full. Oracle7 Release 7.2 (and all higher versions, including Oracle8 and Oracle8*i*) comply with the Entry SQL92 standards, as certified by the National Institute for Standards and Technology (NIST). Oracle is working with ANSI to ensure that future versions of Oracle and PL/SQL comply with the full standard.

Features of PL/SQL

PL/SQL's many different features and capabilities are best illustrated by example. The following sections describe some of the main features of the language.

Basic Features

We will concentrate primarily on the advanced features of PL/SQL throughout this book. However, the following sections provide an introduction to the basic features of the language. For more information, see the *PL/SQL User's Guide and Reference*, or the second edition of this book, *Oracle8 PL/SQL Programming*.

Block Structure

The basic unit in PL/SQL is a *block*. All PL/SQL programs are made up of blocks, which can be nested within each other. Typically, each block performs a logical unit of work in the program, thus separating different tasks from each other. A block has the following structure:

```
DECLARE
    /* Declarative section - PL/SQL variables, types, cursors,
       and local subprograms go here. */
BEGIN
   /* Executable section - procedural and SQL statements go here.
      This is the main section of the block and the only one
      that is required. */
EXCEPTION
   /* Exception-handling section - error-handling statements go
      here. */
END;
```

Only the executable section is required; the declarative and exception-handling sections are optional. The executable section must also contain at least one executable statement. The different sections of the block separate different functions of a PL/SQL program.

The design for PL/SQL is modeled after the Ada third-generation language. Many of the constructs available in Ada can also be found in PL/SQL, including the block structure. Other Ada features found in PL/SQL include exception handling, the syntax for declaring procedures and functions, and packages.

Error Handling

The exception-handling section of the block is used to respond to runtime errors encountered by your program. By separating the error-handling code from the main body of the program, the structure of the program itself is clear. For example, the following PL/SQL block demonstrates an exception-handling section that logs the error received along with the current time and the user who encountered the error:

```
-- Available online as Error.sql
DECLARE
  v_ErrorCode NUMBER;              -- Code for the error
  v_ErrorMsg  VARCHAR2(200);    -- Message text for the error
  v_CurrentUser VARCHAR2(8);     -- Current database user
  v_Information VARCHAR2(100); -- Information about the error
BEGIN
  /* Code that processes some data here */
EXCEPTION
  WHEN OTHERS THEN
    -- Assign values to the log variables, using built-in
    -- functions.
```

```
v_ErrorCode := SQLCODE;
v_ErrorMsg := SQLERRM;
v_CurrentUser := USER;
v_Information := 'Error encountered on ' ||
   TO_CHAR(SYSDATE) || ' by database user ' || v_CurrentUser;
-- Insert the log message into log_table.
INSERT INTO log_table (code, message, info)
   VALUES (v_ErrorCode, v_ErrorMsg, v_Information);
END;
```

NOTE
The previous example, like many others in the book, can be found in the online distribution. For more information, see "Included CD-ROM," later in this chapter.

Variables and Types

Information is transmitted between PL/SQL and the database with *variables.* A variable is a storage location that can be read from or assigned to by the program. In the previous example, **v_CurrentUser**, **v_ErrorCode**, and **v_Information** are all variables. Variables are declared in the declarative section of the block.

Every variable has a specific *type* associated with it. The type defines what kind of information the variable can hold. PL/SQL variables can be of the same type as database columns:

```
DECLARE
   v_StudentName VARCHAR2(20);
   v_CurrentDate DATE;
   v_NumberCredits NUMBER(3);
```

or they can be of additional types:

```
DECLARE
   v_LoopCounter BINARY_INTEGER;
   v_CurrentlyRegistered BOOLEAN;
```

PL/SQL also supports user-defined types such as tables and records. User-defined types allow you to customize the structure of the data your program manipulates:

```
DECLARE
   TYPE t_StudentRecord IS RECORD (
   FirstName  VARCHAR2(10),
   LastName   VARCHAR2(10),
   CurrentCredits NUMBER(3)
   );
   v_Student t_StudentRecord;
```

Looping Constructs

PL/SQL supports different kinds of loops. A *loop* allows you to execute the same sequence of statements repeatedly. For example, the following block uses a *simple loop* to insert the numbers 1 through 50 into **temp_table**:

```
-- Available online as SimpleLoop.sql
DECLARE
  v_LoopCounter BINARY_INTEGER := 1;
BEGIN
  LOOP
    INSERT INTO temp_table (num_col)
      VALUES (v_LoopCounter);
    v_LoopCounter := v_LoopCounter + 1;
    EXIT WHEN v_LoopCounter > 50;
  END LOOP;
END;
```

Another type of loop, a *numeric FOR loop*, can be used as well. This looping construct provides a simpler syntax. We can accomplish the same thing as the preceding example with this:

```
-- Available online as NumericLoop.sql
BEGIN
  FOR v_LoopCounter IN 1..50 LOOP
    INSERT INTO temp_table (num_col)
      VALUES (v_LoopCounter);
  END LOOP;
END;
```

Cursors

A *cursor* is used to process multiple rows retrieved from the database (with a SELECT statement). Using a cursor, your program can step through the set of rows returned one at a time, processing each one. For example, the following block will retrieve the first and last names of all students in the database:

```
-- Available online as CursorLoop.sql
DECLARE
  v_FirstName VARCHAR2(20);
  v_LastName  VARCHAR2(20);
  -- Cursor declaration.  This defines the SQL statement to
  -- return the rows.
  CURSOR c_Students IS
```

```
    SELECT first_name, last_name
      FROM students;
BEGIN
  -- Begin cursor processing.
  OPEN c_Students;
  LOOP
    -- Retrieve one row.
    FETCH c_Students INTO v_FirstName, v_LastName;
    -- Exit the loop after all rows have been retrieved.
    EXIT WHEN c_Students%NOTFOUND;
    /* Process data here */
  END LOOP;
  -- End processing.
  CLOSE c_Students;
END;
```

Advanced Features

The following sections provide examples of some of the advanced features that we will be discussing in more detail in later chapters. These features build on the basic PL/SQL features.

Procedures and Functions

Procedures and functions (together known as *subprograms*) are a special type of PL/SQL block that can be stored in the database in compiled form, and then called from a subsequent block. For example, the following statement creates a procedure **PrintStudents**, which will echo the first and last name of all the students in the specified major to the screen, using the DBMS_OUTPUT package:

```
-- Available online as part of PrintStudents.sql
CREATE OR REPLACE PROCEDURE PrintStudents(
  p_Major IN students.major%TYPE) AS

  CURSOR c_Students IS
    SELECT first_name, last_name
      FROM students
      WHERE major = p_Major;
BEGIN
  FOR v_StudentRec IN c_Students LOOP
    DBMS_OUTPUT.PUT_LINE(v_StudentRec.first_name || ' ' ||
                         v_StudentRec.last_name);
  END LOOP;
END;
```

Once this procedure is created and stored in the database, we can call it with a block similar to the following:

```
-- Available online as part of PrintStudents.sql
SQL> BEGIN
  2    PrintStudents('Computer Science');
  3  END;
  4  /
Scott Smith
Joanne Junebug
Shay Shariatpanahy
```

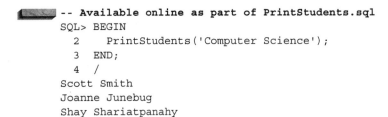

NOTE
The output from DBMS_OUTPUT is available in SQL*Plus by using the SET SERVEROUTPUT ON command. For more information, see Chapter 2.

Packages

Subprograms, along with variables and types, can be grouped together into a *package*. A package has two parts—the specification and body. Together, they allow related objects to be stored together in the database. For example, the **RoomsPkg** package contains procedures that insert a new room, and delete a room from the **rooms** table:

```
-- Available online as RoomsPkg.sql
CREATE OR REPLACE PACKAGE RoomsPkg AS
  PROCEDURE NewRoom(p_Building rooms.building%TYPE,
                    p_RoomNum rooms.room_number%TYPE,
                    p_NumSeats rooms.number_seats%TYPE,
                    p_Description rooms.description%TYPE);

  PROCEDURE DeleteRoom(p_RoomID IN rooms.room_id%TYPE);
END RoomsPkg;

CREATE OR REPLACE PACKAGE BODY RoomsPkg AS
  PROCEDURE NewRoom(p_Building rooms.building%TYPE,
                    p_RoomNum rooms.room_number%TYPE,
                    p_NumSeats rooms.number_seats%TYPE,
                    p_Description rooms.description%TYPE) IS
  BEGIN
    INSERT INTO rooms
      (room_id, building, room_number, number_seats, description)
      VALUES
      (room_sequence.NEXTVAL, p_Building, p_RoomNum, p_NumSeats,
       p_Description);
  END NewRoom;
```

```
PROCEDURE DeleteRoom(p_RoomID IN rooms.room_id%TYPE) IS
BEGIN
  DELETE FROM rooms
    WHERE room_id = p_RoomID;
END DeleteRoom;
END RoomsPkg;
```

Dynamic SQL

Through dynamic SQL, a PL/SQL application can build a SQL statement at runtime
and execute it. There are two different dynamic SQL methods—the DBMS_SQL
package, available with PL/SQL 2.1 and higher, and native dynamic SQL, available
with Oracle8*i* and higher. The **DropTable** procedure is written using the DBMS_SQL
package, and will drop the table specified:

```
-- Available online as part of DropTable.sql
CREATE OR REPLACE PROCEDURE DropTable(p_Table IN VARCHAR2) AS
  v_SQLString VARCHAR2(100);
  v_Cursor BINARY_INTEGER;
  v_ReturnCode BINARY_INTEGER;
BEGIN
  -- Build the string based on the input parameter.
  v_SQLString := 'DROP TABLE ' || p_Table;

  -- Open the cursor.
  v_Cursor := DBMS_SQL.OPEN_CURSOR;

  -- Parse and execute the statement.
  DBMS_SQL.PARSE(v_Cursor, v_SQLString, DBMS_SQL.NATIVE);
  v_ReturnCode := DBMS_SQL.EXECUTE(v_Cursor);

  -- Close the cursor.
  DBMS_SQL.CLOSE_CURSOR(v_Cursor);
END DropTable;
```

With Oracle8*i* and higher, we can rewrite **DropTable** using native dynamic
SQL, as follows:

```
-- Available online as part of DropTable.sql
CREATE OR REPLACE PROCEDURE DropTable(p_Table IN VARCHAR2) AS
  v_SQLString VARCHAR2(100);
BEGIN
  -- Build the string based on the input parameter.
  v_SQLString := 'DROP TABLE ' || p_Table;

  EXECUTE IMMEDIATE v_SQLString;
END DropTable;
```

Object Types

Oracle8 (with PL/SQL 8) supports object types. An object type has attributes and methods, and can be stored in a database table. The following example creates an object type:

```
-- Available online as part of ch12/objTypes.sql
CREATE OR REPLACE TYPE Student AS OBJECT (
    ID                NUMBER(5),
    first_name        VARCHAR2(20),
    last_name         VARCHAR2(20),
    major             VARCHAR2(30),
    current_credits   NUMBER(3),

    -- Returns the first and last names, separated by a space.
    MEMBER FUNCTION FormattedName
      RETURN VARCHAR2,
    PRAGMA RESTRICT_REFERENCES(FormattedName, RNDS, WNDS, RNPS, WNPS),

    -- Updates the major to the specified value in p_NewMajor.
    MEMBER PROCEDURE ChangeMajor(p_NewMajor IN VARCHAR2),
    PRAGMA RESTRICT_REFERENCES(ChangeMajor, RNDS, WNDS, RNPS, WNPS),

    -- Updates the current_credits by adding the number of
    -- credits in p_CompletedClass to the current value.
    MEMBER PROCEDURE UpdateCredits(p_CompletedClass IN Class),
    PRAGMA RESTRICT_REFERENCES(UpdateCredits, RNDS, WNDS, RNPS, WNPS),

    -- ORDER function used to sort students.
    ORDER MEMBER FUNCTION CompareStudent(p_Student IN Student)
      RETURN NUMBER
);

CREATE OR REPLACE TYPE BODY Student AS
  MEMBER FUNCTION FormattedName
    RETURN VARCHAR2 IS
  BEGIN
    RETURN first_name || ' ' || last_name;
  END FormattedName;

  MEMBER PROCEDURE ChangeMajor(p_NewMajor IN VARCHAR2) IS
  BEGIN
    major := p_NewMajor;
  END ChangeMajor;

  MEMBER PROCEDURE UpdateCredits(p_CompletedClass IN Class) IS
  BEGIN
    current_credits := current_credits +
    p_CompletedClass.num_credits;
  END UpdateCredits;
```

```
ORDER MEMBER FUNCTION CompareStudent(p_Student IN Student)
  RETURN NUMBER IS
BEGIN
  -- First compare by last names
  IF p_Student.last_name = SELF.last_name THEN
    -- If the last names are the same, then compare first names.
    IF p_Student.first_name < SELF.first_name THEN
      RETURN 1;
    ELSIF p_Student.first_name > SELF.first_name THEN
      RETURN -1;
    ELSE
      RETURN 0;
    END IF;
  ELSE
    IF p_Student.last_name < SELF.last_name THEN
      RETURN 1;
    ELSE
      RETURN -1;
    END IF;
  END IF;
END CompareStudent;
END;
```

Collections

PL/SQL collections are similar to arrays in other 3GLs. PL/SQL provides three different types of collections: index-by tables (2.0 and higher), nested tables (8.0 and higher), and varrays (8.0 and higher). The following example illustrates various types of collections.

```
-- Available online as Collections.sql
DECLARE
  TYPE t_IndexBy IS TABLE OF NUMBER
    INDEX BY BINARY_INTEGER;
  TYPE t_Nested IS TABLE OF NUMBER;
  TYPE t_Varray IS VARRAY(10) OF NUMBER;

  v_IndexBy t_IndexBy;
  v_Nested t_Nested;
  v_Varray t_Varray;
BEGIN
  v_IndexBy(1) := 1;
  v_IndexBy(2) := 2;
  v_Nested := t_Nested(1, 2, 3, 4, 5);
  v_Varray := t_Varray(1, 2);
END;
```

Built-In Packages

In addition to the features supplied with the PL/SQL language, Oracle provides a number of built-in packages that provide additional functionality. We will be discussing these in detail throughout the course of this book, and they are summarized in Appendix A (on the CD-ROM that accompanies this book). The major built-in packages that we will cover are described in the following table:

Package	Description
DBMS_ALERT	Database alerts, allows intersession communication
DBMS_JOB	Job scheduling services
DBMS_LOB	Large object manipulations
DBMS_PIPE	Database pipes, allows intersession communication
DBMS_SQL	Dynamic SQL
UTL_FILE	Text file input and output

In general, the DBMS_* packages are available only in the server, while the UTL_* packages are available in both server- and client-side PL/SQL. (Some client environments, such as Oracle Forms, provide additional packages as well.)

Conventions Used in This Book

I use several conventions throughout the remainder of the book, which are discussed here. These include the icons used to delineate differences between PL/SQL versions, how I refer to the Oracle documentation, and the location for the online examples.

PL/SQL and Oracle Versions

PL/SQL is contained within the Oracle server. The first version of PL/SQL, 1.0, was released with Oracle version 6. Oracle7 contains PL/SQL 2.*x*. With Oracle8, the PL/SQL version number was increased to 8 as well. Oracle8*i* (which corresponds to 8.1) consequently contains PL/SQL version 8.1. Each subsequent release of the database contains an associated version of PL/SQL, as illustrated in Table 1-1. This table also describes the major new features incorporated in each release. This book

Oracle Version	PL/SQL Version	Features Added or Changed
6	1.0	Initial version
7.0	2.0	CHAR datatype changed to fixed length Stored subprograms (procedures, functions, packages, and triggers) User-defined composite types—tables and records Intersession communication with the DBMS_PIPE and DBMS_ALERT packages Output in SQL*Plus or Server Manager with the DBMS_OUTPUT package
7.1	2.1	User-defined subtypes Ability to use user-defined functions in SQL statements Dynamic PL/SQL with the DBMS_SQL package
7.2	2.2	Cursor variables User-defined constrained subtypes Ability to schedule PL/SQL batch processing with the DBMS_JOB package
7.3	2.3	Enhancements to cursor variables (allow fetch on server, and weakly typed) File I/O with the UTL_FILE package PL/SQL table attributes and tables of records Triggers stored in compiled form
8.0	8.0	Object types and methods Collection types—nested tables and varrays Advanced Queuing option External procedures LOB enhancements
8.1	8.1	Native dynamic SQL Java external routines Invoker's rights NOCOPY parameters Autonomous transactions Bulk operations

TABLE 1-1. *Oracle and PL/SQL Features by Version Number*

discusses PL/SQL versions 2.0 through 8.1. Features available only in specific releases are highlighted by icons like these:

 This paragraph discusses a feature available with PL/SQL 2.1 and higher, such as the DBMS_SQL package.

 This paragraph discusses a feature available with PL/SQL 2.2 and higher, such as cursor variables.

 This paragraph discusses a feature available with PL/SQL 2.3 and higher, such as the UTL_FILE package.

 This paragraph discusses a feature available with PL/SQL 8.0 and higher, such as object types.

 This paragraph discusses a feature available with PL/SQL 8.1 and higher, such as native dynamic SQL.

It is important to be aware of the PL/SQL release you are using so you can take advantage of the appropriate features. When you connect to the database, the initial string will contain the database version. For example,

```
Connected to:
Oracle8 Enterprise Edition Release 8.0.6.0.0 - Production
With the Objects option
PL/SQL Release 8.0.6.0.0 - Production
```

and

```
Connected to:
Oracle8i Enterprise Edition Release 8.1.5.0.0 - Production
With the Partitioning and Java options
PL/SQL Release 8.1.5.0.0 - Production
```

are both valid initial strings. Note that the PL/SQL release corresponds to the database release.

The majority of the examples in this book were done with Oracle 8.0.6, running on a Solaris system. The Oracle8i examples were written with Oracle8i version 8.1.5, also on Solaris. All of the screen shots were taken under Windows 95 or Windows NT connecting to a database on the server.

Oracle Documentation

In many sections of the book, I refer you to the Oracle documentation for more information. Because the names of the manuals change with versions, I generally use a shortened version. For example, the *Oracle Server Reference* refers to the *Oracle7 Server Reference*, the *Oracle8 Server Reference*, or the *Oracle8i Server Reference*, depending on which version of Oracle you are using.

Included CD-ROM

The CD-ROM accompanying this book has several different kinds of information on it:

- The code for the examples used in the book. This code can also be found on Osborne/McGraw-Hill's Oracle Press Web page at **http://www.osborne.com**.

- Trial versions of five PL/SQL development tools, from different vendors. For more information, see Chapters 2 and 3.

- Online versions of Chapters 15, 16, and Appendixes A–C. Some screenshots from Chapter 2 are also included.

For more information on the CD-ROM contents, see the **readme.html** file in the root directory.

Example Locations

The examples included in the online distribution are identified by a comment on the first line indicating the filename. All of these examples are in the directory named **code** on the CD (and the Web page as well), in a subdirectory with the chapter number. For example, consider the following looping example, which we saw earlier in this chapter in "Looping Constructs":

```
-- Available online as SimpleLoop.sql
DECLARE
  v_LoopCounter BINARY_INTEGER := 1;
BEGIN
  LOOP
    INSERT INTO temp_table (num_col)
      VALUES (v_LoopCounter);
    v_LoopCounter := v_LoopCounter + 1;
    EXIT WHEN v_LoopCounter > 50;
  END LOOP;
END;
```

This example can be found online in the file **code/ch01/simple.sql**. The file **code/readme.html** describes all of the examples.

Example Tables

The examples used in this book operate on a common set of database tables that implement a registration system for a college. There are three main tables: **students**, **classes**, and **rooms**. These contain the main entities necessary for the system. In addition to these main tables, the **registered_students** table contains information about students who have signed up for classes. The following sections detail the structure of these tables, with the SQL necessary to create them.

NOTE
These tables can all be created using the
relTables.sql script, found in the online distribution.
The Oracle8 tables can be found in objTables.sql.
Both scripts are located in the code subdirectory.
This section documents the relational tables
only—see objTables.sql for the object versions.

Sequences

The **student_sequence** sequence is used to generate unique values for the primary key of **students**, and the **room_sequence** sequence is used to generate unique values for the primary key of **rooms**.

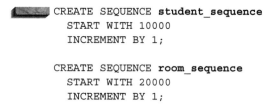

```
CREATE SEQUENCE student_sequence
   START WITH 10000
   INCREMENT BY 1;

CREATE SEQUENCE room_sequence
   START WITH 20000
   INCREMENT BY 1;
```

students

The **students** table contains information about students attending the school.

```
CREATE TABLE students (
   id                NUMBER(5) PRIMARY KEY,
   first_name        VARCHAR2(20),
   last_name         VARCHAR2(20),
   major             VARCHAR2(30),
   current_credits   NUMBER(3)
   );

INSERT INTO students (id, first_name, last_name, major,
                     current_credits)
   VALUES (student_sequence.NEXTVAL, 'Scott', 'Smith',
          'Computer Science', 11);

INSERT INTO students (id, first_name, last_name, major,
                     current_credits)
   VALUES (student_sequence.NEXTVAL, 'Margaret', 'Mason',
          'History', 4);
```

```
INSERT INTO students (id, first_name, last_name, major,
                 current_credits)
  VALUES (student_sequence.NEXTVAL, 'Joanne', 'Junebug',
      'Computer Science', 8);

INSERT INTO students (id, first_name, last_name, major,
                 current_credits)
  VALUES (student_sequence.NEXTVAL, 'Manish', 'Murgratroid',
      'Economics', 8);

INSERT INTO students(id, first_name, last_name, major,
                 current_credits)
  VALUES(student_sequence.NEXTVAL, 'Patrick', 'Poll',
      'History', 4);

INSERT INTO students(id, first_name, last_name, major,
                 current_credits)
  VALUES (student_sequence.NEXTVAL, 'Timothy', 'Taller',
      'History', 4);

INSERT INTO students(id, first_name, last_name, major,
                 current_credits)
  VALUES (student_sequence.NEXTVAL, 'Barbara', 'Blues',
      'Economics', 7);

INSERT INTO students(id, first_name, last_name, major,
                 current_credits)
  VALUES (student_sequence.NEXTVAL, 'David', 'Dinsmore',
      'Music', 4);

INSERT INTO students(id, first_name, last_name, major,
                 current_credits)
  VALUES (student_sequence.NEXTVAL, 'Ester', 'Elegant',
      'Nutrition', 8);

INSERT INTO students(id, first_name, last_name, major,
                 current_credits)
  VALUES (student_sequence.NEXTVAL, 'Rose', 'Riznit',
      'Music', 7);

INSERT INTO STUDENTS(id, first_name, last_name, major,
                 current_credits)
  VALUES (student_sequence.NEXTVAL, 'Rita', 'Razmataz',
      'Nutrition', 8);

INSERT INTO students(id, first_name, last_name, major,
                 current_credits)
  VALUES (student_sequence.NEXTVAL, 'Shay', 'Shariatpanahy',
      'Computer Science', 3);
```

major_stats
The **major_stats** table holds statistics generated about different majors.

```
CREATE TABLE major_stats (
  major            VARCHAR2(30),
  total_credits  NUMBER,
  total_students NUMBER);

INSERT INTO major_stats (major, total_credits, total_students)
  VALUES ('Computer Science', 22, 3);

INSERT INTO major_stats (major, total_credits, total_students)
  VALUES ('History', 12, 3);

INSERT INTO major_stats (major, total_credits, total_students)
  VALUES ('Economics', 15, 2);

INSERT INTO major_stats (major, total_credits, total_students)
  VALUES ('Music', 11, 2);

INSERT INTO major_stats (major, total_credits, total_students)
  VALUES ('Nutrition', 16, 2);
```

rooms
The **rooms** table holds information about the classrooms available.

```
CREATE TABLE rooms (
  room_id          NUMBER(5) PRIMARY KEY,
  building         VARCHAR2(15),
  room_number      NUMBER(4),
  number_seats     NUMBER(4),
  description      VARCHAR2(50)
  );

INSERT INTO rooms (room_id, building, room_number, number_seats,
                   description)
  VALUES (room_sequence.NEXTVAL, 'Building 7', 201, 1000,
          'Large Lecture Hall');

INSERT INTO rooms (room_id, building, room_number, number_seats,
                   description)
  VALUES (room_sequence.NEXTVAL, 'Building 6', 101, 500,
          'Small Lecture Hall');

INSERT INTO rooms (room_id, building, room_number, number_seats,
                   description)
  VALUES (room_sequence.NEXTVAL, 'Building 6', 150, 50,
          'Discussion Room A');
```

```
INSERT INTO rooms (room_id, building, room_number, number_seats,
                description)
  VALUES (room_sequence.NEXTVAL, 'Building 6', 160, 50,
        'Discussion Room B');

INSERT INTO rooms (room_id, building, room_number, number_seats,
                description)
  VALUES (room_sequence.NEXTVAL, 'Building 6', 170, 50,
        'Discussion Room C');

INSERT INTO rooms (room_id, building, room_number, number_seats,
                description)
  VALUES (room_sequence.NEXTVAL, 'Music Building', 100, 10,
        'Music Practice Room');

INSERT INTO rooms (room_id, building, room_number, number_seats,
                description)
  VALUES (room_sequence.NEXTVAL, 'Music Building', 200, 1000,
        'Concert Room');

INSERT INTO rooms (room_id, building, room_number, number_seats,
                description)
  VALUES (room_sequence.NEXTVAL, 'Building 7', 300, 75,
        'Discussion Room D');

INSERT INTO rooms (room_id, building, room_number, number_seats,
                description)
  VALUES (room_sequence.NEXTVAL, 'Building 7', 310, 50,
        'Discussion Room E');
```

classes

The **classes** table describes the classes available for students to take.

```
CREATE TABLE classes (
    department      CHAR(3),
    course          NUMBER(3),
    description     VARCHAR2(2000),
    max_students    NUMBER(3),
    current_students NUMBER(3),
    num_credits     NUMBER(1),
    room_id         NUMBER(5),
    CONSTRAINT classes_department_course
      PRIMARY KEY (department, course),
    CONSTRAINT classes_room_id
      FOREIGN KEY (room_id) REFERENCES rooms (room_id)
    );
```

```
INSERT INTO classes(department, course, description, max_students,
                    current_students, num_credits, room_id)
   VALUES ('HIS', 101, 'History 101', 30, 11, 4, 20000);

INSERT INTO classes(department, course, description, max_students,
                    current_students, num_credits, room_id)
   VALUES ('HIS', 301, 'History 301', 30, 0, 4, 20004);

INSERT INTO classes(department, course, description, max_students,
                    current_students, num_credits, room_id)
   VALUES ('CS', 101, 'Computer Science 101', 50, 0, 4, 20001);

INSERT INTO classes(department, course, description, max_students,
                    current_students, num_credits, room_id)
   VALUES ('ECN', 203, 'Economics 203', 15, 0, 3, 20002);

INSERT INTO classes(department, course, description, max_students,
                    current_students, num_credits, room_id)
   VALUES ('CS', 102, 'Computer Science 102', 35, 3, 4, 20003);

INSERT INTO classes(department, course, description, max_students,
                    current_students, num_credits, room_id)
   VALUES ('MUS', 410, 'Music 410', 5, 4, 3, 20005);

INSERT INTO classes(department, course, description, max_students,
                    current_students, num_credits, room_id)
   VALUES ('ECN', 101, 'Economics 101', 50, 0, 4, 20007);

INSERT INTO classes(department, course, description, max_students,
                    current_students, num_credits, room_id)
   VALUES ('NUT', 307, 'Nutrition 307', 20, 2, 4, 20008);

INSERT INTO classes(department, course, description, max_students,
                    current_students, num_credits, room_id)
   VALUES ('MUS', 100, 'Music 100', 100, 0, 3, NULL);
```

registered_students

The **registered_students** table contains information about the classes students are currently taking.

```
CREATE TABLE registered_students (
   student_id NUMBER(5) NOT NULL,
   department CHAR(3)   NOT NULL,
   course     NUMBER(3) NOT NULL,
   grade      CHAR(1),
   CONSTRAINT rs_grade
     CHECK (grade IN ('A', 'B', 'C', 'D', 'E')),
   CONSTRAINT rs_student_id
```

```
    FOREIGN KEY (student_id) REFERENCES students (id),
  CONSTRAINT rs_department_course
    FOREIGN KEY (department, course)
    REFERENCES classes (department, course)
  );

INSERT INTO registered_students (student_id, department, course,
                                grade)
  VALUES (10000, 'CS', 102, 'A');

INSERT INTO registered_students (student_id, department, course,
                                grade)
  VALUES (10002, 'CS', 102, 'B');

INSERT INTO registered_students (student_id, department, course,
                                grade)
  VALUES (10003, 'CS', 102, 'C');

INSERT INTO registered_students (student_id, department, course,
                                grade)
  VALUES (10000, 'HIS', 101, 'A');

INSERT INTO registered_students (student_id, department, course,
                                grade)
  VALUES (10001, 'HIS', 101, 'B');

INSERT INTO registered_students (student_id, department, course,
                                grade)
  VALUES (10002, 'HIS', 101, 'B');

INSERT INTO registered_students (student_id, department, course,
                                grade)
  VALUES (10003, 'HIS', 101, 'A');

INSERT INTO registered_students (student_id, department, course,
                                grade)
  VALUES (10004, 'HIS', 101, 'C');

INSERT INTO registered_students (student_id, department, course,
                                grade)
  VALUES (10005, 'HIS', 101, 'C');

INSERT INTO registered_students (student_id, department, course,
                                grade)
  VALUES (10006, 'HIS', 101, 'E');

INSERT INTO registered_students (student_id, department, course,
                                grade)
  VALUES (10007, 'HIS', 101, 'B');
```

```
INSERT INTO registered_students (student_id, department, course,
                                 grade)
   VALUES (10008, 'HIS', 101, 'A');

INSERT INTO registered_students (student_id, department, course,
                                 grade)
   VALUES (10009, 'HIS', 101, 'D');

INSERT INTO registered_students (student_id, department, course,
                                 grade)
   VALUES (10010, 'HIS', 101, 'A');

INSERT INTO registered_students (student_id, department, course,
                                 grade)
   VALUES (10008, 'NUT', 307, 'A');

INSERT INTO registered_students (student_id, department, course,
                                 grade)
   VALUES (10010, 'NUT', 307, 'A');

INSERT INTO registered_students (student_id, department, course,
                                 grade)
   VALUES (10009, 'MUS', 410, 'B');

INSERT INTO registered_students (student_id, department, course,
                                 grade)
   VALUES (10006, 'MUS', 410, 'E');

INSERT INTO registered_students (student_id, department, course,
                                 grade)
   VALUES (10011, 'MUS', 410, 'B');

INSERT INTO registered_students (student_id, department, course,
                                 grade)
   VALUES (10000, 'MUS', 410, 'B');
```

RS_audit

The **RS_audit** table is used to record changes made to **registered_students**.

```
CREATE TABLE RS_audit (
    change_type    CHAR(1)      NOT NULL,
    changed_by     VARCHAR2(8)  NOT NULL,
    timestamp      DATE         NOT NULL,
    old_student_id NUMBER(5),
    old_department CHAR(3),
```

```
old_course       NUMBER(3),
old_grade        CHAR(1),
new_student_id   NUMBER(5),
new_department   CHAR(3),
new_course       NUMBER(3),
new_grade        CHAR(1)
);
```

log_table
The **log_table** table is used to record Oracle errors.

```
CREATE TABLE log_table (
   code            NUMBER,
   message         VARCHAR2(200),
   info            VARCHAR2(100)
);
```

temp_table
The **temp_table** table is used to store temporary data that is not necessarily relevant to the other information.

```
CREATE TABLE temp_table (
   num_col    NUMBER,
   char_col   VARCHAR2(60)
);
```

connect_audit
The **connect_audit** table is used by examples in Chapter 6 to record connects to and disconnects from the database.

```
CREATE TABLE connect_audit (
   user_name   VARCHAR2(30),
   operation   VARCHAR2(30),
   timestamp   DATE);
```

debug_table
The **debug_table** table is used by the **Debug** package in Chapter 3 to hold PL/SQL debugging information.

```
CREATE TABLE debug_table (
   linecount   NUMBER,
   debug_str   VARCHAR2(100)
);
```

source and destination

The **source** and **destination** table are used by one of the debugging examples in Chapter 3.

```
CREATE TABLE source (
   key NUMBER(5),
   value VARCHAR2(50)  );

CREATE TABLE destination (
   key NUMBER(5),
   value NUMBER);
```

Summary

In this chapter, we saw a broad overview of PL/SQL, including the purpose of the language and the major features. We also discussed the importance of PL/SQL and database versions and how they correspond. The chapter concluded with a description of the accompanying CD and the example tables used in this book. In the next two chapters, we will discuss various development, debugging, and execution environments for PL/SQL.

CHAPTER
2

PL/SQL Development
and Execution
Environments

L/SQL blocks can be run from various environments, each of which has different properties and capabilities. In this chapter, we will discuss the locations where a PL/SQL engine can be found. We will also discuss different environments available for developing PL/SQL applications, including both Oracle tools and the tools available from third parties.

Application Models and PL/SQL

A database application can be divided into three parts:

- The user interface, which is responsible for the application's look and feel. This layer handles the input from the user and displays the application output.

- The application logic, which controls the work done by the application.

- The database, which stores the application data persistently and reliably.

There are two different models for designing an application that apportion these parts into different locations.

In order to compile and run a PL/SQL block, you need to submit it to the PL/SQL engine. Similar to a Java virtual machine, the *PL/SQL engine* consists of both the compiler and runtime system. With development tools available from Oracle and other vendors, PL/SQL can be used at any of the application layers, and PL/SQL engines can exist in different places.

The Two-Tier Model

The two-tier, or client-server, model is a traditional one for application design. Here, there are two portions of the application—the client and the server. The client handles the user interface, while the server contains the database. The application logic is split between the client and the server. There is a PL/SQL engine on the server and, in some cases, on the client as well.

PL/SQL in the Server

PL/SQL has been available in the database server since version 6 of Oracle, and the server is the original location for a PL/SQL engine. Since the database server also processes SQL statements, this means that both SQL statements and PL/SQL blocks can be sent to the database and processed. A client application, written using either Oracle's development tools or tools by another vendor, can issue both SQL statements and PL/SQL blocks to the server. SQL*Plus is an example of such a client application in which SQL statements and PL/SQL blocks entered interactively at the SQL prompt are sent to the server for execution.

For example, suppose we enter the following in SQL*Plus while connected to the server:

```
-- Available online as SQL_PLSQL.sql
SQL> CREATE OR REPLACE PROCEDURE ServerProcedure AS
  2    BEGIN
  3      NULL;
  4    END ServerProcedure;
  5    /
Procedure created.

SQL> DECLARE
  2      v_StudentRecord students%ROWTYPE;
  3      v_Counter BINARY_INTEGER;
  4    BEGIN
  5      v_Counter := 7;
  6
  7      SELECT *
  8        INTO v_StudentRecord
  9        FROM students
 10        WHERE id = 10001;
 11
 12      ServerProcedure;
 13
 14    END;
 15    /
PL/SQL procedure successfully completed.

SQL> UPDATE classes
  2      SET max_students = 70
  3      WHERE department = 'HIS'
  4      AND course = 101;
1 row updated.
```

NOTE
The previous example, like many in this book, can be found on the included CD. Examples that are on the CD are indicated with a comment like "-- Available online as xxx.sql," *where* xxx.sql *is the filename on the CD. For more information, including a description of all the online files, see the **readme.html** file in the **code** directory.*

Figure 2-1 illustrates this scenario. The client application issues both a PL/SQL block (which contains both procedural and SQL statements, including a call to a server-side stored procedure), and a separate SQL statement to the server. Both the PL/SQL block and the SQL statement are sent over the network to the server. Once there, the SQL statement is sent directly to the SQL statement executor contained in the server, while the PL/SQL block is sent to the PL/SQL engine, which parses the entire block. During execution of the block, the PL/SQL engine executes the procedural statements (such as the assignment and the stored procedure call). But it sends any SQL statements inside the block (such as the SELECT statement) to the same SQL statement executor.

PL/SQL on the Client

In addition to the PL/SQL engine on the server, several of Oracle's development tools contain a PL/SQL engine. The development tool itself runs on the client, not the server. The PL/SQL engine also runs on the client. With client-side PL/SQL, procedural statements within PL/SQL blocks are run on the client and not sent to the server. As an example, Oracle Forms (bundled as part of Oracle Developer) contains a separate PL/SQL engine. Other tools in this suite, such as Oracle Reports, also contain a PL/SQL engine. This engine is different from the PL/SQL on the server. PL/SQL blocks are contained within a client-side application written using these tools. An Oracle Forms application, for example, contains triggers and procedures. These are executed on the client, and only the SQL statements within them, and calls to server-side stored subprograms, are sent to the server for processing. The local PL/SQL engine on the client processes the procedural statements, as illustrated in Figure 2-2.

Standalone SQL statements issued by the application (the UPDATE statement) are sent directly over the network to the SQL statement executor on the server, as before. However, the client processes PL/SQL blocks locally. Any procedural statements (such as the assignment) can be processed without network traffic. SQL statements within PL/SQL blocks (such as the SELECT statement) are sent to the SQL executor, and calls to server-side stored subprograms are sent to the server-side PL/SQL engine.

ORACLE PRECOMPILERS   You can use the Oracle precompilers such as Pro*C/C++ and Pro*COBOL to create applications that execute PL/SQL in the server. The resultant applications do not contain a PL/SQL engine. Thus, both SQL and PL/SQL statements issued by the application are sent to the server for processing.

The precompilers themselves, however, do contain a PL/SQL engine within them. This is used during precompilation to verify the syntax and semantics of anonymous blocks within the application code. The precompilers are unique among Oracle's development tools in this respect.

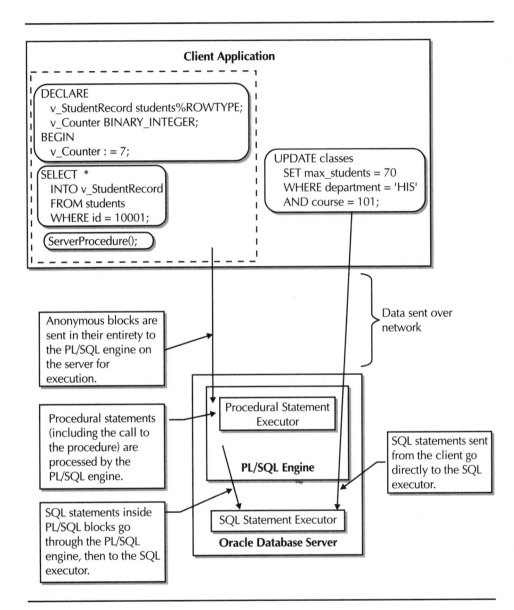

FIGURE 2-1. *PL/SQL engine on the server*

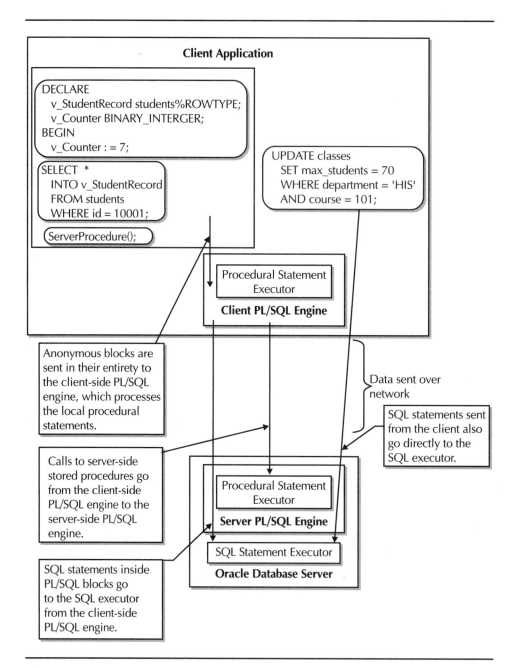

FIGURE 2-2. *PL/SQL engine on the client*

Communication Between Engines

In the scenario illustrated in Figure 2-2, there are two separate PL/SQL engines that communicate with each other. For example, a trigger within a form (running in client-side PL/SQL) can call a stored procedure within the database (running in server-side PL/SQL). Communications such as these take place through remote procedure calls. A similar mechanism is used to communicate between PL/SQL engines in two different servers, through database links.

In this situation, PL/SQL objects in different engines can depend on each other. This type of relationship works the same way as PL/SQL objects in the same database, with some caveats. For more information, see Chapter 5.

In general, the two PL/SQL engines may be different versions. Oracle Developer version 1.2, for example, uses PL/SQL version 1, while the server uses PL/SQL version 2 (or 8 if Oracle8). This implies that features contained in PL/SQL version 2 and higher, such as user-defined tables and records and fixed-length CHAR datatypes, among others, might not be available in the client-side PL/SQL engine. Although Oracle Developer version 2 and higher contain PL/SQL version 8, there could still be version differences between the engines, and, thus, different features would be available in each.

The Three-Tier Model

In a three-tier model, the user interface, application logic, and database storage are split into three separate parts. The client in this model is typically thin, such as a browser. The application logic is entirely contained within one layer, known as the application server. In this environment, the PL/SQL engine is generally found in the server only.

The Oracle Application Server (OAS) can function as a complete application server. Through the PL/SQL cartridge, you can execute stored procedures on the server and return the results as HTML pages. This is facilitated by the PL/SQL Web Toolkit, which is part of OAS. This situation is illustrated by Figure 2-3. For more information on the PL/SQL cartridge and the Web Toolkit, see the Oracle documentation.

PL/SQL Development Tools

There are many different tools that allow you to develop and debug a PL/SQL application, each with advantages and disadvantages. The tools that we will discuss in detail are described in Table 2-1. As the table indicates, SQL*Plus is provided by Oracle Corporation with the server, and the remainder of the tools are available from third-party vendors. Trial versions of the third-party tools are included on the CD packaged with this book. We will examine these tools in the following sections. In Chapter 3, we will examine the debugging features of the tools in more detail.

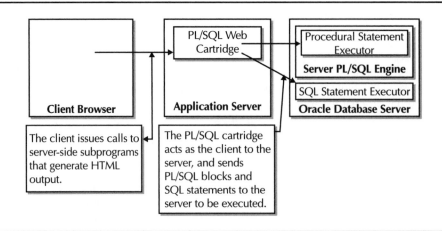

FIGURE 2-3. *The three-tier model*

NOTE
*The tools that are included on the CD-ROM can be found in the **Development Tools** directory. For more information, see the **readme.html** file on the root level of the CD.*

Tool	Vendor	Web Site	Included on CD?
SQL*Plus™	Oracle Corporation	www.oracle.com	No
Rapid SQL™	Embarcadero Technologies, Inc.	www.embarcadero.com	Yes
XPEDITER/SQL™	Compuware	www.compuware.com	Yes
SQL Navigator™	Quest Software	www.quest.com	Yes
TOAD™	Quest Software	www.quest.com or www.toadsoft.com	Yes
SQL-Programmer™	Sylvain Faust International	www.sfi-software.com	Yes

TABLE 2-1. *PL/SQL Development Environments*

For consistency, each of the following discussions takes place in a schema that has several examples of different types of PL/SQL objects. This allows us to see how each tool works in the same environment. The schema contains the objects described in Table 2-2, and can be created by running the files indicated after running the **relTables.sql** setup script. The online file **Setup.sql** can also be used to run each of the subsequent files. Note that the CREATE LIBRARY system privilege is required to create the external procedures and functions.

NOTE
*In the following sections, there are screenshots for each of the tools. Due to space constraints in this book, some of the screenshots can be found on the CD-ROM that accompanies this book. For more information, see **ch02ScreenShots.html** in the **Online Chapters** directory.*

SQL*Plus

SQL*Plus is perhaps the simplest of the PL/SQL development tools. It allows the user to enter SQL statements and PL/SQL blocks interactively from a prompt. These statements are sent directly to the database, and the results are returned to the screen. It is a character mode environment, and there is no local PL/SQL engine.

Generally, SQL*Plus is shipped along with the Oracle server, and is available as part of a standard Oracle installation. For more information on SQL*Plus and its commands not covered in this section, see the *SQL*Plus User's Guide and Reference.*

Object Name	Object Type	Script to Run
AddNewStudent	Procedure	ch04/AddNewStudent.sql
AlmostFull	Function	ch04/AlmostFull.sql
ModeTest	Procedure	ch04/ModeTest.sql
ClassPackage	Package and Package Body	ch04/ClassPackage.sql
Point	Object Type and Type Body	ch12/Point.sql
OutputString	External Procedures and Functions	ch10/OutputString.sql

TABLE 2-2.   *Sample Schema*

SQL*Plus commands are not case-sensitive. For example, all of the following commands declare bind variables:

```
SQL> VARIABLE v_Num NUMBER
SQL> variable v_Char char(3)
SQL> vaRIAbLe v_Varchar VarCHAR2(5)
```

Connecting to the Database

Before you can issue any SQL or PL/SQL statements in SQL*Plus, you must connect to the server. This can be done in one of two ways:

- By passing a userid and password and/or connect string on the SQL*Plus command line

- By using the CONNECT statement once you are in SQL*Plus

As the following example illustrates, if you do not specify a password, then SQL*Plus will prompt you for it and will not echo the input to the screen.

```
$ sqlplus example/example
SQL*Plus: Release 8.0.6.0.0 - Production on Wed Nov 3 10:29:11 1999
(c) Copyright 1999 Oracle Corporation.  All rights reserved.

Connected to:
Oracle8 Enterprise Edition Release 8.0.6.0.0 - Production
With the Objects option
PL/SQL Release 8.0.6.0.0 - Production

SQL> exit
Disconnected from Oracle8 Enterprise Edition Release 8.0.6.0.0 -
Production
With the Objects option
PL/SQL Release 8.0.6.0.0 - Production
$ sqlplus example
SQL*Plus: Release 8.0.6.0.0 - Production on Wed Nov 3 10:29:15 1999
(c) Copyright 1999 Oracle Corporation.  All rights reserved.
Enter password:

Connected to:
Oracle8 Enterprise Edition Release 8.0.6.0.0 - Production
With the Objects option
PL/SQL Release 8.0.6.0.0 - Production

SQL> connect example/example
Connected.
SQL> connect example/example@v806_tcp
Connected.
```

Manipulating Blocks in SQL*Plus

When you execute a SQL statement in SQL*Plus, the semicolon terminates the statement. The semicolon is not part of the statement itself—it is the statement terminator. When SQL*Plus reads the semicolon, it knows that the statement is complete and sends it to the database. On the other hand, with a PL/SQL block, the semicolon is a syntactic part of the block itself—it is not a statement terminator. When you enter the DECLARE or BEGIN keyword, SQL*Plus detects this and knows that you are running a PL/SQL block rather than a SQL statement. But SQL*Plus still needs to know when the block has ended. This is done with a forward slash, which is short for the SQL*Plus RUN command.

Note the slash after the PL/SQL block that updates the **registered_students** table in Figure 2-4. The SELECT statement after the block does not need the slash because the semicolon is present. (You can use a slash instead of the semicolon for SQL statements as well, if desired.)

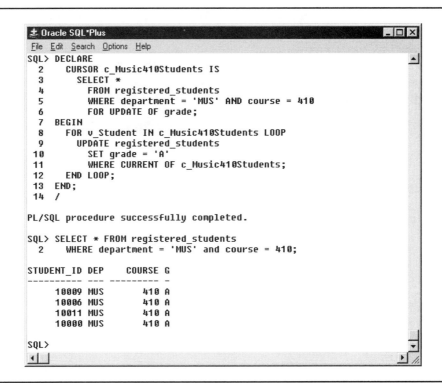

FIGURE 2-4. *PL/SQL in SQL*Plus*

Substitution and Bind Variables

Because PL/SQL is designed to be a server-side language, it does not have any built-in capabilities for input from the user and output to the screen. File I/O can be done through the UTL_FILE package (PL/SQL 2.3 and higher; see Chapter 7 for details), and Oracle8 can read external files through the BFILE interface (see Chapters 15 and 16 on the CD-ROM included with this book for details). In addition, limited screen output can be done with the DBMS_OUTPUT package, in concert with SQL*Plus (see Chapter 3 for details).

None of these methods provide a way to receive input from the user. This is typically the responsibility of the environment that issued the PL/SQL. For example, a Pro*C program can accept input using the C I/O library, and pass this to PL/SQL.

SQL*Plus has two different types of variables, which can be used to accept input from the user and store information across multiple executions—substitution and bind variables.

SUBSTITUTION VARIABLES   Substitution variables are delineated by the ampersand (&) character in a PL/SQL block or SQL statement. (The character can be changed using the SET DEFINE command.) SQL*Plus will perform a complete textual substitution of the variable before the PL/SQL block or SQL statement is sent to the server, similar to the behavior of C macros.

Figure 2-5 illustrates the use of substitution variables. The same block is run twice, each time initializing **v_StudentID** to a different value. The user inputs the values 10004 and 10005, and they are textually replaced in the block for **&student_id**.

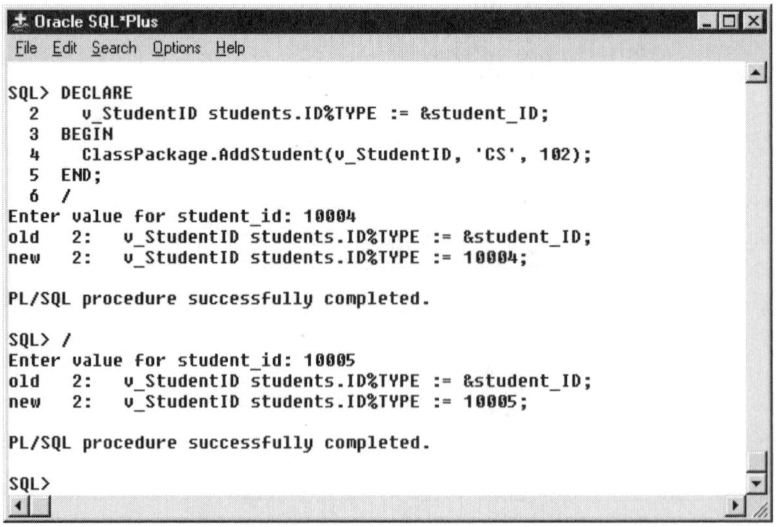

FIGURE 2-5.   *SQL*Plus substitution variables*

It is important to note that no memory is actually allocated for substitution variables. SQL*Plus replaces the substitution variable with the value you input before the block is sent to the database for execution. Because of this, substitution variables can be used for input only. Bind variables (discussed in the next section), however, can be used for input or output.

TIP
Suppose you enter the following SQL statement from the SQL> prompt:

```
SQL> SELECT *
       FROM students
       WHERE first_name = &first_name;
```

*In this case, when SQL*Plus prompts you for a value, you must include the single quotes, such as 'SCOTT'. Compare this to the following statement:*

```
SQL> SELECT *
       FROM students
       WHERE first_name = '&first_name';
```

Now, you don't enter the quotes, since they are already part of the statement. Depending on what you are substituting, quotes may or may not be necessary.

BIND VARIABLES   As we saw in the last section, there is no memory allocated for substitution variables. However, SQL*Plus can allocate memory that can be used inside PL/SQL blocks and SQL statements. Because this storage is allocated outside the block, it can be used for more than one block or statement in succession, and it can be printed after a block completes. This storage is known as a *bind variable*, illustrated in the online screenshots as Figure CD2-1. The **v_Count** bind variable is allocated using the SQL*Plus command VARIABLE. Note that this command is valid only from the SQL prompt, and not inside a PL/SQL block. Inside the block, the bind variable is delimited by the leading colon rather than an ampersand. After the block, the PRINT command shows the value of the variable. The types valid for SQL*Plus bind variables include VARCHAR2, CHAR, and NUMBER. REFCURSOR is available with SQL*Plus 3.2 and higher, and NCHAR, NVARCHAR2, CLOB, and NCLOB are available with SQL*Plus 8.0 and higher. If the length isn't specified for bind variables of type VARCHAR2, CHAR, NCHAR, or NVARCHAR2, the length defaults to 1. NUMBER bind variables *cannot* be constrained by a precision or scale.

VARIABLES AND DATABASE OBJECTS   Because substitution variables are replaced before the block is sent to the server, they can be used for syntactic portions of SQL commands and for database objects. Bind variables cannot be used in this manner. This is illustrated by the following SQL*Plus session.

```
-- Available online as Variables.sql
SQL> SELECT &columns
  2    FROM classes;
Enter value for columns: department, course
old   1: SELECT &columns
new   1: SELECT department, course

DEP    COURSE
---    ---------
HIS       101
HIS       301
CS        101
ECN       203
CS        102
MUS       410
ECN       101
NUT       307
MUS       100

9 rows selected.
SQL> SELECT first_name, last_name
  2    FROM students
  3    WHERE &where_clause;
Enter value for where_clause: ID = 10001
old   3:   WHERE &where_clause
new   3:   WHERE ID = 10001

FIRST_NAME          LAST_NAME
------------------  -------------------
Margaret            Mason

SQL> -- But a bind variable cannot be used in this manner:
SQL> VARIABLE where_clause VARCHAR2(100)
SQL>
SQL> BEGIN
  2    :where_clause := 'WHERE ID = 10001';
  3  END;
  4  /

PL/SQL procedure successfully completed.
SQL> PRINT :where_clause

WHERE_CLAUSE
-------------------------------------------------------------------
```

```
WHERE ID = 10001

SQL> SELECT first_name, last_name
  2     FROM students
  3     WHERE :where_clause;
   WHERE :where_clause
                      *
ERROR at line 3:
ORA-00920: invalid relational operator
```

You can use dynamic SQL to build SQL statements and PL/SQL blocks at runtime, and use PL/SQL variables for syntactic portions of the statements. For more information, see Chapter 8.

Calling Stored Procedures with EXECUTE

A stored procedure call must be made from the executable or exception-handling section of a PL/SQL block. SQL*Plus provides a useful shorthand for this syntax—the EXECUTE command. All that EXECUTE does is take its arguments, put BEGIN before them, and END; after. A semicolon is added after the procedure call as well. The resulting block is then submitted to the database. For example, if we enter

```
SQL> EXECUTE ClassPackage.AddStudent(10006, 'CS', 102)
```

from the SQL prompt, the PL/SQL block

```
BEGIN ClassPackage.AddStudent(10006, 'CS', 102); END;
```

would actually be sent to the database. A semicolon is optional after the EXECUTE command. This is true of all the SQL*Plus commands—if a semicolon is present, it is ignored. Like PRINT or VARIABLE, EXECUTE is a SQL*Plus command and thus is not valid inside a PL/SQL block.

TIP
The EXECUTE command does not store the generated anonymous block in the SQL buffer, as it would have been if the anonymous block were entered directly.

Using Files

SQL*Plus can save the current PL/SQL block or SQL statement to a file, and this file can then be read back in and executed. This useful feature is valuable both during development of a PL/SQL program and later execution of it. For example, you can store a CREATE OR REPLACE command in a file. This way, any modifications to the procedure can be done to the file. In order to save the changes in the database, you can simply read the file into SQL*Plus. Files can contain more than one command as well.

The SQL*Plus GET command reads a file from disk into the local buffer. A forward slash will then run it, as if it had been entered directly from the keyboard. If the file contains a slash at the end, however, it can be read in and run using the at sign (@) shortcut. For example, assume that the file **File.sql** contains the following lines:

```
-- Available online as File.sql
BEGIN
  FOR v_Count IN 1..10 LOOP
    INSERT INTO temp_Table (num_col, char_col)
      VALUES (v_Count, 'Hello World!');
  END LOOP;
END;
/

SELECT * FROM temp_table;
```

We can now execute this file from the SQL prompt with

```
SQL> @File
```

The output from this is shown in the online screenshots as Figure CD2-2. The SET ECHO ON command (the first command in the figure) tells SQL*Plus to echo the contents of the file to the screen as they are read from the file.

Using the SHOW ERRORS Command

When a stored subprogram is created, information about it is stored in the data dictionary. Specifically, any compile errors are stored in the **user_errors** data dictionary view. SQL*Plus provides a useful command, SHOW ERRORS, which will query this view and report the errors. Figure CD2-3 in the online screenshots illustrates this. SHOW ERRORS can be used after SQL*Plus reports this message:

```
Warning: Procedure created with compilation errors.
```

Rapid SQL

Rapid SQL, produced by Embarcadero Technologies, is a GUI development environment that has the following features, among others:

- Auto-formatting of PL/SQL and SQL statements
- A PL/SQL debugger

- Support for Oracle8 object types and table partitions

- SQL job scheduling

- Project management

- Support for Windows Active Scripting

- Support for third-party version control systems

- Integrated database development and Web programming

For more information on installing and using Rapid SQL Pro, see the online help.

Connecting to the Database

When you first start Rapid SQL, you will get a window similar to Figure 2-6. The pane on the left allows you to explore database objects, sorted by datasource. The pane on

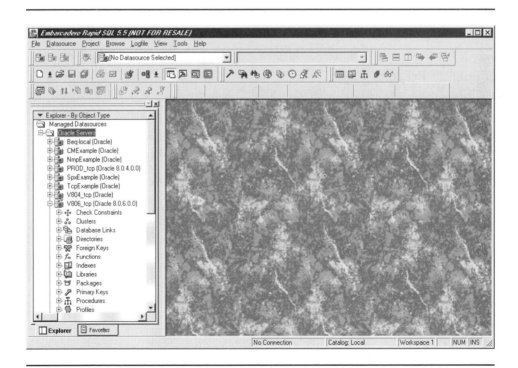

FIGURE 2-6. *Rapid SQL main window*

the right is the working pane, which can show different types of objects as you work with them. A *datasource* records all pertinent information about a remote database, such as the type of database, userid, password, and connect information. The first time Rapid SQL is run, it will automatically discover available datasources for you by searching the SQL*Net or Net8 configuration for your machine. Double-clicking a particular datasource will bring up a dialog box allowing you to enter a userid and password for that connection, as shown in the online screenshots as Figure CD2-4. You can also add new datasources through the Datasource menu.

If you choose, Rapid SQL will remember the userid and password, and will not prompt you again for that datasource. You can have multiple connections open at one time.

Browsing Database Objects

Once you have established a connection to the database, you can browse the available objects in the Explorer pane. Clicking a type of object will expand the list to include those objects, and you can further examine individual objects in the list. Double-clicking a particular object will bring up the SQL or PL/SQL that creates that object. For example, Figure 2-7 shows packages and tables in the Explorer and the DDL for the **classes** table in the working area.

Types of Editors

Rapid SQL has two different types of windows that allow you to enter SQL statements and PL/SQL blocks, each suitable for different tasks:

- An SQL editor is a general editor, suitable for SQL DML and DDL statements, as well as anonymous PL/SQL blocks and CREATE statements.

- A DDL editor allows you to choose the type of object to create, and automatically fills it in with the structure.

The editors can be chosen from the File | New submenu. Figure CD2-5 (in the online screenshots) shows a PL/SQL editor with an anonymous block. Clicking the green triangle will send the block to the server for execution.

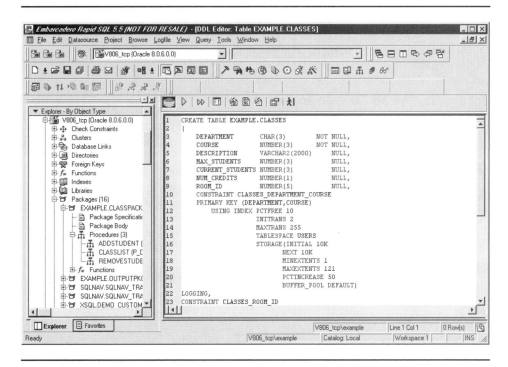

FIGURE 2-7.   *Exploring the* **classes** *table*

Auto-Formatting

Any editor can auto-format SQL and PL/SQL statements. Auto-formatting includes indentation and the case of various syntactic elements. This is a very useful feature, and allows you to easily format PL/SQL blocks according to your particular style guidelines. Figure CD2-6 (in the online screenshots) shows the options for the auto-formatter.

Viewing Errors

After submitting a PL/SQL block to the server, any errors can be displayed by clicking the Errors tool. The object is also shown with an X in the Explorer, since it is not valid. This is illustrated in the online screenshots by Figure CD2-7. Any errors will be shown in a pane below the PL/SQL text. Clicking a particular error will advance the cursor to the location for that error.

Job Scheduling
Rapid SQL incorporates the Microsoft Job Scheduler (available with Windows 98 or NT), which allows you to run jobs at certain times, independent of Rapid SQL Pro itself.

Integrated Web Development
Rapid SQL also has the capability to edit Java code and HTML pages, through additional types of editors. For more information, see the online documentation.

XPEDITER/SQL

XPEDITER/SQL is published by Compuware Corporation. It is a GUI development environment, which has the following features, among others:

- Auto-formatting of PL/SQL and SQL statements

- A PL/SQL debugger

- Support for Oracle8 object types

- Project management

- Support for debugging and tracing of any application

- Support for third-party version control systems

Connecting to the Database
When you first start XPEDITER/SQL, it will prompt you for a database connection. You can store profiles for different connections, each of which records the userid and connect string. By specifying the userid as "userid/password," the password can be stored as well. This dialog box is illustrated by Figure CD2-8 in the online screenshots. More than one connection can be active at one time.

Server-Side Setup
In order to use XPEDITER/SQL properly, a server-side setup is necessary. This will create a database user that contains tables that store information necessary to XPEDITER/SQL. This can be done during installation, or can be done after the program is installed through use of the Database Setup Wizard, shown in the online screenshots as Figure CD2-9. The wizard allows you to install, de-install, or upgrade the server-side objects for multiple databases.

Browsing Database Objects

The Object Browser window is used to view information about database objects, including session privileges. You can open different browsers for the same connection, if desired, but each browser can show information on only one connection. An object browser is shown in Figure 2-8. The left pane shows a tree that allows you to choose the type and owner of the object desired. The right pane shows information about the object, including whether or not it has been compiled with debug information and dependency information. (Objects can be compiled with or without debug information by choosing Object | Debug On or Object | Debug Off.)

Editing Database Objects

Double-clicking a particular object in the browser will open it in a SQL Notepad window. SQL Notepad windows are used to edit all types of database objects,

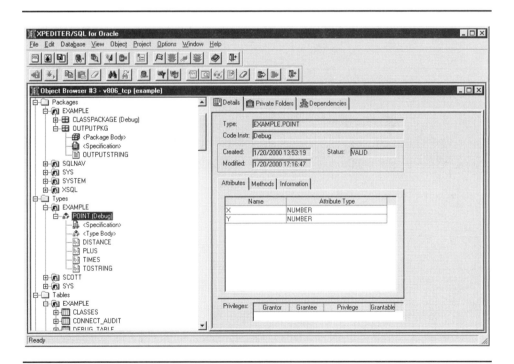

FIGURE 2-8.   *Browsing the **Point** object type*

including PL/SQL stored subprograms and anonymous blocks. For example, Figure 2-9 shows the **Point** type specification in a Notepad. PL/SQL code is automatically formatted. The SQL in a Notepad can be run by clicking the red triangle button, and can be debugged by clicking the green triangle button.

Showing Errors

Compile errors for an object can be viewed by clicking the SQL Errors tab in the bottom pane of the SQL Notepad. This will show the errors for the current object or block, if any. Clicking a particular error will scroll the text of the procedure to the appropriate line, as well. The errors for the **TooManyErrors** procedure are shown in the online screenshots as Figure CD2-10. Invalid objects are also indicated in the Object Browser.

Using Templates

An additional useful feature of XPEDITER/SQL is the Template Editor. This window, available from the Tools | Template Editor submenu when a SQL Notepad is active,

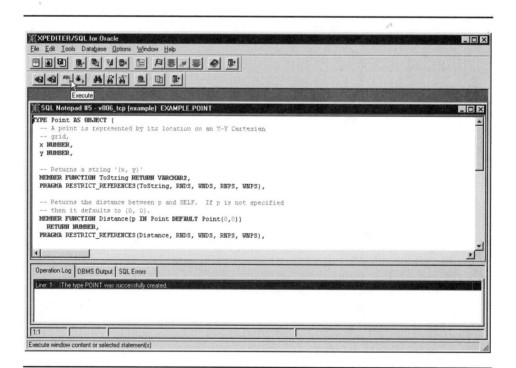

FIGURE 2-9. *Editing Point*

allows you to insert predefined portions of PL/SQL code into the active Notepad. In addition to the syntax for creating new procedures, functions, triggers, packages, and types, the Template Editor contains calls to commonly used built-in packages, such as DBMS_SQL or DBMS_OUTPUT. The Template Editor is shown in the online screenshots as Figure CD2-11. Double-clicking a particular template will copy the text to the Notepad window.

DBPartner

The final feature of XPEDITER/SQL that we will discuss is DBPartner. This utility allows you to capture the SQL from any program, and edit or debug it from XPEDITER/SQL. In this way, you can potentially tune or debug programs when the source code is unavailable.

SQL Navigator

SQL Navigator is published by Quest Software. It is a GUI development environment that offers the following features:

- Auto-formatting of PL/SQL and SQL statements

- A PL/SQL debugger

- Database browser

- Support for Oracle8 object types and Oracle8*i* types

- Code templates

- Support for third-party version control systems

Connecting to the Database

Like XPEDITER/SQL, SQL Navigator asks for a database connection when it is first started. Connection profiles are stored automatically for later use, but the password is not stored. The window used to establish the connection is shown in the online screenshots as Figure CD2-12. If you don't connect to a database upon startup, then you will be prompted with this same dialog box upon opening an editing or browsing window. SQL Navigator supports multiple connections to different databases simultaneously.

Setting Up Server-Side Objects

Many of the options within SQL Navigator require that a user SQLNAV be created on the server. The Server Side Installation Wizard, shown in the online screenshots as Figure CD2-13, aids in creating the necessary user and objects. This wizard can be run as part of the installation, and also after installation by selecting Tools |

Server Side Installation Wizard. Server-side installation is necessary for explain plan support, team programming, third-party version control, and support for SQL Navigator Tuner.

Browsing Database Objects

The DB Navigator window is used to browse objects in the database. It presents a tree view from which you can choose the type and owner of the desired objects. One of the unique features of this database browser is the use of filters. A *filter*, as its name suggests, will only show certain types of objects. There are many predefined filters available, and you can create your own as well. The Navigator shown in Figure 2-10 has three filters active.

SQL Navigator also supports Oracle8*i* Java stored procedures (JSPs) in the database browser, if you are connected to an Oracle8*i* database. In this case, extra entries for Java classes, sources, and resources will appear in the tree. You cannot edit the Java code from within SQL Navigator, but you can compile sources that are

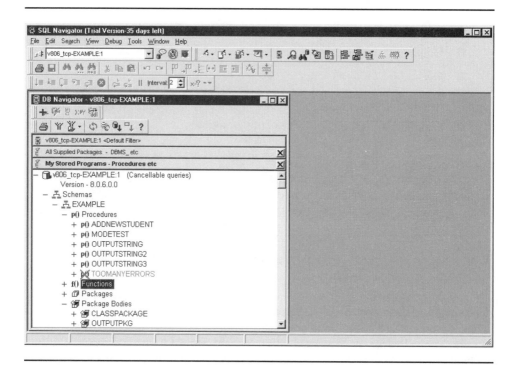

FIGURE 2-10. *DB Navigator with filters*

already present in the database. For more information on using JSPs in Oracle8*i*, see Chapter 10.

Editing Database Objects

There are three different kinds of editing windows available with SQL Navigator:

■ The SQL Editor, which can contain either a single SQL statement or a script.

■ The Trigger Editor, which is used to create or edit database triggers. The Oracle8 instead-of trigger type is supported.

■ The Stored Program Editor, which is used to create or edit stored PL/SQL code.

The appropriate editor will be opened when you click an object in the DB Navigator, or you can open them directly using the toolbar. Figure 2-11 shows the **AlmostFull** function in a Stored Program Editor. PL/SQL code is automatically highlighted in editing windows.

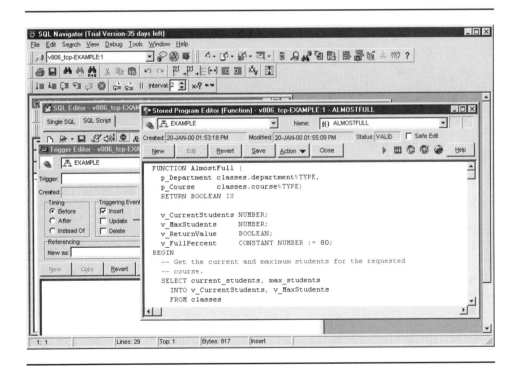

FIGURE 2-11. *Editing AlmostFull*

Showing Errors

If there are errors during the compilation of a PL/SQL object, they will be shown when you compile the object from a Stored Program Editor. Clicking an error highlights the source line, and double-clicking an error will bring up a window with the cause and action from the Oracle documentation. The errors for the **TooManyErrors** procedure are shown in the online screenshots as Figure CD2-14.

Code Templates

The Code Assistant, available on the Tools menu, provides a library of commonly used PL/SQL and SQL constructs. Highlighting a particular construct will bring up a description in the Code Assistant Information window, and double-clicking will copy it to an available editing window, where it can be customized. The Code Assistant is shown in the online screenshots as Figure CD2-15.

TOAD

TOAD (Tool for Oracle Application Developers) was originally developed separately from SQL Navigator, but is now produced by Quest Software along with SQL Navigator. Consequently, the two tools share some features, including the licensing mechanism. However, there are differences, as we will see. TOAD has the following features:

- Auto-formatting of PL/SQL and SQL statements
- A PL/SQL debugger
- Database browser
- Support for Oracle8 object types
- Code templates
- Support for third-party version control systems

TOAD is designed to be a lightweight, but still powerful, development environment. It has much smaller disk and memory requirements than the other tools.

Connecting to the Database

TOAD can support multiple database connections at any point. When you first start the application, it prompts you to connect with the dialog box shown in the online screenshots as Figure CD2-16. Further connections can be made from the File | New Connection command. Once a connection is established, it will remain active until you explicitly close it by selecting File | Close Connection. Passwords are stored in the connection profiles.

One unique feature of the way that TOAD manages connections is that the connection associated with any window can be changed dynamically. This allows you to work with multiple servers at the same time, while keeping the number of windows to a minimum. A given work window can be associated with only one session at a time, however.

Browsing Database Objects

There are two different kinds of database browsers available with TOAD—the Schema Browser and Object Browser. The Schema Browser, shown in Figure 2-12, allows you to select Oracle7 types such as tables, procedures, and packages. Instead of a tree structure like the browsers in the other tools we have examined, the Schema Browser has tabs to select the type of objects, which are then shown in the pane on the left. The right pane shows details about the object. You can also compile or drop objects from this browser.

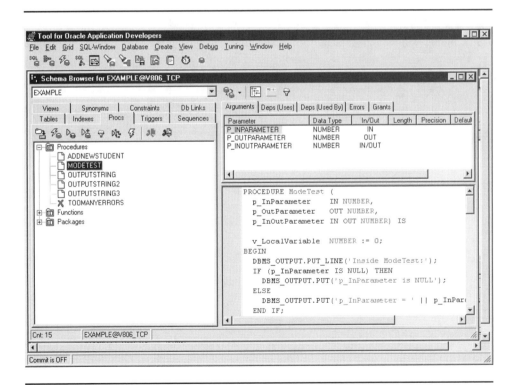

FIGURE 2-12. *The Schema Browser*

The Object Browser, on the other hand, is used solely to examine Oracle8 object types and type bodies. Like the Schema Browser, it allows you to examine and modify the properties of object types and type bodies. An Object Browser with the type body of the **Point** object is shown in the online screenshots as Figure CD2-17.

Editing Database Objects

TOAD has two types of editing windows: a SQL Edit Window and a Stored Procedure Edit window. As their names suggest, SQL Edit windows are used to edit single SQL statements or SQL scripts, while Stored Procedure Edit windows are used to edit stored procedures, functions, packages, and triggers. From a Stored Procedure Edit window, you can compile, run, or debug the procedure shown. Figure 2-13 shows the **OutputString** procedure, which happens to be an external routine implemented in C, in a Stored Procedure Edit window. Stored Procedure Edit windows can be loaded from database objects or files, or can be used to create new objects.

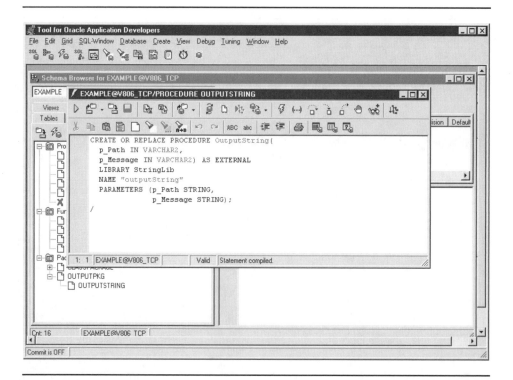

FIGURE 2-13. *The Stored Procedure Edit window*

Showing Errors
If you attempt to compile a procedure with errors, the errors will be shown in an error pane at the bottom of the Stored Procedure Edit window. As you click between the errors using the blue triangle buttons, the relevant lines of source are highlighted, as shown in the online screenshots by Figure CD2-18. Errors can also be viewed in a Schema Browser for invalid objects.

Code Templates
TOAD supports code templates for commonly used PL/SQL and SQL constructs. Rather than entering them graphically, however, you can use a keyboard shortcut. Entering the keyboard shortcut in an edit window, followed by CTRL-SPACEBAR, will replace the shortcut with the full construct. The templates can be viewed from the Editor options window, as shown in the online screenshots by Figure CD2-19. You can also edit the existing templates or add your own.

SQL-Programmer
The final GUI development tool that we will examine is SQL-Programmer, by Sylvain Faust International. It supports the following features:

- Auto-formatting of PL/SQL and SQL statements

- A PL/SQL debugger

- Database browser

- Support for Oracle8 object types

- Code templates

- Support for third-party version control systems

- Scripting of database objects

Connecting to the Database
SQL-Programmer supports multiple simultaneous connections to different databases. The connection dialog box is shown in the online screenshots as Figure CD2-20. Passwords are not stored in connection profiles, but you can store different profiles for different servers. This dialog box also shows the current connections that are open.

Browsing Database Objects
The SQL-Explorer window allows you to browse through the database objects, sorted by schema and object type. If there is more than one connection active, a single SQL-Explorer can view objects from both connections. Figure 2-14

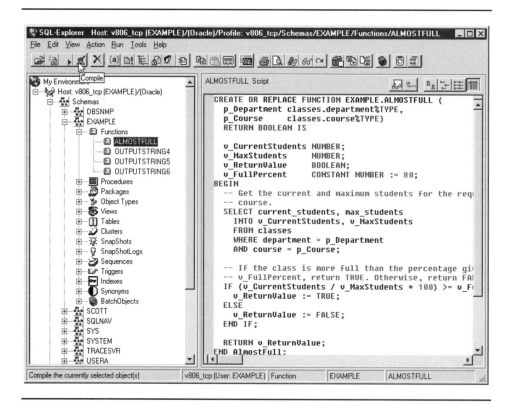

FIGURE 2-14. *The SQL-Explorer*

demonstrates a SQL-Explorer with the **AlmostFull** function. From the SQL-Explorer, you can not only view attributes of the object (such as GRANTs made, synonyms, and so on), but you can also compile the object, or drop it.

Editing Database Objects

Double-clicking a particular object in the SQL-Explorer will bring it up in a SQL-Programmer Development Window, or SPDW. An SPDW allows you to query or modify detailed information about the object within it. The SPDW for **AlmostFull**, including the arguments, is shown in Figure 2-15. You can execute a procedure directly from an SPDW, in which case you will be prompted for the values of any input parameters that will be used in the anonymous block.

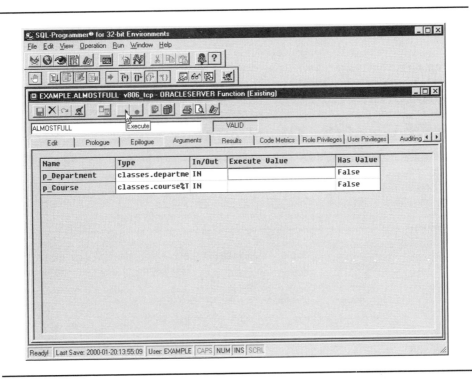

FIGURE 2-15. *AlmostFull* in an SPDW

Showing Errors

If a procedure has compile errors, then the SPDW will show the errors in an error
pane below the text, as we can see in the online screenshots as Figure CD2-21.
Double-clicking a particular error will highlight the relevant section of the code
in the pane above it. Note also that the SPDW indicates that the procedure is invalid.

Code Templates

SQL-Programmer has templates available for creating new objects. When you
create a new object from the SQL-Explorer, it will automatically be filled in with the
appropriate template. The available templates can be specified from the Options menu.
Figure CD2-22 in the online screenshots shows the default template for a procedure.
Note that it includes suggested comments in addition to the procedure code itself.

Scripting

The scripting interface allows you to create a script for any combination of database objects. This script will contain code to automatically re-create the objects on any other server. Thus, scripts provide a good mechanism to copy individual objects, or entire schemas, between databases. The scripting interface is shown in the online screenshots as Figure CD2-23.

Summary of the Development Tools

None of the tools that we have discussed in this chapter have a client-side PL/SQL engine. They all can be used to develop and debug PL/SQL applications. A comparison between some of the major features can be found in Table 2-3. For

Feature	SQL*Plus	Rapid SQL	XPEDITER/ SQL	SQL Navigator	TOAD	SQL- Programmer
Availability	Shipped with the server	Sold separately	Sold separately	Sold separately	Sold separately	Sold separately
GUI environment	No	Yes	Yes	Yes	Yes	Yes
Object browser	No	Yes	Yes	Yes	Yes	Yes
Code templates	No	Yes	Yes	Yes	Yes	Yes
Project management	No	Yes	Yes	No	No	No
Code formatting	No	Yes	Yes	Yes	Yes	Yes
Job scheduling	No	Yes	No	No	No	No
Version control	No	Yes	Yes	Yes	Yes	Yes
Support for Oracle8 types	Yes	Yes	Yes	Yes	Yes	Yes
Support for Oracle8*i* types	Yes	Yes	No	Yes	No	No
Server-side setup required	No	No	Yes	Yes	No	No
Simultaneous connections	No	Yes	No	Yes	Yes	Yes

TABLE 2-3. *Comparison of PL/SQL Development Tools*

more information about any of these development tools, consult the online help available with each, as well as the vendor's Web site listed in Table 2-1.

The tools that support version control generally do so through the use of third-party source control systems. Different development tools support different source control systems. Again, see the online help for each tool for details.

Summary

In this chapter, we have examined six different development environments for creating PL/SQL applications. These included SQL*Plus from Oracle, Rapid SQL from Embarcadero Technologies, XPEDITER/SQL from Compuware, SQL Navigator and TOAD from Quest Software, and SQL-Programmer from Sylvain-Faust International. With the exception of SQL*Plus, which is available with every Oracle release, trial versions of the tools can be found on the accompanying CD. In the next chapter, we will examine the debugging features of each of these environments.

CHAPTER
3

Tracing and Debugging

ery few programs perform correctly the first time they are written. Also, the requirements for a program often change during development, and the program must be rewritten. In either case, the program needs to be tested thoroughly to make sure that it is working properly and performing as expected. In this chapter, we will discuss several techniques for testing and debugging PL/SQL programs, including both non-graphical techniques and various graphical PL/SQL debuggers. We will also examine the tracing and profiling tools available with Oracle8*i*.

Problem Diagnosis

Every bug is different from the last, which is what makes debugging and testing a challenge. You can reduce the occurrences of bugs through testing and QA analysis during development, but if you do program development for a while, you will almost certainly have to find the bugs and errors in your own or somebody else's code.

Debugging Guidelines

Even though every bug is different, and there could be many fixes for any given bug, the process of finding and fixing bugs can be defined. Over the past few years of debugging both my own and other programmers' code, I have developed several guidelines for determining the cause of a problem. These guidelines can be applied to development in any programming language, not just PL/SQL.

Find the Place Where the Error Occurs

Obvious though it may seem, finding the place where the error occurs is crucial to fixing coding problems. If you have a large, complicated program that simply fails, the first step is to determine exactly where the failure is occurring. This is not necessarily an easy task, depending on the complexity of the code. The easiest way to find the source of an error is to trace the program as it runs, examining the values of the data structures to determine what went wrong.

Define Exactly What Is Wrong

Once you know where the problem happens, you need to define exactly what the problem is. Is an Oracle error returned? Does a calculation return the wrong result? Does the wrong data get inserted into the database? In order to fix a bug, it is necessary to know how the bug manifests itself.

Reduce the Program to a Simple Test Case

A good strategy to follow when you don't know where the error is occurring is to reduce the program to a simple test case. Start cutting out parts of the code and rerun the program. If the error still occurs, you know that the section you removed did not cause the error. If the error goes away, examine the section that was removed.

Remember that one area of your code may have the bug, but the problem may manifest itself in another part of the code. For example, a procedure may return an incorrect value, but the returned value is not actually used until later in the main program. The problem here is not the main program (where the error appears to be) but in the procedure. Cutting out the procedure call and replacing it with a direct assignment to the returned value would reveal the source of the problem. We will examine this particular case later in this chapter.

Establish a Testing Environment

Ideally, testing and debugging is not done in a production environment. It is a good idea to maintain a testing environment that duplicates production as much as possible—the same database structure but with less data, for example. This way you can develop and test newer versions of your application without affecting the production version that is already running. If a problem occurs in production, try reproducing the problem in test first. This follows the previous principle of reducing the problem to a smaller test case. A test case may involve more than just the code—PL/SQL is very dependent on the database structure and the contents of the data, and these should be reduced as well.

The Debug Package

PL/SQL is designed primarily for manipulation of data stored in an Oracle database. The structure of the language is based on this use and it performs admirably. For practical purposes, however, we need some additional tools to help write and debug programs.

In the next sections, we will examine in detail different methods of debugging PL/SQL code. Each section focuses on a different problem and uses a different method to isolate the problem following the guidelines just given. Each section will first describe the general debugging method, then give a description of the problem to be solved. We will discuss both nongraphical and graphical debugging techniques. In the course of solving the nongraphical problems, we will develop different versions of a debugging package, **Debug**, which you can use in your own programs. Depending on your environment and needs, the different capabilities of each package will be useful.

Nongraphical Debugging Techniques

Although there are many graphical debuggers available for PL/SQL (we will examine them later in this chapter), there are times where simple text-based debugging is helpful. GUI-based tools are not always available, or may not be able to be set up for complicated PL/SQL runtime environments. The two techniques we will discuss in this chapter—inserting into a test table, and printing to the screen—are simple and require no additional software beyond the capabilities of PL/SQL itself.

Inserting into a Test Table

The simplest method of debugging is to insert the values of local variables into a temporary table as the program is running. When the program has completed, you can query the table to determine the values of the variables. This method requires the least effort to implement and will work regardless of the execution environment, since it simply involves extra INSERT statements.

Problem I

Suppose we want to write a function that will return the average grade for each class, based on the currently registered students. We could write this function as follows:

```
-- Available online as AverageGrade1.sql
CREATE OR REPLACE FUNCTION AverageGrade (
/* Determines the average grade for the class specified. Grades are
   stored in the registered_students table as single characters
   A through E. This function will return the average grade, again,
   as a single letter. If there are no students registered for
   the class, an error is raised. */
p_Department IN VARCHAR2,
p_Course IN NUMBER) RETURN VARCHAR2 AS

  v_AverageGrade VARCHAR2(1);
  v_NumericGrade NUMBER;
  v_NumberStudents NUMBER;

  CURSOR c_Grades IS
    SELECT grade
      FROM registered_students
      WHERE department = p_Department
      AND course = p_Course;
BEGIN
  /* First we need to see how many students there are for
     this class. If there aren't any, we need to raise an error. */
  SELECT COUNT(*)
    INTO v_NumberStudents
    FROM registered_students
    WHERE department = p_Department
      AND course = p_Course;

  IF v_NumberStudents = 0 THEN
    RAISE_APPLICATION_ERROR(-20001, 'No students registered for ' ||
```

```
        p_Department || ' ' || p_Course);
  END IF;

  /* Since grades are stored as letters, we can't use the AVG
     function directly on them. Instead, we can use the DECODE
     function to convert the letter grades to numeric values,
     and take the average of those. */
  SELECT AVG(DECODE(grade, 'A', 5,
                           'B', 4,
                           'C', 3,
                           'D', 2,
                           'E', 1))
    INTO v_NumericGrade
    FROM registered_students
    WHERE department = p_Department
    AND course = p_Course;

  /* v_NumericGrade now contains the average grade, as a number from
     1 to 5. We need to convert this back into a letter. The DECODE
     function can be used here as well. Note that we are selecting
     the result into v_AverageGrade rather than assigning to it,
     because the DECODE function is only legal in a SQL statement. */
  SELECT DECODE(ROUND(v_NumericGrade), 5, 'A',
                                       4, 'B',
                                       3, 'C',
                                       2, 'D',
                                       1, 'E')
    INTO v_AverageGrade
    FROM dual;

  RETURN v_AverageGrade;
END AverageGrade;
```

Suppose the contents of **registered_students** looks like this:

```
SQL> select * from registered_students;
STUDENT_ID DEP    COURSE G
---------- ---    --------- -
     10000 CS        102 A
     10002 CS        102 B
     10003 CS        102 C
     10000 HIS       101 A
     10001 HIS       101 B
     10002 HIS       101 B
     10003 HIS       101 A
     10004 HIS       101 C
     10005 HIS       101 C
```

```
     10006 HIS        101 E
     10007 HIS        101 B
     10008 HIS        101 A
     10009 HIS        101 D
     10010 HIS        101 A
     10008 NUT        307 A
     10010 NUT        307 A
     10009 MUS        410 B
     10006 MUS        410 E
     10011 MUS        410 B
     10000 MUS        410 B
20 rows selected.
```

NOTE
*registered_students is populated with these 20 rows
by the **relTables.sql** script, available online. For more
information on **relTables.sql**, see Chapter 1.*

Four classes have students registered in them: Computer Science 102, History 101, Nutrition 307, and Music 410. So we can call **AverageGrade** with these four classes. Any other classes should raise the error "No students registered." A sample SQL*Plus output is shown here:

```
-- Available online as callAG.sql
SQL> VARIABLE v_AveGrade VARCHAR2(1)
SQL> exec :v_AveGrade := AverageGrade('HIS', 101)
PL/SQL procedure successfully completed.

SQL> print v_AveGrade
V_AVEGRADE
-------------------------------
B

SQL> exec :v_AveGrade := AverageGrade('NUT', 307)
PL/SQL procedure successfully completed.

SQL> print v_AveGrade
V_AVEGRADE
-------------------------------
A

SQL> exec :v_AveGrade := AverageGrade('MUS', 410)
PL/SQL procedure successfully completed.

SQL> print v_AveGrade
```

```
V_AVEGRADE
-------------------------------
C

SQL> exec :v_AveGrade := AverageGrade('CS', 102)
begin :v_AveGrade := AverageGrade('CS', 102); end;
*
ERROR at line 1:
ORA-20001: No students registered for CS 102
ORA-06512: at "EXAMPLE.AVERAGEGRADE", line 29
```

The last call illustrates the bug. The ORA-20001 error is returned, even though students are registered for Computer Science 102.

PROBLEM 1: THE DEBUG PACKAGE The version of **Debug** that we will use to find this bug is shown next. The **Debug.Debug** procedure is the main procedure in the package. It takes two parameters—a description and a variable. These are concatenated and inserted into the **debug_table** table. The **Debug.Reset** procedure should be called at the start of the program to initialize the table and the internal line counter (it is also called by the package initialization code). The line counter is necessary to ensure that the rows in **debug_table** will be selected in the order in which they were inserted.

```
-- Available online as Debug1.sql
CREATE OR REPLACE PACKAGE Debug AS
   /* First version of the debug package. This package works
      by inserting into the debug_table table. In order to see
      the output, select from debug_table in SQL*Plus with:
   SELECT debug_str FROM debug_table ORDER BY linecount; */

   /* This is the main debug procedure. p_Description will be
      concatenated with p_Value, and inserted into debug_table. */
   PROCEDURE Debug(p_Description IN VARCHAR2, p_Value IN VARCHAR2);

   /* Resets the Debug environment. Reset is called when the
      package is instantiated for the first time, and should be
      called to delete the contents of debug_table for a new
      session. */
   PROCEDURE Reset;
END Debug;

CREATE OR REPLACE PACKAGE BODY Debug AS
   /* v_LineCount is used to order the rows in debug_table. */
   v_LineCount NUMBER;

   PROCEDURE Debug(p_Description IN VARCHAR2, p_Value IN VARCHAR2) IS
```

```
BEGIN
  INSERT INTO debug_table (linecount, debug_str)
    VALUES (v_LineCount, p_Description || ': ' || p_Value);
  COMMIT;
  v_LineCount := v_LineCount + 1;
END Debug;

PROCEDURE Reset IS
BEGIN
  v_LineCount := 1;
  DELETE FROM debug_table;
END Reset;

BEGIN /* Package initialization code */
  Reset;
END Debug;
```

NOTE
*The **debug_table** table is created by **relTables.sql**
with the following:*

```
CREATE TABLE debug_table (
  linecount   NUMBER PRIMARY KEY,
  debug_str   VARCHAR2(200));
```

PROBLEM 1: USING THE DEBUG PACKAGE   In order to determine the
problem with **AverageGrade**, we need to look at the value of the variables used by
the procedure. We do this by adding debugging statements in the code. With this
version of **Debug**, we need to call **Debug.Reset** at the start of **AverageGrade** and
Debug.Debug whenever we want to look at a variable. The modified version is
given next. Some of the comments have been removed for brevity.

```
-- Available online as AverageGrade2.sql
CREATE OR REPLACE FUNCTION AverageGrade (
  p_Department IN VARCHAR2,
  p_Course IN NUMBER) RETURN VARCHAR2 AS

  v_AverageGrade VARCHAR2(1);
  v_NumericGrade NUMBER;
  v_NumberStudents NUMBER;

  CURSOR c_Grades IS
    SELECT grade
      FROM registered_students
      WHERE department = p_Department
      AND course = p_Course;
```

```
BEGIN
  Debug.Reset;
  Debug.Debug('p_Department', p_Department);
  Debug.Debug('p_Course', p_Course);

  /* First we need to see how many students there are for
     this class. If there aren't any, we need to raise an
     error. */
  SELECT COUNT(*)
    INTO v_NumberStudents
    FROM registered_students
    WHERE department = p_Department
    AND course = p_Course;

  Debug.Debug('After select, v_NumberStudents', v_NumberStudents);

  IF v_NumberStudents = 0 THEN
    RAISE_APPLICATION_ERROR(-20001, 'No students registered for ' ||
      p_Department || ' ' || p_Course);
  END IF;

  SELECT AVG(DECODE(grade, 'A', 5,
                           'B', 4,
                           'C', 3,
                           'D', 2,
                           'E', 1))
    INTO v_NumericGrade
    FROM registered_students
    WHERE department = p_Department
      AND course = p_Course;

  SELECT DECODE(ROUND(v_NumericGrade), 5, 'A',
                                       4, 'B',
                                       3, 'C',
                                       2, 'D',
                                       1, 'E')
    INTO v_AverageGrade
    FROM dual;

  RETURN v_AverageGrade;
END AverageGrade;
```

Now we can call **AverageGrade** again and select from the **debug_table** afterwards to see the results:

```
SQL> EXEC :v_AveGrade := AverageGrade('CS', 102)
begin :v_AveGrade := AverageGrade('CS', 102); end;
```

```
     *
ERROR at line 1:
ORA-20001: No students registered for CS 102
ORA-06512: at "EXAMPLE.AVERAGEGRADE", line 25
ORA-06512: at line 1

SQL> SELECT debug_str FROM debug_table ORDER BY linecount;
DEBUG_STR
----------------------------------------------------------
p_Department: CS
p_Course: 102
After select, v_NumberStudents: 0
```

We have verified that **v_NumberStudents** is in fact 0, which explains why we are getting the ORA-20001 error. This narrows the problem down to the SELECT statement, which isn't matching any rows. We therefore need to examine the WHERE clause of this statement in more detail:

```
SELECT COUNT(*)
    INTO v_NumberStudents
    FROM registered_students
    WHERE department = p_Department
    AND course = p_Course;
```

The debug output seems to show the correct values for **p_Department** and **p_Course**, but there could be trailing white space after each line, so this output may be deceiving. Let's change the calls to **Debug.Debug** to put quotes around **p_Department** and **p_Course**. This will reveal any leading or trailing spaces.

```
-- Available online as AverageGrade3.sql
CREATE OR REPLACE FUNCTION AverageGrade
   ...
BEGIN
  Debug.Reset;
  Debug.Debug('p_Department', '''' || p_Department || '''');
  Debug.Debug('p_Course', '''' || p_Course || '''');

  /* First we need to see how many students there are for
     this class. If there aren't any, we need to raise an error. */
  SELECT COUNT(*)
    INTO v_NumberStudents
    FROM registered_students
    WHERE department = p_Department
      AND course = p_Course;

  Debug.Debug('After select, v_NumberStudents', v_NumberStudents);
  ...
```

Now when we run **AverageGrade** and query **debug_table**, we get the following result:

```
SQL> EXEC :v_AveGrade := AverageGrade('CS', 102)
begin :v_AveGrade := AverageGrade('CS', 102); end;
  *
ERROR at line 1:
ORA-20001: No students registered for CS 102
ORA-06512: at "EXAMPLE.AVERAGEGRADE", line 25
ORA-06512: at line 1

SQL> SELECT debug_str FROM debug_table ORDER BY linecount;
DEBUG_STR
------------------------------------------------------------
p_Department: 'CS'
p_Course: '102'
After select, v_NumberStudents: 0
```

We can see that **p_Department** doesn't have a trailing space. This is the problem. The **department** column of **registered_students** is defined as CHAR(3), but **p_Department** is a VARCHAR2. This means that the database column contains 'CS ' (with a trailing space), which explains why the SELECT statement doesn't return any rows. Thus **v_NumberStudents** is assigned 0.

TIP

The built-in function DUMP can be used to examine the exact contents of a database column. For example, we can determine the contents of the **department** *column in* **registered_students** *with*

```
SQL> SELECT DISTINCT DUMP(department)
  2     FROM registered_students
  3     WHERE department = 'CS';

DUMP(DEPARTMENT)
--------------------------------------
Typ=96 Len=3: 67,83,32
```

The type is 96, indicating CHAR, and the last byte in the column is 32, which is the ASCII code for a space (the actual byte value will vary depending on the database character set). This tells us that the column is blank-padded. The datatype codes are described in the Oracle SQL Reference.

One fix for this problem is to change the type of **p_Department** to CHAR:

```
CREATE OR REPLACE FUNCTION AverageGrade (
    p_Department IN CHAR,
    p_Course IN NUMBER) RETURN VARCHAR2 AS
    ...
BEGIN
    ...
END AverageGrade;
```

After doing this, we get the correct result for **AverageGrade**:

```
SQL> EXEC :v_AveGrade := AverageGrade('CS', 102)
PL/SQL procedure successfully completed.

SQL> print v_AveGrade
V_AVEGRADE
-------------------------------
B
```

This works because both values in the WHERE clause are now CHAR and blank-padded character comparison semantics are used, resulting in the match.

TIP
*Had we used the %TYPE attribute in the function declaration, the type of **p_Department** would have been correct. This is another reason why using %TYPE is advisable. Also, since the return value of **AverageGrade** is a character string of length 1, and It will always be 1, we can use the fixed-length type CHAR for the RETURN clause as well. The declaration of **AverageGrade** would therefore look like this:*

```
-- Available online as part of AverageGrade4.sql
CREATE OR REPLACE FUNCTION AverageGrade (
    p_Department IN registered_students.department%TYPE,
    p_Course IN registered_students.course%TYPE) RETURN CHAR AS

    v_AverageGrade CHAR(1);
    v_NumericGrade NUMBER;
    v_NumberStudents NUMBER;
    ...
BEGIN
    ...
END AverageGrade;
```

PROBLEM I: COMMENTS   This version of **Debug** is very simple. All it does is insert into **debug_table**, but we were still able to use it to find the bug in **AverageGrade**. There are some advantages to this technique:

■   Since **Debug** doesn't rely on anything but SQL, it can be used from any environment. The SELECT statement that shows the output can be run from SQL*Plus or another tool.

■   **Debug** is simple, so it doesn't add too much overhead to the procedure being debugged.

There are also disadvantages:

■   **AverageGrade** raised an exception in the preceding example. This causes any SQL done by the program to be rolled back. Thus the COMMIT in **Debug.Debug** is required to ensure that the inserts into **debug_table** are not rolled back as well. This can cause a problem if other work in the procedure being debugged shouldn't be committed. This commit will also invalidate any SELECT FOR UPDATE cursors that may be open. (With Oracle8*i*, **Debug.Debug** could be written as an autonomous transaction, which would solve this problem. See Chapter 11 for more details.)

■   As currently written, **Debug** won't work properly if more than one session is using it simultaneously. The SELECT statement will return the results from both sessions. This could be fixed by modifying both the **Debug** package and **debug_table** to include a column uniquely identifying the session.

We will resolve the disadvantages of this version of **Debug** by using the DBMS_OUTPUT package, described in the upcoming section.

Printing to the Screen

The first version of **Debug**, which we saw in the last section, essentially implemented a limited version of I/O (to a database table, not to the screen directly). PL/SQL has no input/output capability built into the language. This was an intentional design decision, since the ability to print out the values of variables and data structures is not required to manipulate data stored in the database. It is, however, a very useful debugging tool. As a result, output capability was added starting with PL/SQL 2.0 through the built-in package DBMS_OUTPUT. We will use DBMS_OUTPUT in the second version of **Debug**, described in this section.

TIP
*PL/SQL still doesn't have input capability built into the language, but SQL*Plus substitution variables (as we saw in Chapter 2) can be used to overcome this to a limited extent. PL/SQL 2.3 and above has a package UTL_FILE, which is used to read from and write to operating system files. Chapter 7 will examine UTL_FILE in detail, including a version of **Debug** that writes the output to a file.*

The DBMS_OUTPUT Package

Before we discuss the debugging problem for this section, we need to examine DBMS_OUTPUT in some detail. This package, like other DBMS packages, is owned by the Oracle user SYS. The script that creates DBMS_OUTPUT grants the EXECUTE permission on the package to PUBLIC and creates a public synonym for it. This means that any Oracle user can call the routines in DBMS_OUTPUT without having to prefix the package name with SYS.

How does DBMS_OUTPUT work? Two basic operations, GET and PUT, are implemented through procedures in the package. A PUT operation takes its argument and places it into an internal buffer for storage. A GET operation reads from this buffer and returns the contents as an argument to the procedure. There is also an ENABLE procedure that sets the size of the buffer.

The PUT routines in the package are PUT, PUT_LINE, and NEW_LINE. The GET routines are GET_LINE and GET_LINES. ENABLE and DISABLE control the buffer.

PUT AND PUT_LINE   The syntax for the PUT and PUT_LINE calls is

```
PROCEDURE PUT(a VARCHAR2);
PROCEDURE PUT(a NUMBER);
PROCEDURE PUT(a DATE);

PROCEDURE PUT_LINE(a VARCHAR2);
PROCEDURE PUT_LINE(a NUMBER);
PROCEDURE PUT_LINE(a DATE);
```

where *a* is the argument to be placed in the buffer. Note that these procedures are overloaded by the type of the parameter (overloading is discussed in Chapter 4). Because of the three different versions of PUT and PUT_LINE, the buffer can contain values of types VARCHAR2, NUMBER, and DATE. They are stored in the buffer in their original format.

The buffer is organized into lines, each of which can have a maximum of 255 bytes. PUT_LINE appends a newline character after its argument, signaling the end of a line. PUT does not. PUT_LINE is equivalent to calling PUT and then calling NEW_LINE.

NEW_LINE   The syntax for the NEW_LINE call is

    PROCEDURE NEW_LINE;

NEW_LINE puts a newline character into the buffer, signaling the end of a line. There is no limit to the number of lines in the buffer. The total size of the buffer is limited to the value specified in ENABLE, however.

GET_LINE   The syntax for GET_LINE is

    PROCEDURE GET_LINE(*line* OUT VARCHAR2, *status* OUT INTEGER);

where *line* is a character string that will contain one line of the buffer, and *status* indicates whether the line was retrieved successfully. The maximum length of a line is 255 bytes. If the line was retrieved, *status* will be 0; if there are no more lines in the buffer, it will be 1.

NOTE
Although the maximum size of a buffer line is 255 bytes, the output variable line can be more than 255 characters. The buffer line can consist of DATE values, for example. These take up 7 bytes of storage in the buffer but are usually converted to character strings with length greater than 7.

GET_LINES   The GET_LINES procedure has an argument that is an index-by table. The table type and procedure syntax are

    TYPE CHARARR IS TABLE OF VARCHAR2(255)
       INDEX BY BINARY_INTEGER;
    PROCEDURE GET_LINES(*lines* OUT CHARARR,
                        numlines IN OUT INTEGER);

where *lines* is an index-by table that will contain multiple lines from the buffer, and *numlines* indicates how many lines are requested. On input to GET_LINES, *numlines* specifies the requested number of lines. On output, *numlines* will contain the actual number of lines returned, which will be less than or equal to the number requested. GET_LINES is designed to replace multiple calls to GET_LINE.

The CHARARR type is also defined in the DBMS_OUTPUT package. Therefore, if you want to call GET_LINES explicitly in your code, you need to declare a variable of type DBMS_OUTPUT.CHARARR. For example,

```
-- Available online as part of DBMSOutput.sql
DECLARE
  /* Demonstrates using PUT_LINE and GET_LINE. */
  v_Data       DBMS_OUTPUT.CHARARR;
  v_NumLines   NUMBER;
BEGIN
  -- Enable the buffer first.
  DBMS_OUTPUT.ENABLE(1000000);

  -- Put some data in the buffer first, so GET_LINES will
  -- retrieve something.
  DBMS_OUTPUT.PUT_LINE('Line One');
  DBMS_OUTPUT.PUT_LINE('Line Two');
  DBMS_OUTPUT.PUT_LINE('Line Three');

  -- Set the maximum number of lines that we want to retrieve.
  v_NumLines := 3;

  /* Get the contents of the buffer back. Note that v_Data is
     declared of type DBMS_OUTPUT.CHARARR, so that it matches
     the declaration of DBMS_OUTPUT.GET_LINES. */
  DBMS_OUTPUT.GET_LINES(v_Data, v_NumLines);

  /* Loop through the returned buffer, and insert the contents
     into temp_table. */
  FOR v_Counter IN 1..v_NumLines LOOP
    INSERT INTO temp_table (char_col)
      VALUES (v_Data(v_Counter));
  END LOOP;
END;
```

NOTE
GET_LINE and GET_LINES retrieve from the buffer and return character strings only. When a GET operation is performed, the contents of the buffer will be converted to a character string according to the default datatype conversion rules. If you want to specify a format for the conversion, use an explicit TO_CHAR call on the PUT, rather than the GET.

ENABLE AND DISABLE   The syntax for the ENABLE and DISABLE calls is

PROCEDURE ENABLE (*buffer_size* IN INTEGER DEFAULT 20000);

PROCEDURE DISABLE;

where *buffer_size* is the initial size of the internal buffer, in bytes. The default size is 20,000 bytes, and the maximum size is 1,000,000 bytes. Later, arguments to PUT or PUT_LINE will be placed in this buffer. They are stored in their internal format, taking up as much space in the buffer as their structure dictates. If DISABLE is called, the contents of the buffer are purged, and subsequent calls to PUT and PUT_LINE have no effect.

Using DBMS_OUTPUT

The DBMS_OUTPUT package itself does not contain any mechanism for printing. Essentially, it simply implements a first in, first out data structure. Having said that, how can we use DBMS_OUTPUT for printing? SQL*Plus and Server Manager both have an option known as SERVEROUTPUT. In addition, many third-party products (including the graphical development and debugging tools) have an option that allows the display of DBMS_OUTPUT data. With this option on, SQL*Plus will automatically call DBMS_OUTPUT.GET_LINES when a PL/SQL block concludes and print the results, if any, to the screen. This is illustrated in Figure 3-1.

The SQL*Plus command SET SERVEROUTPUT ON implicitly calls DBMS_OUTPUT.ENABLE, which sets up the internal buffer. Optionally, you can specify a size with

SET SERVEROUTPUT ON SIZE *buffer_size*

where *buffer_size* will be used as the initial size of the buffer (the argument to DBMS_OUTPUT.ENABLE). With SERVEROUTPUT on, SQL*Plus will call DBMS_OUTPUT.GET_LINES *after* the PL/SQL block has completed. This means that the output will be echoed to the screen when the block has finished and *not* during execution of the block. This is normally not a problem when DBMS_OUTPUT is used for debugging.

CAUTION
*DBMS_OUTPUT is designed to be used primarily for debugging. It is not meant for general reporting. If you need to customize the output from your queries, it is better to use tools such as Oracle Reports rather than DBMS_OUTPUT and SQL*Plus.*

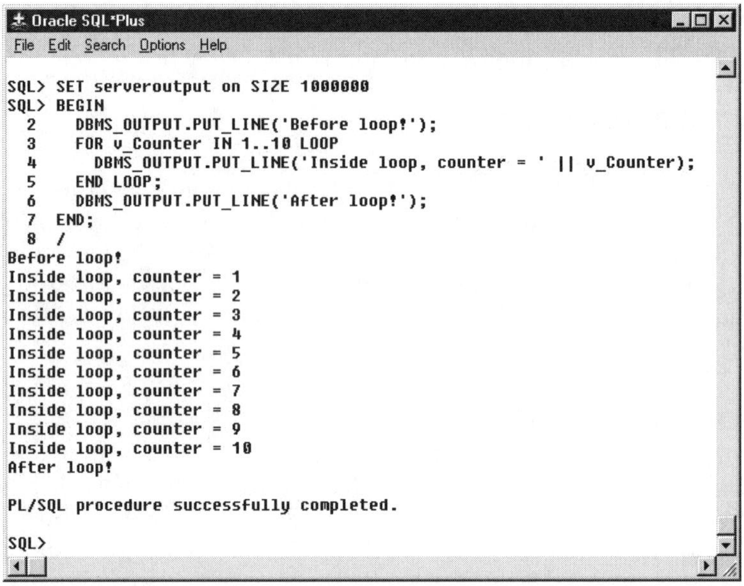

FIGURE 3-1. *Using SERVEROUTPUT and PUT_LINE*

The internal buffer does have a maximum size (specified in DBMS_OUTPUT.ENABLE), and each line has a maximum length of 255 bytes. As a result, calls to DBMS_OUTPUT.PUT, DBMS_OUTPUT.PUT_LINE, and DBMS_OUTPUT.NEW_LINE can raise either

```
ORA-20000: ORU-10027: buffer overflow,
          limit of <buf_limit> bytes.
```

or

```
ORA-20000: ORU-10028: line length overflow,
          limit of 255 bytes per line.
```

The message depends on which limit is exceeded.

TIP

It is a good idea always to specify a buffer length in the SET SERVEROUTPUT ON command. Although the default value for DBMS_OUTPUT.ENABLE is 20,000 bytes, SQL*Plus will call DBMS_OUTPUT.ENABLE with a size of 2,000 if you don't specify an explicit size in SET SERVEROUTPUT ON.

Problem 2

The **students** table has a column for the current number of credits for which the student is registered, and **registered_students** contains information about which students are in which classes. If a student changes his or her registration (and hence the information in **registered_students** changes), we need to update the **current_credits** column in **students**. We can do this by writing the **CountCredits** function, which will count the total credits for which a student is registered, as follows:

```
-- Available online as CountCredits1.sql
CREATE OR REPLACE FUNCTION CountCredits (
  /* Returns the number of credits for which the student
     identified by p_StudentID is currently registered */
  p_StudentID IN students.ID%TYPE)
  RETURN NUMBER AS

  v_TotalCredits NUMBER;   -- Total number of credits
  v_CourseCredits NUMBER; -- Credits for one course
  CURSOR c_RegisteredCourses IS
    SELECT department, course
      FROM registered_students
      WHERE student_id = p_StudentID;
BEGIN
  FOR v_CourseRec IN c_RegisteredCourses LOOP
    -- Determine the credits for this class.
    SELECT num_credits
      INTO v_CourseCredits
      FROM classes
      WHERE department = v_CourseRec.department
      AND course = v_CourseRec.course;
```

```
    -- Add it to the total so far.
    v_TotalCredits := v_TotalCredits + v_CourseCredits;
  END LOOP;

  RETURN v_TotalCredits;
END CountCredits;
```

Since **CountCredits** doesn't modify any database or package state, we can call it directly from a SQL statement (with PL/SQL 2.1 or higher). (Calling functions from SQL statements is discussed in Chapter 5.) We can therefore determine the current number of credits for all students by selecting from the **students** table. We get the following result:

```
SQL> SELECT ID, CountCredits(ID) "Total Credits"
  2    FROM students;
       ID Total Credits
--------- -------------
    10000
    10001
    10002
    10003
    10004
    10005
    10006
    10007
    10008
    10009
    10010
    10011
12 rows selected.
```

There is no output for **CurrentCredits**, which means that the function is returning NULL. This is not the correct result.

PROBLEM 2: THE DEBUG PACKAGE   We will use the DBMS_OUTPUT package to find the bug in **CountCredits**. To do this, we can use the following version of **Debug**. It has the same interface as the first version of **Debug**, which we saw in the previous section, so we only have to change the package body.

```
-- Available online as Debug2.sql
CREATE OR REPLACE PACKAGE BODY Debug AS
  PROCEDURE Debug(p_Description IN VARCHAR2,
                  p_Value IN VARCHAR2) IS
  BEGIN
    DBMS_OUTPUT.PUT_LINE(p_Description || ': ' || p_Value);
```

```
    END Debug;

    PROCEDURE Reset IS
    BEGIN
      /* Disable the buffer first, then enable it with the
       * maximum size. Since DISABLE purges the buffer, this
       * ensures that we will have a fresh buffer whenever
       * Reset is called.
       */
      DBMS_OUTPUT.DISABLE;
      DBMS_OUTPUT.ENABLE(1000000);
    END Reset;

BEGIN /* Package initialization code */
  Reset;
END Debug;
```

We no longer use **debug_table**; instead, we use DBMS_OUTPUT. As
a result, this version of **Debug** will work only in tools that automatically call
DBMS_OUTPUT.GET_LINES and print the buffer contents (such as SQL*Plus).
SERVEROUTPUT also needs to be on before using **Debug**.

PROBLEM 2: USING THE DEBUG PACKAGE   CountCredits is returning a
NULL result. Let's verify this, as well as what value we are adding to **v_TotalCredits**
in the loop. We do this by adding **Debug** calls:

```
-- Available online as CountCredits2.sql
CREATE OR REPLACE FUNCTION CountCredits (
  /* Returns the number of credits for which the student
     identified by p_StudentID is currently registered */
  p_StudentID IN students.ID%TYPE)
  RETURN NUMBER AS

  v_TotalCredits NUMBER;   -- Total number of credits
  v_CourseCredits NUMBER; -- Credits for one course
  CURSOR c_RegisteredCourses IS
    SELECT department, course
      FROM registered_students
      WHERE student_id = p_StudentID;
BEGIN
  Debug.Reset;
  FOR v_CourseRec IN c_RegisteredCourses LOOP
    -- Determine the credits for this class.
    SELECT num_credits
      INTO v_CourseCredits
      FROM classes
```

```
      WHERE department = v_CourseRec.department
      AND course = v_CourseRec.course;

    Debug.Debug('Inside loop, v_CourseCredits', v_CourseCredits);
    -- Add it to the total so far.
    v_TotalCredits := v_TotalCredits + v_CourseCredits;
  END LOOP;

    Debug.Debug('After loop, returning', v_TotalCredits);
    RETURN v_TotalCredits;
END CountCredits;
```

We now get the following output:

```
SQL> VARIABLE v_Total NUMBER
SQL> SET SERVEROUTPUT ON
SQL> exec :v_Total := CountCredits(10006);
Inside loop, v_CourseCredits: 4
Inside loop, v_CourseCredits: 3
After loop, returning:
PL/SQL procedure successfully completed.

SQL> print v_Total
  V_TOTAL
---------

SQL>
```

NOTE
*We are testing **CountCredits** with a SQL*Plus
bind variable rather than selecting the value of the
function from the **students** table. This is because
CountCredits now calls DBMS_OUTPUT, which is
not considered to be a pure function. If we were to
use **CountCredits** inside a SQL statement, we would
get the "ORA-6571: Function does not guarantee
not to update database" error. (Oracle8*i* removes
this restriction.) See Chapter 5 for more information
on this error and calling stored functions from SQL
statements.*

Based on this **Debug** output, it looks like the number of credits calculated for
each class is correct: the loop was executed twice, with four and three credits
returned each time. But clearly, this isn't being added to the total properly. Let's
add some more debugging statements:

```
-- Available online as CountCredits3.sql
CREATE OR REPLACE FUNCTION CountCredits (
  /* Returns the number of credits for which the student
     identified by p_StudentID is currently registered */
  p_StudentID IN students.ID%TYPE)
  RETURN NUMBER AS

  v_TotalCredits NUMBER;   -- Total number of credits
  v_CourseCredits NUMBER; -- Credits for one course
  CURSOR c_RegisteredCourses IS
    SELECT department, course
      FROM registered_students
      WHERE student_id = p_StudentID;
BEGIN
  Debug.Reset;
  Debug.Debug('Before loop, v_TotalCredits', v_TotalCredits);
  FOR v_CourseRec IN c_RegisteredCourses LOOP
    -- Determine the credits for this class.
    SELECT num_credits
      INTO v_CourseCredits
      FROM classes
      WHERE department = v_CourseRec.department
      AND course = v_CourseRec.course;

    Debug.Debug('Inside loop, v_CourseCredits', v_CourseCredits);
    -- Add it to the total so far.
    v_TotalCredits := v_TotalCredits + v_CourseCredits;
    Debug.Debug('Inside loop, v_TotalCredits', v_TotalCredits);
  END LOOP;

  Debug.Debug('After loop, returning', v_TotalCredits);
  RETURN v_TotalCredits;
END CountCredits;
```

The output from this latest version of **CountCredits** is

```
SQL> EXEC :v_Total := CountCredits(10006);
Before loop, v_TotalCredits:
Inside loop, v_CourseCredits: 4
Inside loop, v_TotalCredits:
Inside loop, v_CourseCredits: 3
Inside loop, v_TotalCredits:
After loop, returning:
PL/SQL procedure successfully completed.
```

We can see the problem from this output. Notice that **v_TotalCredits** is NULL before the loop starts and remains NULL during the loop. This is because we didn't initialize **v_TotalCredits** in the declaration. We can fix this with the final version of **CountCredits**, which also has the debugging statements removed:

```
-- Available online as CountCredits4.sql
CREATE OR REPLACE FUNCTION CountCredits (
  /* Returns the number of credits for which the student
     identified by p_StudentID is currently registered */
  p_StudentID IN students.ID%TYPE)
  RETURN NUMBER AS

v_TotalCredits NUMBER := 0;   -- Total number of credits
v_CourseCredits NUMBER;       -- Credits for one course
  CURSOR c_RegisteredCourses IS
    SELECT department, course
      FROM registered_students
      WHERE student_id = p_StudentID;
BEGIN
  FOR v_CourseRec IN c_RegisteredCourses LOOP
    -- Determine the credits for this class.
    SELECT num_credits
      INTO v_CourseCredits
      FROM classes
      WHERE department = v_CourseRec.department
      AND course = v_CourseRec.course;

    -- Add it to the total so far.
    v_TotalCredits := v_TotalCredits + v_CourseCredits;
  END LOOP;

  RETURN v_TotalCredits;
END CountCredits;
```

The output from this is as follows:

```
SQL> EXEC :v_Total := CountCredits(10006);
PL/SQL procedure successfully completed.
SQL> print v_Total
  V_TOTAL
---------
        7
SQL> SELECT ID, CountCredits(ID) "Total Credits"
  2    FROM students;
       ID Total Credits
--------- -------------
    10000            11
    10001             4
```

```
10002            8
10003            8
10004            4
10005            4
10006            7
10007            4
10008            8
10009            7
10010            8
10011            3
12 rows selected.
```

We can see that **CountCredits** is working properly now, both for the single student example and for the entire table. If a variable is not initialized when it is declared, it is assigned the nonvalue NULL. The NULL value is maintained throughout the addition operation, according to the rules for evaluating NULL expressions.

PROBLEM 2: COMMENTS   This version of **Debug** has different features from the first version. Namely, we have eliminated the dependency on **debug_table**. This gives us several advantages:

- There is no worry about multiple database sessions interfering with each other, since each session will have its own DBMS_OUTPUT internal buffer.

- We no longer have to issue a COMMIT inside **Debug.Debug**.

- As long as SERVEROUTPUT is on, no additional SELECT statement is necessary to see the output. Also, we can turn off debugging by simply setting SERVEROUTPUT off. If SERVEROUTPUT is off, the debugging information will still be logged to the DBMS_OUTPUT buffer, but will not be printed to the screen.

On the other hand, there are still some things to be aware of with this version:

- If we are not using a tool like SQL*Plus or Server Manager, the debugging output will not be printed to the screen automatically. The package can still be used from other PL/SQL execution environments (such as Pro*C or Oracle Forms), but you may have to call DBMS_OUTPUT.GET_LINE or DBMS_OUTPUT.GET_LINES explicitly and display the results yourself.

- The amount of debugging output is limited by the size of the DBMS_OUTPUT buffer. This affects both the size of each line and the total size of the buffer. If you find that there is too much output and the buffer is not large enough, the first version of **Debug** may be a better option.

PL/SQL Debuggers

As of this writing, there are several PL/SQL development tools available that include an integrated debugger. A tool like this is very valuable, since it allows you to step through PL/SQL code line by line and examine the values of variables as the program executes. You can also set breakpoints at various points, as well as watch the value of specific variables.

General Comments About PL/SQL Debuggers

Using graphical debugging tools has several advantages over the nongraphical techniques that we examined initially, namely,

■ We don't need to add any debugging code to the application; we simply run it in a controlled debugging environment.

■ Since the code doesn't have to be changed, recompiled, and then run to see different variables, it is more convenient to debug.

■ All of the tools provide an integrated development environment, with browsing and editing features.

However, there are some situations where a graphical debugging environment may not be effective. For example, the GUI tools are not supported on all platforms. In these cases, the nongraphical techniques, or the tracing and profiling tools that we will examine later in this chapter, may be more effective.

In the next sections, we will examine the debugging features of the GUI tools that we first saw in Chapter 2 and are also included on the CD. The debugging features of each product are summarized in Table 3-1. For more information on any of the tools, see the online documentation.

Problem 3

Consider the following procedure:

```
-- Available online as CreditLoop1.sql
CREATE OR REPLACE PROCEDURE CreditLoop AS
   /* Inserts the student ID numbers and their current credit
      values into temp_table. */
   v_StudentID students.ID%TYPE;
   v_Credits   students.current_credits%TYPE;
   CURSOR c_Students IS
     SELECT ID
```

```
      FROM students;
BEGIN
  OPEN c_Students;
  LOOP
    FETCH c_Students INTO v_StudentID;
    v_Credits := CountCredits(v_StudentID);
    INSERT INTO temp_table (num_col, char_col)
      VALUES (v_StudentID, 'Credits = ' || TO_CHAR(v_Credits));
    EXIT WHEN c_Students%NOTFOUND;
  END LOOP;
  CLOSE c_Students;
END CreditLoop;
```

Feature	Rapid SQL	XPEDITER/ SQL	SQL Navigator	TOAD	SQL-Programmer
Animate	No	Yes	No	No	No
Watchpoints	Yes	Yes	Yes	Yes	Yes
Automatically show current variables	Yes	Yes	Yes	No	No
Stop on exceptions	No	Yes	No	Yes	Yes
Change values of variables during run	Yes, watchpoints only	Yes	Yes	No	Yes
Server-side install necessary to debug	No	Yes	Yes	No	No
Debug anonymous blocks	No	Yes	No	No	No
Attach to external process	No	Yes (through DBPartner)	Yes	No	No

TABLE 3-1. *PL/SQL Debugger Comparison*

CreditLoop simply records the number of credits for each student in **temp_table**. It calls **CountCredits** (which we saw in the previous section) to determine the total number of credits per student. When running **CreditLoop** and querying **temp_table** in SQL*Plus, we get

```
-- Available online as callCL.sql
SQL> EXEC CreditLoop;
PL/SQL procedure successfully completed.
SQL> SELECT *
  2    FROM temp_table
  3    ORDER BY num_col;

  NUM_COL CHAR_COL
--------- ----------------
    10000 Credits = 11
    10001 Credits = 4
    10002 Credits = 8
    10003 Credits = 8
    10004 Credits = 4
    10005 Credits = 4
    10006 Credits = 7
    10007 Credits = 4
    10008 Credits = 8
    10009 Credits = 7
    10010 Credits = 8
    10011 Credits = 3
    10011 Credits = 3
13 rows selected.
```

The problem is that the last two rows are inserted twice—there are two rows for student ID 10011 and one row for all the others.

Problem 3: Debugging with Rapid SQL

The first step in debugging a stored procedure in Rapid SQL is to open it in a PL/SQL editor window. We can then debug it by either selecting Debug | Start Debugging, or by clicking on the Debug PL/SQL icon, as shown in Figure 3-2. Doing this will cause Rapid SQL to initialize a debugging session and set up the environment as shown in Figure 3-3.

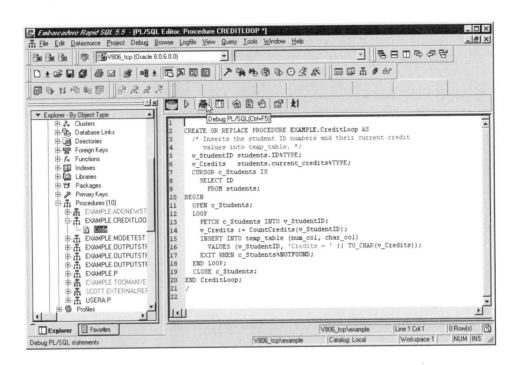

FIGURE 3-2. *Preparing to debug* **CreditLoop**

A debugging session includes four extra windows, which are automatically opened and docked by Rapid SQL at the bottom of the screen:

- **The Watch window**, which will show the values of variables in which you are interested, whether or not they are in scope. You can highlight a variable in the editor window, and drag it onto the Watch window to watch it.

- **The Variables window**, which will always show the values of the variables that are currently in scope.

■ **The Call Stack window**, which shows which line is currently executing, as well as the complete PL/SQL call stack at any point.

■ **The Dependency Tree window**, which shows the dependencies of the current object. Figure 3-3 shows that **CreditLoop** depends on **CountCredits**, for example.

In addition, the editing window shows an arrow next to the current line. We can start the procedure by clicking on the Step Into button on the toolbar. At this point, we need to set a breakpoint. We can then run the procedure until this point, and look at the local variables in the Variables window. Breakpoints are set by clicking on the desired line, and then by clicking the Insert or Remove Break button. For **CreditLoop**, we want to break at line 13, right after the FETCH statement, as shown in Figure 3-4. Once the breakpoint is set, we can run the procedure up until the

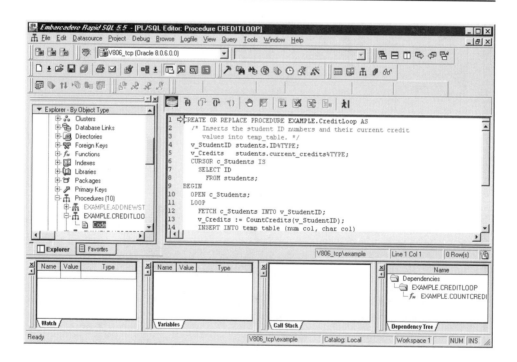

FIGURE 3-3.   *Initial **CreditLoop** debugging session*

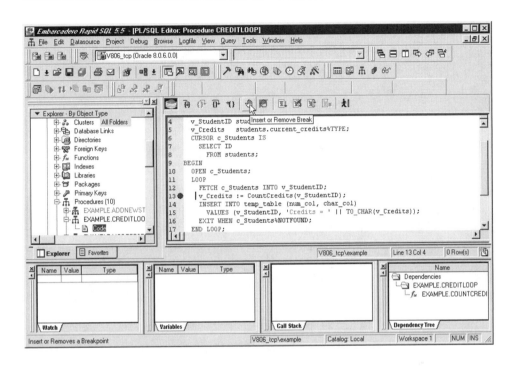

FIGURE 3-4. *Setting a breakpoint*

breakpoint by clicking on the Go button. Figure 3-5 shows the results after stopping at the breakpoint. We have fetched the first row and so **v_StudentID** is 10000, while **v_Credits** is NULL. This is what we expect.

From here, we can continue to step through the code (by clicking on Go) and see **v_StudentID** after each FETCH. As we do this, we can see **v_StudentID** changing, as it should. This continues until the last FETCH, which happens to return student ID 10011. We insert this value into **temp_table** and then loop again. However, the next FETCH doesn't change the value of **v_StudentID**—it is still 10011. Thus, it gets inserted twice. After the second INSERT, the loop exits because **c_Students%NOTFOUND** becomes TRUE. This points out the problem, namely that the EXIT statement should be immediately after the FETCH. We can modify **CreditLoop** in the PL/SQL editor

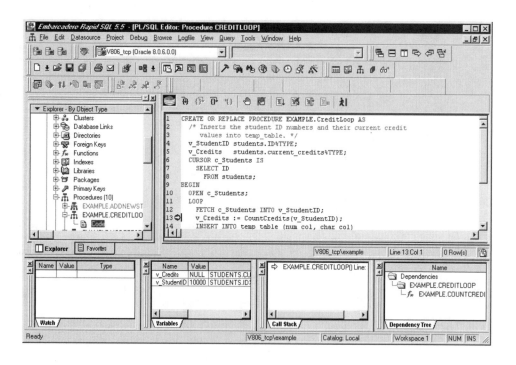

FIGURE 3-5. *Stopped at the breakpoint*

and then test it again to ensure that it behaves properly. The correct version is shown
in Figure 3-6 and is also available online as **CreditLoop2.sql**.

Now that we have fixed the problem, we can test the procedure again from
SQL*Plus. The output is shown here:

```
-- Available online as callCL.sql
SQL> EXEC CreditLoop
PL/SQL procedure successfully completed.

SQL> SELECT * FROM temp_table
  2    ORDER BY num_col;
  NUM_COL CHAR_COL
--------- ------------------------------
```

```
    10000 Credits = 11
    10001 Credits = 4
    10002 Credits = 8
    10003 Credits = 8
    10004 Credits = 4
    10005 Credits = 4
    10006 Credits = 7
    10007 Credits = 4
    10008 Credits = 8
    10009 Credits = 7
    10010 Credits = 8
    10011 Credits = 3
12 rows selected.
```

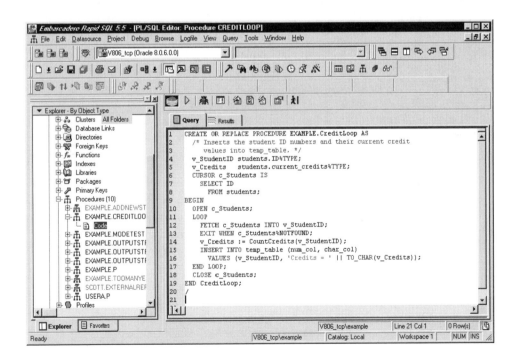

FIGURE 3-6. *Correct version of* ***CreditLoop***

Problem 3: Comments

A cursor fetch loop always executes the FETCH statement until it returns NO_DATA_FOUND (tested with the %NOTFOUND attribute in **CreditLoop**). Once %NOTFOUND returns TRUE, the loop should be exited, as no additional data will have been fetched. The output variable (**v_StudentID** in **CreditLoop**) will contain the values they had in the previous iteration of the loop.

TIP

You can use a cursor FOR loop instead, which will implicitly open the cursor, fetch once each time through the loop, and close the cursor at the end.

Problem 4

If a cursor is stored in a package, it will persist beyond the life of a particular packaged subprogram call. This enables us to write a routine that will fetch a number of rows at a time from the cursor. This is exactly what the **StudentFetch** package is designed to do.

```
-- Available online as StudentFetch1.sql
CREATE OR REPLACE PACKAGE StudentFetch AS
  TYPE t_Students IS TABLE OF students%ROWTYPE
    INDEX BY BINARY_INTEGER;

  -- Opens the cursor for processing.
  PROCEDURE OpenCursor;

  -- Closes the cursor.
  PROCEDURE CloseCursor;

  -- Returns up to p_BatchSize rows in p_Students, and returns
  -- TRUE as long as there are still rows to be fetched.
  FUNCTION FetchRows(p_BatchSize IN NUMBER := 5,
                     p_Students OUT t_Students)
    RETURN BOOLEAN;

  -- Prints p_BatchSize rows from p_Students.
  PROCEDURE PrintRows(p_BatchSize IN NUMBER,
                      p_Students IN t_Students);
END StudentFetch;

CREATE OR REPLACE PACKAGE BODY StudentFetch AS
```

```
  CURSOR c_AllStudents IS
    SELECT *
      FROM students
      ORDER BY ID;

  -- Opens the cursor for processing.
  PROCEDURE OpenCursor IS
  BEGIN
    OPEN c_AllStudents;
  END OpenCursor;

  -- Closes the cursor.
  PROCEDURE CloseCursor IS
  BEGIN
    CLOSE c_AllStudents;
  END CloseCursor;

  -- Returns up to p_BatchSize rows in p_Students, and returns
  -- TRUE as long as there are still rows to be fetched.
  FUNCTION FetchRows(p_BatchSize IN NUMBER := 5,
                     p_Students OUT t_Students)
    RETURN BOOLEAN IS
    v_Finished BOOLEAN := TRUE;
  BEGIN
    FOR v_Count IN 1..p_BatchSize LOOP
      FETCH c_AllStudents INTO p_Students(v_Count);
      IF c_AllStudents%NOTFOUND THEN
        v_Finished := FALSE;
        EXIT;
      END IF;
    END LOOP;
    RETURN v_Finished;
  END FetchRows;

  -- Prints p_BatchSize rows from p_Students.
  PROCEDURE PrintRows(p_BatchSize IN NUMBER,
                      p_Students IN t_Students) IS
  BEGIN
    FOR v_Count IN 1..p_BatchSize LOOP
      DBMS_OUTPUT.PUT('ID: ' || p_Students(v_Count).ID);
      DBMS_OUTPUT.PUT(' Name: ' || p_Students(v_Count).first_name);
      DBMS_OUTPUT.PUT_LINE(' ' || p_Students(v_Count).last_name);
    END LOOP;
  END PrintRows;
END StudentFetch;
```

Each time we call **StudentFetch.FetchRows**, it should return the next batch of rows. The following SQL*Plus session illustrates how it works.

```
-- Available online as callSF1.sql
SQL> DECLARE
  2      v_BatchSize NUMBER := 5;
  3      v_Students StudentFetch.t_Students;
  4  BEGIN
  5      StudentFetch.OpenCursor;
  6      WHILE StudentFetch.FetchRows(v_BatchSize, v_Students) LOOP
  7          StudentFetch.PrintRows(v_BatchSize, v_Students);
  8      END LOOP;
  9      StudentFetch.CloseCursor;
 10  END;
 11  /
ID: 10000 Name: Scott Smith
ID: 10001 Name: Margaret Mason
ID: 10002 Name: Joanne Junebug
ID: 10003 Name: Manish Murgatroid
ID: 10004 Name: Patrick Poll
ID: 10005 Name: Timothy Taller
ID: 10006 Name: Barbara Blues
ID: 10007 Name: David Dinsmore
ID: 10008 Name: Ester Elegant
ID: 10009 Name: Rose Riznit
PL/SQL procedure successfully completed.
```

However, there is a problem—we didn't fetch all of the rows in **students**. We returned 10 rows, but there are actually 12.

Problem 4: Debugging with XPEDITER/SQL

We will use the XPEDITER/SQL debugger to solve this problem. First, we need to load the calling block in a Debugger window. We do this by opening it in a Notepad window, and clicking on the Debug button, as shown in Figure 3-7. The resulting Debugger window is shown in Figure 3-8.

We can now step through the code, until we get to **FetchRows**. Here, we want to set a breakpoint at line 27, to see when **v_Finished** gets set to FALSE. We do this by double-clicking on the line number. The breakpoint is shown in Figure 3-9. We

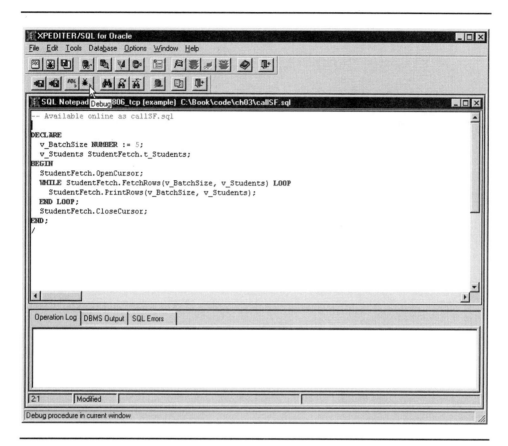

FIGURE 3-7. *Preparing to debug the calling block*

are now ready to run until we get to the breakpoint. Rather than just running, however, we can use the Animate feature of XPEDITER/SQL. This will automatically step through the program line by line until the breakpoint, at an adjustable speed. The situation when we reach the breakpoint is shown in Figure 3-10, after the animation completes.

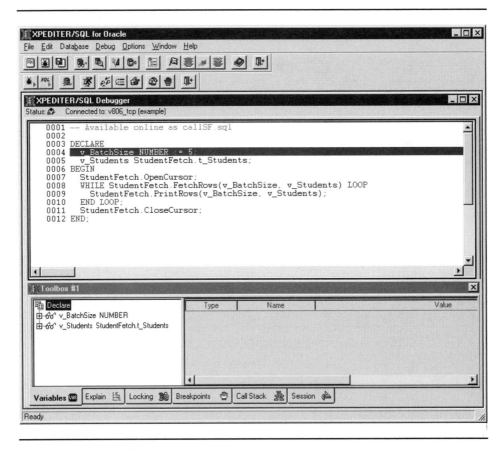

FIGURE 3-8. *Calling block in a Debugger window*

The problem is now clear. We can see from the previous animation, and from the fact that **v_Count** is currently 3 (the local variables are shown in the Toolbox window of Figure 3-10), that we have actually fetched two rows in this call to **FetchRows**. At this point we will set **v_Finished** to FALSE and return it immediately. But the calling block will not print out these extra rows, because it will only call **PrintRows** if **FetchRows** returned TRUE.

Fixing this requires two changes. First, **FetchRows** needs to return the actual number of rows retrieved, as follows:

```
-- Available online as part of StudentFetch2.sql
  -- Returns up to p_BatchSize rows in p_Students, and returns
  -- TRUE as long as there are still rows to be fetched.
```

```
-- The actual number of rows fetched is returned in p_BatchSize.
FUNCTION FetchRows(p_BatchSize IN OUT NUMBER,
                   p_Students OUT t_Students)
  RETURN BOOLEAN IS
  v_Finished BOOLEAN := TRUE;
BEGIN
  FOR v_Count IN 1..p_BatchSize LOOP
    FETCH c_AllStudents INTO p_Students(v_Count);
    IF c_AllStudents%NOTFOUND THEN
      v_Finished := FALSE;
      p_BatchSize := v_Count - 1;
      EXIT;
    END IF;
  END LOOP;
  RETURN v_Finished;
END FetchRows;
```

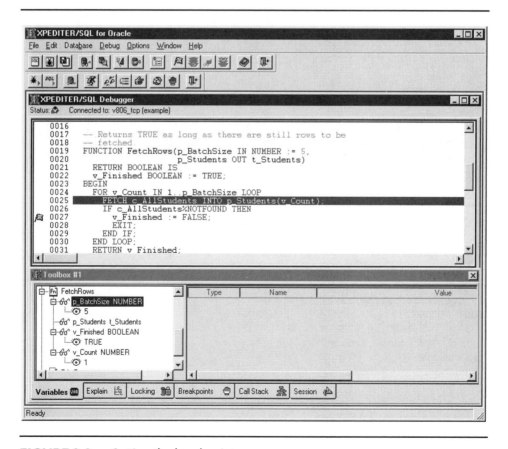

FIGURE 3-9. *Setting the breakpoint*

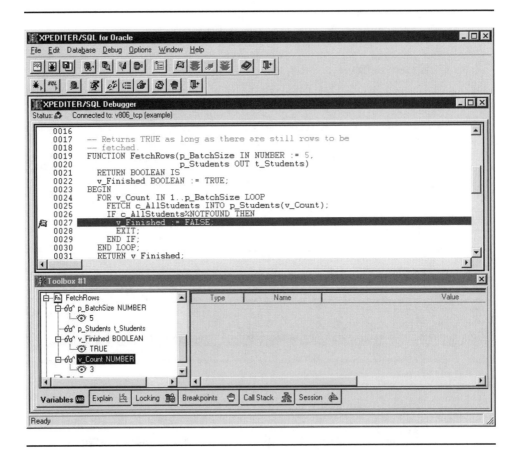

FIGURE 3-10. *Stopped at the breakpoint*

Second, we need to call **PrintRows** after the last fetch, as shown here:

```
-- Available online as callSF2.sql
SQL> DECLARE
  2    v_BatchSize NUMBER := 5;
  3    v_Students StudentFetch.t_Students;
  4  BEGIN
```

```
 5    StudentFetch.OpenCursor;
 6    WHILE StudentFetch.FetchRows(v_BatchSize, v_Students) LOOP
 7      StudentFetch.PrintRows(v_BatchSize, v_Students);
 8    END LOOP;
 9    -- Print any extra rows from the last batch.
10    IF v_BatchSize != 0 THEN
11      StudentFetch.PrintRows(v_BatchSize, v_Students);
12    END IF;
13    StudentFetch.CloseCursor;
14  END;
15  /
ID: 10000 Name: Scott Smith
ID: 10001 Name: Margaret Mason
ID: 10002 Name: Joanne Junebug
ID: 10003 Name: Manish Murgatroid
ID: 10004 Name: Patrick Poll
ID: 10005 Name: Timothy Taller
ID: 10006 Name: Barbara Blues
ID: 10007 Name: David Dinsmore
ID: 10008 Name: Ester Elegant
ID: 10009 Name: Rose Riznit
ID: 10010 Name: Rita Razmataz
ID: 10011 Name: Shay Shariatpanahy
PL/SQL procedure successfully completed.
```

Problem 4: Comments

At first glance, this fetch loop looks very similar to the one we examined in Problem 3. However, each fetch can return from up to five rows, rather than up to one. With array fetch loops like this, it is necessary to process any remaining rows even after the end-of-fetch condition is reached.

Problem 5

The mathematical *Fibonacci sequence* is a sequence of numbers such that $Fib(n) = Fib(n-1) + Fib(n-2)$. $Fib(0)$ is defined to be 0, and $Fib(1)$ is defined to be 1. This defines a sequence as follows:

0, 1, 1, 2, 3, 5, 8, 13, ...

We can write a function in PL/SQL that will calculate the *n*th Fibonacci number as follows:

```
-- Available online as part of Fibonacci.sql
CREATE OR REPLACE FUNCTION Fib(n IN BINARY_INTEGER)
  RETURN BINARY_INTEGER AS
BEGIN
  RETURN Fib(n - 1) + Fib(n - 2);
END Fib;
```

However, when we run this function from SQL*Plus, it doesn't return, and will eventually crash with an out-of-memory error.

Problem 5: Debugging with SQL Navigator

We will use the SQL Navigator debugger to solve this problem. Like the other PL/SQL debuggers, we could directly debug **Fib** entirely within SQL Navigator, simply by opening the function in a Stored Program Editor and stepping into it, as shown in Figure 3-11. This would bring up a dialog box asking for the initial value of *n*, and would construct an anonymous block to call the function.

Instead, we are going to call **Fib** from a SQL*Plus window and attach to the session from SQL Navigator. This feature is similar to the ability of some C debuggers to attach to a running process and debug it. In order to do this with PL/SQL, the calling application must first call two subprograms in the DBMS_DEBUG package to enable the debugger to attach to it, as shown by the following SQL*Plus session:

```
-- Available online as part of attachFib.sql
SQL> -- First initialize the debugger
SQL> ALTER SESSION SET PLSQL_DEBUG = TRUE;
Session altered.
SQL> DECLARE
  2     v_DebugID VARCHAR2(30);
  3  BEGIN
  4     v_DebugID := DBMS_DEBUG.INITIALIZE('DebugMe');
  5     DBMS_DEBUG.DEBUG_ON;
  6  END;
  7  /
PL/SQL procedure successfully completed.
```

The ALTER SESSION statement tells the PL/SQL compiler to compile future anonymous blocks with the DEBUG option. DBMS_DEBUG.INITIALIZE takes a string that identifies this session to the server, and DBMS_DEBUG.DEBUG_ON

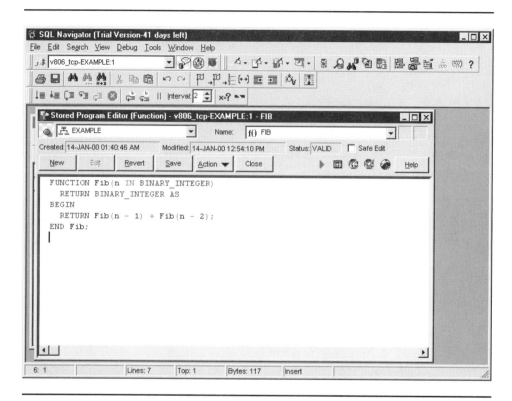

FIGURE 3-11. *Preparing to debug **Fib** directly*

tells the server that the next block will contain a call that is to be debugged. We do this by issuing a call to **Fib**, as follows:

```
SQL> -- And now execute the call to Fib.  This will hang until you
SQL> -- attach to this session in SQL Navigator.
SQL> exec DBMS_OUTPUT.PUT_LINE(Fib(3));
```

We can now attach to the session in SQL Navigator, by choosing Debug |
Attach External Session. This will bring up a dialog box asking for the identifier used
in the INTIALIZE call, as shown in Figure 3-12. Once we enter this, the Execution
Status window opens, with the call stack showing the anonymous block that we ran

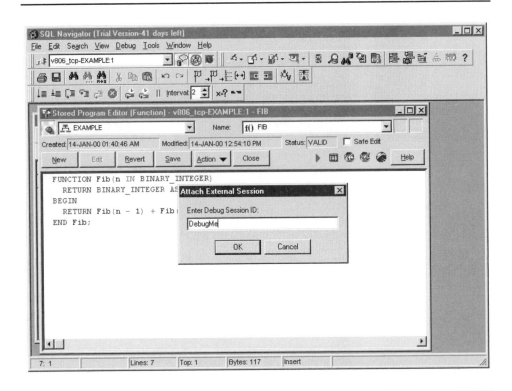

FIGURE 3-12. *Attaching to the session*

from SQL*Plus. We can now step into this block and continue debugging **Fib**. This is shown in Figure 3-13.

We are now ready to set a watchpoint for *n*, and continue stepping through the program. The watchpoint is set by highlighting the variable, right-clicking on it, and choosing Add Watchpoint from the context menu. We can now step through the function and see what happens to *n* as it runs. The value after several runs is shown in Figure 3-14, which illustrates the problem.

There is no stopping condition in **Fib**. The first call will subtract 1 from *n*, and recursively call **Fib** again. This call will also subtract 1, and call once more. This continues, subtracting from *n* and adding another call to the stack, until we run out

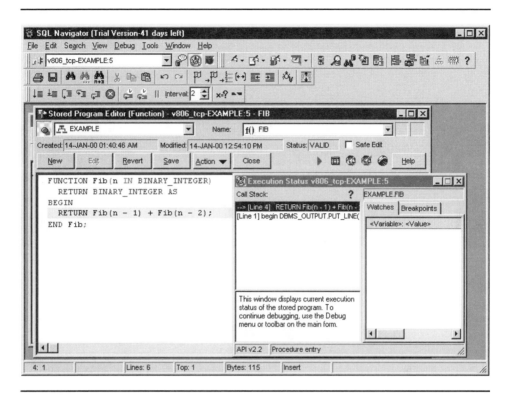

FIGURE 3-13. *Stepped into* **Fib**

of memory. The fix for this problem is to add a stopping condition to **Fib**, as illustrated by the following:

```
-- Available online as part of Fibonacci.sql
CREATE OR REPLACE FUNCTION Fib(n IN BINARY_INTEGER)
  RETURN BINARY_INTEGER AS
BEGIN
  IF n = 0 OR n = 1 THEN
    RETURN n;
  ELSE
    RETURN Fib(n - 1) + Fib(n - 2);
  END IF;
END Fib;
```

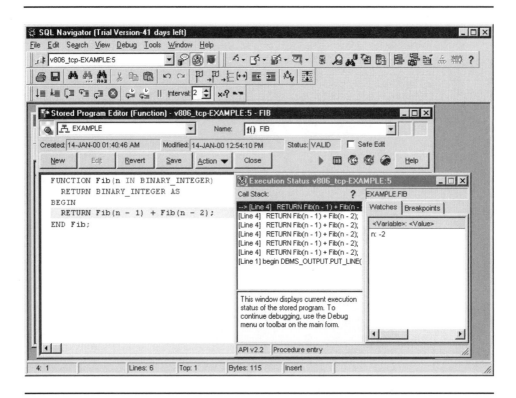

FIGURE 3-14. *Negative argument*

The previous version does return the correct result, as the following SQL*Plus session shows.

```
-- Available online as part of Fibonacci.sql
SQL> BEGIN
  2     -- Some calls to Fib.
  3     FOR v_Count IN 1..10 LOOP
  4       DBMS_OUTPUT.PUT_LINE(
  5         'Fib(' || v_Count || ') is ' || Fib(v_Count));
  6     END LOOP;
  7   END;
  8   /
Fib(1) is 1
Fib(2) is 1
Fib(3) is 2
```

```
Fib(4) is 3
Fib(5) is 5
Fib(6) is 8
Fib(7) is 13
Fib(8) is 21
Fib(9) is 34
Fib(10) is 55
PL/SQL procedure successfully completed.
```

Problem 5: Comments

Recursive functions can provide a simple and elegant solution to problems, provided that they have the correct stopping condition. Without this, they will run until memory is exhausted.

Even with a stopping condition, however, recursive functions are generally not the most efficient way to solve a particular problem, because they involve repeated function calls. We will examine an iterative version of **Fib** later in this chapter (in "PL/SQL-Based Profiling"), which demonstrates this.

Problem 6

In many cases, the problem with a PL/SQL program is not with the program itself but with the data on which it operates. For example, consider the following SQL script, which copies data from the **source** to **destination** table:

```
-- Available online as CopyTables.sql
CREATE OR REPLACE PROCEDURE CopyTables AS
  v_Key    source.key%TYPE;
  v_Value source.value%TYPE;

  CURSOR c_AllData IS
    SELECT *
      FROM source;
BEGIN
  OPEN c_AllData;

  LOOP
    FETCH c_AllData INTO v_Key, v_Value;
    EXIT WHEN c_AllData%NOTFOUND;

    INSERT INTO destination (key, value)
      VALUES (v_Key, TO_NUMBER(v_Value));
  END LOOP;

  CLOSE c_AllData;
END CopyTables;
```

The **source** and **destination** tables are created with

```
-- Available online as part of relTables.sql
CREATE TABLE source (
  key NUMBER(5),
  value VARCHAR2(50));

CREATE TABLE destination (
  key NUMBER(5),
  value NUMBER);
```

Note that the **value** column of **source** is VARCHAR2, but the **value** column of **destination** is NUMBER. Suppose we then populate **source** with the following PL/SQL block, which will insert 500 rows. Of these, 499 have a legal string (which can be converted into a NUMBER). However, one row (chosen at random, using the **Random** package from Chapter 4) has an illegal value.

```
-- Available online as populate.sql
DECLARE
  v_RandomKey source.key%TYPE;
BEGIN
  -- First fill up the source table with legal values.
  FOR v_Key IN 1..500 LOOP
    INSERT INTO source (key, value)
      VALUES (v_Key, TO_CHAR(v_Key));
  END LOOP;

  -- Now, pick a random number between 1 and 500, and update that
  -- row to an illegal value.
  v_RandomKey := Random.RandMax(500);
  UPDATE source
    SET value = 'Oops, not a number!'
    WHERE key = v_RandomKey;

  COMMIT;
END;
```

If we call **CopyTables** now, we will get an ORA-1722 error:

```
SQL> exec CopyTables
begin CopyTables; end;
*
ERROR at line 1:
ORA-01722: invalid number
ORA-06512: at "EXAMPLE.COPYTABLES", line 15
ORA-06512: at line 1
```

Clearly, the error is occurring on the INSERT statement. The question is, which value is bad? We can use a debugger to determine this.

Problem 6: TOAD Debugger

In order to run a PL/SQL procedure with the TOAD debugger, you must run it from a Stored Procedure Edit/Compile window. Figure 3-15 shows **CopyTables** open in such a window. We can then step into the function by choosing Debug | Trace Into or clicking the Trace Into button on the debugging toolbar. This will start the procedure and stop at the first line, as shown in Figure 3-16.

The next step is to set watchpoints for the two local variables, **v_Key** and **v_Value**. This is done by highlighting the variable and clicking on the Add Watch button, as shown in Figure 3-17. The values of both variables are NULL, since we haven't fetched into them yet. We can now continue execution. TOAD will

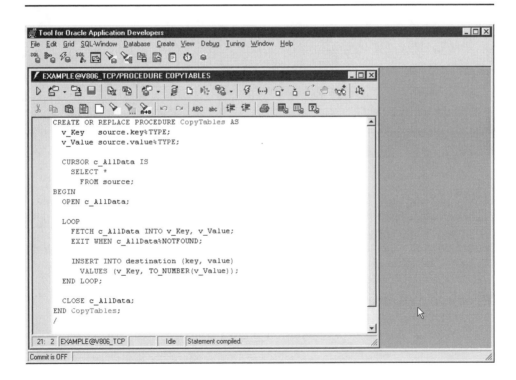

FIGURE 3-15. *CopyTables in an Edit/Compile window*

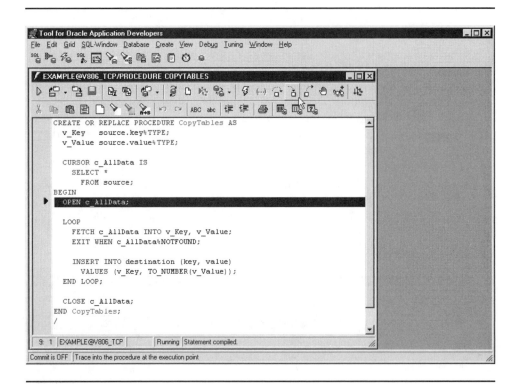

FIGURE 3-16. *Stopped at the first line*

automatically stop the procedure when the error is raised, as shown in Figure 3-18. When we continue execution, the values of the local variables will be shown in the Watch window. This tells us that the bad data is at key 434 (in this case), as illustrated by Figure 3-19.

Problem 6: Comments

Although this is a simple example, data can be invalid in more complicated or subtle ways, depending on your application. In this case, the data was of the wrong

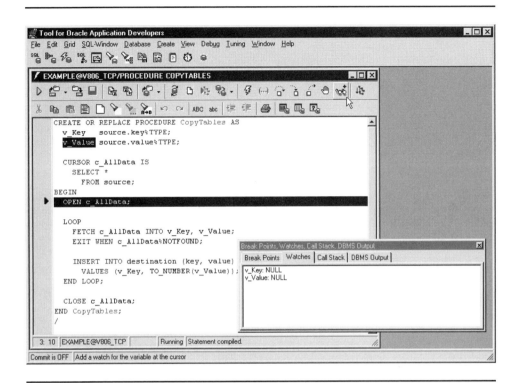

FIGURE 3-17. *Adding watchpoints*

type and thus couldn't be converted. It is also possible for the data to be out of range, for example. Note that invalid data may not always raise an exception; depending on your error handling and the nature of the inconsistency, you may get different results.

It is important to note, however, that in this case the PL/SQL code is fine. The problem is not with the code, it is with the data on which the code operates. Thus you may be able to find the incorrect data by querying the tables directly rather than debugging the program.

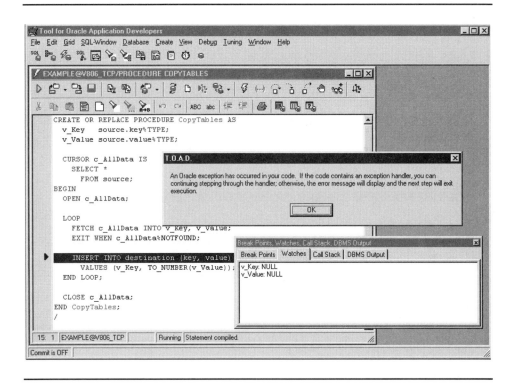

FIGURE 3-18. *Stopped at the error*

Problem 7

Consider the following procedure:

```
-- Available online as RSLoop1.sql
CREATE OR REPLACE PROCEDURE RSLoop AS
  v_RSRec registered_students%ROWTYPE;
  CURSOR c_RSGrades IS
    SELECT *
      FROM registered_students
      ORDER BY grade;
BEGIN
  -- Loop over the cursor to determine the last row.
  FOR v_RSRec IN c_RSGrades LOOP
```

```
      NULL;
   END LOOP;

   -- And print it out.
   DBMS_OUTPUT.PUT_LINE(
      'Last row selected has ID ' || v_RSRec.student_id);
END RSLoop;
```

RSLoop will query the **registered_students** table (sorted by grade), and report the ID of the last row fetched. However, when we run it, we get a NULL result:

```
SQL> exec RSLoop;
Last row selected has ID
PL/SQL procedure successfully completed.
```

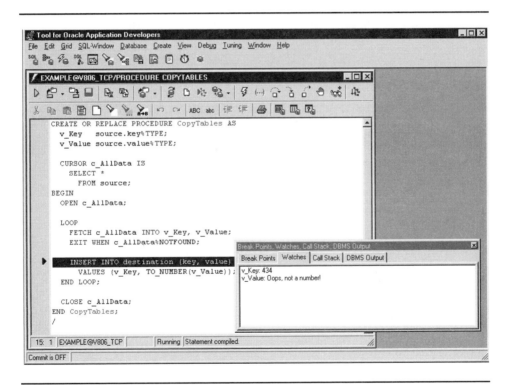

FIGURE 3-19. *Bad data*

Problem 7: Debugging with SQL-Programmer

The first step in debugging this problem is to open **RSLoop** in a Development window, as shown in Figure 3-20. We can then step into the code using the Step Into button, as Figure 3-21 illustrates.

The next step is to set a watchpoint on **v_RSRec**. We do this by highlighting the variable in the code, and dragging it to the Watchpoint window, as in Figure 3-22. The value is NULL, since we just started the procedure. As we step through the code, we should see the value of **v_RSRec** changing each time through the loop. But it remains NULL, as we can see in Figure 3-23, which also contains a watchpoint for the value of the cursor itself, showing that we are at row 8, but **v_RSRec** is still NULL.

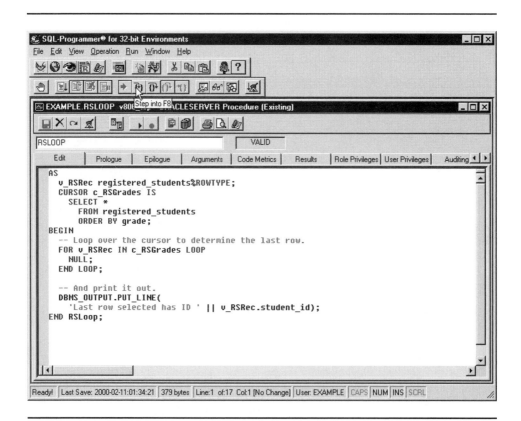

FIGURE 3-20. *Preparing to debug **RSLoop***

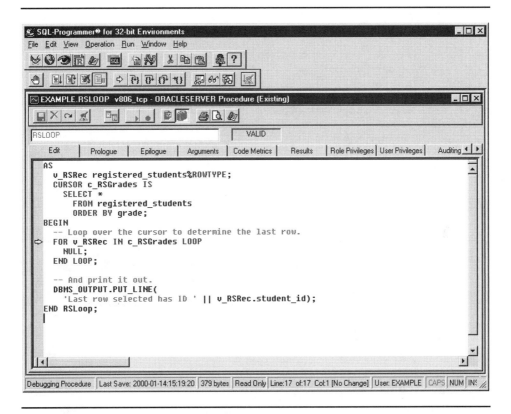

FIGURE 3-21. *Stopped at the first line*

Why does the loop not assign to **v_RSRec**? The problem is that the loop declares an implicit variable, also called **v_RSRec**. Inside the loop, the implicitly declared variable hides the explicit variable, and thus it doesn't get assigned. One fix is to change the loop to an explicit FETCH loop, which will use the explicit variable, as shown next:

```
-- Available online as RSLoop2.sql
CREATE OR REPLACE PROCEDURE RSLoop AS
  v_RSRec registered_students%ROWTYPE;
  CURSOR c_RSGrades IS
    SELECT *
```

```
      FROM registered_students
      ORDER BY grade;
BEGIN
  -- Loop over the cursor to determine the last row.
  OPEN c_RSGrades;
  LOOP
      FETCH c_RSGrades INTO v_RSRec;
      EXIT WHEN c_RSGrades%NOTFOUND;
  END LOOP;
  CLOSE c_RSGrades;

  -- And print it out.
  DBMS_OUTPUT.PUT_LINE(
    'Last row selected has ID ' || v_RSRec.student_id);
END RSLoop;
```

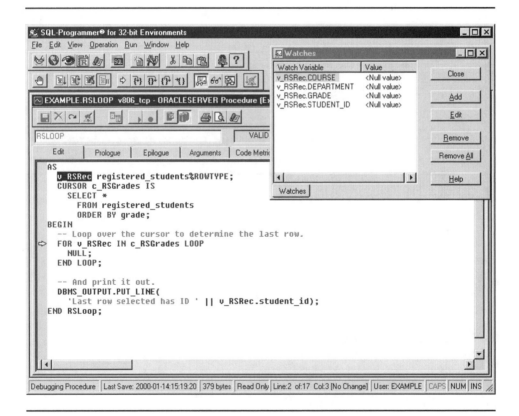

FIGURE 3-22. *Watching v_RSRec*

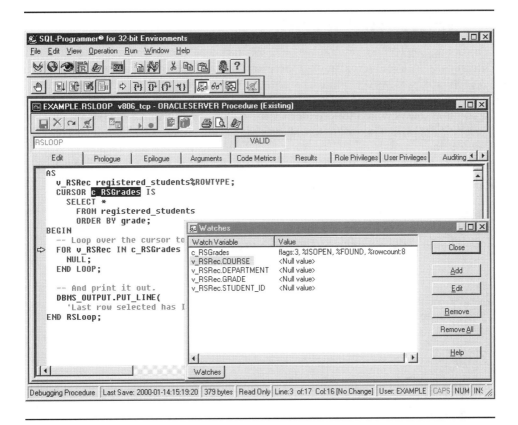

FIGURE 3-23. *v_RSRec still NULL*

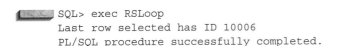

```
SQL> exec RSLoop
Last row selected has ID 10006
PL/SQL procedure successfully completed.
```

Problem 7: Comments

Implicitly declared loop variables (both records for cursor FOR loops and loop counters for numeric FOR loops) are only in scope for the duration of the loop. They will hide any other variable of the same name while inside the loop. We could also have fixed the previous problem by renaming the implicit variable, and then assigning it to the explicit variable each time through the loop.

Tracing and Profiling

The debugging techniques that we have examined so far are useful to pinpoint specific bugs in your application. However, they are not as helpful for all kinds of problems, such as performance issues. To rectify this, PL/SQL provides several different kinds of tracing and profiling tools. *Tracing* an application produces a report that shows which subprograms were called and which exceptions were raised. *Profiling* extends the information that tracing provides to include timing information.

Event-based PL/SQL tracing was first made available with Oracle7 Release 7.3.4. Tracing through a PL/SQL API is available with Oracle8*i* Release 1 (8.1.5), and profiling is available with Oracle8*i* Release 2 (8.1.6). We will examine these methods in the following sections.

All of the examples in subsequent sections use the procedures and packages found in the code that follows. The **Random** package can be found in Chapter 4.

```
-- Available online as traceDemo.sql
-- Returns fib(n), equivalent to fib(n-1) + fib(n-2).
CREATE OR REPLACE FUNCTION RecursiveFib(n IN BINARY_INTEGER)
  RETURN BINARY_INTEGER AS
BEGIN
  IF n = 0 OR n = 1 THEN
    RETURN n;
  ELSE
    RETURN RecursiveFib(n - 1) + RecursiveFib(n - 2);
  END IF;
END RecursiveFib;


CREATE OR REPLACE FUNCTION IterativeFib(n IN BINARY_INTEGER)
RETURN BINARY_INTEGER AS
  v_Result BINARY_INTEGER;
  v_Sum1 BINARY_INTEGER := 1;
  v_Sum2 BINARY_INTEGER := 1;
BEGIN
  IF n = 1 OR n = 2 THEN
    RETURN 1;
  ELSE
    FOR v_Count IN 2..n - 1 LOOP
      v_Result := v_Sum1 + v_Sum2;
      v_Sum2 := v_Sum1;
      v_Sum1 := v_Result;
    END LOOP;
    RETURN v_Result;
  END IF;
END IterativeFib;
```

```
CREATE OR REPLACE PROCEDURE RaiseIt(p_Exception IN NUMBER) AS
  e_MyException EXCEPTION;
BEGIN
  IF p_Exception = 0 THEN
    NULL;
  ELSIF p_Exception < 0 THEN
    RAISE e_MyException;
  ELSIF p_Exception = 1001 THEN
    RAISE INVALID_CURSOR;
  ELSIF p_Exception = 1403 THEN
    RAISE NO_DATA_FOUND;
  ELSIF p_Exception = 6502 THEN
    RAISE VALUE_ERROR;
  ELSE
    RAISE_APPLICATION_ERROR(-20001, 'Exception ' || p_Exception);
  END IF;
END RaiseIt;

CREATE OR REPLACE PROCEDURE CallRaise(p_Exception IN NUMBER := 0) AS
BEGIN
  RaiseIt(p_Exception);
EXCEPTION
  WHEN OTHERS THEN
    NULL;
END CallRaise;

CREATE OR REPLACE PROCEDURE RandomRaise(p_NumCalls IN NUMBER := 1) AS
  v_Case NUMBER;
BEGIN
  FOR v_Count IN 1..p_NumCalls LOOP
    v_Case := Random.RandMax(6);
    IF v_Case = 1 THEN
      CallRaise(-1);
    ELSIF v_Case = 2 THEN
      CallRaise(0);
    ELSIF v_Case = 3 THEN
      CallRaise(1001);
    ELSIF v_Case = 4 THEN
      CallRaise(1403);
    ELSIF v_Case = 5 THEN
      CallRaise(6502);
    ELSE
      CallRaise(v_Case);
    END IF;
  END LOOP;
END RandomRaise;
```

```
CREATE OR REPLACE PROCEDURE CallMe1 AS
BEGIN
  NULL;
END CallMe1;

CREATE OR REPLACE PROCEDURE CallMe2 AS
BEGIN
  NULL;
END CallMe2;

CREATE OR REPLACE PROCEDURE CallMe3 AS
BEGIN
  NULL;
END CallMe3;

CREATE OR REPLACE PACKAGE CallMe AS
  PROCEDURE One;
  PROCEDURE Two;
  PROCEDURE Three;
END CallMe;

CREATE OR REPLACE PACKAGE BODY CallMe AS
  PROCEDURE One IS
  BEGIN
    NULL;
  END One;

  PROCEDURE Two IS
  BEGIN
    NULL;
  END Two;

  PROCEDURE Three IS
  BEGIN
    NULL;
  END Three;
END CallMe;

CREATE OR REPLACE PROCEDURE RandomCalls(p_NumCalls IN NUMBER := 1) AS
  v_Case NUMBER;
BEGIN
  FOR v_Count IN 1..p_NumCalls LOOP
    v_Case := Random.RandMax(6);
    IF v_Case = 1 THEN
      CallMe1;
    ELSIF v_Case = 2 THEN
     CallMe2;
    ELSIF v_Case = 3 THEN
```

```
      CallMe3;
    ELSIF v_Case = 4 THEN
       CallMe.One;
    ELSIF v_Case = 5 THEN
       CallMe.Two;
    ELSE
       CallMe.Three;
    END IF;
  END LOOP;
END RandomCalls;
```

Event-Based Tracing

This type of tracing is enabled or disabled based on the setting of a database event. A *database event* is a debugging tool available in both the RDBMS and PL/SQL. There are two ways of setting an event:

- In a particular session, with the ALTER SESSION statement. The syntax is

    ALTER SESSION SET EVENTS *'event event_string'*;

    where *event* is the event number, and *event_string* describes how the particular event is to be set. With this method, the event will be set only for this particular session, and will not affect other database sessions.

- For the entire database instance, with a parameter in the database initialization file (init.ora). The syntax is

    event="*event event_string*"

    where *event* is the event number, and *event_string* describes how the particular event is to be set. With this method, the event will be set for all database sessions after the database is shut down and restarted.

Different events can turn on different kinds of tracing. In all cases, the trace information is written to the session trace file, found in the directory identified by the USER_DUMP_DEST database initialization file parameter.

TIP
*If you don't know the value of USER_DUMP_DEST, you can determine it by querying the **v$database_parameters** data dictionary view, or by using the SHOW PARAMETERS command in Server Manager or SQL*Plus 8i and higher.*

Since additional information will be written to the trace file, setting these events can adversely affect performance. Database events are used for many other purposes besides the specific events described in this section. Setting additional events can have additional consequences, and should be done only under the direction of Oracle Support Services.

Tracing Specific Errors

Setting an event equal to a specific error number will cause the database to dump information to the trace file when that error is raised. Among other things, the trace file will contain the current SQL statement and call stack when the error was raised. To set an event for this purpose, the event string should be

> *event_num* trace name errorstack

where *event_num* is the desired error. For example, suppose we issue the following anonymous block:

```
-- Available online as event6502.sql
SQL> -- First set the events in the session
SQL> ALTER SESSION SET EVENTS '6502 trace name errorstack';
Session altered.
SQL> -- And then raise ORA-6502
SQL> BEGIN
  2     RaiseIt(6502);
  3  END;
  4  /
BEGIN
*
ERROR at line 1:
ORA-06502: PL/SQL: numeric or value error
ORA-06512: at "EXAMPLE.RAISEIT", line 13
ORA-06512: at line 2
```

This will produce a trace file that will contain lines similar to the following:

```
*** SESSION ID:(7.4) 2000-01-10 17:54:08.710
*** 2000-01-10 17:54:08.710
ksedmp: internal or fatal error
ORA-06502: PL/SQL: numeric or value error
Current SQL statement for this session:
BEGIN
  RaiseIt(6502);
END;
----- PL/SQL Call Stack -----
  object      line  object
  handle    number  name
802da2a0         2  anonymous block
```

The trace file indicates that the current SQL statement is the anonymous block that calls **RaiseIt**. The trace file also contains a PL/SQL call stack, which also indicates that the anonymous block is the culprit. However, the real error was raised inside **RaiseIt**, not in the block. Why doesn't the call stack have the complete PL/SQL stack at the time of the error? To answer this, we have to examine further how the trace file is generated.

When a PL/SQL block is sent to the server for execution, the shadow process receives it and detects that it is a PL/SQL block. At this point, it is sent to the PL/SQL engine for execution, rather than the SQL statement executor. When the PL/SQL engine returns, any results are sent back to the client. If the PL/SQL engine returns with an error (as in the previous case), the server will dump information to the trace file if there is an event set. By the time this happens, the error will have been propagated out from any inner procedure to the anonymous block. Thus, the call stack indicates only the anonymous block.

NOTE

Trace files generated in this manner contain other information as well, such as the C call stack and register dump, which are generally not helpful in pinpointing the source of an error in your PL/SQL code. They are useful to Oracle Support to help in pinpointing errors in Oracle code, however.

Call and Exception Tracing

This level of tracing is available with Oracle7 Release 7.3.4, and Oracle8 Release 8.0.5 and higher. It is not available with Oracle8 releases prior to 8.0.5.

Event-based call and exception tracing allows you to trace three occurrences of interest to PL/SQL—calls to stored subprograms, raised exceptions, and the value of bind variables. This type of tracing can either dump the output directly to the trace file when the specified event occurs, or the tracing data can be stored in a circular buffer, which is dumped only on certain conditions. Using the circular buffer is helpful to limit the size of large trace files.

EVENT LEVELS   To enable call and exception tracing, you use event 10938. The syntax for the event string is

    10938 trace name context level *level_num*

where *level_num* is the bitwise OR of the values in the following table.

Trace Name	Hex Value	Decimal Value	Description
TRACE_ACALL	0x0001	1	Trace all calls
TRACE_ECALL	0x0002	2	Trace enabled calls
TRACE_AEXCP	0x0004	4	Trace all exceptions
TRACE_EEXCP	0x0008	8	Trace enabled exceptions
TRACE_CIRCULAR	0x0010	16	Use circular buffer
TRACE_BIND_VARS	0x0020	32	Trace bind variables

An *enabled call* is a subprogram that has been compiled with the DEBUG option, and an *enabled exception* is an exception raised from an enabled subprogram (see "Enabled Calls and Exceptions" for details). In order to compute the desired level, take the bitwise OR of the desired trace types (equivalent to the sum of the decimal values). For example:

- Level 17 (ACALL | CIRCULAR) will trace all calls, using the buffer.

- Level 22 (ECALL | AEXCP | CIRCULAR) will trace enabled calls and all exceptions, using the buffer.

- Level 32 (BIND_VARS) will trace bind variables, without using the buffer.

- Level 53 (ACALL | AEXCP | CIRCULAR | BIND_VARS) will yield the maximum level of tracing, using the buffer.

- Level 37 (ACALL | AEXCP | BIND_VARS) will yield the maximum level of tracing, without using the buffer.

Suppose we issue the following SQL to the database:

```
-- Available online as AllCallsExceptions.sql
SQL> -- Enable tracing of all calls and all exceptions.  5 is the
SQL> -- bitwise OR of 0x01 and 0x04.
SQL> ALTER SESSION SET EVENTS '10938 trace name context level 5';
Session altered.

SQL> -- Anonymous block which raises some exceptions.
SQL> BEGIN
  2    CallRaise(1001);
  3    RaiseIt(-1);
  4  END;
  5  /
BEGIN
*
ERROR at line 1:
ORA-06510: PL/SQL: unhandled user-defined exception
```

```
ORA-06512: at "EXAMPLE.RAISEIT", line 7
ORA-06512: at line 3
```

This produces output like the following in the trace file:

```
----------- PL/SQL TRACE INFORMATION -----------
Levels set :  1    4
Trace:  ANONYMOUS BLOCK: Stack depth = 1
Trace:    PROCEDURE EXAMPLE.CALLRAISE: Call to entry at line 3 Stack depth = 2
Trace:     PROCEDURE EXAMPLE.RAISEIT: RAISEIT Stack depth = 3
Trace:      Pre-defined exception - OER 1001 at line 9 of PROCEDURE EXAMPLE.RAISEIT:
Trace:    PROCEDURE EXAMPLE.RAISEIT: RAISEIT Stack depth = 2
Trace:     User defined exception at line 7 of PROCEDURE EXAMPLE.RAISEIT:
```

Each call to the server will produce output similar to this, with the following characteristics:

- At the beginning of the trace info, the line "PL/SQL TRACE INFORMATION" is printed, followed by the trace levels currently set. Levels 1 and 4 in the example indicate that TRACE_ACALL and TRACE_AEXCP have been enabled.

- After these introductory lines, a line will appear in the trace file when a tracing event occurs. In the previous example, both TRACE_ACALL and TRACE_AEXCP have been enabled. Thus, there are entries each time a subprogram is entered, as well as entries for the raised exceptions.

- For subprogram calls, the stack depth is also printed. The text itself is also indented to match the stack depth. As the depth increases, the length of the lines in the trace file increases as well. Lines in the trace file are limited to 512 characters, which also limits the maximum stack depth.

- Exceptions are printed to the trace file as soon as they are raised, whether they are handled in that block or a containing block.

We will see more examples of the different kinds of tracing output in the following sections.

ENABLED CALLS AND EXCEPTIONS   Enabled subprograms have been compiled with the DEBUG option. There are two ways of doing this. The first is to issue the statement

```
ALTER SESSION SET PLSQL_DEBUG = TRUE;
```

after which any PL/SQL blocks or subprograms will be compiled with DEBUG. You can also recompile a stored subprogram with

```
ALTER [PROCEDURE | FUNCTION | PACKAGE BODY | TYPE BODY] object_name
    COMPILE DEBUG;
```

Anonymous blocks can be compiled with DEBUG only by issuing the ALTER SESSION statement. For example, if we issue the following SQL statements to the database:

```
-- Available online as EnabledCallsExceptions.sql
SQL> -- Enable tracing of enabled calls and exceptions.  10 is the
SQL> -- bitwise OR of 0x02 and 0x08.
SQL> ALTER SESSION SET EVENTS '10938 trace name context level 10';
Session altered.

SQL> ALTER PROCEDURE RaiseIt COMPILE DEBUG;
Procedure altered.

SQL> -- Anonymous block which raises some exceptions.
SQL> BEGIN
  2    CallRaise(1001);
  3    RaiseIt(-1);
  4  END;
  5  /
BEGIN
*
ERROR at line 1:
ORA-06510: PL/SQL: unhandled user-defined exception
ORA-06512: at "EXAMPLE.RAISEIT", line 7
ORA-06512: at line 3
```

RaiseIt is the only block that is enabled. Thus, the trace file only shows the following:

```
----------- PL/SQL TRACE INFORMATION -----------
Levels set :  2    8
Trace:    PROCEDURE EXAMPLE.RAISEIT: RAISEIT Stack depth = 3
Trace:      Pre-defined exception - OER 1001 at line 9 of PROCEDURE EXAMPLE.RAISEIT:
Trace:    PROCEDURE EXAMPLE.RAISEIT: RAISEIT Stack depth = 2
Trace:      User defined exception at line 7 of PROCEDURE EXAMPLE.RAISEIT:
```

The only entries are those that come from **RaiseIt**. If an exception is raised from a un-enabled block (not compiled with debug), it will not be shown.

TRACING CALLS TO PACKAGED SUBPROGRAMS
When calling a packaged subprogram, the specific subprogram within the package is not shown in the trace file. For example, suppose we issue the following anonymous block in SQL*Plus:

```
-- Available online as PackagedCalls.sql
SQL> -- Enable tracing of all calls and all exceptions.  5 is the
SQL> -- bitwise OR of 0x01 and 0x04.
SQL> ALTER SESSION SET EVENTS '10938 trace name context level 5';
Session altered.

SQL> -- Anonymous block which calls packaged procedures.
SQL> BEGIN
```

```
  2      CallMe.One;
  3      CallMe.Two;
  4      CallMe.Three;
  5   END;
  6   /
PL/SQL procedure successfully completed.
```

The previous block will produce trace output similar to the following.

```
------------ PL/SQL TRACE INFORMATION -----------
Levels set :  1    4
Trace:  ANONYMOUS BLOCK: Stack depth = 1
Trace:    PACKAGE BODY EXAMPLE.CALLME: Call to entry at line 4 Stack depth = 2
Trace:    PACKAGE BODY EXAMPLE.CALLME: Call to entry at line 9 Stack depth = 2
Trace:    PACKAGE BODY EXAMPLE.CALLME: Call to entry at line 14 Stack depth = 2
```

Only the name of the package body is present for each entry line. However, the line information is also present, which can be used to identify the specific packaged subprogram.

BIND VARIABLES   Bind variable information is included when the TRACE_BIND_VARS bit is set. This will add a line to the trace file for each occurrence of a bind variable when PL/SQL gets the bind information. The bind variable information will be printed whether or not the block is enabled. The following SQL*Plus session shows a PL/SQL block that contains bind variables.

```
-- Available online as BindVariables.sql
SQL> -- First set up the variables
SQL> VARIABLE v_String1 VARCHAR2(20);
SQL> VARIABLE v_String2 VARCHAR2(20);
SQL> BEGIN
  2      :v_String1 := 'Hello';
  3      :v_String2 := ' World!';
  4   END;
  5   /
PL/SQL procedure successfully completed.

SQL> -- Enable tracing for all calls and bind variables.
SQL> ALTER SESSION SET EVENTS '10938 trace name context level 33';
Session altered.
SQL> BEGIN
  2      DBMS_OUTPUT.PUT_LINE(:v_String1 || :v_String2);
  3   END;
  4   /
Hello World!
PL/SQL procedure successfully completed.
```

This produces a trace file similar to the following.

```
------------ PL/SQL TRACE INFORMATION -----------
Levels set :  1    32
Trace: ANONYMOUS BLOCK: Stack depth = 1
op: GBVAR; pos: 1; buf: 10bd7b8; len: 5; ind: 0; bfl: 20;
```

```
op: GBVAR; pos: 2; buf: 10bd7d8; len: 7; ind: 0; bfl: 20;
Trace:   PACKAGE BODY SYS.DBMS_OUTPUT: Call to entry at line 1 Stack depth = 2
Trace:    PACKAGE BODY SYS.DBMS_OUTPUT: Call to entry at line 1 Stack depth = 3
Trace:     PACKAGE BODY SYS.STANDARD: Call to entry at line 793 Stack depth = 4
Trace:     PACKAGE BODY SYS.STANDARD: ICD vector index = 45 Stack depth = 4
Trace:      PACKAGE BODY SYS.STANDARD: Call to entry at line 564 Stack depth = 5
```

In addition to the calls to DBMS_OUTPUT (which in turn makes calls to package STANDARD), the trace shows that PL/SQL received two bind variables using the pseudo-opcode GBVAR.

TIP

This type of tracing does not show the value of the bind variable, only its type and length. You can get the values of bind variables by setting event 10046 to level 4. This event will also generate SQL_TRACE info. See "SQL Tracing" later in this chapter for more details.

USING THE CIRCULAR BUFFER   When tracing calls, especially for long-running programs, the trace file can get quite large. Usually, only the last portion of the file is useful for debugging, as it will contain the latest information. In order to rectify this, PL/SQL provides a circular buffer. Instead of sending the output directly to the trace file, the output is instead sent to the buffer. When the buffer fills up, subsequent output starts over at the beginning of the buffer. Thus, it always holds the last portion of the tracing data. The buffer can then be dumped out to the trace file on various conditions. The circular buffer is controlled by three parameters and events:

- The TRACE_CIRCULAR bit must be set with the 10938 event. This sends the trace output to the buffer, rather than the file directly.

- The size of the circular buffer is set with event 10940, using the event string

    10940 trace name context level *buffer_size*

    where *buffer_size* is the size of the buffer, in K. The default is 8K. This event can be set either with an ALTER SESSION statement, or with a setting in the database initialization file.

- The conditions on which the buffer is dumped to the file are specified by the _PLSQL_DUMP_BUFFER_EVENTS database initialization parameter (note the initial underscore). This should be set to a comma-separated, all-uppercase list of events, with no spaces between each one. The available events are listed in the following table:

Dumping Event	Description
ON_EXIT	The buffer will be dumped whenever the PL/SQL interpreter exits, such as the end of a call.
error number	The buffer will be dumped whenever the specified error occurs. This must be a runtime error, not a PL/SQL compile error.
ALL_EXCEPTIONS	The buffer will be dumped whenever an error occurs.

The following list demonstrates some valid settings for this parameter:

■ _PLSQL_DUMP_BUFFER_EVENTS="1,6502,1001" will dump the buffer whenever the ORA-1, ORA-1001, or ORA-6502 errors are raised.

■ _PLSQL_DUMP_BUFFER_EVENTS="ON_EXIT,6502" will dump the buffer when the interpreter exits and whenever the ORA-6502 error is raised.

■ _PLSQL_DUMP_BUFFER_EVENTS="ALL_EXCEPTIONS,ON_EXIT" will dump the buffer when the interpreter exits and whenever any error is raised.

Pseudo-Code Tracing

This level of tracing is available with all PL/SQL versions. It will echo all of the PL/SQL pseudo-code operations to the trace file as they are executed, along with the current line of source code, if available. Pseudo-code operations are similar to assembly language instructions—they are what PL/SQL code is compiled into, and are executed by the runtime engine. Although the pseudo-codes themselves are not documented, this type of tracing is useful to determine what lines of PL/SQL are being executed. The pseudo-code instructions themselves are also useful for Oracle Support for debugging problems.

Pseudo-code tracing is enabled by setting event 10928 to any level above 0, with the following event string syntax:

    10928 trace name context level 1

The event can be set at the session level with ALTER SESSION, or for the entire database with an entry in the initialization file. It does not use the circular buffer, so all of the tracing output will go to the file. This can result in large files, so be sure there is enough disk space available.

NOTE
The maximum size of trace files can be set using the MAX_DUMP_FILE_SIZE initialization parameter. When the trace file reaches this size, no further output is done.

For example, consider the following anonymous block:

```
-- Available online as PseudoCode.sql
ALTER SESSION SET EVENTS '10928 trace name context level 1';

BEGIN
  CallMe1;
  CallMe2;
  CallRaise(100);
END;
```

Executing this block in SQL*Plus will produce output in the trace file similar to the following.

```
*** SESSION ID:(12.4415) 2000-03-03 13:45:11.164
Entry #1
00001: ENTER     44, 0, 1, 1
00009: INFR      DS[0]+36
  Frame Desc Version = 1, Size = 19
    # of locals = 1
    TC_SSCALAR: FP+8, d=FP+16, n=FP+40
<source not available>
00014: INSTB    1, STPROC
00018: XCAL     1, 1
Entry #1
EXAMPLE.CALLME1: 00001: ENTER    4, 0, 1, 1
[Line 4]
[Line 4] END CallMe1;
EXAMPLE.CALLME1: 00009: RET
<source not available>
00023: INSTB    2, STPROC
00027: XCAL     2, 1
Entry #1
EXAMPLE.CALLME2: 00001: ENTER    4, 0, 1, 1
[Line 3]    NULL;
EXAMPLE.CALLME2: 00009: RET
<source not available>
00032: CVTIN    HS+0 =100=, FP+8
00037: INSTB    4, STPROC
00041: MOVA     FP+8, FP+4
00046: XCAL     4, 1
Entry #1
EXAMPLE.CALLRAISE: 00001: ENTER    8, 0, 1, 1
```

```
[Line 3]    RaiseIt(p_Exception);
EXAMPLE.CALLRAISE: 00009: INSTB     2, STPROC
EXAMPLE.CALLRAISE: 00013: MOVA      AP[4], FP+4
EXAMPLE.CALLRAISE: 00018: XCAL      2, 1
Entry #1
EXAMPLE.RAISEIT: 00001: ENTER     228, 0, 1, 1
EXAMPLE.RAISEIT: 00009: INFR      DS[0]+120
  Frame Desc Version = 1, Size = 52
    # of locals = 6
    TC_SSCALAR: FP+16, d=FP+80, n=FP+104
    TC_SSCALAR: FP+24, d=FP+108, n=FP+132
    TC_SSCALAR: FP+32, d=FP+136, n=FP+160
    TC_SSCALAR: FP+40, d=FP+164, n=FP+188
    TC_SSCALAR: FP+48, d=FP+192, n=FP+216
    TC_VCHAR: FP+60, d=FP+220, n=FP+224, mxl=4000, CS_IMPLICIT
[Line 4]    IF p_Exception = 0 THEN
EXAMPLE.RAISEIT: 00014: CVTIN     HS+0 =0=, FP+16
EXAMPLE.RAISEIT: 00019: CMP3N     AP[4], FP+16, PC+22 =00041:=
EXAMPLE.RAISEIT: 00029: BRNE      PC+12 =00041:=
[Line 6]    ELSIF p_Exception < 0 THEN
EXAMPLE.RAISEIT: 00041: CVTIN     HS+0 =0=, FP+24
EXAMPLE.RAISEIT: 00046: CMP3N     AP[4], FP+24, PC+27 =00073:=
EXAMPLE.RAISEIT: 00056: BRGE      PC+17 =00073:=
[Line 8]    ELSIF p_Exception = 1001 THEN
EXAMPLE.RAISEIT: 00073: CVTIN     HS+8 =1001=, FP+32
EXAMPLE.RAISEIT: 00078: CMP3N     AP[4], FP+32, PC+27 =00105:=
EXAMPLE.RAISEIT: 00088: BRNE      PC+17 =00105:=
[Line 10]   ELSIF p_Exception = 1403 THEN
EXAMPLE.RAISEIT: 00105: CVTIN     HS+16 =1403=, FP+40
EXAMPLE.RAISEIT: 00110: CMP3N     AP[4], FP+40, PC+27 =00137:=
EXAMPLE.RAISEIT: 00120: BRNE      PC+17 =00137:=
[Line 12]   ELSIF p_Exception = 6502 THEN
EXAMPLE.RAISEIT: 00137: CVTIN     HS+24 =6502=, FP+48
EXAMPLE.RAISEIT: 00142: CMP3N     AP[4], FP+48, PC+27 =00169:=
EXAMPLE.RAISEIT: 00152: BRNE      PC+17 =00169:=
[Line 15]    RAISE_APPLICATION_ERROR(-20001, 'Exception ' || p_Exception);
EXAMPLE.RAISEIT: 00169: CVTNC     AP[4], FP+60
EXAMPLE.RAISEIT: 00174: CONC3     HS+32='Exception '=, FP+60, FP+56
EXAMPLE.RAISEIT: 00181: INSTS     2
EXAMPLE.RAISEIT: 00184: INSTB     2, SPEC
EXAMPLE.RAISEIT: 00188: MOVA      HS+56, FP+4
EXAMPLE.RAISEIT: 00193: MOVA      FP[56], FP+8
EXAMPLE.RAISEIT: 00198: MOVA      HS+0, FP+12
EXAMPLE.RAISEIT: 00203: ICAL      2, 1, 1, 3
Exception handler: OTHER Line 3-3.  PC 9-28.
[Line 6]     NULL;
EXAMPLE.CALLRAISE: 00029: CLREX
EXAMPLE.CALLRAISE: 00030: BRNCH     PC+6 =00036:=
EXAMPLE.CALLRAISE: 00036: RET
00051: RET
Entry #1
00001: ENTER    212, 0, 1, 1
00009: INFR     DS[0]+32
  Frame Desc Version = 1, Size = 29
```

```
      # of locals = 1
      _TC_iVCHAR: FP+32, d=FP+196, n=FP+208, mxl=0, CS_IMPLICIT
      # of bind proxies = 1
      _TC_iVCHAR: FP+12, d=FP+52, n=FP+192, ubn(mxl)=128, CS_IMPLICIT
<source not available>
00014: GBVAR     SQLT_CHR(1), 1, FP+12
00021: INSTS     4
00024: INSTB     4, SPEC_BODY
00028: MOVA      FP+12, FP+4
00033: MOVA      FP+32, FP+8
00038: XCAL      4, 1
Entry #1
SYS.DBMS_APPLICATION_INFO: 00001: ENTER      12, 1, 1, 1
[shrink-wrapped frame]
SYS.DBMS_APPLICATION_INFO: 00009: MOVA       AP[4], FP+4
SYS.DBMS_APPLICATION_INFO: 00014: MOVA       AP[8], FP+8
SYS.DBMS_APPLICATION_INFO: 00019: ICAL       0, 7, 1, 2
SYS.DBMS_APPLICATION_INFO: 00028: RET
00043: RET
```

Along with the pseudo-codes themselves, the output shows the line of source that was compiled into the pseudo-codes, when possible. The trace file depicts the following sequence of events:

1. Entrance into the anonymous block. This is indicated by the ENTER instruction. The code for the block is not shown, because it has not been stored in the database, indicated by the **<source not available>** line.

2. Entrance into **CallMe1** and immediate return. We can see the actual lines of source code here, since **CallMe1** is stored in the database. After this, another **<source not available>** line is shown, indicating a return to the anonymous block.

3. Entrance into **CallMe2** and immediate return. Again, we can see the lines of source code, and return to the anonymous block.

4. Entrance into **CallRaise** and then into **RaiseIt**. The source code is shown each time.

5. Stepping through the IF THEN statement of **RaiseIt**, with the associated pseudo-codes for each test. This stops at the call to RAISE_APPLICATION_ERROR and the entry into the exception handler.

6. Exit from the exception handler and the anonymous block.

7. We now see that SQL*Plus itself has issued another PL/SQL block, with a call to DBMS_APPLICATION_INFO. The source code for this package is not shown, since it has been wrapped. We can see the pseudo-codes, however. (Note that not all versions of SQL*Plus will issue this call, so you may not see this output.)

The meaning of some of the pseudo-codes is described in Table 3-2. Even without knowing exactly what each does, however, this level of tracing can show the progress of a PL/SQL program.

SQL Tracing

By setting SQL_TRACE to TRUE in a session with

```
ALTER SESSION SET SQL_TRACE = TRUE;
```

information about all SQL statements and PL/SQL blocks sent to the server is dumped to the trace file. (The tkprof utility can then be used to format this information into a more readable form.) This same information can be achieved through event 10046, with the event string:

    10046 trace name context forever, level *level_num*

Pseudo-Code	Description
BR*	Pseudo-codes beginning with BR (such as BRNE) are branch instructions.
CALL, XCAL, SCAL, ICALL	Call to a procedure, either in the current block or external to the block. Depending on the location of the called procedure, different pseudo-codes are used.
ENTER	Entrance into a stack frame (such as the start of anonymous block or procedure).
GBVAR, SBVAR,GBCR	Processing of a PL/SQL bind variable.
MOV*	Pseudo-codes beginning with MOV signify the movement of data from one location to another, as in an assignment.
RET	Return from a stack frame.

TABLE 3-2. *PL/SQL Pseudo-Codes*

The levels that can be set for this event are shown in the following table:

Trace Level	Description
1	Same as SQL_TRACE
4	Level 1 + bind variable information
8	Level 1 + wait information (useful for spotting latch waits, can also be used to detect full table scans)
12	Level 1 + bind variable and wait information

Unlike the bind variable tracing that we examined earlier as part of the circular buffer tracing, this tracing will show information about all bind variables sent to the server, not just those inside PL/SQL blocks. Furthermore, the values of the variables themselves are also shown.

For example, suppose we issue the following from SQL*Plus:

```
-- Available online as SQLTrace.sql
SQL> -- First set up the variables
SQL> VARIABLE v_String1 VARCHAR2(20);
SQL> VARIABLE v_String2 VARCHAR2(20);
SQL>
SQL> BEGIN
  2    :v_String1 := 'Hello';
  3    :v_String2 := ' World!';
  4  END;
  5  /
PL/SQL procedure successfully completed.

SQL> -- Turn on SQL tracing (including bind variable information)
SQL> ALTER SESSION SET EVENTS '10046 trace name context forever, level 4';
Session altered.

SQL> BEGIN
  2    DBMS_OUTPUT.PUT_LINE(:v_String1 || :v_String2);
  3  END;
  4  /
Hello World!
PL/SQL procedure successfully completed.
```

This block will produce output similar to the following.

```
PARSING IN CURSOR #1 len=61 dep=0 uid=28 oct=47 lid=28 tim=0 hv=2809072883
ad='801d40b4'
BEGIN
  DBMS_OUTPUT.PUT_LINE(:v_String1 || :v_String2);
END;
END OF STMT
PARSE #1:c=0,e=0,p=0,cr=0,cu=0,mis=0,r=0,dep=0,og=4,tim=0
```

```
BINDS #1:
bind 0: dty=1 mxl=32(20) mal=00 scl=00 pre=00 oacflg=03 oacfl2=10 size=64
         offset=0    bfp=010bf728 bln=32 avl=05 flg=05
   value="Hello"
bind 1: dty=1 mxl=32(20) mal=00 scl=00 pre=00 oacflg=03 oacfl2=10 size=0
         offset=32   bfp=010bf748 bln=32 avl=07 flg=01
   value=" World!"
EXEC #1:c=0,e=0,p=0,cr=0,cu=0,mis=0,r=1,dep=0,og=4,tim=0
=====================
PARSING IN CURSOR #2 len=52 dep=0 uid=28 oct=47 lid=28 tim=0 hv=4201917273
ad='8010fdac'
begin dbms_output.get_lines(:lines, :numlines); end;
END OF STMT
PARSE #2:c=0,e=0,p=0,cr=0,cu=0,mis=0,r=0,dep=0,og=4,tim=0
BINDS #2:
bind 0: dty=1 mxl=2000(255) mal=25 scl=00 pre=00 oacflg=43 oacfl2=10 size=2000
         offset=0    bfp=010c63a0 bln=255 avl=00 flg=05
bind 1: dty=2 mxl=22(02) mal=00 scl=00 pre=00 oacflg=01 oacfl2=0 size=24
         offset=0    bfp=010bf750 bln=22 avl=02 flg=05
   value=25
EXEC #2:c=0,e=0,p=0,cr=0,cu=0,mis=0,r=1,dep=0,og=4,tim=0
=====================
PARSING IN CURSOR #1 len=53 dep=0 uid=28 oct=47 lid=28 tim=0 hv=583813323
ad='80355540'
begin DBMS_APPLICATION_INFO.SET_MODULE(:1,NULL); end;
END OF STMT
PARSE #1:c=0,e=0,p=0,cr=0,cu=0,mis=0,r=0,dep=0,og=4,tim=0
BINDS #1:
bind 0: dty=1 mxl=128(08) mal=00 scl=00 pre=00 oacflg=21 oacfl2=0 size=128
         offset=0    bfp=010bf6e8 bln=128 avl=08 flg=05
   value="SQL*Plus"
APPNAME mod='SQL*Plus' mh=3669949024 act='' ah=4029777240
EXEC #1:c=0,e=0,p=0,cr=0,cu=0,mis=0,r=1,dep=0,og=4,tim=0
```

In addition to the anonymous block issued by the script, the tracing also shows two additional blocks submitted by SQL*Plus itself (one to retrieve and display the DBMS_OUTPUT information, and the other to DBMS_APPLICATION_INFO). All three of these blocks contain bind variables. The information shown for a bind variable in this type of tracing is shown in Table 3-3. Most of the fields shown are for internal use, but the **dty**, **mxl**, and **value** fields are generally the most useful.

Combining Trace Events

All of the event-based tracing that we have examined in the previous sections produces output in the same trace file. Thus, if more than one event is set, the output from each will be interleaved. For example, we can combine call tracing with pseudo-code tracing with the following:

```
-- Available online as CombinedTracing.sql
SQL> -- Set both the pseudo-code and call tracing events.
SQL> ALTER SESSION SET EVENTS '10928 trace name context level 1';
```

```
Session altered.

SQL> ALTER SESSION SET EVENTS '10938 trace name context level 1';
Session altered.

SQL> -- Make some random calls.
SQL> BEGIN
  2     RandomCalls(3);
  3  END;
  4  /
PL/SQL procedure successfully completed.
```

Field	Description
bind	Position being bound (starting from 0).
dty	Datatype. These correspond to the OCI datatypes found in the **ocidfn.h** header file.
mxl	Maximum length of the bind variable. Note that this may be bigger than the requested length for character strings, to ease sharing of cursor data in the shared pool. The requested length is in parentheses.
mal	Array length for array binds.
scl	Scale.
pre	Precision.
oacflg, oacfl2	Internal flags.
size	Total size of grouped bind buffers.
offset	Offset into grouped bind buffers.
bfp	Address of the bind buffer.
bln	Length of the bind buffer.
avl	Actual variable length.
flg	Internal flags.
value	Value of the variable, if known.

TABLE 3-3. *Fields in Bind Variable Tracing*

A portion of the resulting trace file is shown next. Note that this shows both types of tracing information.

```
------------ PL/SQL TRACE INFORMATION -----------
Levels set :  1
Entry #1
00001: ENTER    44, 0, 1, 1
Trace:  ANONYMOUS BLOCK: Stack depth = 1
00009: INFR     DS[0]+36
  Frame Desc Version = 1, Size = 19
    # of locals = 1
    TC_SSCALAR: FP+8, d=FP+16, n=FP+40
<source not available>
00014: CVTIN    HS+0 =3=, FP+8
00019: INSTB    2, STPROC
00023: MOVA     FP+8, FP+4
00028: XCAL     2, 1
Entry #1
EXAMPLE.RANDOMCALLS: 00001: ENTER    312, 0, 1, 1
Trace:   PROCEDURE EXAMPLE.RANDOMCALLS: Call to entry at line 4 Stack depth = 2
...
Trace:    PACKAGE BODY EXAMPLE.RANDOM: Call to entry at line 3 Stack depth = 3
EXAMPLE.RANDOM: 00009: INFR     DS[0]+92
...
[Line 6]      IF v_Case = 1 THEN
EXAMPLE.RANDOMCALLS: 00072: CVTIN     HS+0 =1=, FP+52
EXAMPLE.RANDOMCALLS: 00077: CMP3N     FP+12, FP+52, PC+31 =00108:=
EXAMPLE.RANDOMCALLS: 00087: BRNE      PC+21 =00108:=
[Line 7]       CallMe1;
EXAMPLE.RANDOMCALLS: 00093: INSTB    3, STPROC
EXAMPLE.RANDOMCALLS: 00097: XCAL     3, 1
Entry #1
EXAMPLE.CALLME1: 00001: ENTER    4, 0, 1, 1
Trace:    PROCEDURE EXAMPLE.CALLME1: Call to entry at line 3 Stack depth = 3
[Line 3]    NULL;
EXAMPLE.CALLME1: 00009: RET
```

PL/SQL-Based Tracing

Oracle **8** and higher — The call and exception tracing available through event 10938 is available through PL/SQL in Oracle8*i* with the DBMS_TRACE package. Future enhancements to the tracing will be through the package, rather than through the event. DBMS_TRACE with Oracle8*i* Release 1 (8.1.5) essentially provides the same type of tracing as the event-based tracing, while Oracle8*i* Release 2 (8.1.6) significantly enhances the tracing capabilities.

DBMS_TRACE in 8.1.5

There are three procedures in DBMS_TRACE in 8.1.5—SET_PLSQL_TRACE, CLEAR_PLSQL_TRACE, and PLSQL_TRACE_VERSION.

SET_PLSQL_TRACE SET_PLSQL_TRACE enables tracing in the current session, and starts dumping information directly to the trace file. It is defined with

PROCEDURE SET_PLSQL_TRACE(*trace_level* IN INTEGER);

where *trace_level* specifies what is to be traced. It is computed the same way as the level for event 10938 that we examined earlier, namely the sum of the desired tracing features. The available features are described in the following table. (The values are the same as for event 10938.)

Trace Name	Value	Description
TRACE_ALL_CALLS	1	Trace all subprogram calls
TRACE_ENABLED_CALLS	2	Trace only enabled calls (those compiled with DEBUG)
TRACE_ALL_EXCEPTIONS	4	Trace all exceptions
TRACE_ENABLED_EXCEPTIONS	8	Trace only exceptions raised in enabled subprograms

The trace names are defined as constants in the package header, and thus can be used directly in a call to SET_PLSQL_TRACE. For example, suppose we issue the following statements to the database:

```
-- Available online as AllCallsExceptions815.sql
SQL> -- Enable tracing of all calls and all exceptions.
SQL> BEGIN
  2    DBMS_TRACE.SET_PLSQL_TRACE(
  3      DBMS_TRACE.TRACE_ALL_CALLS +
  4      DBMS_TRACE.TRACE_ALL_EXCEPTIONS);
  5  END;
  6  /
PL/SQL procedure successfully completed.

SQL> -- Anonymous block which raises some exceptions.
SQL> BEGIN
  2    CallRaise(1001);
  3    RaiseIt(-1);
  4  END;
  5  /
BEGIN
*
ERROR at line 1:
ORA-06510: PL/SQL: unhandled user-defined exception
```

```
ORA-06512: at "EXAMPLE.RAISEIT", line 7
ORA-06512: at line 3
```

This block will produce the following output in the trace file. This is the same output as the event 10938 tracing.

```
------------ PL/SQL TRACE INFORMATION -----------
Levels set :  1    4
Trace:  ANONYMOUS BLOCK: Stack depth = 1
Trace:    PROCEDURE EXAMPLE.CALLRAISE: Call to entry at line 3 Stack depth = 2
Trace:     PROCEDURE EXAMPLE.RAISEIT: Call to entry at line 4 Stack depth = 3
Trace:      Pre-defined exception - OER 1001 at line 9 of PROCEDURE EXAMPLE.RAISEIT:
Trace:    PROCEDURE EXAMPLE.RAISEIT: Call to entry at line 4 Stack depth = 2
Trace:     User defined exception at line 7 of PROCEDURE EXAMPLE.RAISEIT:
```

CLEAR_PLSQL_TRACE   The CLEAR_PLSQL_TRACE procedure is used to turn off tracing for the session. Statements executed after this call will not be traced. It is defined with

```
PROCEDURE CLEAR_PLSQL_TRACE;
```

and takes no parameters.

PLSQL_TRACE_VERSION   This procedure returns the major and minor versions of the DBMS_TRACE package. The major and minor versions are also defined as constants in the package header. It is defined with

```
PROCEDURE PLSQL_TRACE_VERSION(major OUT BINARY_INTEGER,
                              minor OUT BINARY_INTEGER);
```

where *major* is the major version, and *minor* is the minor version. It returns the following when run against Oracle8*i* Release 8.1.5:

```
-- Available online as traceVersion.sql
SQL> DECLARE
  2     v_MajorVersion BINARY_INTEGER;
  3     v_MinorVersion BINARY_INTEGER;
  4  BEGIN
  5     DBMS_TRACE.PLSQL_TRACE_VERSION(v_MajorVersion, v_MinorVersion);
  6     DBMS_OUTPUT.PUT_LINE(
  7        'Trace major version: ' || v_MajorVersion);
  8     DBMS_OUTPUT.PUT_LINE(
  9        'Trace minor version: ' || v_MinorVersion);
 10  END;
 11  /
```

```
Trace major version: 1
Trace minor version: 0
PL/SQL procedure successfully completed.
```

DBMS_TRACE in 8.1.6

Unlike the 8.1.5 version of DBMS_TRACE and the event-based tracing, the output from DBMS_TRACE in 8.1.6 is stored in database tables, rather than dumped to a file. This provides a much more persistent and reliable storage. There are also more types of trace events, and some additional subprograms in DBMS_TRACE.

TRACE EVENTS   The available trace events for 8.1.6 are listed in Table 3-4. These include all of the events available in release 8.1.5. They are used the same way in SET_PLSQL_TRACE.

Trace Event	Value	Description
TRACE_ALL_CALLS	1	Trace all subprogram calls
TRACE_ENABLED_CALLS	2	Trace only enabled calls (those compiled with DEBUG)
TRACE_ALL_EXCEPTIONS	4	Trace all exceptions
TRACE_ENABLED_EXCEPTIONS	8	Trace only exceptions raised in enabled subprograms
TRACE_ALL_SQL	32	Trace all SQL statements executed
TRACE_ENABLED_SQL	64	Trace SQL statements executed from enabled subprograms
TRACE_ALL_LINES	128	Trace all lines of code (including a call to or return from a procedure)
TRACE_ENABLED_LINES	256	Trace lines of code in enabled subprograms
TRACE_STOP	16384	Stop tracing
TRACE_PAUSE	4096	Pause tracing
TRACE_RESUME	8192	Continue tracing
TRACE_LIMIT	16	Limit the amount of tracing

TABLE 3-4.   *DBMS_TRACE Trace Events*

PAUSING AND RESUMING TRACING   Collection of trace data can be paused by using the procedure PAUSE_PLSQL_TRACE, and resumed again by using RESUME_PLSQL_TRACE, both of which take no arguments.

Tracing can also be paused by issuing SET_PLSQL_TRACE with a *trace_level* equal to TRACE_PAUSE, and resumed by setting *trace_level* to TRACE_RESUME.

LIMITING TRACE DATA   Similar to the circular buffer available with event-based tracing, PL/SQL-based tracing can also keep only the most recent records. There are two methods of doing this. The first is with the LIMIT_PLSQL_TRACE procedure, defined with

    PROCEDURE LIMIT_PLSQL_TRACE(*limit* IN BINARY_INTEGER := 8192);

Approximately *limit* records will be kept (the most recent ones). Earlier trace records will be overwritten. The limit is approximate because it is not checked for each trace occurrence, but at most 1,000 additional records beyond limit will be logged.

The second method is by passing TRACE_LIMIT as *trace_level* in SET_PLSQL_TRACE, and by setting event 10940 (which was used to limit the size of the circular buffer for event-based tracing). In this case, the trace limit will be set to 1,023 × the level set by event 10940.

TRACE COMMENTS   Each trace run can have a comment associated with it, through the COMMENT_PLSQL_TRACE procedure, defined as follows:

    PROCEDURE COMMENT_PLSQL_TRACE(*comment* IN VARCHAR2);

where *comment* is the desired comment. It is limited to 2,047 characters.

VERSION VERIFICATION   If the database version has been upgraded or downgraded without reloading the appropriate version of the DBMS_TRACE package, problems can occur. This can be checked with the INTERNAL_VERSION_CHECK function, defined with

    FUNCTION INTERNAL_VERSION_CHECK
      RETURN BINARY_INTEGER;

The return value is 0 if the versions match, 1 if they do not. If this function returns 1, then you should reload the DBMS_TRACE package before using it.

RUN NUMBERS   Each time you start a trace run, a unique run number is generated. This can be returned by the GET_PLSQL_TRACE_RUNNUMBER function, defined with

```
FUNCTION GET_PLSQL_TRACE_RUNNUMBER
   RETURN BINARY_INTEGER;
```

TRACE TABLES   Tracing data is kept in two tables, **plsql_trace_runs**, and **plsql_trace_events**. They are created by the **tracetab.sql** script, found in $ORACLE_HOME/rdbms/admin on Unix systems. Both tables are owned by SYS, and thus access to them must be GRANTed to other users if desired.

General information about each trace run is kept in **plsql_trace_runs**, which has the following structure:

Column	Datatype	Description
runid	NUMBER	Unique run ID
run_date	DATE	Time the run was started
run_owner	VARCHAR2(31)	Account that started the run
run_comment	VARCHAR2(2047)	User-supplied comment
run_comment1	VARCHAR2(2047)	Additional comment. Note that COMMENT_PLSQL_TRACE will modify only **run_comment**, so this column needs to be modified manually.
run_end	DATE	Time the run ended
run_flags	VARCHAR2(2047)	Flags used for the run
related_run	NUMBER	Used for relating runs on the client and server
run_system_info	VARCHAR2(2047)	Currently unused
spare1	VARCHAR2(256)	Currently unused

The **plsql_trace_events** table records detailed trace data. Each row in the table corresponds to a trace event. It has the following structure:

Column	Datatype	Description
runid	NUMBER	Run ID
event_seq	NUMBER	Event ID
event_time	DATE	Time of this event
related_event	NUMBER	ID of a related event

Column	Datatype	Description
event_kind	VARCHAR2(31)	Type of event
event_unit_dblink	VARCHAR2(31)	Database link for the current library unit
event_unit_owner	VARCHAR2(31)	Owner of the current library unit
event_unit	VARCHAR2(31)	Name of the current library unit
event_unit_kind	VARCHAR2(31)	Kind of the current library unit
event_line	NUMBER	Current line
event_proc_name	VARCHAR2(31)	Current procedure name, if any
stack_depth	NUMBER	Current stack depth
proc_name	VARCHAR2(31)	Name of a called procedure
proc_dblink	VARCHAR2(31)	Database link for a called procedure
proc_owner	VARCHAR2(31)	Owner of a called procedure
proc_unit	VARCHAR2(31)	Library unit called
proc_unit_kind	VARCHAR2(31)	Kind of procedure called
proc_line	NUMBER	Line of procedure called
proc_params	VARCHAR2(2047)	Procedure parameters
icd_index	NUMBER	Index of the ICD for calls to PL/SQL internal routines
user_excp	NUMBER	Number of a user-defined exception
excp	NUMBER	Number of a predefined exception
event_comment	VARCHAR2(2047)	Comment for this event

The kind of tracing event is listed in the **event_kind** column. The values in this column have meanings described in the following table. The symbolic name is a constant defined in the DBMS_TRACE package header.

Symbolic Name	Value	Description
PLSQL_TRACE_START	38	Start of tracing
PLSQL_TRACE_STOP	39	End of tracing
PLSQL_TRACE_SET_FLAGS	40	Trace options changed

Symbolic Name	Value	Description
PLSQL_TRACE_PAUSE	41	Tracing paused
PLSQL_TRACE_RESUME	42	Tracing resumed
PLSQL_TRACE_ENTER_VM	43	Entrance into the runtime engine
PLSQL_TRACE_EXIT_VM	44	Exit from the runtime engine
PLSQL_TRACE_BEGIN_CALL	45	Call to a standalone procedure
PLSQL_TRACE_ELAB_SPEC	46	Call to a package specification
PLSQL_TRACE_ELAB_BODY	47	Call to a package body
PLSQL_TRACE_ICD	48	Call to an internal PL/SQL routine
PLSQL_TRACE_RPC	49	Call to a remote procedure
PLSQL_TRACE_END_CALL	50	End of a call, and return to the calling block
PLSQL_TRACE_NEW_LINE	51	New line of PL/SQL code
PLSQL_TRACE_EXCP_RAISED	52	Exception raised
PLSQL_TRACE_EXCP_HANDLED	53	Exception handled
PLSQL_TRACE_SQL	54	SQL statement executed
PLSQL_TRACE_BIND	55	Bind variable processed
PLSQL_TRACE_USER	56	User-defined trace event
PLSQL_TRACE_NODEBUG	57	Events skipped because the module was not compiled debug

EXAMPLES   Examples of DBMS_TRACE can be found at the Web site for this book, accessible from **www.osborne.com**.

PL/SQL-Based Profiling

Oracle **8i** and higher   Along with the PL/SQL-based tracing that we discussed in the past sections, Oracle8i Release 2 (8.1.6) provides a profiler through the DBMS_PROFILER package. Tracing, as we have seen, provides information about events that occur during the execution of a PL/SQL program, such as calls to procedures or raised exceptions. Profiling, on the other hand, is used to time the execution of the program. You can collect information about the minimum, maximum, and total time spent executing each line of PL/SQL code. This information can then be rolled up to the library unit level or application level.

NOTE
Several of the development tools examined earlier in this chapter, including Rapid SQL, SQL Navigator, and SQL Programmer, provide a graphical interface to the profiler. See the online documentation for more details.

DBMS_PROFILER Subprograms

The subprograms available in DBMS_PROFILER are summarized in Table 3-5 and described in more detail in the following sections. Each subprogram is available as both a function and a procedure. The functions return a BINARY_INTEGER value indicating success or failure, while the procedures will raise the appropriate exception if a failure occurs. The return codes are defined in the package header and are listed in the following table.

Return Code	Value	Description
SUCCESS	0	Function executed successfully
ERROR_PARAM	1	Function called with an incorrect parameter
ERROR_IO	2	Error writing to the profiler tables
ERROR_VERSION	-1	Mismatch between the package version and database software

Subprogram	Description
START_PROFILER	Starts a profiler run
STOP_PROFILER	Stops a profiler run and flushes the data to the tables
PAUSE_PROFILER	Pauses the collection of data
RESUME_PROFILER	Continues after a pause
FLUSH_DATA	Flushes the collected data to the tables
GET_VERSION	Returns the version of the profiler package
INTERNAL_VERSION_CHECK	Verifies that the software and database version match
ROLLUP_UNIT	Rolls up data for the specified library unit
ROLLUP_RUN	Rolls up the data for the entire run

TABLE 3-5. *DBMS_PROFILER Subprograms*

Similar to DBMS_TRACE with Oracle8*i* 8.1.6, profiling data is written to database tables. We will examine those tables in "DBMS_PROFILER Tables," later in this chapter.

START_PROFILER   START_PROFILER starts the collection of profiling data and can return the current run number. It is defined as follows:

```
FUNCTION START_PROFILER(run_comment IN VARCHAR2 := SYSDATE,
                        run_comment1 IN VARCHAR2 := '',
                        run_number OUT BINARY_INTEGER)
  RETURN BINARY_INTEGER;
PROCEDURE  START_PROFILER(run_comment IN VARCHAR2 := SYSDATE,
                        run_comment1 IN VARCHAR2 := '',
                        run_number OUT BINARY_INTEGER);
FUNCTION START_PROFILER(run_comment IN VARCHAR2 := SYSDATE,
                        run_comment1 IN VARCHAR2 := '')
  RETURN BINARY_INTEGER;
PROCEDURE  START_PROFILER(run_comment IN VARCHAR2 := SYSDATE,
                        run_comment1 IN VARCHAR2 := '');
```

run_comment and *run_comment1* can be used to describe this profiler run and will be stored in the profiler tables. The current run number is returned in *run_number*. Note that if you use the versions that don't return the run number, the only way to determine it is to query the tables.

STOP_PROFILER   STOP_PROFILER will stop collection of profiler data, and flush it to the tables. It is defined with

```
FUNCTION STOP_PROFILER RETURN BINARY_INTEGER;
PROCEDURE STOP_PROFILER;
```

and takes no parameters.

PAUSE_PROFILER   PAUSE_PROFILER will stop collection of profiler data temporarily. It does not flush it to the tables. It is defined with

```
FUNCTION PAUSE_PROFILER RETURN BINARY_INTEGER;
PROCEDURE PAUSE_PROFILER;
```

RESUME_PROFILER   RESUME_PROFILER will restart the collection of profiler data after a pause. It is defined with

```
FUNCTION RESUME_PROFILER RETURN BINARY_INTEGER;
PROCEDURE RESUME_PROFILER;
```

FLUSH_DATA   FLUSH_DATA will flush the collected data to the profiler tables. Unless the data is flushed with either FLUSH_DATA or STOP_PROFILER, it will not be saved. FLUSH_DATA is defined with

```
FUNCTION FLUSH_DATA RETURN BINARY_INTEGER;
PROCEDURE FLUSH_DATA;
```

GET_VERSION   The GET_VERSION procedure will return the major and minor versions of the profiler package. The major and minor versions are defined in the package header as well. GET_VERSION is defined with

```
PROCEDURE GET_VERSION(major OUT BINARY_INTEGER,
                       minor OUT BINARY_INTEGER);
```

The major version is returned in *major*, and the minor version in *minor*.

INTERNAL_VERSION_CHECK   Just like DBMS_TRACE, if the database version has been upgraded or downgraded without reloading the appropriate version of the DBMS_PROFILER package, problems can occur. This can be checked with the INTERNAL_VERSION_CHECK function, defined with

```
FUNCTION INTERNAL_VERSION_CHECK
  RETURN BINARY_INTEGER;
```

The return value is 0 if the versions match, 1 if they do not. If this function returns 1, then you should reload the DBMS_PROFILER package before using it.

ROLLUP_UNIT   The ROLLUP_UNIT procedure will compute the total time spent executing a particular program unit. It is defined with

```
PROCEDURE ROLLUP_UNIT(run IN NUMBER, unit IN NUMBER);
```

where *run* is the run number, and *unit* is the unit number. Each program unit is assigned a unique number for each run, and this can be determined by querying the profiler tables.

ROLLUP_RUN   ROLLUP_RUN will compute the total time spent for a given run. It is defined with

    PROCEDURE ROLLUP_RUN(*run* IN NUMBER);

where *run* is the run number.

DBMS_PROFILER Tables

Profiler data is stored in three database tables. The tables can be created with the **proftab.sql** file, found in $ORACLE_HOME/rdbms/admin on Unix systems. The tables are described in the following sections.

PLSQL_PROFILER_RUNS   The **plsql_profiler_runs** table stores information about each profiler run. It has the following structure:

Column	Datatype	Description
runid	NUMBER	Unique ID for this run.
related_run	NUMBER	Run ID for related run. This is used for correlating runs on the client and server.
run_owner	VARCHAR2(32)	User who started the run.
run_date	DATE	Start time of the run.
run_comment	VARCHAR2(2047)	User-specified comment for this run, passed to START_PROFILER.
run_total_time	NUMBER	Total time for this run.
run_system_info	VARCHAR2(2047)	Currently unused.
run_comment1	VARCHAR2(2047)	Additional comment, also passed to START_PROFILER.
spare1	VARCHAR2(256)	Currently unused.

PLSQL_PROFILER_UNITS   The **plsql_profiler_units** table stores information about each program unit executed during the run. It has the following structure:

Column	Datatype	Description
runid	NUMBER	Unique ID for this run
unit_number	NUMBER	Unique ID for this program unit
unit_type	VARCHAR2(32)	Type of program unit
unit_owner	VARCHAR2(32)	Owner of this program unit
unit_name	VARCHAR2(32)	Name of this program unit
unit_timestamp	DATE	Timestamp for this program unit; can be used to detect changes
total_time	NUMBER	Total time spent executing this program unit
spare1	NUMBER	Currently unused
spare2	NUMBER	Currently unused

PLSQL_PROFILER_DATA   The **plsql_profiler_data** table provides the lowest level of detail for profiling, namely information about each line of PL/SQL code. It has the following structure:

Column	Datatype	Description
runid	NUMBER	Unique run ID
unit_number	NUMBER	Unique unit ID
line#	NUMBER	Line number within unit
total_occur	NUMBER	Number of times this line was executed for this run
total_time	NUMBER	Total time spent executing this line
min_time	NUMBER	Minimum time spent executing this line
max_time	NUMBER	Maximum time spent executing this line
spare1	NUMBER	Currently unused
spare2	NUMBER	Currently unused

Column	Datatype	Description
spare3	NUMBER	Currently unused
spare4	NUMBER	Currently unused

Examples

Examples of DBMS_PROFILER can be found at the Web site for this book, accessible from **www.osborne.com**.

Summary

In this chapter, we have examined different techniques for debugging PL/SQL code, ranging from text-based techniques such as DBMS_OUTPUT and inserting into a debugging table to full GUI debuggers. Depending on your environment and needs, different methods may be appropriate. As we examined each of these debugging methods, we also discussed seven common PL/SQL errors and how to avoid them. We also discussed the tracing and profiling tools available with various PL/SQL versions.

PART

II

Non-Object Features

CHAPTER

4

Creating Subprograms and Packages

here are two main kinds of PL/SQL blocks: anonymous and named. An anonymous block (beginning with either DECLARE or BEGIN) is compiled each time it is issued. It also is not stored in the database, and cannot be called directly from other PL/SQL blocks. The constructs that we will look at in this and the next two chapters—procedures, functions, packages, and triggers—are all named blocks and thus do not have these restrictions. They can be stored in the database and run when appropriate. In this chapter, we will explore the syntax of creating procedures, functions, and packages. In Chapter 5, we will examine how to use them and some of their implications. Chapter 6 focuses on database triggers.

Procedures and Functions

PL/SQL procedures and functions behave very much like procedures and functions in other 3GLs (third-generation languages). They share many of the same properties. Collectively, procedures and functions are also known as *subprograms*. As an example, the following code creates a procedure in the database:

```
-- Available online as part of AddNewStudent.sql
CREATE OR REPLACE PROCEDURE AddNewStudent (
  p_FirstName  students.first_name%TYPE,
  p_LastName   students.last_name%TYPE,
  p_Major      students.major%TYPE) AS
BEGIN
  -- Insert a new row in the students table. Use
  -- student_sequence to generate the new student ID, and
  -- 0 for current_credits.
  INSERT INTO students (ID, first_name, last_name,
                        major, current_credits)
    VALUES (student_sequence.nextval, p_FirstName, p_LastName,
            p_Major, 0);
END AddNewStudent;
```

NOTE
*The **students** table, along with the other relational tables described in Chapter 1, can be created using the **relTables.sql** script, available online.*

Once this procedure is created, we can call it from another PL/SQL block:

```
-- Available online as part of AddNewStudent.sql
BEGIN
  AddNewStudent('Zelda', 'Zudnik', 'Computer Science');
END;
```

This example illustrates several notable points:

■ The **AddNewStudent** procedure is created first with the CREATE OR REPLACE PROCEDURE statement. When a procedure is created, it is first compiled, then stored in the database in compiled form. This compiled code can then be run later from another PL/SQL block. (The source code for the procedure is also stored. See "Stored Subprograms and the Data Dictionary" in Chapter 5 for more information.)

■ When the procedure is called, parameters can be passed. In the preceding example, the new student's first name, last name, and major are passed to the procedure at run time. Inside the procedure, the parameter **p_FirstName** will have the value 'Zelda', **p_LastName** will have the value 'Zudnik', and **p_Major** will have the value 'Computer Science', since these literals are passed to the procedure when it is called.

■ A procedure call is a PL/SQL statement by itself. It is not called as part of an expression. When a procedure is called, control passes to the first executable statement inside the procedure. When the procedure finishes, control resumes at the statement following the procedure call. In this regard, PL/SQL procedures behave the same as procedures in other 3GLs. Functions are called as part of an expression, as we will see later in this section.

■ A procedure is a PL/SQL block, with a declarative section, executable section, and exception handling section. As in an anonymous block, only the executable section is required. **AddNewStudent** only has an executable section.

Subprogram Creation

Similar to other data dictionary objects, subprograms are created using the CREATE statement. Procedures are created with CREATE PROCEDURE, and functions are created with CREATE FUNCTION. We will examine the details of these statements in the following sections.

Creating a Procedure

The basic syntax for the CREATE [OR REPLACE] PROCEDURE statement is

```
CREATE [OR REPLACE] PROCEDURE procedure_name
  [ (argument [{IN | OUT | IN OUT}] type,
    ...
    argument [{IN | OUT | IN OUT}] type) ] {IS | AS}
procedure_body
```

where *procedure_name* is the name of the procedure to be created, *argument* is the name of a procedure parameter, *type* is the type of the associated parameter, and *procedure_body* is a PL/SQL block that makes up the code of the procedure. See "Subprogram Parameters," later in this chapter, for information on procedure and function parameters, and the meaning of the IN, OUT, and IN OUT keywords.

Oracle**8***i*
and higher

Oracle8*i* adds an additional optional keyword to each parameter—NOCOPY. This is discussed later in this chapter in "Passing Parameters by Reference and by Value."

In order to change the code of a procedure, the procedure must be dropped and then re-created. Since this is a common operation while the procedure is under development, the OR REPLACE keywords allow this to be done in one operation. If the procedure exists, it is dropped first, without a warning message. (To drop a procedure, use the DROP PROCEDURE command, described in the "Dropping Procedures and Functions" section later in this chapter.) If the procedure does not already exist, then it is simply created. If the procedure exists and the OR REPLACE keywords are not present, the CREATE statement will return the Oracle error "ORA-955: name is already used by an existing object."

As with other CREATE statements, creating a procedure is a DDL operation, so an implicit COMMIT is done both before and after the procedure is created. Either the IS or the AS keyword can be used—they are equivalent.

THE PROCEDURE BODY   The body of a procedure is a PL/SQL block with declarative, executable, and exception sections. The declarative section is located between the IS or AS keyword and the BEGIN keyword. The executable section (the only one that is required) is located between the BEGIN and EXCEPTION keywords. The exception section is located between the EXCEPTION and END keywords.

TIP
There is no DECLARE keyword in a procedure or function declaration. The IS or AS keyword is used instead. This syntax originally comes from Ada, on which PL/SQL is based.

The structure of a procedure therefore looks like this:

```
CREATE OR REPLACE PROCEDURE procedure_name [parameter_list] AS
   /* Declarative section is here */
BEGIN
```

```
   /* Executable section is here */
EXCEPTION
   /* Exception section is here */
END [procedure_name];
```

The procedure name can optionally be included after the final END statement in the procedure declaration. If there is an identifier after the END, it must match the name of the procedure.

TIP
It is good style to include the procedure name in the final END statement, both because it emphasizes the END, which matches the CREATE statement, and because it enables the PL/SQL compiler to flag mismatched BEGIN-END pairs as early as possible.

Creating a Function

A function is very similar to a procedure. Both take parameters, which can be of any mode (parameters and modes are described later in this chapter, in "Subprogram Parameters"). Both are different forms of PL/SQL blocks, with a declarative, executable, and exception section. Both can be stored in the database or declared within a block. (Procedures and functions not stored in the database are discussed in Chapter 5, in "Subprogram Locations.") However, a procedure call is a PL/SQL statement by itself, while a function call is called as part of an expression. For example, the following function returns TRUE if the specified class is 80 percent full or more, and FALSE otherwise:

```
-- Available online as AlmostFull.sql
CREATE OR REPLACE FUNCTION AlmostFull (
   p_Department classes.department%TYPE,
   p_Course     classes.course%TYPE)
   RETURN BOOLEAN IS

   v_CurrentStudents NUMBER;
   v_MaxStudents     NUMBER;
   v_ReturnValue     BOOLEAN;
   v_FullPercent     CONSTANT NUMBER := 80;
BEGIN
   -- Get the current and maximum students for the requested
   -- course.
```

```
SELECT current_students, max_students
  INTO v_CurrentStudents, v_MaxStudents
  FROM classes
  WHERE department = p_Department
  AND course = p_Course;

-- If the class is more full than the percentage given by
-- v_FullPercent, return TRUE. Otherwise, return FALSE.
IF (v_CurrentStudents / v_MaxStudents * 100) >= v_FullPercent THEN
  v_ReturnValue := TRUE;
ELSE
  v_ReturnValue := FALSE;
END IF;

RETURN v_ReturnValue;
END AlmostFull;
```

The **AlmostFull** function returns a boolean value. It can be called from the following PL/SQL block. Note that the function call is not a statement by itself—it is used as part of the IF statement inside the loop.

```
-- Available online as callFunction.sql
SQL> DECLARE
  2     CURSOR c_Classes IS
  3       SELECT department, course
  4         FROM classes;
  5  BEGIN
  6     FOR v_ClassRecord IN c_Classes LOOP
  7       -- Output all the classes which don't have very much room
  8       IF AlmostFull(v_ClassRecord.department,
  9                     v_ClassRecord.course) THEN
 10         DBMS_OUTPUT.PUT_LINE(
 11           v_ClassRecord.department || ' ' ||
 12           v_ClassRecord.course || ' is almost full!');
 13       END IF;
 14     END LOOP;
 15  END;
 16  /
MUS 410 is almost full!
PL/SQL procedure successfully completed.
```

FUNCTION SYNTAX   The syntax for creating a stored function is very similar to the syntax for a procedure. It is

```
CREATE [OR REPLACE] FUNCTION function_name
  [(argument [{IN | OUT | IN OUT}] type,
   ...
   argument [{IN | OUT | IN OUT}] type)]
  RETURN return_type {IS | AS}
  function_body
```

where *function_name* is the name of the function, *argument* and *type* are the same as for procedures, *return_type* is the type of the value that the function returns, and *function_body* is a PL/SQL block containing the code for the function.

Similar to procedures, the argument list is optional. In this case, there are no parentheses either in the function declaration or in the function call. However, the function return type is required, since the function call is part of an expression. The type of the function is used to determine the type of the expression containing the function call.

Oracle **8i** and higher | Like procedures, the NOCOPY keyword is available with Oracle8*i* for function parameters. See "Passing Parameters by Reference and by Value" later in this chapter for details.

THE RETURN STATEMENT   Inside the body of the function, the RETURN statement is used to return control to the calling environment with a value. The general syntax of the RETURN statement is

```
RETURN expression;
```

where *expression* is the value to be returned. When RETURN is executed, *expression* will be converted to the type specified in the RETURN clause of the function definition, if it is not already of that type. At this point, control immediately returns to the calling environment.

There can be more than one RETURN statement in a function, although only one of them will be executed. It is an error for a function to end without executing a RETURN. The following example illustrates multiple RETURN statements in one function. Even though there are five different RETURN statements in the function, only one of them is executed. Which one is executed depends on how full the class specified by **p_Department** and **p_Course** is.

```
-- Available online as ClassInfo.sql
CREATE OR REPLACE FUNCTION ClassInfo(
  /* Returns 'Full' if the class is completely full,
     'Some Room' if the class is over 80% full,
     'More Room' if the class is over 60% full,
     'Lots of Room' if the class is less than 60% full, and
```

```
         'Empty' if there are no students registered. */
   p_Department classes.department%TYPE,
   p_Course     classes.course%TYPE)
   RETURN VARCHAR2 IS

   v_CurrentStudents NUMBER;
   v_MaxStudents     NUMBER;
   v_PercentFull     NUMBER;
BEGIN
   -- Get the current and maximum students for the requested
   -- course.
   SELECT current_students, max_students
     INTO v_CurrentStudents, v_MaxStudents
     FROM classes
     WHERE department = p_Department
     AND course = p_Course;

   -- Calculate the current percentage.
   v_PercentFull := v_CurrentStudents / v_MaxStudents * 100;

   IF v_PercentFull = 100 THEN
     RETURN 'Full';
   ELSIF v_PercentFull > 80 THEN
     RETURN 'Some Room';
   ELSIF v_PercentFull > 60 THEN
     RETURN 'More Room';
   ELSIF v_PercentFull > 0 THEN
     RETURN 'Lots of Room';
   ELSE
     RETURN 'Empty';
   END IF;
END ClassInfo;
```

When used in a function, the RETURN statement must have an expression associated with it. RETURN can also be used in a procedure, however. In this case, it has no arguments, which causes control to pass back to the calling environment immediately. The current values of the formal parameters declared as OUT or IN OUT are passed back to the actual parameters, and execution continues from the statement following the procedure call. (See "Subprogram Parameters," later in this chapter, for more information on parameters.)

Dropping Procedures and Functions

Similar to dropping a table, procedures and functions can also be dropped. This removes the procedure or function from the data dictionary. The syntax for dropping a procedure is

```
DROP PROCEDURE procedure_name;
```

and the syntax for dropping a function is

```
DROP FUNCTION function_name;
```

where *procedure_name* is the name of an existing procedure, and *function_name* is the name of an existing function. For example, the following statement drops the **AddNewStudent** procedure:

```
DROP PROCEDURE AddNewStudent;
```

If the object to be dropped is a function, you must use DROP FUNCTION, and if the object is a procedure, you must use DROP PROCEDURE. Like CREATE, DROP is a DDL command, so an implicit COMMIT is done both before and after the statement. If the subprogram does not exist, the DROP statement will raise the error "ORA-4043: object does not exist."

Subprogram Parameters

As in other 3GLs, you can create procedures and functions that take parameters. These parameters can have different modes, and may be passed by value or by reference. We will examine how to do this in the next few sections.

Parameter Modes

Given the **AddNewStudent** procedure shown earlier, we can call this procedure from the following anonymous PL/SQL block:

```
-- Available online as callANS.sql
DECLARE
  -- Variables describing the new student
  v_NewFirstName  students.first_name%TYPE := 'Cynthia';
  v_NewLastName   students.last_name%TYPE := 'Camino';
  v_NewMajor      students.major%TYPE := 'History';
BEGIN
  -- Add Cynthia Camino to the database.
  AddNewStudent(v_NewFirstName, v_NewLastName, v_NewMajor);
END;
```

The variables declared in the preceding block (**v_NewFirstName**, **v_NewLastName**, **v_NewMajor**) are passed as arguments to **AddNewStudent**. In this context, they are known as *actual parameters*, while the parameters in the procedure declaration (**p_FirstName**, **p_LastName**, **p_Major**) are known as *formal parameters*. Actual parameters contain the values passed to the procedure when it is called, and they receive results from the procedure when it returns (depending on the mode). The values of the actual parameters are the ones that will be used in the procedure. The formal parameters are the placeholders for the values of the actual parameters. When the procedure is called, the formal parameters are assigned the values of the actual parameters. Inside the procedure, they are referred to by the formal parameters. When the procedure returns, the actual parameters are assigned the values of the formal parameters. These assignments follow the normal rules for PL/SQL assignment, including type conversion, if necessary.

Formal parameters can have three modes—IN, OUT, or IN OUT. (Oracle 8i adds the NOCOPY modifier, described in "Using NOCOPY," later in this chapter.) If the mode is not specified for a formal parameter, it defaults to IN. The differences between each mode are described in Table 4-1 and illustrated in the following example:

Mode	Description
IN	The value of the actual parameter is passed into the procedure when the procedure is invoked. Inside the procedure, the formal parameter acts like a PL/SQL constant—it is considered *read-only* and cannot be changed. When the procedure finishes and control returns to the calling environment, the actual parameter is not changed.
OUT	Any value the actual parameter has when the procedure is called is ignored. Inside the procedure, the formal parameter acts like an uninitialized PL/SQL variable, and thus has a value of NULL. It can be read from and written to. When the procedure finishes and control returns to the calling environment, the contents of the formal parameter are assigned to the actual parameter. (In Oracle8i, this behavior can be altered by using the NOCOPY modifier—see "Passing Parameters by Reference and by Value," later in this chapter.)
IN OUT	This mode is a combination of IN and OUT. The value of the actual parameter is passed into the procedure when the procedure is invoked. Inside the procedure, the formal parameter acts like an initialized variable, and can be read from and written to. When the procedure finishes and control returns to the calling environment, the contents of the formal parameter are assigned to the actual parameter (subject to NOCOPY in Oracle8i, as for IN).

TABLE 4-1. *Parameter Modes*

NOTE
*The **ModeTest** example shows legal and illegal*
PL/SQL assignments. If you remove the comments
from the illegal statements, you will receive
compilation errors.

```
-- Available online as ModeTest.sql
CREATE OR REPLACE PROCEDURE ModeTest (
  p_InParameter    IN NUMBER,
  p_OutParameter   OUT NUMBER,
  p_InOutParameter IN OUT NUMBER) IS

  v_LocalVariable  NUMBER := 0;
BEGIN
  DBMS_OUTPUT.PUT_LINE('Inside ModeTest:');
  IF (p_InParameter IS NULL) THEN
    DBMS_OUTPUT.PUT('p_InParameter is NULL');
  ELSE
    DBMS_OUTPUT.PUT('p_InParameter = ' || p_InParameter);
  END IF;

  IF (p_OutParameter IS NULL) THEN
    DBMS_OUTPUT.PUT('  p_OutParameter is NULL');
  ELSE
    DBMS_OUTPUT.PUT('  p_OutParameter = ' || p_OutParameter);
  END IF;

  IF (p_InOutParameter IS NULL) THEN
    DBMS_OUTPUT.PUT_LINE('  p_InOutParameter is NULL');
  ELSE
    DBMS_OUTPUT.PUT_LINE('  p_InOutParameter = ' ||
                         p_InOutParameter);
  END IF;

  /* Assign p_InParameter to v_LocalVariable. This is legal,
     since we are reading from an IN parameter and not writing
     to it. */
  v_LocalVariable := p_InParameter;  -- Legal

  /* Assign 7 to p_InParameter. This is ILLEGAL, since we
     are writing to an IN parameter. */
  -- p_InParameter := 7;  -- Illegal

  /* Assign 7 to p_OutParameter. This is legal, since we
     are writing to an OUT parameter. */
  p_OutParameter := 7;  -- Legal
```

```
    /* Assign p_OutParameter to v_LocalVariable. In Oracle7 version
       7.3.4, and Oracle8 version 8.0.4 or higher (including 8i),
       this is legal.  Prior to 7.3.4, it is illegal to read from an
       OUT parameter. */
    v_LocalVariable := p_OutParameter;   -- Possibly illegal

    /* Assign p_InOutParameter to v_LocalVariable. This is legal,
       since we are reading from an IN OUT parameter. */
    v_LocalVariable := p_InOutParameter;   -- Legal

    /* Assign 8 to p_InOutParameter. This is legal, since we
       are writing to an IN OUT parameter. */
    p_InOutParameter := 8;   -- Legal

    DBMS_OUTPUT.PUT_LINE('At end of ModeTest:');
    IF (p_InParameter IS NULL) THEN
      DBMS_OUTPUT.PUT('p_InParameter is NULL');
    ELSE
      DBMS_OUTPUT.PUT('p_InParameter = ' || p_InParameter);
    END IF;

    IF (p_OutParameter IS NULL) THEN
      DBMS_OUTPUT.PUT('  p_OutParameter is NULL');
    ELSE
      DBMS_OUTPUT.PUT('  p_OutParameter = ' || p_OutParameter);
    END IF;

    IF (p_InOutParameter IS NULL) THEN
      DBMS_OUTPUT.PUT_LINE('  p_InOutParameter is NULL');
    ELSE
      DBMS_OUTPUT.PUT_LINE('  p_InOutParameter = ' ||
                            p_InOutParameter);
    END IF;

END ModeTest;
```

NOTE

It is illegal to read from OUT parameters in Oracle versions prior to 7.3.4 and in 8.0.3, but legal in Oracle8 version 8.0.4 and higher. See "Reading from OUT Parameters," later in this chapter, for more details.

PASSING VALUES BETWEEN FORMAL AND ACTUAL PARAMETERS

We can call **ModeTest** with the following block:

```
-- Available online as part of callMT.sql
DECLARE
  v_In NUMBER := 1;
  v_Out NUMBER := 2;
  v_InOut NUMBER := 3;
BEGIN
  DBMS_OUTPUT.PUT_LINE('Before calling ModeTest:');
  DBMS_OUTPUT.PUT_LINE('v_In = ' || v_In ||
                    ' v_Out = ' || v_Out ||
                    ' v_InOut = ' || v_InOut);

  ModeTest(v_In, v_Out, v_InOut);

  DBMS_OUTPUT.PUT_LINE('After calling ModeTest:');
  DBMS_OUTPUT.PUT_LINE('  v_In = ' || v_In ||
                    ' v_Out = ' || v_Out ||
                    ' v_InOut = ' || v_InOut);
END;
```

This produces output as follows:

```
Before calling ModeTest:
v_In = 1  v_Out = 2  v_InOut = 3
Inside ModeTest:
p_InParameter = 1  p_OutParameter is NULL  p_InOutParameter = 3
At end of ModeTest:
p_InParameter = 1  p_OutParameter = 7  p_InOutParameter = 8
After calling ModeTest:
v_In = 1  v_Out = 7  v_InOut = 8
```

This output shows that the OUT parameter has been initialized to NULL inside the procedure. Also, the values of the IN and IN OUT formal parameters at the end of the procedure have been copied back to the actual parameters when the procedure ends.

NOTE
If the procedure raises an exception, then the values of IN OUT and OUT formal parameters are not copied to their corresponding actual parameters (subject to NOCOPY in Oracle8i). See "Exceptions Raised Inside Subprograms," later in this chapter.

LITERALS OR CONSTANTS AS ACTUAL PARAMETERS   Because of this copying, the actual parameter which corresponds to an IN OUT or OUT parameter must be a variable, and cannot be a constant or expression. There must be a location where the returned value can be stored. For example, we can replace **v_In** with a literal when we call **ModeTest**:

```
-- Available online as part of callMT.sql
DECLARE
  v_Out NUMBER := 2;
  v_InOut NUMBER := 3;
BEGIN
  ModeTest(1, v_Out, v_InOut);
END;
```

But if we replace **v_Out** with a literal, we get the following illegal example:

```
-- Available online as part of callMT.sql
SQL> DECLARE
  2     v_InOut NUMBER := 3;
  3   BEGIN
  4     ModeTest(1, 2, v_InOut);
  5   END;
  6   /
DECLARE
*
ERROR at line 1:
ORA-06550: line 4, column 15:
PLS-00363: expression '2' cannot be used as an assignment target
ORA-06550: line 4, column 3:
PL/SQL: Statement ignored
```

COMPILATION CHECKS   The PL/SQL compiler will check for legal assignments when the procedure is created. For example, if we remove the comments on the assignment to **p_InParameter**, **ModeTest** generates the following error if we attempt to compile it:

```
PLS-363: expression 'P_INPARAMETER' cannot be used as an
         assignment target
```

READING FROM OUT PARAMETERS   Prior to version 7.3.4 and in 8.0.3, it is illegal to read from an OUT parameter in a procedure. If we attempt to compile **ModeTest** against an 8.0.3 database, for example, we receive the following error:

```
PLS-00365: 'P_OUTPARAMETER' is an OUT parameter and cannot be read
```

Oracle Version	Legal to Read OUT Parameters?
Prior to 7.3.4	No
7.3.4	Yes
8.0.3	No
8.0.4 and higher	Yes

TABLE 4-2.   *The Legality of Reading OUTs*

One workaround for this issue is to declare OUT parameters as IN OUT. Table 4-2 shows which Oracle versions allow reading from OUT parameters and which do not.

Constraints on Formal Parameters

When a procedure is called, the values of the actual parameters are passed in, and they are referred to using the formal parameters inside the procedure. The constraints on the variables are passed as well, as part of the parameter passing mechanism. In a procedure declaration, it is illegal to constrain CHAR and VARCHAR2 parameters with a length, and NUMBER parameters with a precision and/or scale, as the constraints will be taken from the actual parameters. For example, the following procedure declaration is illegal and will generate a compile error:

```
-- Available online as part of ParameterLength.sql
CREATE OR REPLACE PROCEDURE ParameterLength (
  p_Parameter1 IN OUT VARCHAR2(10),
  p_Parameter2 IN OUT NUMBER(3,1)) AS
BEGIN
  p_Parameter1 := 'abcdefghijklm';
  p_Parameter2 := 12.3;
END ParameterLength;
```

The correct declaration for this procedure would be

```
-- Available online as part of ParameterLength.sql
CREATE OR REPLACE PROCEDURE ParameterLength (
  p_Parameter1 IN OUT VARCHAR2,
  p_Parameter2 IN OUT NUMBER) AS
BEGIN
  p_Parameter1 := 'abcdefghijklmno';
  p_Parameter2 := 12.3;
END ParameterLength;
```

So, what are the constraints on **p_Parameter1** and **p_Parameter2**? They come from the actual parameters. If we call **ParameterLength** with

```
-- Available online as part of ParameterLength.sql
DECLARE
  v_Variable1 VARCHAR2(40);
  v_Variable2 NUMBER(7,3);
BEGIN
  ParameterLength(v_Variable1, v_Variable2);
END;
```

then **p_Parameter1** will have a maximum length of 40 (coming from the actual parameter **v_Variable1**) and **p_Parameter2** will have precision 7 and scale 3 (coming from the actual parameter **v_Variable2**). It is important to be aware of this. Consider the following block, which also calls **ParameterLength**:

```
-- Available online as part of ParameterLength.sql
DECLARE
  v_Variable1 VARCHAR2(10);
  v_Variable2 NUMBER(7,3);
BEGIN
  ParameterLength(v_Variable1, v_Variable2);
END;
```

The only difference between this block and the prior one is that **v_Variable1**, and hence **p_Parameter1**, has a length of 10 rather than 40. Since **ParameterLength** assigns a character string of length 15 to **p_Parameter1** (and hence **v_Variable1**), there is not enough room in the string. This will result in the following Oracle errors when the procedure is called:

```
ORA-06502: PL/SQL: numeric or value error
ORA-06512: at "EXAMPLE.PARAMETERLENGTH", line 5
ORA-06512: at line 5
```

The source of the error is not in the procedure, it is in the code that calls the procedure. In addition, the ORA-6502 is a runtime error, not a compile error. Thus the block compiled successfully, and the error was actually raised when the procedure returned and the PL/SQL engine attempted to copy the actual value 'abcdefghijklmno' into the formal parameter.

TIP
In order to avoid errors such as ORA-6502,
document any constraint requirements of the
actual parameters when the procedure is created.
This documentation should consist of comments
stored with the procedure, and should include a
description of what the procedure does, in addition
to any parameter definitions.

%TYPE AND PROCEDURE PARAMETERS   Although formal parameters
cannot be declared with constraints, they can be constrained by using %TYPE. If a
formal parameter is declared using %TYPE, and the underlying type is constrained,
then the constraint will be on the formal parameter rather than the actual parameter.
If we declare **ParameterLength** with

```
-- Available online as part of ParameterLength.sql
CREATE OR REPLACE PROCEDURE ParameterLength (
  p_Parameter1 IN OUT VARCHAR2,
  p_Parameter2 IN OUT students.current_credits%TYPE) AS
BEGIN
  p_Parameter2 := 12345;
END ParameterLength;
```

p_Parameter2 will be constrained with precision of 3, since that is the precision
of the **current_credits** column. Even if we call **ParameterLength** with an actual
parameter of enough precision, the formal precision is taken. Thus the following
example will generate the ORA-6502 error:

```
-- Available online as part of ParameterLength.sql
SQL> DECLARE
  2     v_Variable1 VARCHAR2(1);
  3     -- Declare v_Variable2 with no constraints
  4     v_Variable2 NUMBER;
  5  BEGIN
  6     -- Even though the actual parameter has room for 12345, the
  7     -- constraint on the formal parameter is taken and we get
  8     -- ORA-6502 on this procedure call.
  9     ParameterLength(v_Variable1, v_Variable2);
 10  END;
 11  /
DECLARE
*
```

```
ERROR at line 1:
ORA-06502: PL/SQL: numeric or value error: number precision too large
ORA-06512: at "EXAMPLE.PARAMETERLENGTH", line 5
ORA-06512: at line 9
```

Exceptions Raised Inside Subprograms

If an error occurs inside a subprogram, an exception is raised. This exception may
be user-defined or predefined. If the procedure has no exception handler for this
error (or if an exception is raised from within a handler), control immediately passes
out of the procedure to the calling environment, in accordance with the exception
propagation rules (see *the PL/SQL User's Guide* for more details). However, in this
case, the values of OUT and IN OUT formal parameters are *not* returned to the
actual parameters. The actual parameters will have the same values as they would
have had, as if the procedure not been called. For example, suppose we create the
following procedure:

```
-- Available online as part of RaiseError.sql
/* Illustrates the behavior of unhandled exceptions and
 * OUT variables. If p_Raise is TRUE, then an unhandled
 * error is raised. If p_Raise is FALSE, the procedure
 * completes successfully.
 */
CREATE OR REPLACE PROCEDURE RaiseError (
  p_Raise IN BOOLEAN,
  p_ParameterA OUT NUMBER) AS
BEGIN
  p_ParameterA := 7;

  IF p_Raise THEN
    /* Even though we have assigned 7 to p_ParameterA, this
     * unhandled exception causes control to return immediately
     * without returning 7 to the actual parameter associated
     * with p_ParameterA.
     */
    RAISE DUP_VAL_ON_INDEX;
  ELSE
    -- Simply return with no error. This will return 7 to the
    -- actual parameter.
    RETURN;
  END IF;
END RaiseError;
```

If we call **RaiseError** with the following block:

```
-- Available online as part of RaiseError.sql
DECLARE
  v_TempVar NUMBER := 1;
```

```
BEGIN
  DBMS_OUTPUT.PUT_LINE('Initial value: ' || v_TempVar);
  RaiseError(FALSE, v_TempVar);
  DBMS_OUTPUT.PUT_LINE('Value after successful call: ' ||
                       v_TempVar);

  v_TempVar := 2;
  DBMS_OUTPUT.PUT_LINE('Value before 2nd call: ' || v_TempVar);
RaiseError(TRUE, v_TempVar);
EXCEPTION
  WHEN OTHERS THEN
    DBMS_OUTPUT.PUT_LINE('Value after unsuccessful call: ' ||
                         v_TempVar);
END;
```

we get the following output:

```
Initial value: 1
Value after successful call: 7
Value before 2nd call: 2
Value after unsuccessful call: 2
```

Before the first call to **RaiseError**, **v_TempVar** contained 1. The first call was successful, and **v_TempVar** was assigned the value 7. The block then changed **v_TempVar** to 2 before the second call to **RaiseError**. This second call did not complete successfully, and **v_TempVar** was unchanged at 2 (rather than being changed to 7 again).

| Oracle **8i** and higher | The semantics of exception handling change when an OUT or IN OUT parameter is declared with the NOCOPY hint. See "Exception Semantics with NOCOPY," later in this chapter, for details. |

Passing Parameters by Reference and by Value

A subprogram parameter can be passed in one of two ways—by reference or by value. When a parameter is passed *by reference*, a pointer to the actual parameter is passed to the corresponding formal parameter. When a parameter is passed *by value*, on the other hand, it is copied from the actual parameter into the formal parameter. Passing by reference is generally faster, since it avoids the copy. This is especially true for collection parameters (tables and varrays, which we will discuss in Chapter 14). By default, PL/SQL will pass IN parameters by reference, and IN OUT and OUT parameters by value. This is done to preserve the exception semantics that we discussed in the previous section, and so that constraints on actual parameters can be verified. Prior to Oracle8i, there is no way to modify this behavior.

USING NOCOPY

 Oracle8*i* includes a compiler hint known as NOCOPY. The syntax for declaring a parameter with this hint is

parameter_name [*mode*] NOCOPY *datatype*

where *parameter_name* is the name of the parameter, *mode* is the parameter mode (IN, OUT, or IN OUT), and *datatype* is the parameter datatype. If NOCOPY is present, then the PL/SQL compiler will try to pass the parameter by reference, rather than by value. NOCOPY is a compiler hint, rather than a directive, so it will not always be taken. The following example illustrates the syntax of NOCOPY:

```
-- Available online as part of NoCopyTest.sql
CREATE OR REPLACE PROCEDURE NoCopyTest (
  p_InParameter    IN NUMBER,
  p_OutParameter   OUT NOCOPY VARCHAR2,
  p_InOutParameter IN OUT NOCOPY CHAR) IS
BEGIN
  NULL;
END NoCopyTest;
```

Using NOCOPY on an IN parameter will generate a compilation error, since IN parameters are always passed by reference and NOCOPY thus doesn't apply.

EXCEPTION SEMANTICS WITH NOCOPY   When a parameter is passed by reference, any modifications to the actual parameter also modify the formal parameter, since both point to the same location. This means that if a procedure exits with an unhandled exception after the formal parameter has been changed, the original value of the actual parameter will be lost. Suppose we modify **RaiseError** to use NOCOPY, as follows:

```
-- Available online as part of NoCopyTest.sql
CREATE OR REPLACE PROCEDURE RaiseError (
  p_Raise IN BOOLEAN,
  p_ParameterA OUT NOCOPY NUMBER) AS
BEGIN
  p_ParameterA := 7;
  IF p_Raise THEN
    RAISE DUP_VAL_ON_INDEX;
  ELSE
    RETURN;
  END IF;
END RaiseError;
```

The only change is that **p_ParameterA** will now be passed by reference, rather than by value. Suppose we call **RaiseError** with the following:

```
-- Available online as part of NoCopyTest.sql
DECLARE
  v_TempVar NUMBER := 1;
BEGIN
  DBMS_OUTPUT.PUT_LINE('Initial value: ' || v_TempVar);
  RaiseError(FALSE, v_TempVar);
  DBMS_OUTPUT.PUT_LINE('Value after successful call: ' ||
                        v_TempVar);

  v_TempVar := 2;
  DBMS_OUTPUT.PUT_LINE('Value before 2nd call: ' || v_TempVar);
  RaiseError(TRUE, v_TempVar);
EXCEPTION
  WHEN OTHERS THEN
    DBMS_OUTPUT.PUT_LINE('Value after unsuccessful call: ' ||
                          v_TempVar);
END;
```

(This is the same block we saw earlier, in "Exceptions Raised Inside Subprograms.") The output of this block, however, is different now:

```
Initial value: 1
Value after successful call: 7
Value before 2nd call: 2
Value after unsuccessful call: 7
```

The actual parameter has been modified both times, even when the exception was raised.

NOCOPY RESTRICTIONS   In some cases, NOCOPY will be ignored, and the parameter will be passed by value. No error is generated in these cases. Remember that NOCOPY is a hint, and the compiler is not obligated to follow it. NOCOPY will be ignored in the following situations:

■ The actual parameter is a member of an index-by table. If the actual parameter is an entire table, however, this restriction does not apply.

■ The actual parameter is constrained by a precision, scale, or NOT NULL constraint. This restriction does not apply to a character parameter constrained by a maximum length, though.

- The actual and formal parameters are both records, and they were declared either implicitly or using %ROWTYPE, and the constraints on the corresponding fields differ.

- Passing the actual parameter requires an implicit datatype conversion.

- The subprogram is involved in a remote procedure call (RPC). An RPC is a procedure call made over a database link to a remote server.

TIP

As the last point above illustrates, if the subprogram is part of an RPC, NOCOPY will be ignored. If you modify an existing application to make some of the calls RPCs, rather than local calls, the exception semantics can change.

BENEFITS OF NOCOPY   The primary advantage of NOCOPY is that it may increase performance. This is especially valuable when passing large PL/SQL tables, as the following example illustrates:

```
-- Available online as CopyFast.sql
CREATE OR REPLACE PACKAGE CopyFast AS
  -- PL/SQL table of students.
  TYPE StudentArray IS
    TABLE OF students%ROWTYPE;

  -- Three procedures which take a parameter of StudentArray, in
  -- different ways.  They each do nothing.
  PROCEDURE PassStudents1(p_Parameter IN StudentArray);
  PROCEDURE PassStudents2(p_Parameter IN OUT StudentArray);
  PROCEDURE PassStudents3(p_Parameter IN OUT NOCOPY StudentArray);

  -- Test procedure.
  PROCEDURE Go;
END CopyFast;

CREATE OR REPLACE PACKAGE BODY CopyFast AS
  PROCEDURE PassStudents1(p_Parameter IN StudentArray) IS
  BEGIN
    NULL;
  END PassStudents1;
```

```
   PROCEDURE PassStudents2(p_Parameter IN OUT StudentArray) IS
   BEGIN
     NULL;
   END PassStudents2;

   PROCEDURE PassStudents3(p_Parameter IN OUT NOCOPY StudentArray) IS
   BEGIN
     NULL;
   END PassStudents3;

   PROCEDURE Go IS
     v_StudentArray StudentArray := StudentArray(NULL);
     v_StudentRec students%ROWTYPE;
     v_Time1 NUMBER;
     v_Time2 NUMBER;
     v_Time3 NUMBER;
     v_Time4 NUMBER;
   BEGIN
     -- Fill up the array with 50,001 copies of David Dinsmore's
     -- record.
     SELECT *
       INTO v_StudentArray(1)
       FROM students
       WHERE ID = 10007;
     v_StudentArray.EXTEND(50000, 1);

     -- Call each version of PassStudents, and time them.
     -- DBMS_UTILITY.GET_TIME will return the current time, in
     -- hundredths of a second.
     v_Time1 := DBMS_UTILITY.GET_TIME;
     PassStudents1(v_StudentArray);
     v_Time2 := DBMS_UTILITY.GET_TIME;
     PassStudents2(v_StudentArray);
     v_Time3 := DBMS_UTILITY.GET_TIME;
     PassStudents3(v_StudentArray);
     v_Time4 := DBMS_UTILITY.GET_TIME;

     -- Output the results.
     DBMS_OUTPUT.PUT_LINE('Time to pass IN: ' ||
                          TO_CHAR((v_Time2 - v_Time1) / 100));
     DBMS_OUTPUT.PUT_LINE('Time to pass IN OUT: ' ||
                          TO_CHAR((v_Time3 -  v_Time2) / 100));
     DBMS_OUTPUT.PUT_LINE('Time to pass IN OUT NOCOPY: ' ||
                          TO_CHAR((v_Time4 - v_Time3) / 100));
   END Go;
END CopyFast;
```

NOTE
This example uses a package to group together related procedures. Packages are described in "Packages," later in this chapter. See Chapter 14 for information on collections and how the EXTEND method is used.

Each of the **PassStudents** procedures does nothing—the procedures simply take a parameter which is a PL/SQL table of students. The parameter is 50,001 records, so it is reasonably large. The difference between the procedures is that **PassStudents1** takes the parameter as an IN, **PassStudents2** as an IN OUT, and **PassStudents3** as IN OUT NOCOPY. Thus, **PassStudents2** should pass the parameter by value and the other two by reference. We can see this by looking at the results of calling **CopyFast.Go**:

```
Time to pass IN: 0
Time to pass IN OUT: 4.28
Time to pass IN OUT NOCOPY: 0
```

Although the actual results may differ on your system, the time for passing the IN OUT parameter by value should be significantly more than passing the IN and IN OUT NOCOPY parameters by reference.

Subprograms with No Parameters
If there are no parameters for a procedure, there are no parentheses in either the procedure declaration or the procedure call. This is also true for functions. The following example illustrates this.

```
-- Available online as noparams.sql
CREATE OR REPLACE PROCEDURE NoParamsP AS
BEGIN
  DBMS_OUTPUT.PUT_LINE('No Parameters!');
END NoParamsP;

CREATE OR REPLACE FUNCTION NoParamsF
  RETURN DATE AS
BEGIN
  RETURN SYSDATE;
END NoParamsF;

BEGIN
  NoParamsP;
  DBMS_OUTPUT.PUT_LINE('Calling NoParamsF on ' ||
    TO_CHAR(NoParamsF, 'DD-MON-YYYY'));
END;
```

With the CALL syntax available with Oracle8*i*, the parentheses are optional.
and higher

Positional and Named Notation

In all of the examples shown so far in this chapter, the actual arguments are associated with the formal arguments by position. Given a procedure declaration such as

```
-- Available online as part of CallMe.sql
CREATE OR REPLACE PROCEDURE CallMe(
  p_ParameterA VARCHAR2,
  p_ParameterB NUMBER,
  p_ParameterC BOOLEAN,
  p_ParameterD DATE) AS
BEGIN
  NULL;
END CallMe;
```

and a calling block such as

```
-- Available online as part of CallMe.sql
DECLARE
  v_Variable1 VARCHAR2(10);
  v_Variable2 NUMBER(7,6);
  v_Variable3 BOOLEAN;
  v_Variable4 DATE;
BEGIN
  CallMe(v_Variable1, v_Variable2, v_Variable3, v_Variable4);
END;
```

the actual parameters are associated with the formal parameters by position: **v_Variable1** is associated with **p_ParameterA**, **v_Variable2** is associated with **p_ParameterB**, and so on. This is known as *positional notation*. Positional notation is more commonly used, and it is also the notation used in other 3GLs such as C.

Alternatively, we can call the procedure using *named notation*:

```
-- Available online as part of CallMe.sql
DECLARE
  v_Variable1 VARCHAR2(10);
  v_Variable2 NUMBER(7,6);
  v_Variable3 BOOLEAN;
  v_Variable4 DATE;
BEGIN
  CallMe(p_ParameterA => v_Variable1,
         p_ParameterB => v_Variable2,
         p_ParameterC => v_Variable3,
         p_ParameterD => v_Variable4);
END;
```

In named notation, the formal parameter and the actual parameter are both included for each argument. This allows us to rearrange the order of the arguments, if desired. For example, the following block also calls **CallMe**, with the same arguments:

```
-- Available online as part of CallMe.sql
DECLARE
  v_Variable1 VARCHAR2(10);
  v_Variable2 NUMBER(7,6);
  v_Variable3 BOOLEAN;
  v_Variable4 DATE;
BEGIN
  CallMe(p_ParameterB => v_Variable2,
         p_ParameterC => v_Variable3,
         p_ParameterD => v_Variable4,
         p_ParameterA => v_Variable1);
END;
```

Positional and named notation can be mixed in the same call as well, if desired. The first arguments must be specified by position, and the remaining arguments can be specified by name. The following block illustrates this method:

```
-- Available online as part of CallMe.sql
DECLARE
  v_Variable1 VARCHAR2(10);
  v_Variable2 NUMBER(7,6);
  v_Variable3 BOOLEAN;
  v_Variable4 DATE;
BEGIN
  -- First 2 parameters passed by position, the second 2 are
  -- passed by name.
  CallMe(v_Variable1, v_Variable2,
         p_ParameterC => v_Variable3,
         p_ParameterD => v_Variable4);
END;
```

Named notation is another feature of PL/SQL that comes from Ada. When should you use positional notation, and when should you use named notation? Neither is more efficient than the other, so the only preference is one of style. Some of the style differences are illustrated in Table 4-3.

I generally use positional notation, as I prefer to write succinct code. It is important to use good names for the actual parameters, however. On the other hand, if the procedure takes a large number of arguments (more than ten is a good measure), then named notation is desirable, since it is easier to match the formal and actual parameters. Procedures with this many arguments are fairly rare, however.

Positional Notation	Named Notation
Relies more on good names for the actual parameters to illustrate what each is used for.	Clearly illustrates the association between the actual and formal parameters.
Names used for the formal and actual parameters are independent; one can be changed without modifying the other.	Can be more difficult to maintain because all calls to the procedure using named notation must be changed if the *names* of the formal parameters are changed.
Can be more difficult to maintain because all calls to the procedure using positional notation must be changed if the *order* of the formal parameters is changed.	The *order* used for the formal and actual parameters is independent; one can be changed without modifying the other.
More succinct than named notation.	Requires more coding, since both the formal and actual parameters are included in the procedure call.
Parameters with default values must be at the end of the argument list.	Allows default values for formal parameters to be used, no matter which parameter has the default.

TABLE 4-3.   *Positional vs. Named Notation*

TIP
The more parameters a procedure has, the more difficult it is to call and make sure that all of the required parameters are present. If you have a significant number of parameters that you would like to pass to or from a procedure, consider defining a record type with the parameters as fields within the record. Then you can use a single parameter of the record type. (Note that if the calling environment is not PL/SQL, then you may not be able to bind a record type, however). PL/SQL has no explicit limit on the number of parameters.

Parameter Default Values

Similar to variable declarations, the formal parameters to a procedure or function can have default values. If a parameter has a default value, it does not have to be passed from the calling environment. If it is passed, the value of the actual parameter will be used instead of the default. A default value for a parameter is included using the syntax:

parameter_name [*mode*] *parameter_type* {:= | DEFAULT} *initial_value*

where *parameter_name* is the name of the formal parameter, *mode* is the parameter mode (IN, OUT, or IN OUT), *parameter_type* is the parameter type (either predefined or user-defined), and *initial_value* is the value to be assigned to the formal parameter by default. Either := or the DEFAULT keyword can be used. For example, we can rewrite the **AddNewStudent** procedure to assign the economics major by default to all new students, unless overridden by an explicit argument:

```
-- Available online as part of default.sql
CREATE OR REPLACE PROCEDURE AddNewStudent (
  p_FirstName    students.first_name%TYPE,
  p_LastName     students.last_name%TYPE,
  p_Major        students.major%TYPE DEFAULT 'Economics') AS
BEGIN
  -- Insert a new row in the students table. Use
  -- student_sequence to generate the new student ID, and
  -- 0 for current_credits.
  INSERT INTO students VALUES (student_sequence.nextval,
    p_FirstName, p_LastName, p_Major, 0);
END AddNewStudent;
```

The default value will be used if the **p_Major** formal parameter does not have an actual parameter associated with it in the procedure call. We can do this with positional notation:

```
-- Available online as part of default.sql
BEGIN
  AddNewStudent('Simon', 'Salovitz');
END;
```

or with named notation:

```
-- Available online as part of default.sql
BEGIN
  AddNewStudent(p_FirstName => 'Veronica',
                p_LastName => 'Vassily');
END;
```

If positional notation is used, all parameters with default values that don't have an associated actual parameter must be at the end of the parameter list. Consider the following example:

```
-- Available online as part of DefaultTest.sql
CREATE OR REPLACE PROCEDURE DefaultTest (
  p_ParameterA NUMBER DEFAULT 10,
  p_ParameterB VARCHAR2 DEFAULT 'abcdef',
  p_ParameterC DATE DEFAULT SYSDATE) AS
BEGIN
  DBMS_OUTPUT.PUT_LINE(
    'A: ' || p_ParameterA ||
    ' B: ' || p_ParameterB ||
    ' C: ' || TO_CHAR(p_ParameterC, 'DD-MON-YYYY'));
END DefaultTest;
```

All three parameters to **DefaultTest** take default arguments. If we wanted to take the default value for **p_ParameterB** only, but specify values for **p_ParameterA** and **p_ParameterC**, we would have to use named notation, as follows:

```
-- Available online as part of DefaultTest.sql
SQL> BEGIN
  2    DefaultTest(p_ParameterA => 7, p_ParameterC => '30-DEC-95');
  3  END;
  4  /
A: 7  B: abcdef  C: 30-DEC-1995
PL/SQL procedure successfully completed.
```

If we wanted to use the default value for **p_ParameterB**, we would also have to use the default value for **p_ParameterC** when using positional notation. When using positional notation, all default parameters for which there are no associated actual parameters must be at the end of the parameter list, as in the following example:

```
-- Available online as part of DefaultTest.sql
SQL> BEGIN
  2    -- Uses the default value for both p_ParameterB and
  3    -- p_ParameterC.
  4    DefaultTest(7);
  5  END;
  6  /
A: 7  B: abcdef  C: 17-OCT-1999
PL/SQL procedure successfully completed.
```

TIP
*When using default values, make them the last
parameters in the argument list if possible. This way,
either positional or named notation can be used.*

Procedures vs. Functions

Procedures and functions share many of the same features:

■ Both can return more than one value via OUT parameters.

■ Both can have declarative, executable, and exception handling sections.

■ Both can accept default values.

■ Both can be called using positional or named notation.

■ Both can accept NOCOPY parameters (Oracle8*i* only).

So when is a function appropriate, and when is a procedure appropriate? It generally depends on how many values the subprogram is expected to return and how those values will be used. The rule of thumb is that if there is more than one return value, use a procedure. If there is only one return value, a function can be used. Although it is legal for a function to have OUT parameters (and thus return more than one value), it is generally considered poor programming style. Functions can also be called from within a SQL statement. (See Chapter 5 for more information.)

Packages

Another Ada feature incorporated in the design of PL/SQL is the *package*. A package is a PL/SQL construct that allows related objects to be stored together. A package has two separate parts—the specification and the body. Each of them is stored separately in the data dictionary. Unlike procedures and functions, which can be contained locally in a block or stored in the database, a package can only be stored; it cannot be local. Besides allowing related objects to be grouped together, packages are useful because they are less restrictive than stored subprograms with respect to dependencies. They also have performance advantages, which we will discuss later in the next chapter.

A package is essentially a named declarative section. Anything that can go in the declarative part of a block can go in a package. This includes procedures, functions, cursors, types, and variables. One advantage of putting these objects into a package is the ability to reference them from other PL/SQL blocks, so packages also provide global variables for PL/SQL.

Package Specification

The *package specification* (also known as the *package header*) contains information about the contents of the package. However, it does not contain the code for any procedures. Consider the following example:

```
-- Available online as part of ClassPackage.sql
CREATE OR REPLACE PACKAGE ClassPackage AS
  -- Add a new student into the specified class.
  PROCEDURE AddStudent(p_StudentID  IN students.id%TYPE,
                       p_Department IN classes.department%TYPE,
                       p_Course     IN classes.course%TYPE);

  -- Removes the specified student from the specified class.
  PROCEDURE RemoveStudent(p_StudentID  IN students.id%TYPE,
                          p_Department IN classes.department%TYPE,
                          p_Course     IN classes.course%TYPE);

  -- Exception raised by RemoveStudent.
  e_StudentNotRegistered EXCEPTION;

  -- Table type used to hold student info.
  TYPE t_StudentIDTable IS TABLE OF students.id%TYPE
    INDEX BY BINARY_INTEGER;

  -- Returns a PL/SQL table containing the students currently
  -- in the specified class.
  PROCEDURE ClassList(p_Department  IN  classes.department%TYPE,
                      p_Course      IN  classes.course%TYPE,
                      p_IDs         OUT t_StudentIDTable,
                      p_NumStudents IN OUT BINARY_INTEGER);
END ClassPackage;
```

ClassPackage contains three procedures, a type, and an exception. The general syntax for creating a package header is

```
CREATE [OR REPLACE] PACKAGE package_name {IS | AS}
    type_definition |
    procedure_specification |
    function_specification |
    variable_declaration |
    exception_declaration |
    cursor_declaration |
    pragma_declaration
END [package_name];
```

where *package_name* is the name of the package. The *elements* within the package (procedure and function specifications, variables, and so on) are the same as they would be in the declarative section of an anonymous block. The same syntax rules apply for a package header as for a declarative section, except for procedure and function declarations. These rules are as follows:

■ Package elements can appear in any order. However, as in a declarative section, an object must be declared before it is referenced. If a cursor contains a variable as part of the WHERE clause, for example, the variable must be declared before the cursor declaration.

■ All types of elements do not have to be present. A package can contain only procedure and function specifications, for example, without declaring any exceptions or types.

■ Any declarations for procedures and functions must be forward declarations. A *forward declaration* simply describes the subprogram and its arguments (if any), but does not include the code. See "Forward Declarations" in Chapter 5 for more information. This rule is different from the declarative section of a block, where both forward declarations and the actual code for procedures or functions may be found. The code which implements the package's procedures and functions is found in the package body.

Package Body

The *package body* is a separate data dictionary object from the package header. It cannot be successfully compiled unless the package header has already been successfully compiled. The body contains the code for the forward subprogram declarations in the package header. It can also contain additional declarations that are global to the package body, but are not visible in the specification. The following example shows the package body for **ClassPackage**:

```
-- Available online as part of ClassPackage.sql
CREATE OR REPLACE PACKAGE BODY ClassPackage AS
  -- Add a new student for the specified class.
  PROCEDURE AddStudent(p_StudentID  IN students.id%TYPE,
                       p_Department IN classes.department%TYPE,
                       p_Course     IN classes.course%TYPE) IS
  BEGIN
    INSERT INTO registered_students (student_id, department, course)
      VALUES (p_StudentID, p_Department, p_Course);
  END AddStudent;
```

```
-- Removes the specified student from the specified class.
PROCEDURE RemoveStudent(p_StudentID  IN students.id%TYPE,
                        p_Department IN classes.department%TYPE,
                        p_Course     IN classes.course%TYPE) IS
BEGIN
  DELETE FROM registered_students
    WHERE student_id = p_StudentID
    AND department = p_Department
    AND course = p_Course;

  -- Check to see if the DELETE operation was successful. If
  -- it didn't match any rows, raise an error.
  IF SQL%NOTFOUND THEN
    RAISE e_StudentNotRegistered;
  END IF;
END RemoveStudent;

-- Returns a PL/SQL table containing the students currently
-- in the specified class.
PROCEDURE ClassList(p_Department IN  classes.department%TYPE,
                    p_Course     IN  classes.course%TYPE,
                    p_IDs        OUT t_StudentIDTable,
                    p_NumStudents IN OUT BINARY_INTEGER) IS

  v_StudentID  registered_students.student_id%TYPE;

  -- Local cursor to fetch the registered students.
  CURSOR c_RegisteredStudents IS
    SELECT student_id
      FROM registered_students
      WHERE department = p_Department
      AND course = p_Course;
BEGIN
  /* p_NumStudents will be the table index. It will start at
   * 0, and be incremented each time through the fetch loop.
   * At the end of the loop, it will have the number of rows
   * fetched, and therefore the number of rows returned in
   * p_IDs.
   */
  p_NumStudents := 0;

  OPEN c_RegisteredStudents;
  LOOP
    FETCH c_RegisteredStudents INTO v_StudentID;
    EXIT WHEN c_RegisteredStudents%NOTFOUND;
```

```
      p_NumStudents := p_NumStudents + 1;
      p_IDs(p_NumStudents) := v_StudentID;
    END LOOP;
  END ClassList;
END ClassPackage;
```

The package body contains the code for the forward declarations in the package header. Objects in the header that are not forward declarations (such as the **e_StudentNotRegistered** exception) can be referenced directly in the package body.

The package body is optional. If the package header does not contain any procedures or functions (only variable declarations, cursors, types, and so on), then the body does not have to be present. This technique is valuable for declaring global variables, since all objects in a package are visible outside the package. (Scope and visibility of packaged elements are discussed in the next section.)

Any forward declaration in the package header must be fleshed out in the package body. The specification for the procedure or function must be the same in both. This includes the name of the subprogram, the names of its parameters, and the mode of the parameters. For example, the following package header does not match the package body, since the body uses a different parameter list for **FunctionA**.

```
-- Available online as packageError.sql
CREATE OR REPLACE PACKAGE PackageA AS
  FUNCTION FunctionA(p_Parameter1 IN NUMBER,
                     p_Parameter2 IN DATE)
    RETURN VARCHAR2;
END PackageA;

CREATE OR REPLACE PACKAGE BODY PackageA AS
  FUNCTION FunctionA(p_Parameter1 IN CHAR)
    RETURN VARCHAR2;
END PackageA;
```

If we try to create **PackageA** as above, we get the following errors for the package body:

```
PLS-00328: A subprogram body must be defined for the forward
           declaration of FUNCTIONA.

PLS-00323: subprogram or cursor 'FUNCTIONA' is declared in a
           package specification and must be defined in the package
           body.
```

Packages and Scope

Any object declared in a package header is in scope and is visible outside the package, by qualifying the object with the package name. For example, we can call **ClassPackage.RemoveStudent** from the following PL/SQL block:

```
BEGIN
   ClassPackage.RemoveStudent(10006, 'HIS', 101);
END;
```

The procedure call is the same as it would be for a stand-alone procedure. The only difference is that it is prefixed by the package name. Packaged procedures can have default parameters, and they can be called using either positional or named notation, just like standalone stored procedures.

This also applies to user-defined types defined in the package. In order to call **ClassList**, for example, we need to declare a variable of type **ClassPackage.t_StudentIDTable** (see Chapter 14 for more information on declaring and using PL/SQL collection types):

```
-- Available online as callCL.sql
DECLARE
  v_HistoryStudents ClassPackage.t_StudentIDTable;
  v_NumStudents     BINARY_INTEGER := 20;
BEGIN
  -- Fill the PL/SQL table with the first 20 History 101
  -- students.
  ClassPackage.ClassList('HIS', 101, v_HistoryStudents,
                       v_NumStudents);

  -- Insert these students into temp_table.
  FOR v_LoopCounter IN 1..v_NumStudents LOOP
    INSERT INTO temp_table (num_col, char_col)
      VALUES (v_HistoryStudents(v_LoopCounter),
              'In History 101');
  END LOOP;
END;
```

Inside the package body, objects in the header can be referenced without the package name. For example, the **RemoveStudent** procedure can reference the exception with simply **e_StudentNotRegistered**, not **ClassPackage.e_StudentNotRegistered**. The fully qualified name can be used if desired, however.

Scope of Objects in the Package Body

As currently written, **ClassPackage.AddStudent** and **ClassPackage.RemoveStudent** simply update the **registered_students** table. This is not really enough, however. They also should update **students** and **classes** to reflect the newly added (or removed) student. We can do this by adding a procedure to the package body, as shown below:

```
-- Available online as part of ClassPackage2.sql
CREATE OR REPLACE PACKAGE BODY ClassPackage AS
  -- Utility procedure that updates students and classes to reflect
  -- the change.  If p_Add is TRUE, then the tables are updated for
  -- the addition of the student to the class.  If it is FALSE,
  -- then they are updated for the removal of the student.
  PROCEDURE UpdateStudentsAndClasses(
      p_Add        IN BOOLEAN,
      p_StudentID IN students.id%TYPE,
      p_Department IN classes.department%TYPE,
      p_Course     IN classes.course%TYPE) IS

    -- Number of credits for the requested class
    v_NumCredits  classes.num_credits%TYPE;
  BEGIN
    -- First determine NumCredits.
    SELECT num_credits
      INTO v_NumCredits
      FROM classes
      WHERE department = p_Department
      AND course = p_Course;

    IF (p_Add) THEN
      -- Add NumCredits to the student's course load
      UPDATE STUDENTS
        SET current_credits = current_credits + v_NumCredits
        WHERE ID = p_StudentID;

      -- And increase current_students
      UPDATE classes
        SET current_students = current_students + 1
        WHERE department = p_Department
        AND course = p_Course;
    ELSE
      -- Remove NumCredits from the students course load
      UPDATE STUDENTS
        SET current_credits = current_credits - v_NumCredits
        WHERE ID = p_StudentID;
```

```
        -- And decrease current_students
      UPDATE classes
        SET current_students = current_students - 1
        WHERE department = p_Department
        AND course = p_Course;
    END IF;
END UpdateStudentsAndClasses;

-- Add a new student for the specified class.
PROCEDURE AddStudent(p_StudentID  IN students.id%TYPE,
                     p_Department IN classes.department%TYPE,
                     p_Course     IN classes.course%TYPE) IS
BEGIN
  INSERT INTO registered_students (student_id, department, course)
    VALUES (p_StudentID, p_Department, p_Course);

  UpdateStudentsAndClasses(TRUE, p_StudentID, p_Department,
                           p_Course);
END AddStudent;

-- Removes the specified student from the specified class.
PROCEDURE RemoveStudent(p_StudentID  IN students.id%TYPE,
                        p_Department IN classes.department%TYPE,
                        p_Course     IN classes.course%TYPE) IS
BEGIN
  DELETE FROM registered_students
    WHERE student_id = p_StudentID
    AND department = p_Department
    AND course = p_Course;

  -- Check to see if the DELETE operation was successful. If
  -- it didn't match any rows, raise an error.
  IF SQL%NOTFOUND THEN
    RAISE e_StudentNotRegistered;
  END IF;

  UpdateStudentsAndClasses(FALSE, p_StudentID, p_Department,
                           p_Course);
END RemoveStudent;

...
END ClassPackage;
```

UpdateStudentsAndClasses is declared global to the package body. Its scope is therefore the package body itself. Consequently, it can be called from other procedures in the body (namely **AddStudent** and **RemoveStudent**), but it is not visible from outside the body.

Overloading Packaged Subprograms

Inside a package, procedures and functions can be *overloaded*. This means that there is more than one procedure or function with the same name, but with different parameters. This is a very useful feature, since it allows the same operation to be applied to objects of different types. For example, suppose we want to add a student to a class either by specifying the student ID or by specifying the first and last names. We could do this by modifying **ClassPackage** as follows:

```
-- Available online as overload.sql
CREATE OR REPLACE PACKAGE ClassPackage AS
  -- Add a new student into the specified class.
  PROCEDURE AddStudent(p_StudentID  IN students.id%TYPE,
                       p_Department IN classes.department%TYPE,
                       p_Course     IN classes.course%TYPE);

  -- Also adds a new student, by specifying the first and last
  -- names, rather than ID number.
  PROCEDURE AddStudent(p_FirstName IN students.first_name%TYPE,
                       p_LastName  IN students.last_name%TYPE,
                       p_Department IN classes.department%TYPE,
                       p_Course     IN classes.course%TYPE);
  ...
END ClassPackage;

CREATE OR REPLACE PACKAGE BODY ClassPackage AS
  -- Add a new student for the specified class.
  PROCEDURE AddStudent(p_StudentID  IN students.id%TYPE,
                       p_Department IN classes.department%TYPE,
                       p_Course     IN classes.course%TYPE) IS
  BEGIN
    INSERT INTO registered_students (student_id, department, course)
      VALUES (p_StudentID, p_Department, p_Course);
  END AddStudent;

  -- Add a new student by name, rather than ID.
  PROCEDURE AddStudent(p_FirstName IN students.first_name%TYPE,
                       p_LastName  IN students.last_name%TYPE,
                       p_Department IN classes.department%TYPE,
                       p_Course     IN classes.course%TYPE) IS
    v_StudentID students.ID%TYPE;
  BEGIN
    /* First we need to get the ID from the students table. */
    SELECT ID
      INTO v_StudentID
      FROM students
      WHERE first_name = p_FirstName
```

```
      AND last_name = p_LastName;

    -- Now we can add the student by ID.
    INSERT INTO registered_students (student_id, department, course)
      VALUES (v_StudentID, p_Department, p_Course);
  END AddStudent;
  ...
END ClassPackage;
```

We can now add a student to Music 410 with either

```
BEGIN
    ClassPackage.AddStudent(10000, 'MUS', 410);
END;
```

or

```
BEGIN
    ClassPackage.AddStudent('Rita', 'Razmataz', 'MUS', 410);
END;
```

Overloading can be a very useful technique, when the same operation can be done on arguments of different types. Overloading is subject to several restrictions, however.

- You cannot overload two subprograms if their parameters differ only in name or mode. The following two procedures cannot be overloaded, for example:

  ```
  PROCEDURE OverloadMe(p_TheParameter IN NUMBER);
  PROCEDURE OverloadMe(p_TheParameter OUT NUMBER);
  ```

- You cannot overload two functions based only on their return type. For example, the following functions cannot be overloaded:

  ```
  FUNCTION OverloadMeToo RETURN DATE;
  FUNCTION OverloadMeToo RETURN NUMBER;
  ```

- Finally, the parameters of overloaded functions must differ by type family—you cannot overload on the same family. For example, since both CHAR and VARCHAR2 are in the same family, you can't overload the following procedures:

  ```
  PROCEDURE OverloadChar(p_TheParameter IN CHAR);
  PROCEDURE OverloadChar(p_TheParameter IN VARCHAR2);
  ```

NOTE
The PL/SQL compiler will actually allow you to create a package that has subprograms that violate the preceding restrictions. However, the runtime engine will not be able to resolve the references and will raise "PLS-307: too many declarations of 'subprogram' match this call."

Object Types and Overloading

Oracle **8** and higher | Packaged subprograms can also be overloaded based on user-defined object types. For example, suppose we create the following two object types:

```
-- Available online as part of objectOverload.sql
CREATE OR REPLACE TYPE t1 AS OBJECT (
  f NUMBER
);

CREATE OR REPLACE TYPE t2 AS OBJECT (
  f NUMBER
);
```

We can now create a package and package body that contains procedures which are overloaded based on the object type of their parameter:

```
-- Available online as part of objectOverload.sql
CREATE OR REPLACE PACKAGE Overload AS
  PROCEDURE Proc(p_Parameter1 IN t1);
  PROCEDURE Proc(p_Parameter1 IN t2);
END Overload;

CREATE OR REPLACE PACKAGE BODY Overload AS
  PROCEDURE Proc(p_Parameter1 IN t1) IS
  BEGIN
    DBMS_OUTPUT.PUT_LINE('Proc(t1): ' || p_Parameter1.f);
  END Proc;

  PROCEDURE Proc(p_Parameter1 IN t2) IS
  BEGIN
    DBMS_OUTPUT.PUT_LINE('Proc(t2): ' || p_Parameter1.f);
  END Proc;
END Overload;
```

As the following example shows, the correct procedure is called based on the type of the argument:

```
-- Available online as part of objectOverload.sql
SQL> DECLARE
  2    v_Obj1 t1 := t1(1);
  3    v_OBj2 t2 := t2(2);
  4  BEGIN
  5    Overload.Proc(v_Obj1);
  6    Overload.proc(v_Obj2);
  7  END;
  8  /
Proc(t1): 1
Proc(t2): 2
PL/SQL procedure successfully completed.
```

For more information on object types and how to use them, see Chapters 12 and 13.

Package Initialization

The first time a packaged subprogram is called, the package is *instantiated*. This means that the package is read from disk into memory, and the compiled code of the called subprogram is run. At this point, memory is allocated for all variables defined in the package. Each session will have its own copy of packaged variables, insuring that two sessions executing subprograms in the same package use different memory locations.

In many cases, initialization code needs to be run the first time the package is instantiated. This can be done by adding an initialization section to the package body, after all other objects, with the syntax

> CREATE OR REPLACE PACKAGE BODY *package_name* {IS | AS}
>
>   ...
> BEGIN
>   *initialization_code*;
> END [*package_name*];

where *package_name* is the name of the package, and *initialization_code* is the code to be run. For example, the following package implements a random number function.

```
-- Available online as Random.sql
CREATE OR REPLACE PACKAGE Random AS
  -- Random number generator.  Uses the same algorithm as the
  -- rand() function in C.

  -- Used to change the seed.  From a given seed, the same
  -- sequence of random numbers will be generated.
  PROCEDURE ChangeSeed(p_NewSeed IN NUMBER);

  -- Returns a random integer between 1 and 32767.
  FUNCTION Rand RETURN NUMBER;

  -- Same as Rand, but with a procedural interface.
  PROCEDURE GetRand(p_RandomNumber OUT NUMBER);

  -- Returns a random integer between 1 and p_MaxVal.
  FUNCTION RandMax(p_MaxVal IN NUMBER) RETURN NUMBER;

  -- Same as RandMax, but with a procedural interface.
  PROCEDURE GetRandMax(p_RandomNumber OUT NUMBER,
                       p_MaxVal IN NUMBER);
END Random;

CREATE OR REPLACE PACKAGE BODY Random AS

  /* Used for calculating the next number. */
  v_Multiplier  CONSTANT NUMBER := 22695477;
  v_Increment   CONSTANT NUMBER := 1;

  /* Seed used to generate random sequence. */
  v_Seed        number := 1;

  PROCEDURE ChangeSeed(p_NewSeed IN NUMBER) IS
  BEGIN
    v_Seed := p_NewSeed;
  END ChangeSeed;

  FUNCTION Rand RETURN NUMBER IS
  BEGIN
    v_Seed := MOD(v_Multiplier * v_Seed + v_Increment,
                (2 ** 32));
    RETURN BITAND(v_Seed/(2 ** 16), 32767);
  END Rand;

  PROCEDURE GetRand(p_RandomNumber OUT NUMBER) IS
  BEGIN
```

```
  -- Simply call Rand and return the value.
  p_RandomNumber := Rand;
END GetRand;

FUNCTION RandMax(p_MaxVal IN NUMBER) RETURN NUMBER IS
BEGIN
  RETURN MOD(Rand, p_MaxVal) + 1;
END RandMax;

PROCEDURE GetRandMax(p_RandomNumber OUT NUMBER,
                     p_MaxVal IN NUMBER) IS
BEGIN
  -- Simply call RandMax and return the value.
  p_RandomNumber := RandMax(p_MaxVal);
END GetRandMax;

BEGIN
  /* Package initialization.  Initialize the seed to the current
     time in seconds. */
  ChangeSeed(TO_NUMBER(TO_CHAR(SYSDATE, 'SSSSS')));
END Random;
```

In order to retrieve a random number, you can simply call **Random.Rand**. The
sequence of random numbers is controlled by the initial seed—the same sequence
is generated for a given seed. Thus, in order to provide more random values, we
need to initialize the seed to a different value each time the package is instantiated.
To accomplish this, the **ChangeSeed** procedure is called from the package
initialization section.

Oracle8 and higher   Oracle8 includes a built-in package DBMS_RANDOM, which can also be
used to provide random numbers. See Appendix A on the CD-ROM included
with this book for more information on the built-in packages.

Summary

We have examined three types of named PL/SQL blocks in this chapter: procedures,
functions, and packages. We discussed the syntax for creating each of these, paying
particular attention to various types of parameter passing. In the next chapter, we
will see more uses of procedures, functions, and packages. Chapter 5 will focus on
types of subprograms, how they are stored in the data dictionary, and calling stored
subprograms from SQL statements. We close the chapter with several new 8*i* features.
In Chapter 6, we will cover a fourth type of named block—database triggers.

CHAPTER
5

Using Subprograms and Packages

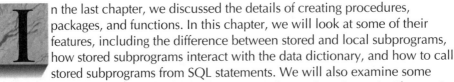

n the last chapter, we discussed the details of creating procedures, packages, and functions. In this chapter, we will look at some of their features, including the difference between stored and local subprograms, how stored subprograms interact with the data dictionary, and how to call stored subprograms from SQL statements. We will also examine some new Oracle8*i* features of stored subprograms. We will examine triggers in Chapter 6.

Subprogram Locations

Subprograms and packages can be stored in the data dictionary, as all of the examples in the previous chapter have shown. The subprogram is created first with the CREATE OR REPLACE command, and then it is called from another PL/SQL block. In addition to this, however, a subprogram can be defined within the declarative section of a block. In this case, it is known as a *local subprogram*. Packages must be stored in the data dictionary and cannot be local.

Stored Subprograms and the Data Dictionary

When a subprogram is created with CREATE OR REPLACE, it is stored in the data dictionary. In addition to the source text, the subprogram is stored in compiled form, which is known as *p-code*. The p-code has all of the references in the subprogram evaluated, and the source code is translated into a form that is easily readable by the PL/SQL engine. When the subprogram is called, the p-code is read from disk, if necessary, and executed. Once it is read from disk, the p-code is stored in the shared pool portion of the system global area (SGA), where it can be accessed by multiple users as needed. Like all of the contents of the shared pool, p-code is aged out of the shared pool according to a least-recently-used algorithm.

P-code is analogous to the object code generated by other 3GL compilers, or to Java bytecodes that can be read by a Java runtime system. Since the p-code has the object references in the subprogram evaluated (this is a property of early binding), executing the p-code is a comparatively inexpensive operation.

Information about the subprogram is accessible through various data dictionary views. The **user_objects** view contains information about all objects owned by the current user, including stored subprograms. This information includes when the object was created and last modified, the type of the object (table, sequence, function, and so on), and the validity of the object. The **user_source** view contains the original source code for the object. The **user_errors** view contains information about compile errors.

Consider the following simple procedure:

```
CREATE OR REPLACE PROCEDURE Simple AS
  v_Counter NUMBER;
```

```
BEGIN
  v_Counter := 7;
END Simple;
```

After this procedure is created, **user_objects** shows it as valid, and **user_source** contains the source code for it. **User_errors** has no rows, since the procedure was compiled successfully. This is illustrated in Figure 5-1.

If, however, we change the code of **Simple** so that it has a compile error (note the missing semicolon), such as

```
CREATE OR REPLACE PROCEDURE Simple AS
  v_Counter NUMBER;
BEGIN
  v_Counter := 7
END Simple;
```

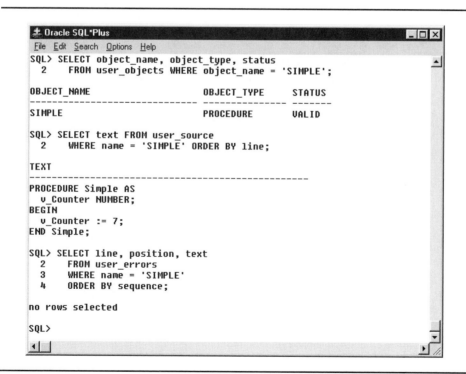

FIGURE 5-1. *Data dictionary views after successful compilation*

and examine the same three data dictionary views (as shown in Figure 5-2), we see several differences. **User_source** still shows the source code for the procedure. However, in **user_objects** the status is listed as 'INVALID' rather than 'VALID', and **user_errors** contains the PLS-103 compilation error.

TIP
*In SQL*Plus, the SHOW ERRORS command will query **user_errors** for you and format the output for readability. It will return information about errors for the last object that you created. You can use SHOW ERRORS after receiving the message "Warning: Procedure created with compilation errors." See Chapter 2 for more information on SQL*Plus and other PL/SQL development environments.*

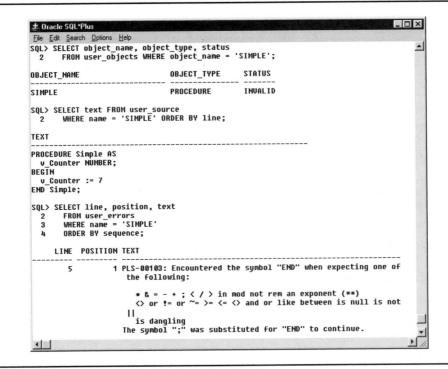

FIGURE 5-2. *Data dictionary views after unsuccessful compilation*

A stored subprogram that is invalid is still stored in the database. However, it cannot be called successfully until the error is fixed. If an invalid procedure is called, the PLS-905 error is raised, as the following example illustrates:

```
SQL> BEGIN Simple; END;
  2  /
BEGIN Simple; END;
      *
ERROR at line 1:
ORA-06550: line 1, column 7:
PLS-00905: object EXAMPLE.SIMPLE is invalid
ORA-06550: line 1, column 7:
PL/SQL: Statement ignored
```

The data dictionary is discussed in more detail in Appendix C, on the CD-ROM that accompanies this book.

Local Subprograms

A local subprogram, declared in the declarative section of a PL/SQL block, is illustrated in the following example:

```
-- Available online as localSub.sql
DECLARE
  CURSOR c_AllStudents IS
    SELECT first_name, last_name
      FROM students;

  v_FormattedName VARCHAR2(50);

  /* Function that will return the first and last name
     concatenated together, separated by a space. */
  FUNCTION FormatName(p_FirstName IN VARCHAR2,
                      p_LastName IN VARCHAR2)
    RETURN VARCHAR2 IS
  BEGIN
    RETURN p_FirstName || ' ' || p_LastName;
  END FormatName;

-- Begin main block.
BEGIN
  FOR v_StudentRecord IN c_AllStudents LOOP
    v_FormattedName :=
      FormatName(v_StudentRecord.first_name,
                 v_StudentRecord.last_name);
```

```
      DBMS_OUTPUT.PUT_LINE(v_FormattedName);
   END LOOP;
END;
```

The **FormatName** function is declared in the declarative section of a block. The function name is a PL/SQL identifier and thus follows the same scope and visibility rules as any other PL/SQL identifier. Specifically, it is only visible in the block in which it is declared. Its scope extends from the point of declaration until the end of the block. No other block can call **FormatName**, since it would not be visible from another block.

Local Subprograms as Part of Stored Subprograms

Local subprograms can also be declared as part of the declarative section of a stored subprogram, as the following example illustrates. In this case, **FormatName** can be called only from within **StoredProc**, since that is the limit of its scope.

```
-- Available online as localStored.sql
CREATE OR REPLACE PROCEDURE StoredProc AS
/* Local declarations, which include a cursor, variable, and a
      function. */
  CURSOR c_AllStudents IS
    SELECT first_name, last_name
      FROM students;

  v_FormattedName VARCHAR2(50);

  /* Function that will return the first and last name
     concatenated together, separated by a space. */
  FUNCTION FormatName(p_FirstName IN VARCHAR2,
                      p_LastName IN VARCHAR2)
    RETURN VARCHAR2 IS
  BEGIN
    RETURN p_FirstName || ' ' || p_LastName;
  END FormatName;

-- Begin main block.
BEGIN
  FOR v_StudentRecord IN c_AllStudents LOOP
    v_FormattedName :=
      FormatName(v_StudentRecord.first_name,
                 v_StudentRecord.last_name);
    DBMS_OUTPUT.PUT_LINE(v_FormattedName);
  END LOOP;
END StoredProc;
```

Location of Local Subprograms

Any local subprogram must be declared at the end of the declarative section. If we were to move **FormatName** above the declaration for **c_AllStudents**, as the following SQL*Plus session illustrates, we would get a compile error.

```
-- Available online as localError.sql
SQL> DECLARE
  2    /* Declare FormatName first. This will generate a compile
  3       error, since all other declarations have to be before
  4       any local subprograms. */
  5    FUNCTION FormatName(p_FirstName IN VARCHAR2,
  6                        p_LastName IN VARCHAR2)
  7      RETURN VARCHAR2 IS
  8    BEGIN
  9      RETURN p_FirstName || ' ' || p_LastName;
 10    END FormatName;
 11
 11    CURSOR c_AllStudents IS
 12      SELECT first_name, last_name
 13        FROM students;
 14
 14    v_FormattedName VARCHAR2(50);
 15  -- Begin main block
 16  BEGIN
 17    NULL;
 18  END;
 19  /
  CURSOR c_AllStudents IS
  *
ERROR at line 11:
ORA-06550: line 11, column 3:
PLS-00103: Encountered the symbol "CURSOR" when expecting one of the
          following:
          begin function package pragma procedure form
```

Forward Declarations

Since the names of local PL/SQL subprograms are identifiers, they must be declared before they are referenced. This is normally not a problem. However, in the case of mutually referential subprograms, this does present a difficulty. Consider the following example:

```
-- Available online as mutual.sql
DECLARE
  v_TempVal BINARY_INTEGER := 5;
```

```
  -- Local procedure A. Note that the code of A calls procedure B.
  PROCEDURE A(p_Counter IN OUT BINARY_INTEGER) IS
  BEGIN
    DBMS_OUTPUT.PUT_LINE('A(' || p_Counter || ')');
    IF p_Counter > 0 THEN
      B(p_Counter);
      p_Counter := p_Counter - 1;
    END IF;
  END A;

  -- Local procedure B. Note that the code of B calls procedure A.
  PROCEDURE B(p_Counter IN OUT BINARY_INTEGER) IS
  BEGIN
    DBMS_OUTPUT.PUT_LINE('B(' || p_Counter || ')');
    p_Counter := p_Counter - 1;
    A(p_Counter);
  END B;
BEGIN
  B(v_TempVal);
END;
```

This example is impossible to compile. Since procedure **A** calls procedure **B**, **B** must be declared prior to **A** so that the reference to **B** can be resolved. Since procedure **B** calls procedure **A**, **A** must be declared prior to **B** so that the reference to **A** can be resolved. Both of these can't be true at the same time. In order to rectify this, we can use a forward declaration. This is simply a procedure name and its formal parameters, which allow mutually referential procedures to exist. Forward declarations are also used in package headers. The following example illustrates this technique:

```
-- Available online as forwardDeclaration.sql
DECLARE
  v_TempVal BINARY_INTEGER := 5;

  -- Forward declaration of procedure B.
  PROCEDURE B(p_Counter IN OUT BINARY_INTEGER);

  PROCEDURE A(p_Counter IN OUT BINARY_INTEGER) IS
  BEGIN
    DBMS_OUTPUT.PUT_LINE('A(' || p_Counter || ')');
    IF p_Counter > 0 THEN
      B(p_Counter);
      p_Counter := p_Counter - 1;
    END IF;
  END A;

  PROCEDURE B(p_Counter IN OUT BINARY_INTEGER) IS
  BEGIN
```

```
      DBMS_OUTPUT.PUT_LINE('B(' || p_Counter || ')');
      p_Counter := p_Counter - 1;
      A(p_Counter);
    END B;
BEGIN
  B(v_TempVal);
END;
```

The output from this block is shown here.

```
B(5)
A(4)
B(4)
A(3)
B(3)
A(2)
B(2)
A(1)
B(1)
A(0)
```

Overloading Local Subprograms

As we saw in Chapter 4, subprograms declared in packages can be overloaded. This is also true for local subprograms, as the following example illustrates:

```
-- Available online as overloadedLocal.sql
DECLARE
  -- Two overloaded local procedures
  PROCEDURE LocalProc(p_Parameter1 IN NUMBER) IS
  BEGIN
    DBMS_OUTPUT.PUT_LINE('In version 1, p_Parameter1 = ' ||
                      p_Parameter1);
  END LocalProc;

  PROCEDURE LocalProc(p_Parameter1 IN VARCHAR2) IS
  BEGIN
    DBMS_OUTPUT.PUT_LINE('In version 2, p_Parameter1 = ' ||
                      p_Parameter1);
  END LocalProc;
BEGIN
  -- Call version 1
  LocalProc(12345);

  -- And version 2
  LocalProc('abcdef');
END;
```

The output from this example is

```
In version 1, p_Parameter1 = 12345
In version 2, p_Parameter1 = abcdef
```

Stored vs. Local Subprograms

Stored subprograms and local subprograms behave differently and they have different properties. When should each be used? I generally prefer to use stored subprograms, and will usually put them in a package. If you develop a useful subprogram, it is likely that you will want to call it from more than one block. In order to do this, the subprogram must be stored in the database. The size and complexity benefits are also usually a factor. The only procedures and functions that I would declare local to a block would tend to be short ones, which are only called from one specific section of the program (their containing block). Local subprograms of this sort are generally used to avoid code duplication within a single block. This usage is similar to C macros. Table 5-1 summarizes the differences between stored and local subprograms.

Stored Subprograms	Local Subprograms
The stored subprogram is stored in compiled p-code in the database; when the procedure is called, it does not have to be compiled.	The local subprogram is compiled as part of its containing block. If the containing block is anonymous and is run multiple times, the subprogram has to be compiled each time.
Stored subprograms can be called from any block submitted by a user who has EXECUTE privileges on the subprogram.	Local subprograms can be called only from the block containing the subprogram.
By keeping the subprogram code separate from the calling block, the calling block is shorter and easier to understand. The subprogram and calling block can also be maintained separately, if desired.	The subprogram and the calling block are one and the same, which can lead to confusion. If a change to the calling block is made, the subprogram will be recompiled as part of the recompilation of the containing block.

TABLE 5-1.   *Stored vs. Local Subprograms*

Stored Subprograms	Local Subprograms
The compiled p-code can be pinned in the shared pool using the DBMS_SHARED_POOL.KEEP packaged procedure.* This can improve performance.	Local subprograms cannot be pinned in the shared pool by themselves.
Standalone stored subprograms cannot be overloaded, but packaged subprograms can be overloaded within the same package.	Local subprograms can be overloaded within the same block.

* The DBMS_SHARED_POOL package is discussed in "Pinning in the Shared Pool," later in this chapter.

TABLE 5-1.   *Stored vs. Local Subprograms* (continued)

Considerations of Stored Subprograms and Packages

Storing subprograms and packages as data dictionary objects has advantages. For example, it allows them to be shared among database users as needed. There are several implications of this, however. These include dependencies among stored objects, how package state is handled, and the privileges necessary to run stored subprograms and packages.

Subprogram Dependencies

When a stored procedure or function is compiled, all of the Oracle objects that it references are recorded in the data dictionary. The procedure is *dependent* on these objects. We have seen that a subprogram that has compile errors is marked as invalid in the data dictionary. A stored subprogram can also become invalid if a DDL operation is performed on one of its dependent objects. The best way to illustrate this is by example. The **AlmostFull** function (defined in Chapter 4) queries the **classes** table. The dependencies of **AlmostFull** are illustrated in Figure 5-3. **AlmostFull** depends on only one object—**classes**. This is indicated by the arrow in the figure.

Now suppose we create a procedure that calls **AlmostFull** and inserts the results into **temp_table**. This procedure is **RecordFullClasses**:

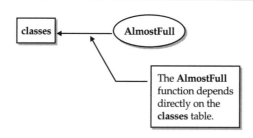

FIGURE 5-3. *AlmostFull dependencies*

```
-- Available online as RecordFullClasses.sql
CREATE OR REPLACE PROCEDURE RecordFullClasses AS
  CURSOR c_Classes IS
    SELECT department, course
      FROM classes;
BEGIN
  FOR v_ClassRecord IN c_Classes LOOP
    -- Record all classes that don't have very much room left
    -- in temp_table.
    IF AlmostFull(v_ClassRecord.department, v_ClassRecord.course)
    THEN
      INSERT INTO temp_table (char_col) VALUES
        (v_ClassRecord.department || ' ' || v_ClassRecord.course ||
        ' is almost full!');
    END IF;
  END LOOP;
END RecordFullClasses;
```

The dependency information is illustrated by the arrows in Figure 5-4. **RecordFullClasses** depends both on **AlmostFull** and on **temp_table**. These are *direct* dependencies, since **RecordFullClasses** refers directly to both **AlmostFull** and **temp_table**. **AlmostFull** depends on **classes**, so **RecordFullClasses** has an *indirect* dependency on **classes**.

If a DDL operation is performed on **classes**, all objects that depend on **classes** (directly or indirectly) are invalidated. Suppose we alter the **classes** table in our example by adding an extra column:

```
ALTER TABLE classes ADD (
  student_rating  NUMBER(2)  -- Difficulty rating from 1 to 10
);
```

This will cause both **AlmostFull** and **RecordFullClasses** to become invalid, since they depend on **classes**. This is illustrated by the SQL*Plus session in Figure 5-5.

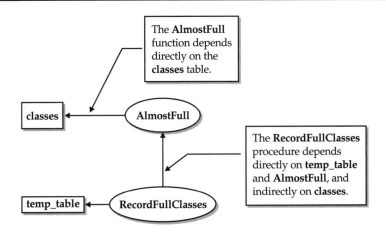

FIGURE 5-4.   *RecordFullClasses* dependencies

```
Oracle SQL*Plus                                                    _ □ ×
File  Edit  Search  Options  Help
SQL> SELECT object_name, object_type, status
  2    FROM user_objects
  3    WHERE object_name IN ('ALMOSTFULL', 'RECORDFULLCLASSES');

OBJECT_NAME                      OBJECT_TYPE      STATUS
-------------------------------- ---------------- -------
RECORDFULLCLASSES                PROCEDURE        VALID
ALMOSTFULL                       FUNCTION         VALID

SQL> ALTER TABLE classes ADD (
  2    student_rating  NUMBER(2)  -- Difficulty rating from 1 to 10
  3  );

Table altered.

SQL> SELECT object_name, object_type, status
  2    FROM user_objects
  3    WHERE object_name IN ('ALMOSTFULL', 'RECORDFULLCLASSES');

OBJECT_NAME                      OBJECT_TYPE      STATUS
-------------------------------- ---------------- -------
RECORDFULLCLASSES                PROCEDURE        INVALID
ALMOSTFULL                       FUNCTION         INVALID

SQL>
```

FIGURE 5-5.   *Invalidation as a result of a DDL operation*

Automatic Recompilation

If a dependent object is invalidated, the PL/SQL engine will automatically attempt to recompile it the next time it is called. Since neither **RecordFullClasses** nor **AlmostFull** references the new column in **classes**, this recompilation will be successful. The SQL*Plus session in Figure 5-6, which continues the session in Figure 5-5, illustrates this.

> **CAUTION**
> *The automatic recompilation can fail (especially if a table description is modified). In this case, the calling block will receive a compilation error. However, this error will occur at runtime, not compile time.*

Packages and Dependencies

As the previous example showed, stored subprograms can be invalidated if their dependent objects are modified. The situation is different for packages, however.

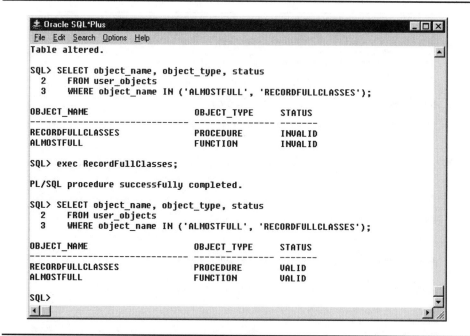

FIGURE 5-6. *Automatic recompilation after invalidation*

Consider the dependency picture for **ClassPackage** (which we saw in Chapter 4) in Figure 5-7. The package body depends on **registered_students** and the package header. But, the package header does not depend on the package body, or on **registered_students**. This is one advantage of packages—we can change the package body without having to change the header. Therefore, other objects that depend on the header won't have to be recompiled at all, since they never get invalidated. If the header is changed, this automatically invalidates the body, since the body depends on the header.

NOTE
There are certain cases in which a change in the package body necessitates a change in the header. For example, if the arguments to a procedure in both the specification and body were changed in the body, then the header would have to be modified to match. The header would not have to be modified if the implementation of a body procedure were changed without affecting its declaration, however. Similarly, if you are using the signature dependency model (described in "How Invalidations Are Determined," later in the chapter), only changes to the signatures of objects in the package specification will invalidate the body. Likewise, if you add an object to a package header (such as a cursor or variable), then the body will be invalidated.

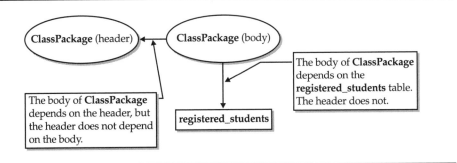

FIGURE 5-7. *ClassPackage dependencies*

We can also see this behavior from the following SQL*Plus session:

```
-- Available online as dependencies.sql
SQL> -- First create a simple table.
SQL> CREATE TABLE simple_table (f1 NUMBER);
Table created.

SQL> -- Now create a packaged procedure that references the table.
SQL> CREATE OR REPLACE PACKAGE Dependee AS
  2     PROCEDURE Example(p_Val IN NUMBER);
  3   END Dependee;
  4   /
Package created.

SQL> CREATE OR REPLACE PACKAGE BODY Dependee AS
  2     PROCEDURE Example(p_Val IN NUMBER) IS
  3     BEGIN
  4        INSERT INTO simple_table VALUES (p_Val);
  5     END Example;
  6   END Dependee;
  7   /
Package body created.

SQL> -- Now create a procedure that references Dependee.
SQL> CREATE OR REPLACE PROCEDURE Depender(p_Val IN NUMBER) AS
  2   BEGIN
  3     Dependee.Example(p_Val + 1);
  4   END Depender;
  5   /
Procedure created.

SQL> -- Query user_objects to see that all objects are valid.
SQL> SELECT object_name, object_type, status
  2     FROM user_objects
  3     WHERE object_name IN ('DEPENDER', 'DEPENDEE',
  4                          'SIMPLE_TABLE');
OBJECT_NAME                      OBJECT_TYPE    STATUS
-------------------------------- -------------- -------
SIMPLE_TABLE                     TABLE          VALID
DEPENDEE                         PACKAGE        VALID
DEPENDEE                         PACKAGE BODY   VALID
DEPENDER                         PROCEDURE      VALID

SQL> -- Change the package body only.  Note that the header is
SQL> -- unchanged.
```

```
SQL> CREATE OR REPLACE PACKAGE BODY Dependee AS
  2    PROCEDURE Example(p_Val IN NUMBER) IS
  3    BEGIN
  4      INSERT INTO simple_table VALUES (p_Val - 1);
  5    END Example;
  6  END Dependee;
  7  /
Package body created.

SQL> -- Now user_objects shows that Depender is still valid.
SQL> SELECT object_name, object_type, status
  2    FROM user_objects
  3    WHERE object_name IN ('DEPENDER', 'DEPENDEE',
  4                          'SIMPLE_TABLE');
OBJECT_NAME                      OBJECT_TYPE     STATUS
------------------------------   -------------   -------
SIMPLE_TABLE                     TABLE           VALID
DEPENDEE                         PACKAGE         VALID
DEPENDEE                         PACKAGE BODY    VALID
DEPENDER                         PROCEDURE       VALID

SQL> -- Even if we drop the table, it only invalidates the
SQL> -- package body.
SQL> DROP TABLE simple_table;
Table dropped.

SQL> SELECT object_name, object_type, status
  2    FROM user_objects
  3    WHERE object_name IN ('DEPENDER', 'DEPENDEE',
  4                          'SIMPLE_TABLE');
OBJECT_NAME                      OBJECT_TYPE     STATUS
------------------------------   -------------   -------
DEPENDEE                         PACKAGE         VALID
DEPENDEE                         PACKAGE BODY    INVALID
DEPENDER                         PROCEDURE       VALID
```

NOTE
*The data dictionary views **user_dependencies**, **all_dependencies**, and **dba_dependencies** directly list the relationships between schema objects. For more information on these views, see Appendix C on the CD-ROM that accompanies this book.*

Figure 5-8 shows the dependencies of the objects created by this script.

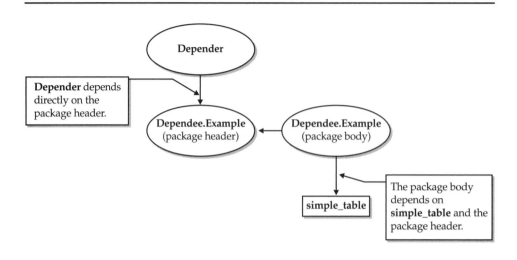

FIGURE 5-8. *More package dependencies*

How Invalidations Are Determined

When an object is altered, its dependent objects are invalidated, as we have seen. If all of the objects are in the same database, the dependent objects are invalidated as soon as the base object is altered. This can be done quickly, since the data dictionary tracks the dependencies. Suppose we create two procedures **P1** and **P2**, as illustrated in Figure 5-9. **P1** depends on **P2**, which means that recompiling **P2** will invalidate **P1**. The SQL*Plus session shown next illustrates this.

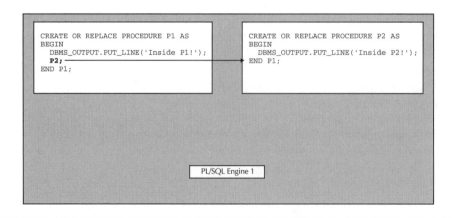

FIGURE 5-9. *P1 and P2 in the same database*

```
-- Available online as part of remoteDependencies.sql
SQL> -- Create two procedures.  P1 depends on P2.
SQL> CREATE OR REPLACE PROCEDURE P2 AS
  2  BEGIN
  3    DBMS_OUTPUT.PUT_LINE('Inside P2!');
  4  END P2;
  5  /
Procedure created.

SQL> CREATE OR REPLACE PROCEDURE P1 AS
  2  BEGIN
  3    DBMS_OUTPUT.PUT_LINE('Inside P1!');
  4    P2;
  5  END P1;
  6  /
Procedure created.

SQL> -- Verify that both procedures are valid.
SQL> SELECT object_name, object_type, status
  2    FROM user_objects
  3    WHERE object_name IN ('P1', 'P2');
OBJECT_NAME                    OBJECT_TYPE     STATUS
------------------------------ --------------- -------
P2                             PROCEDURE       VALID
P1                             PROCEDURE       VALID

SQL> -- Recompile P2, which invalidates P1 immediately.
SQL> ALTER PROCEDURE P2 COMPILE;
Procedure altered.

SQL> -- Query again to see this.
SQL> SELECT object_name, object_type, status
  2    FROM user_objects
  3    WHERE object_name IN ('P1', 'P2');
OBJECT_NAME                    OBJECT_TYPE     STATUS
------------------------------ --------------- -------
P2                             PROCEDURE       VALID
P1                             PROCEDURE       INVALID
```

Suppose, however, that **P1** and **P2** are in different databases, and **P1** calls **P2** over a database link. This situation is illustrated by Figure 5-10. In this case, recompiling **P2** does not immediately invalidate **P1**, as the following SQL*Plus session shows:

```
-- Available online as part of remoteDependencies.sql
SQL> -- Create a database link that points back to the current
SQL> -- instance.
SQL> CREATE DATABASE LINK loopback
  2    USING 'connect_string';
Database link created.

SQL> -- Change P1 to call P2 over the link.
SQL> CREATE OR REPLACE PROCEDURE P1 AS
  2  BEGIN
  3    DBMS_OUTPUT.PUT_LINE('Inside P1!');
  4    P2@loopback;
  5  END P1;
  6  /
Procedure created.

SQL> -- Verify that both are valid.
SQL> SELECT object_name, object_type, status
  2    FROM user_objects
  3    WHERE object_name IN ('P1', 'P2');
OBJECT_NAME                       OBJECT_TYPE        STATUS
------------------------------    ---------------    -------
P2                                PROCEDURE          VALID
P1                                PROCEDURE          VALID

SQL> -- Now when we recompile P2, P1 is not invalidated immediately.
SQL> ALTER PROCEDURE P2 COMPILE;
Procedure altered.

SQL> SELECT object_name, object_type, status
  2    FROM user_objects
  3    WHERE object_name IN ('P1', 'P2');
OBJECT_NAME                       OBJECT_TYPE        STATUS
------------------------------    ---------------    -------
P2                                PROCEDURE          VALID
P1                                PROCEDURE          VALID
```

NOTE

*In this example, the database link is actually a loopback, which points to the same database. The observed behavior, however, is the same as if **P1** and **P2** were actually in separate databases. Using a loopback enables us to query the status of **P1** and **P2** in one SELECT statement.*

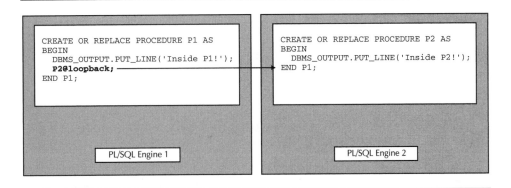

```
CREATE OR REPLACE PROCEDURE P1 AS
BEGIN
   DBMS_OUTPUT.PUT_LINE('Inside P1!');
   P2@loopback;
END P1;
```

```
CREATE OR REPLACE PROCEDURE P2 AS
BEGIN
   DBMS_OUTPUT.PUT_LINE('Inside P2!');
END P1;
```

PL/SQL Engine 1   PL/SQL Engine 2

FIGURE 5-10. *P1 and P2 in different databases*

Why is the behavior different in the remote case? The answer lies in the fact that the data dictionary does not track remote dependencies. It would thus be too expensive to invalidate all the dependent objects, since they could be in different databases (that may or may not even be accessible at the time of the invalidation).

Instead, the validity of remote objects is checked at runtime. When **P1** is called, the remote data dictionary is queried to determine the status of **P2** (if the remote database is inaccessible, then an error is raised). **P1** and **P2** are compared to see if **P1** needs to be recompiled. There are two different methods of comparison—the timestamp and signature methods.

NOTE
*It is not necessary to have a database link to utilize runtime validity checking. If **P1** were in a client-side PL/SQL engine (such as Oracle Forms), and **P2** were in the server, then the situation would be similar, and either the timestamp or signature method would be used. See Chapter 2 for more information about different PL/SQL execution environments.*

TIMESTAMP MODEL   With this model, the timestamps of the last modifications of the two objects are compared. The LAST_DDL_TIME field of **user_objects** contains this timestamp. If the base object has a newer timestamp than the dependent object, the dependent object will be recompiled. There are several issues with this model, however:

- The date comparison does not take the locations of the two PL/SQL engines into account. If they are in different time zones, then the comparison will not be valid.

- Even if the two engines are in the same time zone, the timestamp model can result in unnecessary recompilations. In the previous example, **P2** was simply recompiled, but was not actually changed. **P1** does not really have to be recompiled, but since it has an older timestamp it would be.

- Slightly more serious is when **P1** is contained in a client-side PL/SQL engine, such as Oracle Forms. In this case, it may not be possible to recompile **P1**, since the source for it may not be included with the runtime version of Forms.

 SIGNATURE MODEL   Starting with version 2.3, PL/SQL provides a different method for determining when remote dependent objects need to be recompiled that resolves the issues with the timestamp model. This method is called the "signature model." When a procedure is created, a *signature* is stored in the data dictionary in addition to the p-code. The signature encodes the types and order of the parameters. With this model, the signature of **P2** will change only when the parameters change. When **P1** is compiled the first time, the signature of **P2** is included (rather than the timestamp). Thus, **P1** only needs to be recompiled when the signature of **P2** changes.

In order to use the signature model, the parameter REMOTE_DEPENDENCIES_MODE must be set to SIGNATURE. This is a parameter in the database initialization file. (The name and location of the initialization file, commonly called init.ora, varies depending on your system.) It can also be set interactively. There are three ways of setting this mode:

- Add the line REMOTE_DEPENDENCIES_MODE=SIGNATURE to the database initialization file. The next time the database is started, the mode will be set to SIGNATURE for all sessions.

- Issue the command

  ```
  ALTER SYSTEM SET REMOTE_DEPENDENCIES_MODE = SIGNATURE;
  ```

  This will affect the entire database (all sessions) from the time the statement is issued. You must have the ALTER SYSTEM system privilege to issue this command.

- Issue the command

  ```
  ALTER SESSION SET REMOTE_DEPENDENCIES_MODE = SIGNATURE;
  ```

This will only affect your session. Objects created after this point in the current session will use the signature method.

In all of these options, TIMESTAMP can be used instead of SIGNATURE to get the 2.2 and earlier behavior. TIMESTAMP is the default.

There are several things to be aware of when using the signature method:

■ Signatures don't get modified if the default values of formal parameters are changed. Suppose **P2** has a default value for one of its parameters, and **P1** is using this default value. If the default value in the specification for **P2** is changed, **P1** will not be recompiled by default. The old value for the default parameter will still be used until **P1** is manually recompiled. This applies for IN parameters only.

■ If **P1** is calling a packaged procedure **P2**, and a new overloaded version of **P2** is added to the remote package, the signature is not changed. **P1** will still use the old version (not the new overloaded one) until **P1** is recompiled manually.

■ To manually recompile a procedure, use the command

```
ALTER PROCEDURE procedure_name COMPILE;
```

where *procedure_name* is the name of the procedure to be compiled. For functions, use

```
ALTER FUNCTION function_name COMPILE;
```

And for packages, use either of the following:

```
ALTER PACKAGE package_name COMPILE SPECIFICATION;
ALTER PACKAGE package_name COMPILE BODY;
```

For more information on the signature model, see the *Oracle Server Application Developer's Guide*, release 7.3 or later.

Package Runtime State

When a package is first instantiated, the package p-code is read from disk and put into the shared pool in the SGA. However, the *runtime state* of a package—namely, the packaged variables and cursors—is kept in session memory in the user global area (UGA). This ensures that each session will have its own copy of the package runtime state. As we saw in Chapter 4, variables declared in a package header have global scope. They are visible for any PL/SQL block that has EXECUTE privilege for the package. Since the runtime state is in the UGA, it will persist for the life of the database session. It is initialized when the package is instantiated (the initialization code, if any, is run at this time), and is not freed until the session ends. Even if the package itself is aged out of the shared pool, the package state will persist. The following example illustrates this:

```
-- Available online as PersistPkg.sql
CREATE OR REPLACE PACKAGE PersistPkg AS
  -- Type which holds an array of student ID's.
  TYPE t_StudentTable IS TABLE OF students.ID%TYPE
    INDEX BY BINARY_INTEGER;

  -- Maximum number of rows to return each time.
  v_MaxRows NUMBER := 5;

  -- Returns up to v_MaxRows student ID's.
  PROCEDURE ReadStudents(p_StudTable OUT t_StudentTable,
                         p_NumRows    OUT NUMBER);

END PersistPkg;

CREATE OR REPLACE PACKAGE BODY PersistPkg AS
  -- Query against students.  Since this is global to the package
  -- body, it will remain past a database call.
  CURSOR StudentCursor IS
    SELECT ID
      FROM students
      ORDER BY last_name;

  PROCEDURE ReadStudents(p_StudTable OUT t_StudentTable,
                         p_NumRows    OUT NUMBER) IS
    v_Done BOOLEAN := FALSE;
    v_NumRows NUMBER := 1;
  BEGIN
    IF NOT StudentCursor%ISOPEN THEN
      -- First open the cursor
      OPEN StudentCursor;
    END IF;

    -- Cursor is open, so we can fetch up to v_MaxRows
    WHILE NOT v_Done LOOP
      FETCH StudentCursor INTO p_StudTable(v_NumRows);
      IF StudentCursor%NOTFOUND THEN
        -- No more data, so we're finished.
        CLOSE StudentCursor;
        v_Done := TRUE;
      ELSE
        v_NumRows := v_NumRows + 1;
        IF v_NumRows > v_MaxRows THEN
          v_Done := TRUE;
        END IF;
      END IF;
```

```
        END LOOP;

        -- Return the actual number of rows fetched.
        p_NumRows := v_NumRows - 1;

    END ReadStudents;
END PersistPkg;
```

PersistPkg.ReadStudents will select from the **StudentsCursor** cursor. Since this cursor is declared at the package level (not inside **ReadStudents**), it will remain past a call to **ReadStudents**. We can call **PersistPkg.ReadStudents** with the following block:

```
-- Available online as callRS.sql
DECLARE
    v_StudentTable PersistPkg.t_StudentTable;
    v_NumRows NUMBER := PersistPkg.v_MaxRows;
    v_FirstName students.first_name%TYPE;
    v_LastName students.last_name%TYPE;
BEGIN
    PersistPkg.ReadStudents(v_StudentTable, v_NumRows);
    DBMS_OUTPUT.PUT_LINE(' Fetched ' || v_NumRows || ' rows:');
    FOR v_Count IN 1..v_NumRows LOOP
        SELECT first_name, last_name
            INTO v_FirstName, v_LastName
            FROM students
            WHERE ID = v_StudentTable(v_Count);
        DBMS_OUTPUT.PUT_LINE(v_FirstName || ' ' || v_LastName);
    END LOOP;
END;
```

The output from executing this block three times is shown in Figure 5-11. On each call, different data is returned because the cursor has remained open in between each call.

Serially Reusable Packages

PL/SQL 2.3 and higher let you mark a package as serially reusable. The runtime state of a *serially reusable* package will be kept in the SGA rather than the UGA, and will last only for each database call. A serially reusable package has the syntax

```
PRAGMA SERIALLY_REUSABLE;
```

in the package header (and also the package body, if present). If we modify **PersistPkg** to include this pragma, the output changes. The modified package is shown next, and the output is shown in Figure 5-12.

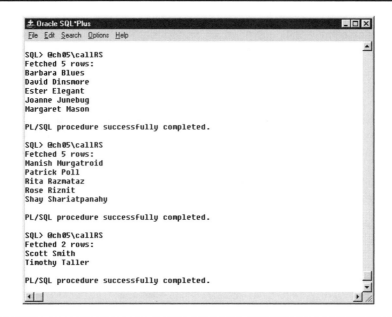

FIGURE 5-11. *Calling ReadStudents*

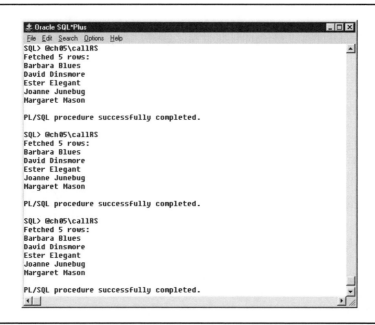

FIGURE 5-12. *Calling a serially reusable ReadStudents*

```
-- Available online as PersistPkg2.sql
CREATE OR REPLACE PACKAGE PersistPkg AS
  PRAGMA SERIALLY_REUSABLE;

  -- Type that holds an array of student IDs.
  TYPE t_StudentTable IS TABLE OF students.ID%TYPE
    INDEX BY BINARY_INTEGER;

  -- Maximum number of rows to return each time.
  v_MaxRows NUMBER := 5;

  -- Returns up to v_MaxRows student IDs.
  PROCEDURE ReadStudents(p_StudTable OUT t_StudentTable,
                         p_NumRows   OUT NUMBER);

END PersistPkg;

CREATE OR REPLACE PACKAGE BODY PersistPkg AS
  PRAGMA SERIALLY_REUSABLE;

  -- Query against students.  Even though this is global to the
  -- package body, it will be reset after each database call,
  -- because the package is now serially reusable.
  CURSOR StudentCursor IS
    SELECT ID
      FROM students
      ORDER BY last_name;
  ...
END PersistPkg;
```

Note the difference between the two versions—the non-serially reusable version will maintain the state of the cursor over database calls, while the serially reusable version resets the state (and thus the output) each time. The differences between serially reusable and non-serially reusable packages are summarized in the following table.

Serially Reusable Packages	Non-Serially Reusable Packages
Runtime state is kept in the SGA, and is freed after every database call.	Runtime state is kept in the UGA, and lasts for the life of the database session.
The maximum memory used is proportional to the number of concurrent users of the package.	The maximum memory used is proportional to the number of concurrently logged-on users, which is typically much higher.

NOTE
The semantics of serially reusable packages remain the same under MTS (multi-threaded server). In an MTS environment, the UGA is actually stored in shared memory so that sessions can be migrated between database server processes. Because of the reduced memory requirements for serially reusable packages, they can be advantageous when using MTS. For more information on configuring and using MTS, see the Oracle documentation.

Dependencies of Package Runtime State

In addition to dependencies between stored objects, dependencies can exist between package state and anonymous blocks. For example, consider the following package:

```
-- Available online as anonymousDependencies.sql
CREATE OR REPLACE PACKAGE SimplePkg AS
  v_GlobalVar NUMBER := 1;
  PROCEDURE UpdateVar;
END SimplePkg;

CREATE OR REPLACE PACKAGE BODY SimplePkg AS
  PROCEDURE UpdateVar IS
  BEGIN
    v_GlobalVar := 7;
  END UpdateVar;
END SimplePkg;
```

SimplePkg contains a package global—**v_GlobalVar**. Suppose we create **SimplePkg** from one database session. Then, in a second session, we call **SimplePkg.UpdateVar** with the following block:

```
BEGIN
  SimplePkg.UpdateVar;
END;
```

Now, back in the first session, we re-create **SimplePkg** by running the creation script again. Finally, we issue the same anonymous block in session 2. We get the following:

```
BEGIN
*
ERROR at line 1:
ORA-04068: existing state of packages has been discarded
ORA-04061: existing state of package "EXAMPLE.SIMPLEPKG" has been
           invalidated
```

```
ORA-04065: not executed, altered or dropped package
        "EXAMPLE.SIMPLEPKG"
ORA-06508: PL/SQL: could not find program unit being called
ORA-06512: at line 2
```

What has happened here? The dependency picture for this situation is shown in Figure 5-13. The anonymous block depends on **SimplePkg**, in the same sense that we have seen earlier. This is a compile-time dependency, in that it is determined when the anonymous block is first compiled. However, there is also a runtime dependency—on the packaged variable, since each session has its own copy of packaged variables. Thus, when **SimplePkg** is recompiled, the runtime dependency is followed, which invalidates the block and raises the ORA-4068 error.

Runtime dependencies exist only on package state. This includes variables and cursors declared in a package. If the package had no global variables, then the second execution of the anonymous block would have succeeded.

Privileges and Stored Subprograms

Stored subprograms and packages are objects in the data dictionary, and as such, they are owned by a particular database user, or schema. Other users can access these objects if they are granted the correct privileges on them. Privileges and roles also come into play when creating a stored object, with regard to the access available inside the subprogram.

EXECUTE Privilege

In order to allow access to a table, the SELECT, INSERT, UPDATE, and DELETE object privileges are used. The GRANT statement gives these privileges to a database user

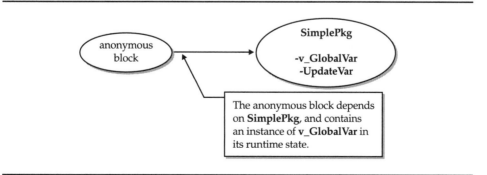

FIGURE 5-13.   *Package global dependencies*

or a role. For stored subprograms and packages, the relevant privilege is EXECUTE. Consider the **RecordFullClasses** procedure, which we examined earlier in this chapter in "Subprogram Dependencies":

```
-- Available online as part of execute.sql
CREATE OR REPLACE PROCEDURE RecordFullClasses AS
  CURSOR c_Classes IS
    SELECT department, course
      FROM classes;
BEGIN
  FOR v_ClassRecord IN c_Classes LOOP
    -- Record all classes that don't have very much room left
    -- in temp_table.
    IF AlmostFull(v_ClassRecord.department, v_ClassRecord.course) THEN
      INSERT INTO temp_table (char_col) VALUES
        (v_ClassRecord.department || ' ' || v_ClassRecord.course ||
         ' is almost full!');
    END IF;
  END LOOP;
END RecordFullClasses;
```

> **NOTE**
> The online example **execute.sql** will first create the users **UserA** and **UserB**, and then create the necessary objects for the examples in this section. You may have to modify the password used for the DBA account in order to get the example to work on your system. You can see the output from running **execute.sql** in **execute.out**, also available online.

Suppose that the objects on which **RecordFullClasses** depends (the function **AlmostFull** and tables **classes** and **temp_table**) are all owned by the database user **UserA**. **RecordFullClasses** is owned by **UserA** as well. If we grant the EXECUTE privilege on **RecordFullClasses** to another database user, say **UserB**, with

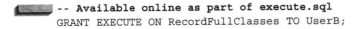

```
-- Available online as part of execute.sql
GRANT EXECUTE ON RecordFullClasses TO UserB;
```

then **UserB** can execute **RecordFullClasses** with the following block. Note that dot notation is used to indicate the schema:

```
-- Available online as part of execute.sql
BEGIN
  UserA.RecordFullClasses;
END;
```

In this scenario, all of the database objects are owned by **UserA**. This situation is illustrated in Figure 5-14. The dotted line signifies the GRANT statement from **UserA** to **UserB**, while the solid lines signify object dependencies. After executing the block of code earlier in this section, the results will be inserted into **UserA.temp_table**.

Now suppose that **UserB** has another table, also called **temp_table**, as illustrated in Figure 5-15. If **UserB** calls **UserA.RecordFullClasses** (by executing the anonymous block shown earlier), which table gets modified? The table in **UserA** does. This concept can be expressed like this:

A subprogram executes under the privilege set of its owner.

Even though **UserB** is calling **RecordFullClasses**, **RecordFullClasses** is owned by **UserA**. Thus the identifier **temp_table** will evaluate to the table belonging to **UserA**, *not* **UserB**.

Oracle **8i** and higher | Note that Oracle8*i* includes a new feature known as "Invoker's rights," which enables you to specify if a procedure executes under the privilege set of its owner or of its caller. See "Invoker's vs. Definer's Rights," later in this chapter, for details.

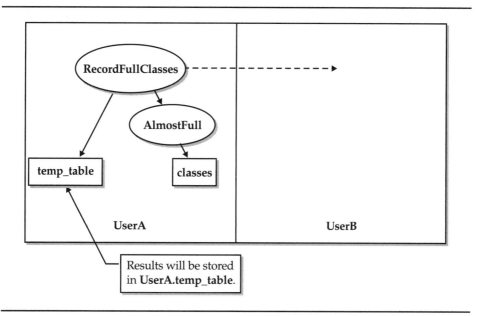

FIGURE 5-14. *Database objects owned by **UserA***

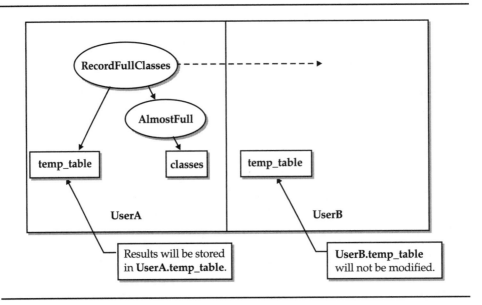

FIGURE 5-15. *temp_table owned by UserB and UserA*

Stored Subprograms and Roles

Let's modify the situation in Figure 5-15 slightly. Suppose **UserA** does not own **temp_table** or **RecordFullClasses**, and these are owned by **UserB**. Furthermore, suppose we have modified **RecordFullClasses** to explicitly refer to the objects in **UserA**. This is illustrated by the following listing and Figure 5-16.

```
-- Available online as part of execute.sql
CREATE OR REPLACE PROCEDURE RecordFullClasses AS
  CURSOR c_Classes IS
    SELECT department, course
      FROM UserA.classes;
BEGIN
  FOR v_ClassRecord IN c_Classes LOOP
    -- Record all classes that don't have very much room left
    -- in temp_table.
    IF UserA.AlmostFull(v_ClassRecord.department,
                        v_ClassRecord.course) THEN
      INSERT INTO temp_table (char_col) VALUES
        (v_ClassRecord.department || ' ' || v_ClassRecord.course ||
         ' is almost full!');
    END IF;
  END LOOP;
END RecordFullClasses;
```

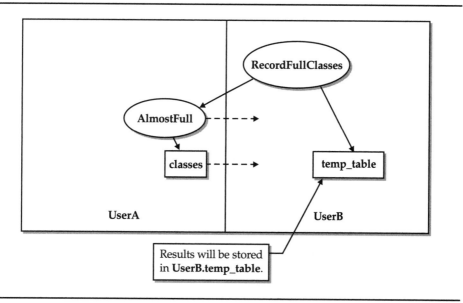

FIGURE 5-16. *RecordFullClasses owned by UserB*

In order for **RecordFullClasses** to compile correctly, **UserA** must have granted the SELECT privilege on **classes** and the EXECUTE privilege on **AlmostFull** to **UserB**. The dotted lines in Figure 5-16 represent this. Furthermore, this grant must be done explicitly and *not* through a role. The following grants, executed by **UserA**, would allow a successful compilation of **UserB.RecordFullClasses**:

```
-- Available online as part of execute.sql
GRANT SELECT ON classes TO UserB;
GRANT EXECUTE ON AlmostFull TO UserB;
```

A grant done through an intermediate role, as in

```
-- Available online as part of execute.sql
CREATE ROLE UserA_Role;
GRANT SELECT ON classes TO UserA_Role;
GRANT EXECUTE ON AlmostFull TO UserA_Role;
GRANT UserA_Role to UserB;
```

will not work. The role is illustrated in Figure 5-17.

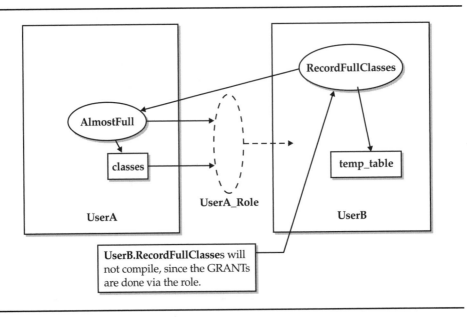

FIGURE 5-17. *Grants done via a role*

So we can clarify the rule in the previous section as follows:

A subprogram executes under the privileges that have been granted explicitly to its owner, not via a role.

If the grants had been done via a role, we would have received PLS-201 errors when we tried to compile **RecordFullClasses**:

```
PLS-201: identifier 'CLASSES' must be declared
PLS-201: identifier 'ALMOSTFULL' must be declared
```

This rule also applies for triggers and packages, which are stored in the database as well. Essentially, *the only objects available inside a stored procedure, function, package, or trigger (from Oracle7.3 and up) are the ones owned by the owner of the subprogram, or explicitly granted to the owner.*

Why is this? To explain this restriction, we need to examine binding. PL/SQL uses early binding—references are evaluated when a subprogram is compiled, not when it is run. GRANT and REVOKE are both DDL statements. They take effect immediately, and the new privileges are recorded in the data dictionary. All database sessions will see the new privilege set. However, this is not necessarily true for roles. A role can be granted to a user, and that user can then choose to disable the role with the SET ROLE command. The distinction is that SET ROLE applies to one database session only, while GRANT and REVOKE apply to all sessions. A role can be disabled in one session but enabled in other sessions.

In order to allow privileges granted via a role to be used inside stored subprograms and triggers, the privileges would have to be checked every time the procedure is run. The privileges are checked as part of the binding process. But early binding means that the privileges are checked at compile time, not runtime. In order to maintain early binding, *all roles are disabled inside stored procedures and triggers.*

Invoker's vs. Definer's Rights

| Oracle **8 i** |
| and higher |

Consider the situation that we examined earlier in this chapter, in "EXECUTE Privilege," and illustrated by Figure 5-15. In this situation, both **UserA** and **UserB** own a copy of **temp_table; and RecordFullClasses**, since it is owned by **UserA**, inserts into **UserA.temp_table**. **RecordFullClasses** is known as a *definer's rights* procedure, since unqualified external references within it are resolved under the privilege set of its owner, or definer.

Oracle8i introduces a different kind of external reference resolution. In an *invoker's rights* subprogram, external references are resolved under the privilege set of the caller, not the owner. An invoker's rights routine is created by using the AUTHID clause. It is valid for standalone subprograms, package specifications, and object type specifications only. Individual subprograms within a package or object type must be all invoker's or definer's, not a mix. The syntax of AUTHID is given here:

```
CREATE [OR REPLACE] FUNCTION function_name
   [parameter_list] RETURN return_type
   [AUTHID {CURRENT_USER | DEFINER}] {IS | AS}
   function_body;
```

```
CREATE [OR REPLACE] PROCEDURE procedure_name
   [parameter_list]
   [AUTHID {CURRENT_USER | DEFINER}] {IS | AS}
   function_body;
```

```
CREATE [OR REPLACE] PACKAGE package_spec_name
   [AUTHID {CURRENT_USER | DEFINER}] {IS | AS}
   package_spec;
```

```
CREATE [OR REPLACE] TYPE type_name
   [AUTHID {CURRENT_USER | DEFINER}] {IS | AS} OBJECT
   type_spec;
```

If CURRENT_USER is specified in the AUTHID clause, the object will have invoker's rights. If DEFINER is specified, then the object will have definer's rights. The default if the AUTHID clause is not present is definer's rights.

For example, the following version of **RecordFullClasses** is an invoker's rights procedure:

```
-- Available online as part of invokers.sql
CREATE OR REPLACE PROCEDURE RecordFullClasses
  AUTHID CURRENT_USER AS

  -- Note that we have to preface classes and AlmostFull with
  -- UserA, since both of these are owned by UserA only.
  CURSOR c_Classes IS
    SELECT department, course
      FROM UserA.classes;
BEGIN
  FOR v_ClassRecord IN c_Classes LOOP
    -- Record all classes that don't have very much room left
    -- in temp_table.
    IF UserA.AlmostFull(v_ClassRecord.department,
                        v_ClassRecord.course) THEN
      INSERT INTO temp_table (char_col) VALUES
        (v_ClassRecord.department || ' ' || v_ClassRecord.course ||
         ' is almost full!');
    END IF;
  END LOOP;
END RecordFullClasses;
```

> **NOTE**
> *The online example **invokers.sql** will first create the users **UserA** and **UserB**, and then create the necessary objects for the examples in this section. You may have to modify the password used for the DBA account in order to get the example to work on your system. You can see the output from running **invokers.sql** in **invokers.out**, also available online.*

If **UserB** executes **RecordFullClasses**, the insert will be done in **UserB.temp_table**. If **UserA** executes it, the insert will be done in **UserA.temp_table**. This is illustrated by the following SQL*Plus session and Figure 5-18.

```
-- Available online as part of invokers.sql
SQL> connect UserA/UserA
Connected.
SQL> -- Call as UserA.  This will insert into UserA.temp_table.
SQL> BEGIN
  2    RecordFullClasses;
  3    COMMIT;
  4  END;
  5  /
```

```
PL/SQL procedure successfully completed.

SQL> -- Query temp_table.  There should be 1 row.
SQL> SELECT * FROM temp_table;
   NUM_COL CHAR_COL
---------- ------------------------------------------------------------
          MUS 410 is almost full!

SQL> -- Connect as UserB.
SQL> -- Now the call to RecordFullClasses will insert into
SQL> -- UserB.temp_table.
SQL> BEGIN
  2    UserA.RecordFullClasses;
  3    COMMIT;
  4  END;
  5  /
PL/SQL procedure successfully completed.

SQL> -- So we should have one row here as well.
SQL> SELECT * FROM temp_table;
   NUM_COL CHAR_COL
---------- ------------------------------------------------------------
          MUS 410 is almost full!
```

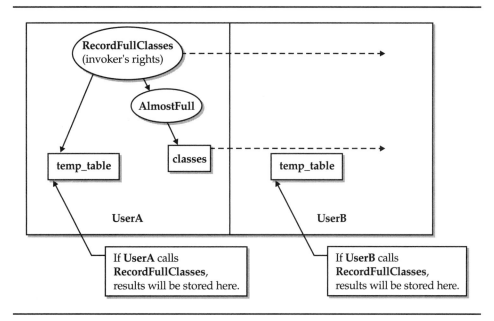

FIGURE 5-18.   *Invoker's rights **RecordFullClasses***

RESOLUTION WITH INVOKER'S RIGHTS   In an invoker's rights routine, external references in SQL statements will be resolved using the caller's privilege set. However, references in PL/SQL statements (such as assignments or procedure calls) are still resolved under the owner's privilege set. This is why, in Figure 5-18, GRANTs need be done only on **RecordFullClasses** and the **classes** table. Since the call to **AlmostFull** is a PL/SQL reference, it will always be done under **UserA**'s privilege set, and thus it does not need to be GRANTed to **UserB**.

However, suppose that the GRANT on **classes** was not done. In this case, **UserA** can successfully compile the procedure, since all of the SQL objects are accessible from **UserA**'s privilege set. But **UserB** will receive an ORA-942 error upon calling **RecordFullClasses**. This is illustrated by Figure 5-19 and the following SQL*Plus session:

```
-- Available online as part of invokers.sql
SQL> connect UserB/UserB
Connected.
SQL> BEGIN
  2    UserA.RecordFullClasses;
  3  END;
  4  /
BEGIN
*
ERROR at line 1:
ORA-00942: table or view does not exist
ORA-06512: at "USERA.RECORDFULLCLASSES", line 7
ORA-06512: at "USERA.RECORDFULLCLASSES", line 10
ORA-06512: at line 2
```

> **NOTE**
> *The error received here is ORA-942, and not PLS-201. It is a database compilation error, but we receive it at runtime.*

ROLES AND INVOKER'S RIGHTS   Suppose the GRANT on **classes** was done via a role, and not directly. Recall from the situation in Figure 5-17 that definer's rights procedures must have all privileges GRANTed explicitly. For invoker's rights routines, however, this is not the case. Since the external references for invoker's rights routines is done at runtime, the current privilege set is available. This implies that privileges GRANTed via a role to the *caller* will be accessible. This is illustrated by the following SQL*Plus session and Figure 5-20.

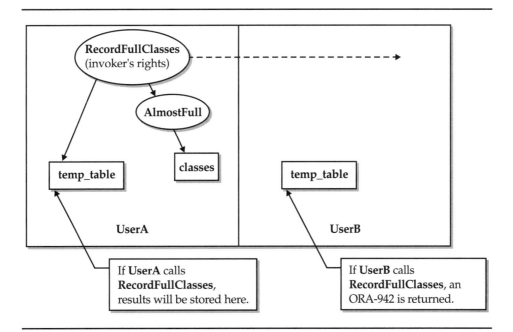

FIGURE 5-19. *Revoked SELECT ON classes*

```
-- Available online as part of invokers.sql
SQL> connect UserA/UserA
Connected.
CREATE ROLE UserA_Role;
Role created.
SQL> GRANT SELECT ON classes TO UserA_Role;
Grant succeeded.
SQL> GRANT UserA_Role TO UserB;
Grant succeeded.
SQL> -- Connect as UserB and call.
SQL> connect UserB/UserB
Connected.
SQL> -- Now the call to RecordFullClasses will succeed.
SQL> BEGIN
  2    UserA.RecordFullClasses;
  3    COMMIT;
  4  END;
  5  /
PL/SQL procedure successfully completed.
```

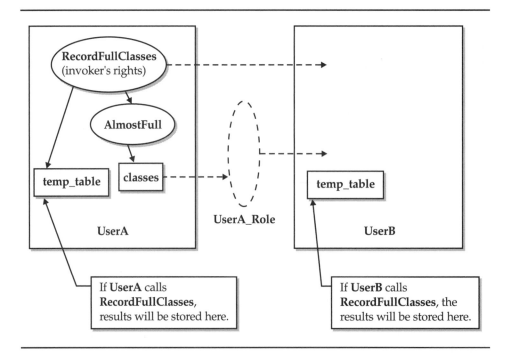

FIGURE 5-20. *Roles and Invoker's rights*

NOTE
References that are resolved at the time of procedure compilation must still be GRANTed directly. Only those references that are resolved at runtime can be GRANTed via a role. This also implies that the SET ROLE command (if executed through dynamic SQL) can be used with runtime references.

EXTERNAL ROUTINES AND INVOKER'S RIGHTS   By default, external routines written in Java (also known as *Java stored procedures*) will have invoker's rights, which is different from the default for PL/SQL routines. This is in accordance with the method invocation model of Java. If you want a Java stored procedure to execute with definer's rights, you can use the AUTHID DEFINER clause on the call specification. See Chapter 10 for more information.

TRIGGERS, VIEWS, AND INVOKER'S RIGHTS   A database trigger will always be executed with definer's rights, and will execute under the privilege set of the schema that owns the triggering table. This is also true for a PL/SQL function that is called from a view. In this case, the function will execute under the privilege set of the view's owner.

Using Stored Functions in SQL Statements

In general, since calls to subprograms are procedural, they cannot be called from SQL statements. PL/SQL 2.1, however, lifted this restriction for stored functions. If a standalone or packaged function meets certain restrictions, it can be called during execution of a SQL statement. This feature is available with PL/SQL 2.1 (Oracle7 Release 7.1) and higher, and has been enhanced for Oracle8*i*.

User-defined functions are called the same way as built-in functions such as TO_CHAR, UPPER, or ADD_MONTHS. Depending on where a user-defined function is used, and what version of Oracle you are running, it must meet different restrictions. These restrictions are defined in terms of purity levels.

Purity Levels

There are four different purity levels for functions. A *purity level* defines what kinds of data structures the function reads or modifies. The available levels are listed in Table 5-2. Depending on the purity level of a function, it is subject to the following restrictions:

- Any function called from a SQL statement cannot modify any database tables (WNDS). (In Oracle8*i*, a function called from a non-SELECT statement can modify database tables. See "Calling Stored Functions from SQL in Oracle8*i*," later in this chapter.)

- In order to be executed remotely (via a database link) or in parallel, a function must not read or write the value of packaged variables (RNPS and WNPS).

- Functions called from the SELECT, VALUES, or SET clauses can write packaged variables. Functions in all other clauses must have the WNPS purity level.

- A function is only as pure as the subprograms it calls. If a function calls a stored procedure that does an UPDATE, for example, the function does not have the WNDS purity level, and thus cannot be used inside a select statement.

- Regardless of their purity level, stored PL/SQL functions cannot be called from a CHECK constraint clause of a CREATE TABLE or ALTER TABLE command, or be used to specify a default value for a column, because these situations require an unchanging definition.

Purity Level	Meaning	Description
WNDS	Writes no database state	The function does not modify any database tables (using DML statements).
RNDS	Reads no database state	The function does not read any database tables (using the SELECT statement).
WNPS	Writes no package state	The function does not modify any packaged variables (no packaged variables are used on the left side of an assignment or in a FETCH statement).
RNPS	Reads no package state	The function does not examine any packaged variables (no packaged variables appear on the right side of an assignment or as part of a procedural or SQL expression).

TABLE 5-2. *Function Purity Levels*

In addition to the preceding restrictions, a user-defined function must also meet the following requirements to be callable from a SQL statement. Note that all the built-in functions must meet these requirements as well.

■ The function has to be stored in the database, either standalone or as part of a package. It must not be local to another block.

■ The function can take only IN parameters, no IN OUT or OUT.

■ The formal parameters must use only database types, not PL/SQL types such as BOOLEAN or RECORD. Database types include NUMBER, CHAR, VARCHAR2, ROWID, LONG, RAW, LONG RAW, and DATE, as well as the new types introduced for Oracle8*i*.

■ The return type of the function must also be a database type.

■ The function must not end the current transaction with COMMIT or ROLLBACK, or roll back to a savepoint prior to the function execution.

■ It also must not issue any ALTER SESSION or ALTER SYSTEM commands.

As an example, the **FullName** function takes a student ID number as input and returns the concatenated first and last names:

```
-- Available online as part of FullName.sql
CREATE OR REPLACE FUNCTION FullName (
  p_StudentID  students.ID%TYPE)
  RETURN VARCHAR2 IS

  v_Result  VARCHAR2(100);
BEGIN
  SELECT first_name || ' ' || last_name
    INTO v_Result
    FROM students
    WHERE ID = p_StudentID;

  RETURN v_Result;
END FullName;
```

FullName meets all of the restrictions, so we can call it from SQL statements, as the following SQL*Plus session illustrates:

```
-- Available online as part of FullName.sql
SQL> SELECT ID, FullName(ID) "Full Name"
  2    FROM students;
       ID Full Name
--------- ------------------------------
    10000 Scott Smith
    10001 Margaret Mason
    10002 Joanne Junebug
    10003 Manish Murgratroid
    10004 Patrick Poll
    10005 Timothy Taller
    10006 Barbara Blues
    10007 David Dinsmore
    10008 Ester Elegant
    10009 Rose Riznit
    10010 Rita Razmataz
    10011 Shay Shariatpanahy
12 rows selected.
SQL> INSERT INTO temp_table (char_col)
  2    VALUES (FullName(10010));
1 row created.
```

RESTRICT_REFERENCES

The PL/SQL engine can determine the purity level of standalone functions. When the function is called from a SQL statement, the purity level is checked. If it does not

meet the restrictions, an error is returned. For packaged functions, however, the
RESTRICT_REFERENCES pragma is required (prior to Oracle8*i*). This pragma
specifies the purity level of a given function, with the syntax

> PRAGMA RESTRICT_REFERENCES(*subprogram_or_package_name*,
>   WNDS [, WNPS] [, RNDS] [, RNPS]);

where *suprogram_or_package_name* is the name of a package, or a packaged
subprogram. (With Oracle8 and higher, you can also use the DEFAULT keyword.
See "DEFAULT Keyword," later in this chapter, for details.) Since WNDS is required
for all functions used in SQL statements, it is also required for the pragma. (This
restriction is relaxed in Oracle8*i*.) The purity levels can be specified in any order.
The pragma goes in the package header, with the specification for the function. For
example, the **StudentOps** package uses RESTRICT_REFERENCES twice:

```
-- Available online as StudentOps.sql
CREATE OR REPLACE PACKAGE StudentOps AS
  FUNCTION FullName(p_StudentID IN students.ID%TYPE)
    RETURN VARCHAR2;
  PRAGMA RESTRICT_REFERENCES(FullName, WNDS, WNPS, RNPS);

  /* Returns the number of History majors. */
  FUNCTION NumHistoryMajors
    RETURN NUMBER;
  PRAGMA RESTRICT_REFERENCES(NumHistoryMajors, WNDS);
END StudentOps;

CREATE OR REPLACE PACKAGE BODY StudentOps AS
  -- Packaged variable to hold the number of history majors.
  v_NumHist NUMBER;

  FUNCTION FullName(p_StudentID IN students.ID%TYPE)
    RETURN VARCHAR2 IS
    v_Result  VARCHAR2(100);
  BEGIN
    SELECT first_name || ' ' || last_name
      INTO v_Result
      FROM students
      WHERE ID = p_StudentID;

    RETURN v_Result;
  END FullName;

  FUNCTION NumHistoryMajors RETURN NUMBER IS
    v_Result NUMBER;
```

```
    BEGIN
      IF v_NumHist IS NULL THEN
        /* Determine the answer. */
        SELECT COUNT(*)
          INTO v_Result
          FROM students
          WHERE major = 'History';
        /* And save it for future use. */
        v_NumHist := v_Result;
      ELSE
        v_Result := v_NumHist;
      END IF;

      RETURN v_Result;
    END NumHistoryMajors;
END StudentOps;
```

NOTE

In Oracle8i, the pragma is no longer required. The PL/SQL engine can verify the purity level of all functions at runtime as needed. For more information, see "Calling Functions from SQL in Oracle8i," later in this chapter.

RATIONALE FOR RESTRICT_REFERENCES   Why is the pragma required for packaged functions, but not for standalone functions? The answer lies in the relationship between the package header and package body. Remember that PL/SQL blocks calling a packaged function will depend only on the package header, and not the body. Furthermore, the body may not even exist when the calling block is created. Consequently, the PL/SQL compiler needs the pragma to determine the purity levels of the packaged function, to verify that it is being used correctly in the calling block. Whenever the package body is subsequently modified (or created for the first time) the function code is also checked against the pragma. The pragma is checked at compile time, not runtime.

Strictly speaking, the PL/SQL engine can verify the purity level at runtime, as it does for standalone functions prior to Oracle8*i*. However, using the pragma means that the engine does not need to verify the level at runtime, which is a performance benefit. Also, it ensures that a given subprogram will not fail when it is called from SQL.

Oracle **8** and higher

DEFAULT KEYWORD   If there is no RESTRICT_REFERENCES pragma associated with a given packaged function, it will not have any purity level asserted. However, with Oracle8 and higher, you can change the default purity level for a package. The DEFAULT keyword is used instead of the subprogram name in the pragma:

```
PRAGMA RESTRICT_REFERENCES(DEFAULT,
    WNDS [, WNPS] [, RNDS] [, RNPS]);
```

Any subsequent subprograms in the package must comply with the purity levels specified. For example, consider the **DefaultPragma** package:

```
-- Available online as DefaultPragma.sql
CREATE OR REPLACE PACKAGE DefaultPragma AS
  FUNCTION f1 RETURN NUMBER;
  PRAGMA RESTRICT_REFERENCES(f1, RNDS, RNPS);

  PRAGMA RESTRICT_REFERENCES(DEFAULT, WNDS, WNPS, RNDS, RNPS);
  FUNCTION f2 RETURN NUMBER;

  FUNCTION f3 RETURN NUMBER;
END DefaultPragma;

CREATE OR REPLACE PACKAGE BODY DefaultPragma AS
  FUNCTION f1 RETURN NUMBER IS
  BEGIN
    INSERT INTO temp_table (num_col, char_col)
      VALUES (1, 'f1!');
    RETURN 1;
  END f1;

  FUNCTION f2 RETURN NUMBER IS
  BEGIN
    RETURN 2;
  END f2;

  -- This function violates the default pragma.
  FUNCTION f3 RETURN NUMBER IS
  BEGIN
    INSERT INTO temp_table (num_col, char_col)
      VALUES (1, 'f3!');
    RETURN 3;
  END f3;
END DefaultPragma;
```

The default pragma (which asserts all four purity levels) will be applied to both **f2** and **f3**. Since **f3** INSERTs into **temp_table**, it violates the pragma. Compiling the above package will return the following errors:

```
PL/SQL: Compilation unit analysis terminated
PLS-00452: Subprogram 'F3' violates its associated pragma
```

INITIALIZATION SECTION   The code in the initialization section of a package can have a purity level as well. The first time any function in the package is called, the initialization section is run. Consequently, a packaged function is only as pure as the initialization section of the containing package. The purity level for a package is also done with RESTRICT_REFERENCES, but with the package name rather than a function name:

```
CREATE OR REPLACE PACKAGE StudentOps AS
   PRAGMA RESTRICT_REFERENCES (StudentOps, WNDS);
...
END StudentOps;
```

OVERLOADED FUNCTIONS   RESTRICT_REFERENCES can appear anywhere in the package specification, after the function declaration. It can apply to only one function definition, however. For overloaded functions, the pragma applies to the nearest definition prior to the pragma. In the following example, each pragma applies to the version of **TestFunc** just prior to it:

```
-- Available online as part of Overload.sql
CREATE OR REPLACE PACKAGE Overload AS
   FUNCTION TestFunc(p_Parameter1 IN NUMBER)
     RETURN VARCHAR2;
   PRAGMA RESTRICT_REFERENCES(TestFunc, WNDS, RNDS, WNPS, RNPS);

   FUNCTION TestFunc(p_ParameterA IN VARCHAR2,
                     p_ParameterB IN DATE)
     RETURN VARCHAR2;
   PRAGMA RESTRICT_REFERENCES(TestFunc, WNDS, RNDS, WNPS, RNPS);
END Overload;

CREATE OR REPLACE PACKAGE BODY Overload AS
   FUNCTION TestFunc(p_Parameter1 IN NUMBER)
     RETURN VARCHAR2 IS
   BEGIN
     RETURN 'Version 1';
   END TestFunc;

   FUNCTION TestFunc(p_ParameterA IN VARCHAR2,
                     p_ParameterB IN DATE)
     RETURN VARCHAR2 IS
   BEGIN
     RETURN 'Version 2';
   END TestFunc;
END Overload;
```

The following SQL*Plus session illustrates that both overloaded versions are callable from SQL:

```
-- Available online as part of Overload.sql
SQL> SELECT Overload.TestFunc(1) FROM dual;
OVERLOAD.TESTFUNC(1)
----------------------------------------------------------
Version 1

SQL> SELECT Overload.TestFunc('abc', SYSDATE) FROM dual;
OVERLOAD.TESTFUNC('ABC',SYSDATE)
----------------------------------------------------------
Version 2
```

TIP

I generally prefer to code the RESTRICT_REFERENCES pragma immediately after each function, so that it is clear to which version it applies.

BUILT-IN PACKAGES   The procedures in the built-in packages supplied with PL/SQL are, in general, not considered pure as of PL/SQL 2.3. This includes DBMS_OUTPUT, DBMS_PIPE, DBMS_ALERT, DBMS_SQL, and UTL_FILE. However, the necessary pragmas were added to these packages in later versions when possible. Table 5-3 shows when the pragmas were added for the more commonly used packages. Since the pragma is not necessary starting with Oracle8*i*, all built-in packaged functions that meet the restrictions can be used in SQL statements as of Oracle8*i*. If you call a built-in packaged function in Oracle8*i* and it does not meet the restrictions, then an error will be raised at runtime.

NOTE

*The pragmas have been added to some of these packages for the RDBMS patch sets, so they may be available in versions prior to the ones listed in Table 5-3. You can check the source for the package header (usually found in the **rdbms/admin** directory under $ORACLE_HOME) to verify the purity level for a particular PL/SQL version.*

Default Parameters

When calling a function from a procedural statement, you can use the default values for formal parameters, if they are present. When calling a function from

Package	Pragma Added as of Version
DBMS_ALERT	N/A—REGISTER contains a COMMIT.
DBMS_JOB	N/A—jobs run in a separate process and thus can't be called from SQL.
DBMS_OUTPUT	7.3.3
DBMS_PIPE	7.3.3
DBMS_SQL	N/A—EXECUTE and PARSE can be used to execute DDL statements, which would cause an implicit COMMIT.
STANDARD	7.3.3 (This includes the RAISE_APPLICATION_ERROR procedure.)
UTL_FILE	8.0.6
UTL_HTTP	7.3.3

TABLE 5-3. *RESTRICT_REFERENCES for Built-In Packages*

a SQL statement, however, all parameters must be specified. Furthermore, you have to use positional notation and not named notation. The following call to **FullName** is illegal:

```
SELECT FullName(p_StudentID => 10000) FROM dual;
```

Calling Functions from SQL in Oracle8*i*

Oracle**8*i***
and higher

As we have seen in the past sections, the RESTRICT_REFERENCES pragma enforces compile-time purity levels. Prior to Oracle8*i*, packaged functions need the pragma in order to be callable from SQL. Oracle8*i*, however, relaxes this restriction. If the pragma is not present, the database will verify the purity level of a function at runtime.

This is especially useful for external routines (those written in Java or C, for example). In this case, the PL/SQL compiler can't check the purity level, since the PL/SQL compiler doesn't actually compile the function. (See Chapter 10 for more information on external routines.) Thus the check has to be performed at runtime.

The check is only performed if the function is called from within an executing SQL statement. If the pragma is present, then the check is not performed. Consequently, using the pragma will save some execution time, and will also serve to document the behavior of the function.

For example, suppose we remove the pragmas from **StudentOps**:

```
-- Available online as part of StudentOps2.sql
CREATE OR REPLACE PACKAGE StudentOps AS
  FUNCTION FullName(p_StudentID IN students.ID%TYPE)
    RETURN VARCHAR2;

  /* Returns the number of History majors. */
  FUNCTION NumHistoryMajors
    RETURN NUMBER;
END StudentOps;
```

We can still call these functions from SQL, as the following SQL*Plus session shows:

```
SQL> SELECT StudentOps.FullName(ID)
  2    FROM students
  3    WHERE major = 'History';
STUDENTOPS.FULLNAME(ID)
-----------------------
Margaret Mason
Patrick Poll
Timothy Taller
SQL> INSERT INTO temp_table (num_col)
  2    VALUES (StudentOps.NumHistoryMajors);
1 row created.
SQL> SELECT * FROM temp_table;
  NUM_COL CHAR_COL
--------- --------
        3
```

If you attempt to call an illegal function from a SQL statement, Oracle8*i* will issue an error such as "ORA-14551: cannot perform a DML operation inside a query," as the following example shows. Consider the **InsertTemp** function:

```
-- Available online as part of InsertTemp.sql
CREATE OR REPLACE FUNCTION InsertTemp(
  p_Num IN temp_table.num_col%TYPE,
  p_Char IN temp_table.char_col%type)
  RETURN NUMBER AS
BEGIN
  INSERT INTO temp_table (num_col, char_col)
    VALUES (p_Num, p_Char);
  RETURN 0;
END InsertTemp;
```

Calling it from within a SELECT statement yields the following results:

```
-- Available online as part of InsertTemp.sql
SQL> SELECT InsertTemp(1, 'Hello')
  2     FROM dual;
SELECT InsertTemp(1, 'Hello')
       *
ERROR at line 1:
ORA-14551: cannot perform a DML operation inside a query
ORA-06512: at "EXAMPLE.INSERTTEMP", line 6
ORA-06512: at line 1
```

TRUST Keyword

Although RESTRICT_REFERENCES is no longer required (and in fact cannot be used for external routines), code written prior to Oracle8*i* may use it. The pragma can also be used to speed processing, as we discussed in the previous section. Thus, you may want to call a function that is declared as pure from a new function that does not have the pragma. To aid this, Oracle8*i* provides an additional keyword that can be used in the pragma, in addition to or instead of the purity levels—TRUST.

If the TRUST keyword is present, then the restrictions listed in the pragma are not enforced. Rather, they are trusted to be true. This allows you to write new code that does not use RESTRICT_REFERENCES, and call the new code from functions that are declared pure. For example, consider the following package:

```
-- Available online as TrustPkg.sql
CREATE OR REPLACE PACKAGE TrustPkg AS
  FUNCTION ToUpper (p_a VARCHAR2) RETURN VARCHAR2 IS
    LANGUAGE JAVA
    NAME 'Test.Uppercase(char[]) return char[]';
    PRAGMA RESTRICT_REFERENCES(ToUpper, WNDS, TRUST);

  PROCEDURE Demo(p_in IN VARCHAR2, p_out OUT VARCHAR2);
  PRAGMA RESTRICT_REFERENCES(Demo, WNDS);
END TrustPkg;

CREATE OR REPLACE PACKAGE BODY TrustPkg AS
  PROCEDURE Demo(p_in IN VARCHAR2, p_out OUT VARCHAR2) IS
  BEGIN
    p_out := ToUpper(p_in);
  END Demo;
END TrustPkg;
```

TrustPkg.ToUpper is an external routine—the body of the function is actually written in Java, and will return its input parameter in all uppercase. (We will see how to do this in Chapter 10.) Since the body is not in PL/SQL, the TRUST keyword is necessary for the pragma. Then, because **ToUpper** is trusted to have the WNDS purity, we can call **ToUpper** from **Demo**.

Calling Functions from DML Statements

Prior to Oracle8*i*, a function called from a DML statement could not update the database (that is, it had to assert the RNDS purity level). With Oracle8*i*, however, this restriction has been relaxed. Now, a function called from a DML statement must not read from nor modify the table(s) being modified by that DML statement, but it can update other tables. For example, consider the **UpdateTemp** function:

```
-- Available online as part of DMLUpdate.sql
CREATE OR REPLACE FUNCTION UpdateTemp(p_ID IN students.ID%TYPE)
  RETURN students.ID%TYPE AS
BEGIN
  INSERT INTO temp_table (num_col, char_col)
    VALUES(p_ID, 'Updated!');
  RETURN p_ID;
END UpdateTemp;
```

Prior to Oracle8*i*, executing the following update statement would raise an error:

```
-- Available online as part of DMLUpdate.sql
UPDATE students
  SET major = 'Nutrition'
  WHERE UpdateTemp(ID) = ID;
```

With Oracle8*i*, however, it succeeds because **UpdateTemp** does not modify **students**, only **temp_table**.

> **NOTE**
> A function called from a parallelized DML statement
> must not modify the database, even tables not
> currently being modified.

Additional Package Features

In this section, we will cover some additional features of packages. These include the ability to pin a package in the shared pool and a discussion about the size of package bodies. For Oracle8*i*, we will discuss the optimization hints DETERMINISTIC and PARALLEL_ENABLE.

Pinning in the Shared Pool

The *shared pool* is the portion of the SGA that contains, among other things, the p-code of compiled subprograms as they are run. The first time a stored subprogram is called, the p-code is loaded from disk into the shared pool. Once the object is no longer referenced, it is free to be aged out. Objects are aged out of the shared pool using a LRU (least recently used) algorithm. See *Oracle Concepts* for more information on the shared pool and how it works.

The DBMS_SHARED_POOL package allows you to pin objects in the shared pool. When an object is *pinned*, it will never be aged out until you request it, no matter how full the pool gets or how often the object is accessed. This can improve performance, as it takes time to reload a package from disk. Pinning an object also helps minimize fragmentation of the shared pool. DBMS_SHARED_POOL has three procedures: DBMS_SHARED_POOL.KEEP, DBMS_SHARED_POOL.UNKEEP, and DBMS_SHARED_POOL.SIZES.

KEEP

The DBMS_SHARED_POOL.KEEP procedure is used to pin objects in the pool. Packages, triggers (in Oracle7 Release 7.3 and higher), sequences, and SQL statements can be pinned. Note that standalone procedures and functions cannot be pinned. KEEP is defined with

```
PROCEDURE KEEP(name VARCHAR2,
              flag CHAR DEFAULT 'P');
```

The parameters are described in the following table. Once an object has been kept, it will not be removed until the database is shut down or the DBMS_SHARED_POOL.UNKEEP procedure is used. Note that DBMS_SHARED_POOL.KEEP does not load the package into the shared pool immediately; rather, it will be pinned the first time it is subsequently loaded.

Parameter	Type	Description
name	VARCHAR2	Name of the object. This can be a package name or the identifier associated with a SQL statement. The SQL identifier is the concatenation of the **address** and **hash_value** fields in the **v$sqlarea** view (by default, selectable only by SYS) and is returned by the SIZES procedure.
flag	CHAR	Determines the type of the object. If *flag* is 'P' (the default), then *name* should match a package name. If *flag* is 'C' (for cursor) then *name* should contain the text of the SQL statement. If 'S', then *name* should be a sequence, and if 'R', then *name* should be a trigger.

UNKEEP

UNKEEP is the only way to remove a kept object from the shared pool. Kept objects are never aged out automatically. UNKEEP is defined with

```
PROCEDURE UNKEEP(name VARCHAR2,
                 flag CHAR DEFAULT 'P');
```

The arguments are the same as for KEEP. If the specified object does not already exist in the shared pool, an error is raised.

SIZES

SIZES will echo the contents of the shared pool to the screen. It is defined with

```
PROCEDURE SIZES(minsize NUMBER);
```

Objects with a size greater than *minsize* will be returned. SIZES uses DBMS_OUTPUT to return the data, so be sure to use SET SERVEROUTPUT ON in SQL*Plus or Server Manager before calling the procedure.

Limits on Package Body Size

The PL/SQL compiler has several internal limits that can affect the size of a PL/SQL block. Generally, package bodies are the largest type of block, and so most often run into one or more of these limits. When an internal compiler limit is reached, the compilation will generally fail with "PLS-123: program too large," although you may also receive a PL/SQL internal error. These limits are

- *Number of nodes in the Diana tree.* The PL/SQL compiler builds an internal tree, known as Diana, that represents the syntactic structure of the block. The Diana is generated during the first phase of the compilation. Prior to Oracle8*i*, the maximum limit on the number of Diana nodes is 2^{15} (32K). Oracle8*i* has increased this limit to 2^{26} (64MB) for package and type bodies. This is generally the limit that most blocks will reach first.

- *Compiler-generated temporary variables.* The maximum number of these is 21K.

- *Number of entrypoints.* A package body can have at most 32K entrypoints, where an *entrypoint* is a procedure or function.

- *Number of strings.* The limit on the number of strings found in a PL/SQL unit is 2^{32}.

Prior to Oracle8*i*, the limit most often encountered is the number of Diana nodes, which is why this limit has been increased. In general, the number of nodes is proportional to the number of source code lines. So, the best way to reduce the size of a package body is to reduce the number of code lines. This is usually done by removing some of the packaged subprograms and placing them in a separate package.

TIP
It is generally a good idea to keep packages small, both for readability and ease of loading.

Optimization Hints

Oracle **8***i* and higher   For Oracle8*i*, there are two additional keywords that can be used in a function declaration—DETERMINISTIC and PARALLEL_ENABLE. These keywords, if present, are used by the optimizer when calling a PL/SQL function to improve performance. Each keyword is placed after the function return type, but before the IS or AS statement, as follows:

```
CREATE [OR REPLACE] FUNCTION function_name
    [parameter_list]
    RETURN return_type
    [DETERMINISTIC]
    [PARALLEL_ENABLE]
    IS | AS
    function_body;
```

If both keywords are specified, they can appear in either order. DETERMINISTIC and PARALLEL_ENABLE can be used for standalone functions, packaged functions, or on methods for object types (see Chapter 13 for more information on object types). If the function is a method or packaged function, the keyword should be on the package or type header, and not on the package or type body.

We will see how these keywords are used in the next two sections.

DETERMINISTIC

A function that always returns the same results given the same input, and does not have any meaningful side effects (such as modifications of packaged variables), is said to be *deterministic*. Deterministic functions are useful because they do not have to be called multiple times if their arguments remain the same. For example, consider the **StudentStatus** function:

```
-- Available online as part of determ.sql
CREATE OR REPLACE FUNCTION StudentStatus(
  p_NumCredits IN NUMBER)
  RETURN VARCHAR2 AS
BEGIN
  IF p_NumCredits = 0 THEN
    RETURN 'Inactive';
  ELSIF p_NumCredits <= 12 THEN
    RETURN 'Part Time';
  ELSE
    RETURN 'Full Time';
  END IF;
END StudentStatus;
```

StudentStatus is deterministic, since it does not modify any package variables and
always returns the same result given the same input. Because of this, we can use the
DETERMINISTIC keyword to indicate to Oracle8*i* that the function is deterministic:

```
-- Available online as part of determ.sql
CREATE OR REPLACE FUNCTION StudentStatus(p_NumCredits IN NUMBER)
  RETURN VARCHAR2
  DETERMINISTIC AS
BEGIN
  IF p_NumCredits = 0 THEN
    RETURN 'Inactive';
  ELSIF p_NumCredits <= 12 THEN
    RETURN 'Part Time';
  ELSE
    RETURN 'Full Time';
  END IF;
END StudentStatus;
```

The PL/SQL compiler will not verify that the function is actually deterministic,
but it will be marked as such. Deterministic functions are useful in the following
situations:

- Any function used in a function-based index must be deterministic.
  Non-deterministic functions can be used in the WHERE clause of SQL
  statements, but you cannot create an index based on them.

- If a materialized view is to be marked ENABLE QUERY REWRITE, then any
  function used in it must be deterministic.

- Functions used in a snapshot or materialized view that is declared REFRESH
  FAST should also be deterministic. This is not required for historical reasons
  (REFRESH FAST snapshots existed prior to deterministic functions), but it is
  recommended.

■ Functions used in the WHERE, ORDER BY, or GROUP BY clause of a SQL
statement should also be deterministic. This also applies to the MAP or
ORDER methods of a SQL type. In general, any function that will be used to
determine the contents of a result set should be deterministic. Once again,
Oracle will not require this, but it is recommended.

DETERMINISTIC FUNCTIONS IN FUNCTION-BASED INDEXES   In
Oracle8*i*, indexes can be created on expressions that call PL/SQL stored functions.
These are known as *function-based indexes*. This allows the index to be used when
the function is called from SQL. For example, consider the following:

```
-- Available online as part of determ.sql
SELECT id
  FROM students
  WHERE SUBSTR(StudentStatus(current_credits), 1, 20) =
    'Part Time';
```

If we look at the execution plan for the SELECT statement, we see

```
Rows     Row Source Operation
-------  ----------------------------------------------------
    12   TABLE ACCESS FULL STUDENTS


Rows     Execution Plan
-------  ----------------------------------------------------
     0   SELECT STATEMENT   GOAL: CHOOSE
    12     TABLE ACCESS (FULL) OF 'STUDENTS'
```

We are doing a full table scan. In order to make this query more efficient, we can
create an index using the function's values. Then, the query can use the index:

```
-- Available online as part of determ.sql
CREATE INDEX students_index ON students
  (SUBSTR(StudentStatus(current_credits), 1, 20))
  COMPUTE STATISTICS;
```

The execution plan for the query now is

```
Rows     Row Source Operation
-------  ----------------------------------------------------
    12   TABLE ACCESS BY INDEX ROWID STUDENTS
    13     INDEX RANGE SCAN (object id 13271)


Rows     Execution Plan
-------  ----------------------------------------------------
     0   SELECT STATEMENT    GOAL: FIRST_ROWS
    12     TABLE ACCESS (FULL) OF 'STUDENTS'
```

NOTE
The owner of the index must be granted the QUERY REWRITE privilege in order to create a function-based index. The GLOBAL REWRITE system privilege allows the grantee to create function-based indexes on tables in other user's schemas. There are also other requirements before the optimizer will use the index. See the Oracle documentation for more details.

PARALLEL_ENABLE

In certain cases, you can use Oracle's parallel execution feature to execute SQL statements in parallel. If these statements call a PL/SQL function, then the function is called by separate processes, each of which will run its own copy of the function to operate on a subset of the rows.

This can cause problems if the function refers to package variables. Each copy of the function will have its packaged variables initialized as if it has just logged in. Thus, it will not see modifications to these variables done earlier by the function. Consequently, any function that reads or modifies packaged variables cannot be parallel enabled. If the statement is a DML statement (instead of a query), then the function can similarly not read from nor modify database state.

Prior to Oracle8*i*, these restrictions were enforced solely by the RESTRICT_REFERENCES pragma. With Oracle8*i*, however, you can use the PARALLEL_ENABLE clause to indicate to the optimizer that the function is parallelizable. This gives you more flexibility to have functions run in parallel than RESTICT_REFERENCES.

Optimization Hints for Non-PL/SQL Functions

Oracle8*i* allows you to create external routines, which are functions written in C or Java that can be called directly from PL/SQL. The DETERMINISTIC and/or PARALLEL_ENABLE clauses can also be used in the PL/SQL call specification for external routines. If so, then the enhancements described in this last section can be used. Of course, since the PL/SQL compiler does not even run on external routines, it is your responsibility to verify that the external routine meet the requirements of DETERMINISTIC or PARALLEL_ENABLE. For more information on external routines, see Chapter 10.

Summary

We have continued our discussion of three types of named PL/SQL blocks in this chapter—procedures, functions, and packages. This discussion included the differences between local and stored subprograms, and how dependencies among stored subprograms work. We also discussed how to call stored subprograms from SQL statements. We closed the chapter with several additional package features. In the next chapter, we will cover a fourth type of named PL/SQL block—database triggers.

CHAPTER

6

Database Triggers

he fourth type of named PL/SQL block is the trigger. Triggers share many of the same characteristics as subprograms, but they have some significant differences. In this chapter, we will examine how to create different types of triggers and discuss some possible applications.

Types of Triggers

Triggers are similar to procedures or functions, in that they are named PL/SQL blocks with declarative, executable, and exception-handling sections. Like packages, triggers must be stored as standalone objects in the database and cannot be local to a block or package. As we have seen in the past two chapters, a procedure is executed explicitly from another block via a procedure call, which can also pass arguments. On the other hand, a trigger is executed implicitly whenever the triggering event happens, and a trigger doesn't accept arguments. The act of executing a trigger is known as *firing* the trigger. The triggering event can be a DML (INSERT, UPDATE, or DELETE) operation on a database table or certain kinds of views. Oracle8i extends this functionality by allowing triggers to fire on a system event, such as database startup or shutdown, and certain kinds of DDL operations. We will discuss the triggering events in detail later in this chapter.

Triggers can be used for many things, including

- Maintaining complex integrity constraints not possible through declarative constraints enabled at table creation

- Auditing information in a table by recording the changes made and who made them

- Automatically signaling other programs that action needs to take place when changes are made to a table

- Publishing information about various events in a publish-subscribe environment

There are three main kinds of triggers—DML, instead-of, and system triggers. In the following sections, we will introduce each kind. We will see more details later in the chapter, in "Creating Triggers."

NOTE
Oracle8i allows triggers to be written in either PL/SQL or other languages that can be called as external routines. See "Trigger Bodies," later in this chapter, for more information, as well as Chapter 10.

DML Triggers

A *DML trigger* is fired by a DML statement, and the type of statement determines the type of the DML trigger. DML triggers can be defined for INSERT, UPDATE, or DELETE operations. They can be fired before or after the operation, and they can also fire on row or statement operations.

As an example, suppose we want to track statistics about different majors, including the number of students registered and the total credits taken. We are going to store these results in the **major_stats** table:

```
-- Available online as part of relTables.sql
CREATE TABLE major_stats (
  major           VARCHAR2(30),
  total_credits   NUMBER,
  total_students NUMBER);
```

In order to keep **major_stats** up-to-date, we can create a trigger on **students** that will update **major_stats** every time **students** is modified. The **UpdateMajorStats** trigger, shown next, does this. After any DML operation on **students**, the trigger will execute. The body of the trigger queries **students** and updates **major_stats** with the current statistics.

```
-- Available online as UpdateMajorStats.sql
CREATE OR REPLACE TRIGGER UpdateMajorStats
  /* Keeps the major_stats table up-to-date with changes made
     to the students table. */
  AFTER INSERT OR DELETE OR UPDATE ON students
DECLARE
  CURSOR c_Statistics IS
    SELECT major, COUNT(*) total_students,
           SUM(current_credits) total_credits
      FROM students
      GROUP BY major;
BEGIN
  /* First delete from major_stats.  This will clear the
     statistics, and is necessary to account for the deletion
     of all students in a given major. */
  DELETE FROM major_stats;

  /* Now loop through each major, and insert the appropriate row into
     major_stats. */
  FOR v_StatsRecord in c_Statistics LOOP
    INSERT INTO major_stats (major, total_credits, total_students)
      VALUES (v_StatsRecord.major, v_StatsRecord.total_credits,
              v_StatsRecord.total_students);
  END LOOP;
END UpdateMajorStats;
```

A statement trigger can be fired for more than one type of triggering statement. For example, **UpdateMajorStats** is fired on INSERT, UPDATE, and DELETE statements. The triggering event specifies one or more of the DML operations that should fire the trigger.

Instead-Of Triggers

 Oracle8 provides an additional kind of trigger. *Instead-of* triggers can be defined on views (either relational or object) only. Unlike a DML trigger, which executes in addition to the DML operation, an instead-of trigger will execute instead of the DML statement that fired it. Instead-of triggers must be row level. For example, consider the **classes_rooms** view:

```
-- Available online as part of insteadOf.sql
CREATE OR REPLACE VIEW classes_rooms AS
  SELECT department, course, building, room_number
  FROM rooms, classes
  WHERE rooms.room_id = classes.room_id;
```

It is illegal to INSERT into this view directly, because it is a join of two tables and the INSERT requires that both underlying tables be modified, as the following SQL*Plus session shows:

```
-- Available online as part of insteadOf.sql
SQL> INSERT INTO classes_rooms (department, course, building,
                                room_number)
  2    VALUES ('MUS', 100, 'Music Building', 200);
INSERT INTO classes_rooms (department, course, building, room_number)
                                                         *
ERROR at line 1:
ORA-01732: data manipulation operation not legal on this view
```

However, we can create an instead-of trigger that does the correct thing for an INSERT, namely, to update the underlying tables:

```
-- Available online as part of insteadOf.sql
CREATE TRIGGER ClassesRoomsInsert
  INSTEAD OF INSERT ON classes_rooms
DECLARE
  v_roomID rooms.room_id%TYPE;
BEGIN
  -- First determine the room ID
  SELECT room_id
    INTO v_roomID
    FROM rooms
    WHERE building = :new.building
    AND room_number = :new.room_number;
```

```
  -- And now update the class
  UPDATE CLASSES
    SET room_id = v_roomID
    WHERE department = :new.department
    AND course = :new.course;
END ClassesRoomsInsert;
```

With the **ClassesRoomsInsert** trigger in place, the INSERT statement succeeds and does the correct thing.

> **NOTE**
> *As currently written, **ClassesRoomsInsert** does not have any error checking. We will rectify this later in this chapter.*

System Triggers

Oracle8*i* provides a third kind of trigger. A *system trigger* fires when a system event, such as database startup or shutdown, occurs, rather than on a DML operation on a table. A system trigger can also be fired on DDL operations, such as table creation. For example, suppose we want to record whenever an object is created. We can do this by creating a table as follows:

```
-- Available online as part of LogCreations.sql
CREATE TABLE ddl_creations (
  user_id          VARCHAR2(30),
  object_type      VARCHAR2(20),
  object_name      VARCHAR2(30),
  object_owner     VARCHAR2(30),
  creation_date DATE);
```

Once this table is available, we can create a system trigger to record the relevant information. The **LogCreations** trigger does just that—after every CREATE operation on the current schema, it records information about the object just created in **ddl_creations**.

```
-- Available online as part of LogCreations.sql
CREATE OR REPLACE TRIGGER LogCreations
  AFTER CREATE ON SCHEMA
BEGIN
  INSERT INTO ddl_creations (user_id, object_type, object_name,
                             object_owner, creation_date)
    VALUES (USER, SYS.DICTIONARY_OBJ_TYPE, SYS.DICTIONARY_OBJ_NAME,
            SYS.DICTIONARY_OBJ_OWNER, SYSDATE);
END LogCreations;
```

Creating Triggers

Regardless of the type, all triggers are created using the same syntax. The general syntax for creating a trigger is

```
CREATE [OR REPLACE] TRIGGER trigger_name
   {BEFORE | AFTER | INSTEAD OF} triggering_event
   referencing_clause
   [WHEN trigger_condition]
   [FOR EACH ROW]
   trigger_body;
```

where *trigger_name* is the name of the trigger, *triggering_event* specifies the event that fires the trigger (possibly including a specific table or view), and *trigger_body* is the main code for the trigger. The *referencing_clause* is used to refer to the data in the row currently being modified with a different name, and the *trigger_condition* in the WHEN clause, if present, is evaluated first. The body of the trigger is executed only when this condition evaluates to TRUE. We will see more examples of different kinds of triggers in the following sections.

NOTE
The trigger body cannot exceed 32K. If you have a trigger that exceeds this size, you can reduce it by moving some of the code to separately compiled packages or stored procedures, and calling these from the trigger body.

Creating DML Triggers

A DML trigger is fired on an INSERT, UPDATE, or DELETE operation on a database table. It can be fired either before or after the statement executes, and can be fired once per affected row, or once per statement. The combination of these factors determines the type of the trigger. There are a total of 12 possible types: 3 statements × 2 timing × 2 levels. For example, all of the following are valid DML trigger types:

- Before update statement level

- After insert row level

- Before delete row level

Table 6-1 summarizes the various options. A trigger can also be fired for more than one kind of DML statement on a given table—INSERT and UPDATE, for example. Any code in the trigger will be executed along with the triggering statement itself, as part of the same transaction.

A table can have any number of triggers defined on it, including more than one of a given DML type. For example, you can define two after delete statement-level triggers. All triggers of the same type will file sequentially. (For more information on the order of trigger firing, see the following section.)

NOTE
Prior to PL/SQL 2.1 (Oracle7 Release 7.1), a table could have only one trigger of each type defined on it, for a maximum of 12. Thus, the COMPATIBLE initialization parameter must be 7.1 or higher to have duplicate triggers of the same type on one table.

The triggering event for a DML trigger specifies the name of the table (and column) on which the trigger will fire. In Oracle8*i*, a trigger can also fire on a column of a nested table. See Chapter 14 for more information.

Category	Values	Comments
Statement	INSERT, DELETE, or UPDATE	Defines which kind of DML statement causes the trigger to fire.
Timing	Before or After	Defines whether the trigger fires before or after the statement is executed.
Level	Row or statement	If the trigger is a row-level trigger, it fires once for each row affected by the triggering statement. If the trigger is a statement-level trigger, it fires once, either before or after the statement. A row-level trigger is identified by the FOR EACH ROW clause in the trigger definition.

TABLE 6-1. *Types of DML Triggers*

Order of DML Trigger Firing

Triggers are fired as the DML statement is executed. The algorithm for executing a DML statement is given here:

1. Execute the before statement-level triggers, if present.

2. For each row affected by the statement:

   a. Execute the before row-level triggers, if present.

   b. Execute the statement itself.

   c. Execute the after row-level triggers, if present.

3. Execute the after statement-level triggers, if present.

To illustrate this, suppose we create all four kinds of UPDATE triggers on the **classes** table—before and after, statement and row level. We will create three before row triggers and two after statement triggers as well, as follows:

```
-- Available online as firingOrder.sql
CREATE SEQUENCE trig_seq
  START WITH 1
  INCREMENT BY 1;

CREATE OR REPLACE PACKAGE TrigPackage AS
  -- Global counter for use in the triggers
  v_Counter NUMBER;
END TrigPackage;

CREATE OR REPLACE TRIGGER ClassesBStatement
  BEFORE UPDATE ON classes
BEGIN
  -- Reset the counter first.
  TrigPackage.v_Counter := 0;

  INSERT INTO temp_table (num_col, char_col)
    VALUES (trig_seq.NEXTVAL,
      'Before Statement: counter = ' || TrigPackage.v_Counter);

  -- And now increment it for the next trigger.
  TrigPackage.v_Counter := TrigPackage.v_Counter + 1;
END ClassesBStatement;

CREATE OR REPLACE TRIGGER ClassesAStatement1
  AFTER UPDATE ON classes
BEGIN
  INSERT INTO temp_table (num_col, char_col)
```

```
      VALUES (trig_seq.NEXTVAL,
        'After Statement 1: counter = ' || TrigPackage.v_Counter);

    -- Increment for the next trigger.
    TrigPackage.v_Counter := TrigPackage.v_Counter + 1;
END ClassesAStatement1;

CREATE OR REPLACE TRIGGER ClassesAStatement2
  AFTER UPDATE ON classes
BEGIN
  INSERT INTO temp_table (num_col, char_col)
    VALUES (trig_seq.NEXTVAL,
      'After Statement 2: counter = ' || TrigPackage.v_Counter);

    -- Increment for the next trigger.
    TrigPackage.v_Counter := TrigPackage.v_Counter + 1;
END ClassesAStatement2;

CREATE OR REPLACE TRIGGER ClassesBRow1
  BEFORE UPDATE ON classes
  FOR EACH ROW
BEGIN
  INSERT INTO temp_table (num_col, char_col)
    VALUES (trig_seq.NEXTVAL,
      'Before Row 1: counter = ' || TrigPackage.v_Counter);

    -- Increment for the next trigger.
    TrigPackage.v_Counter := TrigPackage.v_Counter + 1;
END ClassesBRow1;

CREATE OR REPLACE TRIGGER ClassesBRow2
  BEFORE UPDATE ON classes
  FOR EACH ROW
BEGIN
  INSERT INTO temp_table (num_col, char_col)
    VALUES (trig_seq.NEXTVAL,
      'Before Row 2: counter = ' || TrigPackage.v_Counter);

    -- Increment for the next trigger.
    TrigPackage.v_Counter := TrigPackage.v_Counter + 1;
END ClassesBRow2;

CREATE OR REPLACE TRIGGER ClassesBRow3
  BEFORE UPDATE ON classes
  FOR EACH ROW
BEGIN
  INSERT INTO temp_table (num_col, char_col)
    VALUES (trig_seq.NEXTVAL,
      'Before Row 3: counter = ' || TrigPackage.v_Counter);
```

```
  -- Increment for the next trigger.
  TrigPackage.v_Counter := TrigPackage.v_Counter + 1;
END ClassesBRow3;

CREATE OR REPLACE TRIGGER ClassesARow
  AFTER UPDATE ON classes
  FOR EACH ROW
BEGIN
  INSERT INTO temp_table (num_col, char_col)
    VALUES (trig_seq.NEXTVAL,
      'After Row: counter = ' || TrigPackage.v_Counter);

  -- Increment for the next trigger.
  TrigPackage.v_Counter := TrigPackage.v_Counter + 1;
END ClassesARow;
```

Suppose we now issue the following UPDATE statement:

```
UPDATE classes
  SET num_credits = 4
  WHERE department IN ('HIS', 'CS');
```

This statement affects four rows. The before and after statement-level triggers are each executed once, and the before and after row-level triggers are each executed four times. If we then select from **temp_table**, we get the following:

```
-- Available online as part of firingOrder.sql
SQL> SELECT * FROM temp_table
  2    ORDER BY num_col;
 NUM_COL CHAR_COL
-------- ------------------------------------
       1 Before Statement: counter = 0
       2 Before Row 3: counter = 1
       3 Before Row 2: counter = 2
       4 Before Row 1: counter = 3
       5 After Row: counter = 4
       6 Before Row 3: counter = 5
       7 Before Row 2: counter = 6
       8 Before Row 1: counter = 7
       9 After Row: counter = 8
      10 Before Row 3: counter = 9
      11 Before Row 2: counter = 10
      12 Before Row 1: counter = 11
      13 After Row: counter = 12
      14 Before Row 3: counter = 13
      15 Before Row 2: counter = 14
      16 Before Row 1: counter = 15
```

```
17 After Row: counter = 16
18 After Statement 2: counter = 17
19 After Statement 1: counter = 18
```

As each trigger is fired, it will see the changes made by the earlier triggers, as well as any database changes made by the statement so far. This can be seen by the counter value printed by each trigger. (See Chapter 5 for more information about using packaged variables.)

The order in which triggers of the same type are fired is not defined. As in the preceding example, each trigger will see changes made by earlier triggers. If the order is important, combine all of the operations into one trigger.

NOTE
When you create a snapshot log for a table, Oracle will automatically create an AFTER ROW trigger for the table, that will update the log after every DML statement. You should be aware of this if you need to create an additional AFTER ROW trigger on that table. There are also additional restrictions on triggers and snapshots. For more information, see Oracle Server Replication.

Correlation Identifiers in Row-Level Triggers

A row-level trigger fires once per row processed by the triggering statement. Inside the trigger, you can access the data in the row that is currently being processed. This is accomplished through two correlation identifiers—**:old** and **:new**. A *correlation identifier* is a special kind of PL/SQL bind variable. The colon in front of each indicates that they are bind variables, in the sense of host variables used in embedded PL/SQL, and indicates that they are not regular PL/SQL variables. The PL/SQL compiler will treat them as records of type

triggering_table%ROWTYPE

where *triggering_table* is the table for which the trigger is defined. Thus, a reference such as

:new.*field*

will be valid only if *field* is a field in the triggering table. The meanings of **:old** and **:new** are described in Table 6-2. Although syntactically they are treated as records, in reality they are not (this is discussed in an upcoming section, "Pseudo-Records"). **:old** and **:new** are also known as *pseudo-records*, for this reason.

Triggering Statement	:old	:new
INSERT	Undefined—all fields are NULL.	Values that will be inserted when the statement is complete.
UPDATE	Original values for the row before the update.	New values that will be updated when the statement is complete.
DELETE	Original values before the row is deleted.	Undefined—all fields are NULL.

TABLE 6-2. *:old* and *:new* Correlation Identifiers

NOTE
:old is undefined for INSERT statements, and *:new* is undefined for DELETE statements. The PL/SQL compiler will not generate an error if you use *:old* in an INSERT or *:new* in a DELETE, but the field values of both will be NULL.

Oracle**8i** and higher   Oracle8*i* defines an additional correlation identifier—**:parent**. If the trigger is defined on a nested table, **:old** and **:new** refer to the rows in the nested table, while **:parent** refers to the current row of the parent table. For more information, see the Oracle documentation.

USING :old AND :new   The **GenerateStudentID** trigger, shown next, uses **:new**. It is a before INSERT trigger, and its purpose is to fill in the **ID** field of **students** with a value generated from the **student_sequence** sequence.

 `-- Available online as part of GenerateStudentID.sql`

```
CREATE OR REPLACE TRIGGER GenerateStudentID
  BEFORE INSERT OR UPDATE ON students
  FOR EACH ROW
BEGIN
  /* Fill in the ID field of students with the next value from
     student_sequence. Since ID is a column in students, :new.ID
     is a valid reference. */
  SELECT student_sequence.NEXTVAL
```

```
    INTO :new.ID
    FROM dual;
END GenerateStudentID;
```

GenerateStudentID actually modifies the value of **:new.ID**. This is one of the useful features of **:new**—when the statement is actually executed, whatever values are in **:new** will be used. With **GenerateStudentID**, we can issue an INSERT statement such as

-- Available online as part of GenerateStudentID.sql
```
INSERT INTO students (first_name, last_name)
  VALUES ('Lolita', 'Lazarus');
```

without generating an error. Even though we haven't specified a value for the primary key column **ID** (which is required), the trigger will supply it. In fact, if we do specify a value for **ID**, it will be ignored, since the trigger changes it. If we issue

-- Available online as part of GenerateStudentID.sql
```
INSERT INTO students (ID, first_name, last_name)
  VALUES (-7, 'Zelda', 'Zoom');
```

the **ID** column will be populated from **student_sequence.NEXTVAL**, rather than containing –7.

As a result of this, you cannot change **:new** in an after row-level trigger, since the statement has already been processed. In general, **:new** is modified only in a before row-level trigger, and **:old** is never modified, only read from.

The **:new** and **:old** records are only valid inside row-level triggers. If you try to reference either inside a statement-level trigger, you will get a compile error. Since a statement-level trigger executes once—even if there are many rows processed by the statement—**:old** and **:new** have no meaning. Which row would they refer to?

PSEUDO-RECORDS   Although **:new** and **:old** are syntactically treated as records of *triggering_table*%ROWTYPE, in reality they are not. As a result, operations that would normally be valid on records are not valid for **:new** and **:old**. For example, they cannot be assigned as entire records. Only the individual fields within them may be assigned. The following example illustrates this:

-- Available online as pseudoRecords.sql
```
CREATE OR REPLACE TRIGGER TempDelete
  BEFORE DELETE ON temp_table
  FOR EACH ROW
DECLARE
  v_TempRec temp_table%ROWTYPE;
```

```
BEGIN
  /* This is not a legal assignment, since :old is not truly
     a record. */
  v_TempRec := :old;

  /* We can accomplish the same thing, however, by assigning
     the fields individually. */
  v_TempRec.char_col := :old.char_col;
  v_TempRec.num_col := :old.num_col;
END TempDelete;
```

In addition, **:old** and **:new** cannot be passed to procedures or functions that take arguments of *triggering_table*%ROWTYPE.

REFERENCING CLAUSE   If desired, you can use the REFERENCING clause to specify a different name for **:old** and **:new**. This clause is found after the triggering event, before the WHEN clause, with the syntax

   REFERENCING [OLD AS :*old_name*] [NEW AS :*new_name*]

In the trigger body, you can use :*old_name* and :*new_name* instead of **:old** and **:new**. Below is an alternate version of the **GenerateStudentID** trigger, which uses REFERENCING to refer to **:new** as **:new_student**.

-- **Available online as part of GenerateStudentID.sql**
```
CREATE OR REPLACE TRIGGER GenerateStudentID
  BEFORE INSERT OR UPDATE ON students
  REFERENCING new AS new_student
  FOR EACH ROW
BEGIN
  /* Fill in the ID field of students with the next value from
     student_sequence. Since ID is a column in students,
     :new_student.ID is a valid reference. */
  SELECT student_sequence.nextval
    INTO :new_student.ID
    FROM dual;
END GenerateStudentID;
```

The WHEN Clause

The WHEN clause is valid for row-level triggers only. If present, the trigger body will be executed only for those rows that meet the condition specified by the WHEN clause. The WHEN clause looks like

WHEN *trigger_condition*

where *trigger_condition* is a Boolean expression. It will be evaluated for each row. The **:new** and **:old** records can be referenced inside *trigger_condition* as well, but the colon is *not* used there. The colon is only valid in the trigger body. For example, the body of the **CheckCredits** trigger is only executed if the current credits being taken by a student are more than 20:

```
CREATE OR REPLACE TRIGGER CheckCredits
  BEFORE INSERT OR UPDATE OF current_credits ON students
  FOR EACH ROW
  WHEN (new.current_credits > 20)
BEGIN
  /* Trigger body goes here. */
END;
```

CheckCredits could also be written as follows:

```
CREATE OR REPLACE TRIGGER CheckCredits
  BEFORE INSERT OR UPDATE OF current_credits ON students
  FOR EACH ROW
BEGIN
  IF :new.current_credits > 20 THEN
    /* Trigger body goes here. */
  END IF;
END;
```

Trigger Predicates: INSERTING, UPDATING, and DELETING

The **UpdateMajorStats** trigger discussed in "DML Triggers," earlier in this chapter, is an INSERT, UPDATE, and DELETE trigger. Inside a trigger of this type (which will fire for different kinds of DML statements), there are three boolean functions that you can use to determine what the operation is. These predicates are INSERTING, UPDATING, and DELETING. Their behavior is described in the following table.

Predicate	Behavior
INSERTING	TRUE if the triggering statement is an INSERT; FALSE otherwise.
UPDATING	TRUE if the triggering statement is an UPDATE; FALSE otherwise.
DELETING	TRUE if the triggering statement is a DELETE; FALSE otherwise.

NOTE
Oracle8i defines additional functions that can be called from within a trigger body, similar to trigger predicates. See "Event Attribute Functions," later in this chapter, for more details.

The **LogRSChanges** trigger uses these predicates to record all changes made to the **registered_students** table. In addition to the change, it records the user who makes the change. The records are kept in the **RS_audit** table, which looks like this:

```
-- Available online as part of relTables.sql
CREATE TABLE RS_audit (
  change_type    CHAR(1)      NOT NULL,
  changed_by     VARCHAR2(8)  NOT NULL,
  timestamp      DATE         NOT NULL,
  old_student_id NUMBER(5),
  old_department CHAR(3),
  old_course     NUMBER(3),
  old_grade      CHAR(1),
  new_student_id NUMBER(5),
  new_department CHAR(3),
  new_course     NUMBER(3),
  new_grade      CHAR(1)
  );
```

LogRSChanges is created with the following:

```
-- Available online as LogRSChanges.sql
CREATE OR REPLACE TRIGGER LogRSChanges
  BEFORE INSERT OR DELETE OR UPDATE ON registered_students
  FOR EACH ROW
DECLARE
  v_ChangeType CHAR(1);
BEGIN
  /* Use 'I' for an INSERT, 'D' for DELETE, and 'U' for UPDATE. */
  IF INSERTING THEN
    v_ChangeType := 'I';
  ELSIF UPDATING THEN
    v_ChangeType := 'U';
  ELSE
    v_ChangeType := 'D';
  END IF;

  /* Record all the changes made to registered_students in
```

```
      RS_audit. Use SYSDATE to generate the timestamp, and
      USER to return the userid of the current user. */
   INSERT INTO RS_audit
     (change_type, changed_by, timestamp,
      old_student_id, old_department, old_course, old_grade,
      new_student_id, new_department, new_course, new_grade)
   VALUES
     (v_ChangeType, USER, SYSDATE,
      :old.student_id, :old.department, :old.course, :old.grade,
      :new.student_id, :new.department, :new.course, :new.grade);
END LogRSChanges;
```

Triggers are commonly used for auditing, as in **LogRSChanges**. While this is available as part of the database, triggers allow for more customized and flexible recording. **LogRSChanges** could be modified, for example, to record changes only made by certain people. It could also check to see if users have permission to make changes and raise an error (with RAISE_APPLICATION_ERROR) if they don't.

Creating Instead-Of Triggers

Oracle **8** and higher Unlike DML triggers, which fire in addition to the INSERT, UPDATE, or DELETE operation (either before or after them), instead-of triggers fire instead of a DML operation. Also, instead-of triggers can be defined only on views, while DML triggers are defined on tables. Instead-of triggers are used in two cases:

■ To allow a view that would otherwise not be modifiable to be modified.

■ To modify the columns of a nested table column in a view.

We will discuss the first case in this section. For more information on nested tables , see Chapter 14.

NOTE
With Oracle8i, Release 8.1.5, instead-of triggers are available only with the Enterprise Edition. They may become available in other editions in future releases.

Modifiable vs. Non-Modifiable Views

A *modifiable view* is one against which you can issue a DML statement. In general, a view is modifiable if it does not contain any of the following:

■ Set operators (UNION, UNION ALL, MINUS)

- Aggregate functions (SUM, AVG, etc.)
- GROUP BY, CONNECT BY, or START WITH clauses
- The DISTINCT operator
- Joins

There are, however, some views that contain joins that are modifiable. In general, a join view is modifiable if the DML operation on it modifies only one base table at a time, and if the DML statement meets the conditions in Table 6-3. (For more information on modifiable vs. non-modifiable join views, see *Oracle Concepts*.) If a view is non-modifiable, then you can write an instead-of trigger on it that does the correct thing, thus allowing it to be modified. An instead-of trigger can also be written on a modifiable view, if additional processing is required.

Table 6-3 refers to key-preserved tables. A table is *key-preserved* if, after a join with another table, the keys in the original table are also keys in the resultant join. For more details on key-preserved tables, see *Oracle8i Application Developer's Guide—Fundamentals*.

Instead-Of Example

Consider the **classes_rooms** view that we saw earlier in "Instead-of Triggers":

```
-- Available online as part of insteadOf.sql
CREATE OR REPLACE VIEW classes_rooms AS
  SELECT department, course, building, room_number
  FROM rooms, classes
  WHERE rooms.room_id = classes.room_id;
```

DML Operation	Permitted If
INSERT	The statement does not refer, implicitly or explicitly, to the columns of a non-key preserved table.
UPDATE	The updated columns map to columns of a key-preserved table.
DELETE	There is exactly one key-preserved table in the join.

TABLE 6-3. *Modifiable Join Views*

As we saw earlier, it is illegal to INSERT into this view. Although it is legal to issue an UPDATE or DELETE against this view, they do not necessarily do the correct thing. For example, a DELETE from **classes_rooms** will delete the corresponding rows from **classes**. What is the correct DML behavior for **classes_rooms**? This could vary, depending on your business rules. Suppose, however, that they have the following meanings:

Operation	Meaning
INSERT	Assign the newly inserted class to the newly inserted room. This results in an update of **classes**.
UPDATE	Change the room assigned to a class. This can result in an update of either **classes** or **rooms**, depending on which columns of **classes_rooms** are updated.
DELETE	Clear the room ID from the deleted class. This results in an update of **classes**, to set the ID to NULL.

The **ClassesRoomsInstead** trigger, shown in the following, enforces the above rules and allows DML operations to be performed correctly against **classes_rooms**.

```
-- Available online as ClassesRoomInstead.sql
CREATE OR REPLACE TRIGGER ClassesRoomsInstead
  INSTEAD OF INSERT OR UPDATE OR DELETE ON classes_rooms
  FOR EACH ROW
DECLARE
  v_roomID rooms.room_id%TYPE;
  v_UpdatingClasses BOOLEAN := FALSE;
  v_UpdatingRooms BOOLEAN := FALSE;

  -- Local function that returns the room ID, given a building
  -- and room number.  This function will raise ORA-20000 if the
  -- building and room number are not found.
  FUNCTION GetRoomID(p_Building IN rooms.building%TYPE,
                     p_Room IN rooms.room_number%TYPE)
    RETURN rooms.room_id%TYPE IS

    v_RoomID rooms.room_id%TYPE;
  BEGIN
    SELECT room_id
      INTO v_RoomID
      FROM rooms
      WHERE building = p_Building
      AND room_number = p_Room;
    RETURN v_RoomID;
```

```
  EXCEPTION
    WHEN NO_DATA_FOUND THEN
      RAISE_APPLICATION_ERROR(-20000, 'No matching room');
  END getRoomID;

  -- Local procedure that checks whether the class identified by
  -- p_Department and p_Course exists.  If not, it raises
  -- ORA-20001.
  PROCEDURE VerifyClass(p_Department IN classes.department%TYPE,
                        p_Course IN classes.course%TYPE) IS
    v_Dummy NUMBER;
  BEGIN
    SELECT 0
      INTO v_Dummy
      FROM classes
      WHERE department = p_Department
      AND course = p_Course;
  EXCEPTION
    WHEN NO_DATA_FOUND THEN
      RAISE_APPLICATION_ERROR(-20001,
        p_Department || ' ' || p_Course || ' doesn''t exist');
  END verifyClass;

BEGIN
  IF INSERTING THEN
    -- This essentially assigns a class to a given room.  The logic
    -- here is the same as the "updating rooms" case below:  First,
    -- determine the room ID:
    v_RoomID := GetRoomID(:new.building, :new.room_number);

      -- And then update classes with the new ID.
      UPDATE CLASSES
        SET room_id = v_RoomID
        WHERE department = :new.department
        AND course = :new.course;


  ELSIF UPDATING THEN
    -- Determine if we are updating classes, or updating rooms.
    v_UpdatingClasses := (:new.department != :old.department) OR
                         (:new.course != :old.course);
    v_UpdatingRooms := (:new.building != :old.building) OR
                       (:new.room_number != :old.room_number);

    IF (v_UpdatingClasses) THEN
      -- In this case, we are changing the class assigned for a
      -- given room.  First make sure the new class exists.
```

```
      VerifyClass(:new.department, :new.course);

   -- Get the room ID,
   v_RoomID := GetRoomID(:old.building, :old.room_number);

   -- Then clear the room for the old class,
   UPDATE classes
     SET room_ID = NULL
     WHERE department = :old.department
     AND course = :old.course;

   -- And finally assign the old room to the new class.
   UPDATE classes
     SET room_ID = v_RoomID
     WHERE department = :new.department
     AND course = :new.course;
  END IF;

  IF v_UpdatingRooms THEN
    -- Here, we are changing the room for a given class.  This
    -- logic is the same as the "inserting" case above, except
    -- that classes is updated with :old instead of :new.
    -- First, determine the new room ID.
    v_RoomID := GetRoomID(:new.building, :new.room_number);

    -- And then update classes with the new ID.
    UPDATE CLASSES
      SET room_id = v_RoomID
      WHERE department = :old.department
      AND course = :old.course;
  END IF;

ELSE
  -- Here, we want to clear the class assigned to the room,
  -- without actually removing rows from the underlying tables.
  UPDATE classes
    SET room_ID = NULL
    WHERE department = :old.department
    AND course = :old.course;
  END IF;
END ClassesRoomsInstead;
```

NOTE
*The FOR EACH ROW clause is optional for
an instead-of trigger. All instead-of triggers are
row level, whether or not the clause is present.*

classes		
Dept.	Course	Room ID
HIS	101	20000
CS	101	20001
ECN	203	20002
CS	102	20003
HIS	301	20004
MUS	410	20005
MUS	100	
ECN	101	20007
NUT	307	20008

rooms		
Room ID	Building	Room Number
20000	Building 7	201
20001	Building 6	101
20002	Building 6	150
20003	Building 6	160
20004	Building 6	170
20005	Music Building	100
20006	Music Building	200
20007	Building 7	300
20008	Building 7	310

classes_rooms			
Dept.	Course	Building	Room Number
HIS	101	Building 7	201
CS	101	Building 6	101
ECN	203	Building 6	150
CS	102	Building 6	160
HIS	301	Building 6	170
MUS	410	Music Building	100
ECN	101	Building 7	300
NUT	307	Building 7	310

FIGURE 6-1.   *Original contents of **classes, rooms**, and **classes_rooms***

ClassesRoomsInstead uses trigger predicates to determine the DML operation being performed, and to take the appropriate action. Figure 6-1 contains the original contents for **classes**, **rooms**, and **classes_rooms**. Suppose we then issue the following INSERT statement:

```
-- Available online as part of ClassesRoomsInstead.sql
INSERT INTO classes_rooms
   VALUES ('MUS', 100, 'Music Building', 200);
```

The trigger causes **classes** to be updated to reflect the new room assignment. This is illustrated by Figure 6-2. Now, suppose we issue the following UPDATE statement:

```
-- Available online as part of ClassesRoomsInstead.sql
UPDATE classes_rooms
   SET department = 'NUT', course = 307
   WHERE building = 'Building 7' AND room_number = 201;
```

classes has been updated again, to reflect the new changes. History 101 now doesn't have a room assigned, and Nutrition 307 has the room originally assigned to History 101. This is illustrated by Figure 6-3. Finally, suppose we issue the following DELETE statement:

```
-- Available online as part of ClassesRoomsInstead.sql
DELETE FROM classes_rooms
   WHERE building = 'Building 6';
```

classes

Dept.	Course	Room ID
HIS	101	20000
CS	101	20001
ECN	203	20002
CS	102	20003
HIS	301	20004
MUS	410	20005
MUS	**100**	**20006**
ECN	101	20007
NUT	307	20008

rooms

Room ID	Building	Room Number
20000	Building 7	201
20001	Building 6	101
20002	Building 6	150
20003	Building 6	160
20004	Building 6	170
20005	Music Building	100
20006	Music Building	200
20007	Building 7	300
20008	Building 7	310

classes_rooms

Dept.	Course	Building	Room Number
HIS	101	Building 7	201
CS	101	Building 6	101
ECN	203	Building 6	150
CS	102	Building 6	160
HIS	301	Building 6	170
MUS	410	Music Building	100
ECN	101	Building 7	300
NUT	307	Building 7	310
MUS	**100**	**Music Building**	**200**

FIGURE 6-2. *Contents after INSERT*

classes

Dept.	Course	Room ID
NUT	**307**	**20000**
CS	101	20001
ECN	203	20002
CS	102	20003
HIS	301	20004
MUS	410	20005
MUS	100	20006
ECN	101	20007
HIS	**101**	

rooms

Room ID	Building	Room Number
20000	Building 7	201
20001	Building 6	101
20002	Building 6	150
20003	Building 6	160
20004	Building 6	170
20005	Music Building	100
20006	Music Building	200
20007	Building 7	300
20008	Building 7	310

classes_rooms

Dept.	Course	Building	Room Number
HIS	101	Building 7	201
CS	101	Building 6	101
ECN	203	Building 6	150
CS	102	Building 6	160
HIS	301	Building 6	170
MUS	410	Music Building	100
ECN	101	Building 7	300
NUT	**307**	**Building 7**	**201**
MUS	100	Music Building	200

FIGURE 6-3. *Contents after UPDATE*

classes		
Dept.	Course	Room ID
NUT	307	20000
CS	101	
ECN	203	
CS	102	
HIS	301	
MUS	410	20005
MUS	100	20006
ECN	101	20007
HIS	101	

rooms		
Room ID	Building	Room Number
20000	Building 7	201
20001	Building 6	101
20002	Building 6	150
20003	Building 6	160
20004	Building 6	170
20005	Music Building	100
20006	Music Building	200
20007	Building 7	300
20008	Building 7	310

classes_rooms			
Dept.	Course	Building	Room Number
MUS	410	Music Building	100
ECN	101	Building 7	300
NUT	307	Building 7	201
MUS	100	Music Building	200

FIGURE 6-4. *Contents after DELETE*

The updates to **classes** now set **room_ID** to NULL for those classes originally in Building 6, as illustrated by Figure 6-4. Note that throughout all the preceding DML statements, **rooms** remained unchanged, and only **classes** was updated.

Creating System Triggers

Oracle **8*i***
and higher

As we have seen in the previous sections, both DML and instead-of triggers fire on (or instead of) DML events, namely, INSERT, UPDATE, or DELETE statements. System triggers, on the other hand, fire on two different kinds of events—DDL or database. *DDL events* include CREATE, ALTER, or DROP statements, while *database events* include startup/shutdown of the server, logon/logoff of a user, and a server error. The syntax for creating a system trigger is as follows:

```
CREATE [OR REPLACE] TRIGGER [schema.]trigger_name
{BEFORE | AFTER}
{ddl_event_list | database_event_list}
ON {DATABASE | [schema.]SCHEMA}
[when_clause]
trigger_body;
```

where *ddl_event_list* is one or more DDL events (separated by the OR keyword), and *database_event_list* is one or more database events (separated by the OR keyword).

Table 6-4 describes the DDL and database events, along with their allowed timings (BEFORE or AFTER). You cannot create an instead-of system trigger. There is no database event for TRUNCATE.

NOTE
You must have the ADMINISTER DATABASE TRIGGER system privilege in order to create a system trigger. See "Trigger Privileges," later in this chapter, for more information.

Event	Timings Allowed	Description
STARTUP	AFTER	Fired when an instance is started up.
SHUTDOWN	BEFORE	Fired when an instance is shut down. This event may not fire if the database is shut down abnormally (as in a shutdown abort).
SERVERERROR	AFTER	Fired whenever an error occurs.
LOGON	AFTER	Fired after a user has successfully connected to the database.
LOGOFF	BEFORE	Fired at the start of a user logoff.
CREATE	BEFORE, AFTER	Fired before or after a schema object is created.
DROP	BEFORE, AFTER	Fired before or after a schema object is dropped.
ALTER	BEFORE, AFTER	Fired before or after a schema object is altered.

TABLE 6-4. *System DDL and Database Events*

Database vs. Schema Triggers

A system trigger can be defined at the database level or a schema level. A database-level trigger will fire whenever the triggering event occurs, while a schema-level trigger will fire only when the triggering event occurs for the specified schema. The DATABASE and SCHEMA keywords determine the level for a given system trigger. If the schema is not specified with the SCHEMA keyword, it defaults to the schema that owns the trigger. For example, suppose we create the following trigger while connected as **UserA**:

```
-- Available online as part of DatabaseSchema.sql
CREATE OR REPLACE TRIGGER LogUserAConnects
   AFTER LOGON ON SCHEMA
BEGIN
   INSERT INTO example.temp_table
     VALUES (1, 'LogUserAConnects fired!');
END LogUserAConnects;
```

LogUserAConnects will record in **temp_table** whenever **UserA** connects to the database. We can do likewise for **UserB** by creating the following while connected as **UserB**:

```
-- Available online as part of DatabaseSchema.sql
CREATE OR REPLACE TRIGGER LogUserBConnects
   AFTER LOGON ON SCHEMA
BEGIN
   INSERT INTO example.temp_table
     VALUES (2, 'LogUserBConnects fired!');
END LogUserBConnects;
```

Finally, we can create the following trigger while connected as **example**. **LogAllConnects** will record all connects to the database, because it is a database-level trigger.

```
-- Available online as part of DatabaseSchema.sql
CREATE OR REPLACE TRIGGER LogAllConnects
   AFTER LOGON ON DATABASE
BEGIN
   INSERT INTO example.temp_table
     VALUES (3, 'LogAllConnects fired!');
END LogAllConnects;
```

NOTE
*You must first create **UserA** and **UserB**, and grant the appropriate permissions, before running the previous examples. See **DatabaseSchema.sql** for more details.*

We can now see the effects of the different triggers in the following SQL*Plus session.

```
-- Available online as part of DatabaseSchema.sql
SQL> connect UserA/UserA
Connected.
SQL> connect UserB/UserB
Connected.
SQL> connect example/example
Connected.
SQL>
SQL> SELECT * FROM temp_table;
   NUM_COL CHAR_COL
---------- ----------------------------------------------------------------
         3 LogAllConnects fired!
         2 LogUserBConnects fired!
         3 LogAllConnects fired!
         3 LogAllConnects fired!
         1 LogUserAConnects fired!
```

LogAllConnects has fired three times (once for all three connections), while **LogUserAConnects** and **LogUserBConnects** have only fired once, as expected.

NOTE
STARTUP and SHUTDOWN triggers are relevant only at the database level. It is not illegal to create them at the schema level, but they will not fire.

Event Attribute Functions

Within a system trigger, there are several event attribute functions that are available. Similar to the trigger predicates (INSERTING, UPDATING, and DELETING), they allow a trigger body to get information about the triggering event. Although it is legal to call these functions from other PL/SQL blocks (not necessarily in a system trigger body), they will not always return a valid result. The event attribute functions are described in Table 6-5.

The **LogCreations** trigger, which we saw at the beginning of this chapter, uses some of the attribute functions. Unlike trigger predicates, event attribute functions are standalone PL/SQL functions that are owned by SYS. There are no synonyms defined for them by default, so they must be prefixed by SYS in order to resolve them.

```
-- Available online as part of LogCreations.sql
CREATE OR REPLACE TRIGGER LogCreations
  AFTER CREATE ON SCHEMA
BEGIN
  INSERT INTO ddl_creations (user_id, object_type, object_name,
```

```
                              object_owner, creation_date)
     VALUES (USER, SYS.DICTIONARY_OBJ_TYPE, SYS.DICTIONARY_OBJ_NAME,
             SYS.DICTIONARY_OBJ_OWNER, SYSDATE);
END LogCreations;
```

Attribute Function	Datatype	System Event Applicable For	Description
SYSEVENT	VARCHAR2(20)	All events	Returns the system event that fired the trigger.
INSTANCE_NUM	NUMBER	All events	Returns the current instance number. This will always be 1 unless you are running OPS.
DATABASE_ NAME	VARCHAR2(50)	All events	Returns the current database name.
SERVER_ERROR	NUMBER	SERVERERROR	Takes a single NUMBER argument. Returns the error at the position on the error stack indicated by the argument. The position 1 is the top of the stack.
IS_SERVERERROR	BOOLEAN	SERVERERROR	Takes an error number as an argument, and returns TRUE if the Oracle error indicated is on the error stack.
LOGIN_USER	VARCHAR2(30)	All events	Returns the userid of the user that fired the trigger.
DICTIONARY_ OBJ_TYPE	VARCHAR2(20)	CREATE, DROP, ALTER	Returns the type of dictionary object on which the DDL operation that fired the trigger occurred.

TABLE 6-5.   *Event Attribute Functions*

Attribute Function	Datatype	System Event Applicable For	Description
DICTIONARY_ OBJ_NAME	VARCHAR2(30)	CREATE, DROP, ALTER	Returns the name of the dictionary object on which the DDL operation that fired the trigger occurred.
DICTIONARY_ OBJ_OWNER	VARCHAR2(30)	CREATE, DROP, ALTER	Returns the owner of the dictionary object on which the DDL operation that fired the trigger occurred.
DES_ENCRYPTED_ PASSWORD	VARCHAR2(30)	CREATE or ALTER USER	Returns the DES encrypted password of the user being created or altered.

TABLE 6-5.   *Event Attribute Functions* (continued)

Using the SERVERERROR Event

The SERVERERROR event can be used to track errors that occur in the database. The error code is available inside the trigger through the SERVER_ERROR attribute function. This function allows you to determine the error codes that are on the stack. However, it does not tell you the messages associated with those codes.

This can be remedied with the DBMS_UTILTITY.FORMAT_ERROR_STACK procedure. Although the trigger itself did not cause the error, the error stack is available to PL/SQL through this procedure. This is illustrated by the following example, which will record errors in the following table:

```
-- Available online as part of LogErrors.sql
CREATE TABLE error_log (
  timestamp       DATE,
  username        VARCHAR2(30),
  instance        NUMBER,
  database_name   VARCHAR2(50),
  error_stack     VARCHAR2(2000)
  );
```

We can create a trigger that inserts into **error_log** as follows:

```
-- Available online as part of LogErrors.sql
CREATE OR REPLACE TRIGGER LogErrors
  AFTER SERVERERROR ON DATABASE
BEGIN
  INSERT INTO error_log
    VALUES (SYSDATE, SYS.LOGIN_USER, SYS.INSTANCE_NUM, SYS.
          DATABASE_NAME, DBMS_UTILITY.FORMAT_ERROR_STACK);
END LogErrors;
```

Finally, we can generate some errors and see that **LogErrors** correctly records them. Note that the trigger captures errors in SQL, runtime PL/SQL errors, and compile-time PL/SQL errors.

```
-- Available online as part of LogErrors.sql
SQL> SELECT * FROM non_existent_table;
SELECT * FROM non_existent_table
              *
ERROR at line 1:
ORA-00942: table or view does not exist
SQL> BEGIN
  2    INSERT INTO non_existent_table VALUES ('Hello!');
  3  END;
  4  /
  INSERT INTO non_existent_table VALUES ('Hello!');
              *
ERROR at line 2:
ORA-06550: line 2, column 15:
PLS-00201: identifier 'NON_EXISTENT_TABLE' must be declared
ORA-06550: line 2, column 3:
PL/SQL: SQL Statement ignored
SQL> BEGIN
  2    -- This is a syntax error!
  3    DELETE FROM students
  4  END;
  5  /
END;
*
ERROR at line 4:
ORA-06550: line 4, column 1:
PLS-00103: Encountered the symbol "END" when expecting one of the
following:
. @ ; return RETURNING_ <an identifier>
<a double-quoted delimited-identifier> partition where
```

```
The symbol ";" was substituted for "END" to continue.
SQL> SELECT *
  2    FROM error_log;

TIMESTAMP USERNAME  INSTANCE DATABASE
--------- -------- --------- --------

ERROR_STACK
------------------------------------------------------------
30-AUG-99 EXAMPLE          1 V815
ORA-00942: table or view does not exist

30-AUG-99 EXAMPLE          1 V815
ORA-06550: line 2, column 15:
PLS-00201: identifier 'NON_EXISTENT_TABLE' must be declared
ORA-06550: line 2, column 3:
PL/SQL: SQL Statement ignored

30-AUG-99 EXAMPLE          1 V815
ORA-06550: line 4, column 1:
PLS-00103: Encountered the symbol "END" when expecting one of
 the following:

   . @ ; return RETURNING_ <an identifier>
   <a double-quoted delimited-identifier> partition where
The symbol ";" was substituted for "END" to continue.
```

System Triggers and Transactions

Depending on the triggering event, the transactional behavior of a system trigger
varies. A system trigger will either fire as a separate transaction that is committed
upon successful completion of the trigger, or it will fire as part of the current user
transaction. STARTUP, SHUTDOWN, SERVERERROR, and LOGON triggers all fire
as a separate transaction, while LOGOFF and DDL triggers fire as part of the current
transaction.

It is important to note, however, that the work done by the trigger will generally
be committed regardless. In the case of a DDL trigger, the current transaction (namely,
the CREATE, ALTER, or DROP statement) is automatically committed, which commits
the work in the trigger. The work in a LOGOFF trigger will also be committed as part
of the final transaction in the session.

NOTE
*Because system triggers are generally committed
anyway, declaring them as autonomous will
not have any effect. See Chapter 11 for more
information about autonomous transactions.*

System Triggers and the WHEN Clause

Just like DML triggers, system triggers can use the WHEN clause to specify a condition on the trigger firing. However, there are restrictions on the types of conditions that can be specified for each type of system trigger, namely,

- STARTUP and SHUTDOWN triggers cannot have any conditions.

- SERVERERROR triggers can use the ERRNO test to check for a specific error only.

- LOGON and LOGOFF triggers can check the userid or username with the USERID or USERNAME tests.

- DDL triggers can check the type and name of the object being modified, and can check the userid or username.

Other Trigger Issues

In this section, we will discuss some remaining issues about triggers. These include the namespace for trigger names, various restrictions on using triggers, and different kinds of trigger bodies. The section closes with a discussion of the privileges related to triggers.

Trigger Names

The namespace for trigger names is different from that of other subprograms. A *namespace* is the set of legal identifiers available for use as the names of an object. Procedures, packages, and tables all share the same namespace. This means that, within one database schema, all objects in the same namespace must have unique names. For example, it is illegal to give the same name to a procedure and a package.

Triggers, however, exist in a separate namespace. This means that a trigger can have the same name as a table or procedure. Within one schema, however, a given name can be used for only one trigger. For example, we can create a trigger called **major_stats** on the **major_stats** table, but it is illegal to create a procedure also called **major_stats**, as the following SQL*Plus session shows.

```
-- Available online as samename.sql
SQL> -- Legal, since triggers and tables are in different namespaces.
SQL> CREATE OR REPLACE TRIGGER major_stats
  2    BEFORE INSERT ON major_stats
  3  BEGIN
  4    INSERT INTO temp_table (char_col)
  5      VALUES ('Trigger fired!');
  6  END major_stats;
  7  /
```

```
Trigger created.

SQL> -- Illegal, since procedures and tables are in the same namespace.
SQL> CREATE OR REPLACE PROCEDURE major_stats AS
  2    BEGIN
  3      INSERT INTO temp_table (char_col)
  4        VALUES ('Procedure called!');
  5    END major_stats;
  6    /
CREATE OR REPLACE PROCEDURE major_stats AS
*
ERROR at line 1:
ORA-00955: name is already used by an existing object
```

TIP
Although it is possible to use the same name for a trigger and a table, I don't recommend it. It is better to give each trigger a unique name that identifies its function as well as the table on which it is defined, or prefix triggers with a common sequence of characters (such as TRG_).

Restrictions on Triggers

The body of a trigger is a PL/SQL block. (Oracle8*i* allows other types of trigger bodies—see the next section for details.) Any statement that is legal in a PL/SQL block is legal in a trigger body, subject to the following restrictions:

- A trigger may not issue any transaction control statements—COMMIT, ROLLBACK, SAVEPOINT, or SET TRANSACTION. The PL/SQL compiler will allow a trigger to be created that contains one of these statements, but you will receive an error when the trigger is fired. This is because it is fired as part of the execution of the triggering statement, and is in the same transaction as the triggering statement. When the triggering statement is committed or rolled back, the work in the trigger is committed or rolled back as well. (In Oracle8*i*, you can create a trigger that executes as an autonomous transaction, in which case the work in the trigger can be committed or rolled back independent of the state of the triggering statement. See Chapter 11 for more information about autonomous transactions.)

- Likewise, any procedures or functions that are called by the trigger body cannot issue any transaction control statements (unless they are also declared as autonomous in Oracle8*i*).

■ The trigger body cannot declare any LONG or LONG RAW variables. Also, **:new** and **:old** cannot refer to a LONG or LONG RAW column in the table for which the trigger is defined.

■ In Oracle8 and higher, code in a trigger body may reference and use LOB (Large OBject) columns, but it may not modify the values of the columns. This is also true for object columns.

There are also restrictions on which tables a trigger body may access. Depending on the type of trigger and the constraints on the tables, tables may be mutating. This situation is discussed in detail in "Mutating Tables," later in this chapter.

Trigger Bodies

Oracle **8***i* and higher

Prior to Oracle8*i*, trigger bodies must be PL/SQL blocks. In Oracle8*i*, however, a trigger body can consist of a CALL statement instead. The procedure that is called can be a PL/SQL stored subprogram, or it can be a wrapper for a C or Java routine. This allows you to create triggers in which the functional code is written in Java. For example, suppose we want to record connects and disconnects to the database, in the following table:

```
-- Available online as part of relTables.sql
CREATE TABLE connect_audit (
  user_name  VARCHAR2(30),
  operation  VARCHAR2(30),
  timestamp  DATE);
```

We can use the following package to record connects and disconnects:

```
-- Available online as LogPkg1.sql
CREATE OR REPLACE PACKAGE LogPkg AS
  PROCEDURE LogConnect(p_UserID IN VARCHAR2);
  PROCEDURE LogDisconnect(p_UserID IN VARCHAR2);
END LogPkg;

CREATE OR REPLACE PACKAGE BODY LogPkg AS
  PROCEDURE LogConnect(p_UserID IN VARCHAR2) IS
  BEGIN
    INSERT INTO connect_audit (user_name, operation, timestamp)
      VALUES (p_USerID, 'CONNECT', SYSDATE);
  END LogConnect;

  PROCEDURE LogDisconnect(p_UserID IN VARCHAR2) IS
  BEGIN
    INSERT INTO connect_audit (user_name, operation, timestamp)
```

```
            VALUES (p_USerID, 'DISCONNECT', SYSDATE);
    END LogDisconnect;
END LogPkg;
```

Both **LogPkg.LogConnect** and **LogPkg.LogDisconnect** take a username as an argument, and insert a row into **connect_audit**. Finally, we can call them from a LOGON and LOGOFF trigger as follows:

```
-- Available online as LogConnects.sql
CREATE OR REPLACE TRIGGER LogConnects
  AFTER LOGON ON DATABASE
  CALL LogPkg.LogConnect(SYS.LOGIN_USER)
/

CREATE OR REPLACE TRIGGER LogDisconnects
  BEFORE LOGOFF ON DATABASE
  CALL LogPkg.LogDisconnect(SYS.LOGIN_USER)
/
```

> **NOTE**
> *Since **LogConnects** and **LogDisconnects** are system triggers on the database (as opposed to a schema), you must have the ADMINISTER DATABASE TRIGGER system privilege to create them.*

The trigger body for both **LogConnects** and **LogDisconnects** is simply a CALL statement, which indicates the procedure to be executed. The current user is passed as the only argument. In the preceding example, the target of the CALL is a standard PL/SQL packaged procedure. However, it could just as easily be a wrapper for a C or Java external routine. For example, suppose we load the following Java class into the database:

```
// Available online as Logger.java
import java.sql.*;
import oracle.jdbc.driver.*;

public class Logger {
  public static void LogConnect(String userID)
  throws SQLException {
    // Get default JDBC connection
    Connection conn = new OracleDriver().defaultConnection();

    String insertString =
      "INSERT INTO connect_audit (user_name, operation, timestamp)" +
```

```
          "  VALUES (?, 'CONNECT', SYSDATE)";

    // Prepare and execute a statement that does the insert
    PreparedStatement insertStatement =
      conn.prepareStatement(insertString);
    insertStatement.setString(1, userID);
    insertStatement.execute();
  }

  public static void LogDisconnect(String userID)
  throws SQLException {
    // Get default JDBC connection
    Connection conn = new OracleDriver().defaultConnection();

    String insertString =
      "INSERT INTO connect_audit (user_name, operation, timestamp)" +
      "  VALUES (?, 'DISCONNECT', SYSDATE)";

    // Prepare and execute a statement that does the insert
    PreparedStatement insertStatement =
      conn.prepareStatement(insertString);
    insertStatement.setString(1, userID);
    insertStatement.execute();
  }
}
```

If we then create **LogPkg** as a wrapper for this class,

```
-- Available online as LogPkg2.sql
CREATE OR REPLACE PACKAGE LogPkg AS
  PROCEDURE LogConnect(p_UserID IN VARCHAR2);
  PROCEDURE LogDisconnect(p_UserID IN VARCHAR2);
END LogPkg;

CREATE OR REPLACE PACKAGE BODY LogPkg AS
  PROCEDURE LogConnect(p_UserID IN VARCHAR2) IS
    LANGUAGE JAVA
    NAME 'Logger.LogConnect(java.lang.String)';

  PROCEDURE LogDisconnect(p_UserID IN VARCHAR2) IS
    LANGUAGE JAVA
    NAME 'Logger.LogDisconnect(java.lang.String)';
END LogPkg;
```

we can use the same triggers to achieve the desired effect. See Chapter 10 for more information about external routines, including how to load Java procedures into the database.

NOTE
*Trigger predicates such as INSERTING, UPDATING, and DELETING, and the **:old** and **:new** correlation identifiers (and **:parent**), can be used only if the trigger body is a complete PL/SQL block and not a CALL statement.*

Trigger Privileges

There are five system privileges that apply to triggers, which are described in Table 6-6. In addition to these, the owner of a trigger must have the necessary object privileges on the objects referenced by the trigger. Since a trigger is a compiled object (since Oracle7 Release 7.3), these privileges must be granted directly, and not through a role.

System Privilege	Description
CREATE TRIGGER	Allows the grantee to create a trigger in his/her own schema.
CREATE ANY TRIGGER	Allows the grantee to create triggers in any schema except SYS. It is not recommended to create triggers on data dictionary tables.
ALTER ANY TRIGGER	Allows the grantee to enable, disable, or compile database triggers in any schema except SYS. Note that if the grantee does not have CREATE ANY TRIGGER, he/she cannot change trigger code.
DROP ANY TRIGGER	Allows the grantee to drop database triggers in any schema except SYS.
ADMINISTER DATABASE TRIGGER	Allows the grantee to create or alter a system trigger on the database (as opposed to the current schema). The grantee must also have either CREATE TRIGGER or CREATE ANY TRIGGER.

TABLE 6-6. *System Privileges Related to Triggers*

Triggers and the Data Dictionary

Similar to stored subprograms, certain data dictionary views contain information about triggers and their status. These views are updated whenever a trigger is created or dropped.

Data Dictionary Views

When a trigger is created, its source code is stored in the data dictionary view **user_triggers**. This view includes the trigger body, WHEN clause, triggering table, and the trigger type. For example, the following query returns information about **UpdateMajorStats**:

```
SQL> SELECT trigger_type, table_name, triggering_event
  2    FROM user_triggers
  3    WHERE trigger_name = 'UPDATEMAJORSTATS';
TRIGGER_TYPE      TABLE_NAME      TRIGGERING_EVENT
----------------  --------------  -------------------------
AFTER STATEMENT   STUDENTS        INSERT OR UPDATE OR DELETE
```

For more information on data dictionary views, see Appendix C on the CD-ROM that accompanies this book.

Dropping and Disabling Triggers

Similar to procedures and packages, triggers can be dropped. The command to do this has the syntax

    DROP TRIGGER *triggername*;

where *triggername* is the name of the trigger to be dropped. This permanently removes the trigger from the data dictionary. Similar to subprograms, the OR REPLACE clause can be specified in the trigger CREATE statement. In this case, the trigger is dropped first, if it already exists.

Unlike procedures and packages, however, a trigger can be disabled without dropping it. When a trigger is disabled, it still exists in the data dictionary but is never fired. To disable a trigger, use the ALTER TRIGGER statement,

    ALTER TRIGGER *triggername* {DISABLE | ENABLE};

where *triggername* is the name of the trigger. All triggers are enabled by default when they are created. ALTER TRIGGER can disable, and then reenable, any trigger. For example, the following code disables and then reenables **UpdateMajorStats**:

```
SQL> ALTER TRIGGER UpdateMajorStats DISABLE;
Trigger altered.

SQL> ALTER TRIGGER UpdateMajorStats ENABLE;
Trigger altered.
```

All triggers for a particular table can be enabled or disabled using the ALTER TABLE command as well, by adding the ENABLE ALL TRIGGERS or the DISABLE ALL TRIGGERS clause. For example:

```
SQL> ALTER TABLE students
  2    ENABLE ALL TRIGGERS;
Table altered.

SQL> ALTER TABLE students
  2    DISABLE ALL TRIGGERS;
Table altered.
```

The **status** column of **user_triggers** contains either 'ENABLED' or 'DISABLED,' indicating the current status of a trigger. Disabling a trigger does not remove it from the data dictionary, like dropping it would do.

Trigger P-Code

When a package or subprogram is stored in the data dictionary, the compiled p-code is stored in addition to the source code for the object. This is also true for triggers. This means that triggers can be called without recompilation, and that dependency information is stored. Thus, they can be automatically invalidated in the same manner as packages and subprograms. When a trigger is invalidated, it will be recompiled the next time it is fired.

Prior to Oracle7 Release 7.3, however, this was not the case for triggers. The only item stored in the data dictionary in those versions is the source code for the trigger, not the p-code. As a result, the trigger would be compiled each time it is read from the dictionary. This doesn't have any effect on the way triggers are defined and used, but it can have an effect on trigger performance.

Mutating Tables

There are restrictions on the tables and columns that a trigger body may access. In order to define these restrictions, it is necessary to understand mutating and constraining tables. A *mutating table* is a table that is currently being modified by a DML statement. For a trigger, this is the table on which the trigger is defined. Tables that may need to be updated as a result of DELETE CASCADE referential integrity constraints are also mutating. (For more information on referential integrity constraints, see the *Oracle Server Reference*.) A *constraining table* is a table that might need to be read from for a referential integrity constraint. To illustrate these definitions, consider the **registered_students** table, which is created with this:

```
-- Available online as part of relTables.sql
CREATE TABLE registered_students (
  student_id NUMBER(5) NOT NULL,
  department CHAR(3)   NOT NULL,
  course     NUMBER(3) NOT NULL,
  grade      CHAR(1),
  CONSTRAINT rs_grade
    CHECK (grade IN ('A', 'B', 'C', 'D', 'E')),
  CONSTRAINT rs_student_id
    FOREIGN KEY (student_id) REFERENCES students (id),
  CONSTRAINT rs_department_course
    FOREIGN KEY (department, course)
    REFERENCES classes (department, course)
);
```

Registered_students has two declarative referential integrity constraints. As such, both **students** and **classes** are constraining tables for **registered_students**. Because of the constraints, **classes** and **students** also need to be modified and/or queried by the DML statement. Also, **registered_students** itself is mutating during execution of a DML statement against it.

SQL statements in a trigger body may not

- Read from or modify any mutating table of the triggering statement. This includes the triggering table itself.

- Read from or modify the primary, unique, or foreign key columns of a constraining table of the triggering table. They may, however, modify the other columns if desired.

These restrictions apply to all row-level triggers. They apply for statement triggers only when the statement trigger would be fired as a result of a DELETE CASCADE operation.

NOTE

If an INSERT statement affects only one row, then the before and after row triggers for that row do not treat the triggering table as mutating. This is the only case where a row-level trigger may read from or modify the triggering table. Statements such as

```
INSERT INTO table SELECT ...
```

always treat the triggering table as mutating, even if the subquery returns only one row.

As an example, consider the **CascadeRSInserts** trigger, shown next. Even though it modifies both **students** and **classes**, it is legal because the columns in **students** and **classes** that are modified are not key columns. In the next section, we will examine an illegal trigger.

```
-- Available online as CascadeRSInserts.sql
CREATE OR REPLACE TRIGGER CascadeRSInserts
  /* Keep the registered_students, students, and classes
     tables in synch when an INSERT is done to registered_students. */
  BEFORE INSERT ON registered_students
  FOR EACH ROW
DECLARE
  v_Credits classes.num_credits%TYPE;
BEGIN
  -- Determine the number of credits for this class.
  SELECT num_credits
    INTO v_Credits
    FROM classes
    WHERE department = :new.department
    AND course = :new.course;

  -- Modify the current credits for this student.
  UPDATE students
    SET current_credits = current_credits + v_Credits
    WHERE ID = :new.student_id;

  -- Add one to the number of students in the class.
  UPDATE classes
    SET current_students = current_students + 1
    WHERE department = :new.department
    AND course = :new.course;
END CascadeRSInserts;
```

Mutating Table Example

Suppose we want to limit the number of students in each major to five. We could accomplish this with a before insert or update row-level trigger on **students**, given here:

-- Available online as part of **LimitMajors.sql**

```
CREATE OR REPLACE TRIGGER LimitMajors
  /* Limits the number of students in each major to 5.
     If this limit is exceeded, an error is raised through
     raise_application_error. */
  BEFORE INSERT OR UPDATE OF major ON students
  FOR EACH ROW
DECLARE
  v_MaxStudents CONSTANT NUMBER := 5;
  v_CurrentStudents NUMBER;
BEGIN
  -- Determine the current number of students in this
  -- major.
  SELECT COUNT(*)
    INTO v_CurrentStudents
    FROM students
    WHERE major = :new.major;

  -- If there isn't room, raise an error.
  IF v_CurrentStudents + 1 > v_MaxStudents THEN
    RAISE_APPLICATION_ERROR(-20000,
      'Too many students in major ' || :new.major);
  END IF;
END LimitMajors;
```

At first glance, this trigger seems to accomplish the desired result. However, if we update **students** and fire the trigger, we get

-- Available onilne as part of **LimitMajors.sql**

```
SQL> UPDATE students
  2    SET major = 'History'
  3    WHERE ID = 10003;
UPDATE students
       *
ERROR at line 1:
ORA-04091: table EXAMPLE.STUDENTS is mutating, trigger/function
           may not see it
ORA-06512: at line 7
ORA-04088: error during execution of trigger 'EXAMPLE.LIMITMAJORS'
```

The ORA-4091 error results because **LimitMajors** queries its own triggering table, which is mutating. ORA-4091 is raised when the trigger is fired, not when it is created.

Workaround for the Mutating Table Error

Students is mutating only for a row-level trigger. This means that we cannot query it in a row-level trigger, but we can in a statement-level trigger. However, we cannot simply make **LimitMajors** into a statement trigger, since we need to use the value of **:new.major** in the trigger body. The solution for this is to create two triggers—a row and a statement level. In the row-level trigger, we record the value of **:new.major**, but we don't query **students**. The query is done in the statement-level trigger and uses the value recorded in the row trigger.

How do we record this value? One way is to use a PL/SQL table inside a package. This way, we can save multiple values per update. Also, each session gets its own instantiation of packaged variables, so we don't have to worry about simultaneous updates by different sessions. This solution is implemented with the **student_data** package and the **RLimitMajors** and **SLimitMajors** triggers:

```
-- Available online as part of mutating.sql
CREATE OR REPLACE PACKAGE StudentData AS
  TYPE t_Majors IS TABLE OF students.major%TYPE
    INDEX BY BINARY_INTEGER;
  TYPE t_IDs IS TABLE OF students.ID%TYPE
    INDEX BY BINARY_INTEGER;

  v_StudentMajors t_Majors;
  v_StudentIDs    t_IDs;
  v_NumEntries    BINARY_INTEGER := 0;
END StudentData;

CREATE OR REPLACE TRIGGER RLimitMajors
  BEFORE INSERT OR UPDATE OF major ON students
  FOR EACH ROW
BEGIN
  /* Record the new data in StudentData. We don't make any
     changes to students, to avoid the ORA-4091 error. */
  StudentData.v_NumEntries := StudentData.v_NumEntries + 1;
  StudentData.v_StudentMajors(StudentData.v_NumEntries) :=
    :new.major;
  StudentData.v_StudentIDs(StudentData.v_NumEntries) := :new.id;
END RLimitMajors;

CREATE OR REPLACE TRIGGER SLimitMajors
```

```
    AFTER INSERT OR UPDATE OF major ON students
DECLARE
  v_MaxStudents      CONSTANT NUMBER := 5;
  v_CurrentStudents NUMBER;
  v_StudentID        students.ID%TYPE;
  v_Major            students.major%TYPE;
BEGIN
  /* Loop through each student inserted or updated, and verify
     that we are still within the limit. */
  FOR v_LoopIndex IN 1..StudentData.v_NumEntries LOOP
    v_StudentID := StudentData.v_StudentIDs(v_LoopIndex);
    v_Major := StudentData.v_StudentMajors(v_LoopIndex);

    -- Determine the current number of students in this major.
    SELECT COUNT(*)
      INTO v_CurrentStudents
      FROM students
      WHERE major = v_Major;

    -- If there isn't room, raise an error.
    IF v_CurrentStudents > v_MaxStudents THEN
      RAISE_APPLICATION_ERROR(-20000,
        'Too many students for major ' || v_Major ||
        ' because of student ' || v_StudentID);
    END IF;
  END LOOP;

  -- Reset the counter so the next execution will use new data.
  StudentData.v_NumEntries := 0;
END LimitMajors;
```

NOTE
*Be sure to drop the incorrect **LimitMajors** trigger*
before running the preceding script.

We can now test this series of triggers by updating **students** until we have too
many history majors:

```
-- Available online as part of mutating.sql
SQL> UPDATE students
  2    SET major = 'History'
  3    WHERE ID = 10003;
1 row updated.
```

```
SQL> UPDATE students
  2    SET major = 'History'
  3    WHERE ID = 10002;
1 row updated.

SQL> UPDATE students
  2    SET major = 'History'
  3    WHERE ID = 10009;
UPDATE students
  *
ERROR at line 1:
ORA-20000: Too many students for major History because of student 10009
ORA-06512: at "EXAMPLE.SLIMITMAJORS", line 19
ORA-04088: error during execution of trigger 'EXAMPLE.SLIMITMAJORS'
```

This is the desired behavior. This technique can be applied to occurrences of ORA-4091 when a row-level trigger reads from or modifies a mutating table. Instead of doing the illegal processing in the row-level trigger, we defer the processing to an after statement-level trigger, in which it is legal. The packaged PL/SQL tables are used to store the rows that were changed.

There are several things to note about this technique:

- The PL/SQL tables are contained in a package so that they will be visible to both the row- and the statement-level trigger. The only way to ensure that variables are global is to put them in a package.

- A counter variable, **StudentData.v_NumEntries**, is used. This is initialized to zero when the package is created. It is incremented by the row-level trigger. The statement-level trigger references it and then resets it to zero after processing. This is necessary so that the next UPDATE statement issued by this session will have the correct value.

- The check in **SLimitMajors** for the maximum number of students had to be changed slightly. Since this is now an after statement trigger, **v_CurrentStudents** will hold the number of students in the major after the insert or update, not before. Thus, the check for **v_CurrentStudents + 1**, which we did in **LimitMajors**, is replaced by **v_CurrentStudents**.

- A database table could have been used instead of PL/SQL tables. I don't recommend this technique, since simultaneous sessions issuing an UPDATE would interfere with each other (in Oracle8*i* you could use a temporary table, however). Packaged PL/SQL tables are unique among sessions, which avoids the problem.

Summary

As we have seen, triggers are a valuable addition to PL/SQL and Oracle. They can be used to enforce data constraints that are much more complex than normal referential integrity constraints. Oracle8*i* extends triggers to events beyond DML operations on a table or view, as well. Triggers complete our discussion of named PL/SQL blocks in the past three chapters. The next type of named PL/SQL block that we will see is an object type body, described in Chapter 13. In the next chapter, we move on to some of the built-in packages in PL/SQL.

CHAPTER 7

Database Jobs and File I/O

he next built-in packages provided with PL/SQL that we will examine are DBMS_JOB and UTL_FILE. The DBMS_JOB package, available with PL/SQL 2.2 and higher, allows stored procedures to be run periodically by the system, without user intervention. The UTL_FILE package, available with PL/SQL 2.3 and higher, adds the ability to read from and write to operating system files. These packages extend PL/SQL and provide functions that are available with other third-generation languages.

Database Jobs

| PL/SQL **2.2** and higher |

With PL/SQL 2.2 and higher, you can schedule PL/SQL routines to run at specified times. This is done with the DBMS_JOB package, which implements *job queues*. A job is run by submitting it to a job queue, along with parameters specifying how often the job should be run. Information about currently executing jobs, and the success or failure of previously submitted jobs, is available in the data dictionary (see "Viewing Jobs in the Data Dictionary" later in this chapter for more details). For more information about database jobs, see the *Server Administrator's Guide*, release 7.2 or later.

| Oracle **8** and higher |

Note that Oracle Advanced Queuing, available with Oracle8 and higher, enhances the queuing capabilities of PL/SQL well beyond what DBMS_JOB provides. For more information, see the Oracle documentation.

Background Processes

An Oracle instance is made up of various processes running on the system. Different processes are in charge of running different aspects of the database, such as reading database blocks into memory, writing blocks back to disk, and archiving data to offline storage. In addition to the processes that manage the database, there are processes known as the SNP processes. These background processes handle the automatic refreshing of snapshots, and they manage the job queues accessed through DBMS_JOB.

SNP processes run in the background, like other database processes. Unlike other database processes, however, if an SNP process fails, Oracle restarts it without affecting the rest of the database. If other database processes fail, they generally bring down the database. Periodically, an SNP process will wake up and check for a job. If a job is due to be run, the SNP process will execute it and then go back to sleep. A given process can be running only one job at a time. In Oracle7, there can be a maximum of ten SNP processes (numbered SNP0 through SNP9), so a maximum of ten database jobs can be running simultaneously. In Oracle8, this limit has been increased to 36 SNP processes, SNP0 through SNP9 and SNPA through SNPZ.

Two parameters in the database initialization (init.ora) file control the behavior of the SNP processes. They are JOB_QUEUE_PROCESSES and JOB_QUEUE_INTERVAL, and are described in Table 7-1. Note that if JOB_QUEUE_PROCESSES is set to zero, no jobs will be executed. Since each process will sleep for JOB_QUEUE_INTERVAL seconds before checking for new jobs, JOB_QUEUE_INTERVAL specifies the minimum amount of time between job executions. Neither of these parameters is dynamically modifiable with ALTER SYSTEM or ALTER SESSION, so you must alter the initialization file and *bounce* (shut down and start up) the database to change their values.

NOTE
The initialization parameter JOB_QUEUE_KEEP_CONNECTIONS, available in Oracle 7.2, has become obsolete with Oracle 7.3 and higher. The physical connections are managed automatically starting in release 7.3.

Running a Job

There are two ways of running a job—submitting it to a job queue, or forcing it to run immediately. When a job is submitted to a job queue, an SNP process will run it when it is scheduled. If specified, this job can then be run automatically thereafter. If a job is run immediately, it is run only once.

Parameter	Default Value	Range of Values	Description
JOB_QUEUE_PROCESSES	0	0..10 (0..36 in Oracle8)	How many processes to start.
JOB_QUEUE_INTERVAL	60	1..3600	Interval between wake-ups of the process. The process will sleep for the specified number of seconds before checking for a new job.

TABLE 7-1. *Job Initialization Parameters*

SUBMIT

A job is submitted to the job queue with the SUBMIT procedure. SUBMIT is defined as

PROCEDURE SUBMIT(*job* OUT BINARY_INTEGER,
                  what IN VARCHAR2,
                  next_date IN DATE DEFAULT SYSDATE,
                  interval IN VARCHAR2 DEFAULT NULL,
                  no_parse IN BOOLEAN DEFAULT FALSE);

The parameters for SUBMIT are described in the following table:

Parameter	Type	Description
job	BINARY_INTEGER	Job number. When the job is created, a number is assigned to it. As long as the job exists, its job number will remain the same. Job numbers are unique across an instance.
what	VARCHAR2	PL/SQL code that makes up the job. Typically, this is a call to a stored procedure.
next_date	DATE	Date when the job will next run.
interval	VARCHAR2	Function that calculates the time at which the job will run again. The function must evaluate to either a future point in time or NULL.
no_parse	BOOLEAN	If TRUE, the job code will not be parsed until the first time it is executed. If FALSE (the default), the job code is parsed when it is submitted. Setting this to TRUE can be useful if the database objects referenced by the job do not yet exist, but you still want to submit it. (They must exist by the time the job is run.)

Note that Oracle8*i* allows jobs to be run in specific instances in an Oracle Parallel Server (OPS) environment. To accomplish this, DBMS_JOB.SUBMIT has two additional parameters—*instance* and *force*. These are discussed in "Instance Affinity," later in this chapter.

For example, suppose we create a procedure **TempInsert** with

 `-- Available online as part of TempInsert.sql`

```
CREATE SEQUENCE temp_seq
  START WITH 1
  INCREMENT BY 1;

CREATE OR REPLACE PROCEDURE TempInsert AS
BEGIN
  INSERT INTO temp_table (num_col, char_col)
    VALUES (temp_seq.nextval,
            TO_CHAR(SYSDATE, 'DD-MON-YYYY HH24:MI:SS'));  COMMIT;
END TempInsert;
```

We can have **TempInsert** run every 90 seconds with the following SQL*Plus script:

`-- Available online as part of TempInsert.sql`

```
SQL> VARIABLE v_JobNum NUMBER
SQL> BEGIN
  2    DBMS_JOB.SUBMIT(:v_JobNum, 'TempInsert;', SYSDATE,
  3                      'sysdate + (90/(24*60*60))');
  4    COMMIT;
  5  END;
  6  /
PL/SQL procedure successfully completed.

SQL> print v_JobNum
  V_JOBNUM
---------
        2
```

NOTE
It is important to commit the transaction in which you call DBMS_JOB.SUBMIT. The job will not be run until you do. This is because SUBMIT records the job information by inserting a row in a data dictionary table, and the SNP process queries this table to see if there are any jobs to be run. Since the INSERT and the SELECT are done by different sessions, the COMMIT is required.

If the initialization parameter JOB_QUEUE_PROCESSES is set to 0, you can still issue the SUBMIT command with no errors. However, the job will not run. Consequently, in order to see the results put into **temp_table** by **TempInsert**, you must have JOB_QUEUE_PROCESSES set to at least 1. If JOB_QUEUE_INTERVAL is set to the default (60 seconds), then the job may not run after 90 seconds. Then, 90 seconds after the previous time it has run, it will be marked as ready to run. However, it will not actually be run until a SNP process wakes up, which could take another 60 seconds. So, it could take as long as 150 seconds before the job will run again. For example, the following is sample output from **temp_table** after the job has run three times:

```
SQL> SELECT * FROM temp_table;
   NUM_COL CHAR_COL
--------- ------------------------
         1 25-APR-1999 18:18:59
         2 25-APR-1999 18:21:02
         3 25-APR-1999 18:23:05
```

In this case, 123 seconds elapsed between the first and second execution, and between the second and third executions.

NOTE
*The SUBMIT call above will cause **TempInsert** to run until the database is shut down, or until the job is removed with the REMOVE call, described in "Removing a Job," later in this chapter.*

JOB NUMBERS   The job number is assigned to the job when it is first submitted. Job numbers are generated from the sequence SYS.JOBSEQ. Once a job number is assigned to a job, it will never change unless the job is removed and then resubmitted.

CAUTION
Jobs can be exported and imported, like other database objects. This does not change the job number. If you try to import a job whose number already exists, you will receive an error, and the job cannot be imported. In this case, simply resubmit the job, which will generate a new job number. You can also use the USER_EXPORT procedure, described in "Exporting Jobs," later in this chapter.

JOB DEFINITIONS   The *what* parameter specifies the code for the job. Jobs generally consist of stored procedures, and *what* should be a string that calls the procedure. We will see the exact format of the string later in this section. This procedure can have any number of parameters. All parameters should be IN parameters, since there aren't any actual parameters that could receive the value of an OUT or IN OUT formal parameter. The only exceptions to this rule are the special identifiers *next_date* and *broken*, described next.

CAUTION
Once the job is submitted, it will be run by one of the SNP processes in the background. In order to see the results, be sure to code a COMMIT at the end of the job procedure. If the job code does not issue a COMMIT, then the transaction is automatically rolled back when the session running it ends.

There are three special identifiers that are valid in a job definition, as listed in Table 7-2. *job* is an IN parameter, so the job can only read this value. *next_date* and *broken* are IN OUT parameters, so the job itself can modify them.

Identifier	Type	Description
job	BINARY_INTEGER	Evaluates to the number of the current job.
next_date	DATE	Evaluates to the date when the job will next run. If a job sets this to NULL, the job will be removed from the queue.
broken	BOOLEAN	Evaluates to the job status—TRUE if the job is broken, FALSE otherwise. If a job sets this to TRUE, then it will be marked as broken in the job queue, but will not be removed.

TABLE 7-2.   *Job Control Identifiers*

Suppose we modify **TempInsert** as follows:

```
-- Available online as part of TempInsert1.sql
CREATE OR REPLACE PROCEDURE TempInsert
  (p_NextDate IN OUT DATE) AS
  v_SeqNum    NUMBER;
  v_StartNum  NUMBER;
  v_SQLErr    VARCHAR2(60);
BEGIN
  SELECT temp_seq.NEXTVAL
    INTO v_SeqNum
    FROM dual;

  -- See if this is the first time we're called.
  BEGIN
    SELECT num_col
      INTO v_StartNum
      FROM temp_table
      WHERE char_col = 'TempInsert Start';

    -- We've been called before, so insert a new value.
    INSERT INTO temp_table (num_col, char_col)
      VALUES (v_SeqNum,
              TO_CHAR(SYSDATE, 'DD-MON-YYYY HH24:MI:SS'));

  EXCEPTION
    WHEN NO_DATA_FOUND THEN
      -- First time we're called.  First clear out the table.
      DELETE FROM temp_table;

      -- And now insert.
      INSERT INTO temp_table (num_col, char_col)
        VALUES (v_SeqNum, 'TempInsert Start');
  END;

  -- If we've been called more than 5 times, exit.
  IF v_SeqNum - V_StartNum > 5 THEN
    p_NextDate := NULL;
    INSERT INTO temp_table (num_col, char_col)
      VALUES (v_SeqNum, 'TempInsert End');

  END IF;

  COMMIT;
EXCEPTION
  WHEN OTHERS THEN
    -- Record the error in temp_table.
```

```
    v_SQLErr := SUBSTR(SQLERRM, 1, 60);
    INSERT INTO temp_table (num_col, char_col)
      VALUES (temp_seq.NEXTVAL, v_SQLErr);

    -- Exit the job.
    p_NextDate := NULL;

    COMMIT;
END TempInsert;
```

and submit it with

 `-- Available online as part of TempInsert1.sql`
```
BEGIN
  DBMS_JOB.SUBMIT(:v_JobNum, 'TempInsert(next_date);', SYSDATE,
                  'SYSDATE + (60/(24*60*60))');
  COMMIT;
END;
```

then the job will run every 60 seconds, and automatically remove itself from the job queue (by setting **p_NextDate** to NULL) when it has been called more than five times. Sample output from **temp_table** is shown below.

> **NOTE**
> *Be sure to remove any previous jobs calling*
> **TempInsert** *before running this example, using*
> *DBMS_JOB.REMOVE.*

```
SQL> SELECT * FROM temp_table ORDER BY num_col;
NUM_COL CHAR_COL
-------- ------------------------------------
      1 TempInsert Start
      2 25-APR-1999 18:45:37
      3 25-APR-1999 18:46:38
      4 25-APR-1999 18:47:40
      5 25-APR-1999 18:48:41
      6 25-APR-1999 18:49:43
      7 25-APR-1999 18:50:44
      7 TempInsert End
```

By returning the value of *next_date* (and/or *broken*) a job can remove itself from the queue when desired.

The *what* parameter is a VARCHAR2 character string. As a result, any character literals that should be used in the call to the job procedure should be delimited by two single quotes. The procedure call should also be terminated with a semicolon. For example, if we create a procedure with a declaration as follows:

```
CREATE OR REPLACE PROCEDURE Test(p_InParameter IN VARCHAR2);
```

we could submit it with the following *what* string:

```
'Test(''This is a character string'');'
```

EXECUTION INTERVALS   The *next_date* parameter specifies the first time the job will be run after the SUBMIT call, and the parameter is evaluated the first time the job is run. Just before the job itself is executed, the function given by *interval* is evaluated. If the job is successful, the result returned by *interval* becomes the new *next_date* (assuming the job itself hasn't specified it). If the job is successful and *interval* evaluates to NULL, the job is deleted from the queue. The expression given by *interval* is passed as a character string, but should evaluate to a date. Some common expressions and their effects are described here:

Interval Value	Result
'SYSDATE + 7'	Exactly seven days from the last execution. If the job is initially submitted on Tuesday, then the next run will be the following Tuesday. If the second run fails, and it then runs successfully on Wednesday, subsequent runs will be on Wednesdays.
'NEXT_DAY(TRUNC(SYSDATE), ''FRIDAY'') + 12/24'	Every Friday at noon. Note the use of the two single quotes around the literal 'FRIDAY' within the string.
SYSDATE + 1/24	Every hour.

RUN

The DBMS_JOB.RUN procedure will run a job immediately. It is defined with

```
RUN(job IN BINARY_INTEGER);
```

The job must already have been created by calling SUBMIT. Regardless of the current status of the job, it is run immediately by the current process. Note that the job is *not* run by an SNP background process.

CAUTION

DBMS_JOB.RUN will reinitialize the current session's packages. This is done so that the job will have a consistent environment in which to run, like it would have had if it been run by a SNP process.

Other DBMS_JOB Subprograms

We will discuss the remainder of the routines in DBMS_JOB in this section. Table 7-3 describes the subprograms available. There is one additional routine contained in the package header for DBMS_JOB - ISUBMIT. This routine is used internally by various procedures to enter a job with a specific job number.

Subprogram	Description
SUBMIT	Submits a new job into the queue, to be run by an SNP process.
ISUBMIT	Used internally to enter a job with a specific job number. You should not use this routine directly in your code—use SUBMIT instead.
RUN	Forces a specified job to run by the current process.
REMOVE	Removes a job from the queue.
BROKEN	Marks a job as broken or not broken.
CHANGE	Changes any of the configurable fields for a job.
WHAT	Changes the *what* field
NEXT_DATE	Changes the *next_date* field
INTERVAL	Changes the *interval* field.
INSTANCE	In 8*i* and higher, changes the *instance* field.
USER_EXPORT	Returns the text of the call needed to re-create a job
CHECK_PRIVS	Ensures that a given job number is accessible

TABLE 7-3. *DBMS_JOB Subprograms*

Removing a Job

As we have seen earlier in this chapter, a job can remove itself from the job queue by setting *next_date* to NULL. You can also remove a job from the queue explicitly with the REMOVE procedure:

    REMOVE(*job* IN BINARY_INTEGER);

where the only parameter is the job number. If the *next_date* for a job evaluates to NULL (either because the job has set it or *interval* evaluates to NULL), then the job will be removed after it has finished executing. If the job is currently running when REMOVE is called, it will be removed from the queue after it has finished.

Broken Jobs

Oracle will automatically attempt to run a job again if it fails. The job will be run again starting one minute after the first failure. If that attempt also fails, the next attempt is two minutes later. The interval doubles each time, to four minutes, then to eight, and so on. If the retry interval exceeds the execution interval specified for the job, the execution interval is used. Once the job fails 16 times, it is marked as broken. Broken jobs will not be run again automatically.

    You can run a broken job with RUN, however. If that call succeeds, then the failure count is reset to zero and the job is marked as not broken. The BROKEN procedure can also be used to change the status of a job. It is defined with

    BROKEN(*job* IN BINARY_INTEGER,
            broken IN BOOLEAN,
            next_date IN DATE DEFAULT SYSDATE);

The parameters are described here:

Parameter	Type	Description
job	BINARY_INTEGER	Job number of the job whose status will be changed.
broken	BOOLEAN	New status of the job. If TRUE, the job is marked as broken. If FALSE, the job is marked as not broken and will be run next at the time specified by *next_date*.
next_date	DATE	Date at which the job will be run next. Defaults to SYSDATE.

Altering a Job

The parameters for a job can be altered after the job has been submitted. This is done using one of the following procedures:

```
PROCEDURE CHANGE(job IN BINARY_INTEGER,
                    what IN VARCHAR2 DEFAULT NULL,
                    next_date IN DATE DEFAULT NULL,
                    interval  IN VARCHAR2 DEFAULT NULL);


PROCEDURE WHAT(job IN BINARY_INTEGER,
                    what IN VARCHAR2);


PROCEDURE NEXT_DATE(job IN BINARY_INTEGER,
                    next_date IN DATE);


PROCEDURE INTERVAL(job IN BINARY_INTEGER,
                    interval  IN VARCHAR2);
```

The CHANGE procedure is used to alter more than one job characteristic at once, and the WHAT, NEXT_DATE, and INTERVAL procedures are used to change the characteristic identified by their respective arguments.

All the arguments behave the same as they do in the SUBMIT procedure. If you change *what* using CHANGE or WHAT, then the current environment becomes the new execution environment for the job. For more information on job environments, see "Job Execution Environments," later in this chapter.

Instance Affinity

| Oracle**8i** |
| and higher |

When running with OPS (Oracle Parallel Server), you can specify which instance should run a given job. This is known as *instance affinity*. The instance can be specified with the INSTANCE procedure, defined with

```
PROCEDURE INSTANCE(job IN BINARY_INTEGER,
                    instance IN BINARY_INTEGER,
                    force IN BOOLEAN DEFAULT FALSE);
```

where *instance* is the number of the instance that is to run the job. If *instance* is DBMS_JOB.ANY_INSTANCE (zero), job affinity is altered and any available instance can execute the job, regardless of the value of *force*. If *instance* is positive and the *force* parameter is FALSE, job affinity is altered only if the specified instance is running. If the instance is not running, or *instance* is not valid, Oracle8i returns the error "ORA-23428: job associated instance number string is not valid."

Instance affinity is supported in other DBMS_JOB subprograms, as well. For example, the SUBMIT procedure also has the *instance* and *force* parameters:

```
PROCEDURE SUBMIT(job OUT BINARY_INTEGER,
                what IN VARCHAR2,
                next_date IN DATE DEFAULT SYSDATE,
                interval IN VARCHAR2 DEFAULT NULL,
                no_parse IN BOOLEAN DEFAULT FALSE,
                instance IN BINARY_INTEGER DEFAULT ANY_INSTANCE,
                force IN BOOLEAN DEFAULT FALSE);
```

Both *instance* and *force* behave the same as they do for DBMS_JOB.INSTANCE. The CHANGE procedure is likewise enhanced for 8*i*:

```
PROCEDURE CHANGE(job IN  BINARY_INTEGER,
                 what IN  VARCHAR2 DEFAULT NULL,
                 next_date IN  DATE DEFAULT NULL,
                 interval  IN  VARCHAR2 DEFAULT NULL,
                 instance IN BINARY_INTEGER DEFAULT NULL,
                 force IN BOOLEAN DEFAULT FALSE);
```

Again, *instance* and *force* behave the same.
Finally, DBMS_JOB.RUN has the *force* parameter:

```
PROCEDURE RUN(job IN BINARY_INTEGER,
             force IN BOOLEAN DEFAULT FALSE);
```

If *force* is TRUE, then the job can be run only if DBMS_JOB.RUN is called from within the specified instance.

Exporting Jobs
The USER_EXPORT procedure will return the text necessary to re-create the given job:

```
PROCEDURE USER_EXPORT(job in BINARY_INTEGER,
                      mycall IN OUT VARCHAR2);
```

For example, if we call USER_EXPORT on the job submitted by the second version of **TempInsert** (earlier in this chapter), it will return the following:

```
-- Available online as jobExport.sql
SQL> DECLARE
  2     v_JobText VARCHAR2(2000);
  3  BEGIN
  4    DBMS_JOB.USER_EXPORT(:v_JobNum, v_JobText);
  5    DBMS_OUTPUT.PUT_LINE(v_JobText);
```

```
  6  END;
  7  /
dbms_job.isubmit(job=>10,what=>'TempInsert(next_date);',next
_date=>to_date('1999-03-29:00:07:37','YYYY-MM-DD:HH24:MI:SS'
),interval=>'sysdate + (5/(24*60*60))',no_parse=>TRUE);
```

The job must be currently in the queue, otherwise USER_EXPORT will return the error "ORA-23421: job number *job_num* is not a job in the job queue."

TIP
USER_EXPORT returns a call to DBMS_JOB.ISUBMIT, not DBMS_JOB.SUBMIT. If you want to re-create the job with the same job number, you can use ISUBMIT. However, this is usually unnecessary, and I recommend using SUBMIT instead. This will resubmit the job and generate a new job number. USER_EXPORT is called automatically by the export utility to generate the code necessary to reimport the job later.

Checking Job Privileges

The CHECK_PRIVS procedure does two things: it verifies that a given job number exists, and locks the row in the data dictionary so that you can safely modify it. It is defined with

    PROCEDURE CHECK_PRIVS(*job* IN BINARY_INTEGER);

where *job* is the job number. If the job number does not exist, or it was not submitted by the current user, then Oracle will raise the error "ORA-23421: job number *job_num* is not a job in the job queue."

Viewing Jobs in the Data Dictionary

Several data dictionary views record information about jobs. **dba_jobs** and **user_jobs** return information about a job, such as *what, next_date*, and *interval*. Information about the execution environment is also included. The **dba_jobs_running** view describes the jobs that are currently running. These views are described in Appendix C, found on the CD-ROM that accompanies this book.

Job Execution Environments

When you submit a job to a queue, the current environment is recorded. This includes the settings of NLS parameters such as NLS_DATE_FORMAT. The settings recorded at job creation will be used whenever the job is run. These settings will be changed if the *what* characteristic is changed using CHANGE or WHAT.

NOTE
A job can change its environment by issuing the ALTER SESSION command via the DBMS_SQL package (or native dynamic SQL in Oracle8i). If this is done, it will only affect the current execution of the job, not future executions. The DBMS_SQL package and native dynamic SQL are described in Chapter 8.

A job will run under the default privilege set of its submitter, with no roles enabled. If you need to enable a role from within the job, you can use dynamic SQL to issue the SET ROLE command. Of course, if the job consists of a stored procedure, all roles will be disabled regardless.

A job can only be run by the submitter. There are no permissions per se associated with jobs; EXECUTE permission on the package itself is the only database permission necessary.

File I/O

 As we have seen, PL/SQL does not have input and output capability built into the language itself, but does have this functionality through supplied packages. I/O to the screen has been implemented with the DBMS_OUTPUT package, described in Chapter 3. PL/SQL 2.3 extends I/O to text files, with the UTL_FILE package. There is no way to output directly to a binary file with this version of UTL_FILE.

 Oracle8 allows binary files to be read by using BFILEs, which are a special form of external LOB. BFILEs are discussed, along with the other LOB types, in Chapters 15 and 16 on the CD-ROM included with this book. However, even with Oracle8*i*, UTL_FILE cannot be used to manipulate binary files.

This section describes how UTL_FILE works. Three complete examples at the end of the section demonstrate the usage of the package.

Security

Client-side PL/SQL has a package similar to UTL_FILE, known as TEXT_IO. There are different security issues on the client than on the server, however. Files created with the client-side TEXT_IO package can be placed anywhere on the client, subject to operating system privileges. There are no privileges associated with PL/SQL or the database itself for client-side file I/O. We will discuss the security implications of UTL_FILE in this section.

Database Security

On the server, a more rigorous security mechanism is needed. This is implemented by restricting the directories that UTL_FILE can access to certain *accessible directories*. The accessible directories are specified by the UTL_FILE_DIR parameter in the database initialization file. Each accessible directory is indicated by a line such as

UTL_FILE_DIR = *directory_name*

in the initialization file. The specification of *directory_name* will vary, depending on the operating system. If the operating system is case sensitive, then *directory_name* is case sensitive. For example, the following entries are legal for a Unix system, assuming that the directories specified actually exist:

UTL_FILE_DIR = /tmp
UTL_FILE_DIR = /home/oracle/output_files

In order to access a file with UTL_FILE, the directory name and the filename are passed as separate parameters to the FOPEN function. The directory name is compared against the accessible files list. If it is found, then the operation is allowed, subject to the operating system security constraints described in the next section. If the directory name specified by FOPEN is not accessible, an error is returned. Subdirectories of accessible directories are not allowed, unless the subdirectory is also listed explicitly as accessible. Given the preceding accessible directories, Table 7-4 describes legal and illegal directory/filename pairs.

NOTE
Even if the operating system is not case sensitive, the comparison between the specified directory and the accessible directories is always case sensitive.

If the initialization file contains

```
UTL_FILE_DIR = *
```

then database permissions are disabled. This makes all directories accessible to UTL_FILE.

Directory Name	Filename	Comment
/tmp	myfile.out	Legal
/home/oracle/output_files	students.list	Legal
/tmp/1995	january.results	Illegal—subdirectory /tmp/1995 is not accessible
/home/oracle	output_files/classes.list	Illegal—subdirectory passed as part of the filename
/TMP	myfile.out	Illegal—case different

TABLE 7-4. *Legal and Illegal File Specifications*

> **CAUTION**
> *Turning off database permissions should be done very carefully. Oracle does not recommend that you use this option in production systems, since it can circumvent operating system permissions. In addition, do not use "." (the current directory on Unix systems) as part of the accessible directories list. Always use explicit directory paths.*

Operating System Security

The file I/O operations that are performed by UTL_FILE will be done as the Oracle user. (The Oracle user is the owner of the files that are used to run the database, and also the owner of the processes that make up a database instance.) Consequently, the Oracle user has to have operating system privileges to read from and write to all of the accessible directories. If the Oracle user does not have privileges for an accessible directory, then any operations in that directory will be prohibited by the operating system.

Any files created by UTL_FILE will be owned by the Oracle user and created with the default operating system privileges for the Oracle user. If it is necessary for other users to access these files outside of UTL_FILE, then the system administrator should change the permissions on the files.

CAUTION
It is also good security practice to prohibit write operations on directories in the accessible directory list. The only user who should be given write permission on accessible directories should be the Oracle user.

Exceptions Raised by UTL_FILE

If a procedure or function in UTL_FILE encounters an error, it will raise an exception. The possible exceptions are listed in Table 7-5. Note that these exceptions include eight that are defined in UTL_FILE, and two predefined exceptions (NO_DATA_FOUND and VALUE_ERROR). The UTL_FILE exceptions can be caught by name or by an OTHERS exception handler. The predefined exceptions can be identified by their SQLCODE values (namely 1403 or 6502) as well.

Opening and Closing Files

All of the operations in UTL_FILE use a file handle. The *file handle* is a value that you use in PL/SQL to identify the file, similar to the cursor ID in DBMS_SQL. All file handles have the type UTL_FILE.FILE_TYPE. File handles are returned by FOPEN, and passed as IN parameters to the other subprograms in UTL_FILE.

FOPEN

FOPEN opens a file for input or output. A given file can be opened for input only or output only at any time. A file cannot be used for both input and output simultaneously. FOPEN is defined with

```
FUNCTION FOPEN(location IN VARCHAR2,
               filename IN VARCHAR2,
               open_mode IN VARCHAR2)
    RETURN FILE_TYPE;
```

Exception	Raised When	Raised By
INVALID_PATH	Directory or filename is invalid or not accessible.	FOPEN
INVALID_MODE	Invalid string specified for file mode.	FOPEN
INVALID_FILEHANDLE	File handle does not specify an open file.	FCLOSE, GET_LINE, PUT, PUT_LINE, NEW_LINE, PUTF, FFLUSH
INVALID_OPERATION	File could not be opened as requested, perhaps because of operating system permissions. Also raised when attempting a write operation on a file opened for read, or a read operation on a file opened for write.	GET_LINE, PUT, PUT_LINE, NEW_LINE, PUTF, FFLUSH
INVALID_MAXLINESIZE	Specified maximum line size is too large or too small. Available in 8.0.5 and higher only.	FOPEN
READ_ERROR	Operating system error occurred during a read operation.	GET_LINE
WRITE_ERROR	Operating system error occurred during a write operation.	PUT, PUT_LINE, PUTF, NEW_LINE, FFLUSH, FCLOSE, FCLOSE_ALL
INTERNAL_ERROR	Unspecified internal error.	All functions
NO_DATA_FOUND	End of file reached during a read.	GET_LINE
VALUE_ERROR	Input line too large for buffer specified in GET_LINE.	GET_LINE

TABLE 7-5. *Exceptions Raised by UTL_FILE*

The directory path specified must already exist—FOPEN will not create it. It will, however, overwrite an existing file if the mode is 'w'. The parameters and return value for FOPEN are described here:

Parameter	Type	Description
location	VARCHAR2	Directory path where the file is located. If this directory is not in the accessible directories list, UTL_FILE.INVALID_PATH is raised.
filename	VARCHAR2	Name of the file to be opened. If the mode is 'w', any existing file is overwritten.
open_mode	VARCHAR2	Mode to be used. Valid values are: 'r' Read text 'w' Write text 'a' Append text This parameter is not case-sensitive. If 'a' is specified and the file does not exist, it is created with 'w' mode.
return value	UTL_FILE.FILE_TYPE	File handle to be used in subsequent functions.

FOPEN can raise any of the following exceptions:

- UTL_FILE.INVALID_PATH

- UTL_FILE.INVALID_MODE

- UTL_FILE.INVALID_OPERATION

- UTL_FILE.INTERNAL_ERROR

FOPEN with max_linesize

With Oracle8 version 8.0.5 and higher, UTL_FILE includes an additional overloaded version of FOPEN:

```
FUNCTION FOPEN(location IN VARCHAR2,
              filename IN VARCHAR2,
              open_mode IN VARCHAR2,
              max_linesize IN BINARY_INTEGER)
   RETURN FILE_TYPE;
```

The *location, filename,* and *open_mode* parameters behave as the first version of FOPEN. *max_linesize* is used to specify the maximum line size for the file. It can range from 1 to 32,767. If it is not specified, then the maximum line size is 1,024. If *max_linesize* is less than 1 or greater than 32,767, the UTL_FILE.INVALID_MAXLINESIZE exception is raised.

FCLOSE

When you are finished reading from or writing to a file, it should be closed with FCLOSE. This frees the resources used by UTL_FILE to operate on the file. FLCOSE is defined with

        PROCEDURE FCLOSE(*file_handle* IN OUT FILE_TYPE);

where the only parameter is the file handle. Any pending changes that have yet to be written to the file are done before the file is closed. If there is an error while writing, UTL_FILE.WRITE_ERROR is raised. If the file handle does not point to a valid open file, UTL_FILE.INVALID_FILEHANDLE is raised.

IS_OPEN

This boolean function returns TRUE if the specified file is open, FALSE if not. IS_OPEN is defined as

        FUNCTION IS_OPEN(*file_handle* IN FILE_TYPE)
            RETURN BOOLEAN;

There could still be operating system errors if the file is used, even if IS_OPEN returns TRUE.

FCLOSE_ALL

FCLOSE_ALL will close all open files. It is meant to be used for clean-up, especially in an error handler. The procedure is defined as

        PROCEDURE FCLOSE_ALL;

and does not take any parameters. Any pending changes will be flushed before the files are closed. Because of this, FCLOSE_ALL can raise UTL_FILE.WRITE_ERROR if an error occurs during the write operation.

CAUTION
*FCLOSE_ALL will close the files and free the
resources used by UTL_FILE. However, it does not
mark the files as closed—IS_OPEN will still return
TRUE after an FCLOSE_ALL. Any read or write
operations on files after FCLOSE_ALL will fail
unless the file is reopened with FOPEN.*

File Output

Five procedures are used to output data to a file: PUT, PUT_LINE, NEW_LINE,
PUTF, and FFLUSH. PUT, PUT_LINE, and NEW_LINE behave very much like
their counterparts in the DBMS_OUTPUT package, discussed in Chapter 3. The
maximum size for an output record is 1,023 bytes (unless a different value is
specified with FOPEN). This includes a byte for the newline character.

PUT

PUT will output the specified string to the specified file. The file should have been
opened for write operations. PUT is defined with

```
PROCEDURE PUT(file_handle IN FILE_TYPE,
              buffer IN VARCHAR2);
```

PUT will not append a newline character in the file. You must use PUT_LINE or
NEW_LINE to include the line terminator in the file. If there is an operating system
error during the write operation, UTL_FILE.WRITE_ERROR is raised. The parameters
for PUT are described here:

Parameter	Type	Description
file_handle	UTL_FILE.FILE_TYPE	File handle returned by FOPEN. If this is not a valid handle, UTL_FILE.INVALID_FILEHANDLE is raised.
buffer	VARCHAR2	Text string to be output to the file. If the file was not opened in 'w' or 'a' mode, UTL_FILE.INVALID_OPERATION is raised.

NEW_LINE

NEW_LINE writes one or more line terminators to the specified file. It is defined with

PROCEDURE NEW_LINE(*file_handle* IN FILE_TYPE,
                   lines IN NATURAL := 1);

The line terminator is system dependent—different operating systems will use different terminators. If there is an operating system error during the write, UTL_FILE.WRITE_ERROR is raised. The parameters for NEW_LINE are described here:

Parameter	Type	Description
file_handle	UTL_FILE.FILE_TYPE	File handle returned by FOPEN. If this is not valid, UTL_FILE.INVALID_FILEHANDLE is raised.
lines	NATURAL	Number of line terminators to output. The default value is 1, which outputs a single newline. If the file was not opened in 'w' or 'a' mode, UTL_FILE.INVALID_OPERATION is raised.

PUT_LINE

PUT_LINE outputs the specified string to the specified file, which must have been opened for write operations. After the string is output, the platform-specific newline character is output. PUT_LINE is defined with

PROCEDURE PUT_LINE(*file_handle* IN FILE_TYPE,
                   buffer IN VARCHAR2);

The parameters for PUT_LINE are described in the following table. Calling PUT_LINE is equivalent to calling PUT followed by NEW_LINE to output the newline. If there is an operating system error during the write, UTL_FILE.WRITE_ERROR is raised.

Parameter	Type	Description
file_handle	UTL_FILE.FILE_TYPE	File handle returned by FOPEN. If this is not a valid handle, UTL_FILE.INVALID_FILEHANDLE is raised.

Parameter	Type	Description
buffer	VARCHAR2	Text string to be output to the file. If the file was not opened in 'w' or 'a' mode, UTL_FILE.INVALID_ OPERATION is raised.

PUTF
PUTF is similar to PUT, but it allows the output string to be formatted. PUTF is a limited version of the C function *printf()* and has syntax similar to *printf()*. PUTF is defined with

```
PROCEDURE PUTF(file_handle IN FILE_TYPE,
               format IN VARCHAR2,
               arg1 IN VARCHAR2 DEFAULT NULL,
               arg2 IN VARCHAR2 DEFAULT NULL,
               arg3 IN VARCHAR2 DEFAULT NULL,
               arg4 IN VARCHAR2 DEFAULT NULL,
               arg5 IN VARCHAR2 DEFAULT NULL);
```

Note that *arg1* through *arg5* have default parameters, which means that they are optional. The *format* string contains regular text, along with two special characters %s and \n. Each occurrence of %s in the format string is replaced with one of the optional arguments. Each occurrence of \n is replaced by a newline character. The parameters are described in the table after the example. As with PUT and PUT_LINE, if there is an operating system error during the write, UTL_FILE.WRITE_ERROR is raised.

For example, if we were to execute the block

```
DECLARE
    v_OutputFile UTL_FILE.FILE_TYPE;
    v_Name VARCHAR2(10) := 'Scott';
BEGIN
    v_OutputFile := UTL_FILE.FOPEN(...);
    UTL_FILE.PUTF(v_OutputFile,
      'Hi there!\nMy name is %s, and I am a %s major.\n',
      v_Name, 'Computer Science');
    FCLOSE(v_OutputFile);
END;
```

the output file would contain the lines

```
Hi There!
My name is Scott, and I am a Computer Science major.
```

Parameter	Type	Description
file_handle	UTL_FILE.FILE_TYPE	File handle returned by FOPEN. If this is not a valid handle, UTL_FILE.INVALID_FILEHANDLE is raised.
format	VARCHAR2	Format string containing regular text and possibly the special formatting characters '%s' or '\n'. If the file was not opened in 'w' or 'a' mode, UTL_FILE.INVALID_OPERATION is raised.
arg1 ... arg5	VARCHAR2	One to five optional arguments. Each argument will be substituted for the corresponding '%s' format character. If there are more '%s' characters than arguments, the empty string (NULL) is substituted for the format character.

FFLUSH

The data output with PUT, PUT_LINE, PUTF, or NEW_LINE is normally buffered. When the buffer is full, it is then physically output to the file. FFLUSH forces the buffer to be immediately written to the specified file. Note that only lines in the buffer that end with a NEW_LINE are output—any final PUTs will remain in the buffer. It is defined with

    PROCEDURE FFLUSH(*file_handle* IN FILE_TYPE);

FFLUSH can raise any of the following exceptions:

- UTL_FILE.INVALID_FILEHANDLE
- UTL_FILE.INVALID_OPERATION
- UTL_FILE.WRITE_ERROR

File Input

GET_LINE is used to read from a file, rather than to write to it. One line of text is read from the specified file and returned in the *buffer* parameter. The newline character is not included in the return string. GET_LINE is defined with

    PROCEDURE GET_LINE(*file_handle* IN FILE_TYPE,
                       buffer OUT VARCHAR2);

When the last line is read from the file, NO_DATA_FOUND is raised. If the line does not fit into the buffer supplied as an actual parameter, VALUE_ERROR is raised. Reading an empty line will return an empty string (NULL). If an operating system error occurs during the read, UTL_FILE.READ_ERROR is raised. The maximum size of the input line is 1,022 bytes (unless a different size has been specified with the *max_linesize* parameter of FOPEN). The parameters are described here:

Parameter	Type	Description
file_handle	UTL_FILE.FILE_TYPE	File handle returned by FOPEN. If this is not a valid handle, UTL_FILE.INVALID_FILEHANDLE is raised.
buffer	VARCHAR2	Buffer into which the line will be written. If the file was not opened for reading ('r'), then UTL_FILE.INVALID_OPERATION is raised.

Examples

This section describes three examples using UTL_FILE. The first is another implementation of the **Debug** package, which we have already seen in Chapter 3. The second example reads student information from a file and loads the table. The third example prints transcripts.

Debug Package

Our first usage of UTL_FILE is to implement a debugging package. Since DBMS_OUTPUT doesn't print the results until the block is finished (as we discussed in Chapter 3), UTL_FILE can provide a more immediate output. The package follows.

```
-- Available online as Debug.sql
CREATE OR REPLACE PACKAGE Debug AS
  /* Global variables to hold the name of the debugging file and
     directory. */
  v_DebugDir VARCHAR2(50) := '/tmp';
  v_DebugFile VARCHAR2(20) := 'debug.out';

  /* Call Debug to output a line consisting of:
     p_Description: p_Value
     to the debugging file. */
  PROCEDURE Debug(p_Description IN VARCHAR2,
                  p_Value IN VARCHAR2);

  /* Closes the debugging file first, then calls FileOpen to
```

```
      set the packaged variables and open the file with the new
      parameters. */
   PROCEDURE Reset(p_NewFile IN VARCHAR2 := v_DebugFile,
                  p_NewDir IN VARCHAR2 := v_DebugDir);

   /* Sets the packaged variables to p_NewFile and p_NewDir, and
      opens the debugging file. */
   PROCEDURE FileOpen(p_NewFile IN VARCHAR2 := v_DebugFile,
                      p_NewDir IN VARCHAR2 := v_DebugDir);

/* Closes the debugging file. */
   PROCEDURE FileClose;
END Debug;

CREATE OR REPLACE PACKAGE BODY Debug AS
   v_DebugHandle UTL_FILE.FILE_TYPE;

   PROCEDURE Debug(p_Description IN VARCHAR2,
                   p_Value IN VARCHAR2) IS
BEGIN
   IF NOT UTL_FILE.IS_OPEN(v_DebugHandle) THEN
       FileOpen;
   END IF;
    /* Output the info, and flush the file. */
    UTL_FILE.PUTF(v_DebugHandle, '%s: %s\n',
                  p_Description, p_Value);
    UTL_FILE.FFLUSH(v_DebugHandle);
   EXCEPTION
     WHEN UTL_FILE.INVALID_OPERATION THEN
       RAISE_APPLICATION_ERROR(-20102,
                               'Debug: Invalid Operation');
     WHEN UTL_FILE.INVALID_FILEHANDLE THEN
       RAISE_APPLICATION_ERROR(-20103,
                               'Debug: Invalid File Handle');
     WHEN UTL_FILE.WRITE_ERROR THEN
       RAISE_APPLICATION_ERROR(-20104,
                               'Debug: Write Error');
     WHEN UTL_FILE.INTERNAL_ERROR THEN
       RAISE_APPLICATION_ERROR(-20104,
                               'Debug: Internal Error');
   END Debug;

   PROCEDURE Reset(p_NewFile IN VARCHAR2 := v_DebugFile,
                   p_NewDir IN VARCHAR2 := v_DebugDir) IS
BEGIN

    /* Make sure the file is closed first. */
```

```
      IF UTL_FILE.IS_OPEN(v_DebugHandle) THEN
        FileClose;
      END IF;

    FileOpen(p_NewFile,p_NewDir);

  END Reset;

  PROCEDURE FileOpen(p_NewFile IN VARCHAR2 := v_DebugFile,
                     p_NewDir  IN VARCHAR2 := v_DebugDir) IS
  BEGIN
      /* Open the file for writing. */
    v_DebugHandle := UTL_FILE.FOPEN(p_NewDir, p_NewFile, 'w');

    /* Set the packaged variables to the values just passed in. */
    v_DebugFile := p_NewFile;
    v_DebugDir := p_NewDir;
  EXCEPTION
    WHEN UTL_FILE.INVALID_PATH THEN
      RAISE_APPLICATION_ERROR(-20100, 'Open: Invalid Path');
    WHEN UTL_FILE.INVALID_MODE THEN
      RAISE_APPLICATION_ERROR(-20101, 'Open: Invalid Mode');
    WHEN UTL_FILE.INVALID_OPERATION THEN
      RAISE_APPLICATION_ERROR(-20101, 'Open: Invalid Operation');
    WHEN UTL_FILE.INTERNAL_ERROR THEN
      RAISE_APPLICATION_ERROR(-20101, 'Open: Internal Error');
  END FileOpen;

  PROCEDURE FileClose IS
  BEGIN
    UTL_FILE.FCLOSE(v_DebugHandle);
  EXCEPTION
    WHEN UTL_FILE.INVALID_FILEHANDLE THEN
      RAISE_APPLICATION_ERROR(-20300,
                              'Close: Invalid File Handle');
    WHEN UTL_FILE.WRITE_ERROR THEN
      RAISE_APPLICATION_ERROR(-20301,
                              'Close: Write Error');
    WHEN UTL_FILE.INTERNAL_ERROR THEN
      RAISE_APPLICATION_ERROR(-20302,
                              'Close: Internal Error');
  END FileClose;
END Debug;
```

Using **Debug** is straightforward. The packaged variables **v_DebugDir** and **v_DebugFile** specify the location and name of the output file. If you call **Debug.Debug** first, then the file will be opened with these values. In order to change the values, you can call **Debug.FileOpen**, which will reset the packaged variables and open the file, or **Debug.Reset**, which will close the file first. **Debug.FileClose** will close the file when you have finished. For example, if we execute the following block,

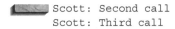

```
-- Available online as CallDebug.sql
BEGIN
  Debug.Debug('Scott', 'First call');
  Debug.Reset('debug2.out', '/tmp');
  Debug.Debug('Scott', 'Second call');
  Debug.Debug('Scott', 'Third call');
  Debug.FileClose;
END;
```

then **/tmp/debug.out** will contain the line

```
Scott: First call
```

and **/tmp/debug2.out** will contain

```
Scott: Second call
Scott: Third call
```

TIP
Note the exception handlers for the various routines. They identify which errors were actually raised, and by which procedures. This is a good technique to follow when using UTL_FILE.

Student Loader

The **LoadStudents** procedure will insert into **students** based on the contents of the file that is passed to it. The file is comma-delimited, which means that each record is contained on one line, with commas used to separate the fields. This is a common format for text files. **LoadStudents** is created with

```
-- Available online as LoadStudents.sql
CREATE OR REPLACE PROCEDURE LoadStudents (
  /* Loads the students table by reading a comma-delimited file.
     The file should have lines that look like

     first_name,last_name,major

     The student ID is generated from student_sequence.
     The total number of rows inserted is returned by
```

```
    p_TotalInserted. */
  p_FileDir  IN VARCHAR2,
  p_FileName IN VARCHAR2,
  p_TotalInserted IN OUT NUMBER) AS

  v_FileHandle UTL_FILE.FILE_TYPE;
  v_NewLine  VARCHAR2(100);  -- Input line
  v_FirstName students.first_name%TYPE;
  v_LastName students.last_name%TYPE;
  v_Major students.major%TYPE;
  /* Positions of commas within input line. */
  v_FirstComma NUMBER;
  v_SecondComma NUMBER;

BEGIN
  -- Open the specified file for reading.
  v_FileHandle := UTL_FILE.FOPEN(p_FileDir, p_FileName, 'r');

  -- Initialize the output number of students.
  p_TotalInserted := 0;

  -- Loop over the file, reading in each line.  GET_LINE will
  -- raise NO_DATA_FOUND when it is done, so we use that as the
  -- exit condition for the loop.
  LOOP
    BEGIN
      UTL_FILE.GET_LINE(v_FileHandle, v_NewLine);
    EXCEPTION
      WHEN NO_DATA_FOUND THEN
        EXIT;
    END;

    -- Each field in the input record is delimited by commas.  We
    -- need to find the locations of the two commas in the line
    -- and use these locations to get the fields from v_NewLine.
    -- Use INSTR to find the locations of the commas.
    v_FirstComma := INSTR(v_NewLine, ',', 1, 1);
    v_SecondComma := INSTR(v_NewLine, ',', 1, 2);

    -- Now we can use SUBSTR to extract the fields.
    v_FirstName := SUBSTR(v_NewLine, 1, v_FirstComma - 1);
    v_LastName := SUBSTR(v_NewLine, v_FirstComma + 1,
                    v_SecondComma - v_FirstComma - 1);
    v_Major := SUBSTR(v_NewLine, v_SecondComma + 1);

    -- Insert the new record into students.
    INSERT INTO students (ID, first_name, last_name, major)
      VALUES (student_sequence.nextval, v_FirstName,
```

```
                    v_LastName, v_Major);

    p_TotalInserted := p_TotalInserted + 1;
  END LOOP;

  -- Close the file.
  UTL_FILE.FCLOSE(v_FileHandle);

  COMMIT;
EXCEPTION
  -- Handle the UTL_FILE exceptions meaningfully, and make sure
  -- that the file is properly closed.
  WHEN UTL_FILE.INVALID_OPERATION THEN
    UTL_FILE.FCLOSE(v_FileHandle);
    RAISE_APPLICATION_ERROR(-20051,
                            'LoadStudents: Invalid Operation');
  WHEN UTL_FILE.INVALID_FILEHANDLE THEN
    UTL_FILE.FCLOSE(v_FileHandle);
    RAISE_APPLICATION_ERROR(-20052,
                            'LoadStudents: Invalid File Handle');
  WHEN UTL_FILE.READ_ERROR THEN
    UTL_FILE.FCLOSE(v_FileHandle);
    RAISE_APPLICATION_ERROR(-20053,
                            'LoadStudents: Read Error');
  WHEN UTL_FILE.INVALID_PATH THEN
    UTL_FILE.FCLOSE(v_FileHandle);
    RAISE_APPLICATION_ERROR(-20054,
                            'LoadStudents: Invalid Path');
  WHEN UTL_FILE.INVALID_MODE THEN
    UTL_FILE.FCLOSE(v_FileHandle);
    RAISE_APPLICATION_ERROR(-20055,
                            'LoadStudents: Invalid Mode');
  WHEN UTL_FILE.INTERNAL_ERROR THEN
    UTL_FILE.FCLOSE(v_FileHandle);
    RAISE_APPLICATION_ERROR(-20056,
                            'LoadStudents: Internal Error');
  WHEN VALUE_ERROR THEN
    UTL_FILE.FCLOSE(v_FileHandle);
    RAISE_APPLICATION_ERROR(-20057,
                            'LoadStudents: Value Error');
  WHEN OTHERS THEN
    UTL_FILE.FCLOSE(v_FileHandle);
    RAISE;
END LoadStudents;
```

A sample input file for **LoadStudents** could look like:

```
-- Available online as students.txt
Scott,Smith,Computer Science
Margaret,Mason,History
Joanne,Junebug,Computer Science
Manish,Murgratroid,Economics
Patrick,Poll,History
Timothy,Taller,History
Barbara,Blues,Economics
David,Dinsmore,Music
Ester,Elegant,Nutrition
Rose,Riznit,Music
Rita,Razmataz,Nutrition
Shay,Shariatpanahy,Computer Science
```

NOTE

LoadStudents uses the *student_sequence* sequence to determine the student ID. If this sequence has been re-created after the *students* table has been loaded, it could return a value which is already in *students*. In this case, the primary key constraint for *students* would be violated.

Printing Transcripts

This example illustrates how to use UTL_FILE to print student transcripts. We first need the **CalculateGPA** procedure:

```
-- Available online as CalculateGPA.sql
CREATE OR REPLACE PROCEDURE CalculateGPA (
  /* Returns the grade point average for the student identified
     by p_StudentID in p_GPA. */
  p_StudentID IN students.ID%TYPE,
  p_GPA OUT NUMBER) AS

  CURSOR c_ClassDetails IS
    SELECT classes.num_credits, rs.grade
      FROM classes, registered_students rs
      WHERE classes.department = rs.department
      AND classes.course = rs.course
      AND rs.student_id = p_StudentID;
```

```
    v_NumericGrade NUMBER;
    v_TotalCredits NUMBER := 0;
    v_TotalGrade NUMBER := 0;

BEGIN
    FOR v_ClassRecord in c_ClassDetails LOOP
        -- Determine the numeric value for the grade.
        SELECT DECODE(v_ClassRecord.grade, 'A', 4,
                                            'B', 3,
                                            'C', 2,
                                            'D', 1,
                                            'E', 0)
          INTO v_NumericGrade
          FROM dual;

        v_TotalCredits := v_TotalCredits + v_ClassRecord.num_credits;
        v_TotalGrade := v_TotalGrade +
                        (v_ClassRecord.num_credits * v_NumericGrade);
    END LOOP;

    p_GPA := v_TotalGrade / v_TotalCredits;
END CalculateGPA;
```

PrintTranscript itself is created with

```
-- Available online as PrintTranscript.sql
CREATE OR REPLACE PROCEDURE PrintTranscript (
    /* Outputs a transcript to the indicated file for the indicated
       student. The transcript will consist of the classes for which
       the student is currently registered and the grade received
       for each class. At the end of the transcript, the student's
       GPA is output. */
    p_StudentID IN students.ID%TYPE,
    p_FileDir IN VARCHAR2,
    p_FileName IN VARCHAR2) AS

    v_StudentGPA NUMBER;
    v_StudentRecord  students%ROWTYPE;
    v_FileHandle UTL_FILE.FILE_TYPE;
    v_NumCredits NUMBER;

    CURSOR c_CurrentClasses IS
        SELECT *
          FROM registered_students
          WHERE student_id = p_StudentID;

BEGIN
```

```
-- Open the output file in append mode.
v_FileHandle := UTL_FILE.FOPEN(p_FileDir, p_FileName, 'a');

SELECT *
  INTO v_StudentRecord
  FROM students
  WHERE ID = p_StudentID;

-- Output header information.  This consists of the current
-- date and time, and information about this student.

UTL_FILE.PUTF(v_FileHandle, 'Student ID: %s\n',
  v_StudentRecord.ID);
UTL_FILE.PUTF(v_FileHandle, 'Student Name: %s %s\n',
  v_StudentRecord.first_name, v_StudentRecord.last_name);
UTL_FILE.PUTF(v_FileHandle, 'Major: %s\n',
  v_StudentRecord.major);
UTL_FILE.PUTF(v_FileHandle, 'Transcript Printed on: %s\n\n\n',
  TO_CHAR(SYSDATE, 'Mon DD,YYYY HH24:MI:SS'));

UTL_FILE.PUT_LINE(v_FileHandle, 'Class   Credits Grade');
UTL_FILE.PUT_LINE(v_FileHandle, '------- ------- -----');
FOR v_ClassesRecord in c_CurrentClasses LOOP
  -- Determine the number of credits for this class.
  SELECT num_credits
    INTO v_NumCredits
    FROM classes
    WHERE course = v_ClassesRecord.course
    AND department = v_ClassesRecord.department;

  -- Output the info for this class.
  UTL_FILE.PUTF(v_FileHandle, '%s %s %s\n',
    RPAD(v_ClassesRecord.department || ' '   ||
        v_ClassesRecord.course, 7),
    LPAD(v_NumCredits, 7),
    LPAD(v_ClassesRecord.grade, 5));
END LOOP;

-- Determine the GPA.
CalculateGPA(p_StudentID, v_StudentGPA);

-- Output the GPA.
UTL_FILE.PUTF(v_FileHandle, '\n\nCurrent GPA: %s\n',
  TO_CHAR(v_StudentGPA, '9.99'));

-- Close the file.
UTL_FILE.FCLOSE(v_FileHandle);
```

```
EXCEPTION
  -- Handle the UTL_FILE exceptions meaningfully, and make sure
  -- that the file is properly closed.
  WHEN UTL_FILE.INVALID_OPERATION THEN
    UTL_FILE.FCLOSE(v_FileHandle);
    RAISE_APPLICATION_ERROR(-20061,
                            'PrintTranscript: Invalid Operation');
  WHEN UTL_FILE.INVALID_FILEHANDLE THEN
    UTL_FILE.FCLOSE(v_FileHandle);
    RAISE_APPLICATION_ERROR(-20062,
                            'PrintTranscript: Invalid File Handle');
  WHEN UTL_FILE.WRITE_ERROR THEN
    UTL_FILE.FCLOSE(v_FileHandle);
    RAISE_APPLICATION_ERROR(-20063,
                            'PrintTranscript: Write Error');
  WHEN UTL_FILE.INVALID_MODE THEN
    UTL_FILE.FCLOSE(v_FileHandle);
    RAISE_APPLICATION_ERROR(-20064,
                            'PrintTranscript: Invalid Mode');
  WHEN UTL_FILE.INTERNAL_ERROR THEN
    UTL_FILE.FCLOSE(v_FileHandle);
    RAISE_APPLICATION_ERROR(-20065,
                            'PrintTranscript: Internal Error');
END PrintTranscript;
```

Given the following contents of **registered_students** (created by **relTables.sql**):

```
SQL> select * from registered_students;
STUDENT_ID DEP     COURSE G
---------- ---     --------- -
     10000 CS         102 A
     10002 CS         102 B
     10003 CS         102 C
     10000 HIS        101 A
     10001 HIS        101 B
     10002 HIS        101 B
     10003 HIS        101 A
     10004 HIS        101 C
     10005 HIS        101 C
     10006 HIS        101 E
     10007 HIS        101 B
     10008 HIS        101 A
     10009 HIS        101 D
     10010 HIS        101 A
     10008 NUT        307 A
     10010 NUT        307 A
```

```
       10009 MUS        410 B
       10006 MUS        410 E
       10011 MUS        410 B
       10000 MUS        410 B
20 rows selected.
```

if we call **PrintTranscript** for students 10000 and 10009, we get the following two output files:

```
Student ID: 10000
Student Name: Scott Smith
Major: Computer Science
Transcript Printed on: Apr 26,1999 22:24:07


Class   Credits Grade
------- ------- -----
CS  102       4     A
HIS 101       4     A
MUS 410       3     B


Current GPA:  3.73
```

```
Student ID: 10009
Student Name: Rose Riznit
Major: Music
Transcript Printed on: Apr 26,1999 22:24:31


Class   Credits Grade
------- ------- -----
HIS 101       4     D
MUS 410       3     B


Current GPA:  1.86
```

Summary

We have examined two utility packages in this chapter: DBMS_JOB and UTL_FILE. Database jobs allow procedures to be automatically run by the database at predefined times. UTL_FILE adds file I/O capability to PL/SQL, subject to security issues on the server. Each of these utilities provides useful functionality that is not inherent in the language.

CHAPTER

8

Dynamic SQL

ne of the original design decisions for PL/SQL involved the use of early binding. The main consequence of this decision was that original releases of PL/SQL could contain DML (Data Manipulation Language) statements only—no DDL (Data Definition Language). Furthermore, the structure of all of the SQL statements within a PL/SQL block had to be known at compile time. Dynamic SQL, however, lifts this restriction. PL/SQL 2.1 (with Oracle7 Release 7.1) provided the first implementation of dynamic SQL—the DBMS_SQL package. DBMS_SQL has been enhanced for Oracle8. Oracle8i improves the situation even more by providing native dynamic SQL integrated within the language. We will discuss both of these dynamic SQL implementations in this chapter, including a comparison between them.

Using SQL in PL/SQL

The only SQL statements allowed directly in a PL/SQL application are DML and transaction control statements. The other types of statements—DDL, session, and system control—are illegal. EXPLAIN PLAN, although classified as DML, is also illegal. In order to explain why this is the case, we need to look at the way PL/SQL is designed.

In general, a programming language can bind variables in two ways—early or late. *Binding* a variable is the process of identifying the storage location associated with an identifier in the program. In PL/SQL, binding also involves checking the database for permission to access the object referenced. A language that uses *early binding* does the bind during the compile phase, while a language that uses *late binding* postpones the bind until runtime. Early binding means that the compile phase will take longer (since the work of binding has to be done), but execution will be faster, since the bind has already been completed. Late binding shortens the compile time but lengthens the execution time.

PL/SQL was intentionally designed to use early binding. This decision was made so that execution of a block would be as fast as possible, because all of the database objects have been verified by the compiler. This makes sense, since PL/SQL blocks can be stored in the database via procedures, functions, packages, triggers, and object types (Oracle8 and higher). As we have seen in Chapters 4 through 6, these objects are stored in compiled form, so that, when needed, they can be loaded from the database into memory and run. As a result of this design decision, DDL statements are prohibited directly in PL/SQL. Since a DDL statement will modify a database object, the permissions must be validated again. Validating the permissions would require that the identifiers be bound, and this has already been done during the compile.

To further illustrate this, consider the following hypothetical PL/SQL block:

```
BEGIN
  CREATE TABLE temp_table (
    num_value   NUMBER,
    char_value  CHAR(10));
  INSERT INTO temp_table (num_value, char_value)
    VALUES (10, 'Hello');
END;
```

In order to compile this, the **temp_table** identifier needs to be bound. This process will check to see whether this table exists. However, the table won't exist until the block is run. But since the block can't even compile, there is no way that it can run.

DML and transaction control statements are the only SQL statements that don't have the potential to modify schema objects or permissions on schema objects, thus they are the only legal SQL statements in PL/SQL.

NOTE
The fact that roles are disabled inside definer's rights stored subprograms and triggers is also a consequence of early binding. See Chapter 5 for more information.

Static vs. Dynamic SQL

All of the PL/SQL we have seen so far in this book has been *static*. This means that the structure of the statement is known at compile time. For example, consider the following PL/SQL block:

```
DECLARE
  v_Department classes.department%TYPE := 'ECN';
  v_NumCredits classes.num_credits%TYPE := 5;
BEGIN
  UPDATE classes
    SET num_credits = v_NumCredits
    WHERE department = v_Department;
END;
```

The UPDATE statement in this block is an example of a static SQL statement. When the block is compiled, we know that the statement is an UPDATE, that it references the **num_credits** and **department** columns in **classes**, and exactly what the WHERE clause specifies. In contrast, consider the following block.

```
DECLARE
    v_SQLString    VARCHAR2(100);
    v_SetClause    VARCHAR2(100);
    v_WhereClause  VARCHAR2(100);
BEGIN
    v_SetClause := 'SET num_credits = :num_credits WHERE ';
    v_WhereClause := 'department = :department';
    v_SQLString := 'UPDATE classes ' || v_SetClause || v_WhereClause;
    DoIt(v_SQLString);
END;
```

This block won't run as written, because the **DoIt** procedure needs to be created. **DoIt** could be written using dynamic SQL, and would thus be able to execute *dynamic* SQL statements. Dynamic statements have fewer restrictions—many of the things that need to be known at compile time don't need to be determined until runtime. The entire SQL statement can be determined at runtime, if desired.

Dynamic SQL allows you to issue DDL, session, and system control statements from PL/SQL. With dynamic SQL, the SQL statement is created dynamically at runtime, and then parsed and executed. Since the statement doesn't actually get created until runtime, the PL/SQL compiler doesn't have to bind the identifiers in the statement, which allows the block to compile. We could use dynamic SQL to execute the CREATE TABLE statement in the preceding block, for example. However, the INSERT statement would fail to compile since the table wouldn't exist until the block is run. The solution to this problem is to use dynamic SQL to execute the INSERT statement as well.

There are two different methods for executing dynamic SQL using PL/SQL. The first is DBMS_SQL, a package supplied with PL/SQL 2.1 and higher. For Oracle8, it has been enhanced with new features, including array processing. Oracle8*i* provides the second method—native dynamic SQL. With native dynamic SQL, the dynamic control statements are built directly into the language, and thus are significantly faster than DBMS_SQL. In the next two sections, we will see an overview of each of these methods. We will examine them in detail in the remainder of the chapter.

Overview of DBMS_SQL

 The algorithm for executing a statement using DBMS_SQL consists of the following steps:

1. Put the SQL statement or PL/SQL block into a string.

2. Parse the string using DBMS_SQL.PARSE.

3. Bind any input variables using DBMS_SQL.BIND_VARIABLE.

4. If the statement is DML or DDL, execute it using DBMS_SQL.EXECUTE, and then retrieve any output bind variables with DBMS_SQL.VARIABLE_VALUE, if necessary. If the statement is a query, continue with step 5.

5. If the statement is a query, define the output variables with DBMS_SQL.DEFINE_COLUMN.

6. Execute the query with DBMS_SQL.EXECUTE, and fetch the results with DBMS_SQL.FETCH_ROWS and DBMS_SQL.COLUMN_VALUE.

As an example, the **RecreateTempTable** procedure first drops, and then creates a table called **temp_table**, with the table description passed into it.

CAUTION
In order to run this example, you must have the CREATE TABLE and DROP TABLE system privileges granted directly, rather than via a role. See "Privileges and Roles with Dynamic SQL," later in this chapter, for more information.

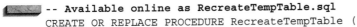

```
-- Available online as RecreateTempTable.sql
CREATE OR REPLACE PROCEDURE RecreateTempTable (
  /* Drops temp_table and re-creates it. The table description
   * is passed in with p_Description, and should be the contents
   * of the CREATE TABLE statement, after the table name. For
   * example, the following is a legal call:
   *
   *   RecreateTempTable('(num_col NUMBER, char_col VARCHAR2(2000))');
   */
  p_Description IN VARCHAR2) IS

  v_Cursor       NUMBER;
  v_CreateString VARCHAR2(100);
  v_DropString   VARCHAR2(100);
BEGIN
  /* Open the cursor for processing. */
  v_Cursor := DBMS_SQL.OPEN_CURSOR;

  /* Drop the table first. */
  v_DropString := 'DROP TABLE temp_table';

  /* Parse and execute the 'DROP TABLE' command.  Since this is a
   * DDL statement, DBMS_SQL.PARSE does both operations.  Trap the
```

```
  * ORA-942 error in case the table doesn't yet exist.
  */
BEGIN
  -- DBMS_SQL.NATIVE is a constant defined in the package header.
  DBMS_SQL.PARSE(v_Cursor, v_DropString, DBMS_SQL.NATIVE);
EXCEPTION
  WHEN OTHERS THEN
    IF SQLCODE != -942 THEN
      RAISE;
    END IF;
END;

/* Now re-create it. We need to create the CREATE TABLE string
 * first, then parse and execute it.  Again, since it is a DDL
 * statement, the DBMS_SQL.PARSE call does both operations.
 */
v_CreateString := 'CREATE TABLE temp_table ' || p_Description;
DBMS_SQL.PARSE(v_Cursor, v_CreateString, DBMS_SQL.NATIVE);

/* Close the cursor, now that we are finished. */
DBMS_SQL.CLOSE_CURSOR(v_Cursor);
EXCEPTION
  WHEN OTHERS THEN
    -- Close the cursor first, then reraise the error so it is
    -- propagated to the calling block.
    DBMS_SQL.CLOSE_CURSOR(v_Cursor);
    RAISE;
END RecreateTempTable;
```

From this example, we can observe several things:

- The string that is parsed can be a constant, such as **v_DropString**, or it can be created dynamically by the program using string functions such as concatenation (**v_CreateString** is done this way).

- Error handling is the same as static SQL—errors are raised as exceptions, and handled by exception handlers. One difference is that we can now get compile errors (such as ORA-942) at runtime. With static SQL, these would be caught during compile time, before the block starts to run.

- We have more direct control of cursor processing, including when cursors are opened and closed. It is necessary to close any cursors that we open, even if an error is raised. The call to DBMS_SQL.CLOSE_CURSOR in the exception handler guarantees this.

The flowchart in Figure 8-1 illustrates the order in which the calls to DBMS_SQL are typically made.

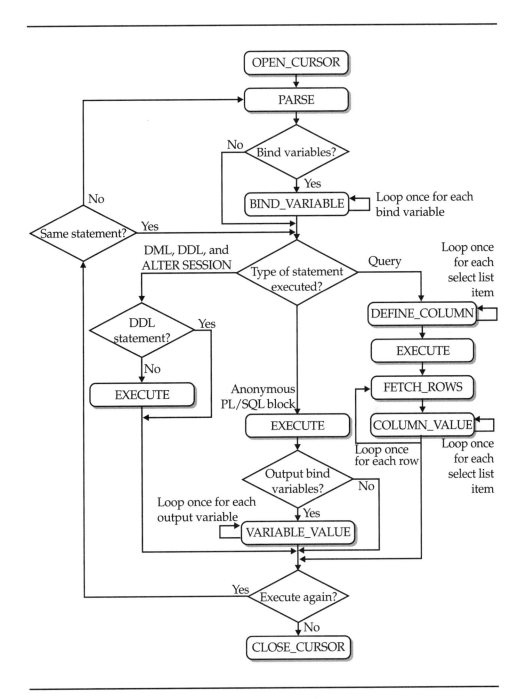

FIGURE 8-1. *The flow of execution in DBMS_SQL*

Three different kinds of statements can be processed with DBMS_SQL: DML, DDL, and ALTER SESSION statements; queries; and anonymous PL/SQL blocks. Each type is executed with different procedures. Brief descriptions of each of the procedures follow, with more detailed explanations later in this chapter, in "Using DBMS_SQL."

NOTE
Transaction control statements (COMMIT and ROLLBACK) can be executed with DBMS_SQL as well. They are executed with the same procedures as DML, DDL, or ALTER SESSION statements.

OPEN_CURSOR   Like static SQL, every SQL statement is executed within a cursor. For dynamic PL/SQL, you control the cursor processing. OPEN_CURSOR returns a cursor ID number that is used to identify the context area in which the statement will be processed. All subsequent calls will use this cursor ID.

PARSE   Parsing a statement involves sending it to the kernel, where the syntax and semantics of the statement are identified and verified. If the statement is a query, the execution plan is also determined at this point. If the statement is a DDL statement, then it is executed now as well.

BIND_VARIABLE   Binding a variable to a placeholder is similar to the binding process PL/SQL uses for static SQL. A placeholder is a special identifier in the statement string. Binding is the act of associating this placeholder with an actual variable and telling DBMS_SQL the type and length of the variable. Binding is done for input variables in SQL statements, and for both input and output variables in PL/SQL statements.

DEFINE_COLUMN   Defining a select list item is similar to binding an input variable. The variables in this case are the results of a query. DEFINE_COLUMN identifies the type and length of the PL/SQL variables that will receive the data when it is retrieved by FETCH_ROWS. DEFINE_COLUMN is used for select list items (the results of queries) only, while BIND_VARIABLE is used for input or output variables (placeholders in statements).

EXECUTE   For a non-query, EXECUTE will carry out the statement and return the number of rows processed. For a query, EXECUTE will determine the active set (which is the set of rows that match the WHERE clause in the query). The data is then fetched with FETCH_ROWS. For all statements, bind variables are examined at EXECUTE time.

FETCH_ROWS   Each call to FETCH_ROWS will return more data from the server. The data will be converted into the datatypes specified by DEFINE_COLUMN. EXECUTE_AND_FETCH combines the execute and fetch operations in one call.

VARIABLE_VALUE   This routine is used to determine the value of a bind variable if it is modified by the statement. This is only used when the statement is a PL/SQL block (perhaps calling a stored procedure).

COLUMN_VALUE   After calling FETCH_ROWS, COLUMN_VALUE is used to actually return the data. It takes variables of the same type specified in DEFINE_COLUMN. COLUMN_VALUE should only be used for queries.

CLOSE_CURSOR   When processing is complete, the cursor is closed. This frees all resources used by the cursor.

Overview of Native Dynamic SQL

Oracle **8i** and higher   Like DBMS_SQL, the SQL statement or PL/SQL block that you execute with native dynamic SQL must first be put into a string. However, the methods differ after that. Rather than separating out the cursor control statements, native dynamic SQL handles the cursor for non-query SQL and PL/SQL blocks automatically, using the EXECUTE IMMEDIATE statement. Single-row queries can be executed with EXECUTE IMMEDIATE as well. For multiple-row queries, you use the OPEN FOR statement to associate a cursor variable with a dynamically created string. For example, we can write **RecreateTempTable** using native dynamic SQL as follows:

```
-- Available online as nativeRT.sql
CREATE OR REPLACE PROCEDURE RecreateTempTable (
  /* Drops temp_table and re-creates it. The table description
     is passed in with p_Description, and should be the contents
     of the CREATE TABLE statement, after the table name. For
     example, the following is a legal call:

     RecreateTempTable('(num_col NUMBER, char_col VARCHAR2(2000))');
  */
  p_Description IN VARCHAR2) IS

  v_CreateString  VARCHAR2(100);
  v_DropString    VARCHAR2(100);
BEGIN
  /* Drop the table first. */
  v_DropString := 'DROP TABLE temp_table';
```

```
/* Execute the 'DROP TABLE' command. Trap the ORA-942 error in
   case the table doesn't yet exist. */
BEGIN
  EXECUTE IMMEDIATE v_DropString;
EXCEPTION
  WHEN OTHERS THEN
    IF SQLCODE != -942 THEN
      RAISE;
    END IF;
END;

/* Now re-create it. We need to create the CREATE TABLE
   string first, then we can execute it. */
v_CreateString := 'CREATE TABLE temp_table ' || p_Description;
EXECUTE IMMEDIATE v_CreateString;
END RecreateTempTable;
```

CAUTION
*Just as in DBMS_SQL, you must have the
CREATE TABLE and DROP TABLE system privileges
granted directly, rather than through a role. See
"Privileges and Roles with Dynamic SQL," later in
this chapter, for more details.*

We can observe the following from this example:

- The commands for native dynamic SQL are built into the language, and thus you don't need to use procedure calls.

- Similar to DBMS_SQL, error handling is handled through exceptions.

- Since the cursors are managed automatically, we don't have to explicitly open and close them, at least for non-query statements. As we will see, processing queries with native dynamic SQL is done the same way as for static SQL—with an explicit cursor.

Using DBMS_SQL

PL/SQL 2.1 and higher This section discusses in detail the steps necessary for executing various kinds of SQL statements using DBMS_SQL. We will start by examining DML, DDL, and ALTER SESSION statements. Processing for queries is described in the "Executing Queries" section, and processing for anonymous PL/SQL blocks is described in the "Executing PL/SQL" section.

NOTE
The discussion in the following three sections describes DBMS_SQL for PL/SQL versions 2.1 through 2.3. Oracle8 provides enhancements to several of the procedures discussed in these sections. These enhancements are discussed in "DBMS_SQL Enhancements for Oracle8 and Oracle8i," later in this chapter.

Executing DML, DDL, and ALTER SESSION Statements

The following steps are required for DML, DDL, and ALTER SESSION statements:

1. Open the cursor (OPEN_CURSOR).

2. Parse the statement (PARSE).

3. Bind any input variables (BIND_VARIABLE). Note that DDL and ALTER SESSION statements cannot have bind variables.

4. Execute the statement (EXECUTE).

5. Close the cursor (CLOSE_CURSOR).

NOTE
Oracle8 introduces the RETURNING clause, which allows a DML statement to also return values. This can be handled using the COLUMN_VALUE routine after the statement has been executed, similar to the processing for PL/SQL blocks. For more information, see "The RETURNING Clause" in the section "DBMS_SQL Enhancements for Oracle8 and Oracle8i," later in this chapter.

Open the Cursor

Every SQL statement or PL/SQL block (static or dynamic) is executed within a cursor. For static SQL, the PL/SQL engine handles the cursor processing for most statements. You can control the processing for queries with the OPEN and CLOSE commands.

Dynamic SQL is no different. Each call to OPEN_CURSOR returns an integer, which is the cursor ID number. This ID is used in subsequent calls. More than one

SQL statement can be executed sequentially within the same cursor, or the same statement can be executed multiple times.

Every call to OPEN_CURSOR should be matched by a call to CLOSE_CURSOR, to free the resources used by the cursor. OPEN_CURSOR is defined with

    OPEN_CURSOR RETURN INTEGER;

It takes no parameters.

Parse the Statement

When the statement is parsed, it is sent to the server. The server checks the syntax and semantics of the statement, and returns an error (via a raised exception) if the statement has a parse error. The execution plan for the statement is determined at PARSE time as well. The equivalent call in OCI7, **oparse**, optionally allows the parse to be deferred. In OCI8, there is no explicit parse call, but the parse is deferred automatically. Deferring the parse reduces network traffic by buffering the statement until execute time, when the statement is parsed. This results in only one network round-trip. However, DBMS_SQL does not support deferred parsing. This is generally not an issue, since the entire PL/SQL block can be executed on the server (perhaps in a stored procedure), thus requiring no network round-trips.

If the statement is a DDL command, then it is executed at PARSE time as well. PARSE is defined with

    PROCEDURE PARSE(c IN INTEGER,
                    statement IN VARCHAR2,
                    language_flag IN INTEGER);

The parameters for PARSE are described as follows:

Parameter	Type	Description
c	INTEGER	ID number for a cursor in which to parse the statement. The cursor must already have been opened with OPEN_CURSOR.
statement	VARCHAR2	SQL statement to be parsed. It should not include the trailing semicolon, since the semicolon is not part of DML or DDL statements. (The semicolon is necessary if the statement is an anonymous PL/SQL block.)

Parameter	Type	Description
language_flag	INTEGER	Determines how the statement is treated. SQL statements can be executed with version 6 or version 7 behavior. This parameter has three possible values: V6 = Version 6 behavior V7 = Oracle7 behavior NATIVE = Behavior for the database to which the program is connected

The *language_flag* parameter specifies version 6 or version 7 behavior with the packaged constants DBMS_SQL.V6, DBMS_SQL.V7, or DBMS_SQL.NATIVE. There is no DBMS_SQL.V8 parameter for Oracle8 or Oracle8*i*—Oracle8 and Oracle8*i* behave the same as Oracle7 in this respect.

The main difference between V6 and V7 behavior is with the handling of CHAR variables and columns. In Oracle6, CHAR columns were variable length, while CHAR is a fixed-length type in Oracle7 and higher. Thus, if you execute a CREATE TABLE with a CHAR column, and *language_flag* is DBMS_SQL.V6, the table will actually be created with a VARCHAR2 column.

Bind Any Input Variables

Binding associates placeholders in the statement with actual PL/SQL variables. A placeholder is identified by a colon in front of the identifier. For example, the statement

```
INSERT INTO temp_table (num_col, char_col)
  VALUES (:number_value, :char_value);
```

has two placeholders—**:number_value** and **:char_value**. The names of the placeholders are not significant. If the same placeholder name is used more than once in the statement, the same value will be bound for all occurrences. If there are no placeholders in the statement, then no binds are necessary.

The BIND_VARIABLE procedure is used for the bind. It identifies placeholders by name. For example, we could bind the placeholders in the preceding INSERT statement with

```
DBMS_SQL.BIND_VARIABLE(v_CursorID, ':number_value', -7);
DBMS_SQL.BIND_VARIABLE(v_CursorID, ':char_value', 'Hello');
```

NOTE
*The colon in the bind variable name is optional.
However, for the sake of consistency, all of the
examples in this chapter do include the colon.
This is consistent with placeholders used in other
dynamic methods, such as OCI or the precompilers.*

The length and datatype of the actual variable are also determined by
BIND_VARIABLE, through a set of overloaded calls. The following call is used
to bind NUMBERs:

    PROCEDURE BIND_VARIABLE(*c* IN INTEGER,
                            name IN VARCHAR2,
                            value IN **NUMBER**);

These are used for binding VARCHAR2s:

    PROCEDURE BIND_VARIABLE(*c* IN INTEGER,
                            name IN VARCHAR2,
                            value IN **VARCHAR2**);

    PROCEDURE BIND_VARIABLE(*c* IN INTEGER,
                            name IN VARCHAR2,
                            value IN **VARCHAR2**,
                            out_value_size IN INTEGER);

This call is used for binding DATEs:

    PROCEDURE BIND_VARIABLE(*c* IN INTEGER,
                            name IN VARCHAR2,
                            value IN **DATE**);

The following are used for binding CHARs. Their names are different because
PL/SQL does not allow overloading on CHAR & VARCHAR2.

    PROCEDURE BIND_VARIABLE_CHAR(*c* IN INTEGER,
                                 name IN VARCHAR2,
                                 value IN **CHAR**);

```
PROCEDURE BIND_VARIABLE_CHAR(c IN INTEGER,
                            name IN VARCHAR2,
                            value IN CHAR,
                            out_value_size IN INTEGER);
```

Likewise, these are used for binding RAWs:

```
PROCEDURE BIND_VARIABLE_RAW(c IN INTEGER,
                           name IN VARCHAR2,
                           value IN RAW);
```

```
PROCEDURE BIND_VARIABLE_RAW(c IN INTEGER,
                           name IN VARCHAR2,
                           value IN RAW,
                           out_value_size IN INTEGER);
```

This call is used for binding MLSLABELs:

```
PROCEDURE BIND_VARIABLE (c IN INTEGER,
                        name IN VARCHAR2,
                        value IN MLSLABEL);
```

Finally, this call is used for binding ROWIDs:

```
PROCEDURE BIND_VARIABLE_ROWID(c IN INTEGER,
                             name IN VARCHAR2,
                             value IN ROWID);
```

NOTE
Oracle8 adds additional BIND_VARIABLE calls for the LOB types, and the BIND_VARIABLE_ROWID call has been removed for Oracle8i. For more information, see "DBMS_SQL Enhancements for Oracle8 and Oracle8i," later in this chapter.

The various parameters for these calls are described in the following table.

Parameter	Type	Description
c	INTEGER	ID for a cursor. This cursor should have been previously opened with OPEN_CURSOR and have had a statement parsed with PARSE.
name	VARCHAR	Name of the placeholder for which this variable will be bound. The colon should be included.
value	NUMBER, CHAR, VARCHAR2, DATE, ROWID, RAW, MLSLABEL	Data that will actually be bound. The type and length of this variable are retrieved as well. The data in this variable will be converted if necessary.
out_value_size	INTEGER	Optional parameter for VARCHAR2, CHAR, and RAW binds only. If specified, this is the maximum expected OUT value size, in bytes. If this parameter is not specified, the size of *value* is used. *Out_value_size* should only be specified when executing an anonymous PL/SQL block, when the bind variable could be written to. For input variables, the size of *value* won't change. For more information, see "Executing PL/SQL," later in this chapter.

Execute the Statement

The EXECUTE function is used to execute the statement. It returns the number of rows processed. The return value of EXECUTE is valid only for DML statements. For queries (and anonymous PL/SQL blocks), the value is undefined and should be ignored. For DDL statements, EXECUTE is a no-op since the statement was executed at the call to PARSE. EXECUTE is a function, so it needs to be called as part of an expression, rather than as a standalone statement. It is defined with

FUNCTION EXECUTE(*c* IN INTEGER) RETURN INTEGER;

The parameters and return value are described here:

Parameter	Type	Description
c	INTEGER	Cursor ID for the cursor containing the statement to be executed. The cursor should have already been opened, a statement parsed in it, and any placeholders bound.
return value	INTEGER	Number of rows processed by the statement. This is analogous to the %ROWCOUNT cursor attribute, and is defined only when the statement executed is an INSERT, UPDATE, or DELETE.

Close the Cursor

The cursor should be closed when processing is complete. This frees the resources allocated by the cursor and signals that it will no longer be used. After a cursor is closed, it can no longer be used unless it is reopened. The syntax for CLOSE_CURSOR is

    PROCEDURE CLOSE_CURSOR(c IN OUT INTEGER);

The value passed into CLOSE_CURSOR should be a valid cursor ID. After the call, the actual parameter is set to NULL, indicating that the cursor is closed.

Examples

In this section, we will see examples of using DBMS_SQL to execute DML and ALTER SESSION statements. We will also summarize the differences for executing DDL statements.

DML STATEMENTS   The **UpdateClasses** procedure updates the number of credits for classes in the specified department. Although this procedure could have been written using static SQL, this example illustrates the necessary steps for processing.

```
-- Available online as dynamicDML.sql
CREATE OR REPLACE PROCEDURE UpdateClasses(
  /* Uses DBMS_SQL to update the classes table, setting the number of
   * credits for all classes in the specified department to the
   * specified number of credits.
   */
  p_Department  IN classes.department%TYPE,
  p_NewCredits  IN classes.num_credits%TYPE,
```

```
    p_RowsUpdated OUT INTEGER) AS

  v_CursorID   INTEGER;
  v_UpdateStmt VARCHAR2(100);
BEGIN
  -- Open the cursor for processing.
  v_CursorID := DBMS_SQL.OPEN_CURSOR;

  -- Determine the SQL string.
  v_UpdateStmt :=
    'UPDATE classes
       SET num_credits = :nc
       WHERE department = :dept';

  -- Parse the statement.
  DBMS_SQL.PARSE(v_CursorID, v_UpdateStmt, DBMS_SQL.NATIVE);

  -- Bind p_NewCredits to the placeholder :nc.  This overloaded
  -- version of BIND_VARIABLE will bind p_NewCredits as a NUMBER,
  -- since that is how it is declared.
  DBMS_SQL.BIND_VARIABLE(v_CursorID, ':nc', p_NewCredits);

  -- Bind p_Department to the placeholder :dept.  This overloaded
  -- version of BIND_VARIABLE will bind p_Department as a CHAR, since
  -- that is how it is declared.
  DBMS_SQL.BIND_VARIABLE_CHAR(v_CursorID, ':dept', p_Department);

  -- Execute the statement.
  p_RowsUpdated := DBMS_SQL.EXECUTE(v_CursorID);

  -- Close the cursor.
  DBMS_SQL.CLOSE_CURSOR(v_CursorID);
EXCEPTION
  WHEN OTHERS THEN
    -- Close the cursor, then raise the error again.
    DBMS_SQL.CLOSE_CURSOR(v_CursorID);
    RAISE;
END UpdateClasses;
```

The following SQL*Plus excerpt shows the results of **UpdateClasses**.

```
-- Available online as callUC.sql
SQL> SELECT department, course, num_credits
  2    FROM classes
  3    WHERE department = 'CS';
```

```
DEP     COURSE NUM_CREDITS
---   --------- -----------
CS        101           4
CS        102           4

SQL> DECLARE
  2      v_RowsUpdated NUMBER;
  3   BEGIN
  4      UpdateClasses('CS', 5, v_RowsUpdated);
  5      DBMS_OUTPUT.PUT_LINE(v_RowsUpdated || ' rows updated.');
  6   END;
  7   /
2 rows updated.
PL/SQL procedure successfully completed.

SQL> SELECT department, course, num_credits
  2      FROM classes
  3      WHERE department = 'CS';

DEP     COURSE NUM_CREDITS
---   --------- -----------
CS        101           5
CS        102           5
```

ALTER SESSION STATEMENTS   Executing an ALTER SESSION statement through DBMS_SQL is very similar to executing a DML statement, except that bind variables are not allowed in ALTER SESSION statements, so calls to BIND_VARIABLE are not necessary. (Transaction control statements have the same restriction as well, so they are also executed with no BIND_VARIABLE calls.) For example, the following procedure can be used to execute an arbitrary ALTER SESSION statement:

```
-- Available online as part of dynamicAS.sql
CREATE OR REPLACE PROCEDURE AlterSession(
  p_SessionString IN VARCHAR2) AS

  v_CursorID INTEGER;
  v_Dummy INTEGER;
BEGIN
  v_CursorID := DBMS_SQL.OPEN_CURSOR;

  DBMS_SQL.PARSE(v_CursorID, p_SessionString, DBMS_SQL.NATIVE);
  v_Dummy := DBMS_SQL.EXECUTE(v_CursorID);
END AlterSession;
```

The following SQL*Plus session illustrates how **AlterSession** works.

```
-- Available online as part of dynamicAS.sql
SQL> SELECT SYSDATE FROM dual;
SYSDATE
-----------------------------
11-SEP-99

SQL> DECLARE
  2    v_SQLString VARCHAR2(100);
  3  BEGIN
  4    v_SQLString := 'ALTER SESSION SET NLS_DATE_FORMAT = ' ||
  5      '''Mon DD, YYYY HH24:MI:SS''';
  6    AlterSession(v_SQLString);
  7  END;
  8  /
PL/SQL procedure successfully completed.

SQL>
SQL> SELECT SYSDATE FROM dual;

SYSDATE
-----------------------------
Sep 11, 1999 19:28:40
```

DDL STATEMENTS   As we have seen in this section, the processing for a DDL statement is slightly different from the processing for a DML statement. There are two differences between DDL and DML processing:

■ Since bind variables are illegal in a DDL statement, no call to BIND_VARIABLE is necessary after the parse. This is the same as ALTER SESSION and transaction control statements.

■ DDL statements are actually executed on the PARSE call. The EXECUTE call is not necessary—if it is included, then it has no effect.

Other than these two details, processing DDL statements is the same as DML statements—open the cursor (DBMS_SQL.OPEN_CURSOR), parse the statement—which also executes it (DBMS_SQL.PARSE)—and close the cursor (DBMS_SQL.CLOSE_CURSOR). For more information on executing DDL statements with dynamic SQL, see "DDL and Dynamic SQL," later in this chapter. See the **RecreateTempTable** example earlier in this chapter for an example of executing a DDL statement.

Executing Queries

The process for executing queries with DBMS_SQL is the same as executing DML, DDL, and ALTER SESSION statements, until the call to EXECUTE. Before the execute, you need to define the types and lengths of the select list items with DEFINE_COLUMN. After the execute, you call FETCH_ROWS and COLUMN_VALUE to retrieve the results. The steps for queries are, therefore,

1. Open a cursor (OPEN_CURSOR).

2. Parse the statement (PARSE).

3. Bind any input variables (BIND_VARIABLE).

4. Define the select list items (DEFINE_COLUMN).

5. Execute the query (EXECUTE).

6. Fetch the rows (FETCH_ROWS).

7. Return the results to PL/SQL variables (COLUMN_VALUE).

8. Close the cursor (CLOSE_CURSOR).

The steps that are the same as we've seen before (OPEN_CURSOR, PARSE, BIND_VARIABLE, EXECUTE, and CLOSE_CURSOR) behave the same way as we've seen for DML and DDL statements. The remainder of this section examines in detail only those calls we have not yet seen, or those that have different ramifications.

Parse the Statement

PARSE behaves the same as the DML case, but the string for a query needs to meet certain restrictions. It is important that the statement be a single SELECT, and not a SELECT embedded in a PL/SQL block. If the query is inside a block, it is processed according to the rules for PL/SQL blocks, which are described in the upcoming section, "Executing PL/SQL." In addition, the query should not have an INTO clause. Instead of this clause, we use the DEFINE_COLUMN and COLUMN_VALUE procedures. Finally, as for DML or DDL statements, the trailing semicolon should not be included, since it is not a syntactic part of the statement. For example, all of the following queries are legal strings for use with DBMS_SQL.PARSE:

```
SELECT * FROM students
```

```
SELECT COUNT(*) "Number of Students", department || course
  FROM registered_students
  WHERE department IN (:d1, :d2)
```

```
GROUP BY department || course

SELECT FullName(ID), ID
  FROM students
  WHERE ID = :student_id
```

Define the Select List Items

The define process is very similar to the bind, except that input variables need to be bound, while only the select list items in a query need to be defined. The DEFINE_COLUMN procedure specifies the type and length for the PL/SQL variables into which the select list items will be fetched. Each select list item will be converted into the type of its associated PL/SQL variable.

Unlike BIND_VARIABLE placeholders, select list items are identified by position, not by name. The first position is number 1, the second is number 2, and so on. For example, if the query

```
SELECT first_name, last_name, current_credits
  FROM students
```

were parsed, the DEFINE_COLUMN calls could look like this:

```
DECLARE
    v_FirstName     students.first_name%TYPE,
    v_LastName      students.last_name%TYPE,
    v_CurrentCredits students.num_credits%TYPE,
    v_CursorID      INTEGER;
BEGIN
    ...
    DBMS_SQL.DEFINE_COLUMN(v_CursorID, 1, v_FirstName, 20);
    DBMS_SQL.DEFINE_COLUMN(v_CursorID, 2, v_LastName, 20);
    DBMS_SQL.DEFINE_COLUMN(v_CursorID, 3, v_CurrentCredits);
    ...
END;
```

Similar to BIND_VARIABLE, DEFINE_COLUMN is overloaded on the type of the output variable. The following call is used for defining NUMBERs:

> PROCEDURE DEFINE_COLUMN(*c* IN INTEGER,
>   *position* IN INTEGER,
>   *column* IN **NUMBER**);

This call is used for defining VARCHAR2s:

```
PROCEDURE DEFINE_COLUMN(c IN INTEGER,
                        position IN INTEGER,
                        column IN VARCHAR2,
                        column_size IN INTEGER);
```

This call is used for defining CHARs:

```
PROCEDURE DEFINE_COLUMN_CHAR(c IN INTEGER,
                             position IN INTEGER,
                             column IN CHAR,
                             column_size IN INTEGER);
```

This is used for defining RAWs:

```
PROCEDURE DEFINE_COLUMN_RAW(c IN INTEGER,
                            position IN INTEGER,
                            column IN RAW,
                            column_size IN INTEGER);
```

NOTE
*The DEFINE_COLUMN calls for VARCHAR2,
CHAR, and RAW require the* column_size
*parameter. This is needed because the PL/SQL
engine needs to know the maximum length of
these variables at runtime. Unlike NUMBER,
DATE, MLSLABEL, and ROWID, these types
do not have a fixed length known in advance
by the PL/SQL compiler.*

Here is the call for defining DATEs:

```
PROCEDURE DEFINE_COLUMN(c IN INTEGER,
                        position IN INTEGER,
                        column IN DATE);
```

The following call is used for defining MLSLABELs:

```
PROCEDURE DEFINE_COLUMN(c IN INTEGER,
                        position IN INTEGER,
                        column IN MLSLABEL);
```

And, finally, here is the call used for defining ROWIDs:

```
PROCEDURE DEFINE_COLUMN_ROWID (c IN INTEGER,
                                     position IN INTEGER,
                                     column IN ROWID);
```

NOTE
Oracle8 adds additional DEFINE_COLUMN calls for the LOB types, and the DEFINE_COLUMN_ROWID call has been removed for Oracle8i. For more information, see "DBMS_SQL Enhancements for Oracle8 and Oracle8i," later in this chapter.

The parameters for these calls are very similar to those for BIND_VARIABLE, and are listed here:

Parameter	Type	Description
c	INTEGER	Cursor ID. The cursor should already have a query parsed and any input variables bound.
position	INTEGER	Position of the item in the select list. The first select list item is at position 1.
column	NUMBER, VARCHAR2, CHAR, DATE, MLSLABEL, RAW, ROWID	Variable that defines the type and length of the output variable. The variable itself isn't necessarily important, but its type and length are. Usually, however, the same variables are used in DEFINE_COLUMN and COLUMN_VALUE.
column_size	INTEGER	Maximum expected size of the output data. This is required for types whose lengths are not known in advance by the PL/SQL engine.

Fetch the Rows
The rows in the active set of the query are fetched into a buffer by FETCH_ROWS. COLUMN_VALUE is then called to retrieve the actual data from this buffer into PL/SQL variables. FETCH ROWS is defined with

FUNCTION FETCH_ROWS(*c* IN INTEGER) RETURN INTEGER;

The only parameter is the cursor ID. FETCH_ROWS returns the number of rows returned. Typically, FETCH_ROWS and COLUMN_VALUE are called repeatedly in a loop until FETCH_ROWS returns zero.

TIP
The exit condition for the loop is when FETCH_ROWS returns zero, not the NO_DATA_FOUND exception or the %NOTFOUND cursor attribute.

The EXECUTE and the first call to FETCH_ROWS can be combined in one call—EXECUTE_AND_FETCH. When used against a remote database, this can save a network trip and thus improve performance. The syntax for EXECUTE_AND_FETCH is

FUNCTION EXECUTE_AND_FETCH(*c* IN INTEGER,
                             exact IN BOOLEAN DEFAULT FALSE)
    RETURN INTEGER;

The parameters are as follows:

Parameter	Type	Description
c	INTEGER	Cursor ID. The cursor should already have a query parsed in it, any input variables bound, and the output variables defined.
exact	BOOLEAN	If TRUE, the TOO_MANY_ROWS exception is raised if the query returns more than one row. Even if the exception is raised, the rows are still fetched and can be retrieved.
return value	INTEGER	The number of rows fetched so far. This is similar to FETCH_ROWS. If the return value is zero, the query did not match any rows.

Return the Results to PL/SQL Variables

Once the data is retrieved into the local buffer by FETCH_ROWS or EXECUTE_AND_FETCH, use COLUMN_VALUE to get the data into PL/SQL variables. Typically, the same variables used in DEFINE_COLUMN are used in

COLUMN_VALUE. Each call to DEFINE_COLUMN should be matched by a call to COLUMN_VALUE.

COLUMN_VALUE should be called only after a successful FETCH_ROWS or EXECUTE_AND_FETCH. If the prior FETCH did not return any rows (indicated by FETCH returning zero), COLUMN_VALUE will set the output variable to NULL.

Similar to BIND_VARIABLE and DEFINE_COLUMN, COLUMN_VALUE is overloaded on the type of the output variable. These are the calls used for NUMBERs:

```
PROCEDURE COLUMN_VALUE(c IN INTEGER,
                       position IN INTEGER,
                       value OUT NUMBER);

PROCEDURE COLUMN_VALUE(c IN INTEGER,
                       position IN INTEGER,
                       value OUT NUMBER,
                       column_error OUT NUMBER,
                       actual_length OUT INTEGER);
```

These are used for VARCHAR2s:

```
PROCEDURE COLUMN_VALUE(c IN INTEGER,
                       position IN INTEGER,
                       value OUT VARCHAR2);

PROCEDURE COLUMN_VALUE(c IN INTEGER,
                       position IN INTEGER,
                       value OUT VARCHAR2,
                       column_error OUT NUMBER,
                       actual_length OUT INTEGER);
```

The following calls are used for DATEs:

```
PROCEDURE COLUMN_VALUE(c IN INTEGER,
                       position IN INTEGER,
                       value OUT DATE);

PROCEDURE COLUMN_VALUE(c IN INTEGER,
                       position IN INTEGER,
                       value OUT DATE,
                       column_error OUT NUMBER,
                       actual_length OUT INTEGER);
```

These are used for CHARs:

```
PROCEDURE COLUMN_VALUE_CHAR(c IN INTEGER,
                           position IN INTEGER,
                           value OUT CHAR);

PROCEDURE COLUMN_VALUE_CHAR(c IN INTEGER,
                           position IN INTEGER,
                           value OUT CHAR,
                           column_error OUT NUMBER,
                           actual_length OUT INTEGER);
```

These are the calls used for RAWs:

```
PROCEDURE COLUMN_VALUE_RAW(c IN INTEGER,
                          position IN INTEGER,
                          value OUT RAW);

PROCEDURE COLUMN_VALUE_RAW(c IN INTEGER,
                          position IN INTEGER,
                          value OUT RAW,
                          column_error OUT NUMBER,
                          actual_length OUT INTEGER);
```

These are for MLSLABELs:

```
PROCEDURE COLUMN_VALUE(c IN INTEGER,
                      position IN INTEGER,
                      value OUT MLSLABEL);

PROCEDURE COLUMN_VALUE(c IN INTEGER,
                      position IN INTEGER,
                      value OUT MLSLABEL,
                      column_error OUT NUMBER,
                      actual_length OUT INTEGER);
```

Finally, these calls are used for ROWIDs:

```
PROCEDURE COLUMN_VALUE_ROWID(c IN INTEGER,
                            position IN INTEGER,
                            value OUT ROWID);
```

```
PROCEDURE COLUMN_VALUE_ROWID(c IN INTEGER,
                            position IN INTEGER,
                            value OUT ROWID,
                            column_error OUT NUMBER,
                            actual_length OUT INTEGER);
```

NOTE
Oracle8 adds additional COLUMN_VALUE calls for the LOB types, and the COLUMN_VALUE_ROWID call has been removed for Oracle8i. For more information, see "DBMS_SQL Enhancements for Oracle8 and Oracle8i," later in this chapter.

The parameters for these calls are described in the following table.

Parameter	Type	Description
c	INTEGER	Cursor ID. The cursor should have had a query parsed, and any placeholders bound, and have been executed and fetched.
position	INTEGER	Relative position within the select list. Similar to DEFINE_COLUMN, the first select list item is at position 1.
value	NUMBER, DATE, MLSLABEL, CHAR, VARCHAR2, RAW, ROWID	Output variable. The contents of the buffer for this row and column will be returned in this variable. If the type of *value* differs from the type specified in DEFINE_COLUMN, the error "ORA-6562: type of OUT argument must match type of column or bind variable" is raised, which is equivalent to the exception DBMS_SQL.INCONSISTENT_TYPES.
column_error	NUMBER	Column-level error code. If specified, this variable will return errors such as "ORA-1406: fetched column value is truncated." The code is returned as a negative value, similar to SQLCODE. The error will also be raised as an exception, but *column_error* allows you to determine which column caused the error. If the column was retrieved successfully, *column_error* is zero.

Parameter	Type	Description
actual_length	INTEGER	If specified, this variable will contain the original length of the column (before it was returned). This is useful if the output variable is not long enough and was truncated (which would raise the ORA-1406 error).

Example

The **DynamicQuery** procedure places the first names, last names, and majors for the students passed to it into **temp_table**. Although this procedure could have been written using static SQL, it illustrates the processing necessary for queries in DBMS_SQL.

```
-- Available online as DynamicQuery.sql
CREATE OR REPLACE PROCEDURE DynamicQuery (
  /* Uses DBMS_SQL to query the students table, and puts the
   * results in temp_table. The first names, last names, and
   * majors are inserted for up to two majors input.
   */
  p_Major1 IN students.major%TYPE DEFAULT NULL,
  p_Major2 IN students.major%TYPE DEFAULT NULL) AS

  v_CursorID   INTEGER;
  v_SelectStmt VARCHAR2(500);
  v_FirstName  students.first_name%TYPE;
  v_LastName   students.last_name%TYPE;
  v_Major      students.major%TYPE;
  v_Dummy      INTEGER;

BEGIN
  -- Open the cursor for processing.
  v_CursorID := DBMS_SQL.OPEN_CURSOR;

  -- Create the query string.
  v_SelectStmt := 'SELECT first_name, last_name, major
                   FROM students
                   WHERE major IN (:m1, :m2)
                   ORDER BY major, last_name';

  -- Parse the query.
  DBMS_SQL.PARSE(v_CursorID, v_SelectStmt, DBMS_SQL.NATIVE);

  -- Bind the input variables.
```

```
DBMS_SQL.BIND_VARIABLE(v_CursorID, ':m1', p_Major1);
DBMS_SQL.BIND_VARIABLE(v_CursorID, ':m2', p_Major2);

-- Define the select list items.
DBMS_SQL.DEFINE_COLUMN(v_CursorID, 1, v_FirstName, 20);
DBMS_SQL.DEFINE_COLUMN(v_CursorID, 2, v_LastName, 20);
DBMS_SQL.DEFINE_COLUMN(v_CursorID, 3, v_Major, 30);

-- Execute the statement. We don't care about the return
-- value, but we do need to declare a variable for it.
v_Dummy := DBMS_SQL.EXECUTE(v_CursorID);

-- This is the fetch loop.
LOOP
  -- Fetch the rows into the buffer, and also check for the exit
  -- condition from the loop.
  IF DBMS_SQL.FETCH_ROWS(v_CursorID) = 0 THEN
    EXIT;
  END IF;

  -- Retrieve the rows from the buffer into PL/SQL variables.
  DBMS_SQL.COLUMN_VALUE(v_CursorID, 1, v_FirstName);
  DBMS_SQL.COLUMN_VALUE(v_CursorID, 2, v_LastName);
  DBMS_SQL.COLUMN_VALUE(v_CursorID, 3, v_Major);

  -- Insert the fetched data into temp_table.
  INSERT INTO temp_table (char_col)
    VALUES (v_FirstName || ' ' || v_LastName || ' is a ' ||
            v_Major || ' major.');
END LOOP;

-- Close the cursor.
DBMS_SQL.CLOSE_CURSOR(v_CursorID);

-- Commit our work.
COMMIT;
EXCEPTION
  WHEN OTHERS THEN
    -- Close the cursor, then raise the error again.
    DBMS_SQL.CLOSE_CURSOR(v_CursorID);
    RAISE;
END DynamicQuery;
```

The output from **DynamicQuery** in SQL*Plus is

```
-- Available online as callDQ.sql
SQL> exec DynamicQuery('History', 'Computer Science')
```

```
PL/SQL procedure successfully completed.

SQL> SELECT char_col FROM temp_table;

CHAR_COL
-------------------------------------------------------
Joanne Junebug is a Computer Science major.
Shay Shariatpanahy is a Computer Science major.
Scott Smith is a Computer Science major.
Margaret Mason is a History major.
Patrick Poll is a History major.
Timothy Taller is a History major.
6 rows selected.
```

Executing PL/SQL

The third and final type of statement that can be executed with dynamic SQL is an anonymous PL/SQL block. One possible use of this statement type would be to call a stored procedure. PL/SQL processing is similar to the processing for DML, DDL, or ALTER SESSION statements, in that there is no fetch loop. PL/SQL blocks also can have bind variables. Unlike a DML, DDL, or ALTER SESSION statement, however, a PL/SQL block can assign to the bind variables. In this case, an additional call, VARIABLE_VALUE (similar to COLUMN_VALUE) is used to get their output values after the block has been executed. Here is the sequence of calls:

1. Open the cursor (OPEN_CURSOR).

2. Parse the statement (PARSE).

3. Bind both input and output bind variables (BIND_VARIABLE).

4. Execute the statement (EXECUTE).

5. Retrieve the value of any output variables (COLUMN_VALUE).

6. Close the cursor (CLOSE_CURSOR).

As in the previous section, we will only examine those calls that have different implications, or are used only for processing anonymous PL/SQL blocks. The other calls behave the same as we've already seen.

Parse the Statement

The string passed to PARSE should contain an entire anonymous PL/SQL block (or CALL statement in Oracle8*i*). The trailing semicolon after the final END *is* included, since it is a syntactic part of the block. (It is not needed for queries, DML, or DDL statements because the semicolon is not a syntactic part of those statements—it is simply the statement terminator.) The block can contain placeholders, which are bound with BIND_VARIABLE. If they are used as output variables (OUT parameters from a stored procedure, for example), then their new value can be retrieved after the block is executed with VARIABLE_VALUE. The following are all legal strings that can be passed to PARSE:

```
BEGIN :placeholder := 7; END;

DECLARE
  v_Numeric   NUMBER := :p1;
  v_Character VARCHAR2(50) := :p2;
BEGIN
  INSERT INTO temp_table VALUES (v_Numeric, v_Character);
END;

BEGIN
  SELECT first_name, last_name
    INTO :first_name, :last_name
    FROM students
    WHERE ID = :id;
END;
```

> **CAUTION**
> *Don't use the - - comments inside a PL/SQL block executed with DBMS_SQL. The double dash symbol comments out the following characters, up to a newline. However, since the entire block is within one string, the rest of the block will be commented out. Use the C-style /* and */ comments instead.*

Retrieve the Value of Any Output Variables

After the statement has been executed, the value of any output variables can be retrieved with VARIABLE_VALUE. Similar to a query, the value is stored in a buffer first by EXECUTE, and retrieved from this buffer with VARIABLE_VALUE. Only those bind variables that are used as output variables need to be retrieved. Typically, the same variables used in BIND_VARIABLE are used in VARIABLE_VALUE, but this is not required.

Like BIND_VARIABLE and COLUMN_VALUE, VARIABLE_VALUE is overloaded by the type of the output variable. The following call is used for NUMBERs:

```
PROCEDURE VARIABLE_VALUE(c IN NUMBER,
                         name IN VARCHAR2,
                         value OUT NUMBER);
```

This call is used for VARCHAR2s:

```
PROCEDURE VARIABLE_VALUE(c IN NUMBER,
                         name IN VARCHAR2,
                         value OUT VARCHAR2);
```

Here is the call used for DATEs:

```
PROCEDURE VARIABLE_VALUE(c IN NUMBER,
                         name IN VARCHAR2,
                         value OUT DATE);
```

This call is used for CHARs:

```
PROCEDURE VARIABLE_VALUE_CHAR(c IN NUMBER,
                              name IN VARCHAR2,
                              value OUT CHAR);
```

The following is used for RAWs:

```
PROCEDURE VARIABLE_VALUE_RAW(c IN NUMBER,
                             name IN VARCHAR2,
                             value OUT RAW);
```

This is the call used for MLSLABELs:

```
PROCEDURE VARIABLE_VALUE(c IN NUMBER,
                         name IN VARCHAR2,
                         value OUT MLSLABEL);
```

And here is the call used for ROWIDs:

```
PROCEDURE VARIABLE_VALUE_ROWID(c IN NUMBER,
                               name IN VARCHAR2,
                               value OUT ROWID);
```

NOTE
Oracle8 adds additional VARIABLE_VALUE calls for the LOB types, and the VARIABLE_VALUE_ROWID call has been removed for Oracle8i. For more information, see "DBMS_SQL Enhancements for Oracle8 and Oracle8i," later in this chapter.

The parameters for these calls are listed in the following table.

Parameter	Type	Description
c	INTEGER	Cursor ID. The cursor should already have been opened, had a PL/SQL block parsed in it, had any placeholders bound, and been executed.
name	VARCHAR2	Name of the placeholder (including the colon) whose value is to be retrieved.
value	NUMBER, CHAR, VARCHAR2, DATE, ROWID, MLSLABEL, RAW	Output variable to receive the result. If the type of value does not match the type used in BIND_VARIABLE, the error "ORA-6562: type of OUT argument must match type of column or bind variable" is raised, which is equivalent to the DBMS_SQL.INCONSISTENT_TYPES exception. This is similar to the behavior of COLUMN_VALUE.

Example

The **DynamicPLSQL** procedure executes a PL/SQL block that queries **students**. Note that we have to pass the maximum length for the output placeholders **:first_name** and **:last_name**. They don't have a value before the block is run, and thus the maximum length can't be determined automatically.

```
-- Available online as DynamicPLSQL.sql
CREATE OR REPLACE PROCEDURE DynamicPLSQL (
  /* Executes a PL/SQL block dynamically. The block
   * selects from students, and uses p_StudentID as an
   * input placeholder.
   */
  p_StudentID IN students.ID%TYPE) IS

  v_CursorID  INTEGER;
  v_BlockStr  VARCHAR2(500);
  v_FirstName students.first_name%TYPE;
  v_LastName  students.last_name%TYPE;
  v_Dummy     INTEGER;

BEGIN
```

```
  -- Open the cursor for processing.
  v_CursorID := DBMS_SQL.OPEN_CURSOR;

  -- Create the string containing the PL/SQL block.
  -- In this string, the :first_name and :last_name
  -- placeholders are output variables, and :ID is an
  -- input variable.
  v_BlockStr :=
    'BEGIN
       SELECT first_name, last_name
         INTO :first_name, :last_name
         FROM students
         WHERE ID = :ID;
     END;';

  -- Parse the statement.
  DBMS_SQL.PARSE(v_CursorID, v_BlockStr, DBMS_SQL.NATIVE);

  -- Bind the placeholders to the variables. Note that we
  -- do this for both the input and output variables.
  -- We pass the maximum length for :first_name and
  -- :last_name.
  DBMS_SQL.BIND_VARIABLE(v_CursorID, ':first_name', v_FirstName, 20);
  DBMS_SQL.BIND_VARIABLE(v_CursorID, ':last_name', v_LastName, 20);
  DBMS_SQL.BIND_VARIABLE(v_CursorID, ':ID', p_StudentID);

  -- Execute the statement. We don't care about the return
  -- value, but we do need to declare a variable for it.
  v_Dummy := DBMS_SQL.EXECUTE(v_CursorID);

  -- Retrieve the values for the output variables.
  DBMS_SQL.VARIABLE_VALUE(v_CursorID, ':first_name', v_FirstName);
  DBMS_SQL.VARIABLE_VALUE(v_CursorID, ':last_name', v_LastName);

  -- And print them out.
  DBMS_OUTPUT.PUT('ID: ' || p_StudentID || ' ');
  DBMS_OUTPUT.PUT_LINE(v_FirstName || ' ' || v_LastName);

  -- Close the cursor.
  DBMS_SQL.CLOSE_CURSOR(v_CursorID);
EXCEPTION
  WHEN OTHERS THEN
    -- Close the cursor, then raise the error again.
    DBMS_SQL.CLOSE_CURSOR(v_CursorID);
    RAISE;
END DynamicPLSQL;
```

The following SQL*Plus session shows the output from **DynamicPLSQL**.

-- Available online as callDP.sql

```
SQL> exec DynamicPLSQL(10010)
ID: 10010 Rita Razmataz
PL/SQL procedure successfully completed.

SQL> exec DynamicPLSQL(10003)
ID: 10003 Manish Murgatroid
PL/SQL procedure successfully completed.
```

Using out_value_size

When using BIND_VARIABLE for an output character variable, it is important to provide a value for the *out_value_size* parameter. Suppose we modify the bind calls in **DynamicPLSQL** as follows:

-- Available online as part of dynamicError.sql

```
   -- Bind the placeholders to the variables. Note that we
   -- do this for both the input and output variables.
   -- Do not pass the maximum length for v_FirstName and
   -- v_LastName.
   DBMS_SQL.BIND_VARIABLE(v_CursorID, ':first_name', v_FirstName);
   DBMS_SQL.BIND_VARIABLE(v_CursorID, ':last_name', v_LastName);
   DBMS_SQL.BIND_VARIABLE(v_CursorID, ':ID', p_StudentID);
```

Now when we run **DynamicPLSQL** we receive ORA-6502:

-- Available online as part of dynamicError.sql

```
SQL> exec DynamicPLSQL(10010)
begin DynamicPLSQL(10010); end;

*
ERROR at line 1:
ORA-06502: PL/SQL: numeric or value error
ORA-06512: at "EXAMPLE.DYNAMICPLSQL", line 49
ORA-06512: at line 1
```

Why is this? The answer lies in how Oracle processes bind variables in general. Bind variables are not examined until the statement is actually executed. At this time, the actual length of the variable is determined, based on the value of the variable. In **DynamicPLSQL**, both **v_FirstName** and **v_LastName** are not initialized by the program. This results in the bind variables being assigned a length of zero. Thus, when the VARIABLE_VALUE call attempts to assign a value back to

v_FirstName, the error is raised. If the *out_value_size* parameter is passed to BIND_VARIABLE, as in the original example, then this length is used instead of the actual length of the variable.

An alternative is to initialize the bind variables to a string with the maximum length, as follows:

```
-- Available online as part of dynamicError.sql
   -- Bind the placeholders to the variables. Note that we
   -- do this for both the input and output variables.
   -- First initialize both variables to their maximum
   -- lengths.
   v_FirstName := '12345678901234567890';
   v_LastName := '12345678901234567890';
   DBMS_SQL.BIND_VARIABLE(v_CursorID, ':first_name', v_FirstName);
   DBMS_SQL.BIND_VARIABLE(v_CursorID, ':last_name', v_LastName);
   DBMS_SQL.BIND_VARIABLE(v_CursorID, ':ID', p_StudentID);
```

This will also allow the execution of **DynamicPLSQL** to succeed.

DBMS_SQL Enhancements for Oracle8 and Oracle8*i*

Oracle **8** and higher

There are several enhancements to the DBMS_SQL package for Oracle8 and Oracle8*i*. These include the ability to parse large SQL strings, use of array processing, the ability to bind and define large objects, enhancements to handle the RETURNING clause, CALL statement, and use of the DESCRIBE_COLUMNS procedure. All of the examples in this section require Oracle8. The CALL statement requires Oracle8*i*.

Parsing Large SQL Strings

Because the maximum length of a PL/SQL VARCHAR is 32,767 bytes and the *statement* parameter of the PARSE call is a VARCHAR, this limits the maximum size of a SQL statement that can be executed using DBMS_SQL. (A SQL statement itself has no explicit limit on its total length.) This restriction is lifted with the following alternative to the PARSE call:

PROCEDURE DBMS_SQL.PARSE(*c* IN INTEGER,
                          ***statement* IN VARCHAR2S**,
                          lb IN INTEGER,
                          ub IN INTEGER,
                          lfflg IN BOOLEAN,
                          language_flag IN INTEGER);

The VARCHAR2S type is defined with

```
TYPE VARCHAR2S IS TABLE OF VARCHAR2(256)
    INDEX BY BINARY_INTEGER;
```

Because the SQL statement is now passed in a PL/SQL index-by table, statements of arbitrary length (up to the maximum size limit of the server) can be parsed. The parameters to this version of PARSE are described in the following table. (See Chapter 14 for more information about index-by tables and other collection types.)

Parameter	Type	Description
c	INTEGER	Cursor ID.
statement	DBMS_SQL.VARCHAR2S	String to be parsed. The string should be broken up into pieces, each of which has a maximum length of 256 characters.
lb	INTEGER	Lower bound in the statement table.
ub	INTEGER	Upper bound in the statement table.
lfflg	BOOLEAN	If TRUE, insert a linefeed after each element in the statement table.
language_flag	INTEGER	Determines how Oracle handles the statement. Behaves the same as before.

In order to use this version of PARSE, copy the statement into the statement index-by table, putting each section of the statement into consecutive elements of the table, from element lb to element ub. The DBMS_SQL package will then combine these into a full statement that would look like this:

```
statement(lb) || statement(lb + 1) || ... || statement(ub)
```

For example, we could rewrite the parse section of **DynamicPLSQL** as follows:

```
-- Available online as part of dynamicParse.sql
CREATE OR REPLACE PROCEDURE DynamicPLSQL (
   p_StudentID IN students.ID%TYPE) IS

   v_CursorID  INTEGER;
```

```
   v_BlockStr   DBMS_SQL.VARCHAR2S;
   ...
BEGIN
  -- Open the cursor for processing.
  v_CursorID := DBMS_SQL.OPEN_CURSOR;

  -- Create the string containing the PL/SQL block.
  -- In this string, the :first_name and :last_name
  -- placeholders are output variables, and :ID is an
  -- input variable.
  v_BlockStr(1) := 'BEGIN';
  v_BlockStr(2) := 'SELECT first_name, last_name';
  v_BlockStr(3) := '  INTO :first_name, :last_name';
  v_BlockStr(4) := '    FROM students';
  v_BlockStr(5) := '    WHERE ID = :ID;';
  v_BlockStr(6) := 'END;';

  -- Parse the statement.
  DBMS_SQL.PARSE(v_CursorID, v_BlockStr, 1, 6, TRUE,
                 DBMS_SQL.NATIVE);
...
END DynamicPLSQL;
```

DBMS_SQL Array Processing

Array processing adds the ability to process large amounts of data with a single SQL statement. For example, you could insert 100 rows into the database with a single round-trip from the client to the server. Without array processing, the same operation would take 100 round-trips. Even if the PL/SQL block is executing on the server, array processing will save context switches between the PL/SQL and SQL engines.

Array processing is done in DBMS_SQL with the BIND_ARRAY (used for batch inserts, updates, and deletes) and DEFINE_ARRAY (used for batch queries) procedures.

| Oracle **8i** |
| and higher |

Note that Oracle8i introduces a feature known as bulk binds, which allows array processing with static SQL. It is not available with dynamic SQL as of Oracle8i Release 8.1.5. For more information, see Chapter 11.

BIND_ARRAY   The BIND_ARRAY procedure operates very similar to BIND_VARIABLE, and takes similar arguments. The variable to be bound, however, is a PL/SQL index-by table rather than a scalar variable. The allowed types are

```
TYPE NUMBER_TABLE IS TABLE OF NUMBER
   INDEX BY BINARY_INTEGER;
```

```
TYPE VARCHAR2_TABLE IS TABLE OF VARCHAR2(2000)
   INDEX BY BINARY_INTEGER;

TYPE DATE_TABLE IS TABLE OF DATE
   INDEX BY BINARY_INTEGER;

TYPE BLOB_TABLE IS TABLE OF BLOB
   INDEX BY BINARY_INTEGER;

TYPE CLOB_TABLE IS TABLE OF CLOB
   INDEX BY BINARY_INTEGER;

TYPE BFILE_TABLE IS TABLE OF BFILE
   INDEX BY BINARY_INTEGER;
```

The other difference between BIND_ARRAY and BIND_VARIABLE is that BIND_ARRAY can take the range of values in the PL/SQL table to bind. Thus, BIND_ARRAY is overloaded on the type of the table, and also on the table indices:

```
PROCEDURE BIND_ARRAY(c IN INTEGER,
                     name IN VARCHAR2,
                     table_variable IN table_datatype);

PROCEDURE BIND_ARRAY(c IN INTEGER,
                     name IN VARCHAR2,
                     table_variable IN table_datatype,
                     index1 IN INTEGER,
                     index2 IN INTEGER);
```

The parameters for BIND_VARIABLE are described in the following table.

Parameter	Datatype	Description
c	INTEGER	Cursor ID.
name	VARCHAR2	Name of the placeholder in the statement.
table_variable	One of NUMBER_TABLE, VARCHAR2_TABLE, DATE_TABLE, BLOB_TABLE, CLOB_TABLE, BFILE_TABLE	PL/SQL table that contains the data to be bound.

Parameter	Datatype	Description
index1	INTEGER	Index of the table element that is the low bound of the range to be bound.
index2	INTEGER	Index of the table element that is the upper bound of the range to be bound.

If *index1* and *index2* are not specified, then the entire index-by table will be used. If more than one index-by table is bound to the same statement (for different placeholders) with different sizes, then the size of the smallest table will be used. An example using both BIND_ARRAY and DEFINE_ARRAY can be found in the next section.

DEFINE_ARRAY   Similar to BIND_ARRAY, the DEFINE_ARRAY procedure operates like DEFINE_COLUMN, except that it takes index-by table arguments. The table types are the same as those used by BIND_VARIABLE. The syntax is

```
PROCEDURE DEFINE_ARRAY(c IN INTEGER,
                    position IN INTEGER,
                    table_variable IN table_datatype,
                    cnt IN INTEGER,
                    indx IN INTEGER);
```

The parameters are described in the following table.

Parameter	Datatype	Description
c	INTEGER	Cursor ID.
position	INTEGER	Position within the select list of this column. The first column has position 1.
table_variable	One of NUMBER_TABLE, VARCHAR2_TABLE, DATE_TABLE, BLOB_TABLE, CLOB_TABLE, BFILE_TABLE	PL/SQL table variable in which the data will be placed by a subsequent FETCH_ROWS statement.
cnt	INTEGER	Maximum number of rows that will be retrieved by each call to FETCH_ROWS.

Parameter	Datatype	Description
indx	INTEGER	Starting index of the result set. At most, *cnt* rows will be written into *table_variable*, starting with index *indx*.

See the next section for an example using both BIND_ARRAY and DEFINE_ARRAY.

ARRAY PROCESSING EXAMPLE The **CopyRegisteredStudents** procedure will make a copy of the **registered_students** table, with the name of the new table passed in.

```
-- Available online as CopyRegisteredStudents.sql
CREATE OR REPLACE PROCEDURE CopyRegisteredStudents(
  p_NewName IN VARCHAR2) AS
  /* Creates a new table, with a name given by p_NewName, with the
   * same structure as registered_students.  The contents of
   * registered_students are then read into PL/SQL tables, and
   * inserted into the new table.
   */
  v_BatchSize CONSTANT INTEGER := 5;
  v_IDs DBMS_SQL.NUMBER_TABLE;
  v_Departments DBMS_SQL.VARCHAR2_TABLE;
  v_Courses DBMS_SQL.NUMBER_TABLE;
  v_Grades DBMS_SQL.VARCHAR2_TABLE;

  v_Cursor1 INTEGER;
  v_Cursor2 INTEGER;
  v_ReturnCode INTEGER;
  v_NumRows INTEGER;
  v_SQLStatement VARCHAR2(200);
  v_SelectStmt VARCHAR2(200);
  v_InsertStmt VARCHAR2(200);

BEGIN
  v_Cursor1 := DBMS_SQL.OPEN_CURSOR;
  v_Cursor2 := DBMS_SQL.OPEN_CURSOR;

  -- First drop the new table.  Ignore ORA-942 (table or view does
  -- not exist) error.
  BEGIN
    v_SQLStatement := 'DROP TABLE ' || p_NewName;
    DBMS_SQL.PARSE(v_Cursor1, v_SQLStatement, DBMS_SQL.NATIVE);
  EXCEPTION
```

```
      WHEN OTHERS THEN
        IF SQLCODE != -942 THEN
          RAISE;
        END IF;
  END;

  -- Create the new table.
  v_SQLStatement := 'CREATE TABLE ' || p_NewName || '(';
  v_SQLStatement := v_SQLStatement || 'student_id NUMBER(5),';
  v_SQLStatement := v_SQLStatement || 'department CHAR(3),';
  v_SQLStatement := v_SQLStatement || 'course NUMBER(3),';
  v_SQLStatement := v_SQLStatement || 'grade CHAR(1))';
  DBMS_SQL.PARSE(v_Cursor1, v_SQLStatement, DBMS_SQL.V7);

  -- Parse both the select and insert statements.
  v_SelectStmt := 'SELECT * FROM registered_students';
  v_InsertStmt := 'INSERT INTO ' || p_NewName || ' VALUES ';
  v_InsertStmt :=
    v_InsertStmt || '(:ID, :department, :course, :grade)';
  DBMS_SQL.PARSE(v_Cursor1, v_SelectStmt, DBMS_SQL.V7);
  DBMS_SQL.PARSE(v_Cursor2, v_InsertStmt, DBMS_SQL.V7);

  -- Use DEFINE_ARRAY to specify the output variables for the select.
  DBMS_SQL.DEFINE_ARRAY(v_Cursor1, 1, v_IDs, v_BatchSize, 1);
  DBMS_SQL.DEFINE_ARRAY(v_Cursor1, 2, v_Departments, v_BatchSize, 1);
  DBMS_SQL.DEFINE_ARRAY(v_Cursor1, 3, v_Courses, v_BatchSize, 1);
  DBMS_SQL.DEFINE_ARRAY(v_Cursor1, 4, v_Grades, v_BatchSize, 1);

  -- Execute the select statement.
  v_ReturnCode := DBMS_SQL.EXECUTE(v_Cursor1);

  -- This is the fetch loop.  Each call to FETCH_ROWS will retrieve
  -- v_BatchSize rows of data.  The loop is over when FETCH_ROWS
  -- returns a value < v_BatchSize.
  LOOP
    v_NumRows := DBMS_SQL.FETCH_ROWS(v_Cursor1);
    DBMS_SQL.COLUMN_VALUE(v_Cursor1, 1, v_IDs);
    DBMS_SQL.COLUMN_VALUE(v_Cursor1, 2, v_Departments);
    DBMS_SQL.COLUMN_VALUE(v_Cursor1, 3, v_Courses);
    DBMS_SQL.COLUMN_VALUE(v_Cursor1, 4, v_Grades);

    -- If this is the last fetch, then FETCH_ROWS will return less
    -- than v_BatchSize rows.  However, there could still be rows
    -- returned, and there are exactly v_NumRows number of them.
    -- Thus we need to use v_NumRows instead of v_BatchSize in these
    -- binds.

    -- The special case of v_NumRows = 0 needs to be checked here.
```

```
        -- This means that the previous fetch returned all the remaining
        -- rows and therefore we are done with the loop.
        IF v_NumRows = 0 THEN
          EXIT;
        END IF;

        -- Use BIND_ARRAY to specify the input variables for the insert.
        -- Only elements 1..v_NumRows will be used.
        DBMS_SQL.BIND_ARRAY(v_Cursor2, ':ID', v_IDs, 1, v_NumRows);
        DBMS_SQL.BIND_ARRAY(v_Cursor2, ':department', v_Departments, 1,
                      v_NumRows);
        DBMS_SQL.BIND_ARRAY(v_Cursor2, ':course', v_Courses, 1,
                      v_NumRows);
        DBMS_SQL.BIND_ARRAY(v_Cursor2, ':grade', v_Grades, 1, v_NumRows);

        -- Execute the insert statement.
        v_ReturnCode := DBMS_SQL.EXECUTE(v_Cursor2);

        -- Exit condition for the loop.  Note that the loop processing
        -- has been done before we check this.
        EXIT WHEN v_NumRows < v_BatchSize;
      END LOOP;

      -- Commit the INSERTs into the new table.
      COMMIT;

      DBMS_SQL.CLOSE_CURSOR(v_Cursor1);
      DBMS_SQL.CLOSE_CURSOR(v_Cursor2);
    END CopyRegisteredStudents;
```

NOTE
*The semantics of FETCH_ROWS change slightly when doing an array fetch. The EXIT WHEN statement of the fetch loop is done only after the rows have been inserted into the new table, not immediately after the FETCH_ROWS statement. (Compare this fetch loop to the one in **DynamicQuery** earlier in this chapter.) This is necessary because there may still be rows left to process after FETCH_ROWS returns less than the requested amount of rows. This condition indicates that all rows have been fetched from the database, but they may not all have been processed yet.*

Binding Large Objects

Oracle8 introduced large objects, which can store up to 4GB of character or binary data (see Chapters 15 and 16 on the CD-ROM included with this book for more information on using LOBs). Consequently, the BIND_VARIABLE, DEFINE_COLUMN, COLUMN_VALUE, and VARIABLE_VALUE subprograms are all overloaded to accept BLOB, CLOB, or BFILE arguments, as well as the other datatypes that we saw earlier. For example, here are the new overloaded calls for BIND_VARIABLE:

```
PROCEDURE BIND_VARIABLE(c IN INTEGER,
                             name IN VARCHAR2,
                             value IN CLOB CHARACTER SET ANY_CS);


PROCEDURE BIND_VARIABLE(c IN INTEGER,
                             name IN VARCHAR2,
                             value IN BLOB);


PROCEDURE BIND_VARIABLE(c IN INTEGER,
                             name IN VARCHAR2,
                             value IN BFILE);
```

The following example illustrates the use of these calls.

```
-- Available online as DynamicLOB.sql
CREATE OR REPLACE PROCEDURE DynamicLOB AS
  /* Uses DBMS_SQL to manipulate rows in the lobdemo table. */

  v_InsertCursor INTEGER;
  v_QueryCursor  INTEGER;
  v_InsertStmt VARCHAR2(500);
  v_QueryStmt  VARCHAR2(500);
  v_Dummy      INTEGER;
  v_CLOB       CLOB;
  v_BLOB       BLOB;
  v_Key        NUMBER;
  v_StringVal  VARCHAR2(100);
  v_RawVal     RAW(100);
BEGIN
  -- Open the cursors for processing.
  v_InsertCursor := DBMS_SQL.OPEN_CURSOR;
  v_QueryCursor := DBMS_SQL.OPEN_CURSOR;
```

```
-- First insert a row with empty LOB values.
v_InsertStmt :=
  'INSERT INTO lobdemo (key, clob_col, blob_col) ' ||
  ' VALUES (:key, :clob_col, :blob_col)';
DBMS_SQL.PARSE(v_InsertCursor, v_InsertStmt, DBMS_SQL.NATIVE);

v_Key := 1;
v_CLOB := EMPTY_CLOB();
v_BLOB := EMPTY_BLOB();

-- Bind the input variables.
DBMS_SQL.BIND_VARIABLE(v_InsertCursor, ':key', v_Key);
DBMS_SQL.BIND_VARIABLE(v_InsertCursor, ':clob_col', v_CLOB);
DBMS_SQL.BIND_VARIABLE(v_InsertCursor, ':blob_col', v_BLOB);

-- Execute the insert.
v_Dummy := DBMS_SQL.EXECUTE(v_InsertCursor);

-- Now retrieve the locators back from the table, so we can
-- use DBMS_LOB to modify them.
v_QueryStmt :=
  'SELECT clob_col, blob_col' ||
  ' FROM lobdemo' ||
  ' WHERE key = :key';
DBMS_SQL.PARSE(v_QueryCursor, v_QueryStmt, DBMS_SQL.NATIVE);

-- Bind the input variable, and define the output columns.
DBMS_SQL.BIND_VARIABLE(v_QueryCursor, ':key', v_Key);
DBMS_SQL.DEFINE_COLUMN(v_QueryCursor, 1, v_CLOB);
DBMS_SQL.DEFINE_COLUMN(v_QueryCursor, 2, v_BLOB);

-- Execute and fetch.
v_Dummy := DBMS_SQL.EXECUTE_AND_FETCH(v_QueryCursor);

-- Retrieve the locators from the table.
DBMS_SQL.COLUMN_VALUE(v_QueryCursor, 1, v_CLOB);
DBMS_SQL.COLUMN_VALUE(v_QueryCursor, 2, v_BLOB);

-- Use DBMS_LOB to copy data into each of the LOBs.
v_StringVal :=
  'abcdefghijklmnopqrstuvwxyzABCDEFGHIJKLMNOPQRSTUVWXYZ';
v_RawVal := HEXTORAW('000102030405060708090A0B0C0D0E0F' ||
                    'FFFEFDFCFBFAF9F8F7F6F5F4F3F2F1F0');

DBMS_LOB.WRITE(v_CLOB, LENGTH(v_StringVal), 1, v_StringVal);
DBMS_LOB.WRITE(v_BLOB, UTL_RAW.LENGTH(v_RawVal), 1, v_RawVal);
v_Key := 2;
```

```
-- And now insert them into row 2, using the first cursor.
DBMS_SQL.BIND_VARIABLE(v_InsertCursor, ':key', v_Key);
DBMS_SQL.BIND_VARIABLE(v_InsertCursor, ':clob_col', v_CLOB);
DBMS_SQL.BIND_VARIABLE(v_InsertCursor, ':blob_col', v_BLOB);
v_Dummy := DBMS_SQL.EXECUTE(v_InsertCursor);

-- Close the cursors.
DBMS_SQL.CLOSE_CURSOR(v_InsertCursor);
DBMS_SQL.CLOSE_CURSOR(v_QueryCursor);
EXCEPTION
  WHEN OTHERS THEN
    -- Close the cursor, then raise the error again.
    DBMS_SQL.CLOSE_CURSOR(v_InsertCursor);
    DBMS_SQL.CLOSE_CURSOR(v_QueryCursor);
    RAISE;
END DynamicLOB;
```

NOTE
*Because the locators queried from row 1 are used
for the insert into row 2, both rows will end up with
the same data. For more information, see Chapter 16
on the CD-ROM included with this book.*

The RETURNING Clause

The RETURNING clause allows you to return information in the same server call as
a DML statement. For example, we can determine the rowid of a newly INSERTed
row without a separate query with the following:

-- **Available online as part of dynamicReturning.sql**

```
SQL> DECLARE
  2     v_RowidString VARCHAR2(100);
  3     v_NumVal NUMBER := 1;
  4     v_StringVal VARCHAR2(20) := 'rowid';
  5  BEGIN
  6     INSERT INTO temp_table VALUES (v_NumVal, v_StringVal)
  7        RETURNING ROWID INTO v_RowidString;
  8     DBMS_OUTPUT.PUT_LINE('ROWID of new row is: ' || v_RowidString);
  9  END;
 10  /
ROWID of new row is: AAAAvRAAFAAAAAwAAG
PL/SQL procedure successfully completed.
```

How do we execute this statement using DBMS_SQL? It is done similar to the
processing for an anonymous PL/SQL block, where the value returned is an output

bind variable. Thus, we retrieve it with VARIABLE_VALUE after the statement has been executed:

```
-- Available online as part of dynamicReturning.sql
SQL> DECLARE
  2     v_RowidString VARCHAR2(100);
  3     v_CursorID INTEGER;
  4     v_NumVal NUMBER := 1;
  5     v_StringVal VARCHAR2(20) := 'rowid';
  6     v_SQLString VARCHAR2(100);
  7     v_ReturnCode NUMBER;
  8  BEGIN
  9     v_SQLString :=
 10        'INSERT INTO temp_table VALUES (:n, :c) ' ||
 11          'RETURNING ROWID INTO :r';
 12     v_CursorID := DBMS_SQL.OPEN_CURSOR;
 13     DBMS_SQL.PARSE(v_CursorID, v_SQLString, DBMS_SQL.NATIVE);
 14     DBMS_SQL.BIND_VARIABLE(v_CursorID, ':n', v_NumVal);
 15     DBMS_SQL.BIND_VARIABLE(v_CursorID, ':c', v_StringVal);
 16     DBMS_SQL.BIND_VARIABLE(v_CursorID, ':r', v_RowidString, 100);
 17     v_ReturnCode := DBMS_SQL.EXECUTE(v_CursorID);
 18     DBMS_SQL.VARIABLE_VALUE(v_CursorID, ':r', v_RowidString);
 19     DBMS_OUTPUT.PUT_LINE('ROWID of new row is: '|| v_RowidString);
 20  END;
 21  /
ROWID of new row is: AAADmSAAFAAAC7jAAB
PL/SQL procedure successfully completed.
```

> **CAUTION**
> *Due to a bug in Oracle8, the previous block will return an ORA-1427 error if run against Oracle8 Release 8.0.6 or earlier. It is fixed in Oracle8i. The workaround is to put the INSERT statement into a PL/SQL block, as follows:*

```
v_SQLString :=
  'BEGIN ' ||
  '  INSERT INTO temp_table VALUES (:n, :c) ' ||
  '    RETURNING ROWID INTO :r ' ||
  'END;';
```

CALL Statements

Oracle8*i* adds an additional way to call a stored procedure or function—the CALL statement. You can use DBMS_SQL to execute a CALL statement as well. The processing is the same as for an anonymous PL/SQL block, namely, open the cursor (OPEN_CURSOR), bind any input or output variables (BIND_VARIABLE), execute the call (EXECUTE), retrieve the output variables (VARIABLE_VALUE), and close the cursor (CLOSE_CURSOR). The only difference is that the string that is parsed contains the CALL statement, rather than an anonymous block. The following example illustrates this process. For more information on the CALL statement, see Chapter 11.

```
-- Available online as DynamicCall.sql
CREATE OR REPLACE PACKAGE DynamicCall AS
  PROCEDURE DoInsert(p_NumCol IN temp_table.num_col%TYPE,
                     p_CharCol IN temp_table.char_col%TYPE);

  PROCEDURE Go;
END DynamicCall;

CREATE OR REPLACE PACKAGE BODY DynamicCall AS
  PROCEDURE DoInsert(p_NumCol IN temp_table.num_col%TYPE,
                     p_CharCol IN temp_table.char_col%TYPE) IS
  BEGIN
    INSERT INTO temp_table (num_col, char_col)
      VALUES (p_NumCol, p_CharCol);
  END DoInsert;

  PROCEDURE Go IS
    v_CallStmt VARCHAR2(100);
    v_CursorID INTEGER;
    v_NumCol temp_table.num_col%TYPE;
    v_CharCol temp_table.char_col%TYPE;
    v_Dummy INTEGER;
  BEGIN
    -- Open the cursor
    v_CursorID := DBMS_SQL.OPEN_CURSOR;

    v_CallStmt := 'CALL DynamicCall.DoInsert(:num_col, :char_col)';
    DBMS_SQL.PARSE(v_CursorID, v_CallStmt, DBMS_SQL.NATIVE);
```

```
      v_NumCol := 123;
      v_CharCol := 'I like CALL statements!';
      DBMS_SQL.BIND_VARIABLE(v_CursorID, ':num_col', v_NumCol);
      DBMS_SQL.BIND_VARIABLE(v_CursorID, ':char_col', v_CharCol);
      v_Dummy := DBMS_SQL.EXECUTE(v_CursorID);
      DBMS_SQL.CLOSE_CURSOR(v_CursorID);
EXCEPTION
   WHEN OTHERS THEN
      -- Close the cursor, then raise the error again.
      DBMS_SQL.CLOSE_CURSOR(v_CursorID);
      RAISE;

   END Go;
END DynamicCall;
```

The output from **DynamicCall.Go** is shown next. Note that the string that is parsed does not contain a trailing semicolon.

```
SQL> exec DynamicCall.Go
PL/SQL procedure successfully completed.

SQL> SELECT *
  2      FROM temp_table;

  NUM_COL CHAR_COL
--------- -------------------------------------
      123 I like CALL statements!
```

Describing the Select List

If a SELECT statement is completely dynamic, the program may not know anything about the columns it will return at compile time. The DESCRIBE_COLUMNS procedure can provide this information. DESCRIBE_COLUMNS can be called any time after a query is parsed. The syntax of the procedure and its types are as follows:

```
TYPE DESC_REC IS RECORD (
  col_type    BINARY_INTEGER := 0;
  col_max_len BINARY_INTEGER := 0;
  col_name      VARCHAR2(32) := '';
  col_name_len BINARY_INTEGER := 0;
  col_schema_name VARCHAR2(32) := '';
  col_schema_name_len BINARY_INTEGER := 0;
  col_precision BINARY_INTEGER := 0;
  col_scale  BINARY_INTEGER := 0;
  col_charsetid BINARY_INTEGER := 0;
  col_charsetform  BINARY_INTEGER := 0;
  col_null_ok  BOOLEAN := TRUE);
```

```
TYPE DESC_TAB IS TABLE OF DESC_REC
  INDEX BY BINARY_INTEGER;

PROCEDURE DBMS_SQL.DESCRIBE_COLUMNS(c IN INTEGER,
                                    col_cnt OUT INTEGER,
                                    dest_t OUT DESC_TYPE);
```

The parameters for DESCRIBE_COLUMNS are described in the following table.

Parameter	Type	Description
c	INTEGER	Cursor ID
col_cnt	INTEGER	Number of columns in the select list
desc_t	DESC_TYPE	PL/SQL table containing column description information

The fields in the DESC_REC type have the following meanings:

Field	Type	Description
col_type	BINARY_INTEGER	Type code for the column being described. The codes are listed in Table 8-1.
col_max_len	BINARY_INTEGER	Maximum length of the column.
col_name	VARCHAR2(32)	Name of the column.
col_name_len	BINARY_INTEGER	Length of the column name.
col_schema_name	VARCHAR2(32)	Name of the schema in which the column type was defined (valid for object types only).
col_schema_name_len	BINARY_INTEGER	Length of the schema name.
col_precision	BINARY_INTEGER	Precision of the column. Valid only for NUMBER columns.
col_scale	BINARY_INTEGER	Scale of the column. Valid only for NUMBER columns.
col_charsetid	BINARY_INTEGER	Character set ID of the column.
col_charsetform	BINARY_INTEGER	Character set form of the column.
col_null_ok	BOOLEAN	TRUE if the column allows NULLs, FALSE otherwise.

Code	Description
1	VARCHAR2
2	NUMBER
8	LONG
12	DATE
23	RAW
24	LONG RAW
11	ROWID
96	CHAR
106	MLSLABEL
109	USER DEFINED[1]
111	REF[1]
112	CLOB
113	BLOB
114	BFILE
208	UROWID[2]

[1] Oracle8 and higher

[2] Oracle8*i* and higher

TABLE 8-1.   *Internal Datatype Codes*

As an example of DESCRIBE_COLUMNS, the following **DescribeTable** procedure will take a table name as input, and then output (using DBMS_OUTPUT) a description of the table to the screen.

```
-- Available online as DescribeTable.sql
CREATE OR REPLACE PROCEDURE DescribeTable(p_Table IN VARCHAR2) AS
  v_Cursor        INTEGER;
  v_SQLStatement  VARCHAR2(100);
  v_DescribeInfo  DBMS_SQL.DESC_TAB;
  v_DRec          DBMS_SQL.DESC_REC;
  v_ReturnCode    INTEGER;
  v_NumColumns    INTEGER;
```

```
    FUNCTION ConvertDatatype (v_Datatype IN NUMBER)
      RETURN VARCHAR2 IS
      v_Output VARCHAR2(20);
    BEGIN
      SELECT DECODE(v_Datatype, 1, 'VARCHAR2',
                                2, 'NUMBER',
                                8, 'LONG',
                                11, 'ROWID',
                                12, 'DATE',
                                23, 'RAW',
                                24, 'LONG RAW',
                                96, 'CHAR',
                                102, 'REF CURSOR',
                                106, 'MLSLABEL',
                                109, 'USER DEFINED',
                                111, 'REF',
                                112, 'CLOB',
                                113, 'BLOB',
                                114, 'BFILE',
                                208, 'UROWID',
                                'OTHER')

      RETURN v_Output;
    END ConvertDatatype;

  BEGIN
    v_Cursor := DBMS_SQL.OPEN_CURSOR;

    -- Parse a select statement for the table.
    -- We don't need to execute it.
    v_SQLStatement := 'SELECT * FROM ' || p_Table;
    DBMS_SQL.PARSE(v_Cursor, v_SQLStatement, DBMS_SQL.V7);

    -- Describe the statement, which will give us a table description.
    DBMS_SQL.DESCRIBE_COLUMNS(v_Cursor,  v_NumColumns, v_DescribeInfo);

    -- Output header info.
    DBMS_OUTPUT.PUT_LINE('Description of ' || p_Table || ':');
    DBMS_OUTPUT.PUT('Column Name     Datatype Length Precision Scale ');
    DBMS_OUTPUT.PUT_LINE('Null?');
    DBMS_OUTPUT.PUT('--------------- -------- ------ --------- ----- ');
    DBMS_OUTPUT.PUT_LINE('-----');

    -- Loop over the columns, outputting the describe info for each.
    FOR v_Col IN 1..v_NumColumns LOOP
      v_DRec := v_DescribeInfo(v_Col);
      DBMS_OUTPUT.PUT(RPAD(v_DRec.col_name, 16));
      DBMS_OUTPUT.PUT(RPAD(ConvertDatatype(v_DRec.col_type), 9));
```

```
   DBMS_OUTPUT.PUT(RPAD(v_DRec.col_max_len, 7));
   DBMS_OUTPUT.PUT(RPAD(v_DRec.col_precision, 10));
   DBMS_OUTPUT.PUT(RPAD(v_DRec.col_scale, 6));
   IF v_DescribeInfo(v_Col).col_null_ok THEN
     DBMS_OUTPUT.NEW_LINE;
   ELSE
     DBMS_OUTPUT.PUT_LINE('NOT NULL');
   END IF;
 END LOOP;

END DescribeTable;
```

NOTE
*Some of the datatype codes used in **DescribeTable**
(and in Table 8-1) are different from the codes
used by OCI.*

The output from **DescribeTable** is illustrated by the following SQL*Plus session.

```
-- Available online as callDT.sql
SQL> exec DescribeTable('students')
Description of students:
Column Name      Datatype      Length Precision Scale Null?
---------------  ------------  ------ --------- ----- -----
ID               NUMBER        22     5         0     NOT NULL
FIRST_NAME       VARCHAR2      20     0         0
LAST_NAME        VARCHAR2      20     0         0
MAJOR            VARCHAR2      30     0         0
CURRENT_CREDITS  NUMBER        22     3         0
PL/SQL procedure successfully completed.

SQL> CREATE TABLE describe_test1 (
  2      f1 VARCHAR2(100),
  3      f2 NUMBER(7, 4),
  4      f3 LONG NOT NULL,
  5      f4 DATE,
  6      f5 RAW(50),
  7      f6 ROWID);
Table created.

SQL> exec DescribeTable('describe_test1')
Description of describe_test1:
Column Name      Datatype      Length Precision Scale Null?
---------------  ------------  ------ --------- ----- -----
F1               VARCHAR2      100    0         0
F2               NUMBER        22     7         4
```

```
F3              LONG        0       0        0       NOT NULL
F4              DATE        7       0        0
F5              RAW         50      0        0
F6              ROWID       16      0        0
PL/SQL procedure successfully completed.

SQL> CREATE TABLE describe_test2 (
  2     f1 LONG RAW,
  3     f2 CHAR(123),
  4     f3 MLSLABEL,
  5     f4 CLOB,
  6     f5 BLOB,
  7     f6 BFILE);
Table created.

SQL> exec DescribeTable('describe_test2');
Description of describe_test2:
Column Name     Datatype     Length Precision Scale Null?
--------------- ------------ ------ --------- ----- -----
F1              LONG RAW     0       0         0
F2              CHAR         123     0         0
F3              MLSLABEL     4       0         0
F4              CLOB         86      0         0
F5              BLOB         86      0         0
F6              BFILE        530     0         0
PL/SQL procedure successfully completed.

SQL> CREATE TYPE testType1 AS
  2    TABLE OF VARCHAR2(10);
  3  /
Type created.

SQL> CREATE TYPE testType2 AS
  2    VARRAY(800) OF DATE;
  3  /
Type created.

SQL> CREATE TYPE testType3 AS OBJECT (
  2    myAttribute NUMBER(1)
  3  );
  4  /
Type created.

SQL> CREATE TABLE describe_test3 (
  2     f1 UROWID,
  3     f2 testType1,
  4     f3 testType2,
  5     f4 testType3,
```

```
  6   f5 REF testType3)
  7   NESTED TABLE f2 STORE AS f2_tab;
Table created.
```

```
SQL> exec DescribeTable('describe_test3');
Description of describe_test3:
Column Name     Datatype      Length Precision Scale Null?
--------------- ------------- ------ --------- ----- -----
F1              UROWID        4000   0               0
F2              USER DEFINED  36     0               0
F3              USER DEFINED  3900   0               0
F4              USER DEFINED  40     0               0
F5              REF           50     0               0
PL/SQL procedure successfully completed.
```

Miscellaneous Procedures

There are additional procedures in DBMS_SQL that are used for fetching LONG data, and for additional error handling. With the exception of DEFINE_COLUMN_LONG and COLUMN_VALUE_LONG, these procedures are available in all versions of the DBMS_SQL package.

Fetching LONG Data

Since a LONG column can hold up to 2GB of data, and a PL/SQL LONG can hold only 32K, DBMS_SQL has the ability to fetch LONG data in more manageable pieces. This is done through two procedures—DEFINE_COLUMN_LONG and COLUMN_VALUE_LONG. These procedures are available starting with PL/SQL 2.2.

They are used in the same way as DEFINE_COLUMN and COLUMN_VALUE, except that COLUMN_VALUE_LONG is typically called in a loop to fetch all of the pieces.

DEFINE_COLUMN_LONG   The syntax for DEFINE_COLUMN_LONG is

PROCEDURE DEFINE_COLUMN_LONG(c IN INTEGER,
                                    position IN INTEGER);

The parameters are described here:

Parameter	Type	Description
c	INTEGER	Cursor ID. The cursor should have been opened and parsed with a query that contains a LONG column. Any placeholders should have been bound as well.
position	INTEGER	Relative position within the select list of the LONG item. The first select list item is at position 1.

COLUMN_VALUE_LONG   The syntax for COLUMN_VALUE_LONG is

PROCEDURE COLUMN_VALUE_LONG(c IN INTEGER,
$\qquad\qquad\qquad\qquad$ *position* IN INTEGER,
$\qquad\qquad\qquad\qquad$ *length* IN INTEGER,
$\qquad\qquad\qquad\qquad$ *offset* IN INTEGER,
$\qquad\qquad\qquad\qquad$ *value* OUT VARCHAR2,
$\qquad\qquad\qquad\qquad$ *value_length* OUT INTEGER);

The parameters are described here:

Parameter	Type	Description
c	INTEGER	Cursor ID. The cursor should have been opened, a query parsed, input placeholders bound, the long column defined with DEFINE_COLUMN_LONG and other columns with DEFINE_COLUMN, executed, and fetched.
position	INTEGER	Relative position within the select list of the LONG item. The first select list item is at position 1.
length	INTEGER	Length in bytes of this segment.
offset	INTEGER	Byte offset within the data at which the piece starts. The piece will be *length* bytes long. A zero *offset* indicates the first piece.
value	VARCHAR2	Output variable to receive this piece.
value_length	INTEGER	Actual returned length of the piece. When *value_length* < *length*, the total column value has been retrieved.

It is most efficient to start at the beginning of the LONG value and fetch from there, rather than starting in the middle or the end. Each call to COLUMN_VALUE_ LONG will return a piece of the LONG value, starting at *offset*, that is *length* bytes long. The piece is returned in *value*, and the length of the piece in *value_length*. If *value_length* is less than *length*, the end of the data has been reached.

Additional Error Functions

These functions can be used for additional error reporting and management of DBMS_SQL cursors. Some of the calls are only valid in certain places, and these are noted in the descriptions.

LAST_ERROR_POSITION   This function returns the byte offset within the SQL statement where an error occurred. This is most useful for parse errors such as "ORA-911: invalid character." The function is defined with

    FUNCTION LAST_ERROR_POSITION RETURN INTEGER;

This function should be called only after a PARSE call, before any other calls to DBMS_SQL. In addition, it should only be used if the PARSE was unsuccessful.

LAST_ROW_COUNT   This function returns the cumulative count of the number of rows fetched so far from a cursor, similar to the %ROWCOUNT cursor attribute. It is defined with

    FUNCTION LAST_ROW_COUNT RETURN INTEGER;

It should be called after FETCH_ROWS or EXECUTE_AND_FETCH. If LAST_ROW_COUNT is called after EXECUTE, but before the first FETCH_ROWS, it will always return zero, since no rows have been retrieved yet.

LAST_ROW_ID   This function returns the rowid of the last row processed. It is defined with

    FUNCTION LAST_ROW_ID RETURN ROWID;

It should be called after FETCH_ROWS or EXECUTE_AND_FETCH. The value is not defined after the EXECUTE of a query, since no rows have been retrieved yet. It is also not defined after the EXECUTE of a DML statement, since a DML statement can process many rows.
    In the case of an array fetch, LAST_ROW_ID will return the rowid of the final row retrieved.

LAST_SQL_FUNCTION_CODE   This function returns the function code for the SQL statement currently being executed. The function codes are subject to change between releases. A list of function codes for your version can be found in the *Programmer's Guide to the Oracle Call Interfaces*. The syntax is

    FUNCTION LAST_SQL_FUNCTION_CODE RETURN INTEGER;

This function can be called immediately after the EXECUTE call. If used at another time, the return value is undefined.

IS_OPEN   This boolean function returns TRUE if the cursor identified by *c* is already open and FALSE if not. It is defined with

FUNCTION IS_OPEN(*c* IN INTEGER) RETURN BOOLEAN;

We can use this function in our error handling to make it more robust:

```
DECLARE
   v_CursorID INTEGER;
   ...
BEGIN
   ...
EXCEPTION
   WHEN OTHERS THEN
      IF DBMS_SQL.IS_OPEN(v_CursorID) THEN
         DBMS_SQL.CLOSE_CURSOR(v_CursorID);
      END IF;
      RAISE;
END;
```

Using Native Dynamic SQL

Oracle **8i**
and higher

This section discusses in detail the steps to process different types of statements with native dynamic SQL. Unlike DBMS_SQL, there are only two different execution models—one for non-query statements (including DML, DDL, ALTER SESSION, transaction control, and anonymous PL/SQL blocks), and one for queries. Non-queries (and queries that return a single row) use the EXECUTE IMMEDIATE statement, while queries generally use the OPEN FOR statement.

Executing Non-query Statements and PL/SQL Blocks

The EXECUTE IMMEDIATE statement will parse and immediately execute a dynamic SQL statement or anonymous block. It is defined as follows:

EXECUTE IMMEDIATE *sql_string*
    [INTO *define_list*]
    [USING *bind_list*];

where *sql_string* contains the SQL to execute. The string can be either a PL/SQL VARCHAR2 variable or a literal. The INTO clause is used to execute single-row queries, and is discussed in "Executing Queries," later in this chapter. The USING clause is used to pass bind variables to, and receive results from, the statement. EXECUTE IMMEDIATE takes the place of the DBMS_SQL routines OPEN_CURSOR, PARSE, BIND_VARIABLE, EXECUTE, VARIABLE_VALUE, and CLOSE_CURSOR.

Statements Without Bind Variables

For DDL statements, anonymous PL/SQL blocks, ALTER SESSION statements, and DML statements that do not have bind variables, you simply put the SQL statement into a string and execute it with EXECUTE IMMEDIATE. At this point, the statement will be parsed and executed. The following block illustrates several EXECUTE IMMEDIATE statements.

```
-- Available online as execImmediate.sql
SQL> DECLARE
  2    v_SQLString   VARCHAR2(200);
  3    v_PLSQLBlock  VARCHAR2(200);
  4  BEGIN
  5    -- First create a temporary table, using a literal.  Note that
  6    -- there is no trailing semicolon in the string.
  7    EXECUTE IMMEDIATE
  8      'CREATE TABLE execute_table (col1 VARCHAR(10))';
  9
  9    -- Insert some rows using a string.  Again, there is no
 10    -- trailing semicolon inside the string.
 11    FOR v_Counter IN 1..10 LOOP
 12      v_SQLString :=
 13        'INSERT INTO execute_table
 14            VALUES (''Row ' || v_Counter || ''')';
 15      EXECUTE IMMEDIATE v_SQLString;
 16    END LOOP;
 17
 17    -- Print out the contents of the table using an anonymous
 18    -- PL/SQL block.  Here we put the entire block into a single
 19    -- string (including the semicolon).
 20    v_PLSQLBLock :=
 21      'BEGIN
 22        FOR v_Rec IN (SELECT * FROM execute_table) LOOP
 23          DBMS_OUTPUT.PUT_LINE(v_Rec.col1);
 24        END LOOP;
 25      END;';
 26
 26    -- And now we execute the anonymous block.
 27    EXECUTE IMMEDIATE v_PLSQLBlock;
 28
 28    -- Finally, drop the table.
 29    EXECUTE IMMEDIATE 'DROP TABLE execute_table';
 30  END;
 31  /
```

```
Row 1
Row 2
Row 3
Row 4
Row 5
Row 6
Row 7
Row 8
Row 9
Row 10
PL/SQL procedure successfully completed.
```

As the previous example illustrates, the rules for the SQL string used in EXECUTE IMMEDIATE are the same as for DBMS_SQL.PARSE. Namely, if the string is a SQL statement, it should not have the trailing semicolon; and if it is an anonymous PL/SQL block, it should include the trailing semicolon.

Statements with Bind Variables

DML statements that have placeholders are executed with the USING clause. The *bind_list* in the clause specifies the list of PL/SQL variables that will be bound to the placeholders (in the same sense as DBMS_SQL.BIND_VARIABLE), using this syntax:

> EXECUTE IMMEDIATE *sql_statement*
> USING [IN | OUT | IN OUT] *bind1,*
>   [IN | OUT | IN OUT] *bind2,*
>
>   ...
>   [IN | OUT | IN OUT] *bindn;*

Each of *bind1...bindn* should correspond with a placeholder in *sql_statement*. The following example illustrates some examples of the USING clause.

```
-- Available online as execBind.sql
DECLARE
  v_SQLString  VARCHAR2(1000);
  v_PLSQLBlock VARCHAR2(1000);

  CURSOR c_EconMajor IS
    SELECT *
      FROM students
      WHERE major = 'Economics';
BEGIN
  -- Insert ECN 103 into classes, using a string for the SQL
  -- statement.
  v_SQLString :=
    'INSERT INTO CLASSES (department, course, description,
                          max_students, current_students,
```

```
                               num_credits)
           VALUES (:dep, :course, :descr, :max_s, :cur_s, :num_c)';

  -- Execute the INSERT, using literal values.
  EXECUTE IMMEDIATE v_SQLString USING
    'ECN', 103, 'Economics 103', 10, 0, 3;

  -- Register all of the Economics majors for the new class.
  FOR v_StudentRec IN c_EconMajor LOOP
    -- Here we have a literal SQL statement, but PL/SQL variables
    -- in the USING clause.
    EXECUTE IMMEDIATE
        'INSERT INTO registered_students
           (student_ID, department, course, grade)
         VALUES (:id, :dep, :course, NULL)'
      USING v_StudentRec.ID, 'ECN', 103;

    -- Update the number of students for the class, using an
    -- anonymous PL/SQL block.
    v_PLSQLBlock :=
      'BEGIN
         UPDATE classes SET current_students = current_students + 1
         WHERE department = :d and course = :c;
       END;';

    EXECUTE IMMEDIATE v_PLSQLBlock USING 'ECN', 103;
  END LOOP;
END;
```

There are a number of things to note about the proper use of the USING clause:

- Every placeholder in the SQL string must have a corresponding bind variable in the USING clause. They are bound by position, not by name. (This isn't entirely true for anonymous PL/SQL blocks—see "Duplicate Placeholders," later in this section, for details).

- Like DBMS_SQL, the names of the placeholders themselves are not significant. They can even match the names of their corresponding columns, as **:course** does in the previous example. However, you cannot use a reserved word for a placeholder.

- Numeric or string literals or PL/SQL variables can be used in the USING clause. However, the boolean literals TRUE and FALSE are not allowed. Likewise, the NULL literal is also illegal (see "Passing NULL Bind Variables," later in this section, for a workaround).

■ Bind variables can be of any SQL datatype, including collections, LOBs, and object type instances. PL/SQL specific types such as index-by tables are not allowed, however.

■ Bulk binds are not available with native dynamic SQL. See Chapter 11 for more information about bulk binds.

NOTE
There is no separate PARSE step, as there is for DBMS_SQL. This means that if you execute a statement repeatedly (such as the INSERT and anonymous block in the previous example), it will be sent to the SQL engine for parse each time. Parses after the first one, however, will be soft parses, since the statement will already be in the shared pool.

BIND VARIABLE MODES   Similar to the formal parameters to a subprogram, bind variables in the USING clause can be either IN, IN OUT, or OUT (see Chapter 4 for more information about parameter modes and their meanings). If the mode is not specified (as in the example in the previous section), then it defaults to IN. You can use the OUT mode for the RETURNING clause of an UPDATE or DELETE statement, for example. IN or IN OUT variables can also be used in a dynamic call to a stored procedure or anonymous PL/SQL block that has output parameters. The following example illustrates some different uses of bind variable modes.

```
-- Available online as bindMode.sql
CREATE OR REPLACE PROCEDURE PrintStudents
  (v_NumStudents IN OUT NUMBER) AS
  -- Prints out the names of up to v_NumStudents students.  Upon
  -- return, v_NumStudents will contain the number printed.

  v_LocalCount NUMBER := 0;
  v_StudentName VARCHAR2(100);
  CURSOR c_StudentNames IS
    SELECT first_name || ' ' || last_name
      FROM students
      ORDER BY ID;
BEGIN
  OPEN c_StudentNames;
  FOR v_Count IN 1..v_NumStudents LOOP
    FETCH c_StudentNames INTO v_StudentName;
    IF c_StudentNames%NOTFOUND THEN
```

```
      EXIT;
    END IF;

    -- Found a student.  Output it, and increment v_LocalCount.
    DBMS_OUTPUT.PUT_LINE(v_Studentname);
    v_LocalCount := v_LocalCount + 1;
  END LOOP;

  CLOSE c_StudentNames;
  v_NumStudents := v_LocalCount;
END PrintStudents;

DECLARE
  v_PLSQLBlock VARCHAR2(1000);

  v_Building rooms.building%TYPE;
  v_RoomNum  rooms.room_number%TYPE;
  v_RoomID   rooms.room_ID%TYPE := 20006;
  v_NumStudents NUMBER;
BEGIN
  -- Delete room 20006 dynamically, and print out the building and
  -- room number afterward.  Note that v_Building and v_RoomNum are
  -- OUT bind variables, but v_RoomID is the default (IN).
  EXECUTE IMMEDIATE
    'DELETE FROM rooms WHERE room_id = :ID
       RETURNING building, room_number INTO :building, :room_num'
    USING v_RoomID, OUT v_Building, OUT v_RoomNum;

  DBMS_OUTPUT.PUT_LINE('Deleted Room ' || v_RoomNum || ' in ' ||
                       v_Building);

  -- Call NumStudents with some different values.  Here v_NumStudents
  -- is IN OUT, to match the formal parameter of PrintStudents.
  v_PLSQLBlock := 'BEGIN PrintStudents(:num); END;';

  v_NumStudents := 4;
  DBMS_OUTPUT.PUT_LINE('Calling PrintStudents with 4:');
  EXECUTE IMMEDIATE v_PLSQLBlock USING IN OUT v_NumStudents;
  DBMS_OUTPUT.PUT_LINE('Returned value is ' || v_NumStudents);

  v_NumStudents := 20;
  DBMS_OUTPUT.PUT_LINE('Calling PrintStudents with 20:');
  EXECUTE IMMEDIATE v_PLSQLBlock USING IN OUT v_NumStudents;
  DBMS_OUTPUT.PUT_LINE('Returned value is ' || v_NumStudents);
END;
```

The output from the previous example in SQL*Plus is

```
Deleted Room 200 in Music Building
Calling PrintStudents with 4:
  Scott Smith
  Margaret Mason
  Joanne Junebug
  Manish Murgatroid
Returned value is 4
Calling PrintStudents with 20:
  Scott Smith
  Margaret Mason
  Joanne Junebug
  Manish Murgatroid
  Patrick Poll
  Timothy Taller
  Barbara Blues
  David Dinsmore
  Ester Elegant
  Rose Riznit
  Rita Razmataz
  Shay Shariatpanahy
Returned value is 12
```

PASSING NULL BIND VALUES   It is illegal to use the literal NULL directly in a USING clause. This can easily be worked around, however, by declaring a local variable instead. For example, if we execute the following block,

```
-- Available online as part of execNULL.sql
DECLARE
  v_SQLString VARCHAR2(1000);
BEGIN
  v_SQLString :=
    'INSERT INTO temp_table (num_col, char_col) VALUES
      (:n, :c)';

  EXECUTE IMMEDIATE v_SQLString USING 1, NULL;
END;
```

we will receive the error "PLS-00457: in USING clause, expressions have to be of SQL types."

The workaround is to declare a local variable, and either assign NULL to it, or use the default value. The following block, for example, will successfully insert into **temp_table**:

```
-- Available online as part of execNULL.sql
DECLARE
  v_SQLString VARCHAR2(1000);
  v_NullVar VARCHAR2(10);
BEGIN
  v_SQLString :=
    'INSERT INTO temp_table (num_col, char_col) VALUES
      (:n, :c)';

  EXECUTE IMMEDIATE v_SQLString USING 1, v_NulLVar;
END;
```

DUPLICATE PLACEHOLDERS   For statements that are not anonymous PL/SQL blocks, binds are done by position, as we have seen. For example, suppose we create the following table:

```
-- Available online as part of dupHolders.sql
CREATE TABLE duplicates (
  f1 NUMBER,
  f2 NUMBER,
  f3 NUMBER,
  f4 NUMBER);
```

Any EXECUTE IMMEDIATE statement with duplicate placeholders should also duplicate the corresponding variables in the USING clause, as illustrated by this example:

```
-- Available online as part of dupHolders.sql
SQL> DECLARE
  2    v_InsertStmt VARCHAR2(100);
  3    v_f1 NUMBER := 1;
  4    v_f2 NUMBER := 2;
  5    v_f3 NUMBER := 3;
  6  BEGIN
  7    v_InsertStmt :=
  8      'INSERT INTO duplicates VALUES (:a, :b, :c, :a)';
  9
  9    EXECUTE IMMEDIATE v_InsertStmt
 10      USING v_f1, v_f2, v_f3, v_f1;
 11  END;
 12  /
PL/SQL procedure successfully completed.

SQL> SELECT *
  2    FROM duplicates;

        F1        F2        F3        F4
--------- --------- --------- ---------
         1         2         3         1
```

However, only unique placeholders in an anonymous PL/SQL block are bound by position. Any duplicate placeholder in an anonymous block will be bound with a single variable in the USING clause, as illustrated by the following:

```
-- Available online as part of dupHolders.sql
SQL> DECLARE
  2     v_InsertStmt VARCHAR2(100);
  3     v_f1 NUMBER := 4;
  4     v_f2 NUMBER := 5;
  5     v_f3 NUMBER := 6;
  6  BEGIN
  7     v_InsertStmt :=
  8       'BEGIN ' ||
  9       '  INSERT INTO duplicates VALUES (:a, :b, :c, :a); ' ||
 10       'END;';
 11
 11     EXECUTE IMMEDIATE v_InsertStmt
 12       USING v_f1, v_f2, v_f3;
 13  END;
 14  /
PL/SQL procedure successfully completed.

SQL> SELECT *
  2    FROM duplicates;

    F1        F2        F3        F4
--------- --------- --------- ---------
     1         2         3         1
     4         5         6         4
```

Executing Queries

To process a query using native dynamic SQL, you use the OPEN FOR statement to associate a cursor variable with a SQL string. A *cursor variable* is a reference type, and can be opened for different queries. A static cursor, on the other hand, can be opened for only one query, which is part of the declaration. The syntax for OPEN FOR is

    OPEN *cursor_variable* FOR *sql_string*l

where *sql_string* is the query for which *cursor_variable* is to be opened.
    Cursor variables are declared by first defining the type, and then declaring the variable of that type. They were first introduced in Oracle7 Release 7.2, where only strongly typed cursor variables were allowed. A *strongly typed* cursor variable can be opened for only one return type, as the following example illustrates.

```
-- Available online as cursorVariables.sql
SQL> DECLARE
```

```
 2    -- This is a strongly typed ref cursor type.  It can be
 3    -- opened only for a query that returns rooms%ROWTYPE.
 4    TYPE t_RoomsCur IS REF CURSOR RETURN rooms%ROWTYPE;
 5
 5    -- Now that the type is declared, we can declare a cursor
 6    -- variable of that type.
 7    v_RoomsCur t_RoomsCur;
 8
 8    v_Rooms rooms%ROWTYPE;
 9  BEGIN
10    -- Open v_RoomsCur for a query.
11    OPEN v_RoomsCur FOR
12      SELECT *
13        FROM rooms
14        WHERE building = 'Building 7';
15
15    -- We can now loop through and fetch the rows.
16    LOOP
17      FETCH v_RoomsCur INTO v_Rooms;
18      EXIT WHEN v_RoomsCur%NOTFOUND;
19      DBMS_OUTPUT.PUT_LINE('Fetched Room #' || v_Rooms.room_number ||
20                           ' in Building 7 from v_RoomsCur');
21    END LOOP;
22
22    CLOSE v_RoomsCur;
23
23    -- We can now open the same variable for a different query,
24    -- which also returns rooms%ROWTYPE.
25    OPEN v_RoomsCur FOR
26      SELECT *
27        FROM rooms
28        WHERE number_seats > 100;
29
29    -- And fetch again.
30    LOOP
31      FETCH v_RoomsCur INTO v_Rooms;
32      EXIT WHEN v_RoomsCur%NOTFOUND;
33      DBMS_OUTPUT.PUT_LINE('Fetched ' || v_Rooms.building || ',' ||
34                           ' Room #' || v_Rooms.room_number ||
35                           ' from v_RoomsCur');
36    END LOOP;
37
37    CLOSE v_RoomsCur;
38  END;
39  /
Fetched Room #201 in Building 7 from v_RoomsCur
Fetched Room #300 in Building 7 from v_RoomsCur
Fetched Room #310 in Building 7 from v_RoomsCur
```

```
Fetched Building 7, Room #201 from v_RoomsCur
Fetched Building 6, Room #101 from v_RoomsCur
Fetched Music Building, Room #200 from v_RoomsCur
PL/SQL procedure successfully completed.
```

A *weakly typed* cursor variable (available since Oracle7 Release 7.3), on the other hand, can be opened for any return type. The following example illustrates this.

```
-- Available online as part of cursorVariables.sql
SQL> DECLARE
  2    -- This is a weakly typed ref cursor type, which can be
  3    -- opened for any query.
  4    TYPE t_Cursor IS REF CURSOR;
  5
  5    v_Cursor t_Cursor;
  6
  6    v_Student students%ROWTYPE;
  7    v_Class classes%ROWTYPE;
  8  BEGIN
  9    -- First open v_Cursor for a query on students.
 10    OPEN v_Cursor FOR
 11      SELECT *
 12        FROM students
 13        WHERE current_credits >= 8;
 14
 14    LOOP
 15      FETCH v_Cursor INTO v_Student;
 16      EXIT WHEN v_Cursor%NOTFOUND;
 17
 17      DBMS_OUTPUT.PUT_LINE(
 18        v_Student.first_name || ' ' || v_Student.last_name ||
 19        ' has ' || v_Student.current_credits || ' credits.');
 20
 20    END LOOP;
 21
 21    CLOSE v_Cursor;
 22
 22    -- And now open it for a query on classes.
 23    OPEN v_Cursor FOR
 24      SELECT *
 25        FROM classes
 26        WHERE department = 'ECN';
 27    DBMS_OUTPUT.PUT_LINE('The Economics classes are: ');
 28    LOOP
 29      FETCH v_Cursor INTO v_Class;
 30      EXIT WHEN v_Cursor%NOTFOUND;
```

```
31
31        DBMS_OUTPUT.PUT_LINE(v_Class.description);
32      END LOOP;
33
33      CLOSE v_Cursor;
34    END;
35    /
Scott Smith has 11 credits.
Joanne Junebug has 8 credits.
Manish Murgatroid has 8 credits.
Ester Elegant has 8 credits.
Rita Razmataz has 8 credits.
The Economics classes are:
Economics 101
Economics 203
PL/SQL procedure successfully completed.
```

Cursor variables have the following properties:

- They can be passed to and from PL/SQL stored subprograms.

- Cursor attributes such as %NOTFOUND can be applied to them.

- OCI and precompiler programs can allocate a cursor variable on the client, and pass it to the server as a bind variable. The server can then return an opened cursor variable for fetching on the client.

- Cursor variables can be opened for queries with bind variables, but the entire query must be known at compile time.

For more information on cursor variables, see the Oracle documentation.

Multi-Row Queries

Native dynamic SQL works by allowing a weakly typed cursor variable to be opened for a query that is determined at runtime, and passing bind variables as needed. The same syntax is used as for static SQL, except that the OPEN FOR statement takes a string rather than a hard-coded SQL statement. This is illustrated by the following procedure, which returns an opened cursor variable using the supplied WHERE clause:

```
-- Available online as part of NativeDynamic.sql
CREATE OR REPLACE PACKAGE NativeDynamic AS
  TYPE t_RefCur IS REF CURSOR;

  -- Selects from students using the supplied WHERE clause,
  -- and returns the opened cursor variable.
```

```
    FUNCTION StudentsQuery(p_WhereClause IN VARCHAR2)
      RETURN t_RefCur;

END NativeDynamic;

CREATE OR REPLACE PACKAGE BODY NativeDynamic AS
  -- Selects from students using the supplied WHERE clause,
  -- and returns the opened cursor variable.
  FUNCTION StudentsQuery(p_WhereClause IN VARCHAR2)
    RETURN t_RefCur IS
    v_ReturnCursor t_RefCur;
    v_SQLStatement VARCHAR2(500);
  BEGIN
    -- Build the query using the supplied WHERE clause
    v_SQLStatement := 'SELECT * FROM students ' || p_WhereClause;

    -- Open the cursor variable, and return it.
    OPEN v_ReturnCursor FOR v_SQLStatement;
    RETURN v_ReturnCursor;
  END StudentsQuery;
END NativeDynamic;
```

We can call **NativeDynamic.StudentsQuery** with the following block.

```
-- Available online as part of NativeDynamic.sql
SQL> DECLARE
  2    v_Student students%ROWTYPE;
  3    v_StudentCur NativeDynamic.t_RefCur;
  4  BEGIN
  5    -- Call StudentsQuery to open the cursor for students with
  6    -- even IDs.
  7    v_StudentCur :=
  8      NativeDynamic.StudentsQuery('WHERE MOD(id, 2) = 0');
  9
  9    -- Loop through the opened cursor, and print out the results.
 10    DBMS_OUTPUT.PUT_LINE('The following students have even IDs:');
 11    LOOP
 12      FETCH v_StudentCur INTO v_Student;
 13      EXIT WHEN v_StudentCur%NOTFOUND;
 14      DBMS_OUTPUT.PUT_LINE('  ' || v_Student.id || ': ' ||
 15                            v_Student.first_name || ' ' ||
 16                            v_Student.last_name);
 17    END LOOP;
 18    CLOSE v_StudentCur;
 19  END;
 20  /
The following students have even IDs:
```

```
10000: Scott Smith
10002: Joanne Junebug
10004: Patrick Poll
10006: Barbara Blues
10008: Ester Elegant
10010: Rita Razmataz
PL/SQL procedure successfully completed.
```

The OPEN FOR statement has the following guidelines when used with native dynamic SQL:

- The query in the SQL string has the same restrictions as the string used in DBMS_SQL.PARSE, namely, it should not have a trailing semicolon or an INTO clause.

- The cursor variable should be weakly typed. Attempting to open a strongly typed cursor variable for a dynamic query will raise the Oracle error "PLS-455: cursor cannot be used in dynamic SQL OPEN statement."

QUERIES WITH BIND VARIABLES   Queries with bind variables are executed with the USING clause of the OPEN FOR statement, defined with

> OPEN *cursor_variable* FOR *sql_string*
>   USING *bind__list*;

where *bind_list* is the same as for the EXECUTE IMMEDIATE statement, except that all binds must be IN. The unique variables in *bind_list* will be bound to placeholders in *sql_string* by position, just like EXECUTE IMMEDIATE. This is illustrated by the following.

```
-- Available online as part of NativeDynamic.sql
CREATE OR REPLACE PACKAGE NativeDynamic AS
  TYPE t_RefCur IS REF CURSOR;

  . . .

  -- Selects from students based on the supplied major,
  -- and returns the opened cursor variable.
  FUNCTION StudentsQuery2(p_Major IN VARCHAR2)
    RETURN t_RefCur;
END NativeDynamic;

CREATE OR REPLACE PACKAGE BODY NativeDynamic AS
  . . .
```

```
-- Selects from students based on the supplied major,
-- and returns the opened cursor variable.
FUNCTION StudentsQuery2(p_Major IN VARCHAR2)
  RETURN t_RefCur IS
  v_ReturnCursor t_RefCur;
  v_SQLStatement VARCHAR2(500);
BEGIN
  v_SQLStatement := 'SELECT * FROM students WHERE major = :m';

  -- Open the cursor variable, and return it.
  OPEN v_ReturnCursor FOR v_SQLStatement USING p_Major;
  RETURN v_ReturnCursor;
END StudentsQuery2;
END NativeDynamic;
```

The output from **NativeDynamic.StudentsQuery2** is shown by the following:

```
-- Available online as part of NativeDynamic.sql
SQL> DECLARE
  2    v_Student students%ROWTYPE;
  3    v_StudentCur NativeDynamic.t_RefCur;
  4  BEGIN
  5    -- Call StudentsQuery2 to open the cursor for music majors.
  6    v_StudentCur :=
  7      NativeDynamic.StudentsQuery2('Music');
  7
  8    -- Loop through the opened cursor, and print out the results.
  9    DBMS_OUTPUT.PUT_LINE('The following students are music majors:');
 10    LOOP
 11      FETCH v_StudentCur INTO v_Student;
 12      EXIT WHEN v_StudentCur%NOTFOUND;
 13      DBMS_OUTPUT.PUT_LINE('  ' || v_Student.id || ': ' ||
 14                            v_Student.first_name || ' ' ||
 15                            v_Student.last_name);
 16    END LOOP;
 17    CLOSE v_StudentCur;
 18  END;
 19  /
The following students are music majors:
  10007: David Dinsmore
  10009: Rose Riznit
PL/SQL procedure successfully completed.
```

Once the cursor variable is opened, it is processed the same whether or not it contained bind variables.

Single-Row Queries

If you know that a query will return only one row, you can execute it using the
EXECUTE IMMEDIATE statement rather than OPEN FOR. This is done by including
an INTO clause, as follows:

> EXECUTE IMMEDIATE *sql_string*
> INTO *define_list*
> [USING *bind_list*];

where *define_list* is either a comma-separated list of output variables, or a PL/SQL
record whose fields match the select list of the query. The query must return exactly
one row, or an error is raised. The following block illustrates this use of EXECUTE
IMMEDIATE.

```
-- Available online as part of NativeDynamic.sql
SQL> DECLARE
  2     v_SQLQuery VARCHAR2(200);
  3     v_Class classes%ROWTYPE;
  4     v_Description classes.description%TYPE;
  5  BEGIN
  6     -- First select into a single variable.
  7     v_SQLQuery :=
  8       'SELECT description ' ||
  9       '  FROM classes ' ||
 10       '  WHERE department = ''ECN''' ||
 11       '  AND course = 203';
 12
 12     EXECUTE IMMEDIATE v_SQLQuery
 13       INTO v_Description;
 14
 14     DBMS_OUTPUT.PUT_LINE('Fetched ' || v_Description);
 15
 15     -- Now select into a record, using a bind variable.
 16     v_SQLQuery :=
 17       'SELECT * ' ||
 18       '  FROM classes ' ||
 19       '  WHERE description = :description';
 20     EXECUTE IMMEDIATE v_SQLQuery
 21       INTO v_Class
 22       USING v_Description;
 23
 23     DBMS_OUTPUT.PUT_LINE(
 24       'Fetched ' || v_Class.department || ' ' || v_Class.course);
 25
 25     -- Fetch more than one row, which will raise ORA-1422.
```

```
26    v_SQLQuery := 'SELECT * FROM classes';
27    EXECUTE IMMEDIATE v_SQLQuery
28      INTO v_Class;
29  END;
30  /
Fetched Economics 203
Fetched ECN 203
DECLARE
*
ERROR at line 1:
ORA-01422: exact fetch returns more than requested number of rows
ORA-06512: at line 27
```

This example illustrates the following points:

■ The query string itself does not contain the INTO clause—it is part of the EXECUTE IMMEDIATE statement itself.

■ If the query returns more than one row, the ORA-1422 error is raised.

■ Any binds in the statement are IN only.

Common Issues

There are several issues common to both DBMS_SQL and native dynamic SQL. These include privileges and roles, guidelines for DDL statements (including bind variables) and the ALTER SESSION command, and cursor control. This section will conclude with a comparison between DBMS_SQL and native dynamic SQL.

Privileges and Roles with Dynamic SQL

Several issues arise with privileges when using DBMS_SQL and native dynamic SQL. These include the privilege to execute the DBMS_SQL package itself, and the way roles interact with DBMS_SQL and native dynamic SQL.

Privileges Required for DBMS_SQL

In order to use DBMS_SQL, you need the EXECUTE privilege on the DBMS_SQL package itself. Like the other DBMS packages, DBMS_SQL is owned by SYS. The install script that creates the package typically grants EXECUTE on the package to PUBLIC, so all users will have access to the package. You may want to revoke this privilege from PUBLIC and grant it only to select users.

Roles and Dynamic SQL

In addition to execute privilege on DBMS_SQL, you also need the necessary privileges to perform the operation that you are trying to perform using dynamic

SQL. For example, consider the following anonymous block, which uses both dynamic methods to create two tables:

```
-- Available online as part of dynamicRole.sql
SQL> DECLARE
  2    v_CreateString1 VARCHAR2(100) :=
  3      'CREATE TABLE dbms_sql_table (f1 NUMBER)';
  4    v_CreateString2 VARCHAR2(100) :=
  5      'CREATE TABLE native_table (f1 NUMBER)';
  6    v_Dummy INTEGER;
  7    v_CursorID INTEGER;
  8  BEGIN
  9    v_CursorID := DBMS_SQL.OPEN_CURSOR;
 10    DBMS_SQL.PARSE(v_CursorID, v_CreateString1, DBMS_SQL.NATIVE);
 11    DBMS_SQL.CLOSE_CURSOR(v_CursorID);
 12
 12    EXECUTE IMMEDIATE v_CreateString2;
 13  END;
 14  /
PL/SQL procedure successfully completed.

SQL> desc dbms_sql_table
 Name                             Null?    Type
 ------------------------------- -------- ----
 F1                                        NUMBER

SQL> desc native_table
 Name                             Null?    Type
 ------------------------------- -------- ----
 F1                                        NUMBER
```

Creating a table requires the CREATE TABLE system privilege, which is typically GRANTed to the user through the RESOURCE role. However, as we discuss in Chapter 5, all roles are disabled inside stored procedures (except when using invoker's rights in Oracle8*i*). Suppose, therefore, that we try to create the table using a stored procedure rather than an anonymous block:

```
-- Available online as part of dynamicRole.sql
CREATE OR REPLACE PROCEDURE CreateDynamicTables(
  p_Method IN VARCHAR2) AS
  v_CreateString1 VARCHAR2(100) :=
    'CREATE TABLE dbms_sql_table (f1 NUMBER)';
  v_CreateString2 VARCHAR2(100) :=
    'CREATE TABLE native_table (f1 NUMBER)';
  v_Dummy INTEGER;
  v_CursorID INTEGER;
BEGIN
  IF p_Method = 'DBMS_SQL' THEN
    v_CursorID := DBMS_SQL.OPEN_CURSOR;
```

```
      DBMS_SQL.PARSE(v_CursorID, v_CreateString1, DBMS_SQL.NATIVE);
      DBMS_SQL.CLOSE_CURSOR(v_CursorID);
   ELSE
      EXECUTE IMMEDIATE v_CreateString2;
   END IF;
END CreateDynamicTables;
```

If we then call **CreateDynamicTables** from an account that has been GRANTed the RESOURCE role, but not CREATE TABLE directly, we will receive an ORA-1031 error:

```
SQL> exec CreateDynamicTables('DBMS_SQL')
begin CreateDynamicTables('DBMS_SQL'); end;
*
ERROR at line 1:
ORA-01031: insufficient privileges
ORA-06512: at "SYS.DBMS_SYS_SQL", line 487
ORA-06512: at "SYS.DBMS_SQL", line 32
ORA-06512: at "EXAMPLE.CREATEDYNAMICTABLES", line 12
ORA-06512: at line 1

SQL> exec CreateDynamicTables('native')
begin CreateDynamicTables('native'); end;
*
ERROR at line 1:
ORA-01031: insufficient privileges
ORA-06512: at "EXAMPLE.CREATEDYNAMICTABLES", line 15
ORA-06512: at line 1
```

Granting CREATE TABLE directly to the owner of **CreateDynamicTables** will allow the call to succeed.

Now suppose that **CreateDynamicTables** is owned by **UserA**, and **UserA** GRANTs execute privilege on the procedure to **UserB**. This situation is illustrated by Figure 8-2. In this case, does **UserB** need the CREATE TABLE system privilege? No, because **CreateDynamicTables** is owned by **UserA**, and thus executes under the privilege set of **UserA**. When **UserB** calls **UserA.CreateDynamicTables**, the **dbms_sql_table** and **native_table** tables will be created under **UserA**'s schema.

TIP

Whenever you receive the ORA-1031 error when using DBMS_SQL, check the SQL statement or PL/SQL block being executed by DBMS_SQL. Make sure that the user executing this (if an anonymous block), or the owner of the stored procedure (if a stored procedure or package) has the appropriate system and object privileges granted directly, not via a role. This is most likely the cause of the problem.

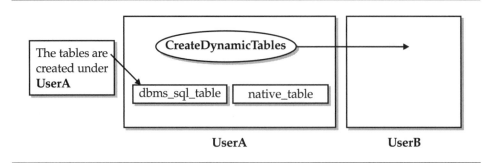

FIGURE 8-2. *CreateDynamicTables owned by UserA*

Invoker's Rights

Oracle **8 i**
and higher

Typically, procedures run under the privilege set of their owners (this is known as *definer's rights*). DBMS_SQL is owned by SYS, which would mean that any commands executed using DBMS_SQL would be run as SYS. Needless to say, this would be a serious security breach. To prevent this, the procedures and functions in DBMS_SQL run under the privilege set of their caller (known as *invoker's rights*), not SYS.

Consider again the situation in Figure 8-2. Here, **CreateDynamicTables** is owned by **UserA** and is a definer's rights procedure. Thus, the two tables will be created in **UserA**'s schema, even if **UserB** calls **CreateDynamicTables**.

Oracle8*i* allows you to create your own procedures that run under the privilege set of their caller, using invoker's rights. This is done by including the AUTHID CURRENT_USER clause in the procedure header. If **CreateDynamicTables** were created as an invoker's rights procedure, and **UserB** were to call it, then the tables would be created under **UserB**'s schema instead of **UserA**'s. This is illustrated by Figure 8-3. For more information on invoker's rights, see Chapter 5.

Invoker's Rights Procedures and Roles

As we saw in the last section, you must have the necessary privileges GRANTed directly and not through a role. This is not the case, however, for invoker's rights routines. This is illustrated by the following, which succeeds even if CREATE TABLE has been GRANTed through a role.

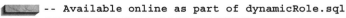 `-- Available online as part of dynamicRole.sql`

```
SQL> CREATE OR REPLACE PROCEDURE CreateDynamicTables(
  2    p_Method IN VARCHAR2)
  3    AUTHID CURRENT_USER AS
  4    v_CreateString1 VARCHAR2(100) :=
```

```
 5       'CREATE TABLE dbms_sql_table (f1 NUMBER)';
 6     v_CreateString2 VARCHAR2(100) :=
 7       'CREATE TABLE native_table (f1 NUMBER)';
 8     v_Dummy INTEGER;
 9     v_CursorID INTEGER;
10   BEGIN
11     IF p_Method = 'DBMS_SQL' THEN
12       v_CursorID := DBMS_SQL.OPEN_CURSOR;
13       DBMS_SQL.PARSE(v_CursorID, v_CreateString1, DBMS_SQL.NATIVE);
14       DBMS_SQL.CLOSE_CURSOR(v_CursorID);
15     ELSE
16       EXECUTE IMMEDIATE v_CreateString2;
17     END IF;
18   END CreateDynamicTables;
19   /
Procedure created.

SQL> exec CreateDynamicTables('DBMS_SQL')
PL/SQL procedure successfully completed.

SQL> exec CreateDynamicTables('native')
PL/SQL procedure successfully completed.

SQL> desc dbms_sql_table
 Name                            Null?    Type
 ------------------------------- -------- ----
 F1                                       NUMBER

SQL> desc native_table
 Name                            Null?    Type
 ------------------------------- -------- ----
 F1                                       NUMBER
```

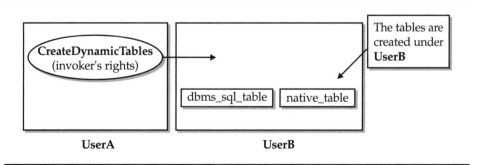

FIGURE 8-3. *Invoker's rights in **CreateDynamicTables***

DDL and Dynamic SQL

There are two issues with dynamic SQL and DDL operations—bind variables and the possibility of deadlock.

DDL and Bind Variables

As we have seen, bind variables are not allowed in DDL statements. DDL statements are executed during the parse phase, and thus the statement is not scanned for placeholders. This can be worked around, however, by dynamically building the SQL string to include the values of the bind variables. Suppose, for example, that we wanted to write a procedure that would allow a user to create a sequence with parameters passed in. We might do this with the following:

```
-- Available online as DynamicSequence.sql
CREATE OR REPLACE PROCEDURE DynamicSequence(
  p_SequenceName IN VARCHAR2,
  p_IncrementBy IN NUMBER := NULL,
  p_StartWith IN NUMBER := NULL,
  p_MaxValue IN NUMBER := NULL,
  p_MinValue IN NUMBER := NULL,
  p_Cycle IN VARCHAR2 := NULL,
  p_Cache IN NUMBER := NULL) AS

  v_CreateStmt VARCHAR2(200);
  v_CursorID INTEGER;
BEGIN
  -- Since we can't use bind variables, build the SQL statement
  -- dynamically based on the input values.
  v_CreateStmt := 'CREATE SEQUENCE ' || p_SequenceName;

  IF p_IncrementBy IS NOT NULL THEN
    v_CreateStmt :=
      v_CreateStmt || ' INCREMENT BY ' || p_IncrementBy;
  END IF;

  IF p_StartWith IS NOT NULL THEN
    v_CreateStmt :=
      v_CreateStmt || ' START WITH ' || p_StartWith;
  END IF;

  IF p_MaxValue IS NOT NULL THEN
    v_CreateStmt :=
      v_CreateStmt || ' MAXVALUE ' || p_MaxValue;
  END IF;
```

```
  IF p_MinValue IS NOT NULL THEN
    v_CreateStmt :=
      v_CreateStmt || ' MINVALUE ' || p_MinValue;
  END IF;

  IF p_Cycle IS NOT NULL THEN
    v_CreateStmt :=
      v_CreateStmt || ' ' || p_Cycle || ' ';
  END IF;

  IF p_Cache IS NOT NULL THEN
    v_CreateStmt :=
      v_CreateStmt || ' CACHE ' || p_Cache;
  END IF;

  -- And now execute it.
  v_CursorID := DBMS_SQL.OPEN_CURSOR;
  DBMS_SQL.PARSE(v_CursorID, v_CreateStmt, DBMS_SQL.NATIVE);
END DynamicSequence;
```

The owner of **DynamicSequence** will need the CREATE SEQUENCE system privilege GRANTed directly as well.

DDL Operations and Deadlock

If you are not careful, using dynamic SQL to execute DDL statements can cause a deadlock situation. For example, a call to a packaged procedure places a lock on the procedure until the call completes. If you try to dynamically drop the package while another user is executing a procedure in that package, a deadlock situation results and the execute of the DROP statement will hang. It will time out after five minutes.

ALTER SESSION and Dynamic SQL

As we have seen, ALTER SESSION statements cannot be executed directly from PL/SQL. However, you can use dynamic SQL to issue them. For example, the following block will only echo the second SQL statement to the trace file:

```
-- Available online as alterSession.sql
DECLARE
  v_RoomRec rooms%ROWTYPE;
  v_StudentRec students%ROWTYPE;
  v_ClassesRec classes%ROWTYPE;
BEGIN
  -- By default, sql_trace is FALSE, so this statement will not
  -- be traced.
  SELECT *
```

```
     INTO v_RoomRec
     FROM rooms
     WHERE room_ID = 20001;

  -- Use dynamic SQL to turn sql_trace on.
  EXECUTE IMMEDIATE 'ALTER SESSION SET SQL_TRACE = TRUE';

  -- This statement will be traced.
  SELECT *
     INTO v_StudentRec
     FROM students
     WHERE ID = 10007;

  -- And now turn it off.
  EXECUTE IMMEDIATE 'ALTER SESSION SET SQL_TRACE = FALSE';

  SELECT *
     INTO v_ClassesRec
     FROM classes
     WHERE department = 'NUT' and course = 307;
END;
```

Certain ALTER SESSION commands, like ALTER SESSION SET SQL_TRACE, do not affect the state of the PL/SQL engine. These are safe to issue from PL/SQL. However, other types of ALTER SESSION commands do affect the PL/SQL engine, and can cause unintended effects. Also, certain types of ALTER SESSION statements (such as NLS parameters) generally do not take effect until after the PL/SQL call completes. The following ALTER SESSION statements can cause these types of effects:

■ ALTER SESSION SET PLSQL_V2_COMPATIBILITY

■ ALTER SESSION SET EVENT

■ ALTER SESSION SET <nls parameter>

Comparison Between DBMS_SQL and Native Dynamic SQL

As we have seen in this chapter, both DBMS_SQL and native dynamic SQL can be used for dynamic SQL processing. Each has certain advantages and disadvantages. The main differences between these methods are described briefly in Table 8-2, and in more detail in the following sections.

Feature	DBMS_SQL	Native Dynamic SQL
Describing the select list	Available with Oracle8 and higher	Not available
Array processing	Available with Oracle8 and higher	Not available
Fetch longs piecewise	Available	Not available
Insert/update of longs piecewise	Not available	Not available
Parse language flag	Available	Not available
Callable from SQL	Not with RESTRICT_REFERENCES	Legal if possible
Handling of object types	Not supported	Supported
Maximum length of a SQL statement	Unlimited through the VARCHAR2S version of DBMS_SQL.PARSE, available with Oracle8 and higher	Limited to the maximum length of a VARCHAR2 variable
Information functions	Available	Not available, but cursor attributes provide some of the functionality
Performance and ease of use	Slower and more complicated	Faster and less complicated
Fetch into records	Not available	Available
Cursor control	Explicit for all statements	Implicit for non-queries, explicit through cursor variables for queries

TABLE 8-2.   *Comparison Between Dynamic Methods*

There are other development tools or interfaces available for Oracle that allow dynamic SQL as well—the precompilers (Pro*C/C++ and Pro*COBOL), OCI, and JDBC. For more information on these tools, see the Oracle documentation.

Describing the Select List

Describing the select list of a query allows you to determine at runtime what kinds of items will be returned—their lengths and datatypes. This feature is available in DBMS_SQL (Oracle8 and higher) through the DESCRIBE_COLUMNS procedure, and is not available in native dynamic SQL. (It is also available through OCI and the precompilers.)

Even with DESCRIBE_COLUMNS, this feature is less useful in DBMS_SQL than it is for dynamic interfaces in other languages. The reason for this has to do with the fact that PL/SQL does not allow the user to dynamically allocate and deallocate memory (in the sense of C's **malloc** and **free** functions). In the precompilers or OCI, after the statement is described, the output variables are often dynamically allocated to fit the size of the expected data. A PL/SQL program would have to simulate this with PL/SQL tables or varrays.

Column information can still be determined from PL/SQL without using DESCRIBE_COLUMNS, however. The **user_tab_columns** data dictionary view contains information about the type and length of database table columns, so a PL/SQL program can query this table to determine the select list structure. This method is not helpful if the select list contains functions, however.

Array Processing

DBMS_SQL, with Oracle8 and higher, allows you to process many rows at once using the BIND_ARRAY and DEFINE_ARRAY procedures. The equivalent for Oracle8i would be bulk binds, which allow you to process many rows at once using static SQL. As of Oracle8i Release 8.1.5, however, bulk binds are not supported for native dynamic SQL, either as input binds or output defines. For more information on bulk binds, see Chapter 11.

Piecewise Operations on LONG Data

The precompilers cannot currently operate on LONG data piecewise. However, OCI can. Many of the calls in DBMS_SQL are implemented by calling the OCI equivalents, which include the **oflng** procedure. This procedure provides the ability to fetch LONG data piecewise and is implemented in DBMS_SQL with the DEFINE_COLUMN_LONG and COLUMN_COLUMN_LONG procedures. It is not available with native dynamic SQL.

Piecewise insertion and update of LONG data is more complicated in OCI and is not currently implemented in DBMS_SQL.

NOTE
Although you cannot insert or update LONG data piecewise in DBMS_SQL (or the precompilers, for that matter), you can manipulate LOB data easily with the DBMS_LOB package. See Chapters 15 and 16 on the CD-ROM included with this book for more information.

Parse Language Flag

The DBMS_SQL.PARSE procedure includes a parameter, *language_flag,* that allows you to specify the behavior of the database parse. If it is DBMS_SQL.V6, then CHAR columns will be treated as variable, rather than fixed, length. This feature is not available with native dynamic SQL. However, this is not a problem because it is designed primarily to preserve compatibility with older Oracle6 databases, and Oracle6 is no longer supported by Oracle.

Callable from SQL

DBMS_SQL.EXECUTE and DBMS_SQL.PARSE do not have the RESTRICT_REFERENCES pragma asserted for them, as they can be used to update database and/or package state. Thus, functions that use DBMS_SQL cannot be called from SQL statements in Oracle8. Oracle8*i*, however, relaxes this restriction to a runtime check. Thus, functions that meet the necessary restrictions (even if they issue dynamic SQL) can be called from SQL statements in Oracle8*i*. For example, consider the following function:

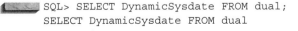

```
-- Available online as part of dynamicFromSQL.sql
CREATE OR REPLACE FUNCTION DynamicSysdate
  RETURN DATE AS

  v_SQLStatement VARCHAR2(100) := 'SELECT SYSDATE FROM dual';
  v_CursorID INTEGER;
  v_ReturnVal DATE;
  v_Dummy INTEGER;
BEGIN
  v_CursorID := DBMS_SQL.OPEN_CURSOR;
  DBMS_SQL.PARSE(v_CursorID, v_SQLStatement, DBMS_SQL.NATIVE);
  DBMS_SQL.DEFINE_COLUMN(v_CursorID, 1, v_ReturnVal);
  v_Dummy := DBMS_SQL.EXECUTE_AND_FETCH(v_CursorID);
  DBMS_SQL.COLUMN_VALUE(v_CursorID, 1, v_ReturnVal);
  DBMS_SQL.CLOSE_CURSOR(v_CursorID);
  RETURN v_ReturnVal;
EXCEPTION
  WHEN OTHERS THEN
    DBMS_SQL.CLOSE_CURSOR(v_CursorID);
    RAISE;
END DynamicSysdate;
```

DynamicSysdate simply returns the current date, which is computed by dynamically selecting it from **dual**. If we call **DynamicSysdate** while connected to an Oracle8 database, we get an ORA-6571 error:

```
SQL> SELECT DynamicSysdate FROM dual;
SELECT DynamicSysdate FROM dual
       *
```

```
ERROR at line 1:
ORA-06571: Function DYNAMICSYSDATE does not guarantee not to update database
```

The same query, however, will work in Oracle8*i*. For more information on calling PL/SQL functions from SQL, including the restrictions, see Chapter 5.

Handling of Object Types

Unlike DBMS_SQL, native dynamic SQL has direct support for object types and large objects. They can be used both as bind variables and as define columns, as the following example illustrates.

```
-- Available online as nativeObjects.sql
SQL> DECLARE
  2      v_Shape Polygon;
  3      v_SQLString VARCHAR2(100);
  4      TYPE t_CurType IS REF CURSOR;
  5      v_Cursor t_CurType;
  6      v_ShapeType shapes.shape_type%TYPE := 'triangle';
  7  BEGIN
  8      -- First select the triangles from the table using native
  9      -- dynamic SQL.
 10      v_SQLString :=
 11        'SELECT shape FROM shapes WHERE shape_type = :shape_type';
 12
 12      OPEN v_Cursor
 13        FOR v_SQLString
 14        USING v_ShapeType;
 15
 15      DBMS_OUTPUT.PUT_LINE('Selected the following shapes:');
 16      LOOP
 17        FETCH v_Cursor INTO v_Shape;
 18        EXIT WHEN v_Cursor%NOTFOUND;
 19
 19        v_Shape.Print;
 20      END LOOP;
 21
 21      CLOSE v_Cursor;
 22
 22      -- Now re-insert the last shape selected back into the
 23      -- table.
 24      v_SQLString :=
 25        'INSERT INTO shapes (key, shape_type, shape) ' ||
 26        ' VALUES (:key, :shape_type, :shape)';
 27      EXECUTE IMMEDIATE v_SQLString
 28        USING 200, 'triangle', v_Shape;
 29  END;
 30  /
```

```
Selected the following shapes:
Polygon Triangle A: Total endpoints: 3
1: (2, 2)
2: (5, 3)
3: (1, 7)
Polygon Triangle B: Total endpoints: 3
1: (0, 0)
2: (0, -10)
3: (3, 1)
Polygon Triangle C: Total endpoints: 3
1: (-2, -2)
2: (-5, -3)
3: (-1, -7)
PL/SQL procedure successfully completed.
```

NOTE
*See Chapters 12 and 13 for more information about using objects in the database, as well as the definition of the **shapes** table and **Polygon** object.*

Maximum Length of a SQL Statement

Because all SQL strings used in native dynamic SQL must be stored in VARCHAR2 variables, the maximum length of a SQL statement that can be executed using native dynamic SQL is limited to the maximum length of a VARCHAR2 variable, namely, 32,767 bytes. DBMS_SQL, on the other hand, can parse and execute arbitrarily long SQL statements, by using the overloaded PARSE call that takes a VARCHAR2S parameter.

Information Functions

DBMS_SQL provides information functions such as LAST_ROW_COUNT and LAST_ROW_ID, which provide more information about the statement currently being executed. Native dynamic SQL has no explicit functions, but you can use cursor attributes to retrieve some of the same information, as illustrated by the following table.

DBMS_SQL Function	Native Dynamic SQL Equivalent
LAST_ERROR_POSITION	None
LAST_ROW_COUNT	%ROWCOUNT
LAST_ROW_ID	None
LAST_SQL_FUNCTION_CODE	None
IS_OPEN	%ISOPEN

For non-queries, the attributes should be applied to the SQL implicit cursor.

Performance and Ease of Use

Because PL/SQL does not yet (as of Oracle8i) provide a user-accessible interface for pointer variables, all fetch operations have to be put into a local buffer and then retrieved with COLUMN_VALUE or VARIABLE_VALUE. These extra calls are not necessary with either OCI or the precompilers, since both of these other methods can pass the addresses of program variables directly to the server. When the statement is executed, the database writes directly into the program variables. No buffer is needed.

Native dynamic SQL does not have these extra calls, and thus is significantly faster.

Fetch into Records

DBMS_SQL has no means of defining PL/SQL records, so it is consequently illegal to fetch a query directly into a record. The individual fields of the record must be defined (using DBMS_SQL.DEFINE_COLUMN) separately. Native dynamic SQL, however, allows you to fetch from the cursor variable directly into a record without listing the fields.

Cursor Control

All operations with DBMS_SQL require explicit cursor control, regardless of the type of statement being executed. Native dynamic SQL, on the other hand, implicitly manages the cursor for non-query statements. Queries, because they use cursor variables, must be explicitly opened and closed.

Summary

In this chapter, we have examined the DBMS_SQL package (available with PL/SQL 2.1 and higher) and native dynamic SQL (available in Oracle8i). Both methods allow dynamic processing of SQL and PL/SQL from a PL/SQL program. Depending on the type of statement being processed (query, DDL, DML, ALTER SESSION, or PL/SQL block), different code paths are used. We also compared and contrasted the two dynamic methods, and discussed tips and techniques for using dynamic SQL in your programs.

CHAPTER

9

Intersession Communication

I n addition to reading and writing into database tables, PL/SQL provides two built-in packages for intersession communication—DBMS_PIPE and DBMS_ALERT. They can be used to send messages between sessions connected to the same database instance. As such, they provide an extremely useful facility that has many applications. In this chapter, we will examine DBMS_PIPE and DBMS_ALERT in detail and compare their behavior so you can choose the appropriate package for your needs.

Oracle **8** and higher

The Oracle8 Advanced Queuing package can also be used for intersession communication. Oracle A/Q has features similar to both DBMS_PIPE and DBMS_ALERT. It also provides a much more scaleable solution. If DBMS_PIPE and DBMS_ALERT do not meet your needs, Oracle A/Q may fit the bill. In addition, enhancements to intersession communication will be made through Advanced Queuing rather than DBMS_PIPE or DBMS_ALERT in the future (although DBMS_PIPE and DBMS_ALERT will continue to be supported). For more information on Advanced Queuing, see the Oracle documentation.

DBMS_PIPE

The DBMS_PIPE package implements database pipes. A *database pipe* is similar to a pipe in other operating systems (such as Unix), but is implemented entirely in Oracle. Thus, a database pipe is independent of operating systems and will work on any platform on which Oracle runs. Different sessions connected to the same Oracle instance can send and receive messages over a pipe. Pipes can have multiple *readers* (sessions that receive the message) and *writers* (sessions that send the message), and a given session can send or receive multiple messages. Readers and writers can be on different machines and can be using different PL/SQL execution environments. All that is required is that they connect to the same Oracle instance, and that they both have the ability to execute PL/SQL blocks.

NOTE
Database pipes are also supported in an OPS (Oracle Parallel Server) system. They are implemented as objects in the shared pool, and thus are shared among OPS instances. A reader and a writer can connect to different instances, but the message will be passed because of the shared pipe. For more information on OPS, see the Oracle documentation.

Pipes are *asynchronous*—they operate independent of transactions. Once a message is sent along a pipe, there is no way of canceling it, even if the transaction that sent it issues a ROLLBACK. Thus, they can be used to implement the functionality of autonomous transactions (transactions that can be committed or rolled back independent of the parent transaction). Autonomous transactions are found in Oracle8*i* and higher. See Chapter 11 for more information.

The DBMS_PIPE API uses a local message buffer to both send and receive messages. The writer packs a series of data items into a local message buffer, and then sends the buffer along the pipe. At the other end, the reader receives the message into its local buffer, and then unpacks the data items from it. For example, the **LogRSInserts** trigger records the inserts into **registered_students**. The changes are sent over a pipe, so the trigger is the writer in this case.

```
-- Available online as LogRSInserts.sql
CREATE OR REPLACE TRIGGER LogRSInserts
  BEFORE INSERT ON registered_students
  FOR EACH ROW
DECLARE
  v_Status INTEGER;
BEGIN

  /* Pack the description into the buffer first. */
  DBMS_PIPE.PACK_MESSAGE('I');

  /* Pack the current user and the timestamp. */
  DBMS_PIPE.PACK_MESSAGE(user);
  DBMS_PIPE.PACK_MESSAGE(sysdate);

  /* Pack the new values. */
  DBMS_PIPE.PACK_MESSAGE(:new.student_ID);
  DBMS_PIPE.PACK_MESSAGE(:new.department);
  DBMS_PIPE.PACK_MESSAGE(:new.course);
  DBMS_PIPE.PACK_MESSAGE(:new.grade);

  /* Send the message over the 'RSInserts' pipe. */
  v_Status := DBMS_PIPE.SEND_MESSAGE('RSInserts');

  /* If the send is unsuccessful, raise an error so the change
     doesn't go through. */
  IF v_Status != 0 THEN
    RAISE_APPLICATION_ERROR(-20010, 'LogRSInserts trigger ' ||
      'couldn''t send the message, status = ' || v_Status);
  END IF;

END LogRSInserts;
```

The trigger is only one component of a logging system, however. It is the writer on the **RSInserts** pipe. We still need a reader. This can be done by the following Pro*C program, which reads from the pipe and writes the changes to an operating system file.

```
/* Available online as LogRSInserts.pc */

/* C and SQL header files */
#include <stdio.h>
EXEC SQL INCLUDE sqlca;

/* Username and password to connect to the database */
char *connectString = "example/example";

/* Status variables used in the calls to DBMS_PIPE */
int    status;
char opCode[5];

/* Variables sent over the pipe - these will be logged. */
char userid[9];
char changeDate[12];
int    studentID;
char department[4];
int    course;
char grade[2];
short gradeInd;

/* File pointer to log file */
FILE *outfile;

/* Error handling function.  Print the error to the screen,
   and exit. */
void sqlerror()
{
  printf("SQL Error!\n");
  printf("%.*s\n", sqlca.sqlerrm.sqlerrml, sqlca.sqlerrm.sqlerrmc);

  EXEC SQL WHENEVER SQLERROR CONTINUE;

  EXEC SQL ROLLBACK WORK RELEASE;

  exit(1);
}

int main()
{
  /* Set up the error handling. */
  EXEC SQL WHENEVER SQLERROR DO sqlerror();

  /* Connect to the database. */
```

```
EXEC SQL CONNECT :connectString;

/* Open the log file. */
outfile = fopen("rs.log", "w");

printf("Successfully connected.  Waiting...\n");

/*
 * Main loop.  The only way we'll break out of the loop is if we
 * receive the 'STOP' message or if an error occurs.
 */
for (;;)
{
  /*
   * Check to see if there is a message on the pipe.  Since the
   * timeout is zero, this call will return immediately if there
   * is no message waiting.
   */
  EXEC SQL EXECUTE
    BEGIN
      :status := DBMS_PIPE.RECEIVE_MESSAGE('RSInserts');
    END;
  END-EXEC;

  if (status == 0)
  {
    /*
     * Successful retrieval of the message.  We now need to get
     * the first data element, to decide what to do with it.
     */
    EXEC SQL EXECUTE
      BEGIN
        DBMS_PIPE.UNPACK_MESSAGE(:opCode);
      END;
    END-EXEC;

    if (!strcmp(opCode, "STOP"))
    {
      /* Stop message received.  Break out of the loop. */
      break;
    }

    /*
     * Retrieve the rest of the message, which consists of the
     * userid, date, and new values.
     */
    EXEC SQL EXECUTE
      DECLARE
        v_ChangeDate DATE;
      BEGIN
```

```
          DBMS_PIPE.UNPACK_MESSAGE(:userid);
          DBMS_PIPE.UNPACK_MESSAGE(v_ChangeDate);
          :changeDate := TO_CHAR(v_ChangeDate, 'DD-MON-YYYY');
          DBMS_PIPE.UNPACK_MESSAGE(:studentID);
          DBMS_PIPE.UNPACK_MESSAGE(:department);
          DBMS_PIPE.UNPACK_MESSAGE(:course);
          DBMS_PIPE.UNPACK_MESSAGE(:grade:gradeInd);
        END;
    END-EXEC;

    if (gradeInd == -1)
      grade[0] = '\0';

    /* Print the data to the log file. */
    fprintf(outfile, "User: %s Changedate: %s",
            userid, changeDate);
    fprintf(outfile, " ID: %d Course: %s %d Grade: %s\n",
            studentID, department, course, grade);
    fflush(outfile);
  }
  else if (status == 1)
  {
    /*
     * The RECEIVE_MESSAGE call timed out.  This means that there
     * was no message waiting.  Sleep for 10 seconds, and then
     * loop back to wait again.
     */
    sleep(10);
    continue;
  }
  else
  {
    /*
     * The RECEIVE_MESSAGE call exited with an error.  Print it,
     * close the file, and exit.
     */
    printf("RECEIVE_MESSAGE Error!  Status = %d\n", status);
    fclose(outfile);
    EXEC SQL ROLLBACK WORK RELEASE;

    exit(1);
  }

} /* End of main loop */

/* Close the file */
fclose(outfile);

/* Disconnect from the database. */
EXEC SQL COMMIT WORK RELEASE;
}
```

NOTE
*Since the previous program does not use EXEC
SQL BEGIN DECLARE SECTION and EXEC SQL
END DECLARE SECTION, it requires Pro*C 2.0
or higher to precompile successfully. The
SQLCHECK=SEMANTICS precompiler option is
also required, since it contains embedded PL/SQL
blocks. See the online file **ch09.mk** for an example
of how to build it.*

Since the write to the pipe is asynchronous, the insert into **registered_
students** will be logged, even if the transaction rolls back. This trigger will thus
log both attempted and actual changes to the database. This is illustrated
by the following example:

```
-- Available online as part of RSInserts.sql
SQL> DECLARE
  2    CURSOR c_EconMajors IS
  3      SELECT ID
  4        FROM students
  5        WHERE major = 'Economics';
  6    v_ID students.ID%TYPE;
  7  BEGIN
  8    OPEN c_EconMajors;
  9    LOOP
 10      FETCH c_EconMajors INTO v_ID;
 11      EXIT WHEN c_EconMajors%NOTFOUND;
 12
 12      INSERT INTO registered_students(student_ID, department, course)
 13        VALUES (v_ID, 'ECN', 203);
 14
 14    END LOOP;
 15    CLOSE c_EconMajors;
 16  END;
 17  /
PL/SQL procedure successfully completed.

SQL> -- Even though we rollback, the INSERTs will still be logged.
SQL> ROLLBACK;
Rollback complete.
```

After running the previous block, the **rs.log** file created by the Pro*C program
will look like the following:

```
User: EXAMPLE   Changedate: 03-DEC-1999 ID: 10003 Course: ECN 203 Grade:
User: EXAMPLE   Changedate: 03-DEC-1999 ID: 10006 Course: ECN 203 Grade:
```

NOTE
*In order to stop the Pro*C program cleanly, we can send the "STOP" message over the pipe. This is done by the following block. For more information on this method, see "Establishing a Communications Protocol," later in this chapter.*

```
-- Available online as part of RSInserts.sql
DECLARE
  v_Status INTEGER;
BEGIN
  -- Send the stop message to the daemon.
  DBMS_PIPE.PACK_MESSAGE('STOP');
  v_Status := DBMS_PIPE.SEND_MESSAGE('RSInserts');
END;
```

Sending a Message

Messages are sent in two steps. First the data is packed into the local message buffer, and then the buffer is sent along the pipe. Data is packed using the PACK_MESSAGE procedure, and the SEND_MESSAGE function sends the buffer along the pipe.

PACK_MESSAGE

The PACK_MESSAGE procedure is overloaded to accept different types of data items. On the receiving end of the pipe, the UNPACK_MESSAGE procedure is similarly overloaded to retrieve the different types. The procedure is defined with

> PROCEDURE PACK_MESSAGE(*item* IN **VARCHAR2**);
> PROCEDURE PACK_MESSAGE(*item* IN **NUMBER**);
> PROCEDURE PACK_MESSAGE(*item* IN **DATE**);
> PROCEDURE PACK_MESSAGE_RAW(*item* IN **RAW**);
> PROCEDURE PACK_MESSAGE_ROWID(*item* IN **ROWID**);

NOTE
PACK_MESSAGE (and thus DBMS_PIPE in general) does not support Oracle8 and Oracle8i object types and REFs. To use these types, you must use Oracle Advanced Queuing.

The size of the buffer is 4,096 bytes. If the total size of the packed data exceeds this value, the error "ORA-6558: Buffer in dbms_pipe package is full. No more items allowed." is raised. In addition to the size of the data itself, each item in the buffer takes 1 byte to represent the datatype, 2 bytes to represent the length, and 1 additional byte to terminate the message. In Oracle8 and higher, 2 bytes are needed for the character set ID, and 1 additional byte for the character set form. So, for Oracle8 the overhead per item is 7 bytes, and for Oracle7 it is 4 bytes. Because the buffer size is limited, there is no way to send LONG or LONG RAW data along a pipe.

 The Oracle8 and higher version of PACK_MESSAGE, which accepts a VARCHAR2 parameter, is defined with

PROCEDURE PACK_MESSAGE(*item* IN VARCHAR2 CHARACTER SET ANY_CS);

This syntax allows PACK_MESSAGE to accept data in different character sets. For more information on NLS and how it interacts with PL/SQL, see the Oracle documentation.

SEND_MESSAGE

Once the local message buffer is filled with one or more calls to PACK_MESSAGE, the contents of the buffer are sent along the pipe with SEND_MESSAGE:

FUNCTION SEND_MESSAGE(*pipename* IN VARCHAR2,
                                   timeout IN INTEGER DEFAULT MAXWAIT,
                                   maxpipesize IN INTEGER DEFAULT 8192)
        RETURN INTEGER;

If the pipe does not yet exist, SEND_MESSAGE will create it. Pipes can also be created with the CREATE_PIPE procedure, which is available in PL/SQL 2.2 and higher and described in "Creating and Managing Pipes," later in this chapter. The parameters for SEND_MESSAGE are described in the following table:

Parameter	Type	Description
pipename	VARCHAR2	Name of the pipe. Pipe names are limited to 30 characters and are not case-sensitive. Names beginning with ORA$ are reserved for use by the database.
timeout	INTEGER	Timeout in seconds. If the message can't be sent for some reason (indicated by the return code), then the call will return after *timeout* seconds. The default value is DBMS_PIPE.MAXWAIT, which is defined as 86,400,000 seconds (1,000 days).

Parameter	Type	Description
maxpipesize	INTEGER	Total size of the pipe, in bytes. Defaults to 8,192 bytes (two messages of the maximum size). The sum of the sizes of all the messages in the pipe cannot exceed this value. (As a message is retrieved with RECEIVE_MESSAGE, it is removed from the pipe.) Once the pipe is created, its maximum size is part of the pipe definition, and it persists as long as the pipe itself persists. Different calls to SEND_MESSAGE can provide different *maxpipesize* values. If the new value provided is larger than the existing size, the pipe size is increased. If the new value provided is smaller, the existing larger value is kept.

The return values for SEND_MESSAGE are described here:

Return Value	Meaning
0	The message was sent successfully. A call to RECEIVE_MESSAGE will retrieve it.
1	The call timed out. This can happen if the pipe is too full for the message, or if a lock on the pipe could not be obtained.
3	The call was interrupted because of an internal error.

Receiving a Message

Three calls in DBMS_PIPE are used to receive the messages sent along a pipe, and then to unpack the messages into the original data items. They are RECEIVE_MESSAGE, NEXT_ITEM_TYPE, and UNPACK_MESSAGE.

RECEIVE_MESSAGE

RECEIVE_MESSAGE is the counterpart to SEND_MESSAGE. It retrieves a message from a pipe and places it into the local message buffer. UNPACK_MESSAGE is then used to retrieve the data from the buffer. RECEIVE_MESSAGE is defined as

FUNCTION RECEIVE_MESSAGE(*pipename* IN VARCHAR2,
                        timeout IN INTEGER DEFAULT MAXWAIT)
    RETURN INTEGER;

Typically, the receiving program issues a RECEIVE_MESSAGE call. If there is no message waiting, RECEIVE_MESSAGE will block until a message is retrieved. This causes the receiving session to sleep until the message is sent along the pipe. The receiving program is very similar to a Unix daemon in that it sleeps until a message is received along the pipe to wake it up. The parameters to RECEIVE_MESSAGE are described here:

Parameter	Type	Description
pipename	VARCHAR2	Name of the pipe. This should be the same pipe name as used in SEND_MESSAGE, subject to the same restrictions (maximum 30 characters, case-insensitive).
timeout	INTEGER	Maximum time, in seconds, to wait for a message. Similar to SEND_MESSAGE, the *timeout* defaults to MAXWAIT (1,000 days). If *timeout* is 0, RECEIVE_MESSAGE returns immediately with a status of 0 (message retrieved) or 1 (time-out).

The return codes for RECEIVE_MESSAGE are described here:

Return Value	Meaning
0	Success. The message was retrieved into the local buffer and can be unpacked with UNPACK_MESSAGE.
1	Timeout. No message was sent along the pipe during the time that RECEIVE_MESSAGE was waiting.
2	The message in the pipe was too large for the buffer. This is an internal error, which should not normally occur.
3	The call was interrupted because of an internal error.

NEXT_ITEM_TYPE
The NEXT_ITEM_TYPE function returns the datatype of the next item in the buffer. Based on this value, you can determine which variable should receive the data. If

you know this in advance, you don't have to use NEXT_ITEM_TYPE. For more information on how this can be set up, see "Establishing a Communications Protocol," later in this chapter. NEXT_ITEM_TYPE is defined with

FUNCTION NEXT_ITEM_TYPE RETURN INTEGER;

The return codes are as follows:

Return Value	Meaning
0	No more items
6	NUMBER
9	VARCHAR2
11	ROWID
12	DATE
23	RAW

NOTE
These are the only types available that can be sent along a database pipe. Specifically, user-defined types such as PL/SQL tables or records (or Oracle8 object types) cannot be sent.

UNPACK_MESSAGE

UNPACK_MESSAGE is the counterpart to PACK_MESSAGE. Like PACK_MESSAGE, it is overloaded on the type of the item to retrieve. It is defined with

PROCEDURE UNPACK_MESSAGE(*item* OUT **VARCHAR2**);
PROCEDURE UNPACK_MESSAGE(*item* OUT **NUMBER**);
PROCEDURE UNPACK_MESSAGE(*item* OUT **DATE**);
PROCEDURE UNPACK_MESSAGE_RAW(*item* OUT **RAW**);
PROCEDURE UNPACK_MESSAGE_ROWID(*item* OUT **ROWID**);

The *item* parameter will receive the data item in the buffer. If there are no more items in the buffer, or if the next item in the buffer is not of the same type as requested, the Oracle errors ORA-6556 or ORA-6559 are raised. Before raising the error, PL/SQL will try to convert the next item to the requested type using the default conversion format.

Like PACK_MESSAGE, the Oracle8 and higher version of
UNPACK_MESSAGE accepts data in different character sets as well. It is
defined with

PROCEDURE UNPACK_MESSAGE(*item* IN VARCHAR2 CHARACTER SET ANY_CS);

Creating and Managing Pipes

The first time a pipe name is referenced in a SEND_MESSAGE call, the
pipe is created implicitly, if it does not already exist. With PL/SQL 2.2 and
higher, pipes can be created and dropped explicitly with the CREATE_PIPE and
REMOVE_PIPE procedures.

Pipes and the Shared Pool

A pipe itself consists of a data structure in the shared pool area of the SGA (system
global area). As such, it does take up space that could be used by other database
objects as they are read from disk. Because of this, pipes are automatically purged
from the shared pool when the space is required. A pipe will only be automatically
purged if it has no waiting messages (although you can explicitly remove a pipe
from the SGA by using the PURGE procedure, described later in this chapter). The
algorithm for doing the purge is the LRU (least recently used) algorithm: At any
given point, the pipe that will be purged is the one that hasn't been used for the
longest amount of time. The maximum size of a pipe, and hence the size of the
data structure in the shared pool, is given by the *maxpipesize* parameter in
SEND_MESSAGE and CREATE_PIPE.

Public vs. Private Pipes

 Pipes created implicitly with SEND_MESSAGE are known as *public* pipes.
Any user who has EXECUTE permission on the DBMS_PIPE package and who
knows the pipe name, can read and write to a public pipe. *Private* pipes, on
the other hand, have restricted access. Access to a private pipe is restricted to the
user who created the pipe, to stored procedures running under the privilege set of
the pipe owner, or to users connected as SYSDBA or INTERNAL.

PL/SQL 2.0 and 2.1 have only public pipes, created implicitly. With PL/SQL 2.2
and higher, private pipes can be created explicitly with the CREATE_PIPE function.
This function is the only way to create a private pipe. It can also be used to create a
public pipe, if desired. Pipes created with CREATE_PIPE remain in the shared pool
until they are explicitly dropped with REMOVE_PIPE, or until the instance is shut
down. They are never purged automatically from the SGA. The following is the
syntax for CREATE_PIPE

```
FUNCTION CREATE_PIPE(pipename IN VARCHAR2,
                     maxpipesize IN INTEGER DEFAULT 8192,
                     private IN BOOLEAN DEFAULT TRUE)
      RETURN INTEGER;
```

CREATE_PIPE will return zero if the pipe was successfully created. If the pipe already exists, and the current user has privileges to access it, a zero is returned and any data already in the pipe remains. If a public pipe exists with the same name, or a private pipe exists with the same name owned by another user, the error "ORA-23322: insufficient privilege to access pipe" is raised and the function does not succeed. The parameters are described here:

Parameter	Type	Description
pipename	VARCHAR2	Name of the pipe to be created. Pipe names are restricted to 30 characters or less. Names beginning with ORA$ are reserved for internal use.
maxpipesize	INTEGER	Maximum pipe size in bytes. This is the same parameter as in SEND_MESSAGE for implicitly created pipes. The default value is 8,192 bytes. If SEND_MESSAGE is called with a higher value for maxpipesize, the pipe size is increased to the new larger value. If SEND_MESSAGE is called with a lower value, the existing higher value is retained.
private	BOOLEAN	TRUE if the pipe should be private, FALSE otherwise. The default is TRUE. Since public pipes are created implicitly by SEND_MESSAGE, there is normally little reason to set private to FALSE.

Pipes created explicitly with CREATE_PIPE are dropped with the REMOVE_PIPE function. If any messages still exist in the pipe when it is removed, they are deleted. Other than shutting down the instance, this is the only way to drop pipes created explicitly. The syntax for REMOVE_PIPE is

```
FUNCTION REMOVE_PIPE(pipename IN VARCHAR)
    RETURN INTEGER;
```

The only parameter is the name of the pipe to be removed. If the pipe exists and the current user has privileges on the pipe, the pipe is removed and the function returns zero. If the pipe does not exist, zero is also returned. If the pipe exists but the current user does not have privileges to access it, ORA-23322 is raised (similar to CREATE_PIPE).

The PURGE Procedure

PURGE will remove the contents of a pipe. The pipe itself will still exist. If it is an implicitly created pipe, since it is now empty, it is eligible to be aged out of the shared pool according to the LRU algorithm. PURGE calls RECEIVE_MESSAGE repeatedly, so the contents of the local message buffer may be overwritten. PURGE is defined with

    PROCEDURE PURGE(*pipename* IN VARCHAR2);

Privileges and Security

Three different levels of security are implemented with the DBMS_PIPE package. The first is the EXECUTE privilege on the package itself. By default, when the package is created, the privilege is not granted to any user. Therefore, only users with the EXECUTE ANY PROCEDURE system privilege will be able to access the DBMS_PIPE package. In order to allow other database users to utilize the package, use GRANT to assign them EXECUTE privileges on the package.

NOTE
The DBA role includes the EXECUTE ANY PROCEDURE system privilege. Consequently, users with the DBA role granted to them (such as SYSTEM) will be able to access DBMS_PIPE from anonymous PL/SQL blocks by default. Since this privilege is granted via a role, they will not be able to access DBMS_PIPE from stored procedures and triggers, since roles are disabled there. For more information on roles and their interaction with stored subprograms, see Chapter 5.

A good method for using this security is to grant the EXECUTE privilege only to certain database users. Then you can design your own package to control access to the underlying pipes. The EXECUTE privilege on this package can then be granted to other users.

The second security method is the pipe name itself. Unless users know the name of a pipe, they cannot send or receive messages along it. You can take advantage of this feature by using randomly generated pipe names, or by making the pipe names specific to the two sessions communicating over the pipe. The latter method can be accomplished with the UNIQUE_SESSION_NAME function and is described in the upcoming section, "Establishing a Communications Protocol."

Private Pipes

The most reliable security method to use, however, is the private pipes available with PL/SQL 2.2. Since a private pipe is available only to the user who created it and users connected as SYSDBA or INTERNAL, access is significantly limited. Even if another user has EXECUTE privileges on the DBMS_PIPE package and knows the name of the pipe, he or she will receive the Oracle error:

 ORA-23322: Insufficient privilege to access pipe

in the situations identified in Table 9-1. Note that the error is raised only when creating or dropping a pipe or trying to send or receive a message. The other calls in DBMS_PIPE do not actually access pipes themselves.

Again, the best way to use private pipes is to create stored procedures or packages that in turn call DBMS_PIPE. Since stored subprograms run under the privilege set of the user who owns them, private pipes can be accessed from stored subprograms.

Procedure or Function	When ORA-23322 Is Raised
CREATE_PIPE	A private pipe with the same name already exists, and the current user does not have privileges to access it. If the current user does have privileges, CREATE_PIPE returns 0 and the pipe ownership is not changed.
SEND_MESSAGE	The current user does not have privileges to access the pipe.
RECEIVE_MESSAGE	The current user does not have privileges to access the pipe.
REMOVE_PIPE	The current user does not have privileges to access the pipe. The pipe will still exist, including any messages currently in it.

TABLE 9-1.   *Situations in Which ORA-23322 Is Raised*

Establishing a Communications Protocol

Using pipes is similar to using other low-level communications packages, such as TCP/IP. You have the flexibility of deciding how the data will be formatted and how it will be sent. In addition, you can decide who will receive the message. In order to use this flexibility properly, however, you should keep in mind the suggestions in the following sections.

Data Formatting

Each message sent over a pipe consists of one or more data items. The data items are inserted into the message buffer using PACK_MESSAGE, and the entire buffer is then sent with SEND_MESSAGE. At the receiving end, the buffer is received with RECEIVE_MESSAGE and the data items are retrieved with NEXT_ITEM_TYPE and UNPACK_MESSAGE.

Typically, the receiving program can do different things based on the contents of the message received. For example, the Pro*C program which implements the back end of the **LogRSInserts** trigger (described earlier in this chapter), uses the first data item to format the message logged to the data file. Essentially, the first data item is an *opcode*, or instruction, which tells the receiving program how to interpret the remainder of the data. Depending on the type of information, there may be different datatypes in the message, or different numbers of data elements.

TIP
It is a good idea to include a STOP instruction in addition to other instructions that you may need. You can use STOP to cause the waiting program to disconnect from the database and exit cleanly. Without a message such as this, the waiting program would have to be killed from the operating system and/or database level, which is not as clean. We will see an example of this in the following section.

Data Addressing

There can be multiple readers and writers for the same pipe. Any given message will be received by exactly one reader, however. Furthermore, it is not defined which reader will actually get it. Because of this, it is best to address your messages to a specific reader program. This can be accomplished by generating a unique pipe name that will be used only by the two sessions involved—one reader and one writer. The UNIQUE_SESSION_NAME function can be used for this. It is defined with

```
FUNCTION UNIQUE_SESSION_NAME RETURN VARCHAR2;
```

Each call to UNIQUE_SESSION_NAME will return a string with a maximum length of 30 characters. Every call from the same database session will return the same string. This string will be unique among all sessions currently connected to the database. If a session disconnects, however, its name can be used by another session at a later point.

UNIQUE_SESSION_NAME can be used as the pipe name, which ensures that the message will go to only one recipient. One method of setting this up is to send the initial message over a pipe with a predefined name. Part of the initial message is the name of the pipe over which to send the response. The receiving program then decodes the initial message and sends the response over this new pipe, which will be used only by these two sessions. Since there is only one reader and one writer for the data pipe, there is no ambiguity about which session will receive the information. We will see an example of this technique in the following section.

Example

This is another version of the **Debug** package, which we first examined in Chapter 3. Similar to the example at the beginning of this chapter, one of the two sessions communicating is a Pro*C program. The **Debug** package itself communicates with this program.

Debug.pc

The program (Debug.pc) is given here:

```
/* Available online as Debug.pc */

/* C and SQL header files */
#include <stdio.h>
EXEC SQL INCLUDE sqlca;

/* Username and password to connect to the database */
char *connectString = "example/example";

/* Status variables used in the calls to DBMS_PIPE */
int status;
char opCode[6];
EXEC SQL VAR opCode IS STRING(6);

/* Variables sent and received along pipes. */
char returnPipeName[31];
EXEC SQL VAR returnPipeName IS STRING(31);

char description[100];
EXEC SQL VAR description IS STRING(100);
```

```
char value[100];
EXEC SQL VAR value IS STRING(100);

/* Error handling function.  Print the error to the screen,
   and exit. */
void sqlerror() {

  printf("SQL Error!\n");
  printf("%.*s\n", sqlca.sqlerrm.sqlerrml, sqlca.sqlerrm.sqlerrmc);

  EXEC SQL WHENEVER SQLERROR CONTINUE;

  EXEC SQL ROLLBACK WORK RELEASE;

  exit(1);
}


int main() {

  /* Set up the error handling. */
  EXEC SQL WHENEVER SQLERROR DO sqlerror();

  /* Connect to the database. */
  EXEC SQL CONNECT :connectString;

  printf("Debug ready for input.\n");

  /* Main loop.  The only way we'll break out of the loop is if
     we receive the 'STOP' message or if an error occurs. */
  for (;;) {
    /* Sleep until a message is received over the 'Debug' pipe.
       The timeout is not specified, so the default will be
       used. */
    EXEC SQL EXECUTE
      BEGIN
        :status := DBMS_PIPE.RECEIVE_MESSAGE('DebugPipe');
      END;
    END-EXEC;

    if (status == 0) {
      /* Successful retrieval of the message.  We now need to get
         the first data element, to decide what to do with it. */
      EXEC SQL EXECUTE
        BEGIN
          DBMS_PIPE.UNPACK_MESSAGE(:opCode);
        END;
      END-EXEC;
```

```
if (!strcmp(opCode, "STOP")) {
  /* STOP message received.  Break out of the loop. */
  break;
} /* End of STOP processing */

else if (!strcmp(opCode, "TEST")) {
  /* TEST message received.  Send back a handshake over the
     same pipe. */
  EXEC SQL EXECUTE
    BEGIN
      DBMS_PIPE.PACK_MESSAGE('Handshake');
      :status := DBMS_PIPE.SEND_MESSAGE('DebugPipe');
    END;
  END-EXEC;

  if (status != 0) {
    /* Error message.  Print it out. */
    printf("Error %d while responding to TEST message\n",
           status);
  }

  /*
   * Sleep for 5 seconds, to give the SQL session a chance
   * to receive the message.
   */
  sleep(5);
} /* End of TEST processing */

else if (!strcmp(opCode, "DEBUG")) {
  /* DEBUG message received.  Unpack the return pipe,
     description, and output value. */
  EXEC SQL EXECUTE
    BEGIN
      DBMS_PIPE.UNPACK_MESSAGE(:returnPipeName);
      DBMS_PIPE.UNPACK_MESSAGE(:description);
      DBMS_PIPE.UNPACK_MESSAGE(:value);
    END;
  END-EXEC;

  /* Echo the debugging info to the screen. */
  printf("%s: %s\n", description, value);

  /* Send the handshake message back. */
  EXEC SQL EXECUTE
    BEGIN
      DBMS_PIPE.PACK_MESSAGE('Processed');
      :status := DBMS_PIPE.SEND_MESSAGE(:returnPipeName);
    END;
```

```
    END-EXEC;

    if (status != 0) {
      /* Error message.  Print it out. */
      printf("Error %d while sending handshake message\n",
             status);
    }
  } /* End of DEBUG processing */
} /* End of successful retrieve of a message */

else if (status == 1) {
  /* The RECEIVE_MESSAGE call timed out.  Loop back to
     wait again. */
  continue;
}

else {
  /* The RECEIVE_MESSAGE call exited with an error.
     Print it, and exit. */
  printf("Main loop RECEIVE_MESSAGE Error. Status = %d\n",
         status);
  EXEC SQL ROLLBACK WORK RELEASE;
  exit(1);
}

}  /* End of main loop */

/* Disconnect from the database. */
EXEC SQL COMMIT WORK RELEASE;
}
```

Debug Package
The **Debug** package itself is defined with

-- Available online as Debug.sql
```
CREATE OR REPLACE PACKAGE Debug AS
  -- Maximum number of seconds to wait for a handshake message.
  v_TimeOut NUMBER := 10;

  -- Main Debug procedure.
  PROCEDURE Debug(p_Description IN VARCHAR2,
                  p_Value       IN VARCHAR2);

  -- Sets up the Debug environment.
  PROCEDURE Reset;

  -- Causes the daemon to exit.
```

```
    PROCEDURE Exit;
END Debug;

CREATE OR REPLACE PACKAGE BODY Debug as

  v_CurrentPipeName VARCHAR2(30);

  PROCEDURE Debug(p_Description IN VARCHAR2,
                 p_Value        IN VARCHAR2) IS
    v_ReturnCode NUMBER;
    v_Handshake  VARCHAR2(10);
  BEGIN
    /* If we don't already have a pipe name, determine one. */
    IF v_CurrentPipeName IS NULL THEN
      v_CurrentPipeName := DBMS_PIPE.UNIQUE_SESSION_NAME;
    END IF;

    /*
     * Send the 'DEBUG' message, along with:
     *   - pipe name for the handshake
     *   - description
     *   - value
     */
    DBMS_PIPE.PACK_MESSAGE('DEBUG');
    DBMS_PIPE.PACK_MESSAGE(v_CurrentPipeName);
    DBMS_PIPE.PACK_MESSAGE(p_Description);
    DBMS_PIPE.PACK_MESSAGE(p_Value);
    v_ReturnCode := DBMS_PIPE.SEND_MESSAGE('DebugPipe');

    IF v_ReturnCode != 0 THEN
      RAISE_APPLICATION_ERROR(-20210,
        'Debug.Debug: SEND_MESSAGE failed with ' || v_ReturnCode);
    END IF;

    -- Wait for the handshake message on the return pipe.
    v_ReturnCode := DBMS_PIPE.RECEIVE_MESSAGE(v_CurrentPipeName);

    IF v_ReturnCode = 1 THEN
        -- Timeout
      RAISE_APPLICATION_ERROR(-20211,
        'Debug.Debug: No handshake message received');
    ELSIF v_ReturnCode != 0 THEN
      -- Other error
      RAISE_APPLICATION_ERROR(-20212,
        'Debug.Debug: RECEIVE_MESSAGE failed with ' ||
        v_ReturnCode);
    ELSE
      -- Check for the handshake message.
```

```
      DBMS_PIPE.UNPACK_MESSAGE(v_Handshake);
    IF v_Handshake = 'Processed' THEN
      -- Output processed.
      NULL;
    ELSE
      -- No handshake
      RAISE_APPLICATION_ERROR(-20213,
        'Debug.Debug: Incorrect handshake message ''' ||
        v_Handshake || ''' received');
    END IF;
  END IF;
END Debug;

/* Check to make sure the daemon is running by sending the test
   message over the pipe.  If not, raise an error. */
PROCEDURE Reset IS
  v_ReturnCode NUMBER;
  v_Handshake VARCHAR2(100);
BEGIN
  DBMS_PIPE.PACK_MESSAGE('TEST');
  v_ReturnCode := DBMS_PIPE.SEND_MESSAGE('DebugPipe');

  IF v_ReturnCode != 0 THEN
    RAISE_APPLICATION_ERROR(-20200,
      'Debug.Reset: SEND_MESSAGE failed with ' || v_ReturnCode);
  END IF;

  -- Sleep for 5 seconds, to give the daemon a chance to reply.
  DBMS_LOCK.SLEEP(5);

  /*
   * The daemon will respond over the same pipe.  If this call
   * times out, or the wrong message is returned, then the daemon
   * isn't ready and we should raise an error.
   */
  v_ReturnCode :=
    DBMS_PIPE.RECEIVE_MESSAGE('DebugPipe', v_TimeOut);
  IF v_ReturnCode = 1 THEN
    -- Timeout
    RAISE_APPLICATION_ERROR(-20201,
      'Debug.Reset: Test message timed out');
  ELSIF v_ReturnCode != 0 THEN
    -- Other error
    RAISE_APPLICATION_ERROR(-20202,
      'Debug.Reset: RECEIVE_MESSAGE failed with ' ||
      v_ReturnCode);
  ELSE
    -- We got a return message, make sure that it is the correct
```

```
        -- one.
      DBMS_PIPE.UNPACK_MESSAGE(v_Handshake);
      IF v_Handshake = 'TEST' THEN
        -- We got back the 'TEST' message that we sent above.
        -- Thus the daemon is not running.
        RAISE_APPLICATION_ERROR(-20203,
          'Debug.Reset: Daemon not running');
      ELSIF v_Handshake != 'Handshake' THEN
        -- We got some other message back.
        RAISE_APPLICATION_ERROR(-20204,
          'Debug.Reset: Reply ''' || v_Handshake ||
          ''' received from test message');
      ELSE
        -- Message sent successfully, do nothing.
        NULL;
      END IF;
    END IF;
  END Reset;

  PROCEDURE Exit IS
    v_ReturnCode NUMBER;
  BEGIN
    -- Send the 'STOP' message.
    DBMS_PIPE.PACK_MESSAGE('STOP');
    v_ReturnCode := DBMS_PIPE.SEND_MESSAGE('DebugPipe');

    IF v_ReturnCode != 0 THEN
      RAISE_APPLICATION_ERROR(-20230,
        'Debug.Exit: SEND_MESSAGE failed with ' || v_ReturnCode);
    END IF;
  END Exit;

END Debug;
```

If we compile the **Debug** deamon and run it, and then issue the following anonymous block,

```
-- Available online as DebugTest.sql
BEGIN
  -- First reset the daemon.
  Debug.Reset;

  -- And print out some messages.
  FOR v_Count IN 1..10 LOOP
    Debug.Debug('Debug Test', 'Count is ' || v_Count);
  END LOOP;
```

```
   -- And then tell the daemon to exit.
   Debug.Exit;

END;
```

we will get the following output from the program.

```
Debug ready for input.
Debug Test: Count is 1
Debug Test: Count is 2
Debug Test: Count is 3
Debug Test: Count is 4
Debug Test: Count is 5
Debug Test: Count is 6
Debug Test: Count is 7
Debug Test: Count is 8
Debug Test: Count is 9
Debug Test: Count is 10
```

The communication between the two sessions is illustrated by Figure 9-1.

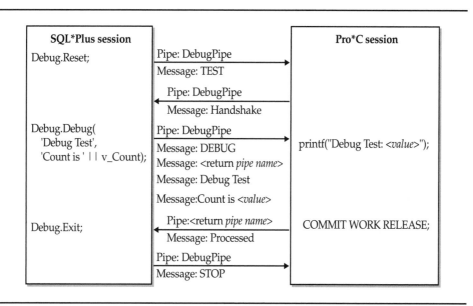

FIGURE 9-1.   *Communication between **Debug** sessions*

Comments

There are several things to note about this version of **Debug**. First of all, the Pro*C program is necessary for the output. When you call **Debug.Debug**, the output will be printed to the screen by the Pro*C program, not by the PL/SQL session. Thus, you should run the program in a separate window from your PL/SQL session. The program is essentially functioning as a daemon—it spends most of its time sleeping, waiting for a message to be sent along the pipe.

OPCODES   The first message sent along **DebugPipe** is the opcode for the daemon. This can be "STOP," "TEST," or "DEBUG." Depending on this opcode, the daemon will respond differently, allowing it to function as a dispatcher. In a more complicated scenario, the daemon could then spawn other processes depending on the opcode, which would then process the data. The daemon itself would then wait for another message.

COMMUNICATIONS PROTOCOL   **Debug.Debug** passes a pipe name as part of the initial message. This pipe name is generated uniquely by UNIQUE_SESSION_NAME. After **Debug.Debug** sends the message, it then listens on this new pipe. This is a very useful technique, since it allows multiple daemons to be running at the same time. The first message will be received by a waiting daemon. The return pipe name will be used by only one session, so it uniquely identifies the session that sent the message. This neatly solves the problem of multiple readers on the same pipe. Once the unique pipe name is established, both sessions can send and receive messages along this new pipe, with the assurance that no other session will be listening.

HANDSHAKE MESSAGES   Both the PL/SQL package and the Pro*C daemon are readers and writers. Consider the "TEST" message, as an example, that **Debug.Debug** sends. The **Debug** package sends a message and then waits for a reply. If the reply times out, we know that the initial message was not received properly. Using handshake messages is a valuable part of a good communications protocol.

SLEEPING   When the daemon is not processing a message, it is waiting for one to be sent. There are two possible ways to implement this wait. The first, which we saw in the daemon for the **LogRSInserts** trigger, is to use the C **sleep()** function. The call to DBMS_PIPE.RECEIVE_MESSAGE in that daemon specified a timeout of zero. The second method is to specify a non-zero timeout, as the **Debug** daemon does. In general, either method can be used.

DBMS_ALERT

The DBMS_ALERT package implements database alerts. An *alert* is a message that is sent when a transaction is committed. Unlike pipes, which are asynchronous, alerts are synchronized with transactions. Alerts are generally used for one-way communication, while a pipe is used for two-way communication.

The sending session issues a SIGNAL call for a particular alert. This call records the fact that the alert has been signaled in the data dictionary, but does not actually send it. When the transaction containing the SIGNAL call commits, the alert is actually sent. If the transaction rolls back, the alert is not sent. The receiving session first registers interest in particular alerts using the REGISTER procedure. Only alerts for which the session has been registered will be received. The receiving session then waits for alerts to be signaled using the WAITONE or WAITANY procedure.

Sending an Alert

Alerts are sent with the SIGNAL procedure, which records the alert information in the data dictionary. The syntax for SIGNAL is

```
PROCEDURE SIGNAL(name IN VARCHAR2,
                 message IN VARCHAR2);
```

SIGNAL takes only two parameters—the name of the alert to be signaled and a message. Alert names have a maximum length of 30 characters and are not case-sensitive. Similar to pipes, alert names beginning with ORA$ are reserved for use by Oracle and should not be used for user applications. The maximum message length is 1,800 bytes.

A given alert can only be in one of two states—signaled or not signaled. The SIGNAL call changes the state of the alert to signaled. This change is recorded in the **dbms_alert_info** data dictionary table, described in "Alerts and the Data Dictionary," later in this chapter. Because of this, only one session can signal an alert at a time. Multiple sessions can signal the same alert. However, the first session will cause the later sessions to block.

When the alert is sent, all sessions currently waiting for that alert will receive the message. If no sessions are currently waiting, the next session to wait for it will receive it immediately.

Receiving an Alert

Receiving an alert involves two steps—registering interest in an alert and then waiting for it. A receiving session will only receive the alerts for which it has registered.

Registering

The REGISTER procedure is used to register interest in a particular alert. A database session can register for as many alerts as desired. The session will remain registered until it disconnects from the database, or until it calls the REMOVE procedure (described in "Unregistering for an Alert") to indicate that it is no longer interested. The REGISTER procedure is defined with

```
PROCEDURE REGISTER(name IN VARCHAR2);
```

The only parameter is the name of the alert. Registering for an alert does not cause the session to block; it only records that this session is interested.

NOTE
REGISTER always performs a COMMIT as part of its processing.

Waiting for One Alert

The WAITONE procedure is used to wait for a particular alert to occur. If this alert has already been signaled, WAITONE returns immediately with a status of 0, indicating that the alert has been received. If the alert is not signaled, then WAITONE will block until either the alert is signaled or it times out. WAITONE is defined with

```
PROCEDURE WAITONE(name IN VARCHAR2,
                  message OUT VARCHAR2,
                  status OUT INTEGER,
                  timeout IN NUMBER DEFAULT MAXWAIT);
```

Similar to RECEIVE_MESSAGE, WAITONE will cause the receiving session to sleep until the alert is signaled, or the timeout occurs.

The same session can both signal an alert, and then wait for it. In this case, be sure to issue a commit between the SIGNAL and the WAITONE call. Otherwise, the WAITONE call will always time out, since the alert would never have been sent. The parameters for WAITONE are described here:

Parameter	Type	Description
name	VARCHAR2	Name of the alert for which to wait. The session should have registered interest in this alert with REGISTER prior to calling WAITONE. Like database pipes, alert names beginning with ORA$ are reserved for internal use.
message	VARCHAR2	Message text included in the SIGNAL call by the sending session. If there were multiple SIGNAL calls for the same alert before the alert was received, only the latest message is retrieved. Earlier messages are discarded.

Parameter	Type	Description
status	INTEGER	Returns an indicator as to whether the alert was received. A value of zero indicates that the alert was received, and a value of one indicates that the call timed out.
timeout	NUMBER	Maximum time to wait before returning, in seconds. If *timeout* is not specified, it defaults to DBMS_ALERT.MAXWAIT, which is defined as 1,000 days. If the alert is not received within *timeout* seconds, the call returns with status one.

Waiting for Any Alert

A session can also wait for any alerts for which it has registered interest to be signaled. This is done with the WAITANY procedure. Unlike WAITONE, WAITANY will return successfully if any of the alerts are signaled, rather than just one. WAITANY is defined with

```
PROCEDURE WAITANY(name OUT VARCHAR2,
                  message OUT VARCHAR2,
                  status OUT INTEGER,
                  timeout IN NUMBER DEFAULT MAXWAIT);
```

The parameters are the same as for WAITONE, with the same meanings. The only difference is that *name* is an OUT parameter and will indicate which alert has actually been signaled.

Again, the same session can both signal an alert and then wait for it with WAITANY. If a COMMIT is not issued between the time the alert is signaled and the WAITANY call, WAITANY will always time out, since the alert will never have been actually sent.

Other Procedures

Three additional procedures are used to manage alerts: REMOVE, REMOVEALL, and SET_DEFAULTS.

Unregistering for an Alert

When a session is no longer interested in an alert, it should unregister for it. This helps free the resources used to signal and receive the alert. Unregistering is accomplished with the REMOVE procedure:

PROCEDURE REMOVE(*name* IN VARCHAR2);

The only parameter is the name of the alert. REMOVE is the counterpart to REGISTER. If you want to unregister from all alerts, you can use the REMOVEALL procedure, which takes no arguments. It will unregister the current session from all alerts. REMOVEALL is called automatically the first time the DBMS_ALERT package is referenced in a session, which ensures that no alerts from prior sessions will affect it.

NOTE
Like REGISTER, REMOVE and REMOVEALL perform a COMMIT.

Polling Intervals

In most cases, Oracle is event driven. This means that a session waiting for something will be notified when that event occurs, rather than having to check in a loop for the event. If a loop is required, it is known as a *polling loop*. The amount of time between each check is known as the *polling interval*. There are two cases in which polling is required for the implementation of alerts:

- If the database is running in parallel server mode, polling is required to check for alerts signaled by another instance. The polling interval for this loop can be set by the SET_DEFAULTS procedure.

- If no registered alerts have been signaled for the WAITANY call, a polling loop is required to check for the signaled alerts. The polling interval starts at 1 second and exponentially increases to a maximum of 30 seconds. This interval is not user configurable.

  The SET_DEFAULTS procedure is defined with

  PROCEDURE SET_DEFAULTS(*polling_interval* IN NUMBER);

The only parameter is the polling interval, in seconds. The default is 5 seconds.

Alerts and the Data Dictionary

Alerts are implemented using a data dictionary table, **dbms_alert_info**. A row gets inserted into this table for each alert that a session registers interest in. If more than one session registers interest in the same alert, a row is inserted for each session. The **dbms_alert_info** table has four columns, with the structure indicated by the following table:

Column	Datatype	Null?	Description
name	VARCHAR2(30)	NOT NULL	Name of the alert that was registered
SID	VARCHAR2(30)	NOT NULL	Session identifier for the session that registered interest
changed	VARCHAR2(1)		Y if the alert is signaled, N if not
message	VARCHAR2(1800)		Message passed with the signal call

We can see how this view works, and the implications it has, by examining the scenario illustrated in Figure 9-2. This figure shows three database sessions and the commands they issue over time. The contents of **dbms_alert_info** are shown at each time as well. Here is a description of events:

- **Time T1**   Session B registers interest in the alert. At this point, a row is inserted into **dbms_alert_info**, recording this. Note that the Changed field reads N, indicating that the alert has not yet been signaled.

- **Time T2**   Session A signals the alert, with message 'Message A.' Since session A hasn't issued a commit, **dbms_alert_info** is unchanged.

- **Time T3**   Session C signals the same alert, with message 'Message C.' Session A hasn't yet committed. Only one session can signal an alert at a time, so the SIGNAL call issued by session C will block.

- **Time T4**   Session A commits. Two things happen now. The SIGNAL issued by session C returns, and A's message is put into **dbms_alert_info**. The Changed field is set to Y, indicating that the alert has been signaled.

- **Time T5**   Session C commits. This *replaces* the message in **dbms_alert_info**. Session A's message is lost.

- **Time T6**   Session B finally decides to wait for the alert. The WAITONE call returns immediately, with 'Message C.' The Changed field is reset to N, indicating that the alert is not signaled anymore.

receiving

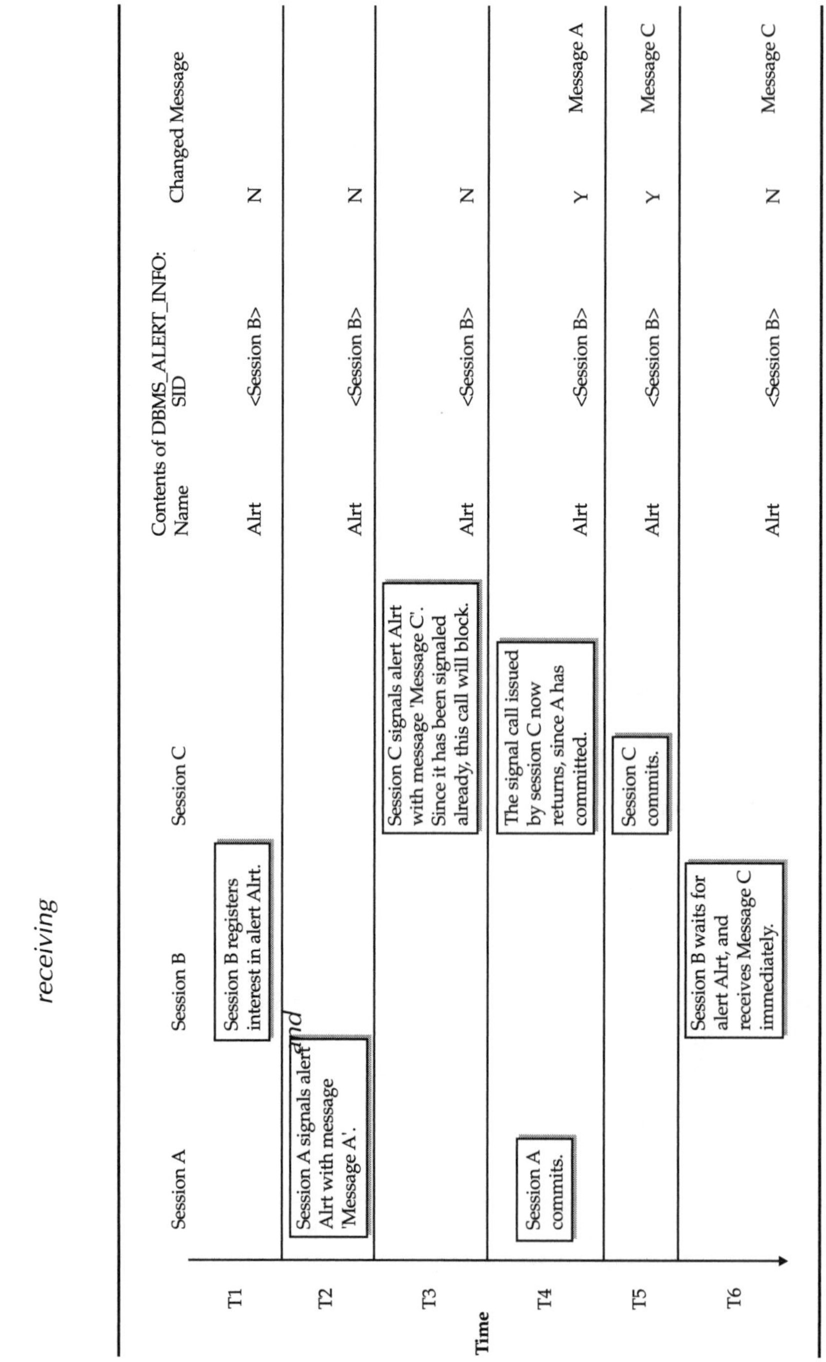

Time	Session A	Session B	Session C	Contents of DBMS_ALERT_INFO: Name	SID	Changed	Message
T1		Session B registers interest in alert Alrt.		Alrt	<Session B>	N	
T2	Session A signals alert Alrt with message 'Message A'.			Alrt	<Session B>	N	
T3			Session C signals alert Alrt with message 'Message C'. Since it has been signaled already, this call will block.	Alrt	<Session B>	N	
T4	Session A commits.		The signal call issued by session C now returns, since A has committed.	Alrt	<Session B>	Y	Message A
T5			Session C commits.	Alrt	<Session B>	Y	Message C
T6		Session B waits for alert Alrt, and receives Message C immediately.		Alrt	<Session B>	N	Message C

FIGURE 9-2. *Signaling*

Comparing DBMS_PIPE and DBMS_ALERT

DBMS_PIPE and DBMS_ALERT have several similarities:

■ Both are implemented as PL/SQL packages. This means that the functionality of either package can be used from any PL/SQL execution environment. For DBMS_PIPE, we examined one such situation—the latest version of **Debug** sends the output to a Pro*C daemon. Both the calling program and the receiving program use PL/SQL, but from different environments.

■ Both packages are designed to do the same thing—send messages between sessions that are connected to the same instance. In general, you can use either package for your application.

■ PL/SQL version 2 does not have a direct means of interfacing with a C program. You can't call a C program from a PL/SQL stored procedure, for example. Prior to Oracle8, the only way around this restriction is to use pipes or alerts to send a message to a waiting C daemon. Oracle8, however, removes this restriction with external routines, described in Chapter 10.

Although both packages accomplish very similar things, there are several differences between their behavior. Depending on your needs, use the package that is most appropriate. Here are the important differences:

■ Alerts are transaction based, while pipes are not. An alert will not be sent until the transaction that contains the DBMS_ALERT.SIGNAL call issues a commit. If the transaction is rolled back, the alert is not sent. Pipes, on the other hand, are asynchronous. As soon as the DBMS_PIPE.SEND_MESSAGE call is issued, the message is sent. There is no way to retrieve it, even if the transaction is rolled back.

■ When an alert is signaled, all sessions that have registered interest in the alert, and are waiting, will receive the message. If there is more than one session waiting on the alert, all of them will receive it. This is different from pipes, where exactly one of the waiting sessions will receive the message. It is not defined which session will receive the message if there is more than one waiting.

■ The methods of sending the information differ as well. Alerts do not have the ability to pass more than a single character string in the message. When a message is sent along a pipe, however, the entire contents of the message buffer are sent. This can include several differing pieces of information, of different types.

■ Because the messages that can be sent with pipes are more complex than alerts, pipes can be easily used for two-way communication. A communications protocol is thus important for good pipe usage. Alerts, on the other hand, are generally used for a single one-way message.

Summary

We have discussed two different mechanisms for intersession communication in this chapter. Database pipes, implemented with the DBMS_PIPE package, allow two-way communication with complex messages. Database alerts, implemented with the DBMS_ALERT package, allow one-way, transaction-based messages. The packages behave differently and are used for different types of applications.

CHAPTER
10

External Routines

L/SQL is a very powerful language with many features, but there are some things for which it is not suited. To help with this, Oracle8 provides the ability to call a C procedure directly from PL/SQL as an external routine. This allows you to use C (which is suited for different tasks than PL/SQL) as part of your PL/SQL application. Oracle8*i* enhances external routines to include Java. In this chapter, we will discuss how external routines work, the necessary requirements, and the difference between C and Java external routines. We will also discuss how to call back to the database from within an external routine.

The Need for External Routines

PL/SQL is especially suited for working with Oracle, due to its integration with SQL. In fact, this is why the language was designed. However, there are other tasks for which other languages are more appropriate. For example, C excels at computation-intensive tasks and integration with the file system and other system devices. Java is an excellent portable language with a well-defined security model that works well for Internet applications. If your application needs to perform tasks that are not well suited for PL/SQL, then another language may be appropriate. In this case, it is necessary to communicate between modules of the application that are written in different languages.

Prior to Oracle8, the only way to communicate between PL/SQL and another language (such as C) was to use the DBMS_PIPE and/or DBMS_ALERT routines. (See Chapter 9 for more information.) This typically required setting up a daemon process written using the Oracle Call Interface (OCI) or the precompilers.

Oracle **8** and higher

Oracle8, however, simplifies this communication through external routines. An *external routine* is a procedure or function written in a language other than PL/SQL, but callable from a PL/SQL program. This is done by publishing the external routine to PL/SQL through a PL/SQL-callable entrypoint (also known as the *wrapper*) that maps to the actual external code. A PL/SQL program then calls the wrapper, which in turn invokes the external code. External routines were first introduced in Oracle8 (where they were known as *external procedures*). In Oracle8, the only supported language for external routines was C. There, the AS EXTERNAL clause was available to create the PL/SQL wrapper.

Oracle **8***i* and higher

Oracle8*i* extends external routines to support Java. PL/SQL wrappers are also extended to include call specifications. A *call specification* is a means of publishing an external routine (regardless of its native language) to PL/SQL. Call specifications use the AS LANGUAGE clause.

NOTE
*A routine in any language that can be called from
C can be used as an external routine. For example,
if you want to create an external routine written in
C++ it would need to have an **extern "C"** wrapper
around it. You can also code an external routine in
C, and then call a routine in another language from
the external routine (provided that it has been linked
properly).*

An External Routine Example

Suppose we want to send e-mail from a PL/SQL application. There is no support for
this built into the language or included packages (except for DBMS_MAIL, which
requires Oracle Office). Thus, this is a good candidate for an external routine, since
both C and Java can send e-mail programmatically. We will see examples of each in
this section.

NOTE
*These examples simply demonstrate the capabilities
of external routines, and do not go into the full detail.
See "C External Routines" and "Java External
Routines," later in this chapter, for a complete
explanation of how to set up and run these examples.*

C Example

The **sendMail** C function, shown next, will send an e-mail message. It takes four
parameters—the subject, message text, e-mail ID of the sender, and e-mail ID of
the recipient, all of which are text strings.

```
/* Available online as sendMail.c */
#include <stdio.h>

/* Set TEMP_FILE to a filename in a directory writable by the
 * Oracle operating system user.
 */
#define TEMP_FILE "/tmp/mail.out"

/* Set MAIL_CMD to the full path of the system mail program.  This
```

```
 * is often /bin/mail or /bin/rmail.
 */
#define MAIL_CMD "/bin/mail"

int sendMail(
  char *subject,                        /* Subject of the message */
  char *message,                         /* Message to be sent */
  char *from,                            /* Email id of the sender */
  char *recipient)                  /* Email id of the recipient */
{
  FILE *tempFP;
  char systemCommand[500];

  /* We will send an email message using the Unix 'mail' command.
   * This requires us to put the message into a file first, then
   * we can use it as input to mail.
   */

  /* First write the subject and message to the file specified in
   * TEMP_FILE.
   */
  tempFP = fopen(TEMP_FILE, "w");
  fprintf(tempFP, "Subject: %s\n", subject);
  fprintf(tempFP, "From: %s\n", from);
  fprintf(tempFP, message);
  fclose(tempFP);

  /* Now build the mail command. */
  sprintf(systemCommand, "%s %s < %s\n",
                      MAIL_CMD, recipient, TEMP_FILE);

  /* And execute it. */
  return system(systemCommand);
}
```

NOTE
You may have to modify the TEMP_FILE and/or MAIL_CMD macros in the code shown previously for your own system.

This example will work only on a Unix system, as it relies on the Unix 'mail' command. It will create a temporary file containing the message text, and then use this file as input to 'mail.' Given the previous routine, we can publish it by creating a PL/SQL wrapper as follows:

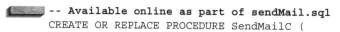
```
-- Available online as part of sendMail.sql
CREATE OR REPLACE PROCEDURE SendMailC (
```

```
    p_Subject IN VARCHAR2,
    p_Message IN VARCHAR2,
    p_From IN VARCHAR2,
    p_Recipient IN VARCHAR2)
AS EXTERNAL
LIBRARY SendMailLibrary
NAME "sendMail"
PARAMETERS (p_Subject STRING,
            p_Message STRING,
            p_From STRING,
            p_Recipient STRING);
```

The **sendMailC** procedure uses the AS EXTERNAL clause, so it will work in both
Oracle8 and Oracle8*i*. Once it is created, we can then call it with an anonymous
block similar to the following:

```
-- Available online as part of sendMail.sql
BEGIN
   SendMailC('Test email from a C external routine',
             'This is the message!',
             'The_PL/SQL_Engine',
             'YOUR_EMAIL_ADDRESS_HERE');
END;
```

> **NOTE**
> *In order for this example to work, you need to
> create the library **SendMailLibrary**, and compile
> **sendMail.c** into a shared object. We will discuss
> these steps in more detail later in this chapter.
> See **sendMail.txt**, available online with the other
> examples from this chapter, for more information on
> how to compile and run the sendMail C example.*

Java Example

Oracle **8i** and higher | Similar to the **sendMail** C function, we can write a Java method that sends
e-mail. The **sendMail** class, shown next, uses the JavaMail API, which is an
extension to the Java JDK. JavaMail, as well as more examples and
documentation, can be downloaded from **java.sun.com**.

```
// Available online as sendMail.java
import java.util.*;
import java.io.*;
import javax.mail.*;
import javax.mail.internet.*;
import javax.activation.*;
```

```java
// This class is based on the msgsendsample.java example found as
// part of the demos for JavaMail 1.1.1.

public class sendMail
{
  /* Set this to the IP address or name of your SMTP mail host.
   * On Unix systems, "localhost" will often work.
   */
  public static String mailhost = "localhost";

  public static void send(
    String subject,             // Subject of the message.
    String message,                // Message to be sent.
    String from,                // Email ID of the sender.
    String recipient)        // Email ID of the recipient.
  {
    // create some properties and get the default Session
    Properties props = new Properties();
    props.put("mail.smtp.host", mailhost);
    Session session = Session.getDefaultInstance(props, null);

    try {
      // create a message
      Message msg = new MimeMessage(session);
      msg.setFrom(new InternetAddress(from));
      InternetAddress[] address = {new InternetAddress(recipient)};
      msg.setRecipients(Message.RecipientType.TO, address);
      msg.setSubject(subject);
      msg.setSentDate(new Date());
      // If the desired charset is known, you can use
      // setText(text, charset)
      msg.setText(message);

      // Send it off
      Transport.send(msg);
    }
    catch (MessagingException mex)
    {
      System.out.println("
        \n--Exception handling in msgsendsample.java");

      mex.printStackTrace();
      System.out.println();
      Exception ex = mex;
      do
```

```
    {
  if (ex instanceof SendFailedException)
  {
    SendFailedException sfex = (SendFailedException)ex;
    Address[] invalid = sfex.getInvalidAddresses();
    if (invalid != null)
    {
      System.out.println("    ** Invalid Addresses");
      if (invalid != null) {
        for (int i = 0; i < invalid.length; i++)
      System.out.println("          " + invalid[i]);
      }
    }
    Address[] validUnsent = sfex.getValidUnsentAddresses();
    if (validUnsent != null)
    {
      System.out.println("    ** ValidUnsent Addresses");
      if (validUnsent != null)
      {
        for (int i = 0; i < validUnsent.length; i++)
      System.out.println("          "+validUnsent[i]);
      }
    }
    Address[] validSent = sfex.getValidSentAddresses();
    if (validSent != null)
    {
      System.out.println("    ** ValidSent Addresses");
      if (validSent != null)
      {
        for (int i = 0; i < validSent.length; i++)
      System.out.println("          "+validSent[i]);
      }
    }
  }
  System.out.println();
    } while ((ex = ((MessagingException)ex).getNextException())
        != null);
  }
 }
}
```

NOTE

*You should modify the **mailhost** variable appropriately for your system.*

We can publish **sendMail.send** by creating a wrapper procedure that uses the AS LANGUAGE clause as follows:

```
-- Available online as part of SendMail.sql
CREATE OR REPLACE PROCEDURE SendMailJava (
   p_Subject IN VARCHAR2,
   p_Message IN VARCHAR2,
   p_From    IN VARCHAR2,
   p_Recipient IN VARCHAR2)
AS LANGUAGE JAVA
   NAME 'sendMail.send(java.lang.String, java.lang.String,
                       java.lang.String, java.lang.String)';
```

Once this is done, and the **sendMail** class loaded into the database, we can call **sendMailJava** with an anonymous block similar to the one here:

```
-- Available online as part of sendMail.sql
BEGIN
   SendMailJava('Test email from a Java stored procedure',
                'This is the message!',
                'The_PL/SQL_Engine',
                'YOUR_EMAIL_ADDRESS_HERE');
END;
```

NOTE
*In order to run this Java example successfully, the class needs to be loaded into the database using the loadjava command, which we will discuss later in this chapter. The **JavaMail** classes need to be loaded as well. See **sendMail.txt**, available online, for more details.*

Architecture of External Routines

Although the syntax for both C and Java external routines is similar, there are significant differences in how they are executed. To illustrate these differences, we need to examine some of the processes that make up an Oracle instance.

Figure 10-1 illustrates the communication between a client process and the Oracle server. The client process communicates with the shadow process via the Oracle Net8 protocol. The shadow process can execute PL/SQL and SQL statements. Together with the other Oracle background processes, PL/SQL subprograms can be loaded from disk storage into the shared pool portion of the SGA and executed. (For more information on how PL/SQL works in the shadow

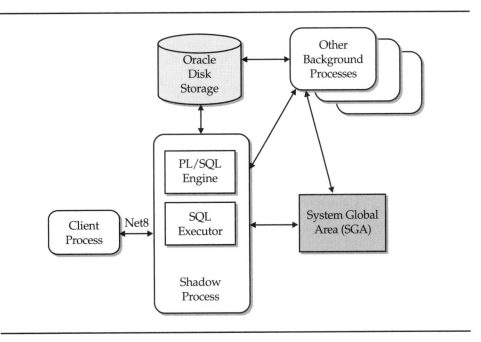

FIGURE 10-1.   *Client and shadow processes*

process, see Chapter 2, and for more information on the processes which make up an Oracle instance, see *Oracle Server Concepts.*)

Depending on the language, external routines execute either in the shadow process, or in a separate process. This architecture is illustrated in Figure 10-2. Java classes are run by Oracle JServer, which is the Java virtual machine contained in Oracle8*i*. Similar to the PL/SQL engine, JServer is within the shadow process and can thus access the SGA directly. A Java external routine therefore runs in a very similar environment to a PL/SQL stored procedure. Java external procedures are also known as *Java stored procedures (JSPs)* for this reason. A C routine, on the other hand, is executed within an external process. When the initial call to a C external routine is made, the Net8 listener spawns a special process known as *extproc*. This process will dynamically load a shared library (or more than one shared library) that contains the C subprogram and then execute it, sending the results back to the shadow process and, in turn, back to the client. Once extproc is spawned, it will persist for the life of the session. In order to execute additional routines, the shadow process and extproc can communicate directly, without going through the listener.

Why is the architecture different for C and Java external routines? C routines can overwrite memory very easily, since there is no protection built into the language,

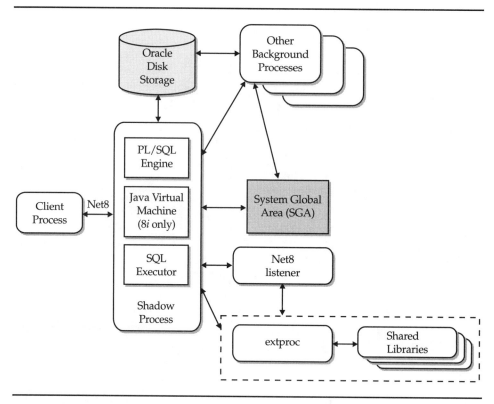

FIGURE 10-2. *Net8 listener and extproc processes*

and any memory location accessible to the operating system process can be written to. If C programs were allowed to run as part of the shadow process, the SGA would be part of the accessible process memory. A C external routine could therefore overwrite information in the SGA and consequently corrupt the database. Java, on the other hand, does not allow this type of memory access. Java classes are thus safe enough to run directly in the shadow process.

There are several things to note about this environment, which illustrate some requirements for using external routines:

■ C external routines must be in a shared library. extproc will dynamically load the library when the procedure is called. If external routines that are in a different library are called later in the session, extproc will also load that library. Thus, external routines are only supported if the underlying operating system supports shared libraries. For example, on Windows NT the external routine would be compiled into a DLL, and on Solaris it would be compiled into a shared object (.so).

■ Analogously, Java external routines must be loaded into the database, using either the loadjava tool or the SQL CREATE OR REPLACE JAVA statement.

■ Each session that calls a C external routine will have its own extproc process spawned by the SQL*Net listener. (On NT, extproc is called as a thread instead of a process, but the idea is similar). In an MTS system, extproc processes will be spawned by the shared server process, and will persist for all sessions using that shared server. Calling a Java stored procedure will not spawn extproc, since it can be run directly in the shadow process or MTS shared server.

■ The listener and extproc must be on the same machine as the database. As we will see in the following sections, the syntax for creating a library data dictionary object has no means for specifying a host name.

■ The external routine can in turn make callbacks to the database to execute additional SQL statements or PL/SQL blocks. C callbacks are done using the Oracle8 Call Interface (OCI) or Pro*C (Oracle8i only), and Java callbacks are done using either JDBC or SQLJ. Both methods are discussed in "Callbacks to the Database," later in this chapter.

■ A given session can call both C and Java external routines in the course of processing.

■ Permission to access a Java stored procedure is done through the database, since a JSP is loaded as a schema object. extproc, however, relies on operating system privileges to access the shared library.

■ Oracle8i can actually call a JSP directly without calling the wrapper. The wrapper is still necessary for compilation, however.

The main differences between C and Java external routines are described in Table 10-1.

C External Routines

We will discuss the steps necessary for creating C external routines in this section. We will also examine the mappings between PL/SQL and C datatypes.

C External Routines	Java External Routines
Run in a separate process (extproc). Thus, they do not have direct memory access to the SGA.	Run in the Java VM contained within the shadow process, which has direct memory access to the SGA.
Must be compiled into a shared library.	Must be loaded into the database.
Can call back to the database to execute SQL through Pro*C (Oracle8*i* only) or OCI.	Can call back to the database to execute SQL through JDBC or SQLJ.
Rely on the operating system to allow extproc access to the shared library.	Rely on database privileges to allow JServer access to the routine.

TABLE 10-1. *C vs. Java External Routines*

Required Steps

In order to call a C external routine, you must complete the following steps:

1. Code the routine in C and compile it into a shared library.

2. Configure the Net8 parameter files and start the listener.

3. Create a library data dictionary object to represent the operating system library.

4. Publish the external routine by creating a PL/SQL wrapper that maps the PL/SQL parameters to C parameters.

We will examine these steps in detail in the following sections.

Coding the Routine

The first step is to write the routine itself. Suppose we want to create an operating system file and write a string to it. We can do this with the **outputString** procedure defined here:

```
/* Available online as part of outputString.c */
#include <stdio.h>

/* Outputs the string contained in message to a file specified by
 * path.  The file will be created if it doesn't exist.
```

```
 */
void outputString(
  char *path,                         /* Complete path of the output file */
  char *message)                                  /* Message to be written */
{
  FILE *file_handle;

  /* Open the file for writing. */
  file_handle = fopen(path, "w");

  /* Output the string followed by a newline. */
  fprintf(file_handle, "%s\n", message);

  /* Close the file. */
  fclose(file_handle);
}
```

Once this file is created, we need to compile it into a shared library. On a Solaris Unix system, we can do this with the command

```
cc -G -o StringLib.so outputString.c
```

which will create the shared library **StringLib.so** in the current directory. The command for doing this on other operating systems will likely vary—consult your operating system and/or compiler documentation for more information.

TIP
*On Unix systems, the Makefile $ORACLE_HOME/
rdbms/demo/demo_rdbms.mk contains targets for
linking shared libraries. The extproc_nocallback
target will build a library that doesn't make
callbacks to the database, and the extproc_callback
target will build a library that does make callbacks.
(Callbacks are discussed later in this chapter in
"Callbacks to the Database.") See demo_rdbms.mk
for more details. The ch10.mk found online uses
demo_rdbms as a template, and you can create
StringLib.so with the command 'make -f ch10.mk
outputString.'*

Configuring the Net8 Listener

The listener needs to be configured only once. Once it is set up and running, the extproc process will be automatically spawned as needed. Configuring the listener requires two files—**listener.ora** and **tnsnames.ora**. Once these files are created, the listener can be started.

The default location for Net8 configuration files will vary depending on your operating system. On Unix, for example, the default location is generally $ORACLE_HOME/network/admin. Other directories, such as /etc, are also checked, depending on the particular operating system you are using. On all Unix systems, the TNS_ADMIN environment variable can be specified to override the default directory. See the Net8 documentation for more information on the configuration files and the TNS_ADMIN environment variable.

LISTENER.ORA   This file specifies the parameters for the listener. It should look something like the following:

```
#Available online as listener.ora
#Sample listener.ora for external routines.
#Replace <<ORACLE_HOME>> with the $ORACLE_HOME directory,
#replace <<LISTENER_KEY>> with an IPC key, and
#replace <<EXTPROC_SID>> with an identifier for extproc.

extproc_listener =
  (ADDRESS_LIST =
    (ADDRESS =
        (PROTOCOL = ipc)
        (KEY = <<LISTENER_KEY>>)
    )
  )

sid_list_extproc_listener =
  (SID_LIST =
    (SID_DESC =
      (SID_NAME = <<EXTPROC_SID>>)
      (ORACLE_HOME = <<ORACLE_HOME>>)
      (PROGRAM = extproc)
)
  )
```

The key thing to note about this configuration file is the (PROGRAM = extproc) section in the SID list. This entry signifies that this connection is to be used to spawn extproc, rather than to connect to a database.

TNSNAMES.ORA   This file is used to specify Net8 connect strings. extproc has a special connect string—extproc_connection_data—that is defined in **tnsnames.ora** similar to the following:

```
#Available online as tnsnames.ora
#Sample tnsnames.ora for external routines.
```

```
#Replace <<LISTENER_KEY>> with an IPC key, and
#replace <<EXTPROC_SID>> with an identifier for extproc.

extproc_connection_data =
  (DESCRIPTION =
    (ADDRESS =
      (PROTOCOL = ipc)
      (KEY = <<LISTENER_KEY>>)
    )
    (CONNECT_DATA =
      (SID = <<EXTPROC_SID>>)
    )
  )
```

The SID specified in the CONNECT_DATA clause of both **tnsnames.ora** and **listener.ora** must be the same. This can be the database SID, but it does not have to be. (For Oracle8*i*, the installer will configure these files automatically to use PLSExtProc as the SID name.) The ADDRESS clause (including the protocol) must be the same for both files as well.

NOTE
*A single listener (or set of listeners) can listen both for external procedures and new database connections. Consequently, the configuration files can include additional database connection descriptions. For more information on additional parameters for **listener.ora** and **tnsnames.ora**, see the Net8 Administrator's Guide.*

STARTING THE LISTENER   The listener is started (and stopped) using the lsnrctl utility (On some systems, the utility is known as lsnrctl80 or lsnrctl81.) This utility is launched from the operating system prompt and has a character mode interface similar to SQL*Plus. Assuming that the **listener.ora** file has been configured like the preceding examples, with PLSExtProc as both the external procedure SID and the IPC key, the following session shows the startup of the listener:

```
$ lsnrctl start extproc_listener

LSNRCTL for Solaris: Version 8.1.5.0.0 - Production on
 09-JUN-99 16:03:27

(c) Copyright 1998 Oracle Corporation.  All rights reserved.

Starting /private/oracle/app/oracle/product/8.1.5/bin/tnslsnr: please
wait
```

```
TNSLSNR for Solaris: Version 8.1.5.0.0 - Production
System parameter file is /private1/surman/book/code/ch10/listener.ora
Log messages written to /private/oracle/app/oracle/product/8.1.5/
network/log/extproc_listener.log
Listening on: (ADDRESS=(PROTOCOL=ipc)(KEY=PLSExtProc))

Connecting to (ADDRESS=(PROTOCOL=ipc)(KEY=PLSExtProc))
STATUS of the LISTENER
-----------------------
Alias                       extproc_listener
Version                     TNSLSNR for Solaris: Version 8.1.5.0.0 -
  Production
Start Date                  09-JUN-99 16:03:28
Uptime                      0 days 0 hr. 0 min. 0 sec
Trace Level                 off
Security                    OFF
SNMP                        OFF
Listener Parameter File     /private1/surman/book/code/ch10/listener.ora
Listener Log File           /private/oracle/app/oracle/product/8.1.5/
network/log/extproc_listener.log
Services Summary...
  PLSExtProc                has 1 service handler(s)
The command completed successfully
```

For more information on using lsnrctl, see the *Net8 Administrator's Guide.*

Creating the Library

A *library* is a data dictionary object that contains information about the operating system location of the shared library on disk. Since the shared library is outside the database, PL/SQL needs something in the database to represent it. Libraries are created using the DDL command CREATE LIBRARY, which has the following syntax:

CREATE LIBRARY *library_name* {IS | AS}
   '*operating_system_path*';

where *library_name* is the name of the new library, and *operating_system_path* is the complete path (including directory) of the shared library on the file system. For example, we can create the library **StringLib** using the following statement:

```
-- Available online as part of OutputString.sql
CREATE LIBRARY StringLib AS
  '/home/surman/book/code/ch10/StringLib.so';
```

A library can be dropped using the DROP LIBRARY command, which has the syntax

DROP LIBRARY *library_name*;

where *library_name* is the name of the library to be dropped.

OPERATING SYSTEM ISSUES   There are a couple of things to note about the shared object on the operating system:

- When a library object is created, the database does not verify that the operating system shared object actually exists. However, if it does not, you will receive an error when trying to call a procedure declared to use the library.

- The shared object does not need to be owned by the same operating system user that runs Oracle, but it does need to be accessible by the Oracle user.

- Likewise, the shared object does not have to be under $ORACLE_HOME, since the library object contains its full path.

PRIVILEGES ON LIBRARIES   In order to create a library, you need the CREATE LIBRARY system privilege, similar to the privileges required for other DDL commands. Once you have created a library, you can allow other users to access it by granting the EXECUTE privilege on it to other users.

LIBRARIES IN THE DATA DICTIONARY   Like other database objects, information about libraries is stored in the data dictionary. Library information is stored in the **user_libraries**, **all_libraries**, and **dba_libraries** tables. The main columns in these tables are described here:

Column	Datatype	Description
library_name	VARCHAR2(30)	Name of the library.
file_spec	VARCHAR2(2000)	Operating system path of the shared library as specified in the CREATE LIBRARY statement.
dynamic	VARCHAR2(1)	If Y, the library is dynamic. If N, it is not. With Oracle8 and Oracle8*i*, only dynamic libraries are supported for external use.
status	VARCHAR2(7)	VALID or INVALID, similar to the status column in other dictionary views.

The following query shows the information about **StringLib**, assuming that it was created as described previously:

```
SQL> SELECT * FROM user_libraries
  2    WHERE library_name = 'STRINGLIB';

LIBRARY_NAME    FILE_SPEC                                        D STATUS
--------------  ----------------------------------------------- - ------
STRINGLIB       /home/surman/book/code/ch10/StringLib.so        Y VALID
```

For more information on the data dictionary and other information stored there, see Appendix C on the CD-ROM that accompanies this book.

Publishing the Routine

In order to call an external routine from PL/SQL, it must be published. This is done by creating a PL/SQL wrapper, which serves several purposes: It maps the PL/SQL parameters to C parameters, it serves as a placeholder so that calling procedures can determine dependencies, and it tells PL/SQL the name of the external library. A wrapper consists of a subprogram specification (including the parameters, if any), followed by the AS EXTERNAL clause (Oracle8) or the AS LANGUAGE clause (Oracle8*i*). The wrapper can be a standalone procedure or function, or part of a package or type body. In Oracle8*i*, wrappers can be in package or type headers as well. The Oracle8 syntax is as follows:

```
{PROCEDURE | FUNCTION} procedure_name [parameter_list]
    AS EXTERNAL
    LIBRARY library_name
    [NAME external_name]
    [LANGUAGE C]
    [CALLING STANDARD {C | PASCAL}]
    [WITH CONTEXT]
    [PARAMETERS (external_parameter_list)];
```

The Oracle8*i* syntax is very similar:

```
{PROCEDURE | FUNCTION} procedure_name [parameter_list]
    AS LANGUAGE C
    LIBRARY library_name
    [NAME external_name]
    [CALLING STANDARD {C | PASCAL}]
    [WITH CONTEXT]
    [PARAMETERS (external_parameter_list)];
```

The appropriate keywords (such as CREATE OR REPLACE for a standalone wrapper) are necessary before the PROCEDURE or FUNCTION keyword. Each of the clauses is described in the following sections.

NOTE
Oracle8i accepts both the AS LANGUAGE and AS EXTERNAL clauses for backwards compatibility. AS LANGUAGE is preferable, however, since it is also used for Java external routines.

LIBRARY   This is the only required clause, and it is used to specify the library that represents the operating system shared library containing the C procedure. This library must either be in the current schema, or you must have EXECUTE privileges on it.

NAME   This clause specifies the name of the C procedure. If it is not specified, it defaults to the name of the PL/SQL wrapper. Note, however, that PL/SQL names are stored in all uppercase, so if the C procedure is lowercase or mixed case, a double-quoted identifier is necessary here.

LANGUAGE   The LANGUAGE clause is used only with the AS EXTERNAL Oracle8 syntax. It is used to specify the language in which the external routine is written. If not specified, it defaults to C, which is the only supported language for external routines for Oracle8. The AS LANGUAGE clause (as opposed to the LANGUAGE C clause in Oracle8) is used in Oracle8*i*.

CALLING STANDARD   The calling standard can be either C or PASCAL. This determines the order in which parameters are placed on the stack. The default is C, which should normally be used for external routines written in C. With the PASCAL calling standard, the external routine is responsible for explicitly popping the stack to retrieve the parameters, and the parameters are reversed. You should use the PASCAL calling standard only if your compiler or operating system generates code that uses it.

WITH CONTEXT   This clause should be used if the external routine will make callbacks to the database. It will add a parameter to the C procedure, which can be used to get the necessary OCI handles. This clause is discussed in detail in "Callbacks to the Database," later in this chapter.

PARAMETERS   The PARAMETERS clause specifies how the PL/SQL parameters of the wrapper are mapped into C parameters for the external routine. If it is not specified, then the default mappings are used. This clause is discussed in detail in the next section, "Parameter Mappings."

The following example is a wrapper procedure for **OutputString**:

```
-- Available online as part of OutputString.sql
CREATE OR REPLACE PROCEDURE OutputString(
  p_Path IN VARCHAR2,
  p_Message IN VARCHAR2) AS EXTERNAL

  LIBRARY StringLib
  NAME "outputString"
  PARAMETERS (p_Path STRING,
              p_Message STRING);
```

After creating this, we can call **OutputString** directly from a PL/SQL block. For example, the following block will create a file called **output.txt** in the /tmp directory, which contains the single line "Hello World!" This is illustrated by the sample SQL*Plus and host session that follows.

```
-- Available online as part of callOS.sql
SQL> BEGIN
  2    OutputString('/tmp/output.txt', 'Hello World!');
  3  END;
  4  /
PL/SQL procedure successfully completed.

SQL> exit
Disconnected from Oracle8i Enterprise Edition Release 8.1.5.0.0 -
 Production
With the Partitioning and Java options
PL/SQL Release 8.1.5.0.0 - Production
$ cat /tmp/output.txt
Hello World!
```

TIP
*The online **callOS.sql** file contains calls to all of the different versions of **OutputString** that we will examine in this chapter.*

The wrapper procedure does not have to be a standalone procedure. For example, it can be part of a package, as the following example illustrates

```
-- Available online as part of OutputString.sql
CREATE OR REPLACE PACKAGE OutputPkg AS
```

```
   PROCEDURE OutputString(p_Path IN VARCHAR2,
                          p_Message IN VARCHAR2);
END OutputPkg;

CREATE OR REPLACE PACKAGE BODY OutputPkg AS
  PROCEDURE OutputString(
    p_Path IN VARCHAR2,
    p_Message IN VARCHAR2) IS EXTERNAL
    LIBRARY StringLib
    NAME "outputString"
    PARAMETERS (p_Path STRING,
                p_Message STRING);
END OutputPkg;
```

We will see more examples of external routines that are not standalone procedures later in this chapter, in "Other Locations for External Routines."

Parameter Mappings

One of the main issues when communicating between two languages is how to convert between datatypes. This is true with external routines as well: You need to specify how the PL/SQL datatypes used for the parameters in the wrapper map to the C datatypes used for the parameters in the external routine. Besides the datatypes themselves, there are other issues that need to be resolved

■ In PL/SQL, any variable can be NULL. C has no concept of NULL (in the SQL or PL/SQL sense), and so an additional variable known as an *indicator* can be passed to indicate whether or not the parameter is NULL.

■ PL/SQL includes datatypes that are not in C, and C includes datatypes that are not in PL/SQL. For example, C has no DATE or BOOLEAN type, while PL/SQL does not distinguish between a one-, two-, and four-byte integer.

■ PL/SQL can accommodate character variables in different character sets. These character sets need to be communicated to C.

■ C needs to know the current and/or maximum length for character strings passed from PL/SQL.

■ PL/SQL needs to know the current and/or maximum length for character strings passed from C.

The PARAMETERS clause is used to resolve all of these concerns, as we will see in this section. It has the following structure:

PARAMETERS (*external_parameter_list*);

The *external_parameter_list* is a list of parameters, each of which has the structure:

{*parameter_name* | SELF | RETURN} *property*
        [BY REFERENCE | VALUE] [*external_datatype*]

where *parameter_name* is the name of the parameter, *external_datatype* is the C datatype to be assigned to this parameter, and *property* is one of INDICATOR, LENGTH, MAXLEN, CHARSETID, and CHARSETFORM. We will examine these clauses in the next sections.

PL/SQL vs. C Datatypes

Since PL/SQL and C do not have the same set of datatypes, Oracle8 and Oracle8*i* provide a default C datatype for each PL/SQL datatype. You can override this default if desired. To facilitate this process, Oracle defines a set of *external datatypes*. An external datatype is a mnemonic for a commonly used C type, or an Oracle-defined type (such as OCILOBLOCATOR). External datatypes can be used in Pro*C or OCI programs, as well as the PARAMETERS clause. Table 10-2 describes the external datatypes that are appropriate for external routines, and Table 10-3 describes the available external datatypes for each PL/SQL datatype. In Table 10-3, the default datatype is in bold.

NOTE
*Oracle8*i *allows you to pass instances of an object type to an external routine. For more information, see the Oracle documentation.*

External Datatype	Description	C Datatype	Notes
CHAR	One-byte quantity, used to store either a character or integer ranging from –128 to +127	char	1
UNSIGNED CHAR	One-byte quantity, used to store integers ranging from 0 to 255	unsigned char	1

TABLE 10-2. *External Datatypes*

External Datatype	Description	C Datatype	Notes
SHORT	Two-byte quantity, used to store an integer ranging from -2^{15} to $+2^{15}-1$	short	1, 2
UNSIGNED SHORT	An unsigned two-byte quantity, used to store an integer ranging from 0 to $+2^{16}$	unsigned short	1, 2
INT	Usually a four-byte quantity, used to store an integer ranging from -2^{31} to $+2^{31}-1$	int	1, 2
UNSIGNED INT	Usually an unsigned four-byte quantity, used to store an integer ranging from 0 to 2^{32}	unsigned int	1, 2
LONG	Usually a four-byte quantity, used to store an integer ranging from -2^{31} to $+2^{31}-1$	long	1, 2
UNSIGNED LONG	Usually an unsigned four-byte quantity, used to store an integer ranging from 0 to 2^{32}	unsigned long	1, 2
SIZE_T	Number of bytes is specified by the operating system and compiler	size_t	1, 2
SB1	Signed one-byte quantity	sb1	3
UB1	Unsigned one-byte quantity	ub1	3
SB2	Signed two-byte quantity	sb2	3
UB2	Unsigned two-byte quantity	ub2	3
SB4	Signed four-byte quantity	sb4	3
UB4	Unsigned four-byte quantity	ub4	3
FLOAT	Four-byte quantity, used to store floating-point numbers	float	1, 2

TABLE 10-2.   *External Datatypes* (continued)

External Datatype	Description	C Datatype	Notes
DOUBLE	Eight-byte quantity, used to store floating-point numbers	double	1, 2
STRING	Used to store variable length null-terminated character strings	char *	1
RAW	Used to store variable length binary strings	unsigned char *	1
OCILOBLOCATOR	Used in OCI functions to manipulate LOBs in the database	OCILobLocator *	4
OCINUMBER	Used in OCI functions to manipulate Oracle NUMBERs	OCINumber *	4,5
OCISTRING	Used in OCI functions to manipulate Oracle strings	OCIString *	4,5
OCIRAW	Used in OCI functions to manipulate Oracle RAWs	OCIRaw *	4,5
OCIDATE	Used in OCI functions to manipulate Oracle DATEs	OCIDate *	4,5
OCICOLL	Used in OCI functions to manipulate collections (varrays and nested tables)	OCIColl *, OCIArray *, or OCITable *	4,5
OCITYPE	Used in OCI functions to manipulate generic object types	OCIType *	4,5,6
TDO	Used in OCI functions to manipulate type descriptor objects (TDOs)	OCIType *	4,5,6
ADT	Used in OCI functions to manipulate Oracle object types.	dvoid *	4,5,6

TABLE 10-2. *External Datatypes* (continued)

Note 1: This is a standard C datatype.

Note 2: The size of this type can vary, depending on the operating system and compiler. Thus it is not always portable.

Note 3: This is an Oracle-defined datatype, which is defined in the header file **oratypes.h**.

Note 4: This is an Oracle-defined datatype, which is defined in the header file **oci.h**.

Note 5: This type can be passed to external routines only with Oracle8*i* and higher

Note 6: Composite Oracle object types are not self-describing. In order to manipulate them with OCI, the type descriptor object (which can be generated with the Oracle Type Translator) is used to describe the attributes of the object type. For more information on using TDOs and OTT, see the Oracle documentation.

TABLE 10-2. *External Datatypes* (continued)

PL/SQL Type	Supported External Datatypes
CHAR, CHARACTER, LONG, ROWID, VARCHAR, VARCHAR2, NVARCHAR, NVARCHAR2	**STRING**, OCISTRING (8*i* only)
BINARY_INTEGER, BOOLEAN, PLS_INTEGER	CHAR, UNSIGNED CHAR, SHORT, UNSIGNED SHORT, **INT**, UNSIGNED INT, LONG, UNSIGNED LONG, SB1, UB1, SB2, UB2, SB4, UB4, SIZE_T
NATURAL, NATURALN, POSITIVE, POSITIVEN, SIGNTYPE	CHAR, UNSIGNED CHAR, SHORT, UNSIGNED SHORT, INT, **UNSIGNED INT**, LONG, UNSIGNED LONG, SB1, UB1, SB2, UB2, SB4, UB4, SIZE_T
FLOAT, REAL	**FLOAT**
DOUBLE PRECISION	**DOUBLE**

TABLE 10-3. *PL/SQL and External Datatype Mappings*

PL/SQL Type	Supported External Datatypes
LONG RAW, RAW	**RAW**
BFILE, BLOB, CLOB, NCLOB	**OCILOBLOCATOR**
NUMBER, DEC, DECIMAL, INT, INTEGER, NUMERIC, SMALLINT	CHAR, UNSIGNED CHAR, SHORT, UNSIGNED SHORT, INT, UNSIGNED INT, LONG, UNSIGNED LONG, SB1, UB1, SB2, UB2, SB4, UB4, SIZE_T, **OCINUMBER**
DATE	**OCIDATE**
Any object type	**ADT**
Collections	**OCICOLL**

Note: The NUMBER, DATE, and object type mappings are available in Oracle8*i* only.

bold = Default external datatype

TABLE 10-3. *PL/SQL and External Datatype Mappings* (continued)

Each entry in the PARAMETERS clause represents a parameter to the C external function. For example, consider the **OutputString** routine, which we examined earlier. The wrapper procedure has a PARAMETERS clause like

```
CREATE OR REPLACE PROCEDURE OutputString(
    p_Path IN VARCHAR2,
    p_Message IN VARCHAR2) AS EXTERNAL
    ...
    PARAMETERS (p_Path STRING,
                p_Message STRING);
```

and the C function is defined with

```
void outputString(
    char *path;                 /* Complete path of the output file */
    char *message;                      /* Message to be written */
{
    ...
```

This clause specifies that **p_Path** and **p_Message** are to be passed to C using the external datatype STRING. According to Table 10-3, this is a legal mapping. Table

10-2 indicates that the proper C datatype is a null-terminated string of type **char ***, and this is how the parameters to the C function are declared. Since the default external datatype for VARCHAR2 is STRING, the PARAMETERS clause could have been omitted in this case.

TIP
I don't recommend omitting the PARAMETERS clause. Besides providing useful documentation about the external routine, the PARAMETERS clause allows you to pass additional information, such as indicators or character string lengths.

Alternatively, consider **outputString2**, which takes an **int** parameter. This parameter indicates the number of times the message should be repeated. The C function is defined with

```
-- Available online as part of outputString.c
/* Outputs the string contained in message to a file specified by
 * path.  The message is repeated num_times times.  The file will
 * be created if it doesn't exist.
 */
  void outputString2(
  char *path;                     /* Complete path of the output file */
  char *message;                          /* Message to be written */
  int   num_times)      /* Number of times the message is repeated */
{
FILE *file_handle;
  int counter;

  /* Open the file for writing. */
  file_handle = fopen(path, "w");

  for (counter = 0; counter < num_times; counter++)
    /* Output the string followed by a newline. */
    fprintf(file_handle, "%s\n", message);

  /* Close the file. */
  fclose(file_handle);
}
```

and the wrapper procedure is defined with

```
-- Available online as part of OutputString.sql
CREATE OR REPLACE PROCEDURE OutputString2(
  p_Path IN VARCHAR2,
```

```
    p_Message IN VARCHAR2,
    p_NumLines IN BINARY_INTEGER) AS EXTERNAL

  LIBRARY StringLib
  NAME "outputString2"
PARAMETERS (p_Path STRING,
            p_Message STRING,
            p_NumLines INT);
```

Note that **p_NumLines** specifies INT as the external datatype.

Parameter Modes

The parameters for the wrapper procedure (and hence for the external routine) can be of any PL/SQL mode—IN, OUT, or IN OUT. As we discussed in Chapter 4, OUT and IN OUT parameters are passed by reference rather than by value. Thus, the associated C parameter must be passed by reference as well. In C, this is done by passing the parameter as a pointer. **OutputString3** illustrates this. Note that **p_NumLinesWritten** is OUT, and thus the associated C parameter is passed as **int ***, rather than **int**. The code for the wrapper and external routine follows.

NOTE
IN parameters can be passed by reference to the C procedure as well, if desired. See the following section, "Using BY REFERENCE and BY VALUE," for more details.

```
-- Available online as part of outputString.c
/* Outputs the string contained in message to a file specified by
 * path.  The message is repeated num_times times.  The file will
 * be created if it doesn't exist.  The number of lines actually
 * written is returned in num_lines_written.
 */
void outputString3(
  char *path,                      /* Complete path of the output file */
  char *message,                         /* Message to be written */
  int   num_times,      /* Number of times the message is repeated */
  int  *num_lines_written)     /* Number of lines actually written */
{

  FILE *file_handle;
  int    counter;

  /* Open the file for writing. */
  file_handle = fopen(path, "w");
```

```
  /* Initialize num_lines_written */
  *num_lines_written = 0;

  for (counter = 0; counter < num_times; counter++)  {
    /* Output the string followed by a newline. */
    fprintf(file_handle, "%s\n", message);
    (*num_lines_written)++;
  }

  /* Close the file. */
  fclose(file_handle);
}
```

```
-- Available online as part of OutputString.sql
CREATE OR REPLACE PROCEDURE OutputString3(
  p_Path IN VARCHAR2,
  p_Message IN VARCHAR2,
  p_NumLines IN BINARY_INTEGER,
  p_NumLinesWritten OUT NATURAL) AS EXTERNAL

  LIBRARY StringLib
  NAME "outputString3"
  PARAMETERS (p_Path STRING,
              p_Message STRING,
              p_NumLines INT,
              p_NumLinesWritten INT);
```

The results of calling **OutputString3** are shown by the following SQL*Plus and host session:

```
-- Available online as part of callOS.sql
SQL> DECLARE
  2     v_NumLinesWritten NATURAL;
  3   BEGIN
  4     OutputString3(p_Path => '/tmp/output.txt',
  5                   p_Message => 'Hello from version 3!',
  6                   p_NumLines => 7,
  7                   p_NumLinesWritten => v_NumLinesWritten);
  8     DBMS_OUTPUT.PUT_LINE('Lines written = ' || v_NumLinesWritten);
  9   END;
 10   /
Lines written = 7
PL/SQL procedure successfully completed.
SQL> exit
Disconnected from Oracle8i Enterprise Edition Release 8.1.5.0.0 -
 Production
With the Partitioning and Java options
```

```
PL/SQL Release 8.1.5.0.0 - Production
$ cat /tmp/output.txt
Hello from version 3!
Hello from version 3!
Hello from version 3!
Hello from version 3!
Hello from version 3!
Hello from version 3!
Hello from version 3!
```

In general, passing a parameter by reference means that the corresponding C argument is a pointer. There are two caveats to this rule, however:

■ A parameter with external datatype STRING (C type char *) or RAW (C type unsigned char *) is always passed by reference, regardless of the associated parameter mode. This is because C has no built-in string datatype, and represents strings as an array of characters. Arrays in C have to be passed by reference.

■ Complex datatypes such as OCINUMBER, OCISTRING, OCIRAW, OCIDATE, OCITYPE, TDO, and ADT are also always passed by reference.

The **ExternalModes** package, shown next, illustrates the behavior of different parameter types and modes. Note that all OUT and IN OUT parameters are passed by reference. The library **ModeLib** referenced by **ExternalModes** is created with

```
-- Available online as part of ExternalModes.sql
CREATE OR REPLACE LIBRARY ModeLib AS
   '/home/surman/book/code/ch10/modelib.so';
```

and the package itself is created with

```
-- Available online as part of ExternalModes.sql
CREATE OR REPLACE PACKAGE ExternalModes AS
   -- This package contains various wrapper routines, each of which
   -- has a corresponding C implementation in externalModes.c.  They
   -- serve to illustrate different kinds of parameter mappings.

   -- Pass some numbers of varying type and mode.
   PROCEDURE NumberP(p_Param1 IN BINARY_INTEGER,
                     p_Param2 OUT BINARY_INTEGER,
                     p_Param3 IN OUT BINARY_INTEGER,
                     p_Param4 IN DOUBLE PRECISION,
                     p_Param5 OUT FLOAT);

   -- Pass some character strings of varying mode.
```

```
      PROCEDURE CharP(p_Param1 IN CHAR,
                      p_Param2 OUT VARCHAR2,
                      p_Param3 IN OUT VARCHAR2);


      -- Pass some LOB locators of varying mode.
      PROCEDURE LobP(p_Param1 IN CLOB,
                     p_Param2 OUT CLOB,
                     p_Param3 IN OUT CLOB);

END ExternalModes;

CREATE OR REPLACE PACKAGE BODY ExternalModes AS
   -- Pass some numbers of varying type and mode.
   PROCEDURE NumberP(p_Param1 IN BINARY_INTEGER,
                     p_Param2 OUT BINARY_INTEGER,
                     p_Param3 IN OUT BINARY_INTEGER,
                     p_Param4 IN DOUBLE PRECISION,
                     p_Param5 OUT FLOAT)
   IS EXTERNAL
     LIBRARY ModeLib
     NAME "NumberP"
     PARAMETERS (p_Param1 INT,      -- IN, passed by value
                 p_Param2 INT,      -- OUT, passed by reference
                 p_Param3 UB4,      -- IN OUT, passed by reference
                 p_Param4 DOUBLE,   -- IN, passed by value
                 p_Param5 FLOAT);   -- OUT, passed by reference

   -- Pass some character strings of varying mode.  Since all of the
   -- parameters have external datatype STRING, they are always
   -- passed by reference regardless of mode.
   PROCEDURE CharP(p_Param1 IN CHAR,
                   p_Param2 OUT VARCHAR2,
                   p_Param3 IN OUT VARCHAR2)
   IS EXTERNAL
     LIBRARY ModeLib
     NAME "CharP"
     PARAMETERS (p_Param1 STRING,   -- IN, passed by reference
                 p_Param2 STRING,   -- OUT, passed by reference
                 p_Param3 STRING);  -- IN OUT, passed by reference

   -- Pass some LOB locators of varying mode.
   PROCEDURE LobP(p_Param1 IN CLOB,
                  p_Param2 OUT CLOB,
                  p_Param3 IN OUT CLOB)
   IS EXTERNAL
     LIBRARY ModeLib
     NAME "LobP"
     WITH CONTEXT
```

```
        PARAMETERS (CONTEXT,
                    p_Param1 OCILOBLOCATOR,   -- IN, passed by value
                    p_Param1 INDICATOR,
                    p_Param2 OCILOBLOCATOR,   -- OUT, passed by
                                              -- reference
                    p_Param2 INDICATOR,
                    p_Param3 OCILOBLOCATOR,   -- IN OUT, passed by
                                              -- reference
                    p_Param3 INDICATOR);
END ExternalModes;
```

NOTE

LobP uses the WITH CONTEXT and INDICATOR clauses, discussed later in this chapter. For more information on using LOBs, see Chapter 15 on the CD-ROM that accompanies this book.

ExternalModes will compile successfully against both Oracle8 and Oracle8i. We can create the corresponding C external routines with the following. See the online file for additional routines, such as the declaration of the **CHECKERROR** macro.

```
/* Available online as part of externalModes.c */
#include <oci.h>
#include <stdio.h>
#include <common_OCI.h>

/* Corresponding PL/SQL parameters:
 *    PARAMETERS (p_Param1 INT,       -- IN
 *                p_Param2 INT,       -- OUT
 *                p_Param3 UB4,       -- IN OUT
 *                p_Param4 DOUBLE,    -- IN
 *                p_Param5 FLOAT);    -- OUT
 */
void numberP(
  int p1,                              /* IN, passed by value */
  int *p2,                       /* OUT, passed by reference */
  ub4 *p3,                    /* IN OUT, passed by reference */
  double p4                            /* IN, passed by value */
  float *p5)                     /* OUT, passed by reference */
{

  /* Just do some simple stuff with the parameters. */
  *p2 = p1 + 7;            /* Reading from IN, assigning to OUT */
  *p3 = *p3 - 50;         /* Reading and writing to IN OUT */
```

```
  *p5 = p4 / 4.5;              /* Reading from IN, assigning to OUT */
}

/* Corresponding PL/SQL parameters:
 *    PARAMETERS(p_Param1 CHAR,        -- IN
 *               p_Param2 VARCHAR2,    -- OUT
 *               p_Param3 VARCHAR2);   -- IN OUT
 */
void charP(
  char *p1,                             /* IN, passed by reference */
  char *p2,                             /* OUT, passed by reference */
  char *p3)                         /* IN OUT, passed by reference */
{

  /* Some string manipulations.  Since we don't know the current
     and max length of the strings, copy at most 10 characters.
     This requires that the input PL/SQL variables be at least 10
     characters in length. */

  /* Reading from IN and IN OUT, assigning to OUT */
  sprintf(p2, "%.5s %.4s", p1, p3);

  /* Assigning to IN OUT */
  sprintf(p3, "new p3");
}

/* Corresponding PL/SQL parameters:
 *    PARAMETERS(CONTEXT,
 *               p_Param1 OCILOBLOCATOR,      -- IN
 *               p_Param1 INDICATOR,
 *               p_Param2 OCILOBLOCATOR,      -- OUT
 *               p_Param2 INDICATOR,
 *               p_Param3 OCILOBLOCATOR,      -- IN OUT
 *               p_Param3 INDICATOR);
 */
void lobP(
  OCIExtProcContext *context,           /* External routine context */
  OCILobLocator   *p1,                    /* IN, passed by value */
  short           p1_ind,                 /* IN, passed by value */
  OCILobLocator   **p2,                 /* OUT, passed by reference */
  short           *p2_ind,              /* OUT, passed by reference */
  OCILobLocator   **p3,             /* IN OUT, passed by reference */
  short           *p3_ind)          /* IN OUT, passed by reference */
  {

  OCIEnv      *envHandle;
  OCISvcCtx   *svcHandle;
```

```
OCIError    *errHandle;

/* Get OCI handles from the external procedure context */
OCIExtProcGetEnv(context, &envHandle, &svcHandle,
                 &errHandle);

/* p2 is an OUT parameter, so it is initialized to NULL.
 * Consequently, we will get an error if we try to use it in an OCI
 * LOB function directly. See the OCI manual for more information
 * on NULL LOB locators.
 */

/* Append p1 to the end of p3. */
CHECKERROR(context, errHandle, OCILobAppend(
  svcHandle,           /* svchp */
  errHandle,           /* errhp */
  *p3,                 /* dst_locp */
  p1));                /* src_locp */


/* Append p3 to the end of itself. */
CHECKERROR(context, errHandle, OCILobAppend(
  svcHandle,           /* svchp */
  errHandle,           /* errhp */
  *p3,                 /* dst_locp */
  *p3));               /* src_locp */
}
```

NOTE

*The **callEM.sql** file, available online, illustrates how to call the subprograms in **ExternalModes**. The online Makefile **ch10.mk** also includes a target **externalModes** to compile **externalModes.c** into the **modelib** shared object.*

Using BY REFERENCE and BY VALUE

As we saw in the **ExternalModes** example in the previous section, by default all scalar IN parameters are passed by value, and IN OUT and OUT parameters by reference. If desired, however, you can pass an IN parameter by reference, which can be faster if the data is long. This is done with the BY REFERENCE clause, as illustrated by the following example:

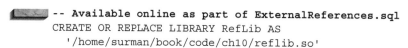

```
-- Available online as part of ExternalReferences.sql
CREATE OR REPLACE LIBRARY RefLib AS
  '/home/surman/book/code/ch10/reflib.so'
```

```
-- Illustrate passing an IN parameter by reference.
CREATE OR REPLACE PROCEDURE ExternalReferences (
     p_Param1 IN BINARY_INTEGER,
     p_Param2 IN BINARY_INTEGER,
     p_Param3 OUT BINARY_INTEGER,
     p_Param4 OUT BINARY_INTEGER)
     AS EXTERNAL
     LIBRARY RefLib
     NAME "externalReferences"
     PARAMETERS (p_Param1 SB4,              -- IN, passed by value
                 p_Param2 BY REFERENCE SB4, -- IN, passed by reference
                 p_Param3 SB4,              -- OUT, passed by reference
                 p_Param4 SB4);             -- OUT, passed by reference
```

p_Param2, although an IN parameter, will be passed by reference. The corresponding C routine is therefore

```
/* Available online as externalReferences.c */
/* Include oci.h for definitions of sb4 types */
#include <oci.h>

/* Corresponding PL/SQL Parameters:
* PARAMETERS (p_Param1 SB4,              -- IN
*             p_Param2 SB4 BY REFERENCE, -- IN
*             p_Param3 SB4,              -- OUT
*             p_Param4 SB4);             -- OUT
*/
void externalReferences(
  sb4  p1,                                /* IN, passed by value */
  sb4 *p2,                                /* IN, passed by reference */
  sb4 *p3,                                /* OUT, passed by reference */
  sb4 *p4)                                /* OUT, passed by reference */
  {

  /* Set p3 = p1 * 2, and p4 = p2 * 3 */
  *p3 = p1 * 2;
  *p4 = *p2 * 3;
}
```

TIP
*The **externalRefs** target in **ch10.mk** can be used to compile **externalReferences.c** into the **reflib** shared object.*

The BY REFERENCE clause should appear after the parameter name, but before the external datatype. You can also use BY VALUE here, which indicates that the parameter is to be passed by value. This is only valid for IN parameters, however. It is an error to pass an IN OUT or OUT parameter by value, since a result has to be returned. Since IN parameters are passed by value by default, the BY VALUE clause can be used to document the behavior of the external routine. For example, we could write **ExternalReferences** as follows instead:

```
-- Available online as part of ExternalReferences.sql
-- Explicitly document the behavior using BY VALUE
CREATE OR REPLACE PROCEDURE ExternalReferences (
  p_Param1 IN BINARY_INTEGER,
  p_Param2 IN BINARY_INTEGER,
  p_Param3 OUT BINARY_INTEGER,
  p_Param4 OUT BINARY_INTEGER)
AS EXTERNAL
LIBRARY RefLib
NAME "externalReferences"
PARAMETERS (
  p_Param1 BY VALUE SB4,        -- IN, passed by value
  p_Param2 BY REFERENCE SB4,    -- IN, passed by reference
  p_Param3 BY REFERENCE SB4,    -- OUT, passed by reference
  p_Param4 BY REFERENCE SB4);   -- OUT, passed by reference
```

TIP
*The online file **callER.sql** contains an example
of calling **ExternalReferences**.*

Parameter Properties

Along with the external datatype, the PARAMETERS clause is used to specify additional information, known as *properties*, for each parameter. Each property maps to another parameter in the C routine (but there is no equivalent parameter in the PL/SQL wrapper). The available properties are described along with their corresponding supported datatypes in Table 10-4. Similar to Table 10-3, the default external datatype for each property is in bold. An example follows the property descriptions.

INDICATOR   An indicator is used to specify whether the associated parameter is NULL. PL/SQL variables can be NULL, while C variables cannot. Thus the indicator is required, since the external procedure may need to know if a parameter is NULL, or the RDBMS may need to know if a returned parameter is NULL. An indicator value of OCI_IND_NULL (defined in the OCI header files to be –1) signifies that the associated parameter is NULL, while an indicator value of OCI_IND_NOTNULL (defined to be 0) signifies that the associated parameter is not NULL.

Property	Supported External Datatypes
INDICATOR	**SHORT**, INT, LONG
LENGTH, MAXLEN	SHORT, UNSIGNED SHORT, **INT**, UNSIGNED INT, LONG, UNSIGNED LONG
CHARSETID, CHARSETFORM	UNSIGNED SHORT, **UNSIGNED INT**, UNSIGNED LONG

bold: Default external datatype

TABLE 10-4.   *Parameter Properties*

For IN parameters, the C routine can check the value of the indicator to determine the NULLness of the associated parameter. The indicator is passed by value, unless BY REFERENCE is used in the parameters clause. Either way, it is considered read-only for IN parameters. For IN OUT or OUT parameters, as well as function return values, the indicator is passed by reference, along with the associated parameter. The C routine should then set the indicator appropriately.

LENGTH AND MAXLEN   LENGTH is used to store the current length, and MAXLEN the maximum length, of a character (CHAR or VARCHAR2) or raw (RAW or LONG RAW) parameter. They are necessary to ensure that an external routine knows the length of input parameters and does not overwrite the space for output parameters.

For IN parameters, the LENGTH property is passed by value (unless BY REFERENCE is used). It is considered read-only in the external routine. MAXLEN does not apply to IN parameters, since they cannot be written to by the routine. For IN OUT or OUT parameters, along with function return values, both LENGTH and MAXLEN are passed by reference, along with their associated parameter. MAXLEN, although passed by reference, is considered read-only. The routine is responsible for setting LENGTH to the correct value for the returned data (which should not exceed MAXLEN).

NOTE

If the returned parameter is NULL, then LENGTH should be specified as zero, and the length of the parameter should also be set to zero. This is done for strings by putting a null byte ('\0') as the first character.

CHARSETID AND CHARSETFORM   These properties are used to specify the character set ID and form, respectively. They are used in NLS environments for CHAR, CLOB, and VARCHAR2 parameters. The equivalent OCI attributes are OCI_ATTR_CHARSET_ID and OCI_ATTR_CHARSET_FORM.

For IN parameters, both properties are passed by value (unless BY REFERENCE is specified). They are passed by reference for IN OUT and OUT parameters and function return values. They are always considered read-only, and cannot be modified by the external routine.

For more information on using these properties in OCI, see the OCI and/or NLS documentation.

EXAMPLE   The **ExternalProps** package contains two external routines that illustrate the use of properties. The SQL code for the package and the C code for the external routines are provided here:

```
-- Available online as ExternalProps.sql
CREATE OR REPLACE LIBRARY PropLib AS
  '/home/surman/book/code/ch10/proplib.so';

CREATE OR REPLACE PACKAGE ExternalProps AS
  PROCEDURE IndicatorP(p_Parameter1 IN BINARY_INTEGER,
                       p_Parameter2 IN OUT VARCHAR2,
                       p_Parameter3 OUT VARCHAR2);

  PROCEDURE LengthP(p_Parameter1 IN VARCHAR2,
                    p_Parameter2 IN OUT VARCHAR2,
                    p_Parameter3 OUT VARCHAR2);
END ExternalProps;

CREATE OR REPLACE PACKAGE BODY ExternalProps AS
  PROCEDURE IndicatorP(p_Parameter1 IN BINARY_INTEGER,
                       p_Parameter2 IN OUT VARCHAR2,
                       p_Parameter3 OUT VARCHAR2)
    IS EXTERNAL
    LIBRARY PropLib
    NAME "indicatorP"
    PARAMETERS (p_Parameter1 INT,
                p_Parameter1 INDICATOR,
                p_Parameter2 STRING,
                p_Parameter2 INDICATOR,
                p_Parameter3 STRING,
                p_Parameter3 INDICATOR);

  PROCEDURE LengthP(p_Parameter1 IN VARCHAR2,
                    p_Parameter2 IN OUT VARCHAR2,
```

```
                        p_Parameter3 OUT VARCHAR2)
    IS EXTERNAL
    LIBRARY PropLib
    NAME "lengthP"
    PARAMETERS(p_Parameter1 STRING,
               p_Parameter1 INDICATOR,
               p_Parameter1 LENGTH,
               p_Parameter2 STRING,
               p_Parameter2 INDICATOR,
               p_Parameter2 LENGTH,
               p_Parameter2 MAXLEN,
               p_Parameter3 STRING,
               p_Parameter3 INDICATOR,
               p_Parameter3 LENGTH,
               p_Parameter3 MAXLEN);
END ExternalProps;
```

```
/* Available online as externalProps.c */
#include <stdio.h>
#include <oci.h>

/* Corresponding PL/SQL Parameters:
 *    PARAMETERS (p_Parameter1 INT,          -- IN
 *                p_Parameter1 INDICATOR,    -- IN
 *                p_Parameter2 STRING,       -- IN OUT
 *                p_Parameter2 INDICATOR,    -- IN OUT
 *                p_Parameter3 STRING,       -- OUT
 *                p_Parameter3 INDICATOR);   -- OUT
 */
void indicatorP(
  int     p1,                    /* p_Parameter1, passed by value */
  short   p1_ind,       /* p_Parameter1 indicator, passed by value */
  char    *p2,                   /* p_Parameter2, passed by reference */
  short   *p2_ind,  /* p_Parameter2 indicator, passed by reference */
  char    *p3,                   /* p_Parameter3, passed by reference */
  short   *p3_ind)  /* p_Parameter3 indicator, passed by reference */
{

  /* If p1 is NULL, then return a string in p2, and NULL in p3.
     Set the output indicators appropriately. */
  if (p1_ind == OCI_IND_NULL)
  {
    strcpy(p2, "p1 was null!");
    *p2_ind = OCI_IND_NOTNULL;
    *p3_ind = OCI_IND_NULL;
  }
  else
```

```
      /* p1 is not NULL.  If p2 is NULL, then return a string in p3. */
      if (*p2_ind == OCI_IND_NULL)
      {
        strcpy(p3, "p1 not null, p2 null!");
        *p3_ind = OCI_IND_NOTNULL;
      }
      else
      {
        /* Append p1 to p2, and return a string in p3 */
        char temp[50];
        strcpy(temp, p2);
        sprintf(p2, "%s: %d", temp, p1);
        strcpy(p3, "p1 not null, p2 not null!");
        *p2_ind = OCI_IND_NOTNULL;
        *p3_ind = OCI_IND_NOTNULL;
      }
}


/* Corresponding PL/SQL parameters:
 *    PARAMETERS(p_Parameter1 STRING,          -- IN
 *               p_Parameter1 INDICATOR,       -- IN
 *               p_Parameter1 LENGTH,          -- IN
 *               p_Parameter2 STRING,          -- IN OUT
 *               p_Parameter2 INDICATOR,       -- IN OUT
 *               p_Parameter2 LENGTH,          -- IN OUT
 *               p_Parameter2 MAXLEN,          -- IN OUT
 *               p_Parameter3 STRING,          -- OUT
 *               p_Parameter3 INDICATOR,       -- OUT
 *               p_Parameter3 LENGTH,          -- OUT
 *               p_Parameter3 MAXLEN);         -- OUT
 */
void lengthP(
  char  *p1,                    /* p_Parameter1, passed by value */
  short  p1_ind,        /* p_Parameter1 indicator, passed by value */
  int    p1_len,           /* p_Parameter1 length, passed by value */
  char  *p2,                   /* p_Parameter2, passed by reference */
  short *p2_ind,     /* p_Parameter2 indicator, passed by reference */
  int   *p2_len,        /* p_Parameter2 length, passed by reference */
  int   *p2_maxlen,/* p_Parameter2 max length, passed by reference */
  char  *p3,                   /* p_Parameter3, passed by reference */
  short *p3_ind,     /* p_Parameter3 indicator, passed by reference */
  int   *p3_len,        /* p_Parameter3 length, passed by reference */
  int   *p3_maxlen)/* p_Parameter3 max length, passed by reference */
{

  /* If p1 is NULL, then return NULL for p2 and p3.  Note that
   * the length of each is set to zero, in addition to the
   * indicators begin set to OCI_IND_NULL.
```

```
 */
if (p1_ind == OCI_IND_NULL)
{
  *p2_ind = OCI_IND_NULL;
  *p2_len = 0;
  p2[0] = '\0';
  *p3_ind = OCI_IND_NULL;
  *p3_len = 0;
  p3[0] = '\0';
}
/* Otherwise, return the length of p1 and p2 in p3.  Make sure
 * to not exceed the max length for p3.  If the length is not
 * long enough, then fill p3 with blanks up to its maximum length.
 */
else
{
  if (*p3_maxlen >= 36)
    sprintf(p3, "p1 len: %2.2d p2 len: %2.2d p2 maxlen: %2.2d",
                p1_len, *p2_len, *p2_maxlen);
  else
  {
    int i;
    for (i = 0; i < *p3_maxlen; i++)
      p3[i] = ' ';
  }
  *p3_len = strlen(p3);
  *p3_ind = OCI_IND_NOTNULL;
}
}
```

The file **callEP.sql**, available online, illustrates some calls to the procedures in **ExternalProps**.

C External Functions

The wrapper for a C external function is created just like the wrapper for a procedure, except that the return value must be specified in the PARAMETERS clause as well. This is done using the RETURN keyword. Properties can be associated with the return value as well, as **OutputString4** shows

```
/* Available online as part of outputString.c */
/* outputString4:
 * Outputs the string contained in message to a file specified by
 * path.  The message is repeated num_times times.  The file will
 * be created if it doesn't exist.  The number of lines actually
 * written is returned.  The NULLness of each parameter is
 * checked.
```

```c
 */
ub2 outputString4(
  char   *path,                 /* Complete path of the output file */
  short  path_ind,                        /* Indicator for path */
  char   *message,                       /* Message to be written */
  short  message_ind,                   /* Indicator for message */
  int    num_times,     /* Number of times the message is repeated */
  short  num_times_ind,                 /* Indicator for num_times */
  short  *retval_ind)              /* Indicator for return value */
{

  FILE *file_handle;
  ub2 counter;

  /* If any of the input parameters are NULL, return NULL and
     don't output anything. */
  if (path_ind == OCI_IND_NULL || message_ind == OCI_IND_NULL ||
      num_times_ind == OCI_IND_NULL) {
    *retval_ind = OCI_IND_NULL;
    return 0;
  }

  /* Open the file for writing. */
  file_handle = fopen(path, "w");

  for (counter = 0; counter < num_times; counter++) {
    /* Output the string followed by a newline. */
    fprintf(file_handle, "%s\n", message);
  }

  /* Close the file. */
  fclose(file_handle);

  /* Set up return values. */
  *retval_ind = OCI_IND_NOTNULL;
  return counter;
}
```

-- **Available online as part of OutputString.sql**
```sql
CREATE OR REPLACE FUNCTION OutputString4(
  p_Path IN VARCHAR2,
  p_Message IN VARCHAR2,
  p_NumLines IN BINARY_INTEGER)
  RETURN NATURAL AS EXTERNAL

  LIBRARY StringLib
  NAME "outputString4"
  PARAMETERS (p_Path STRING,
              p_Path INDICATOR,
```

```
    p_Message STRING,
    p_Message INDICATOR,
    p_NumLines INT,
    p_NumLines INDICATOR,
    RETURN INDICATOR,
    RETURN UB2);
```

The **callOS.sql** file, available online, illustrates how to call **OutputString4** as well as some sample output.

Java External Routines

Oracle **8i**
and higher In this section, we will discuss the steps necessary to create and publish a Java external routine. We will also discuss some of the advantages of running Java stored procedures in the server.

Required Steps

The steps necessary to create a Java external routine are as follows:

1. Code the routine.

2. Load it into the database.

3. Publish the routine by creating a PL/SQL wrapper that maps the PL/SQL parameters to Java parameters.

We will examine these steps in detail in the following sections.

Coding the Routine

As with a C external routine, the first step is to code the Java procedure. Suppose we want to manipulate dates and times with millisecond precision. Oracle DATEs have a precision only to the second, so they can't hold the necessary information. The Java **Date** class, on the other hand, does have millisecond precision, so this is a good candidate for a Java routine. The following class provides some utility functions that operate on date values:

```java
// Available online as DateUtils.java
import java.util.*;
import java.lang.*;
import java.text.*;

class DateUtils
{
    // Initial format string.  This can be changed by calling
```

```java
// setFormatString.
private static String initialFormatString =
  "MM/dd/yyyy HH:mm:ss:SSS";

// Formatter which will convert between Date and String
// values.
private static SimpleDateFormat formatter =
  new SimpleDateFormat(initialFormatString);

// Calendar which will do the date arithmetic.
private static GregorianCalendar calendar =
  new GregorianCalendar();

// Sets the format string used by DateUtils functions.
public static void setFormatString(String inputString)
{
  formatter.applyPattern(inputString);
}

// Returns the internal format string.
public static String getFormatString()
{
  return formatter.toPattern();
}

// Adds numDays to the input value.  numDays can contain a
// fractional day, similar to the Oracle behavior for date
// arithmetic.  This method is accurate to the millisecond.
public static String addDays(String inputString,
                             double numDays)
  throws ParseException
{
  // First convert our input string to a date.
  Date inputDate = formatter.parse(inputString);

  // Our input is in days.  First get the whole days.
  Double d = new Double(numDays);
  int days = (int)numDays;

  // Fraction of a day, as a double.
  double fractionalDays = numDays % 1;
  // Number of seconds, as a double.
  double seconds = (fractionalDays * 24 * 60 * 60);
  // Fraction of a second, as a double.
  double fractionalSeconds = seconds % 1;

  // Number of milliseconds, as a double.
```

```
      double milliseconds = fractionalSeconds * 1000;

      // Do the arithmetic.
      calendar.setTime(inputDate);
      calendar.add(calendar.DAY_OF_YEAR, days);
      calendar.add(calendar.SECOND, (int)seconds);
      calendar.add(calendar.MILLISECOND, (int)milliseconds);

      // And convert for output.
      Date outputDate = calendar.getTime();
      return formatter.format(outputDate);
    }
}
```

The **DateUtils** class provides three public methods: **setFormatString**, **getFormatString**, and **addDays**. **addDays** functions the same way as Oracle DATE arithmetic, except that it is accurate to millisecond precision. The **callDU** class, shown next, shows some sample output from the methods in **DateUtils**.

```
// Available online as callDU.java
import java.lang.*;

class callDU
{
  // Demonstrates some calls to DateUtils.
  public static void main(String args[])
    throws java.text.ParseException
  {
    // First get the initial date format.
    System.out.println("Initial date format: " +
      DateUtils.getFormatString());

    // Initialize our first date value.
    String d = "06/15/1999 00:00:00:000";
    System.out.println("Initial value: " + d);

    // And do some arithmetic!
    String d1 = DateUtils.addDays(d, 1.5);
    System.out.println("Initial value + 1.5 days = " + d1);

    String d2 = DateUtils.addDays(d1, -2.1);
    System.out.println("Subtracting 2.1 days = " + d2);

    String d3 = DateUtils.addDays(d2, 0.01);
    System.out.println("Adding 0.01 days = " + d3);

    // Change the format to put the year first
    DateUtils.setFormatString("yyyy/dd/MM HH:mm:ss:SSS");
    System.out.println("New date format: " +
```

```
        DateUtils.getFormatString());

    // And now do some more
    d = "2000/01/01 00:00:00:000";
    System.out.println("New initial value: " + d);

    d1 = DateUtils.addDays(d, 366);
    System.out.println("Initial value + 366 days = " + d1);
  }
}
```

TIP
*The online **ch10.mk** Makefile can be used to compile and run the classes shown previously, once the necessary modifications to **common.mk** have been made (see the Makefile for details). The command 'make –f ch10.mk DateUtils.class callDU.class' will compile the two files, and 'make –f ch10.mk run-java ENTRY=callDU' will run them.*

The output from **callDU** is

```
Initial date format: MM/dd/yyyy HH:mm:ss:SSS
Initial value: 06/15/1999 00:00:00:000
Initial value + 1.5 days = 06/16/1999 12:00:00:000
Subtracting 2.1 days = 06/14/1999 09:36:00:000
Adding 0.01 days = 06/14/1999 09:50:23:999
New date format: yyyy/dd/MM HH:mm:ss:SSS
New initial value: 2000/01/01 00:00:00:000
Initial value + 366 days = 2001/01/01 00:00:00:000
```

Loading Java Routines into the Database

As we saw earlier in this chapter, C external routines are compiled into a shared object in the operating system, and a library data dictionary object is created to represent them. Java stored procedures, on the other hand, are loaded into the database directly. There is no need for a library object. Either the Java source or compiled class (or both) can be loaded into the database using one of the following methods—the CREATE JAVA statement, or the loadjava utility.

USING CREATE JAVA   CREATE JAVA is a SQL statement that is used to load an individual class into the database. The syntax is

CREATE [OR REPLACE] [AND {RESOLVE | COMPILE} [NOFORCE] JAVA
{{SOURCE | RESOURCE} NAMED [*schema .*] *primary_name* |

```
      CLASS [SCHEMA schema]}
      [invoker_rights_clause]
      [RESOLVER resolver_clause]
      {AS source_text | USING lob_clause;
```

where *schema* is the schema in which to store the Java object and *primary_name* is the name of the Java source or resource. The *invoker_rights_clause* is the same as we saw in Chapter 5. The *resolver_clause* specifies how external references in the Java class are to be resolved. Finally, the text can be found in *source_text* or referenced through a LOB in *lob_clause*. The following example illustrates two different ways of loading Java sources into the database. For more information on using CREATE JAVA, see the *Oracle8i SQL Reference*.

```
-- Available online as part of creJava.sql
-- Load DateUtils using a BFILE.  First we have to create the
-- directory.  Note that the CREATE ANY DIRECTORY system privilege
-- is needed for this to succeed.
CREATE OR REPLACE DIRECTORY ch10 AS
   '/home/surman/book/code/ch10';

-- And now load the class.  This will read the source for the class
-- from the file system, and compile it into the database.
CREATE OR REPLACE AND RESOLVE JAVA SOURCE
   NAMED "DateUtils"
   USING BFILE (ch10, 'DateUtils.java');

-- Here we create a second JSP (Java Stored Procedure), which just
-- echoes the current date format.
CREATE OR REPLACE AND RESOLVE JAVA SOURCE
   NAMED "GetString" AS
   class GetString
   {
     // Simply echos the current date format.
     public static void main(String args[])
       throws java.text.ParseException
     {
       System.out.println("Current date format: " +
         DateUtils.getFormatString());
     }
   };
```

USING LOADJAVA   The CREATE JAVA statement can be used to load a single Java class into the database. However, since Java applications typically consist of many classes, Oracle provides a utility called loadjava that can load multiple classes and resources into the database. loadjava is run from the operating system prompt, and has the syntax

> loadjava [*options*] *files*

where the *options* are listed in Table 10-5, and *files* is a list of Java source files, class files, archives, resources, or properties. For example, the following session shows the results from loading the **callDate** class into the database:

```
$loadjava -user example/example -resolve -verbose callDU.java
initialization complete
loading   : callDU
creating  : callDU
resolver  :
resolving: callDU
```

NOTE
JSP's created with CREATE OR REPLACE JAVA can be dropped with the DROP JAVA statement, and JSP's created with loadjava can be dropped using the dropjava utility.

Option	Description
−u *user/password@connect_string*, −user *user/password@connect_string*	Database account in which the Java objects will be created. The *connect_string* is optional.
−o, −oci8	Uses the JDBC OCI driver to connect. If the *connect_string* is specified in −user, then it must be a valid entry in the *tnsnames.ora* file.
−t, −thin	Uses the JDBC thin driver to connect. The *connect_string* must be of the format "host:port:SID" or a valid Net8 name-value list.
−h, −help	Prints out a help listing of the valid options.
−v, −verbose	Prints extra information as the files are loaded into the database.

TABLE 10-5. *loadjava Options*

Option	Description
−r, −resolve	Resolves external references in all classes after they are loaded.
−a, −andresolve	Resolves external references in all classes as they are loaded.
−f, −force	Forces reloading of classes, even if they are already in the database. Normally, if the class in the database and on the operating system are the same, it is not reloaded.
−s, −synonym	Creates a public synonym for each class as it is loaded. You must have the CREATE PUBLIC SYNONYM system privilege.
−R, −resolver_description, *resolver_description*	Uses *resolver_description* to resolve external references. See the *Java Developer's Guide* for more information about resolvers.
−g *grantlist*, −grant *grantlist*	Grants EXECUTE privilege on the loaded class to the schemas specified in *grantlist*. *grantlist* is a comma-separated list of database users, roles, or to PUBLIC.
−S *schema*, −schema *schema*	Loads the objects into *schema*, rather than the user specified by the −user option. You must have the necessary privileges.
−d, −definer	Creates the class with definer's rights methods, rather than invoker's rights. The default is invoker's. See "Invokers and Definer's Rights," later in this chapter, for more information.
−oracleresolver	Uses the default resolver, which looks for external references first in the user's schema, then in PUBLIC.
−debug	Generates debug information, similar to the −g option of the javac compiler.

TABLE 10-5. *loadjava Options* (continued)

Option	Description
−e *encoding_scheme,* −encoding *encoding_scheme*	Uses the specified encoding scheme (the default is latin1) for the supplied class(es). The encoding scheme will be recorded for future calls as well.

TABLE 10-5. *loadjava Options* (continued)

Publishing the Routine

Publishing a Java method is done the same way as for a C external routine—through a PL/SQL wrapper that uses the AS LANGUAGE clause. The wrapper will publish a single static method in the Java class. Not all of the clauses used for C are required for Java, however. The syntax is

    {PROCEDURE | FUNCTION} procedure_name [plsql_parameter_list]
       AS LANGUAGE JAVA
       [NAME external_name [(java_parameter_list)]];

where *external_name* is the name of the Java method. The *java_parameter_list* describes the parameters to the Java method, analogous to the PARAMETERS clause used for external C routines. Since Java methods can be overloaded, however, the *java_parameter_list* also identifies the particular method in the class. The **DateUtils** package, shown next, contains wrappers for each of the public methods in the **DateUtils** class.

```
-- Available online as DateUtils.sql
CREATE OR REPLACE PACKAGE DateUtils AS
  PROCEDURE SetFormatString(p_NewFormat IN VARCHAR2) IS
    LANGUAGE JAVA
    NAME 'DateUtils.setFormatString(java.lang.String)';

  FUNCTION GetFormatString RETURN VARCHAR2 IS
    LANGUAGE JAVA
    NAME 'DateUtils.getFormatString() return java.lang.String';

  FUNCTION AddDays(p_InputDate VARCHAR2,
                   p_Seconds NUMBER) RETURN VARCHAR2 IS
    LANGUAGE JAVA
    NAME 'DateUtils.addDays (java.lang.String, long)
          return java.lang.String';
END DateUtils;
```

The following SQL*Plus session shows the output from some calls to **DateUtils**. It is the same as the output from the **callDU** class which we examined earlier.

--Available online as callDU.sql

```
SQL> -- Demonstrates some calls to DateUtils.
SQL> DECLARE
  2    v_Date VARCHAR2(25);
  3    v_Date1 VARCHAR2(25);
  4    v_Date2 VARCHAR2(25);
  5    v_Date3 VARCHAR2(25);
  6  BEGIN
  7    -- First get the initial date format.
  8    DBMS_OUTPUT.PUT_LINE('Initial date format: ' ||
  9      DateUtils.GetFormatString());
 10
 11    -- Initialize our first date value.
 12    v_Date := '06/15/1999 00:00:00:000';
 13    DBMS_OUTPUT.PUT_LINE('Initial value: ' || v_Date);
 14
 15    -- And do some arithmetic!
 16    v_Date1 := DateUtils.AddDays(v_Date, 1.5);
 17    DBMS_OUTPUT.PUT_LINE('Initial value + 1.5 days = ' || v_Date1);
 18
 19    v_Date2 := DateUtils.AddDays(v_Date1, -2.1);
 20    DBMS_OUTPUT.PUT_LINE('Subtracting 2.1 days = ' || v_Date2);
 21
 22    v_Date3 := DateUtils.AddDays(v_Date2, 0.01);
 23    DBMS_OUTPUT.PUT_LINE('Adding 0.01 days = ' || v_Date3);
 24
 25    -- Change the format to put the year first
 26    DateUtils.SetFormatString('yyyy/dd/MM HH:mm:ss:SSS');
 27    DBMS_OUTPUT.PUT_LINE('New date format: ' ||
 28      DateUtils.GetFormatString());
 29
 30    -- And now do some more
 31    v_Date := '2000/01/01 00:00:00:000';
 32    DBMS_OUTPUT.PUT_LINE('New initial value: ' || v_Date);
 33
 34    v_Date1 := DateUtils.AddDays(v_Date, 366);
 35    DBMS_OUTPUT.PUT_LINE('Initial value + 366 days = ' || v_Date1);
 36  END;
 37  /
Initial date format: MM/dd/yyyy HH:mm:ss:SSS
Initial value: 06/15/1999 00:00:00:000
Initial value + 1.5 days = 06/16/1999 12:00:00:000
Subtracting 2.1 days = 06/14/1999 09:36:00:000
Adding 0.01 days = 06/14/1999 09:50:23:999
```

```
New date format: yyyy/dd/MM HH:mm:ss:SSS
New initial value: 2000/01/01 00:00:00:000
Initial value + 366 days = 2001/01/01 00:00:00:000
PL/SQL procedure successfully completed.
```

STATIC METHODS   Only static methods of a Java object can be published through a PL/SQL wrapper. This is the case even if the wrapper is part of a PL/SQL type body. This is because all PL/SQL subprograms are considered static—there is only one copy of them in memory at any one point, and they do not take SELF as a parameter. Like static Java methods, they can only call other static methods. The Java code, of course, is free to call other non-static methods by instantiating their containing object. For more information on object types and their methods, see Chapter 12.

FULLY QUALIFIED PARAMETERS   All of the parameters listed for the Java method must be fully qualified, as if there were no import statement. For example, String parameters must be specified with "java.lang.String," as in the previous example. This is also true for any user-specified datatypes that you want to pass to a JSP. Furthermore, all of the parameters in the PL/SQL wrapper must correspond to the parameters for the Java method. The only exception to this rule is for **main** methods, described in the next section.

THE main METHOD   The **main** method of Java classes is similar to the **main** function in a C program—it is the first method called by the virtual machine to start the program. **main** methods always are defined as follows:

```
public static void main (String[] args)
```

where *args* is an array of Java strings. Thus, **main** can take a variable number of arguments, which are typically passed on the command line to the Java VM. So how many arguments does the PL/SQL wrapper have? It can have as many as the **main** method can accept. For example, suppose we load the following class into the database:

```java
// Available online as DemoMain.java
public class DemoMain
{
  // Just loops through its arguments, and prints them out.
  public static void main(String[] args)
  {
    for (int i = 0; i < args.length; i++)
      System.out.println("args[" + i + "]: " + args[i]);
  }
}
```

TIP
*You can use the following loadjava command to load the class shown previously into the **example** schema: "loadjava –user example/example –verbose –resolve DemoMain.java."*

We can create wrappers for this method with different numbers of arguments, as the **DemoMain** package illustrates.

```
-- Available online as part of DemoMain.sql
CREATE OR REPLACE PACKAGE DemoMain AS
   PROCEDURE Main(p1 IN VARCHAR2) IS
      LANGUAGE JAVA
      NAME 'DemoMain.main(java.lang.String[])';

   PROCEDURE Main(p1 IN VARCHAR2, p2 IN VARCHAR2) IS
      LANGUAGE JAVA
      NAME 'DemoMain.main(java.lang.String[])';

   PROCEDURE Main(p1 IN VARCHAR2, p2 IN VARCHAR2, p3 IN VARCHAR2) IS
      LANGUAGE JAVA
      NAME 'DemoMain.main(java.lang.String[])';

   PROCEDURE Main(p1 IN VARCHAR2, p2 IN VARCHAR2, p3 IN VARCHAR2,
                  p4 IN VARCHAR2) IS
      LANGUAGE JAVA
NAME 'DemoMain.main(java.lang.String[])';
END DemoMain;
```

Note that all four overloaded procedures have the same Java specification. If we run this from SQL*Plus, we get the following output. (The CALL statement, available in Oracle8*i* and higher, allows you to call a stored procedure. See Chapter 11 for more details.)

```
-- Available online as part of DemoMain.sql
SQL> CALL DemoMain.Main('One');
args[0]: One
Call completed.

SQL> CALL DemoMain.Main('One', 'Two');
args[0]: One
args[1]: Two
Call completed.

SQL> CALL DemoMain.Main('One', 'Two', 'Three');
args[0]: One
```

```
args[1]: Two
args[2]: Three
Call completed.

SQL> CALL DemoMain.Main('One', 'Two', 'Three', 'Four');
args[0]: One
args[1]: Two
args[2]: Three
args[3]: Four
Call completed.
```

NOTE
*It is necessary to first call DBMS_JAVA.SET_OUTPUT to redirect **System.output** to the DBMS_OUTPUT buffer. See "Redirecting Output," later in this chapter, for details.*

Parameter Mappings

Just like we saw earlier for C external routines, parameters have to be mapped between PL/SQL and Java for Java external routines. Instead of the PARAMETERS clause, the *java_parameter_list* clause in the NAME clause specifies the Java types for the external routine.

PL/SQL vs. Java Datatypes

Table 10-6 lists the valid mappings between PL/SQL types and Java types. There are several things to note about the datatypes that can be passed to a JSP:

- UROWID, BOOLEAN, and the subtypes of NUMBER (INTEGER, REAL) are not supported.

- The mappings to classes in **oracle.sql** are the most optimal. These classes implement the structure of the underlying Oracle types, and thus require no conversions.

- The classes in **oracle.jdbc2** are defined in the JDBC 2.0 specification.

For more information on using these Java types and the **oracle.sql** and **oracle.jdbc2** packages, see the *JDBC Developer's Guide and Reference.* For information on passing objects to Java external routines, see the Oracle documentation.

Parameter Modes

If a parameter is IN OUT or OUT, then it needs to be passed by reference, rather than by value. (This is the same as for C external routines.) For a Java external routine, rather than using the BY REFERENCE clause, the Java parameter should be passed as an array.

Category	PL/SQL Type	Java Type
Character strings	CHAR, NCHAR, LONG, VARCHAR2, NVARCHAR2	oracle.sql.CHAR, java.lang.String, java.sql.Date, java.sql.Time, java.sql.Timestamp, java.lang.Byte, java.lang.Short, java.lang.Integer, java.lang.Long, java.lang.Float, java.lang.Double, java.math.BigDecimal, byte, short, int, long, float, double
Dates	DATE	oracle.sql.DATE, java.sql.Date, java.sql.Time, java.sql.Timestamp, java.lang.String
Numbers	NUMBER	oracle.sql.NUMBER, java.lang.Byte, java.lang.Short, java.lang.Integer, java.lang.Long, java.lang.Float, java.lang.Double, java.math.BigDecimal, byte, short, int, long, float, double
Raw values	RAW, LONG RAW	oracle.sql.RAW, byte[]
Rowids	ROWID	oracle.sql.CHAR, oracle.sql.ROWID, java.lang.String
BFILEs	BFILE	oracle.sql.BFILE
Binary LOBs	BLOB	oracle.sql.BLOB, oracle.jdbc2.Blob
Character LOBs	CLOB, NCLOB	oracle.sql.CLOB, oracle.jdbc2.Clob
Objects	OBJECT	oracle.sql.STRUCT, oracle.sqlJData, oracle.jdbc2.Struct
Object References	REF	oracle.sql.REF, oracle.jdbc2.Ref
Collections	TABLE, VARRAY	oracle.sql.ARRAY, oracle.jdbc2.Array
Any	Any type	oracle.sql.CustomDatum, oracle.sql.Datum

TABLE 10-6. *PL/SQL and Java Datatype Mappings*

To modify the value, the JSP needs to set element 0 of the array. The following example illustrates this. Suppose we load the **JavaModes** class into the database:

```
-- Available online as JavaModes.java
import oracle.sql.*;
import java.sql.*;

class JavaModes
{
  public static void numP(int p1, int[] p2, int[] p3)
  {
    // Assign p2 = p2 + p1, and p3 = p2 * 2
    p3[0] = p2[0] * 2;
    p2[0] = p2[0] + p1;
  }

  public static void charP(String p1, String[] p2, String[] p3)
  {
    // Concatenate p1 on the end of p2, and assign to p3
    p2[0] += p1;
    p3[0] = "Hello, I'm a Java string!";
  }

  public static void dateP(DATE p1, DATE[] p2, DATE[] p3)
    throws SQLException
  {
    // Add 6 months to p2, and set p3 to p1 - 6 months.
    p2[0] = p2[0].addMonths(6);
    p3[0] = p1.addMonths(-6);
  }
}
```

The corresponding PL/SQL wrapper is

```
-- Available online as JavaModes.sql
CREATE OR REPLACE PACKAGE JavaModes AS
  PROCEDURE NumP(p1 IN NUMBER,
                 p2 IN OUT NUMBER,
                 p3 OUT NUMBER) IS
  LANGUAGE JAVA
  NAME 'JavaModes.numP(int, int[], int[])';

  PROCEDURE CharP(p1 IN VARCHAR2,
                  p2 IN OUT VARCHAR2,
                  p3 OUT VARCHAR2) IS
  LANGUAGE JAVA
  NAME 'JavaModes.charP(java.lang.String, java.lang.String[],
        java.lang.String[])';
```

```
    PROCEDURE DateP(p1 IN DATE,
                    p2 IN OUT DATE,
                    p3 OUT DATE) IS
      LANGUAGE JAVA
      NAME 'JavaModes.dateP(oracle.sql.DATE, oracle.sql.DATE[],
            oracle.sql.DATE[])';
  END JavaModes;
```

The following SQL*Plus session shows the output:

```
-- Available online as callJModes.sql
SQL> DECLARE
  2      v_Num1 NUMBER := 10;
  3      v_Num2 NUMBER := 20;
  4      v_Num3 NUMBER;
  5      v_Char1 VARCHAR2(10) := 'abc';
  6      v_Char2 VARCHAR2(20) := 'defghijk';
  7      v_Char3 VARCHAR2(30);
  8      v_Date1 DATE := TO_DATE('04-APR-1971', 'DD-MON-YYYY');
  9      v_Date2 DATE := TO_DATE('29-FEB-2000', 'DD-MON-YYYY');
 10      v_Date3 DATE;
 11   BEGIN
 12      DBMS_OUTPUT.PUT_LINE('Before call to numP:');
 13      DBMS_OUTPUT.PUT_LINE('  v_Num1: ' || v_Num1);
 14      DBMS_OUTPUT.PUT_LINE('  v_Num2: ' || v_Num2);
 15      DBMS_OUTPUT.PUT_LINE('  v_Num3: ' || v_Num3);
 16      JavaModes.NumP(v_Num1, v_Num2, v_Num3);
 17      DBMS_OUTPUT.PUT_LINE('After call to numP:');
 18      DBMS_OUTPUT.PUT_LINE('  v_Num1: ' || v_Num1);
 19      DBMS_OUTPUT.PUT_LINE('  v_Num2: ' || v_Num2);
 20      DBMS_OUTPUT.PUT_LINE('  v_Num3: ' || v_Num3);
 21
 22      DBMS_OUTPUT.PUT_LINE('Before call to charP:');
 23      DBMS_OUTPUT.PUT_LINE('  v_Char1: ' || v_Char1);
 24      DBMS_OUTPUT.PUT_LINE('  v_Char2: ' || v_Char2);
 25      DBMS_OUTPUT.PUT_LINE('  v_Char3: ' || v_Char3);
 26      JavaModes.CharP(v_Char1, v_Char2, v_Char3);
 27      DBMS_OUTPUT.PUT_LINE('After call to charP:');
 28      DBMS_OUTPUT.PUT_LINE('  v_Char1: ' || v_Char1);
 29      DBMS_OUTPUT.PUT_LINE('  v_Char2: ' || v_Char2);
 30      DBMS_OUTPUT.PUT_LINE('  v_Char3: ' || v_Char3);
 31
 32      DBMS_OUTPUT.PUT_LINE('Before call to DateP:');
 33      DBMS_OUTPUT.PUT_LINE('  v_Date1: ' || v_Date1);
 34      DBMS_OUTPUT.PUT_LINE('  v_Date2: ' || v_Date2);
 35      DBMS_OUTPUT.PUT_LINE('  v_Date3: ' || v_Date3);
 36      JavaModes.DateP(v_Date1, v_Date2, v_Date3);
 37      DBMS_OUTPUT.PUT_LINE('After call to DateP:');
```

```
38    DBMS_OUTPUT.PUT_LINE('  v_Date1: ' || v_Date1);
39    DBMS_OUTPUT.PUT_LINE('  v_Date2: ' || v_Date2);
40    DBMS_OUTPUT.PUT_LINE('  v_Date3: ' || v_Date3);
41  END;
42  /
Before call to numP:
  v_Num1: 10
  v_Num2: 20
  v_Num3:
After call to numP:
  v_Num1: 10
  v_Num2: 30
  v_Num3: 40
Before call to charP:
  v_Char1: abc
  v_Char2: defghijk
  v_Char3:
After call to charP:
  v_Char1: abc
  v_Char2: defghijkabc
  v_Char3: Hello, I'm a Java string!
Before call to DateP:
  v_Date1: 04-APR-1971
  v_Date2: 29-FEB-2000
  v_Date3:
After call to DateP:
  v_Date1: 04-APR-1971
  v_Date2: 31-AUG-2000
  v_Date3: 04-OCT-1970
PL/SQL procedure successfully completed.
```

Passing NULLs

Since indicators are valid only for C external routine, there is no way to specify a NULL value for a parameter to a JSP. If the parameter is an object, then a NULL value will be passed as a null object. For numeric parameters (byte, short, int, and so on), a NULL value will be passed as zero, since these types are not Java objects. This is illustrated by the following example. Suppose we load the **JavaNull** class into the database:

```
// Available online as JavaNull.java
class JavaNull
{
  public static void doIt(String p1, int p2, oracle.sql.DATE p3)
  {
    if (p1 == null)
      System.out.println("p1: null");
    else
      System.out.println("p1: " + p1);
```

```
    System.out.println("p2: " + p2);
    if (p3 == null)
      System.out.println("p3: null");
    else
      System.out.println("p3: " + p3.dateValue());
  }
}
```

If we then create a wrapper procedure and call it, we get the output as shown in the following SQL*Plus session.

```
-- Available online as JavaNull.sql
SQL> CREATE OR REPLACE PROCEDURE JavaNull(p1 IN VARCHAR2,
  2                                       p2 IN NUMBER,
  3                                       p3 IN DATE) AS
  4      LANGUAGE JAVA
  5      NAME 'JavaNull.doIt(java.lang.String, int, oracle.sql.DATE)';
  6  /
Procedure created.

SQL> set serveroutput on
SQL> CALL DBMS_JAVA.SET_OUTPUT(2000);
Call completed.

SQL> -- First call with valid values for the parameters
SQL> CALL JavaNull('abcd', 1, SYSDATE);
p1: abcd
p2: 1
p3: 2000-01-06
Call completed.

SQL>
SQL> -- Now pass SQL null.
SQL> CALL JavaNull(null, null, null);
p1: null
p2: 0
p3: null
Call completed.
```

NOTE
*The call to DBMS_JAVA.SET_OUTPUT redirects the output from **System.out.println** to the DBMS_OUTPUT buffer. See "Redirecting Output," later in this chapter, for details.*

Length of Strings

There are no properties associated with parameters to JSPs. As we saw in the previous section, NULL PL/SQL variables are handled by passing either null Java objects, or 0 for numeric types. What then is the equivalent of the LENGTH and MAXLEN properties? For Java strings and byte arrays, you can use the **length()** method to determine the length of IN parameters. However, there is no equivalent to the MAXLEN property. This is illustrated by the **JavaLength** class and corresponding PL/SQL wrapper, shown here:

```
// Available online as JavaLength.java
class JavaLength
{
  // Uppercases the value of inOut, and returns a string of
  // numChars characters in out.
  public static void doIt(int numChars,
                          String[] inOut,
                          String[] out)
  {
    if (inOut[0] == null)
      System.out.println("inOut is null");
    else
      System.out.println("Length of inOut is " + inOut[0].length());

    if (out[0] == null)
      System.out.println("out is null");
    else
      System.out.println("Length of out is " + out[0].length());

    inOut[0] = inOut[0].toUpperCase();
    out[0] = new String();
    for (int i = 1; i <= numChars; i++)
      out[0] += 'a';
  }
}
```

```
-- Available online as part of JavaLength.sql
CREATE OR REPLACE PROCEDURE JavaLength(p_NumChars IN NUMBER,
                                       p_InOut IN OUT VARCHAR2,
                                       p_Out OUT VARCHAR2) AS
  LANGUAGE JAVA
  NAME 'JavaLength.doIt(int, java.lang.String[], java.lang.String[])';
```

Consider the following SQL*Plus session, which calls **JavaLength** with various inputs:

```
-- Available online as part of JavaLength.sql
SQL> DECLARE
  2    v_String1 VARCHAR2(20) := 'abcd';
  3    v_String2 VARCHAR2(30);
```

```
 4  BEGIN
 5     -- First call JavaLength with v_String1, and get back 10
 6     -- characters.
 7     DBMS_OUTPUT.PUT_LINE('Calling JavaLength with v_String1...');
 8     JavaLength(10, v_String1, v_String2);
 9     DBMS_OUTPUT.PUT_LINE('v_String1 = ' || v_String1);
10     DBMS_OUTPUT.PUT_LINE('v_String2 = ' || v_String2);
11
12     -- Now call JavaLength with v_String2, but request more than 30
13     -- characters.
14     DBMS_OUTPUT.PUT_LINE('Calling JavaLength with v_String2...');
15     JavaLength(35, v_String1, v_String2);
16     DBMS_OUTPUT.PUT_LINE('v_String1 = ' || v_String1);
17     DBMS_OUTPUT.PUT_LINE('v_String2 = ' || v_String2);
18  END;
19  /
Calling JavaLength with v_String1...
Length of inOut is 4
out is null
v_String1 = ABCD
v_String2 = aaaaaaaaaa
Calling JavaLength with v_String2...
Length of inOut is 4
out is null
DECLARE
*
ERROR at line 1:
ORA-06502: PL/SQL: numeric or value error: character string buffer
           too small
ORA-06512: at line 15
```

What has happened here? The first call to **JavaLength** succeeds, and illustrates that the length of **inOut** is 4. **out** is null, so there is no way of determining its maximum length. However, the maximum length of the corresponding PL/SQL VARCHAR2 variable **v_String1** is 20, so the assignment of 10 characters to it succeeds. The second call, however, attempts to assign a string of length 35 to a VARCHAR2 of maximum length 30, and thus the ORA-6502 error is raised. Note that the error is not raised inside the JSP itself, but is raised upon return to PL/SQL.

Java External Functions

For a Java external function, the PL/SQL call specification must include the type of the return parameter as well. It is specified after the *java_parameter_list*, as follows:

{PROCEDURE | FUNCTION} *procedure_name* [*plsql_parameter_list*]
   AS LANGUAGE JAVA
   [NAME *external_name* [(*java_parameter_list*)] **return *return_type***];

where *return_type* is the type returned by the function. For example, suppose we load the following simple Java class into the database:

```
// Available online as JReturn.java
class Jreturn
{
  // Simply returns its parameter.
  static public String theFunc(String p)
  {
    return p;
  }
}
```

We can create a call specification for **Jreturn.theFunc** with the following:

```
-- Available online as part of JReturn.sql
CREATE OR REPLACE FUNCTION JReturn(p_Parameter IN VARCHAR2)
  RETURN VARCHAR2 AS
  LANGUAGE JAVA
  NAME 'JReturn.theFunc(java.lang.String) return java.lang.String';
```

TIP

*"return" must be in lowercase and enclosed in the single quotes around the Java specification. If we were to use "RETURN" instead of "return" in the previous listing, Oracle8*i* would raise the following compilation error:*

```
PLS-00311: the declaration of "JReturn.theFunc(java.lang.String)
           RETURN java.lang.string" is incomplete or malformed
```

The following SQL*Plus session shows the output from **JReturn**.

```
-- Available online as part of JReturn.sql
SQL> DECLARE
  2     v_Variable1 VARCHAR2(20) := 'abcdefghijk';
  3     v_Variable2 VARCHAR2(20);
  4  BEGIN
  5     DBMS_OUTPUT.PUT_LINE('Before call: v1 = ' || v_Variable1 ||
  6                          '  v2 = ' || v_Variable2);
  7     v_Variable2 := JReturn(v_Variable1);
  8     DBMS_OUTPUT.PUT_LINE('After call: v1 = ' || v_Variable1 ||
  9                          '  v2 = ' || v_Variable2);
 10  END;
 11  /
Before call: v1 = abcdefghijk  v2 =
After call: v1 = abcdefghijk  v2 = abcdefghijk
PL/SQL procedure successfully completed.
```

Java Stored Procedures and Oracle JServer

There are a number of issues relating to Java stored procedures and Oracle JServer. We will discuss some of them in this section. For more details on running Java in the server, see the *Oracle8i Java Stored Procedures Developer's Guide*.

The Oracle installer will create the DBMS_JAVA package as part of the JServer installation. This package contains a number of utility subprograms that make it easier to work with JSPs and to control the behavior of the Java compiler. Many of the subprograms in DBMS_JAVA are for internal use only. The public subprograms are listed in the following table and described in the following sections.

DBMS_JAVA Subprograms	Description
SET_OUTPUT	Redirects **System.out** and **System.err** to the SQL*Plus DBMS_OUTPUT buffer
GET_COMPILER_OPTION, SET_COMPILER_OPTION, RESET_COMPILER_OPTION	Controls the behavior of the Java compiler
LONGNAME, SHORTNAME	Returns the full Java name for a stored Java object, or the shortened name given the full name
START_DEBUGGING, STOP_DEBUGGING, RESTART_DEBUGGING	Used to control the debug agent, which in concert with the **DebugProxy** class, allows you to debug a server-side JSP

Redirecting Output

When you run a Java program on the client, you can use **System.out** and **System.err** to output to the standard out and standard error streams, respectively. Typically, this output appears on the screen. When running in the server, however, screen output is not available. Instead, calls to **System.out.println** and **System.err.println** will go to the session trace file. The location of this trace file is determined by the USER_DUMP_DEST parameter in the database initialization file. For example, suppose we load the following procedure into the database:

```
// Available online as Output.java
class Output
{
  public static void main(String args[])
  {
    // Print some messages to standard output and standard error.
    System.out.println("This is a message to standard output!");
    System.out.println("Here's another one!");
    System.err.println("This is message to standard error!");
```

```
      System.err.println("This is another one!");
    }
}
```

If we publish **Output.main** with the following wrapper:

```
-- Available online as part of Output.sql
CREATE OR REPLACE PROCEDURE Output AS
  LANGUAGE JAVA
  NAME 'Output.main(java.lang.String[])';
```

and call it, then the output will go to the trace file. However, if we first call the packaged procedure DBMS_JAVA.SET_OUTPUT, and set the SQL*Plus SERVEROUTPUT option, then the output will go to the screen, as illustrated by Figure 10-3.

DBMS_JAVA.SET_OUTPUT is defined with

PROCEDURE SET_OUTPUT(*buffersize* IN NUMBER);

where *buffersize* is the size of the internal buffer. The minimum is 2,000, and the maximum is 1,000,000. DBMS_JAVA.SET_OUTPUT, in combination with SQL*Plus, lets you output to the screen in the same way as the DBMS_OUTPUT package does. In the same manner as DBMS_OUTPUT, **System.out** and **System.err** are buffered, and

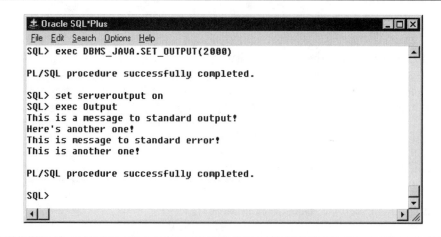

FIGURE 10-3. *Output with DBMS_JAVA.SET_OUTPUT*

when control returns to SQL*Plus (at the conclusion of the block), the contents are printed to the screen. For more information on DBMS_OUTPUT, see Chapter 3.

TIP
*The default buffer size for the SQL*Plus SERVEROUTPUT option is 2000. It is a good idea to use the same value in DBMS_JAVA.SET_OUTPUT and in SQL*Plus.*

Access to System Resources

The Java virtual machine is responsible for controlling access to system resources, such as files on the operating system or network ports. This is done through an instance of **java.lang.SecurityManager.** Oracle JServer implements security through three database roles—JAVASYSPRIV, JAVAUSERPRIV, and JAVADEBUGPRIV. When a JSP attempts to access a system resource, the dynamic ID (generally the current user, or the owner of the JSP if it is created with definer's rights) must have the necessary role GRANTed to them to allow the operation to succeed. If they do not, then JServer will raise a **SecurityException**.

■ JAVASYSPRIV   This role grants the most access, including the privilege to create a subprocess and listen on a network port.

■ JAVAUSERPRIV   This role grants some access, including the privilege to open a socket connection.

■ JAVADEBUGPRIV   This role allows you to debug a Java session. For more information, see "Debugging External Routines," later in this chapter.

FILESYSTEM I/O   I/O access to the filesystem depends on several factors. The policy is as follows:

■ If the current dynamic ID has been granted JAVASYSPRIV, then access to the filesystem is allowed.

■ If the current dynamic ID has been granted JAVAUSERPRIV, then the same rules that apply to the UTL_FILE package apply. Namely, the file being accessed must be in a directory specified by the UTL_FILE_DIR database initialization file parameter. For more information on UTL_FILE_DIR and the UTL_FILE package, see Chapter 7.

■ If the current dynamic ID has not been granted either privilege, then access to the filesystem is not allowed.

JServer Compiler Options

There are three subprograms in DBMS_JAVA that allow you to control the behavior of the Java compiler in JServer. The options that you can set are primarily used for Java stored procedures that are written using SQLJ. They are defined as follows:

```
FUNCTION GET_COMPILER_OPTION(what VARCHAR2,
                                 optionName VARCHAR2)
  RETURN VARCHAR2;
PROCEDURE SET_COMPILER_OPTION(what VARCHAR2,
                              optionName VARCHAR2,
                              value VARCHAR2);
PROCEDURE RESET_COMPILER_OPTION(what VARCHAR2,
                                optionName VARCHAR2);
```

where *what* identifies the package or class name, *optionName* is the compiler option to set, and *value* contains what it is to be set to. GET_COMPILER_OPTION will return the current value of an option for the given package or class, SET_COMPILER_OPTION will set the option for the given package or class to the given value, and RESET_COMPILER_OPTION will reset the option to its default. For more information on the available compiler options, see the *SQLJ Developer's Guide and Reference*.

JSPs and the Data Dictionary

Java stored procedures are stored as data dictionary objects, and as such they have entries in data dictionary views such as **user_objects** and **user_dependencies**. Java sources appear with type JAVA SOURCE in **user_objects**, and Java classes have type JAVA CLASS. The name of the object, however, differs slightly from a PL/SQL stored subprogram:

- The name of Java objects is case-sensitive, unlike PL/SQL objects.

- If the object is in a package (such as **java.lang.String**), the dots are replaced with slashes.

- Since the **object_name** column in **user_objects** is limited to 30 characters, Java objects with longer names are truncated.

For example, suppose we load the following classes into the database:

```
-- Available online as LongName.sql
CREATE OR REPLACE AND RESOLVE JAVA SOURCE
  NAMED "theSource" AS
```

```
   package package1.package2.package3;
   class theClass1
   {
     public static void main(String args[])
     {
       System.out.println("Hi there");
     }
   };

   class theClass2
   {
     public static void main(String args[])
     {
       System.out.println("Hi there");
     }
   };

CREATE OR REPLACE AND RESOLVE JAVA SOURCE
   NAMED "ShortName" AS
   class ShortName
   {
     public static void main(String args[])
     {
       System.out.println("Hi there");
     }
   };
```

This SQL loads two source objects into the database, the first of which contains two classes, and the second of which contains one class. We therefore end up with five Java objects, as shown by the following SQL*Plus session:

```
-- Available online as part of LongName.sql
SQL> SELECT object_name, object_type, status
  2     FROM user_objects
  3     WHERE object_type LIKE 'JAVA%';

OBJECT_NAME                          OBJECT_TYPE         STATUS
------------------------------------ ------------------- -------
/2ba8d92e_theClass2                  JAVA CLASS          VALID
/83751a3e_theClass1                  JAVA CLASS          VALID
ShortName                            JAVA CLASS          VALID
ShortName                            JAVA SOURCE         VALID
theSource                            JAVA SOURCE         VALID

SQL> SELECT name, type, referenced_owner, referenced_name,
  2          referenced_type
  3  FROM user_dependencies
```

```
    4   WHERE name = 'ShortName';
```

```
NAME        TYPE        REFERENCED_OWNER REFERENCED_NAME      REFERENCED_T
---------   ----------  ---------------- -------------------  -----------
ShortName   JAVA CLASS  SYS              java/lang/String     JAVA CLASS
ShortName   JAVA CLASS  SYS              java/lang/System     JAVA CLASS
ShortName   JAVA CLASS  SYS              java/io/PrintStream  JAVA CLASS
ShortName   JAVA CLASS  SYS              java/lang/Object     JAVA CLASS
```

LONG AND SHORT NAMES   In the previous example, the full name for **theClass1** and **theClass2** are too long to fit in **user_objects**. In order to see the full name, we can use DBMS_JAVA.LONGNAME, which is defined with

FUNCTION LONGNAME (*shortname* VARCHAR2) RETURN VARCHAR2;

where *shortname* is the value found in **user_objects**. For example, we can use DBMS_JAVA.LONGNAME to determine the full name of the classes loaded:

-- Available online as part of LongName.sql
```
SQL> SELECT DBMS_JAVA.LONGNAME(object_name) long_name, object_type
  2     FROM user_objects
  3     WHERE object_type LIKE 'JAVA%';
```

```
LONG_NAME                                  OBJECT_TYPE
-----------------------------------------  ------------------
package1/package2/package3/theClass2       JAVA CLASS
package1/package2/package3/theClass1       JAVA CLASS
ShortName                                  JAVA CLASS
ShortName                                  JAVA SOURCE
theSource                                  JAVA SOURCE
```

Likewise, the DBMS_JAVA.SHORTNAME function will return the name used in the data dictionary for a given class. It is defined with

FUNCTION SHORTNAME (*longname* VARCHAR2) RETURN VARCHAR2;

where *longname* is the full name of the class.

For more information on the data dictionary, see Appendix C on the CD-ROM that accompanies this book.

Exceptions Thrown from JSPs

A Java stored procedure can throw an exception if an error condition occurs. If not handled by the external routine (in a try…catch block), then it will be raised in PL/SQL, in much the same way as exceptions propagate between PL/SQL procedures. Suppose we load the following class into the database:

```
// Available online as Throw.java
class Throw
{
  // If message is non-null, an exception will be thrown with the
  // given message.
  public static void doIt(String message)
    throws Exception
  {
    if (message != null)
      throw new Exception(message);
  }
}
```

We can create the call specification for **Throw.DoIt** as follows:

```
-- Available online as part of Throw.sql
CREATE OR REPLACE PROCEDURE Throw(p_Message IN VARCHAR2) AS
  LANGUAGE JAVA
  NAME 'Throw.DoIt(java.lang.String)';
```

The output from calling **Throw** is shown in the following SQL*Plus session:

```
-- Available online as part of Throw.sql
SQL> -- First call Throw without handling the exception
SQL> BEGIN
  2    Throw('A Java error!');
  3  END;
  4  /
BEGIN
*
ERROR at line 1:
ORA-29532: Java call terminated by uncaught Java exception:
java.lang.Exception: A Java error!
ORA-06512: at "EXAMPLE.THROW", line 0
ORA-06512: at line 2
SQL> -- Now handle the exception with a WHEN OTHERS clause
SQL> DECLARE
  2    v_SQLCode NUMBER;
  3    v_SQLErrm VARCHAR2(200);
  4  BEGIN
  5    Throw('A Java error!');
  6  EXCEPTION
  7    WHEN OTHERS THEN
  8      DBMS_OUTPUT.PUT_LINE('Caught exception!');
```

```
 9        v_SQLCode := SQLCODE;
10        v_SQLErrm := SUBSTR(SQLERRM, 1, 200);
11        DBMS_OUTPUT.PUT_LINE('Code: ' || v_SQLCode);
12        DBMS_OUTPUT.PUT_LINE('Message: ' || v_SQLErrm);
13   END;
14   /
Caught exception!
Code: -29532
Message: ORA-29532: Java call terminated by uncaught Java exception:
java.lang.Exception: A Java error!
PL/SQL procedure successfully completed.
```

Any Java exception will be raised as an ORA-29532 error in the calling block. This exception can be handled just like any other PL/SQL exception, as the second block in the previous example illustrates.

NOTE
Unlike C external routines, which can raise specific Oracle errors using service routines (see "C Service Routines" for details), a Java external routine cannot raise a specific Oracle error by error number.

Callbacks to the Database

An external routine can make callbacks to the database to raise errors or issue SQL commands. For C external routines, these are done using the Oracle8 OCI interface. Oracle8*i* adds the ability to use Pro*C for database callbacks. Java external routines can use either JDBC or the SQLJ preprocessor for callbacks. All SQL statements executed from an external routine use the existing connection and transaction established in the calling PL/SQL session.

C Service Routines

Service routines are used to raise exceptions in the database, allocate memory, and retrieve OCI handles to execute SQL statements. All of the service routines take a context as one of their parameters. In C, the context is of type **OCIExtProcContext**, and is indicated by the CONTEXT keyword in the parameter list. The WITH CONTEXT clause is also required.

OCIExtProcRaiseExcp
This service routine raises a predefined exception, similar to the RAISE statement. The C prototype is defined with

> int OCIExtProcRaiseExcp(OCIExtProcContext *with_context,
>   size_t   error_number);

Like RAISE, when you call **OCIExtProcRaiseExcp**, no values are assigned to OUT or IN OUT parameters, and the procedure must return immediately. (Even if the C code does assign a value to OUT or IN OUT parameters after the call to **OCIExtProcRaiseExcp**, these values will not be returned to the PL/SQL session.) **OutputString6** illustrates this service routine by raising ORA-6502 if a NULL value is passed. Note the use of WITH CONTEXT in the PARAMETERS clause.

```
-- Available online as part of outputString.c
/* outputString5:
 * Outputs the string contained in message to a file specified by
 * path.  The message is repeated num_times times.  The file will
 * be created if it doesn't exist.  The number of lines actually
 * written is returned.  The NULLness of each parameter is
 * checked, and ORA-6502 is raised if any input parameter is NULL.
 */
ub2 outputString5(
  OCIExtProcContext *context,          /* External routine context */
  char  *path,                  /* Complete path of the output file */
  short  path_ind,                         /* Indicator for path */
  char  *message,                          /* Message to be written */
  short  message_ind,                      /* Indicator for message */
  int    num_times,      /* Number of times the message is repeated */
  short  num_times_ind,                    /* Indicator for num_times */
  short *retval_ind)
{

  FILE *file_handle;
  ub2 counter;

  /* If any of the input parameters are NULL, raise ORA-6502 and
     return immediately. */
  if (path_ind == OCI_IND_NULL || message_ind == OCI_IND_NULL ||
      num_times_ind == OCI_IND_NULL) {
    OCIExtProcRaiseExcp(context, 6502);
    return 0;
  }

  /* Open the file for writing. */
  file_handle = fopen(path, "w");

  for (counter = 0; counter < num_times; counter++)  {
```

```
      /* Output the string followed by a newline. */
      fprintf(file_handle, "%s\n", message);
   }

   /* Close the file. */
   fclose(file_handle);

   /* Set up return values. */
   *retval_ind = OCI_IND_NOTNULL;
   return counter;
}
```

-- **Available online as part of OutputString.sql**
```
CREATE OR REPLACE FUNCTION OutputString5(
  p_Path IN VARCHAR2,
  p_Message IN VARCHAR2,
  p_NumLines IN BINARY_INTEGER)
  RETURN NATURAL AS EXTERNAL

  LIBRARY StringLib
  NAME "outputString5"
  WITH CONTEXT
  PARAMETERS (CONTEXT,
              p_Path STRING,
              p_Path INDICATOR,
              p_Message STRING,
              p_Message INDICATOR,
              p_NumLines INT,
              p_NumLines INDICATOR,
              RETURN INDICATOR,
              RETURN UB2);
```

The raised error is illustrated by the following SQL*Plus session:

-- **Available online as part of callOS.sql**
```
SQL> DECLARE
  2    v_NumLinesWritten NATURAL;
  3  BEGIN
  4    v_NumLinesWritten :=
  5      OutputString5(p_Path => '/tmp/output.txt',
  6                    p_Message => NULL,
  7                    p_NumLines => 8);
  8    DBMS_OUTPUT.PUT_LINE('Lines written = ' || v_NumLinesWritten);
  9  END;
 10  /
DECLARE
*
ERROR at line 1:
```

```
ORA-06502: PL/SQL: numeric or value error
ORA-06512: at "EXAMPLE.OUTPUTSTRING5", line 0
ORA-06512: at line 4
```

OCIExtProcRaiseExcpWithMsg

This service routine is similar to RAISE_APPLICATION_ERROR. Unlike
OCIExtProcRaiseExcp, it allows you to pass a user-defined message along with
the error. The error number should be between 20,000 and 20,999, just like
RAISE_APPLICATION_ERROR. The prototype is

> int OCIExtProcRaiseExcpWithMsg(OCIExtProcContext *with_context,
>   size_t   error_number,
>   text   *error_message,
>   size_t   len);

If *error_message* is a null-terminated string, then *len* should be zero. Otherwise,
len should be the length of the string. **OutputString6** (in the next section) illustrates
this technique.

OCIExtprocAllocCallMemory

If you need to allocate memory in your external procedure, you can use
OCIExtprocAllocCallMemory. This routine will allocate memory that will last
for the duration of the call, and will be freed automatically by PL/SQL when the
external procedure returns. The prototype is

> dvoid *OCIExtprocAllocCallMemory(OCIExtProcContext *with_context,
>   size_t   amount);

where *amount* is the number of bytes to allocate. **OutputString6** uses this routine to
allocate memory for the error message text.

```
/* Available online as part of outputString.c */
/* outputString6:
 * Outputs the string contained in message to a file specified by
 * path.  The message is repeated num_times times.  The file will
 * be created if it doesn't exist.  The number of lines actually
 * written is returned.  The NULLness of each parameter is
 * checked, and ORA-6502 is raised if any input parameter is NULL.
 * If the file cannot be opened, a user-defined error is returned.
 */
ub2 outputString6(
  OCIExtProcContext *context,              /* External routine context */
```

```
    char   *path,                    /* Complete path of the output file */
    short  path_ind,                        /* Indicator for path */
    char   *message,                        /* Message to be written */
    short  message_ind,                     /* Indicator for message */
    int    num_times,      /* Number of times the message is repeated */
    short  num_times_ind,                   /* Indicator for num_times */
    short  *retval_ind)
{

    FILE *file_handle;
    ub2 counter;
    text *initial_msg = (text *)"Cannot open file ";
    text *error_msg;

    /* If any of the input parameters are NULL, raise ORA-6502 and
       return immediately. */
    if (path_ind == OCI_IND_NULL || message_ind == OCI_IND_NULL ||
        num_times_ind == OCI_IND_NULL)
    {
      OCIExtProcRaiseExcp(context, 6502);
      return 0;
    }

    /* Open the file for writing. */
    file_handle = fopen(path, "w");

    /* Check for success.  If not, raise an error. */
    if (!file_handle)
    {
      /* Allocate space for the error message text, and set it up.
         We do not have to free this memory - PL/SQL will do that
         automatically. */
      error_msg = OCIExtProcAllocCallMemory(context,
                      strlen(path) + strlen(initial_msg) + 1);
      strcpy((char *)error_msg, (char *)initial_msg);
      strcat((char *)error_msg, path);

          OCIExtProcRaiseExcpWithMsg(context, 20001, error_msg, 0);
          return 0;
    }

    for (counter = 0; counter < num_times; counter++)
    {
      /* Output the string followed by a newline. */
      fprintf(file_handle, "%s\n", message);
    }

    /* Close the file. */
```

```
  fclose(file_handle);

  /* Set up return values. */
  *retval_ind = OCI_IND_NOTNULL;
  return counter;
}
```

-- **Available online as part of OutputString.sql**
```
CREATE OR REPLACE FUNCTION OutputString6(
  p_Path IN VARCHAR2,
  p_Message IN VARCHAR2,
  p_NumLines IN BINARY_INTEGER)
  RETURN NATURAL AS EXTERNAL

  LIBRARY StringLib
  NAME "outputString6"
  WITH CONTEXT
  PARAMETERS (CONTEXT,
              p_Path STRING,
              p_Path INDICATOR,
              p_Message STRING,
              p_Message INDICATOR,
              p_NumLines INT,
              p_NumLines INDICATOR,
              RETURN INDICATOR,
              RETURN UB2);
```

The following SQL*Plus session illustrates the error raised by **OutputString6**.

-- **Available online as part of callOS.sql**
```
SQL> DECLARE
  2    v_NumLinesWritten NATURAL;
  3  BEGIN
  4    v_NumLinesWritten :=
  5      OutputString6(p_Path => '/GARBAGE_PATH',
  6                    p_Message => 'Hello from version 6!',
  7                    p_NumLines => 8);
  8    DBMS_OUTPUT.PUT_LINE('Lines written = ' || v_NumLinesWritten);
  9  END;
 10  /
DECLARE
*
ERROR at line 1:
ORA-20001: Cannot open file /GARBAGE_PATH
ORA-06512: at "EXAMPLE.OUTPUTSTRING6", line 0
ORA-06512: at line 4
```

SQLExtProcError

Oracle**8i**
and higher

If you are writing a Pro*C external routine, you can use the **SQLExtProcError** function to raise an error in the calling environment, similar to **OCIExtProcRaiseExcpWithMsg**. In fact, **SQLExtProcError** calls **OCIExtProcRaiseExcpWithMsg** internally. It is defined with

```
void SQLExtProcError(sql_context ctx,
                     char *msg,
                     size_t msglen);
```

The *ctx* parameter here is not the external routine context; rather, it is the Pro*C runtime context. The macro SQL_SINGLE_RCTX, defined in **sqlcpr.h**, can be used for this parameter. For an example, see the Pro*C example in the following section.

Executing SQL in an External Routine

For C external routines, you can use either OCI or Pro*C (Oracle8i only) to execute SQL. Java external routines can use either JDBC or SQLJ. In all cases, you first need to get a handle to the connection used by the calling session. This is done differently for each method. We will examine how each of these methods work in the following sections, each of which implements the external routine corresponding to the following package:

```
-- Available online as part of CallBack.sql
CREATE OR REPLACE LIBRARY CallBackLib AS
   '/home/surman/book/code/ch10/callbacklib.so';

CREATE OR REPLACE PACKAGE CallBack AS
   -- This package contains various wrapper routines, each of which
   -- makes a callback to the database.  They all take the same
   -- two arguments - a number and character string, to be inserted
   -- into temp_table.
   PROCEDURE OCI(p_Num IN BINARY_INTEGER,
                 p_Char IN VARCHAR2) IS
     LANGUAGE C
     LIBRARY CallBackLib
     NAME "OCI"
     WITH CONTEXT
     PARAMETERS(CONTEXT,
                p_Num SB4,
                p_Char STRING);

   PROCEDURE ProC(p_Num IN BINARY_INTEGER,
```

```
                    p_Char IN VARCHAR2) IS
      LANGUAGE C
      LIBRARY CallBackLib
      NAME "ProC"
      WITH CONTEXT
      PARAMETERS(CONTEXT,
                 p_Num SB4,
                 p_Char STRING);

   PROCEDURE JDBC(p_Num IN NUMBER,
                  p_Char IN VARCHAR2) IS
      LANGUAGE JAVA
      NAME 'CallBackJDBC.insert(int, java.lang.String)';

   PROCEDURE SQLJ(p_Num IN NUMBER,
                  p_Char IN VARCHAR2) IS
      LANGUAGE JAVA
      NAME 'CallBackSQLJ.insert(int, java.lang.String)';
END CallBack;
```

TIP

*The **ch10.mk** Makefile contains targets for compiling each of the examples in the following sections. You must have Pro*C installed (and be using Oracle8i) for the Pro*C example. Likewise, you must have SQLJ installed for the SQLJ example. See the Makefile for details.*

OCI

An OCI connection is represented by several handles, including the environment, service context, and error handles. The **OCIExtProcGetEnv** routine will return these handles, given the external routine context. This service routine is defined with

```
sword OCIExtProcGetEnv(OCIExtProcContext *with_context,
                       OCIEnv      **envh,
                       OCISvcCtx   **svch,
                       OCIError    **errh);
```

You can use the returned environment, service context and error handles in subsequent OCI calls that execute SQL statements. These handles can be used only for callbacks to the calling session—they cannot be used for other sessions. For

example, the implementation of the **CallBack.OCI** external routine shown next uses
the handles to insert into **temp_table**:

```
/* Available online as callbackOCI.c */
#include <oci.h>
#include <stdio.h>
/* For CHECKERROR macro */
#define EXTERNAL_ROUTINE

#include <common_OCI.h>


/* Corresponding PL/SQL Parameters:
 * PARAMETERS (CONTEXT,
 *             p_Num SB4,
 *             p_Char STRING);
 */
void OCI(
  OCIExtProcContext *ctx,               /* External routine context */
  sb4                 p_Num,            /* Number to be INSERTed */
  char               *p_Char)           /* String to be INSERTed */
{
  OCIEnv     *envHandle;
  OCISvcCtx  *svcHandle;
  OCIError   *errHandle;
  OCIStmt    *stmtHandle;
  OCIBind    *numBindHandle = (OCIBind *)0;
  OCIBind    *charBindHandle = (OCIBind *)0;

  CONST text *insertStmt =
    (text *)"INSERT INTO temp_table VALUES (:1, :2)";

  /* Get OCI handles from the external procedure context */
  OCIExtProcGetEnv(ctx, &envHandle, &svcHandle,
                   &errHandle);

  /* Allocate the statement handle */
  CHECKERROR(ctx, errHandle, OCIHandleAlloc(
    (dvoid *)envHandle,          /* parenth */
    (dvoid **) &stmtHandle,      /* hndlpp */
    OCI_HTYPE_STMT,              /* type */
    (size_t) 0,                  /* xtramem_sz */
    (dvoid **)0));               /* usrmempp */

  /* Prepare the statement */
  CHECKERROR(ctx, errHandle, OCIStmtPrepare(
    stmtHandle,                  /* stmtp */
    errHandle,                   /* errhp */
```

```
    insertStmt,                     /* stmt */
    (ub4) strlen(insertStmt),       /* stmt_len */
    (ub4) OCI_NTV_SYNTAX,           /* language */
    (ub4) OCI_DEFAULT));            /* mode */

  /* Bind p_Num */
  CHECKERROR(ctx, errHandle, OCIBindByPos(
    stmtHandle,                     /* stmtp */
    &numBindHandle,                 /* bindpp */
    errHandle,                      /* errhp */
    (ub4)1,                         /* position */
    (dvoid *) &p_Num,               /* valuep */
    (sb4) sizeof(p_Num),            /* value_sz */
    SQLT_INT,                       /* dty */
    (dvoid *) NULL,                 /* indp */
    (ub2 *) NULL,                   /* alenp */
    (ub2 *) NULL,                   /* rcodep */
    (ub4) 0,                        /* maxarr_len */
    (ub4 *)NULL,                    /* curelep */
    OCI_DEFAULT));                  /* mode */

  /* Bind p_Char */
  CHECKERROR(ctx, errHandle, OCIBindByPos(
    stmtHandle,                     /* stmtp */
    &charBindHandle,                /* bindpp */
    errHandle,                      /* errhp */
    (ub4) 2,                        /* position */
    (dvoid *) p_Char,               /* valuep */
    (sb4) strlen(p_Char) + 1,       /* value_sz */
    SQLT_STR,                       /* dty */
    (dvoid *) NULL,                 /* indp */
    (ub2 *) NULL,                   /* alenp */
    (ub2 *) NULL,                   /* rcodep */
    (ub4) 0,                        /* maxarr_len */
    (ub4 *)NULL,                    /* curelep */
    OCI_DEFAULT));                  /* mode */

  /* Execute the statement */
  CHECKERROR(ctx, errHandle, OCIStmtExecute(
    svcHandle,                      /* svchp */
    stmtHandle,                     /* stmtp */
    errHandle,                      /* errhp */
    (ub4) 1,                        /* iters */
    (ub4) 0,                        /* rowoff */
    (CONST OCISnapshot *) NULL,     /* snap_in */
    (OCISnapshot *) NULL,           /* snap_out */
    OCI_DEFAULT));                  /* mode */
}
```

NOTE
*See the online file **common_OCI.h** for the definition of the CHECKERROR macro.*

For more information on OCI, see the *Programmer's Guide to the Oracle Call Interface*.

Pro*C

A Pro*C program normally connects to the database with the EXEC SQL CONNECT command. However, this cannot be used to get the database connection used by the PL/SQL session. Instead, Pro*C provides the EXEC SQL REGISTER CONNECT USING command, which takes the external routine context as a parameter. It then sets up the necessary runtime state to execute embedded SQL. The implementation of the **CallBack.ProC** external routine demonstrates this:

```
/* Available online as part of callBackProC.pc */
void ProC(ctx, p_Num, p_Char)
OCIExtProcContext *ctx;
sb4                p_Num;
char               *p_Char;
{
  /* Handle any errors */
  EXEC SQL WHENEVER SQLERROR goto err;

  /* Establish the Pro*C default connection based on the context */
  EXEC SQL REGISTER CONNECT USING :ctx;

  /* And insert! */
  EXEC SQL INSERT INTO temp_table VALUES (:p_Num, :p_Char);

  return;

err:
  /* Raise the error in PL/SQL */
  SQLExtProcError(SQL_SINGLE_RCTX,
                  sqlca.sqlerrm.sqlerrmc,
                  sqlca.sqlerrm.sqlerrml);
  return;
}
```

For more information on using Pro*C, see the *Pro*C/C++ Precompiler Programmer's Guide*.

JDBC

A JSP can issue callbacks through the server-side JDBC driver. Unlike the client-side thin or OCI driver, the server-side driver does not need a user ID and password to connect. Rather, it uses the external routine context. The JDBC Connection object is returned by the **OracleDriver.defaultConnection()** method, as illustrated by the following implementation of **CallBack.JDBC**:

```
// Available online as part of CallBackJDBC.java
class CallBackJDBC {
  public static void insert(int p_Num, String p_Char)
    throws SQLException
  {
      Connection conn = new OracleDriver().defaultConnection();
      PreparedStatement pstmt = conn.prepareStatement(
        "INSERT INTO temp_table VALUES (?, ?)");

      pstmt.setInt(1, p_Num);
      pstmt.setString(2, p_Char);
      pstmt.executeUpdate();
  }
}
```

For more information on using JDBC, see the *JDBC Developer's Guide and Reference*.

SQLJ

SQLJ, like Pro*C, is a preprocessor that simplifies database access from Java. It generates JDBC code as output. A JSP written using SQLJ does not need to make any explicit connection at all. The default SQLJ context is already initialized, based on the external routine context. For example, here is the implementation of **CallBack.SQLJ**:

```
// Available online as part of CallBackSQLJ.sqlj
class CallBackSQLJ {
  public static void insert(int p_Num, String p_Char)
    throws SQLException {

      // Issue the INSERT statement directly, we already have the
      // default connection established.
      #sql {INSERT INTO temp_table VALUES (:p_Num, :p_Char)};
  }
}
```

For more information on SQLJ, see the *SQLJ Developer's Guide and Reference*.

Restrictions on Callbacks

There are several restrictions to keep in mind when issuing SQL statements within an external routine. In general, the following kinds of statements are not allowed.

■ Transaction control statements like COMMIT or ROLLBACK

■ DDL statements which would cause an implicit COMMIT

Furthermore, Pro*C external routines have the following additional restrictions:

■ They must be written in C. C++ external routines are not supported. You can call a C++ routine from the external routine, however, if it has an extern "C" wrapper.

■ While connected using the EXEC SQL REGISTER CONNECT context, additional default connections are not allowed.

■ Multithreaded external routines are not supported. Thus, the EXEC SQL ENABLE THREADS statement will raise a runtime error.

■ The following embedded statements are not allowed: EXEC SQL OBJECT, EXEC SQL LOB, and EXEC TOOLS.

In addition, there are certain OCI calls that are not allowed in an external routine. These are listed in Table 10-7. Along with the calls listed there, polling-mode OCI routines such as **OCIGetPieceInfo** are not supported. Finally, with the routine **OCIHandleAlloc**, the following handle types are not supported:

■ OCI_HTYPE_SERVER

■ OCI_HTYPE_SESSION

■ OCI_HTYPE_SVCCTX

■ OCI_HTYPE_TRANS

Common Issues

We will discuss some issues common to both C and Java external routines in this section. These include external routines that are not standalone procedures, how external routines work with invoker's and definer's rights, and tips for debugging external routines. We will close out the section with some general guidelines and restrictions for external routines.

OCIObjectNew	OCIObjectPin	OCIObjectUnpin
OCIObjectPinCountReset	OCIObjectLock	OCIObjectMarkUpdate
OCIObjectUnmark	OCIObjectUnmarkByRef	OCIObjectAlwaysLatest
OCIObjectNotAlwaysLatest	OCIObjectMarkDeleteByRef	OCIObjectMarkDelete
OCIObjectFlush	OCIObjectFlushRefresh	OCIObjectGetTypeRef
OCIObjectGetObjectRef	OCIObjectExists	OCIObjectIsLocked
OCIObjectIsDirtied	OCIObjectIsLoaded	OCIObjectRefresh
OCIObjectPinTable	OCIObjectArrayPin	OCICacheFlush
OCICacheFlushRefresh	OCICacheRefresh	OCICacheUnpin
OCICacheFree	OCICacheUnmark	OCICacheGetObjects
OCICacheRegister	OCIEnvInit	OCIInitialize
OCIPasswordChange	OCIServerAttach	OCIServerDetach
OCISessionBegin	OCISessionEnd	OCISvcCtxToLda
OCITransCommit	OCITransDetach	OCITransRollback
OCITransStart		

TABLE 10-7. *OCI Calls Not Allowed in an External Routine*

Other Locations for External Routines

External routines can be either procedures (which don't return a value) or functions (which do return a value). The PL/SQL wrapper can be in a package or object type, or can be standalone. In Oracle8*i* the wrapper may be in a package body as well. However, wrappers written using the AS EXTERNAL clause cannot be located in package or type bodies. Table 10-8 summarizes the various locations for the PL/SQL call specification. Given the following C external routine:

```
/* Available online as location.c */
/* A simple external routine, that just returns its first
 * parameter in the second parameter.
 */
void location(
  int p1,
```

```
  int *p2)
{
  *p2 = p1;
}
```

we can create wrappers in various locations, as demonstrated by the following:

```
-- Available online as Location.sql
CREATE OR REPLACE LIBRARY LocationLib AS
   '/home/surman/book/code/ch10/locationlib.so';

-- Standalone procedure
CREATE OR REPLACE PROCEDURE Location(p1 IN BINARY_INTEGER,
                                     p2 OUT BINARY_INTEGER) AS
   LANGUAGE C
   LIBRARY LocationLib
   NAME "location"
   PARAMETERS (p1 INT,
               p2 INT);

-- Package header and package body
CREATE OR REPLACE PACKAGE LocPackage AS
   -- Since this procedure uses the AS EXTERNAL clause, it must be
   -- in the package body.
   PROCEDURE LocBody (p1 IN BINARY_INTEGER,
                      p2 OUT BINARY_INTEGER);

   -- But this can be in the header.
   PROCEDURE LocHeader(p1 IN BINARY_INTEGER,
                       p2 OUT BINARY_INTEGER) IS
     LANGUAGE C
     LIBRARY LocationLib
     NAME "location"
     PARAMETERS (p1 INT,
                 p2 INT);
END LocPackage;

CREATE OR REPLACE PACKAGE BODY LocPackage AS
   PROCEDURE LocBody (p1 IN BINARY_INTEGER,
                      p2 OUT BINARY_INTEGER) IS
     EXTERNAL
     LIBRARY LocationLib
     NAME "location"
     PARAMETERS (p1 INT,
                 p2 INT);
END LocPackage;
```

```
-- Object type header and body
CREATE OR REPLACE TYPE LocType AS OBJECT (
  v_Attribute VARCHAR2(10),

  -- Since this procedure uses the AS EXTERNAL clause, it must be
  -- in the type body.
  MEMBER PROCEDURE LocBody (p1 IN BINARY_INTEGER,
                            p2 OUT BINARY_INTEGER),

  -- But this can be in the header.
  MEMBER PROCEDURE LocHeader(p1 IN BINARY_INTEGER,
                             p2 OUT BINARY_INTEGER) IS
    LANGUAGE C
    LIBRARY LocationLib
    NAME "location"
    PARAMETERS (SELF,
                p1 INT,
                p2 INT)
);

CREATE OR REPLACE TYPE BODY LocType AS
  MEMBER PROCEDURE LocBody (p1 IN BINARY_INTEGER,
                            p2 OUT BINARY_INTEGER) IS
    EXTERNAL
    LIBRARY LocationLib
    NAME "location"
    PARAMETERS (SELF,
                p1 INT,
                p2 INT);
END;
```

Location	Valid in Oracle8?	Valid in Oracle8i?
Standalone (schema level)	Yes	Yes
Package header	Yes	Yes
Package body	No	Yes (AS LANGUAGE clause only)
Type header	Yes	Yes
Type body	No	Yes (AS LANGUAGE clause only)

TABLE 10-8. *Locations for PL/SQL Call Specifications*

NOTE
*For external object type methods, SELF is required
as part of the PARAMETERS clause. Although SELF
is optional for the PL/SQL declaration, it is required
for the C declaration. For more information, see the
Oracle documentation.*

C External Methods
Methods of an object type can be implemented as an external routine, either in
C (Oracle8) or Java (Oracle8*i*). All object type methods take SELF as an implicit
parameter, meaning the current object. For C external methods, SELF must be
passed explicitly. The SELF keyword is used in the PARAMETERS clause to indicate
the position of this parameter. It can take properties as well. For more information,
see the Oracle documentation.

Overloading
If the PL/SQL wrapper is contained in a package or type, it can be overloaded, just
like a regular packaged subprogram. Furthermore, a wrapper can be overloaded
with another wrapper, or with a regular subprogram. For example, the **DemoMain**
package, which we saw earlier in this chapter, overloaded four wrappers. For more
information on overloading, see the Oracle documentation.

RESTRICT_REFERENCES
If an external function is in a package, you can assert the RESTRICT_REFERENCES
pragma to allow it to be used in a SQL statement. (RESTRICT_REFERENCES is not
necessary in Oracle8*i*.) However, the PL/SQL compiler has no way of verifying that
the external function does not violate the pragma, since it is not written in PL/SQL.
It is your responsibility to insure that the external function does not violate the
pragma. If the external function violates the pragma, internal errors can result.

 Oracle8*i* adds the TRUST keyword to RESTRICT_REFERENCES, which
signals to the PL/SQL compiler that the specified function conforms to the
pragma, without having to verify it. This keyword can be used to allow an
external routine to be called from a subprogram that has a purity level asserted.
    For more information on RESTRICT_REFERENCES, including how to use TRUST,
see Chapter 5.

Invoker's and Definer's Rights
As we saw in Chapter 5, PL/SQL stored subprograms can be created with
invoker's or definer's rights, starting with Oracle8*i*. The default is definer's rights,
which means that references to database objects will be done under the privilege

set of the owner of the subprogram. An invoker's rights subprogram, on the other hand, will resolve references under the privilege set of the caller, not the owner.

Invoker's and definer's rights are specified using the AUTHID clause in the CREATE OR REPLACE statement. For C external routines, the AUTHID clause is specified on the PL/SQL wrapper. If it is not specified, then the external routine will default to definer's rights (the same as a PL/SQL subprogram). For Java external routines, the AUTHID clause can be specified on both the wrapper and the JSP itself. The default for the wrapper is definer's, but the default for the JSP is invoker's. This is because the Java execution model conforms more closely to the invoker's rights model. We will see examples of both Java and C invoker's and definer's rights routines in the following sections. Following the examples, Table 10-9 summarizes the behavior.

C Example

Consider the **OCI** external routine, which we saw earlier in this chapter in "Executing SQL in an External Routine." This routine inserted its arguments into **temp_table**. Suppose we have two users, **UserA** and **UserB**, each of which has a copy of **temp_table**. We then create the following three PL/SQL wrappers in **UserA**'s schema, and GRANT execute on all of them to **UserB**:

```
-- Available online as part of CInvoker.sql
CREATE OR REPLACE LIBRARY CallBackLib AS
   '/home/surman/book/code/ch10/callbacklib.so';

-- Default, which for a C external routine is definer's rights
CREATE OR REPLACE PROCEDURE OCIDefault(p_Num IN BINARY_INTEGER,
                                       p_Char IN VARCHAR2) AS
   LANGUAGE C
   LIBRARY CallBackLib
   NAME "OCI"
   WITH CONTEXT
   PARAMETERS (CONTEXT,
               p_Num SB4,
               p_Char STRING);

-- Invoker's rights routine
CREATE OR REPLACE PROCEDURE OCIInvokers(p_Num IN BINARY_INTEGER,
                                        p_Char IN VARCHAR2)
   AUTHID CURRENT_USER AS
   LANGUAGE C
   LIBRARY CallBackLib
   NAME "OCI"
   WITH CONTEXT
   PARAMETERS (CONTEXT,
               p_Num SB4,
```

```
                        p_Char STRING);

-- Definer's rights routine
CREATE OR REPLACE PROCEDURE OCIDefiners(p_Num IN BINARY_INTEGER,
                                        p_Char IN VARCHAR2)
    AUTHID DEFINER AS
    LANGUAGE C
    LIBRARY CallBackLib
    NAME "OCI"
    WITH CONTEXT
    PARAMETERS (CONTEXT,
                p_Num SB4,
                p_Char STRING);

-- GRANT execute on all three to UserB.
GRANT EXECUTE ON OCIDefault TO UserB;
GRANT EXECUTE ON OCIInvokers TO UserB;
GRANT EXECUTE ON OCIDefiners TO UserB;
```

This situation is illustrated by Figure 10-4. In the figure, the dashed arrows signify the GRANTs, and the solid arrows signify dependencies. If we now call the

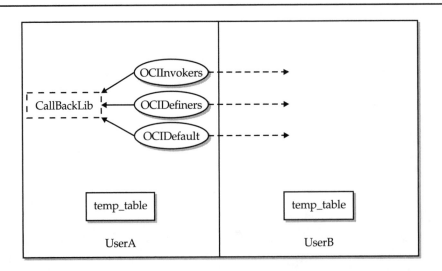

FIGURE 10-4. *Invoker's and definer's C external routines*

three wrappers while connected as **UserB**, **OCIDefault** and **OCIDefiners** will insert into **UserA.temp_table**, while **OCIInvokers** will insert into **UserB.temp_table**. This is illustrated by the following SQL*Plus session:

```
-- Available online as part of CInvoker.sql
SQL> -- Call OCIDefault.  This will insert into UserA's temp_table.
SQL> CALL UserA.OCIDefault(1, 'Calling default as UserB');
Call completed.

SQL> -- Call OCIInvokers.  This will insert into UserB's temp_table.
SQL> CALL UserA.OCIInvokers(2, 'Calling invokers as UserB');
Call completed.

SQL> -- Call OCIDefiners.  This will insert into UserA's temp_table.
SQL> CALL UserA.OCIDefiners(3, 'Calling definers as UserB');
Call completed.

SQL> COMMIT;
Commit complete.

SQL> -- Verify the results.    This should have row 2.
SQL> SELECT * FROM temp_table;

   NUM_COL CHAR_COL
---------- -------------------------------------------------------------
         2 Calling invokers as UserB

SQL> connect UserA/UserA
Connected.
SQL> -- And this should have rows 1 and 3.
SQL> SELECT * FROM temp_table;

   NUM_COL CHAR_COL
---------- -------------------------------------------------------------
         1 Calling default as UserB
         3 Calling definers as UserB
```

Java Example

For Java external routines, the situation is slightly more complicated. Both the JSP itself and the PL/SQL wrapper can specify an AUTHID clause. The JSP will default to invoker's rights, while the wrapper will default to definer's rights. The best way to illustrate this is by example. Consider the following three JSPs, which are loaded into **UserA**'s schema:

```
-- Available online as part of JInvoker.sql
-- Default, which for a JSP is invoker's rights
CREATE OR REPLACE AND RESOLVE JAVA SOURCE
  NAMED JDefault AS
  import java.sql.*;
  import oracle.jdbc.driver.*;
  class JDefault
  {
    public static void insert(int p_Num, String p_Char)
      throws SQLException
    {
      Connection conn = new OracleDriver().defaultConnection();

      PreparedStatement pstmt = conn.prepareStatement(
        "INSERT INTO temp_table VALUES (?, ?)");

      pstmt.setInt(1, p_Num);
      pstmt.setString(2, p_Char);
      pstmt.executeUpdate();
    }
  };

-- Invoker's rights
CREATE OR REPLACE AND RESOLVE JAVA SOURCE
  NAMED JInvokers AUTHID CURRENT_USER AS
  import java.sql.*;
  import oracle.jdbc.driver.*;
  class JInvokers
  {
    public static void insert(int p_Num, String p_Char)
      throws SQLException
    {
      Connection conn = new OracleDriver().defaultConnection();

      PreparedStatement pstmt = conn.prepareStatement(
        "INSERT INTO temp_table VALUES (?, ?)");

      pstmt.setInt(1, p_Num);
      pstmt.setString(2, p_Char);
      pstmt.executeUpdate();
    }
  };
```

```
-- Definer's rights
CREATE OR REPLACE AND RESOLVE JAVA SOURCE
  NAMED JDefiners AUTHID DEFINER AS
  import java.sql.*;
  import oracle.jdbc.driver.*;
  class JDefiners
  {
    public static void insert(int p_Num, String p_Char)
      throws SQLException
    {
      Connection conn = new OracleDriver().defaultConnection();

      PreparedStatement pstmt = conn.prepareStatement(
        "INSERT INTO temp_table VALUES (?, ?)");

      pstmt.setInt(1, p_Num);
      pstmt.setString(2, p_Char);
      pstmt.executeUpdate();
    }
  };
```

NOTE
You can also specify that a JSP have definer's rights by using the –definer option for loadjava. If you don't specify –definer, it defaults to invoker's rights.

We can now create both an invoker's rights and definer's rights PL/SQL wrapper for each of the JSPs, and grant EXECUTE on the wrapper to UserB. These are done with

 -- Available online as part of Jinvokers.sql
```
CREATE OR REPLACE PROCEDURE PInvokersToJDefault(p_Num IN NUMBER,
                                                p_Char IN VARCHAR2)
  AUTHID CURRENT_USER AS
  LANGUAGE JAVA
  NAME 'JDefault.insert(int, java.lang.String)';

CREATE OR REPLACE PROCEDURE PInvokersToJInvokers(p_Num IN NUMBER,
                                                 p_Char IN VARCHAR2)
  AUTHID CURRENT_USER AS
  LANGUAGE JAVA
  NAME 'JInvokers.insert(int, java.lang.String)';

CREATE OR REPLACE PROCEDURE PInvokersToJDefiners(p_Num IN NUMBER,
                                                 p_Char IN VARCHAR2)
  AUTHID CURRENT_USER AS
  LANGUAGE JAVA
```

```
    NAME 'JDefiners.insert(int, java.lang.String)';

CREATE OR REPLACE PROCEDURE PDefinersToJDefault(p_Num IN NUMBER,
                                                p_Char IN VARCHAR2)
    AUTHID DEFINER AS
    LANGUAGE JAVA
    NAME 'JDefault.insert(int, java.lang.String)';

CREATE OR REPLACE PROCEDURE PDefinersToJInvokers(p_Num IN NUMBER,
                                                 p_Char IN VARCHAR2)
    AUTHID DEFINER AS
    LANGUAGE JAVA
    NAME 'JInvokers.insert(int, java.lang.String)';

CREATE OR REPLACE PROCEDURE PDefinersToJDefiners(p_Num IN NUMBER,
                                                 p_Char IN VARCHAR2)
    AUTHID DEFINER AS
    LANGUAGE JAVA
    NAME 'JDefiners.insert(int, java.lang.String)';
```

This situation is illustrated by Figure 10-5. The following SQL*Plus session shows the results of calling each of the wrappers as **UserB**:

```
-- Available online as part of JInvoker.sql
SQL> CALL UserA.PInvokersToJDefault(1,
        'Calling PInvokersToJDefault as UserB');
Call completed.

SQL> CALL UserA.PInvokersToJInvokers(2,
        'Calling PInvokersToJInvokers as UserB');
Call completed.

SQL> CALL UserA.PInvokersToJDefiners(3,
        'Calling PInvokersToJDefiners as UserB');
Call completed.

SQL> CALL UserA.PDefinersToJDefault(4,
        'Calling PDefinersToJDefault as UserB');
Call completed.

SQL> CALL UserA.PDefinersToJInvokers(5,
        'Calling PDefinersToJInvokers as UserB');
Call completed.

SQL> CALL UserA.PDefinersToJDefiners(6,
```

```
       'Calling PDefinersToJDefiners as UserB');
Call completed.

SQL> COMMIT;
Commit complete.

SQL> SELECT * FROM temp_table ORDER BY num_col;
   NUM_COL CHAR_COL
---------- ------------------------------------------------------------
         1 Calling PInvokersToJDefault as UserB
         2 Calling PInvokersToJInvokers as UserB

SQL> connect UserA/UserA
Connected.
SQL> SELECT * FROM temp_table ORDER BY num_col;
   NUM_COL CHAR_COL
---------- ------------------------------------------------------------
         3 Calling PInvokersToJDefiners as UserB
         4 Calling PDefinersToJDefault as UserB
         5 Calling PDefinersToJInvokers as UserB
         6 Calling PDefinersToJDefiners as UserB
```

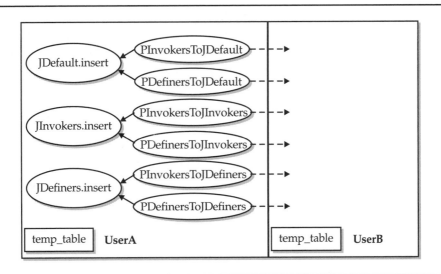

FIGURE 10-5. *Invoker's and definer's Java external routines*

Essentially, the only way in which the JSP will execute with invoker's rights is if both the wrapper and the JSP are specified with invoker's rights. If either is specified with definer's rights, that overrides and the routine is executed under the privilege set of its owner.

Summary

Table 10-9 summarizes the behavior of C and Java external routines with respect to invoker's and definer's rights. Note that if you do not specify an AUTHID clause on either the JSP or the call specification, then both C and Java external routines will default to definer's rights.

NOTE

There are other ways of calling a Java stored procedure than through PL/SQL. If you are using one of these methods (CORBA, for example), then there is no wrapper subprogram, and the AUTHID of the JSP is the only one in effect. For more information, see the Enterprise JavaBeans and CORBA Developer's Guides.

External Routine Dependencies

As we have seen in Chapter 5, stored PL/SQL subprograms can have dependencies on other database objects. These dependencies are tracked by the data dictionary, and the subprograms can be invalidated if their dependent objects change. For

Language	Wrapper Defined as	External Routine Defined as	Results in
C	Invoker's	N/A	Invoker's
	Definer's (default)	N/A	Definer's
Java	Invoker's	Invoker's (default)	Invoker's
	Invoker's	Definer's	Definer's
	Definer's (default)	Definer's	Definer's
	Definer's (default)	Invoker's (default)	Definer's

TABLE 10-9. *Invoker's and Definer's Rights for External Routines*

external routines, however, the dependencies are not tracked in the same manner. Suppose we load the following class into the database:

```java
// Available online as Depender.java
import java.sql.*;
import oracle.jdbc.driver.*;
class Depender
{
  // This procedure simply selects from temp_table, and prints
  // the results to System.out.
  public static void main(String[] args)
    throws SQLException
  {
    String query = "SELECT * FROM temp_table";
    Connection conn = new OracleDriver().defaultConnection();

    PreparedStatement pstmt = conn.prepareStatement(query);
    ResultSet rset = pstmt.executeQuery();
    int rowCount = 0;

    System.out.println("f1\tf2");
    while (rset.next())
    {
      System.out.println(rset.getString(1) + "\t" +
                         rset.getString(2));
      rowCount++;
    }

    System.out.println("Total rows: " + rowCount);
  }
}
```

We can create a call specification for **Depender.main** with the following:

```sql
-- Available online as part of Depender.sql
CREATE OR REPLACE PROCEDURE DependerWrapper AS
  LANGUAGE JAVA
  NAME 'Depender.main(java.lang.String [])';
```

Depender.main queries **temp_table**, so it is dependent on any modifications to it. Likewise, if the arguments to **Depender.main** were to change, **DependerWrapper** might have to be modified, so **DependerWrapper** depends on the JSP. These dependencies, however, are not stored in the data dictionary. However, dependencies among Java classes are recorded. This situation is indicated by Figure 10-6. The dotted lines in the figure represent dependencies that aren't recorded, and the solid lines represent recorded dependencies.

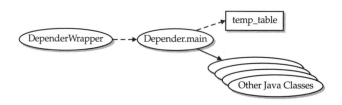

FIGURE 10-6. *Dependencies for **Depender.main** and **DependerWrapper***

What does this mean? Consider the following SQL*Plus session:

```
-- Available online as part of Depender.sql
SQL> SELECT name, type, referenced_name, referenced_type
  2     FROM user_dependencies
  3     WHERE UPPER(name) LIKE 'DEPENDER%';
```

NAME	TYPE	REFERENCED_NAME	REFERENCED_T
DEPENDERWRAPPER	PROCEDURE	SYS_STUB_FOR_PURITY_ANALYSIS	PACKAGE
Depender	JAVA CLASS	java/lang/String	JAVA CLASS
Depender	JAVA CLASS	java/lang/StringBuffer	JAVA CLASS
Depender	JAVA CLASS	java/lang/System	JAVA CLASS
Depender	JAVA CLASS	java/io/PrintStream	JAVA CLASS
Depender	JAVA CLASS	java/sql/Connection	JAVA CLASS
Depender	JAVA CLASS	java/sql/ResultSet	JAVA CLASS
Depender	JAVA CLASS	java/sql/SQLException	JAVA CLASS
Depender	JAVA CLASS	/c4156ac6_OracleDriver	JAVA CLASS
Depender	JAVA CLASS	java/sql/PreparedStatement	JAVA CLASS
Depender	JAVA CLASS	java/lang/Object	JAVA CLASS

```
11 rows selected.
```

This query shows the dependencies for **DependerWrapper** and the Java class. The class depends on a number of other classes, but the wrapper does not depend on the class. This is illustrated further by the following:

```
-- Available online as part of Depender.sql
SQL> SELECT object_name, object_type, status
  2     FROM user_objects
  3     WHERE UPPER(object_name) LIKE 'DEPENDER%';
```

OBJECT_NAME	OBJECT_TYPE	STATUS
DEPENDERWRAPPER	PROCEDURE	**VALID**
Depender	JAVA CLASS	**VALID**

```
SQL>
SQL> ALTER TABLE temp_table MODIFY (num_col NUMBER);

Table altered.
SQL> SELECT object_name, object_type, status
  2     FROM user_objects
  3     WHERE UPPER(object_name) LIKE 'DEPENDER%';


OBJECT_NAME             OBJECT_TYPE          STATUS
-------------------     ------------------   -------
DEPENDERWRAPPER         PROCEDURE            VALID
Depender                JAVA CLASS           VALID
```

Even though we have altered **temp_table**, the class and wrapper are still valid.

Library Dependencies

The dependency between a wrapper and a library, however, is recorded in the data dictionary. Consider the following:

```
-- Available online as part of Depender.sql
CREATE LIBRARY DependLibrary AS
  '/home/surman/ch10/code/dependlib.so';

CREATE OR REPLACE PROCEDURE Depender2 AS
  LANGUAGE C
  NAME "Depender2"
  LIBRARY DependLibrary;
```

If we query the data dictionary, we see that the dependency is there:

```
-- Available online as part of Depender.sql
SQL> SELECT name, type, referenced_name, referenced_type
  2     FROM user_dependencies
  3     WHERE name IN ('DEPENDER2', 'DEPENDLIBRARY');
```

NAME	TYPE	REFERENCED_NAME	REFERENCED_T
DEPENDER2	PROCEDURE	SYS_STUB_FOR_PURITY_ANALYSIS	PACKAGE
DEPENDER2	**PROCEDURE**	**DEPENDLIBRARY**	**UNDEFINED**

This is further demonstrated if we drop the library:

```
-- Available online as part of Depender.sql
SQL> SELECT object_name, object_type, status
  2     FROM user_objects
  3     WHERE object_name IN ('DEPENDER2', 'DEPENDLIBRARY');


OBJECT_NAME             OBJECT_TYPE          STATUS
-------------------     ------------------   -------
```

```
DEPENDLIBRARY          LIBRARY          VALID
DEPENDER2              PROCEDURE        VALID

SQL> DROP LIBRARY DependLibrary;
Library dropped.

SQL> SELECT object_name, object_type, status
  2    FROM user_objects
  3    WHERE object_name IN ('DEPENDER2', 'DEPENDLIBRARY');

OBJECT_NAME            OBJECT_TYPE        STATUS
-------------------    -----------------  -------
DEPENDER2              PROCEDURE          INVALID
```

Dropping the library does in fact invalidate the wrapper. This dependency behavior is summarized in Table 10-10.

Debugging External Routines

As we have seen, external routines are a very useful and powerful feature. However, because we are dealing with different languages (PL/SQL, C, and Java) and the interface between them, debugging external routines can be tricky. Here, we will look at some different methods for debugging external routines.

Call from the Native Language Directly

Perhaps the simplest method of debugging is to call the external routine directly from C or Java, without any PL/SQL at all. If it is a C routine, you can call it from either a statically or dynamically linked program and use the standard C debugger

Depender	Dependent	Recorded in Data Dictionary?
PL/SQL stored subprogram	Database object (such as a table or another stored subprogram)	Yes
PL/SQL wrapper	External routine (C or Java)	No
C external routine	Library object	Yes
Java external routine	Java external routine	Yes
Java external routine	Database object	No

TABLE 10-10. *Dependencies Between Objects*

provided on your system (or other means) to debug the program. If it is a Java routine, you can call it from another class and debug using the Java environment on your system. For example, the following main can be used to call the **sendMail** C routine that we examined at the beginning of this chapter:

```c
/* Available online as sendMailMain.c */
#include <stdio.h>

extern int sendMail(char *, char *, char *, char *);

int main()
{
  char *subject = "Test email from a C routine";
  char *message = "This is a test message from C.\nHello!\n";
  char *from = "The_Operating_System";
  char *to = "YOUR_EMAIL_ADDRESS_HERE";

  printf("Sending C message to %s!\n", to);
  sendMail(subject, message, from, to);
}
```

Likewise, we can use the following Java class to call the **sendMail** Java routine:

```java
// Available online as sendMailMain.java
import java.io.*;

public class sendMailMain
{
  public static void main(String args[])
  {
    String subject = "Test email from Java";
    String message = "This is a test message from Java.\nHello!\n";
    String from = "The_Java_VM";
    String to = "YOUR_EMAIL_ADDRESS_HERE";

    System.out.println("Sending Java message to " + to + "!");
    sendMail.send(subject, message, from, to);
  }
}
```

NOTE
*The **ch10.mk** Makefile available online includes targets to compile and run the previous two examples.*

While this method won't uncover problems relating to the PL/SQL-to-C or PL/SQL-to-Java interface, it can uncover coding errors in the external routine itself.

If the external routine makes database callbacks, then you will need to establish the connection directly, instead of using **OciExtProcGetEnv** for a C routine or **OracleDriver.defaultConnection()** for a Java routine.

Attaching to extproc with a Debugger

In order to step through a C program with a debugger, the program is typically started under control of the debugger. With external routines, however, extproc is started automatically by the Net8 listener. This precludes you from starting it under control of a debugger. The solution to this is to start extproc first (by calling a dummy external routine) and then attach to the running process with the debugger.

NOTE
In order to use this method, your operating system must support a debugger that allows you to attach to a running process. For example, on many Unix systems you can use the gdb debugger.

To facilitate this process, Oracle provides a package called **debug_extproc**. The script to create this package can be found in the PL/SQL demo directory under $ORACLE_HOME and also on the CD accompanying this book. The code for **debug_extproc** is as follows:

```
-- Available online as dbgextp.sql
CREATE OR REPLACE PACKAGE debug_extproc IS
  --
  -- Start up the extproc agent process in the session
  --
  --    Executing this procedure starts up the extproc agent process
  --    in the session allowing one to be able get the PID of the
  --    executing process. This PID is needed to be able to attach
  --    to the running process using a debugger.
  PROCEDURE startup_extproc_agent;
END debug_extproc;

CREATE OR REPLACE LIBRARY debug_extproc_library IS STATIC;

CREATE OR REPLACE PACKAGE BODY debug_extproc IS
  extproc_lib_error EXCEPTION;
  PRAGMA EXCEPTION_INIT (extproc_lib_error, -6520);

  extproc_func_error EXCEPTION;
  PRAGMA EXCEPTION_INIT (extproc_func_error, -6521);
```

```
   PROCEDURE local_startup_extproc_agent IS EXTERNAL
     LIBRARY debug_extproc_library;

   PROCEDURE startup_extproc_agent is
   BEGIN
     -- call a dummy procedure and trap all errors.
     local_startup_extproc_agent;
   EXCEPTION
     -- Ignore any errors if the function or library is not found.
     WHEN extproc_func_error then NULL;
     WHEN extproc_lib_error then NULL;
   END startup_extproc_agent;
END debug_extproc;
```

The steps for using this package are as follows:

1. Make sure that your C program is compiled and linked into the shared library with debug symbols. On Unix systems, this is usually done by passing the –g flag to the compiler.

2. In a SQL*Plus or other connection to the database, call **debug_extproc.startup_extproc_agent**. Although there is no actual C procedure associated with this wrapper procedure, extproc is started. No errors are signaled because of the exception handlers in **startup_extproc_agent**.

3. Determine the operating system process ID of extproc. On Unix, this can be done with a 'ps' command.

4. Start the debugger, and attach to the running process determined in step 3.

5. Set a breakpoint in the function pextproc, and allow the debugger to continue.

6. In the original session, call the PL/SQL wrapper. This will in turn call extproc, which will then stop in pextproc.

7. At this point, the external procedure has been resolved by extproc, so you can set a breakpoint for it. As the symbol will have been dynamically loaded, some debuggers may not immediately recognize it, and you may have to tell the debugger to load the symbols again. (This is done with the 'share' command in gdb.)

8. Continue in the debugger, which will then break in your procedure. You can now step through the external procedure code and debug.

Using the JServer Debug Proxy

A similar problem exists for debugging Java external routines. Normally, a Java debugger (such as jdb) is invoked in the same environment as the Java virtual machine. In the case of JServer, however, the virtual machine is inside the database server. The debugger is typically running on a client workstation. To facilitate debugging, JServer provides the **DebugProxy** class. This class implements the standard **sun.tools.debug.Agent** debugging protocol and allows you to step through a class running on the server. Essentially, the steps are as follows:

1. Start the **DebugProxy**. This will connect to the server, and wait for an agent to make a connection to it.

2. Connect to the server in a separate session and start the agent. This will cause the **DebugProxy** to print out a password.

3. Start the debugger using the password provided.

In the following sections, we will examine these steps in more detail. For more information, see the *Oracle8i Java Developer's Guide*.

STARTING THE PROXY   The **DebugProxy** class is found in the aurora_client.jar archive, typically found in $ORACLE_HOME/lib. Assuming that the archive is in your CLASSPATH, you can start the proxy from the command line as follows:

```
java oracle.aurora.server.tools.DebugProxy
```

The proxy will print out the machine name, IP address, and port number that it is listening on, after which it will wait for a connection.. You can also specify a port using

```
java oracle.aurora.server.tools.DebugProxy -port portnum
```

where *portnum* is the requested port.

STARTING THE AGENT   The debug agent will connect to the proxy. It is called using the START_DEBUGGING procedure in DBMS_JAVA, defined with

```
PROCEDURE START_DEBUGGING(host VARCHAR2,
                          port NUMBER,
                          timeout NUMBER);
```

where *host* and *port* specify where the proxy is listening (output from **DebugProxy**), and *timeout* specifies the time out in seconds. START_DEBUGGING will wait until it times out for you to start a debugging session.

   The agent will run until it is stopped, the debugger disconnects, or the session ends. You can stop the debugging agent manually using DBMS_JAVA.STOP_DEBUGGING:

   PROCEDURE STOP_DEBUGGING;

and can restart the agent (keeping any existing breakpoints) with DBMS_JAVA.RESTART_DEBUGGING:

   PROCEDURE RESTART_DEBUGGING(*timeout* NUMBER);

where *timeout* is the same as before.

NOTE
These procedures require that the user executing them be GRANTed the JAVASYSPRIV role.

CONNECTING THE DEBUGGER   The final step is to start the debugger with the specified password, which was printed out by the session running the **DebugProxy** class. For jdb, this is done by using the -password flag on the command line. The command is different for other debuggers.

Guidelines

There are several things to keep in mind when using external routines, especially C routines:

- Calling an external routine does involve some overhead, especially the first time in a session. For a C routine, a request has to be made to the listener, and extproc needs to be spawned. Therefore, use external routines when the efficiency gained by coding in C outweighs the cost of spawning the process. The initial cost of calling a Java stored procedure is less than calling a C external routine, but the same guideline applies.

- There is no guarantee that the shared library containing the external routine will stay open by extproc between calls. (This is especially true on NT.) Thus, you shouldn't rely on static variables keeping their values between calls. In general, you can't save C state between calls to the external routine.

■ extproc will assume the operating system privileges of the listener that spawned it. Consequently, it is a good idea to start a separate listener for external routines from an account with restricted access. If the listener is running as the Oracle user, for example, then any user with permission to create a library can potentially write a C program that could modify the files under $ORACLE_HOME, possibly corrupting the database.

■ Be sure to write a value to any OUT or IN OUT parameters, as well as the function return value. PL/SQL has no means of checking this, and internal errors can result if these parameters are not assigned.

■ Likewise, do not write to IN parameters or overflow the capacity (as specified by the MAXLEN property) of OUT parameters.

■ Use the LENGTH and INDICATOR properties to handle all cases of character parameters. If you are returning a NULL value, then set the LENGTH parameter to zero.

■ If there is a PRAGMA RESTRICT_REFERENCES statement for the wrapper function, the external function cannot violate the pragma. PL/SQL has no way of checking this, and internal errors can result if the external function modifies the database in violation of the pragma. Oracle8*i* can check the purity level of functions at runtime, so the pragma is not necessary there. For more information, see Chapter 5.

■ The DETERMINISTIC and PARALLEL_ENABLE clauses (available with Oracle8*i*) can also be specified for the PL/SQL call specification. In this case, these keywords apply to the external routine itself and not the wrapper. For more information on these keywords, see Chapter 5.

Restrictions

In addition to the restrictions for callbacks to the database, which we discussed earlier in this chapter, C external routines have the following restrictions (as of Oracle8*i* version 8.1.5):

■ If the underlying platform does not support dynamic linking and shared libraries, then external procedures are not available.

■ The Net8 listener and extproc must run on the same machine as the database. Similarly, you cannot use a database link in the LIBRARY clause to specify a library on a remote database.

■ The only language supported directly by extproc is C. If you want to call another language (besides Java in Oracle8*i*), however, you can write a C external routine to serve as an intermediary. PL/SQL would then call your C routine, which could then call a procedure written in still another language, as long as that procedure is accessible from the shared library.

■ Parameters cannot be PL/SQL cursor variables, records, collections, or object type instances. However, you can retrieve these objects by using a callback to the database in the external routine (subject to the OCI limitations described earlier).

■ The maximum number of parameters that can be passed to a C external routine is 128. This includes parameters used to retrieve properties such as INDICATOR or LENGTH. However, if float or double parameters are passed by reference, then the maximum is less than 128. Each parameter passed like this takes up approximately the space of two parameters passed by value.

In addition, the following restriction applies for Oracle8:

■ The Oracle server cannot be running MTS. extproc needs a dedicated server process with which to communicate.

Summary

In this chapter, we have discussed external routines, which allow a PL/SQL program to directly call a C or Java subprogram. We discussed the differences between C and Java external routines, as well as their similarities. These included how to map PL/SQL datatypes to C or Java datatypes, and the use of properties to get information about the parameters. We also reviewed several methods for debugging external procedures. In the next chapter, we will examine more new PL/SQL features of Oracle8*i*.

CHAPTER
11

Additional
Oracle8i Features

n addition to the many database enhancements, Oracle8i includes various enhancements to PL/SQL. These features improve PL/SQL performance, ease application development, and improve the interface between PL/SQL and other languages. Some of them, such as native dynamic SQL and invoker's rights procedures, we have already examined. In this chapter, we will see the remainder of the new features. We will also examine timing results for the performance enhancements.

Feature Summary

Oracle **8 i**
and higher Table 11-1 describes the new PL/SQL features available in Oracle8i. They can be categorized according to performance, application development, integration with the Web and HTML, and integration with Java. The following sections briefly describe each of the new features.

Performance

The performance features in Oracle8i can be divided into user-visible and transparent features. The user-visible features include profiling, tracing, bulk binds, and NOCOPY parameters. The transparent features include the optimization of package STANDARD, anonymous block execution, RPCs (Remote Procedure Calls), and the RETURNING INTO clause.

User-Visible Features

The user-visible features of Oracle8i consist of new language features and built-in packages. Your application will need to be coded explicitly to use these new features in order to realize their benefits.

PROFILING   The PL/SQL profiler can gather information about a running PL/SQL application. This information can then be used to tune the application for better performance by identifying the bottlenecks. The profiler, implemented through the DBMS_PROFILER package, provides details such as these:

■ The total number of times each line in the application has been executed

■ The total amount of time spent executing that line

■ The minimum and maximum times spent on a particular execution

This information can be rolled up to the procedure, package, or application level. For more information, see Chapter 3.

Area	New Oracle8*i* Feature
Performance	Profiling and tracing Bulk binds NOCOPY parameters Transparent features
Application Development	Debugging enhancements Increase of package body size Purity simplification Pro*C external routine callbacks SQL queries on PL/SQL tables ORA-6502 error message Autonomous transactions Native dynamic SQL Invoker's rights routines DETERMINISTIC and PARALLEL_ENABLE keywords Objects and extensibility enhancements Improved interoperability Temporary LOBs CALL statement Constrained subtypes
Integration with the Web and Java or C external routines	PL/SQL cartridge enhancements UTL_HTTP package Java stored procedures C external routine enhancements

TABLE 11-1. *Oracle8*i *Features*

TRACING   The tracing facilities of PL/SQL have been greatly enhanced for Oracle8*i* as well. Oracle8*i* Release 1 (8.1.5) provides a PL/SQL interface (through the DBMS_TRACE package) to the event-based tracing available with earlier versions. Oracle8*i* Release 2 (8.1.6) extends DBMS_TRACE to trace many additional features, and adds the ability to store the results in database tables rather than a trace file. For more information, see Chapter 3.

BULK BINDS   In many applications, SQL statements are executed from within a PL/SQL loop. For each execution of the SQL statement, the server has to perform a context switch between PL/SQL and SQL. With bulk binds, an entire PL/SQL table of data can be passed to SQL in one statement, eliminating the redundant context switches. For more information, see "Bulk Binds," later in this chapter.

NOCOPY PARAMETERS   The default behavior for parameters with the IN OUT and OUT modes is implemented through data copying. For IN OUT parameters, the data is copied on both the procedure invocation and return. Data is copied only on the return for OUT parameters. This is necessary to preserve the semantics of these modes (mainly to check constraints and retain the original value in case of a raised exception), but it can have a performance impact. The NOCOPY modifier allows the PL/SQL engine to pass a parameter by reference instead of by value when possible, which improves performance. Using NOCOPY does change the exception-handling semantics of IN OUT and OUT parameters, however. For more information on using NOCOPY, see Chapter 5. For some performance comparisons, see "NOCOPY Modifier," later in this chapter.

Transparent Features

In addition to the user-visible features that we discussed in the previous sections, Oracle8*i* includes several enhancements that are transparent to the end user. Many existing applications will simply run with improved performance thanks to these enhancements, and will not need to be recoded. Each of the following PL/SQL application elements have been optimized: package STANDARD, anonymous blocks, RPCs, and the RETURNING clause.

OPTIMIZATION OF PACKAGE STANDARD   The built-in subprograms found in package STANDARD are used heavily in many applications. The built-ins include functions such as TO_CHAR and TO_DATE. The calls in package STANDARD are used in procedural statements, while the SQL engine processes the equivalent calls in SQL statements.

ANONYMOUS BLOCK EXECUTION   OCI and precompiler applications use anonymous blocks with embedded host variables to call PL/SQL. Oracle8*i* has enhancements for these types of applications, including

- ◾ Faster access to elements in array bind variables

- ◾ Optimization of host binds that are used only in SQL statements, but not in the anonymous PL/SQL block itself

- ◾ Elimination of rebinds for bind variables in SQL statements for multiple executions of the anonymous block

RPC EXECUTION   The parameter processing mechanism for remote procedure calls has been improved by removing redundant temporary variables. This is valid for calls between two database servers, as well as between the client and server. The parameters that will benefit the most include large records, object types, and collections.

RETURNING CLAUSE   The RETURNING clause, introduced in Oracle8, allows a DML statement to return certain types of information, such as the rowid of a newly inserted row, in one trip to the server. The runtime support for this clause in PL/SQL has been optimized for Oracle8*i* as well. RETURNING can also be used with bulk queries, described in "BULK COLLECT Clause," later in this chapter. (Use of RETURNING with bulk queries requires application recoding.)

Application Development

The application development features can be divided into debugging and ease-of-use enhancements, plus other new features.

Debugging Enhancements

Oracle8*i* provides APIs for debugging and tracing your application, along with an API for code coverage. They are

- **DBMS_DEBUG**   This package is a low-level interface designed primarily for implementers of PL/SQL development environments. It provides debugging features that can be used in a full-featured debugger.

- **DBMS_TRACE**   This package allows you to trace a PL/SQL application by function, or by exception, which can help in environments in which a debugger is not available.

- **Code Coverage**   This API can be used to develop a code coverage tool. Like DBMS_DEBUG, it is designed primarily for implementers of a PL/SQL development environment. Unlike DBMS_DEBUG and DBMS_TRACE, the API for code coverage is not public.

For more information on these packages and tools that use them, see Chapters 2 and 3.

Ease-of-Use Enhancements

The ease-of-use enhancements can help you design more streamlined applications. They include an increase of the allowable package body size, purity simplification, callbacks from external routines in Pro*C rather than OCI, and the ability to query PL/SQL collections directly from SQL. The ORA-6502 error has also been enhanced to provide more useful error messages, and interoperability between different PL/SQL versions has been improved.

INCREASE OF PACKAGE BODY SIZE   In prior versions of Oracle, PL/SQL blocks were limited in size by internal compiler limits. These were reached in practice most often by package and type bodies, since they tend to be the largest types of PL/SQL blocks. Compiling blocks that were too large would raise "PLS-123: program too large" or other errors. For Oracle8*i*, these limits have been relaxed for package and type bodies to allow larger blocks. Note that the original limits still apply to other types of program units, including standalone subprograms (defined at the schema level with CREATE OR REPLACE) and object and type headers. For more information on the original limits, see Chapter 5.

PURITY SIMPLIFICATION   Originally available in PL/SQL 2.1, the RESTRICT_REFERENCES pragma allowed you to call stored functions directly from SQL statements. The pragma was necessary so that the runtime engine could ensure that the called function did not have any destructive side effects. Oracle8*i* moves the verification from the compiler to the runtime system, which means that the pragma is no longer necessary. This also allows more functions to be called directly from SQL, including external routines written in Java or C. For more information on calling stored functions from SQL, see Chapter 5.

PRO*C EXTERNAL ROUTINE CALLBACKS   External routines (known as external procedures in Oracle8) allow a subprogram written in C to be called directly from PL/SQL. This external routine can in turn make callbacks to the database to execute SQL statements as part of the current transaction. In Oracle8, database callbacks must be written using OCI only, which can be complicated. Oracle8*i* allows external routines to be written using Pro*C and embedded SQL (or a combination of OCI and Pro*C) instead. For more information, see Chapter 10.

SQL QUERIES ON PL/SQL COLLECTIONS   PL/SQL collections (nested tables and varrays) provide a mechanism for grouping related objects together. Oracle8 introduced nested tables and varrays, and allowed them to be both manipulated by PL/SQL and stored in database tables. Collections stored in database tables could be queried using the THE operator. Oracle8*i* improves the syntax of this operation using the TABLE operator instead. See Chapter 14 for more details.

ORA-6502   The most commonly raised error in PL/SQL is the "ORA-6502: numeric or value error" message. This can be raised in many different types of situations, for example, assigning a character string that is too long to a VARCHAR2 or CHAR variable. Because there are so many different possible causes of this error, it can be hard to determine the cause. Oracle8*i* adds additional information to the error message returned with ORA-6502 that identifies the specific error condition. For more information, see "The 'Numeric or Value Error' Message," later in this chapter.

New Application Development Features

In addition to the debugging and ease-of-use enhancements, Oracle8*i* includes the following features for application development: autonomous transactions, native dynamic SQL, invoker's rights routines, the DETERMINISTIC and PARALLEL_ENABLE keywords, and enhancements to objects. Interoperability between different versions of PL/SQL is also enhanced. The following sections briefly describe each of these.

AUTONOMOUS TRANSACTIONS   It is often desirable to issue some SQL statements that will commit or roll back regardless of the state of the current transaction. This could be used to ensure that logging data is always committed, for example. Autonomous transactions give you this capability. An autonomous transaction is started after a parent transaction has begun, and can be committed or rolled back independent of the parent transaction. For more details, see "Autonomous Transactions," later in this chapter.

NATIVE DYNAMIC SQL   Dynamic SQL has been available since PL/SQL Release 2.1 through the DBMS_SQL package. This package allows you to dynamically create and execute SQL and PL/SQL statements at runtime, rather than compile time. Oracle8*i* builds this functionality directly into the language, rather than using a package. Besides the simplified application development, native dynamic SQL is significantly faster than DBMS_SQL because it does not have to go through as much overhead. For more information on native dynamic SQL, see Chapter 8. For a performance comparison between DBMS_SQL and native dynamic SQL, see "Native Dynamic SQL," later in this chapter.

INVOKER'S RIGHTS ROUTINES   An invoker's rights routine will execute under the privilege set of its caller, rather than its definer. This allows you greater flexibility in designing different modules of your application, and how they interact. Java stored procedures also execute with invoker's rights by default. For more information about invoker's rights routines, see Chapter 5.

DETERMINISTIC AND PARALLEL_ENABLE   These two keywords can be used in the declaration of a stored subprogram. The DETERMINISTIC keyword signals to the PL/SQL compiler that the function is deterministic—it always returns the same result given the same input. Deterministic functions can be used in function-based indexes. The PARALLEL_ENABLE keyword signals to the optimizer that the function can be executed in parallel, something that was previously indicated only tangentially by the RNPS and WNPS keywords in the RESTRICT_REFERENCES pragma. For more information on both of these keywords, see Chapter 5.

OBJECTS AND EXTENSIBILITY ENHANCEMENTS   There are several enhancements to the objects functionality of PL/SQL in Oracle8*i*. User-defined operators can be used directly in SQL statements, and by index types. Static methods can be invoked efficiently because they do not have a SELF parameter, and logically are components of the object type rather than of instances of that type. Finally, objects and collections can be passed as parameters to external routines in Oracle8*i*. For more information on objects, see Chapters 12 and 13.

INTEROPERABILITY BETWEEN PL/SQL VERSIONS   PL/SQL subprograms that are stored in an Oracle7 database or an Oracle Developer product containing version 2.3 could call all packaged procedures stored in a remote Oracle8 database. However, they could only call schema-level subprograms that did not use any Oracle8 features. This restriction has been removed in Oracle8*i*—a subprogram in Oracle7, Oracle8, or Oracle Developer can call either a schema-level or a packaged subprogram contained in Oracle8*i*, and the called subprogram can use any new Oracle8*i* feature.

TEMPORARY LOBS   Prior to Oracle8*i*, all LOB data must be stored in database tables before it can be modified. Oracle8*i* adds temporary LOBs to the LOB datatypes. A temporary LOB is stored in memory, and does not persist unless it is explicitly written to the database. Thus, temporary LOBs are useful when LOB data needs to be modified before it can be stored. For more information on LOBs in general, including temporary LOBs, see Chapters 15 and 16 on the CD-ROM included with this book.

THE CALL STATEMENT   Oracle8*i* adds a unified syntax for calling a stored subprogram, either PL/SQL or Java, known as the CALL statement. CALL is a new top-level SQL command that conforms to the SQL standard. For more information, see "The CALL Statement," later in this chapter.

Web and External Routine Integration

Through the PL/SQL cartridge in the Oracle Application Server, PL/SQL procedures can be used to dynamically generate Web content. These capabilities have been enhanced for Oracle8*i*. Oracle JServer, contained as part of Oracle8*i*, allows you to create Java procedures and store them directly in the database. These Java procedures can be called from PL/SQL. C external routines have been enhanced as well.

Web Integration

The UTL_HTTP package and the Oracle Web Toolkit, in conjunction with the PL/SQL Cartridge, are powerful Web development tools. They have been enhanced for Oracle8*i* Release 8.1.5, and will be enhanced further in future versions of Oracle8*i*. For more information on the PL/SQL cartridge, see Chapter 2 and the Oracle documentation.

UTL_HTTP   The UTL_HTTP package can be used to send and receive requests over the network using the HTTP protocol, and to receive the results. It can be used in a stored procedure outside the Application Server, and can access the Internet and/or call PL/SQL cartridges in the Application Server.

THE ORACLE WEB TOOLKIT   The Web Toolkit, which consists of the HTP and HTF packages, in conjunction with the PL/SQL cartridge, allows a procedure running in the server to dynamically generate HTML based on database content.

ORACLE8*i* RELEASE 2 ENHANCEMENTS   Oracle8*i* Release 2 includes more Web-enabled improvements, such as PL/SQL server pages and additional packages to implement various Web protocols (such as TCP and SMTP). For more information, see the Oracle documentation.

Java and C Integration

Oracle8*i* includes a complete Java virtual machine as part of the database server. This allows you to load Java procedures into the database and run them. They execute as part of the database process, just like a PL/SQL procedure. A C external routine, on the other hand, executes in a separate process. Specific PL/SQL enhancements, such as call specifications, DLL caching, and improved parameter mapping, enhance the interface between PL/SQL and external languages. For more information on external routines, see Chapter 10.

CALL SPECIFICATIONS   Call specifications allow you to call a Java stored procedure or C external routine from PL/SQL in a standard way. The AS LANGUAGE clause replaces the AS EXTERNAL clause to accomplish this.

DLL CACHING   For C external routines, the extproc process will now cache up to ten separate DLLs that contain external C code. This means that the external DLLs will not have to be reloaded if the external routines contained within them are re-executed. This feature does not guarantee that static variables in C code will retain their values between calls to external C routines, however.

PARAMETER MAPPING   Oracle8*i* provides support for additional datatype mappings. These allow you to pass any PL/SQL type to a C or Java external routine, including LOBs and collections. They can be manipulated in C using their native types as well.

New Features

In this section, we will discuss in detail the main new features that we haven't yet seen—bulk binds and autonomous transactions. We will also see how the ORA-6502 error has been improved and the syntax of the CALL statement.

Bulk Binds

As we discussed in Chapter 2, SQL statements in PL/SQL blocks are sent to the SQL engine to be executed. The SQL engine can, in turn, send data back to the PL/SQL engine. For example, consider the following block:

```
-- Available online as part of bulkDemo.sql
DECLARE
  TYPE t_Numbers IS TABLE OF temp_table.num_col%TYPE
    INDEX BY BINARY_INTEGER;
  TYPE t_Chars IS TABLE OF temp_table.char_col%TYPE
    INDEX BY BINARY_INTEGER;
  v_Numbers t_Numbers;
  v_Chars t_Chars;
BEGIN
  -- Fill up the arrays with 500 rows.
  FOR v_Count IN 1..500 LOOP
    v_Numbers(v_Count) := v_Count;
    v_Chars(v_Count) := 'Row number ' || v_Count;
  END LOOP;

  -- And insert them into the database.
  FOR v_Count IN 1..500 LOOP
    INSERT INTO temp_table VALUES
      (v_Numbers(v_Count), v_Chars(v_Count));
  END LOOP;
END;
```

When we run this block, 500 rows are inserted into **temp_table**. However, each INSERT is done individually. This results in 500 context switches between PL/SQL and SQL.

Oracle8*i* eliminates all but one of these context switches by passing the entire PL/SQL table to the SQL engine in one step, which is known as a *bulk bind*. Bulk binds are done using the FORALL statement, as in the following block:

```
-- Available online as part of bulkDemo.sql
DECLARE
  TYPE t_Numbers IS TABLE OF temp_table.num_col%TYPE
    INDEX BY BINARY_INTEGER;
  TYPE t_Chars IS TABLE OF temp_table.char_col%TYPE
    INDEX BY BINARY_INTEGER;
  v_Numbers t_Numbers;
  v_Chars t_Chars;
BEGIN
  -- Fill up the arrays with 500 rows.
  FOR v_Count IN 1..500 LOOP
    v_Numbers(v_Count) := v_Count;
    v_Chars(v_Count) := 'Row number ' || v_Count;
  END LOOP;

  -- And insert them into the database using bulk binds.
  FORALL v_Count IN 1..500
    INSERT INTO temp_table VALUES
      (v_Numbers(v_Count), v_Chars(v_Count));
END;
```

NOTE
We will see a quantitative example of the performance improvement between these two blocks in "Performance Comparisons," later in this chapter.

FORALL Clause
The syntax for the FORALL clause is

> FORALL *index_variable* IN *low_bound .. high_bound*
>   *sql_statement*;

where *index_variable*, like the variable used in a numeric FOR loop, is implicitly declared of type BINARY_INTEGER. It is valid only inside the FORALL statement. *low_bound* and *high_bound* specify the range of elements that will be used during the execution of *sql_statement*. The following example illustrates some uses of FORALL.

```
-- Available online as part of FORALL.sql
SQL> DECLARE
  2     TYPE t_Numbers IS TABLE OF temp_table.num_col%TYPE;
  3     TYPE t_Strings IS TABLE OF temp_table.char_col%TYPE;
  4     v_Numbers t_Numbers := t_Numbers(1);
  5     v_Strings t_Strings := t_Strings(1);
  6
  6     -- Prints the total number of rows in temp_table.
  7     PROCEDURE PrintTotalRows(p_Message IN VARCHAR2) IS
  8       v_Count NUMBER;
  9     BEGIN
 10       SELECT COUNT(*)
 11         INTO v_Count
 12         FROM temp_table;
 13       DBMS_OUTPUT.PUT_LINE(p_Message || ': Count is ' || v_Count);
 14     END PrintTotalRows;
 15
 15  BEGIN
 16     -- First delete from temp_table.
 17     DELETE FROM temp_table;
 18
 18     -- Fill up the PL/SQL nested tables with 1000 values.
 19     v_Numbers.EXTEND(1000);
 20     v_Strings.EXTEND(1000);
 21     FOR v_Count IN 1..1000 LOOP
 22       v_Numbers(v_Count) := v_Count;
 23       v_Strings(v_Count) := 'Element #' || v_Count;
 24     END LOOP;
 25
 25     -- Insert all 1000 elements using a single FORALL statement.
 26     FORALL v_Count IN 1..1000
 27       INSERT INTO temp_table VALUES
 28         (v_Numbers(v_Count), v_Strings(v_Count));
 29
 29     -- There should be 1000 rows now.
 30     PrintTotalRows('After first insert');
 31
 31     -- Insert elements 501 through 1000 again.
 32     FORALL v_Count IN 501..1000
 33       INSERT INTO temp_table VALUES
       34          (v_Numbers(v_Count), v_Strings(v_Count));
 35
 35     -- We should now have 1500 rows
 36     PrintTotalRows('After second insert');
 37
 37     -- Update all of the rows.
 38     FORALL v_Count IN 1..1000
 39       UPDATE temp_table
 40         SET char_col = 'Changed!'
```

```
41        WHERE num_col = v_Numbers(v_Count);
42
42    -- Even though there are only 1000 elements, the previous
43    -- statement updated 1500 rows, since the WHERE clause matched
44    -- 2 rows for each of the last 500.
45    DBMS_OUTPUT.PUT_LINE(
46      'Update processed ' || SQL%ROWCOUNT || ' rows.');
47
47    -- Likewise, this DELETE will remove 300 rows
48    FORALL v_Count IN 401..600
49      DELETE FROM temp_table
50        WHERE num_col = v_Numbers(v_Count);
51
51    -- So there should be 1200 left.
52    PrintTotalRows('After delete');
53 END;
54 /
After first insert: Count is 1000
After second insert: Count is 1500
Update processed 1500 rows.
After delete: Count is 1200
PL/SQL procedure successfully completed.
```

There are several things to note about the use of the FORALL clause:

■ It can be used with any collection type—index-by tables, nested tables, or varrays. See Chapter 14 for information on these types.

■ Collection subscripts within the SQL statement cannot be expressions—only the index variable itself can be used directly.

■ The range specified by *low_bound* and *high_bound* must be contiguous, and all the elements in that range must exist. For example, the following block raises an ORA-22160 error:

```
-- Available online as part of FORALL.sql
SQL> DECLARE
  2    TYPE t_Numbers IS TABLE OF NUMBER;
  3    v_Numbers t_Numbers := t_Numbers(1, 2, 3, 4, 5);
  4  BEGIN
  5    -- Delete element 4
  6    v_Numbers.DELETE(4);
  7
  7    -- And try to insert elements 3 through 5.
  8    FORALL v_Count IN 3..5
  9      INSERT INTO temp_table (num_col) VALUES (v_Numbers(v_Count));
 10  END;
 11  /
DECLARE
```

```
*
ERROR at line 1:
ORA-22160: element at index [4] does not exist
ORA-06512: at line 8
```

Transactional Issues

If there is an error processing one of the rows in a bulk DML operation, then only that row is rolled back. The prior rows are still processed. This is the same behavior as bulk operations with OCI or the precompilers, and is illustrated by the following example.

```
-- Available online as part of FORALL.sql
SQL> DECLARE
  2    TYPE t_Strings IS TABLE OF temp_table.char_col%TYPE
  3      INDEX BY BINARY_INTEGER;
  4    TYPE t_Numbers IS TABLE OF temp_table.num_col%TYPE
  5      INDEX BY BINARY_INTEGER;
  6    v_Strings t_Strings;
  7    v_Numbers t_Numbers;
  8  BEGIN
  9    -- Delete from the table, and set up the index-by table.
 10    DELETE FROM temp_table;
 11    FOR v_Count IN 1..10 LOOP
 12      v_Strings(v_Count) := '12345678901234567890123 4567890';
 13      v_Numbers(v_Count) := v_Count;
 14    END LOOP;
 15
 15    FORALL v_Count IN 1..10
 16      INSERT INTO temp_table (num_col, char_col)
 17        VALUES (v_Numbers(v_Count), v_Strings(v_Count));
 18
 18    -- Add an extra character to v_Strings(6).
 19    v_Strings(6) := v_Strings(6) || 'a';
 20
 20    -- This bulk update will fail on the sixth row, but the
 21    -- first 5 rows will still be updated.
 22    FORALL v_Count IN 1..10
 23      UPDATE temp_table
 24        SET char_col = char_col || v_Strings(v_Count)
 25        WHERE num_col = v_Numbers(v_Count);
 26  EXCEPTION
 27    WHEN OTHERS THEN
 28      DBMS_OUTPUT.PUT_LINE('Got exception: ' || SQLERRM);
 29      COMMIT;
 30  END;
 31  /
Got exception: ORA-01401: inserted value too large for column
PL/SQL procedure successfully completed.
```

```
SQL> -- This query should show that the first 5 rows have been
SQL> -- modified.
SQL> SELECT char_col
  2    FROM temp_table
  3    ORDER BY num_col;


CHAR_COL
------------------------------------------------------------
12345678901234567890123456789012345678901234567890
12345678901234567890123456789012345678901234567890
12345678901234567890123456789012345678901234567890
12345678901234567890123456789012345678901234567890
12345678901234567890123456789012345678901234567890
12345678901234567890
12345678901234567890
12345678901234567890
12345678901234567890
12345678901234567890
10 rows selected.
```

BULK COLLECT Clause

The FORALL statement is used for DML operations, as we saw in the previous section. The equivalent statement for a bulk fetch is the BULK COLLECT clause. BULK COLLECT is used as part of the SELECT INTO, FETCH INTO, or RETURNING INTO clauses, and has the following syntax:

    BULK COLLECT INTO *collectionA* [, *collectionB*] [, ...]

This statement will retrieve all of the rows from the query into the indicated collections, as illustrated by the following example.

```
-- Available online as part of BULK_COLLECT.sql
SQL> DECLARE
  2    TYPE t_Numbers IS TABLE OF temp_table.num_col%TYPE;
  3    TYPE t_Strings IS TABLE OF temp_table.char_col%TYPE;
  4    v_Numbers t_Numbers := t_Numbers(1);
  5    v_Strings t_Strings := t_Strings(1);
  6    v_Numbers2 t_Numbers;
  7    v_Strings2 t_Strings;
  8
  8    CURSOR c_char IS
  9      SELECT char_col
 10        FROM temp_table
 11        WHERE num_col > 800
 12        ORDER BY num_col;
```

```
13
13   BEGIN
14     -- First load temp_table with 1500 rows, 500 of which are
15     -- duplicates.
16     v_Numbers.EXTEND(1500);
17     v_Strings.EXTEND(1500);
18     FOR v_Count IN 1..1000 LOOP
19       v_Numbers(v_Count) := v_Count;
20       v_Strings(v_Count) := 'Element #' || v_Count;
21       IF v_Count > 500 THEN
22         v_Numbers(v_Count + 500) := v_Count;
23         v_Strings(v_Count + 500) := 'Element #' || v_Count;
24       END IF;
25     END LOOP;
26
26     DELETE FROM temp_table;
27     FORALL v_Count IN 1..1500
28       INSERT INTO temp_table (num_col, char_col)
29         VALUES (v_Numbers(v_Count), v_Strings(v_Count));
30
30     -- Grab all of the rows back into the nested tables in one
31     -- operation.
32     SELECT num_col, char_col
33       BULK COLLECT INTO v_Numbers, v_Strings
34       FROM temp_table
35       ORDER BY num_col;
36
36     DBMS_OUTPUT.PUT_LINE(
37       'First query fetched ' || v_Numbers.COUNT || ' rows');
38
38     -- The table does not have to be initialized, the BULK COLLECT
39     -- will add elements as needed:
40     SELECT num_col
41       BULK COLLECT INTO v_Numbers2
42       FROM temp_table;
43
43     DBMS_OUTPUT.PUT_LINE(
44       'Second query fetched ' || v_Numbers2.COUNT || ' rows');
45
45     -- We can bulk fetch from a cursor as well.
46     OPEN c_char;
47     FETCH c_char BULK COLLECT INTO v_Strings2;
48     CLOSE c_char;
49
49     DBMS_OUTPUT.PUT_LINE(
50       'Cursor fetch retrieved ' || v_Strings2.COUNT || ' rows');
51
51   END;
52   /
```

```
First query fetched 1500 rows
Second query fetched 1500 rows
Cursor fetch retrieved 400 rows
PL/SQL procedure successfully completed.
```

We can observe the following items about the use of BULK COLLECT:

■   BULK COLLECT can be used for both implicit cursors (SELECT INTO) and explicit cursors (FETCH INTO).

■   The BULK COLLECT operation will fetch the data starting at index 1, and successively overwrite elements in the output collection until it retrieves all the rows.

■   You can BULK COLLECT into a varray, but ORA-22160 will be raised if there is not enough room, as illustrated by the following example:

```
-- Available online as part of BULK_COLLECT.sql
SQL> DECLARE
  2    TYPE t_Numbers IS VARRAY(10) OF temp_table.num_col%TYPE;
  3    v_Numbers t_Numbers;
  4  BEGIN
  5    SELECT num_col
  6      BULK COLLECT INTO v_Numbers
  7      FROM temp_table;
  8  END;
  9  /
DECLARE
*
ERROR at line 1:
ORA-22160: element at index [10] does not exist
ORA-06512: at line 5
```

BULK COLLECT AND RETURNING INTO   BULK COLLECT can be used as part of the RETURNING INTO clause as well, to return information from a DML statement, as the following example illustrates:

```
-- Available online as part of BULK_COLLECT.sql
SQL> DECLARE
  2    TYPE t_Numbers IS TABLE OF temp_table.num_col%TYPE
  3      INDEX BY BINARY_INTEGER;
  4    TYPE t_Strings IS TABLE OF temp_table.char_col%TYPE
  5      INDEX BY BINARY_INTEGER;
  6    v_Numbers t_Numbers;
  7    v_Strings t_Strings;
  8  BEGIN
```

```
 9     -- Delete from the table, and then insert 55 rows.  Also set
10     -- up t_Numbers here.
11     DELETE FROM temp_table;
12     FOR v_Outer IN 1..10 LOOP
13       FOR v_Inner IN 1..v_Outer LOOP
14         INSERT INTO temp_table (num_col, char_col)
15           VALUES (v_Outer, 'Element #' || v_Inner);
16       END LOOP;
17       v_Numbers(v_Outer) := v_Outer;
18     END LOOP;
19
19     -- Delete some of the rows, but save the character data.
20     FORALL v_Count IN 1..5
21       DELETE FROM temp_table
22         WHERE num_col = v_Numbers(v_Count)
23         RETURNING char_col BULK COLLECT INTO v_Strings;
24
24     -- v_Strings now contains 15 rows, which is 1+2+3+4+5.
25     DBMS_OUTPUT.PUT_LINE('After delete:');
26     FOR v_Count IN 1..v_Strings.COUNT LOOP
27       DBMS_OUTPUT.PUT_LINE(
28         '  v_Strings(' || v_Count || ') = ' || v_Strings(v_Count));
29     END LOOP;
30   END;
31   /
After delete:
v_Strings(1) = Element #1
v_Strings(2) = Element #1
v_Strings(3) = Element #2
v_Strings(4) = Element #1
v_Strings(5) = Element #2
v_Strings(6) = Element #3
v_Strings(7) = Element #1
v_Strings(8) = Element #2
v_Strings(9) = Element #3
v_Strings(10) = Element #4
v_Strings(11) = Element #1
v_Strings(12) = Element #2
v_Strings(13) = Element #3
v_Strings(14) = Element #4
v_Strings(15) = Element #5
PL/SQL procedure successfully completed.
```

The %BULK_ROWCOUNT Attribute

When doing bulk operations, it is often useful to know how many rows were affected by each row of the input collections. The SQL%ROWCOUNT cursor attribute will contain the total number of affected rows. Oracle8*i* defines a new attribute—SQL%BULK_ROWCOUNT, which contains the affected rows for each input row. SQL%BULK_ROWCOUNT has the semantics of an index-by table, and SQL%BULK_ROWCOUNT(*i*) contains the number of rows affected by the *i*th input row, as illustrated by the following example:

```
-- Available online as part of FORALL.sql
SQL> DECLARE
  2    TYPE t_Numbers IS TABLE OF temp_table.num_col%TYPE
  3      INDEX BY BINARY_INTEGER;
  4    v_Numbers t_Numbers;
  5  BEGIN
  6    -- Delete from the table, and then insert 120 rows.  Also set
  7    -- up t_Numbers here.
  8    DELETE FROM temp_table;
  9    FOR v_Outer IN 1..15 LOOP
 10      FOR v_Inner IN 1..v_Outer LOOP
 11        INSERT INTO temp_table (num_col, char_col)
 12          VALUES (v_Outer, 'Element #' || v_Inner);
 13      END LOOP;
 14      v_Numbers(v_Outer) := v_Outer;
 15    END LOOP;
 16
 16    -- Delete some of the rows.
 17    FORALL v_Count IN 10..15
 18      DELETE FROM temp_table
 19        WHERE num_col = v_Numbers(v_Count);
 20
 20    DBMS_OUTPUT.PUT_LINE(
 21      'Total number of rows deleted: ' || SQL%ROWCOUNT);
 22    FOR v_Count IN 10..15 LOOP
 23      DBMS_OUTPUT.PUT_LINE(
 24        ' Rows deleted by v_Numbers(' || v_Count || '): ' ||
 25        SQL%BULK_ROWCOUNT(v_Count));
 26    END LOOP;
 27  END;
 28  /
Total number of rows deleted: 75
Rows deleted by v_Numbers(10): 10
Rows deleted by v_Numbers(11): 11
Rows deleted by v_Numbers(12): 12
Rows deleted by v_Numbers(13): 13
Rows deleted by v_Numbers(14): 14
Rows deleted by v_Numbers(15): 15
PL/SQL procedure successfully completed.
```

The indexes of SQL%BULK_ROWCOUNT will be the same as the indexes used in the FORALL statement. Similar to the other cursor attributes, SQL%BULK_

ROWCOUNT cannot be assigned as a whole to other collections, and cannot be passed as a parameter to subprograms.

Autonomous Transactions

Oracle is a transactional database. This means that every SQL operation takes place in the context of a transaction, which is either committed or rolled back as a whole. Prior to Oracle8*i*, there was no way in which some SQL operations within a transaction could be committed independent of the rest of the operations. Oracle8*i* allows this, however, through autonomous transactions. An *autonomous transaction* is a transaction that is started within the context of another transaction, known as the *parent transaction*, but is independent of it. The autonomous transaction can be committed or rolled back regardless of the state of the parent transaction.

PRAGMA AUTONOMOUS_TRANSACTION

The only way to execute an autonomous transaction is from within a PL/SQL block. The block is marked as autonomous by using a pragma in the declarative section, as the following example illustrates:

```
-- Available online as part of autoTrans.sql
CREATE OR REPLACE PROCEDURE Autonomous AS
  PRAGMA AUTONOMOUS_TRANSACTION;
BEGIN
  INSERT INTO temp_table VALUES (-10, 'Hello from Autonomous!');
  COMMIT;
END Autonomous;
```

The pragma indicates to the PL/SQL compiler that this block is to be treated as autonomous. If we call **Autonomous** from the following PL/SQL block,

```
-- Available online as part of autoTrans.sql
BEGIN
  -- Insert into temp_table from the parent transaction.
  INSERT INTO temp_table VALUES (-10, 'Hello from the parent!');

  -- Call Autonomous, which will be independent of this
  -- transaction.
  Autonomous;

  -- Even though we roll back the parent transaction, the insert
  -- done from Autonomous is still committed.
  ROLLBACK;
END;
```

only one row will be in **temp_table**. The INSERT from the parent block has been rolled back along with the rollback of the parent transaction, but the INSERT from the procedure is still committed:

```
-- Available online as part of autoTrans.sql
SQL> SELECT * FROM temp_table WHERE num_col = -10;
  NUM_COL CHAR_COL
--------- ----------------------------------------
      -10 Hello from Autonomous!
```

LOCATION OF THE PRAGMA   PRAGMA AUTONOMOUS_TRANSACTION must appear in the declarative section of the block, and only one pragma is allowed in the block. It can go anywhere in the declarative section, but it is good style to put it at the beginning.

TYPES OF AUTONOMOUS BLOCKS   Not all blocks can be marked as autonomous. Only the following are legal:

- Top-level anonymous blocks

- Local, standalone, and packaged subprograms

- Methods of an object type

- Database triggers

In particular, nested PL/SQL blocks cannot be autonomous. Also, only individual subprograms within a package can be marked as autonomous—the package itself cannot be. The following SQL*Plus session illustrates some valid and invalid locations for the pragma. Note that if the pragma is located in an invalid place, the PLS-710 compile error is raised.

```
-- Available online as autoPragma.sql
SQL> -- The pragma is legal in top-level anonymous blocks:
SQL> DECLARE
  2    PRAGMA AUTONOMOUS_TRANSACTION;
  3  BEGIN
  4    COMMIT;
  5  END;
  6  /
PL/SQL procedure successfully completed.

SQL> -- But it is not legal in nested blocks:
SQL> BEGIN
```

```
  2   DECLARE
  3     PRAGMA AUTONOMOUS_TRANSACTION;
  4   BEGIN
  5     COMMIT;
  6   END;
  7  END;
  8  /
   PRAGMA AUTONOMOUS_TRANSACTION;
         *
ERROR at line 3:
ORA-06550: line 3, column 12:
PLS-00710: PRAGMA AUTONOMOUS_TRANSACTION cannot be declared here

SQL> -- It is valid in both standalone and local subprograms.
SQL> CREATE OR REPLACE PROCEDURE Auto1 AS
  2    PRAGMA AUTONOMOUS_TRANSACTION;
  3
  4    PROCEDURE Local IS
  5      PRAGMA AUTONOMOUS_TRANSACTION;
  6    BEGIN
  7      ROLLBACK;
  8    END Local;
  9  BEGIN
 10    Local;
 11    COMMIT;
 12  END Auto1;
 13  /
Procedure created.
SQL> show errors
No errors.

SQL> -- It is valid in a packaged procedure.
SQL> CREATE OR REPLACE PACKAGE Auto2 AS
  2    PROCEDURE P;
  3  END Auto2;
  4  /
Package created.
SQL> show errors
No errors.

SQL> CREATE OR REPLACE PACKAGE BODY Auto2 AS
  2    PROCEDURE P IS
  3      PRAGMA AUTONOMOUS_TRANSACTION;
  4    BEGIN
  5      COMMIT;
  6    END P;
  7  END Auto2;
  8  /
```

```
Package body created.
SQL> show errors
No errors.

SQL> -- But not valid at the package level.
SQL> CREATE OR REPLACE PACKAGE Auto3 AS
  2    PRAGMA AUTONOMOUS_TRANSACTION;
  3    PROCEDURE P;
  4    PROCEDURE Q;
  5  END Auto3;
  6  /
Warning: Package created with compilation errors.
SQL> show errors
Errors for PACKAGE AUTO3:

LINE/COL ERROR
-------- --------------------------------------------------------------
2/10     PLS-00710: PRAGMA AUTONOMOUS_TRANSACTION cannot be declared
         here
```

Properties of Autonomous Transactions

An autonomous transaction begins with the first SQL statement in an autonomous block, and ends with a COMMIT or ROLLBACK statement. Any transaction control statement can be used in an autonomous transaction, including COMMIT, ROLLBACK, SAVEPOINT, ROLLBACK TO SAVEPOINT, and SET TRANSACTION.

Savepoints are local to the current transaction. Thus, you can't roll back to a savepoint in the parent transaction, as illustrated by the following:

```
-- Available online as autoSavepoints.sql
SQL> CREATE OR REPLACE PROCEDURE AutoProc AS
  2    PRAGMA AUTONOMOUS_TRANSACTION;
  3  BEGIN
  4    ROLLBACK TO SAVEPOINT A;
  5  END AutoProc;
  6  /
Procedure created.

SQL> BEGIN
  2    SAVEPOINT A;
  3    INSERT INTO temp_table (char_col)
  4      VALUES ('Savepoint A!');
  5    -- Even though A is a valid savepoint in the parent
  6    -- transaction, it is not in the autonomous transaction.
  7    -- So this will raise an error.
  8    AutoProc;
  9  END;
 10  /
```

```
BEGIN
*
ERROR at line 1:
ORA-01086: savepoint 'A' never established
ORA-06512: at "EXAMPLE.AUTOPROC", line 4
ORA-06512: at line 8
```

Ending Autonomous Transactions

An autonomous transaction ends with a COMMIT or ROLLBACK statement. It does not end when the block containing it ends. If an autonomous block ends without ending the transaction, an ORA-6519 error is raised and the autonomous transaction is rolled back:

```
-- Available online as part of autoTrans.sql
SQL> DECLARE
  2     PRAGMA AUTONOMOUS_TRANSACTION;
  3  BEGIN
  4     INSERT INTO temp_table (num_col) VALUES (1);
  5  END;
  6  /
DECLARE
*
ERROR at line 1:
ORA-06519: active autonomous transaction detected and rolled back
ORA-06512: at line 4
```

Calling Autonomous Functions from SQL

Functions called from SQL statements must obey rules about modifying database and package state, as we discussed in Chapter 5. However, since an autonomous function by definition does not affect the current transaction, autonomous functions can be called from SQL statements even if they violate the rules for standard functions, as illustrated by the following:

```
-- Available online as autoSQL.sql
SQL> CREATE OR REPLACE FUNCTION LogParam(p1 IN NUMBER)
  2     RETURN NUMBER AS
  3
  3     PRAGMA AUTONOMOUS_TRANSACTION;
  4  BEGIN
  5     -- Insert the parameter into temp_table, then return it.
  6     INSERT INTO temp_table (num_col, char_col)
  7       VALUES (p1, 'Logged!');
  8     COMMIT;
  9     RETURN p1;
 10  END LogParam;
 11  /
```

```
Function created.
SQL> -- This is legal because LogParam is autonomous.
SQL> SELECT LogParam(ID) FROM students;

LOGPARAM(ID)
------------
       10000
       10001
       10002
       10003
       10004
       10005
       10006
       10007
       10008
       10009
       10010
       10011
12 rows selected.

SQL> -- But the rows have been inserted into temp_table.
SQL> SELECT num_col
  2      FROM temp_table
  3      WHERE char_col = 'Logged!';

  NUM_COL
---------
    10000
    10001
    10002
    10003
    10004
    10005
    10006
    10007
    10008
    10009
    10010
    10011
12 rows selected.
```

Autonomous Triggers

Because autonomous triggers run in a separate transaction, they are allowed
to (and, in fact, must) issue a COMMIT or ROLLBACK. This allows you to, for
example, log changes made to the database even if the parent transaction rolls
back. Consider the following trigger, which is similar to the **LogRSChanges** trigger
we examined in Chapter 6.

```
-- Available online as LogRSChanges.sql
CREATE OR REPLACE TRIGGER LogRSChanges
  BEFORE INSERT OR DELETE OR UPDATE ON registered_students
  FOR EACH ROW
DECLARE
  PRAGMA AUTONOMOUS_TRANSACTION;
  v_ChangeType CHAR(1);
BEGIN
  /* Use 'I' for an INSERT, 'D' for DELETE, and 'U' for UPDATE. */
  IF INSERTING THEN
    v_ChangeType := 'I';
  ELSIF UPDATING THEN
    v_ChangeType := 'U';
  ELSE
    v_ChangeType := 'D';
  END IF;

  /* Record all the changes made to registered_students in
     RS_audit. Use SYSDATE to generate the timestamp, and
     USER to return the userid of the current user. */
  INSERT INTO RS_audit
    (change_type, changed_by, timestamp,
     old_student_id, old_department, old_course, old_grade,
     new_student_id, new_department, new_course, new_grade)
  VALUES
    (v_ChangeType, USER, SYSDATE,
     :old.student_id, :old.department, :old.course, :old.grade,
     :new.student_id, :new.department, :new.course, :new.grade);
  COMMIT;
END LogRSChanges;
```

The only difference between this trigger and the original trigger in Chapter 6 is that this version is autonomous, and thus the changes will be logged even if the changes to **registered_students** are rolled back, as illustrated by the following:

```
-- Available online as RSChanges.sql
SQL> -- Delete everybody from Music 410.
SQL> DELETE FROM registered_students
  2    WHERE department = 'MUS'
  3      AND course = 410;
4 rows deleted.

SQL> -- And rollback.
SQL> ROLLBACK;
Rollback complete.

SQL> -- But the changes are still recorded in RS_audit.
```

```
SQL> SELECT change_type, changed_by, timestamp,
  2         old_student_ID, old_department, old_course
  3    FROM RS_audit;

C CHANGED_ TIMESTAMP OLD_STUDENT_ID OLD OLD_COURSE
- -------- --------- -------------- --- ----------
D EXAMPLE  19-JAN-00          10006 MUS        410
D EXAMPLE  19-JAN-00          10011 MUS        410
D EXAMPLE  19-JAN-00          10000 MUS        410
D EXAMPLE  19-JAN-00          10009 MUS        410
```

Autonomous Transactions and ALTER SESSION

Although an autonomous block runs within a different transaction, it still shares the same session as the parent transaction. Thus, any ALTER SESSION statements done by either block will be reflected in both. This is illustrated by the following example:

```
-- Available online as part of autoALTER.sql
SQL> -- Autonomous procedure that inserts the current date into
SQL> -- temp_table, using the current date format.
SQL> CREATE OR REPLACE PROCEDURE InsertDate1(p_Msg IN VARCHAR2) AS
  2    PRAGMA AUTONOMOUS_TRANSACTION;
  3  BEGIN
  4    INSERT INTO temp_table(num_col, char_col)
  5      VALUES (400, p_Msg || ': ' || SYSDATE);
  6    COMMIT;
  7  END InsertDate1;
  8  /
Procedure created.

SQL> -- Autonomous procedure that changes the date format, then
SQL> -- inserts the current date into temp_table using this new
SQL> -- format.
SQL> CREATE OR REPLACE PROCEDURE InsertDate2(p_Msg IN VARCHAR2) AS
  2    PRAGMA AUTONOMOUS_TRANSACTION;
  3  BEGIN
  4    EXECUTE IMMEDIATE
  5      'ALTER SESSION SET NLS_DATE_FORMAT =
  6        ''MM/DD/YYYY HH24:MI:SS''';
  7
  8    INSERT INTO temp_table(num_col, char_col)
  9      VALUES (400, p_Msg || ': ' || SYSDATE);
 10    COMMIT;
 11  END InsertDate2;
 12  /
Procedure created.
```

```
SQL> -- First alter the default date format.
SQL> ALTER SESSION SET NLS_DATE_FORMAT = 'DD-MON-YYYY HH24:MI:SS';
Session altered.

SQL> BEGIN
  2      InsertDate1('First insert');
  3      InsertDate2('Second insert');
  4      InsertDate1('Third insert');
  5  END;
  6  /
PL/SQL procedure successfully completed.

SQL> SELECT char_col
  2      FROM temp_table
  3      WHERE num_col = 400;

CHAR_COL
------------------------------------------------------------
First insert: 19-JAN-2000 13:08:52
Second insert: 01/19/2000 13:08:52
Third insert: 01/19/2000 13:08:52
```

This also implies that if you issue the statement 'ALTER SESSION DISABLE COMMIT IN PROCEDURE,' a COMMIT of an autonomous transaction will still raise an error:

-- **Available online as part of autoALTER.sql**

```
SQL> ALTER SESSION DISABLE COMMIT IN PROCEDURE;
Session altered.

SQL> BEGIN
  2      -- This will still raise an error.
  3      InsertDate1('With COMMIT IN PROCEDURE disabled');
  4      COMMIT;
  5  END;
  6  /
BEGIN
*
ERROR at line 1:
ORA-00034: cannot COMMIT in current PL/SQL session
ORA-06512: at "EXAMPLE.INSERTDATE1", line 6
ORA-06512: at line 3
```

The "Numeric or Value Error" Message

One of the most common errors in PL/SQL is "ORA-6502: numeric or value error." There are lots of different circumstances that raise this error. For example, assigning a character string that is too long to a VARCHAR2 variable will raise ORA-6502. In Oracle8, if we run the following block,

```
-- Available online as part of ora6502.sql
DECLARE
  v_TempVar VARCHAR2(5);
BEGIN
  -- Assign a character string that is too long.
  v_TempVar := 'abcdefghijkl';
END;
```

we get the following errors:

```
ORA-06502: PL/SQL: numeric or value error
ORA-06512: at line 5
```

In Oracle8*i*, however, the same block will return

```
ORA-06502: PL/SQL: numeric or value error: character string buffer
            too small
ORA-06512: at line 5
```

Only the error message text has been changed. The error number remains the same to ensure compatibility with previous versions. The following SQL*Plus session shows some different kinds of ORA-6502 messages.

```
-- Available online as part of ora6502.sql
SQL> DECLARE
  2    v_TempVar NUMBER;
  3  BEGIN
  4    -- Illegal conversion between character and number.
  5    v_TempVar := 'xyz';
  6  END;
  7  /
DECLARE
*
ERROR at line 1:
ORA-06502: PL/SQL: numeric or value error: character to number
           conversion error
ORA-06512: at line 5

SQL> DECLARE
  2    TYPE t_NumTab IS TABLE OF NUMBER
  3      INDEX BY BINARY_INTEGER;
  4    v_TempVAR t_NumTab;
  5  BEGIN
  6    -- NULL key value in an index-by table
```

```
  7     v_TempVAR(NULL) := 4;
  8  END;
  9  /
DECLARE
*
ERROR at line 1:
ORA-06502: PL/SQL: numeric or value error: NULL index table key value
ORA-06512: at line 7
```

```
SQL> DECLARE
  2     v_TempVar NUMBER(2);
  3  BEGIN
  4     -- Number that exceeds precision
  5     v_TempVar := 456;
  6  END;
  7  /
DECLARE
*
ERROR at line 1:
ORA-06502: PL/SQL: numeric or value error: number precision too large
ORA-06512: at line 5
```

The CALL Statement

Oracle8*i* adds a new SQL statement to call stored subprograms, the CALL statement. It can be used to call both PL/SQL and Java subprograms with a PL/SQL wrapper, and has the syntax

> CALL *subprogram_name* ([*argument_list*]) [INTO *host_variable*];

where *subprogram_name* is a standalone or packaged subprogram. It can also be an object type method, and can be at a remote database. The *argument_list* is a comma-separated list of arguments, and *host_variable* is a host variable used to retrieve the return value of functions. The following SQL*Plus session illustrates some uses of the CALL statement.

```
-- Available online as calls.sql
SQL> CREATE OR REPLACE PROCEDURE CallProc1(p1 IN VARCHAR2 := NULL) AS
  2  BEGIN
  3     DBMS_OUTPUT.PUT_LINE('CallProc1 called with ' || p1);
  4  END CallProc1;
  5  /
Procedure created.

SQL> CREATE OR REPLACE PROCEDURE CallProc2(p1 IN OUT VARCHAR2) AS
  2  BEGIN
```

```
  3    DBMS_OUTPUT.PUT_LINE('CallProc2 called with ' || p1);
  4    p1 := p1 || ' returned!';
  5  END CallProc2;
  6  /
Procedure created.

SQL> CREATE OR REPLACE FUNCTION CallFunc(p1 IN VARCHAR2)
  2    RETURN VARCHAR2 AS
  3  BEGIN
  4    DBMS_OUTPUT.PUT_LINE('CallFunc called with ' || p1);
  5    RETURN p1;
  6  END CallFunc;
  7  /
Function created.

SQL> -- Some valid calls direct from SQL.
SQL> CALL CallProc1('Hello!');
CallProc1 called with Hello!
Call completed.

SQL> CALL CallProc1();
CallProc1 called with
Call completed.

SQL> VARIABLE v_Output VARCHAR2(50);
SQL> CALL CallFunc('Hello!') INTO :v_Output;
CallFunc called with Hello!
Call completed.

SQL> PRINT v_Output
V_OUTPUT
----------------------------------------------------------------
Hello!

SQL> CALL CallProc2(:v_Output);
CallProc2 called with Hello!
Call completed.

SQL> PRINT v_Output
V_OUTPUT
----------------------------------------------------------------
Hello! returned!

SQL> -- This is illegal
SQL> BEGIN
  2    CALL CallProc1();
  3  END;
  4  /
```

```
        CALL CallProc1();
            *
ERROR at line 2:
ORA-06550: line 2, column 8:
PLS-00103: Encountered the symbol "CALLPROC1" when expecting one of the
following:
:= . ( @ % ;
The symbol ":=" was substituted for "CALLPROC1" to continue.

SQL> -- But these are legal
SQL> DECLARE
  2     v_Result VARCHAR2(50);
  3   BEGIN
  4     EXECUTE IMMEDIATE 'CALL CallProc1(''Hello from PL/SQL'')';
  5     EXECUTE IMMEDIATE
  6       'CALL CallFunc(''Hello from PL/SQL'') INTO :v_Result'
  7       USING v_Result;
  8   END;
  9   /
CallProc1 called with Hello from PL/SQL
CallFunc called with Hello from PL/SQL
PL/SQL procedure successfully completed.
```

This example illustrates the following points:

■   CALL is a SQL statement. It is not valid inside a PL/SQL block, but is valid when executed using dynamic SQL. (Inside a PL/SQL block, you can call the subprogram using the PL/SQL syntax.)

■   The parentheses are always required, even if the subprogram takes no arguments (or has default values for all the arguments).

■   The INTO clause is used for the output variables of functions only. IN OUT or OUT parameters are specified as part of the *argument_list*.

TIP
SQL*Plus versions earlier than 8.1 do not accept the CALL statement as valid syntax. You can use the EXECUTE SQL*Plus command instead. For more information, see Chapter 2.

Performance Comparisons

In this section, we will compare the performance of Oracle8 and Oracle8*i* with respect to the new features we have discussed, including bulk binds, the NOCOPY

modifier, native dynamic SQL, and some of the transparent enhancements. For the
performance comparisons, we will need to time the execution of a PL/SQL program.
We can use the following package to do this:

```
-- Available online as part of Timing.sql
CREATE OR REPLACE PACKAGE Timing AS
  PROCEDURE StartTiming;
  PROCEDURE StopTiming;
  PROCEDURE PrintElapsed(p_Message IN VARCHAR2);
END Timing;

CREATE OR REPLACE PACKAGE BODY Timing AS
  v_StartTime NUMBER;
  v_EndTime NUMBER;

  PROCEDURE StartTiming IS
  BEGIN
    -- Record the current time in v_StartTime.
    v_StartTime := DBMS_UTILITY.GET_TIME;
  END StartTiming;

  PROCEDURE StopTiming IS
  BEGIN
    -- Record the current time in v_StopTime.
    v_EndTime := DBMS_UTILITY.GET_TIME;
  END StopTiming;

  PROCEDURE PrintElapsed(p_Message IN VARCHAR2) IS
    v_Elapsed NUMBER := (v_EndTime - v_StartTime) / 100;
  BEGIN
    DBMS_OUTPUT.PUT_LINE(
      'Elapsed Time for ' || p_Message || ' is ' ||
      v_Elapsed  || ' seconds.');
  END PrintElapsed;
END Timing;
```

> **NOTE**
> *The **Timing** package uses DBMS_UTILITY.GET_TIME,
> which returns the current time in hundredths of a
> second. For more information on DBMS_UTILITY,
> see Appendix A on the CD-ROM included with
> this book.*

The usage of **Timing** is very simple, as the following SQL*Plus session illustrates.

-- Available online as part of Timing.sql

```
SQL> BEGIN
  2      -- Start timing first.
  3      Timing.StartTiming;
  4
  4      -- Do something that will take some time...
  5      FOR i IN 1..500000 LOOP
  6        NULL;
  7      END LOOP;
  8
  8      -- End the timing
  9      Timing.StopTiming;
 10
 10      -- And print the results!
 11      Timing.PrintElapsed('Timing Test');
 12  END;
 13  /
Elapsed Time for Timing Test is .79 seconds.
```

Bulk Binds

As we saw earlier in this chapter, bulk binds allow you to pass an entire collection of data between PL/SQL and SQL in one operation, rather than binding each row. The following example illustrates the performance benefits of bulk binds:

-- Available online as bulkTiming.sql

```
DECLARE
  c_NumRows CONSTANT NUMBER := 2000;

  TYPE t_Numbers IS TABLE OF temp_table.num_col%TYPE
    INDEX BY BINARY_INTEGER;
  TYPE t_Chars IS TABLE OF temp_table.char_col%TYPE
    INDEX BY BINARY_INTEGER;
  v_Numbers1 t_Numbers;
  v_Numbers2 t_Numbers;
  v_Chars1 t_Chars;
  v_Chars2 t_Chars;

  CURSOR c_TempCursor IS
    SELECT * FROM temp_table;
BEGIN
  -- Fill up v_Numbers1 and v_Chars1 with c_NumRows rows.
  FOR v_Count IN 1..c_NumRows LOOP
    v_Numbers1(v_Count) := v_Count;
    v_Chars1(v_Count) := 'Row number ' || v_Count;
  END LOOP;
```

```
  -- Clear the table and commit, so that we have a clean table and
  -- a clean transaction.
  DELETE FROM temp_table;
  COMMIT;

  -- First insert them individually.
  Timing.StartTiming;
  FOR v_Count IN 1..c_NumRows LOOP
    INSERT INTO temp_table VALUES
      (v_Numbers1(v_Count), v_Chars1(v_Count));
  END LOOP;
  Timing.StopTiming;
  Timing.PrintElapsed('Individual Insert');

  -- Now insert them using bulk binds.
  Timing.StartTiming;
  FORALL v_Count IN 1..c_NumRows
    INSERT INTO temp_table VALUES
      (v_Numbers1(v_Count), v_Chars1(v_Count));
  Timing.StopTiming;
  Timing.PrintElapsed('Bulk Insert');

  -- Select the rows (c_NumRows * 2 of them) individually into
  -- v_Numbers2 and v_Chars2.
  Timing.StartTiming;
  OPEN c_TempCursor;
  FOR v_Count IN 1..c_NumRows * 2 LOOP
    FETCH c_TempCursor
      INTO v_Numbers2(v_Count), v_Chars2(v_Count);
  END LOOP;
  CLOSE c_TempCursor;
  Timing.StopTiming;
  Timing.PrintElapsed('Individual Select');

  -- And now select them using a bulk fetch.
  Timing.StartTiming;
  OPEN c_TempCursor;
  FETCH c_TempCursor
    BULK COLLECT INTO v_Numbers2, v_Chars2;
  CLOSE c_TempCursor;
  Timing.StopTiming;
  Timing.PrintElapsed('Bulk Select');
END;
```

The results of running this block three times in SQL*Plus are shown next, and show the performance advantage of bulk binds.

```
SQL> @ch11\bulkTiming
Elapsed Time for Individual Insert is 3.86 seconds.
Elapsed Time for Bulk Insert is 3.32 seconds.
Elapsed Time for Individual Select is .64 seconds.
Elapsed Time for Bulk Select is .04 seconds.
PL/SQL procedure successfully completed.

SQL> /
Elapsed Time for Individual Insert is 4.87 seconds.
Elapsed Time for Bulk Insert is .11 seconds.
Elapsed Time for Individual Select is .75 seconds.
Elapsed Time for Bulk Select is .05 seconds.
PL/SQL procedure successfully completed.

SQL> /
Elapsed Time for Individual Insert is 3.82 seconds.
Elapsed Time for Bulk Insert is .14 seconds.
Elapsed Time for Individual Select is .56 seconds.
Elapsed Time for Bulk Select is .05 seconds.
PL/SQL procedure successfully completed.
```

NOTE
The timing results here may differ on your system. Using any of these performance features will improve the times, but how much improvement can vary.

NOCOPY Modifier

The NOCOPY modifier, which we examined in detail in Chapter 5, allows the PL/SQL engine to pass certain OUT and IN OUT parameters by reference. The impact is highest when you are passing large records or collections to a procedure, as the following procedure illustrates:

```
-- Available online as part of NoCopyTiming.sql
CREATE OR REPLACE PACKAGE NoCopyTiming AS
  TYPE t_LargeNumbers IS TABLE OF NUMBER;
  TYPE t_LargeChars IS TABLE OF VARCHAR2(50);

  -- This procedure doesn't use NOCOPY, so the parameters will
  -- be passed by value.
  PROCEDURE CallMe(
    p_Parameter1 IN OUT t_LargeNumbers,
    p_Parameter2 IN OUT t_LargeChars);
```

```
     -- This procedure uses NOCOPY, so the parameters will be passed
     -- by reference if possible.
     PROCEDURE CallMeNocopy(
       p_Parameter1 IN OUT NOCOPY t_LargeNumbers,
       p_Parameter2 IN OUT NOCOPY t_LargeChars);
END NoCopyTiming;

CREATE OR REPLACE PACKAGE BODY NoCopyTiming AS
  PROCEDURE CallMe(
     p_Parameter1 IN OUT t_LargeNumbers,
     p_Parameter2 IN OUT t_LargeChars) IS
  BEGIN
     NULL;
  END CallMe;

  PROCEDURE CallMeNocopy(
     p_Parameter1 IN OUT NOCOPY t_LargeNumbers,
     p_Parameter2 IN OUT NOCOPY t_LargeChars) IS
  BEGIN
     NULL;
  END CallMeNocopy;
END NoCopyTiming;
```

NOTE
Collections such as the PL/SQL table used in this
example are described in Chapter 14.

If we call **CallMe** and **CallMeNocopy** with the following block,

```
-- Available online as part of NoCopyTiming.sql
DECLARE
  -- Initialize two variables to one element each.
  v_Nums NoCopyTiming.t_LargeNumbers :=
    NoCopyTiming.t_LargeNumbers(123456);
  v_Chars NoCopyTiming.t_LargeChars :=
    NoCopyTiming.t_LargeChars('abcdefghijklmnopqrstuvwxyz');

  c_NumRows CONSTANT NUMBER := 50000;
BEGIN
  -- Add c_NumRows - 1 elements to each table, by copying the first
  -- element.
  v_Nums.EXTEND(c_NumRows - 1, 1);
  v_Chars.EXTEND(c_NumRows -1, 1);

  -- Call the first procedure, without NOCOPY.
  Timing.StartTiming;
```

```
  NoCopyTiming.CallMe(v_Nums, v_Chars);
  Timing.StopTiming;
  Timing.PrintElapsed('Without NOCOPY');

  -- Call the second procedure, with NOCOPY.
  Timing.StartTiming;
  NoCopyTiming.CallMeNocopy(v_Nums, v_Chars);
  Timing.StopTiming;
  Timing.PrintElapsed('With NOCOPY');
END;
```

we get the following results. NOCOPY is faster because the large arrays do not have to be copied back and forth.

```
Elapsed Time for Without NOCOPY is 2.37 seconds.
Elapsed Time for With NOCOPY is 0 seconds.
PL/SQL procedure successfully completed.

SQL> /
Elapsed Time for Without NOCOPY is 2.31 seconds.
Elapsed Time for With NOCOPY is 0 seconds.
PL/SQL procedure successfully completed.

SQL> /
Elapsed Time for Without NOCOPY is 2.45 seconds.
Elapsed Time for With NOCOPY is 0 seconds.
PL/SQL procedure successfully completed.
```

Native Dynamic SQL

Native dynamic SQL is significantly faster than DBMS_SQL, primarily because it is built into the language itself, and thus does not have to do as many context switches. This is illustrated by the following example:

```
-- Available online as part of dynamicTiming.sql
DECLARE
  v_CursorID INTEGER;
  v_Dummy NUMBER;
  v_SQLStatement VARCHAR2(100) :=
    'INSERT INTO temp_table (num_col) VALUES (:num)';

  c_NumRows CONSTANT NUMBER := 5000;
BEGIN
  -- Clear the table and commit.
  DELETE FROM temp_table;
  COMMIT;
```

```
Timing.StartTiming;
-- Loop c_NumRows times, and insert using DBMS_SQL.
v_CursorID := DBMS_SQL.OPEN_CURSOR;

FOR v_Count IN 1..c_NumRows LOOP
  DBMS_SQL.PARSE(v_CursorID, v_SQLStatement, DBMS_SQL.NATIVE);
  DBMS_SQL.BIND_VARIABLE(v_CursorID, ':num', v_Count);
  v_Dummy := DBMS_SQL.EXECUTE(v_CursorID);
END LOOP;

DBMS_SQL.CLOSE_CURSOR(v_CursorID);

Timing.StopTiming;
Timing.PrintElapsed('DBMS_SQL');

-- Clear the table and commit.
DELETE FROM temp_table;
COMMIT;


-- Do the same insert using native dynamic SQL.
Timing.StartTiming;
FOR v_Count IN 1..c_NumRows LOOP
  EXECUTE IMMEDIATE v_SQLStatement USING v_Count;
END LOOP;
Timing.StopTiming;
Timing.PrintElapsed('Native Dynamic SQL');
END;
```

The results from running the previous block are shown in the following SQL*Plus session:

```
SQL> @ch11\dynamicTiming
Elapsed Time for DBMS_SQL is 11.94 seconds.
Elapsed Time for Native Dynamic SQL is 8.17 seconds.
PL/SQL procedure successfully completed.

SQL> /
Elapsed Time for DBMS_SQL is 10.09 seconds.
Elapsed Time for Native Dynamic SQL is 8.35 seconds.
PL/SQL procedure successfully completed.

SQL> /
Elapsed Time for DBMS_SQL is 13.19 seconds.
Elapsed Time for Native Dynamic SQL is 10.31 seconds.
PL/SQL procedure successfully completed.
```

Summary

Oracle8*i* includes many new features for PL/SQL, both transparent and user visible. In this chapter, we discussed all of the new available enhancements. We discussed bulk binds and autonomous transactions in detail. The chapter concluded with performance comparisons of bulk binds, the NOCOPY modifier, and native dynamic SQL.

PART
III

Object Features
and LOBs

CHAPTER
12

Introduction to Objects

bjects are among the main new features of Oracle8 and PL/SQL 8. In this chapter, we will see how to create and use objects, including methods and constructors. We will also discuss Oracle8*i* enhancements to objects, such as static methods. In the next chapter, we will discuss the implications of storing objects in the database.

Background

Oracle **8** and higher

Before we can introduce Oracle's implementation of objects, we need to discuss the fundamentals of object-oriented design and methodology. A full discussion of this paradigm is beyond the scope of this book; however, we can cover the fundamentals here. Once we understand the fundamentals of this design philosophy, we will discuss Oracle's implementation of object types in the following sections.

Basis of Object-Oriented Programming

Why do we write computer applications? One possible answer to this question is to model the real world. A software system is designed to simulate both the objects that exist in the world, and the interactions between them. Once the objects and interactions are modeled, the application can be used to track how they evolve and automate the processes involved. An order entry system, for example, allows a salesperson to concentrate on making a sale by providing him or her with all the necessary information and then handling the interactions with other departments, such as accounts receivable and shipping.

Consider a university. What are the entities in this world? We have students who communicate with the registrar to sign up for classes. The registrar informs professors of students' registrations for their classes. Professors communicate with students during the class and when they assign grades. The people who run the university bookstore need to know from the professors which books they want for their classes, and then they make the books available to the students. This model is illustrated in Figure 12-1. The circles in the figure represent the entities involved (students, registrar, professors, and the bookstore), and the arrows represent interactions between the entities, such as a student purchasing a book from the bookstore.

This is a reasonable model. By examining the model, we can determine information about the real world. For example, we can see that the registrar is centrally involved because many of the other entities need to communicate with the registrar.

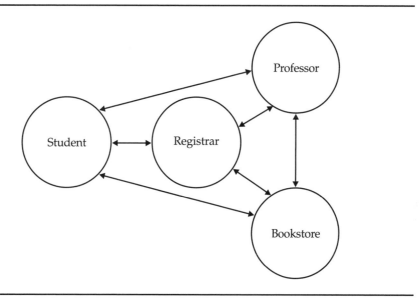

FIGURE 12-1.   *A model of a university*

Object-oriented design essentially turns this model directly into a computer application. Each of the entities is represented by an object in the system. An object represents the attributes of the real-world entity and operations that act on those attributes. Consider the student object represented in Figure 12-2. A student has *attributes*, such as first and last name, major, and current credits. The operations that act on these attributes are also included, such as **ChangeMajor** (which modifies the major) and **UpdateCredits** (which adds credits to the student's record for completed classes). The operations are known as *methods*.

Objects can communicate with each other by invoking methods. For example, the registrar can invoke the **UpdateCredits** method for a particular student after that student has passed a class.

An application can also model a mathematical world, such as a Euclidean geometry system. There, the entities in the world consist of points, which are laid out on an X-Y Cartesian grid. We can also have polygons, which are made up of sets of points. This is illustrated by Figure 12-3. Points and polygons can also be represented by objects, as shown in Figure 12-4. Endpoints can be added to or removed from a polygon using the **InsertPoint** or **RemovePoint** methods. We will see the full definitions of the methods later in this chapter.

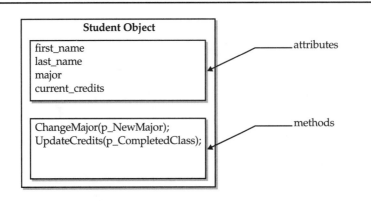

FIGURE 12-2. *A student object*

Abstraction

The attributes and methods of an object neatly implement both data and procedural abstraction, as we covered in Chapter 4's discussion of packages. Ideally, a client

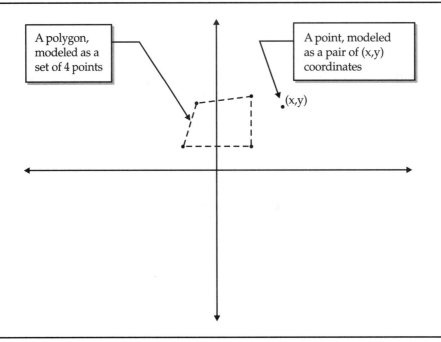

FIGURE 12-3. *Points and polygons*

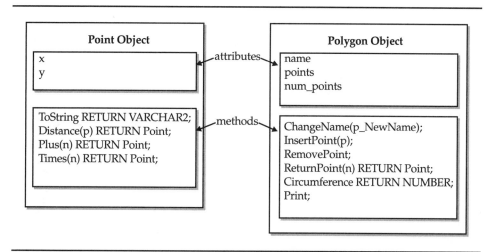

FIGURE 12-4. *A point object and a polygon object*

using a given object manipulates the attributes only through the methods. By doing this, the client application does not have to know the actual implementation of the methods, and can just call them.

Objects vs. Object Instances

It is important to note the difference between an object type itself, and an *instance* of that type. There can be only one object type in a given environment, but many instances of it. An object instance is similar to a variable—each instance has its own memory, and thus its own copy of the attributes. For example, Figure 12-5 illustrates two instances of the **Student** type and an instance of the **Polygon** type. This is analogous to two different PL/SQL records declared of the same type.

Object-Relational Databases

Many object-oriented programming languages are available, including C++ and Java. Programming languages like this allow you to define objects and manipulate them. What they are lacking, however, is persistence—the ability to store and retrieve objects in a safe, consistent way. This is where object-relational databases such as Oracle8 come in. Oracle8 is designed to store and retrieve object data just as it does relational data, by using SQL as the standard way of communicating with the database. In an object-relational database, SQL (and PL/SQL) can be used to manipulate both relational and object data. Both the object definition (in the form of a database type) and object instances (as a row in a table) can be stored in the

---

Student Object 1		Student Object 2	
first_name:	Scott	first_name:	Margaret
last_name:	Smith	last_name:	Mason
major	Computer Science	major	History
current_credits:	4	current_credits:	8

Polygon Object	
name:	almostSquare
num_points:	4
points:	(5, 10), (5, 2.5),
	(-4, 2.5), (-2, 8)

FIGURE 12-5. *Object instances*

database. Oracle8 also provides the advantages of consistent transactional control, secure backup and recovery, excellent query performance, locking and concurrency, and scalability. By combining objects with the relational model, we have the best of both worlds—the power and reliability of a relational database along with the flexibility and modeling capabilities of objects.

In the rest of this chapter, we will see how Oracle8 implements object storage and retrieval. We will discuss how to create objects and methods, and their ramifications. In Chapter 13, we will see how objects can be stored in the database and manipulated using SQL.

NOTE
Objects were introduced first in Oracle8. They have been enhanced for Oracle8i, and we will see these enhancements in this and the next chapter. In both of the objects chapters, the term "Oracle8" refers to both Oracle8 and Oracle8i, except where indicated.

Object Types

Objects are created in Oracle8 with object types. The *object type* describes both the attributes and the methods associated with a particular kind of object. In the next few sections, we will see how to create and use object types.

In Oracle8, before you can use objects, the *Objects option* is required. When you connect to an Oracle8 database, you should see a message something like the following:

```
Oracle8 Enterprise Edition Release 8.0.6.0.0 - Production
With the Partitioning and Objects options
PL/SQL Release 8.0.6.0.0 - Production
```

If you don't see the Objects option in the version information line, it has not been installed. Consequently, you will not be able to create and use object types. If this is the case, the Oracle executable may have to be relinked with the Objects option by using the Oracle installer. Check the installation and user's guide for your system for more information.

Oracle **8***i* and higher   In Oracle8*i*, objects are available in all configurations of the server, so no direct check is necessary. In the rest of this chapter, it is assumed that you either have the objects option available (Oracle8) or are using Oracle8*i*.

Defining Object Types

An object type is similar to a package—it has both a specification and body. The type specification contains the attributes, and forward declarations for the methods. The type body contains the actual code for the methods. The syntax for creating a type specification is as follows; the syntax for creating the type body is in "Methods," later in this chapter.

Object type specifications are defined with the CREATE TYPE ... AS OBJECT statement, the syntax of which is

CREATE [OR REPLACE] TYPE [*schema.*]*type_name*
[AUTHID {CURRENT_USER | DEFINER} AS OBJECT (*attribute_list*,
                                              [*method_list*]);

where *type_name* is the name of the new object type, and *schema* is the owner. In order to create an object type in your own schema, you must have the CREATE TYPE system privilege. Creating a type in another user's schema requires the CREATE ANY TYPE system privilege.

Oracle **8***i* and higher   The AUTHID clause is available in Oracle8*i* and signifies that the methods are executed under the privilege set of the owner, or of their caller. Like a package specification, all of the methods in the object type must execute with the same privilege set. For more information on the AUTHID clause, see Chapter 5.

The *attribute_list* is a comma-separated list of attribute declarations, each of which looks like

attribute_name datatype

where *attribute_name* is the name of an attribute, and *datatype* is either a built-in Oracle datatype, an already defined user-defined datatype, or a reference to an object type (see the next chapter for more information on object references). This is the same syntax as a variable declaration in the declarative section of a block or of a record element. Unlike a record declaration, however, you can't use the %TYPE attribute or initialization clauses.

The *method_list* is a comma-separated list of method declarations. We will examine the syntax for creating methods, including the special MAP and ORDER methods, in "Methods," later in this chapter. Method declarations can include the PRAGMA RESTIRCT_REFERENCES clause (discussed in Chapter 5) as well. Note that at least one attribute is required, but the methods are optional. You cannot create an object type with only methods.

For example, the following statement creates a type that can represent a student:

 `-- Available online as part of objTypes.sql`

```
CREATE OR REPLACE TYPE Student AS OBJECT (
    ID              NUMBER(5),
    first_name      VARCHAR2(20),
    last_name       VARCHAR2(20),
    major           VARCHAR2(30),
    current_credits NUMBER(3)
    ...
    );
```

NOTE
*The object types that we will examine in this chapter are contained in several online files. The **Student**, **Class**, **Room**, and **Address** objects can be found in **objTypes.sql**. The **Point** object is in **Point.sql**, and the **Polygon** object is in **Polygon.sql**. All of these files can be found in the **code/ch12** directory.*

There are several things to note about object types:

- The CREATE TYPE statement is a DDL statement. As such, it can't be used directly in a PL/SQL block. You can, however, use dynamic SQL (either DBMS_SQL or Oracle8*i* native dynamic SQL, described in Chapter 8) to execute the CREATE TYPE statement.

- You must have the CREATE TYPE system privilege (which is part of the RESOURCE role) in order to create an object type.

- Object types are created as data dictionary objects. Consequently, they are created in the current schema, unless a different schema is specified in the CREATE TYPE ... AS OBJECT statement.

- The attributes of the newly created type are specified similar to the fields of a PL/SQL record or the columns of a table in the CREATE TABLE statement.

- Unlike record fields, the attributes of an object type can not be constrained to be NOT NULL, initialized to a default value, or declared using %TYPE.

- Like a PL/SQL record, you can refer to the attributes within an object using dot notation.

- Unlike other object-oriented languages (such as Java or C++), object type attributes are always public. Any user who has EXECUTE privilege on the type can modify the attributes directly.

There are also several restrictions on the datatype of object attributes. Object attributes can be any Oracle8 datatype except

- A LONG or LONG RAW. They can be a LOB type, however.

- Any national language type, such as NCHAR, NVARCHAR2, or NCLOB.

- ROWID or UROWID (UROWID is a new Oracle8*i* type).

- Types available only in PL/SQL but not in the database. These include BINARY_INTEGER, BOOLEAN, PLS_INTEGER, RECORD, and REF CURSOR.

- A type defined with %TYPE or %ROWTYPE.

- Types defined within a PL/SQL package.

The reason for these restrictions is that an object type, as defined for Oracle8, is a data dictionary object. Thus, only features and types available directly to the database are legal. PL/SQL types and constructs like %TYPE are not allowed. These restrictions will likely be lifted in future releases of Oracle, when an object type can be declared local to a PL/SQL block, as well as in the data dictionary. They are still in place for Oracle8*i*, however.

TIP

When creating a type specification (or type body) using SQL*Plus, you must include a forward slash on the line following the type definition to execute the CREATE TYPE ... AS OBJECT statement, similar to executing a PL/SQL block.

Nested Object Types

Subject to the restrictions in the previous section, an attribute of an object type can be any Oracle8 type. This includes other object types. For example, we can create an object type to represent a point as a pair of x and y coordinates as follows:

```
-- Available online as part of Point.sql
CREATE OR REPLACE TYPE Point AS OBJECT (
  -- A point is represented by its location on an X-Y Cartesian
  -- grid.
  x NUMBER,
  y NUMBER
  ...
);
```

Once this is done, we can create a polygon type as follows:

```
-- Available online as part of Polygon.sql
CREATE OR REPLACE TYPE PointList AS
  VARRAY(10) OF Point;

CREATE OR REPLACE TYPE Polygon AS OBJECT (
  name VARCHAR2(50),    -- Name of this object
  num_points INTEGER,   -- Current number of endpoints
  points PointList      -- Collection of endpoints
  ...
);
```

A **Polygon** consists of up to 10 **Points**, stored as a varray. We will examine the **Point** and **Polygon** types in more detail later in this chapter.

> **NOTE**
> *A varray is one type of PL/SQL collection. It is a datatype similar to a C array. We will examine collections, including varrays, in Chapter 14.*

Declaring and Initializing Objects

Just like any other PL/SQL variable, an object is declared simply by placing it syntactically after its type in the declarative section of the block, for example:

```
DECLARE
  v_Student Student;
  v_Point Point;
```

This block declares **v_Student** as an instance of the object type **Student**, and **v_Point** as an instance of the object type **Point**. In accordance with the rules of

PL/SQL, an object instance declared in this manner is initialized to NULL. Note that the entire object is NULL, not necessarily the attributes within it. If an object is NULL in this manner, it is illegal to refer to an attribute within it. NULL issues with objects are described in the upcoming section, "Object NULL vs. Attribute NULL."

Initializing Objects

How then do you initialize objects? This is done with a constructor. A *constructor* is a function that returns an initialized object and takes as arguments the values for the object's attributes. For every object type, Oracle predefines a constructor with the same name as the type. For example, the **Student** constructor would have the following specification:

```
FUNCTION Student(ID IN NUMBER,
                 first_name IN VARCHAR2,
                 last_name IN VARCHAR2,
                 major IN VARCHAR2,
                 current_credits IN NUMBER)
   RETURN Student;
```

NOTE

The constructor is not explicitly defined. However, it can be thought of as having the specification shown previously. The name of the constructor is the same as the name of the object type.

We can therefore create an initialized instance of a **Student**, and refer to its attributes, as follows:

```
-- Available online as objInit.sql
DECLARE
   -- Creates the object instance, with the attributes set.
   v_Student Student := Student(10020, 'Chuck', 'Choltry', NULL, 0);
BEGIN
   -- Modifies the major attribute to 'Music'.  Note the use of
   -- dot notation to refer to the attribute.
   v_Student.major := 'Music';
END;
```

Object NULL vs. Attribute NULL

An object declaration that does not use the constructor creates a NULL object. It is important to note the difference between the NULLness of an object and the NULLness of its attributes. If an object is NULL (this can be described as *atomically*

NULL), it is illegal to refer to the attributes of it. For example, the following block raises the error "ORA-06530: Reference to uninitialized composite":

```
-- Available online as objNULL.sql
SQL> DECLARE
  2    v_Student Student; -- This assigns NULL to v_Student by default
  3    BEGIN
  4      v_Student.ID := 10020;
  5    END;
  6  /
DECLARE
*
ERROR at line 1:
ORA-06530: Reference to uninitialized composite
ORA-06512: at line 4
```

The IS NULL condition can be applied to objects to test whether or not they are NULL. For example, the **AssignName** procedure checks the NULLness of its argument before assigning to it:

```
-- Available online as part of AssignName.sql
CREATE OR REPLACE PROCEDURE AssignName(
  p_Student IN OUT Student,
  p_FirstName IN VARCHAR2,
  p_LastName IN VARCHAR2) AS
BEGIN
  IF p_Student IS NULL THEN
    RAISE_APPLICATION_ERROR(-20000, 'Student is NULL');
  ELSE
    p_Student.first_name := p_FirstName;
    p_Student.last_name := p_LastName;
  END IF;
END AssignName;
```

The output from calling **AssignName** is shown here:

```
-- Available online as part of AssignName.sql
SQL> DECLARE
  2    v_Student Student;
  3    v_SQLErr VARCHAR2(100);
  4    BEGIN
  5      -- v_Student is initialized to NULL by default.  So this
  6      -- call will raise an error.
  7      BEGIN
  8        AssignName(v_Student, 'Joe', 'Blow');
  9      EXCEPTION
 10        WHEN OTHERS THEN
 11          v_SQLErr := SUBSTR(SQLERRM, 1, 100);
```

```
12          DBMS_OUTPUT.PUT_LINE('AssignName raised ' || v_SQLErr);
13     END;
14
14     -- But if we initialize v_Student first, then the call succeeds.
15     v_Student := Student(10020, NULL, NULL, NULL, 0);
16     AssignName(v_Student, 'Joe', 'Blow');
17     DBMS_OUTPUT.PUT_LINE('AssignName succeeded');
18  END;
19  /
AssignName raised ORA-20000: Student is NULL
AssignName succeeded
```

Forward Type Definitions

It is sometimes useful to create a type before you know the attributes and/or
methods that it will contain. You can do this with a *forward type declaration*, which
is similar to a forward declaration of a procedure or method. The syntax is simply

CREATE TYPE *type_name*;

where *type_name* is the name of the type. This is useful for mutually referential
types, and also to allow other types to refer to this one before it is fully fleshed
out. Forward type definitions are very similar to forward subprogram declarations
in packages.

Only types can be declared with forward declarations—other PL/SQL data
dictionary objects, such as triggers, packages, or subprograms, cannot.

Methods

The methods in an object type allow you to act on objects, possibly modifying
their attributes. In the following sections, we will examine the syntax for declaring
methods, and discuss various kinds of methods.

Declaring Methods

In the next two sections, we will discuss the syntax for declaring methods in the
type specification and body.

TYPE SPECIFICATIONS   Recall the syntax for an object type specification
that we examined earlier in this chapter:

CREATE [OR REPLACE] TYPE [*schema.*]*type_name*
   [AUTHID {CURRENT_USER | DEFINER} AS OBJECT (*attribute_list*,
                                 [*method_list*]);

The *method_list* is a comma-separated list of method declarations, each of which can be one of the following:

> [STATIC | MEMBER] PROCEDURE *procedure_spec,*
> [STATIC | MEMBER] FUNCTION *function_spec,*
> [MAP | ORDER] MEMBER FUNCTION *function_spec,*
> *pragma_declaration*

where *function_spec* is a function specification (including the RETURN clause) and *procedure_spec* is a procedure specification, as we saw in Chapter 4. Just like in a package header, method specifications are forward declarations and have no body code. In fact, the only difference between a method specification and a packaged subprogram specification is the STATIC or MEMBER keyword in front of the declaration. STATIC is valid in Oracle8*i* only. See "Static Methods," later in this chapter, for details.

The *method_list* can also contain RESTRICT_REFERENCES pragmas, which enable methods to be called from SQL statements (the pragma is not necessary in Oracle8*i*). For example, we can extend the specification for the **Student** object type as follows:

```
-- Available online as part of objTypes.sql
CREATE OR REPLACE TYPE Student AS OBJECT (
  ID               NUMBER(5),
  first_name       VARCHAR2(20),
  last_name        VARCHAR2(20),
  major            VARCHAR2(30),
  current_credits  NUMBER(3),

  -- Returns the first and last names, separated by a space.
  MEMBER FUNCTION FormattedName
    RETURN VARCHAR2,
  PRAGMA RESTRICT_REFERENCES(FormattedName,
                             RNDS, WNDS, RNPS, WNPS),

  -- Updates the major to the specified value in p_NewMajor.
  MEMBER PROCEDURE ChangeMajor(p_NewMajor IN VARCHAR2),
  PRAGMA RESTRICT_REFERENCES(ChangeMajor,
                             RNDS, WNDS, RNPS, WNPS)
  ...
);
```

There are several things to note about the method declarations in the type specification:

- All of the methods must have the keyword MEMBER or STATIC before the forward declaration. (The STATIC keyword, available with Oracle8*i*, is discussed later in "Static Methods.")

- Instead of a semicolon after each declaration (or pragma), there is a comma. This is true for all elements of the type specification, including the attributes, except for the last one.

- The method declarations must occur after the attribute declarations.

- The MAP and ORDER functions are used to determine the sort order for this object type. These functions are discussed later in "MAP and ORDER Methods."

- The RESTRICT_REFERENCES pragma can be used to enable a method to be called from an SQL statement. The same rules apply when using this pragma for a method as for a subprogram—for more information, see Chapter 5.

TYPE BODIES   Creating a type body is done with the CREATE TYPE BODY command, which is similar to creating a package body. The syntax for creating a type body is

```
CREATE [OR REPLACE] TYPE BODY [schema.]type_name {IS | AS}
  method_body_list
END;
```

where *method_body_list* is a list of method bodies, each of which can be one of the following:

```
[STATIC | MEMBER] PROCEDURE procedure_body
[STATIC | MEMBER] FUNCTION function_body
[MAP | ORDER] MEMBER function_body
```

where *procedure_body* and *function_body* are the implementation of methods defined in the type specification, just like subprograms defined in a package body. For example, we can create the **Student** type body with

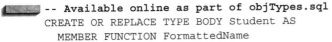 `-- Available online as part of objTypes.sql`
```
CREATE OR REPLACE TYPE BODY Student AS
  MEMBER FUNCTION FormattedName
    RETURN VARCHAR2 IS
```

```
BEGIN
  RETURN first_name || ' ' || last_name;
END FormattedName;

MEMBER PROCEDURE ChangeMajor(p_NewMajor IN VARCHAR2) IS
BEGIN
  major := p_NewMajor;
END ChangeMajor;
  ...
END;
```

Object types are similar to packages in many ways. For example:

- Both promote data abstraction by separating the specification and body into different data dictionary objects. This breaks the dependency chain for object type bodies the same way as it does for package bodies.

- Both create data dictionary objects.

- Method bodies are declared like subprograms in a package body, with a trailing semicolon after each.

However, there are some significant differences:

- A package body can include additional declarations not in the specification. These private declarations are in scope only in the package body. An object type body, on the other hand, can only contain member subprograms.

- Object types are actual PL/SQL types—variables can be declared of a particular object type. A package is a different type of schema object entirely—it groups together related declarations.

- Packages can contain an initialization section; objects cannot. The initial values of the attributes are set using the constructor, described earlier in this chapter in "Declaring and Initializing Objects."

- The END keyword after a type body does not have the name of the type after it. However, the END keyword for each method implementation can have the method name after it.

The complete implementation of the **Point** object type is shown next. It contains two attributes (**x** and **y**, which we've already seen) and four methods.

```
-- Available online as Point.sql
CREATE OR REPLACE TYPE Point AS OBJECT (
  -- A point is represented by its location on an X-Y Cartesian
  -- grid.
  x NUMBER,
  y NUMBER,

  -- Returns a string '(x, y)'
  MEMBER FUNCTION ToString RETURN VARCHAR2,
  PRAGMA RESTRICT_REFERENCES(ToString, RNDS, WNDS, RNPS, WNPS),

  -- Returns the distance between p and the current Point (SELF).
  -- If p is not specified then it defaults to (0, 0).
  MEMBER FUNCTION Distance(p IN Point DEFAULT Point(0,0))
    RETURN NUMBER,
  PRAGMA RESTRICT_REFERENCES(Distance, RNDS, WNDS, RNPS, WNPS),

  -- Returns the sum of p and the current Point.
  MEMBER FUNCTION Plus(p IN Point) RETURN Point,
  PRAGMA RESTRICT_REFERENCES(Plus, RNDS, WNDS, RNPS, WNPS),

  -- Returns current Point * n.
  MEMBER FUNCTION Times(n IN NUMBER) RETURN Point
  PRAGMA RESTRICT_REFERENCES(Times, RNDS, WNDS, RNPS, WNPS)
);

CREATE OR REPLACE TYPE BODY Point AS
  -- Returns a string '(x, y)'
  MEMBER FUNCTION ToString RETURN VARCHAR2 IS
    v_Result VARCHAR2(20);
    v_xString VARCHAR2(8) := SUBSTR(TO_CHAR(x), 1, 8);
    v_yString VARCHAR2(8) := SUBSTR(TO_CHAR(y), 1, 8);
  BEGIN
    v_Result := '(' || v_xString || ', ';
    v_Result := v_Result || v_yString || ')';
    RETURN v_Result;
  END ToString;

  -- Returns the distance between p and the current Point (SELF).
  -- If p is not specified then it defaults to (0, 0).
  MEMBER FUNCTION Distance(p IN Point DEFAULT Point(0,0))
    RETURN NUMBER IS
  BEGIN
    RETURN SQRT(POWER(x - p.x, 2) + POWER(y - p.y, 2));
  END Distance;
```

```
   -- Returns the sum of p and the current Point.
   MEMBER FUNCTION Plus(p IN Point) RETURN Point IS
     v_Result Point;
   BEGIN
     v_Result := Point(x + p.x, y + p.y);
     RETURN v_Result;
   END Plus;

   -- Returns current Point * n.
   MEMBER FUNCTION Times(n IN NUMBER) RETURN Point IS
     v_Result Point;
   BEGIN
     v_Result := Point(x * n, y * n);
     RETURN v_Result;
   END Times;
END;
```

Calling a Method

Although methods are syntactically like packaged subprograms, they are called differently. A stored subprogram is a standalone object and it is called directly from a PL/SQL block. However, each instantiation of an object has its own state. Since an object's methods are used to modify the object's state, the method needs to reference a particular object instance. (This is not the case for static methods, available in Oracle8*i*. See "Static Methods" for details.) So, in order to call a method for a particular instantiation, you use dot notation as follows:

object_name.method_name

where *object_name* is the name of the object variable, and *method_name* is the name of the method. The following SQL*Plus session illustrates calling methods on various **Student** objects.

> **NOTE**
> *If the method has no arguments, it can be called either with no parentheses (like a normal PL/SQL procedure) or with a set of empty parentheses. The following block also illustrates this.*

 -- **Available online as callStud.sql**
```
SQL> DECLARE
  2     v_Student1 Student :=
  3        Student(10020, 'Chuck', 'Choltry', NULL, 0);
  4     v_Student2 Student :=
```

```
 5       Student(10021, 'Denise', 'Davenport', NULL, 0);
 6   BEGIN
 7     -- Change the major of both students.
 8     v_Student1.ChangeMajor('Economics');
 9     v_Student2.ChangeMajor('Computer Science');
10
11     -- Print out Student1's name. Note that there are no
12     -- parentheses in the call to the method.
13     DBMS_OUTPUT.PUT_LINE(v_Student1.FormattedName);
14
15     -- Print out Student2's name. This call has empty parentheses.
16     DBMS_OUTPUT.PUT_LINE(v_Student2.FormattedName());
17   END;
18   /
Chuck Choltry
Denise Davenport
PL/SQL procedure successfully completed.
```

Like a regular procedure, methods can be called with either positional or named notation, and the parameters can have default values. They can also be overloaded on the type and number of arguments. Positional and named notation, default values, and overloading are discussed in Chapters 4 and 5. The following SQL*Plus session illustrates this.

```
-- Available online as callPoint.sql
SQL> DECLARE
 2     v_P1 Point := Point(-1, 5);
 3     v_P2 Point := Point(5, 2);
 4     v_Result Point;
 5   BEGIN
 6     DBMS_OUTPUT.PUT_LINE('p1: ' || v_P1.toString);
 7     DBMS_OUTPUT.PUT_LINE('p2: ' || v_P2.toString);
 8
 9     -- Call distance, specifying the parameter.
10     DBMS_OUTPUT.PUT_LINE('Distance between p1 and p2 = ' ||
11       v_P1.Distance(v_P2));
12
13     -- Call distance without a parameter, which will use the default
14     -- value.
15     DBMS_OUTPUT.PUT_LINE('Distance between p1 and the origin = ' ||
16       v_P1.Distance);
17
18     -- Call times and plus with named notation
19     v_Result := v_P1.Times(n => 2.5);
20     DBMS_OUTPUT.PUT_LINE('p1 * 2.5: ' || v_Result.ToString);
21     v_Result := v_P1.Plus(p => v_P2);
22     DBMS_OUTPUT.PUT_LINE('p1 + p2: ' || v_Result.ToString);
```

```
 23  END;
 24  /
p1: (-1, 5)
p2: (5, 2)
Distance between p1 and p2 = 6.7082039324993690892275210061938287 0632
Distance between p1 and the origin =
   5.0990195135927848300282241090227 8198956
p1 * 2.5: (-2.12313, 10.61567)
p1 + p2: (4, 7)
PL/SQL procedure successfully completed.
```

Passing Objects to Methods

Just as we saw earlier with the **AssignName** procedure, objects can be passed to methods as parameters. For example, suppose we create object types to represent rooms and classes to go along with the **Student** type:

 -- Available online as part of objTypes.sql
```sql
CREATE OR REPLACE TYPE Room AS OBJECT (
  ID              NUMBER(5),
  building        VARCHAR2(15),
  room_number     NUMBER(4),
  number_seats    NUMBER(4),
  description     VARCHAR2(50)
  ...
);

CREATE OR REPLACE TYPE Class AS OBJECT (
  department          CHAR(3),
  course              NUMBER(3),
  description         VARCHAR2(2000),
  max_students        NUMBER(3),
  current_students    NUMBER(3),
  num_credits         NUMBER(1),
  roomP               REF Room
  ...
);
```

NOTE

roomP *is a REF type, which is a pointer to another object, rather than an embedded object. For more information, see Chapter 13.*

We can now add the **UpdateCredits** method to **Student**, as follows:

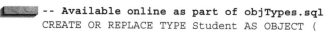 -- Available online as part of objTypes.sql
```sql
CREATE OR REPLACE TYPE Student AS OBJECT (
```

```
  ID                   NUMBER(5),
  first_name           VARCHAR2(20),
  last_name            VARCHAR2(20),
  major                VARCHAR2(30),
  current_credits      NUMBER(3),
  ...
  -- Updates the current_credits by adding the number of
  -- credits in p_CompletedClass to the current value.
  MEMBER PROCEDURE UpdateCredits(p_CompletedClass IN Class),
  PRAGMA RESTRICT_REFERENCES(UpdateCredits, RNDS, WNDS, RNPS, WNPS)
  ...
);

CREATE OR REPLACE TYPE BODY Student AS
  ...
  MEMBER PROCEDURE UpdateCredits(p_CompletedClass IN Class) IS
  BEGIN
    current_credits := current_credits +
                       p_CompletedClass.num_credits;
  END UpdateCredits;
  ...
END;
```

Similarly, we can add methods to the **Polygon** type as follows:

```
-- Available online as part of Polygon.sql
CREATE OR REPLACE TYPE Polygon AS OBJECT (
  name VARCHAR2(50),       -- Name of this object
  num_points INTEGER,      -- Current number of endpoints

  points PointList,        -- Collection of endpoints

  -- Changes the name to p_NewName
  MEMBER PROCEDURE ChangeName(p_NewName IN VARCHAR2),
  PRAGMA RESTRICT_REFERENCES(ChangeName, WNDS, RNDS, WNPS, RNPS),

  -- Inserts p at the end of the Polygon.  If there is no
  -- more room, an error is raised.
  MEMBER PROCEDURE InsertPoint(p IN Point),
  PRAGMA RESTRICT_REFERENCES(InsertPoint, WNDS, RNDS, WNPS, RNPS),

  -- Removes the point at the end.  If there are no endpoints, an
  -- error is raised.  Together, InsertPoint and RemovePoint
  -- act like the push and pop operations on a stack.
  MEMBER PROCEDURE RemovePoint,
  PRAGMA RESTRICT_REFERENCES(RemovePoint, WNDS, RNDS, WNPS, RNPS),

  -- Returns the Point at position n.  If n is not passed (or is
  -- passed as NULL), returns the Point at the top of the list.
```

```
   MEMBER FUNCTION ReturnPoint(n IN NUMBER := NULL)
     RETURN Point,
   PRAGMA RESTRICT_REFERENCES(ReturnPoint, WNDS, RNDS, WNPS, RNPS),

   -- Returns the circumference (distance around the outside) of
   -- this Polygon.
   MEMBER FUNCTION Circumference RETURN NUMBER,
   PRAGMA RESTRICT_REFERENCES (Circumference, WNDS, RNDS, WNPS, RNPS),

   -- Prints out this Polygon in a nice format.
   MEMBER PROCEDURE Print,
   ...
);

CREATE OR REPLACE TYPE BODY Polygon AS
-- Changes the name to p_NewName
  MEMBER PROCEDURE ChangeName(p_NewName IN VARCHAR2) IS
  BEGIN
    name := p_NewName;
  END ChangeName;

  -- Inserts p at the end of the Polygon.  If there is no
  -- more room, an error is raised.
  MEMBER PROCEDURE InsertPoint(p IN Point) IS
  BEGIN
    IF num_points = 10 THEN
      RAISE_APPLICATION_ERROR(-20000,
        'Polygon ' || name || ' already has 10 points');
    END IF;

    IF points IS NULL THEN
      points := PointList(null);
    ELSE
      points.EXTEND;
    END IF;

    num_points := num_points + 1;
    points(num_points) := p;
  END InsertPoint;

  -- Removes the point at the end.  Together, InsertPoint and
  -- RemovePoint act like the push and pop operations on a stack.
  MEMBER PROCEDURE RemovePoint IS
  BEGIN
    IF num_points = 0 THEN
      RAISE_APPLICATION_ERROR(-20001,
        'Polygon ' || name || ' has 0 points');
    END IF;
```

```
    points.TRIM;
    num_points := num_points - 1;
END RemovePoint;

-- Returns the Point at position n.  If n is not passed (or is
-- passed as NULL), returns the Point at the top of the list.
MEMBER FUNCTION ReturnPoint(n IN NUMBER := NULL)
    RETURN Point IS
BEGIN
  IF n IS NULL THEN
    RETURN points(num_points);
  ELSE
    RETURN points(n);
  END IF;
END ReturnPoint;

-- Returns the circumference (distance around the outside) of
-- this Polygon.
MEMBER FUNCTION Circumference RETURN NUMBER IS
    v_Result NUMBER := 0;
    v_Count1 BINARY_INTEGER;
BEGIN
  IF num_points = 0 OR num_points = 1 THEN
    RETURN 0;
  ELSIF num_points = 2 THEN
    RETURN points(0).Distance(points(1));
  ELSE
    v_Count1 := 1;
    FOR v_Count2 IN 2..num_points LOOP
      v_Result := v_Result +
        points(v_Count1).Distance(points(v_Count2));
      v_Count1 := v_Count1 + 1;
    END LOOP;
    v_Result := v_Result + points(num_points).Distance(points(1));
    RETURN v_Result;
  END IF;
END Circumference;

-- Prints out this Polygon in a nice format.
MEMBER PROCEDURE Print IS
BEGIN
  DBMS_OUTPUT.PUT('Polygon ' || name || ':');
  DBMS_OUTPUT.PUT_LINE(' Total endpoints: ' || num_points);
  IF num_points != 0 THEN
    FOR v_Count IN 1..num_points LOOP
      DBMS_OUTPUT.PUT_LINE('   ' || v_Count || ': ' ||
                            points(v_Count).ToString);
    END LOOP;
```

```
        END IF;
    END Print;
    ...
END;
```

The **InsertPoint** method takes a **Point** as an argument. Furthermore, the constructor for **Polygon** takes a **PointList**, which is a varray of **Points**. These are illustrated by the following SQL*Plus session:

```
-- Available online as part of callPoly.sql
SQL> DECLARE
  2    v_Poly Polygon;
  3    v_Points PointList;
  4    v_SQLMesg VARCHAR2(100);
  5  BEGIN
  6    -- First create a new Polygon, without any Points, and print it.
  7    v_Poly := Polygon('My Shape', 0, NULL);
  8    v_Poly.Print;
  9
  9    -- Add 10 Points and print again.
 10    FOR v_Count IN 1..10 LOOP
 11      v_Poly.InsertPoint(Point(v_Count, v_Count));
 12    END LOOP;
 13    v_Poly.Print;
 14
 14    -- Add one more Point.  This should raise an error.
 15    BEGIN
 16      v_Poly.InsertPoint(Point(0, 0));
 17    EXCEPTION
 18      WHEN OTHERS THEN
 19        DBMS_OUTPUT.PUT('Exception raised: ');
 20        v_SQLMesg := SUBSTR(SQLERRM, 1, 100);
 21        DBMS_OUTPUT.PUT_LINE(v_SQLMesg);
 22    END;
 23
 23    -- Remove 9 Points, which should leave us with 1.
 24    FOR v_Count IN 1..9 LOOP
 25      v_Poly.RemovePoint;
 26    END LOOP;
 27    v_Poly.Print;
 28
 28    -- Reinitialize v_Poly using the constructor.  This time, we
 29    -- will pass in a PointList which sets up a square centered
 30    -- on the origin.
 31    v_Points :=
 32      PointList(Point(1, 1), Point(1, -1),
 33                Point(-1, -1), Point(-1, 1));
```

```
34    v_Poly := Polygon('Square', v_Points.COUNT, v_Points);
35    v_Poly.Print;
36
36    -- And print out the circumference of our square.
37    DBMS_OUTPUT.PUT_LINE('Square circumference = ' ||
38                          v_Poly.Circumference);
39  END;
40  /
Polygon My Shape: Total endpoints: 0
Polygon My Shape: Total endpoints: 10
  1: (1, 1)
  2: (2, 2)
  3: (3, 3)
  4: (4, 4)
  5: (5, 5)
  6: (6, 6)
  7: (7, 7)
  8: (8, 8)
  9: (9, 9)
  10: (10, 10)
Exception raised: ORA-20000: Polygon My Shape already has 10 points
Polygon My Shape: Total endpoints: 1
  1: (1, 1)
Polygon Square: Total endpoints: 4
  1: (1, 1)
  2: (1, -1)
  3: (-1, -1)
  4: (-1, 1)
Square circumference = 8
PL/SQL procedure successfully completed.
```

In this example, we use the **Point** and **PointList** predefined constructors to create the objects passed to **InsertPoint** and the **Polygon** constructor.

The SELF Keyword

Consider the **Student.ChangeMajor** method, which we saw earlier in this chapter:

```
MEMBER PROCEDURE ChangeMajor(p_NewMajor IN VARCHAR2) IS
  BEGIN
    major := p_NewMajor;
  END ChangeMajor;
```

This method modifies the **major** attribute of the **Student** for which it is called. Inside the method, therefore, the identifier "major" is bound to the instantiating object. In order to make this clearer, PL/SQL provides a new keyword—SELF.

SELF is automatically bound to the instantiating object inside a method. So we could rewrite **ChangeMajor** as follows:

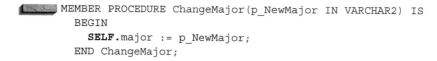

```
MEMBER PROCEDURE ChangeMajor(p_NewMajor IN VARCHAR2) IS
    BEGIN
        SELF.major := p_NewMajor;
    END ChangeMajor;
```

SELF is the first parameter to every member method. It can either be explicitly or implicitly declared. For member functions, SELF is implicitly declared as IN; for procedures, it is declared as IN OUT. The type of SELF is the object type itself in the previous example **Student**. It is an error to declare SELF as other than the first parameter, since it is implicitly declared first for you.

NOTE
When implementing a method as an external C routine, SELF is passed explicitly, both in the PARAMETERS clause and as a parameter to the external routine itself. For more information, see the Oracle documentation.

For the **ChangeMajor** method, the use of SELF is optional, since unqualified references to attributes refer to the current object by default. However, if you want to pass the current object instance, or a reference to it, as an argument to another procedure or method, you need to use SELF, as the following example illustrates. First, we create the **SelfDemo** type specification as follows:

```
-- Available online as part of SelfDemo.sql
CREATE OR REPLACE TYPE SelfDemo AS OBJECT (
    attrib1 NUMBER,
    attrib2 VARCHAR2(10),

    -- Method which will call UpdateSelf to modify the attributes.
    MEMBER PROCEDURE UpdateMe,

    -- Prints the current values of the attributes.
    MEMBER PROCEDURE Print
);
```

We can now create a procedure **UpdateSelf** that will modify the attributes of a **SelfDemo** object passed to it:

```
-- Available online as part of SelfDemo.sql
CREATE OR REPLACE PROCEDURE UpdateSelf(p_Self IN OUT SelfDemo) AS
BEGIN
  p_Self.attrib1 := 10;
  p_Self.attrib2 := 'Updated!';
END UpdateSelf;
```

Next, we can create the type body. The implementation of **UpdateMe** calls **UpdateSelf** and passes SELF as the formal parameter:

```
-- Available online as part of SelfDemo.sql
CREATE OR REPLACE TYPE BODY SelfDemo AS
  -- CallsUpdateSelf to do the work.
  MEMBER PROCEDURE UpdateMe IS
  BEGIN
    UpdateSelf(SELF);
  END UpdateMe;

  -- Prints the current values of the attributes.
  MEMBER PROCEDURE Print IS
  BEGIN
    DBMS_OUTPUT.PUT_LINE('attrib1: ' || attrib1 ||
                         ' attrib2: ''' || attrib2 || '''');
  END Print;
END;
```

Finally, we can call **SelfDemo.UpdateMe**, as the following SQL*Plus session shows:

```
-- Available online as part of SelfDemo.sql
SQL> DECLARE
  2    v_SelfObj SelfDemo := SelfDemo(1, 'Original');
  3  BEGIN
  4    DBMS_OUTPUT.PUT_LINE('Original values:');
  5    v_SelfObj.Print;
  6
  7    -- Call UpdateMe to change the attributes, and print the result.
  8    v_SelfObj.UpdateMe;
  9    DBMS_OUTPUT.PUT_LINE('New values:');
 10    v_SelfObj.Print;
 11  END;
 12  /
Original values:
attrib1: 1  attrib2: 'Original'
New values:
attrib1: 10  attrib2: 'Updated!'
PL/SQL procedure successfully completed.
```

CALLING MEMBER METHODS FROM OTHER METHODS If you want
to call a method from within another method of an object type, then SELF is also
required. For example, suppose we change **UpdateMe** as follows:

```
-- Available online as part of SelfDemo.sql
CREATE OR REPLACE TYPE SelfDemo AS OBJECT (
   ...
   -- Method that will call UpdateSelf to modify the attributes.
   -- If p_Print is TRUE, then Print will be called afterwards.
   MEMBER PROCEDURE UpdateMe(p_Print IN BOOLEAN := FALSE),
   ...
);

CREATE OR REPLACE TYPE BODY SelfDemo AS
   -- CallsUpdateSelf to do the work.
   MEMBER PROCEDURE UpdateMe(p_Print IN BOOLEAN := FALSE) IS
   BEGIN
     UpdateSelf(SELF);
     IF p_Print THEN
       Print;
     END IF;
   END UpdateMe;
   ...
END;
```

Attempting to compile the type body will yield the following errors:

```
LINE/COL ERROR
-------- ----------------------------------------------------------
7/7      PLS-00306: wrong number or types of arguments in call to
         'PRINT'
7/7      PL/SQL: Statement ignored
```

This can be fixed by changing **UpdateMe** to call Print with SELF:

```
-- Available online as part of SelfDemo.sql
MEMBER PROCEDURE UpdateMe(p_Print IN BOOLEAN := FALSE) IS
  BEGIN
    UpdateSelf(SELF);
    IF p_Print THEN
      SELF.Print;
    END IF;
  END UpdateMe;
```

Static Methods

Oracle **8i**
and higher As we saw earlier in "Calling a Method," SELF is passed in implicitly to each member method call. The member method can therefore modify the values of the current object. Oracle8i introduces another kind of method—a static method. Unlike nonstatic member methods, a *static method* is invoked on the object type itself, rather than an instance of it, using the syntax:

> *object_type_name.method_name*

where *object_type_name* is the name of the type, and *method_name* is a method declared with the STATIC keyword, rather than the MEMBER keyword.

Since a static method does not have an object instance passed into it, it cannot refer to any attributes of the current object. It can, however, refer to attributes of a new object or an object passed as a parameter. Likewise, SELF cannot be passed explicitly to a static method. This is illustrated by the following example. Suppose we create a type header as follows:

```
-- Available online as part of StaticDemo.sql
CREATE OR REPLACE TYPE StaticDemo AS OBJECT (
  attribute1 NUMBER,
  attribute2 NUMBER,

  STATIC PROCEDURE Static1,
  STATIC FUNCTION Static2(p_Obj IN StaticDemo)
    RETURN StaticDemo
);
```

Both of the methods **Static1** and **Static2** are static methods, and thus cannot refer directly to **attribute1** or **attribute2**. If they do, then Oracle8i will raise the PLS-588 error and the type body will not compile.

```
-- Available online as part of StaticDemo.sql
SQL> CREATE OR REPLACE TYPE BODY StaticDemo AS
  2    -- This method will not compile, since it refers to unqualified
  3    -- attributes.
  4    STATIC PROCEDURE Static1 IS
  5    BEGIN
  6      attribute1 := 7;
  7      DBMS_OUTPUT.PUT_LINE(attribute2);
  8    END Static1;
  9
  9    -- This is legal, since we don't refer to attributes without a
```

```
10     -- specific object reference first.
11     STATIC FUNCTION Static2(p_Obj IN StaticDemo)
12       RETURN StaticDemo IS
13       v_Result StaticDemo := StaticDemo(0, 0);
14     BEGIN
15       v_Result.attribute1 := p_Obj.attribute1 + 1;
16       v_Result.attribute2 := p_Obj.attribute2 - 1;
17       RETURN v_Result;
18     END Static2;
19   END;
20   /
Warning: Type Body created with compilation errors.
SQL> show errors
Errors for TYPE BODY STATICDEMO:

LINE/COL ERROR
-------- -------------------------------------------------------------
6/5      PLS-00588: unqualified instance attribute references allowed
         only in member methods
6/5      PL/SQL: Statement ignored
7/5      PL/SQL: Statement ignored
7/26     PLS-00588: unqualified instance attribute references allowed
         only in member methods
```

USING STATIC METHODS AS INITIALIZERS   The default constructor for
an object, as we have seen, takes all of the attributes as parameters. This is not
always convenient, as you may want to initialize some attributes in a different
manner. This is a good use for a static method that takes the desired parameters and
returns an initialized object as needed. For example, suppose we want to create
Polygons that are squares. We can create a static method **CreateSquare** that does
this as follows:

```
-- Available online as part of Polygon.sql
CREATE OR REPLACE TYPE Polygon AS OBJECT (
  name VARCHAR2(50),    -- Name of this object
  num_points INTEGER,   -- Current number of endpoints
  points PointList,     -- Collection of endpoints
  ...
  -- Static method (only works on Oracle8i).  This returns a
  -- new Polygon that has 4 endpoints, centered around p_Center.
  STATIC FUNCTION CreateSquare(
    p_Name       IN VARCHAR2,
    p_SideLength IN NUMBER,
    p_Center     IN Point DEFAULT Point(0,0))
    RETURN Polygon
);
```

```
CREATE OR REPLACE TYPE BODY Polygon AS
  ...
  STATIC FUNCTION CreateSquare(
    p_Name       IN VARCHAR2,
    p_SideLength IN NUMBER,
    p_Center     IN Point DEFAULT Point(0,0))
    RETURN Polygon IS

    v_UpperLeft Point;
    v_UpperRight Point;
    v_LowerLeft Point;
    v_LowerRight Point;
    v_HalfLength NUMBER;
  BEGIN
    -- First calculate each of the four corners.  These are computed
    -- by adding or subtracting (p_SideLength / 2, p_SideLength /2)
    -- from p_Center.
    v_HalfLength := p_SideLength / 2;
    v_UpperLeft := p_Center.Plus(Point(-v_HalfLength, v_HalfLength));
    v_UpperRight := p_Center.Plus(Point(v_HalfLength, v_HalfLength));
    v_LowerLeft := p_Center.Plus(Point(-v_HalfLength, -v_HalfLength));
    v_LowerRight := p_Center.Plus(Point(v_HalfLength, -v_HalfLength));

    -- And now we can create a Polygon to return.
    RETURN Polygon(p_Name, 4,
      PointList(v_UpperLeft, v_UpperRight,
                v_LowerRight, v_LowerLeft));
  END CreateSquare;
END;
```

CreateSquare is demonstrated by the following SQL*Plus session. Note that we call **CreateSquare** as **Polygon.CreateSquare**, referring to the object type itself, rather than an instance of it.

```
-- Available online as part of callPoly.sql
SQL> DECLARE
  2    v_Poly Polygon;
  3  BEGIN
  4    -- Create a square centered around the origin, with sides of
  5    -- length 3.
  6    v_Poly := Polygon.CreateSquare('Square A', 3);
  7    v_Poly.Print;
  8    DBMS_OUTPUT.PUT_LINE(
  9      'Circumference = ' || v_Poly.Circumference);
 10
 10    -- Create another square centered around (1, 2) with sides of
 11    -- length 7.
```

```
12    v_Poly := Polygon.CreateSquare('Square B', 7, Point(1, 2));
13    v_Poly.Print;
14    DBMS_OUTPUT.PUT_LINE(
15      'Circumference = ' || v_Poly.Circumference);
16  END;
17  /
Polygon Square A: Total endpoints: 4
 1: (-1.5, 1.5)
 2: (1.5, 1.5)
 3: (1.5, -1.5)
 4: (-1.5, -1.5)
Circumference = 12
Polygon Square B: Total endpoints: 4
 1: (-2.5, 5.5)
 2: (4.5, 5.5)
 3: (4.5, -1.5)
 4: (-2.5, -1.5)
Circumference = 28
PL/SQL procedure successfully completed.
```

TIP

Although Oracle8 Release 8.0 does not have static methods, you can still create useful initializers for object types. But instead of creating them as part of the object type itself, you can create them as separate packaged procedures. That way, you don't have to have an object first to call them.

MAP and ORDER Methods

The Oracle predefined types all have an implicit ordering. Given two VARCHAR2 variables, for example, you can determine if one is less than, greater than, or equal to the other. Without this, it would be impossible to sort values of the given datatype. Object types, on the other hand, have no implicit ordering.

This can be remedied, however, through the use of MAP and ORDER methods. Besides allowing direct comparisons between objects, they can be used to sort objects stored in the database, as we will see in Chapter 13.

MAP METHODS   A MAP method is a function that returns a scalar type. When Oracle needs to sort a list of objects or compare two objects, it can call the MAP function to convert the object to a type that can be sorted. The method thus acts like a hash function. For example, consider the **Room** object that we saw earlier in this chapter:

-- Available online as part of objTypes.sql

```
CREATE OR REPLACE TYPE Room AS OBJECT (
  ID           NUMBER(5),
  building     VARCHAR2(15),
  room_number  NUMBER(4),
  number_seats NUMBER(4),
  description  VARCHAR2(50)
  ...
);
```

We can create a MAP method for **Room** that returns the ID, as follows:

-- Available online as part of objTypes.sql

```
CREATE OR REPLACE TYPE Room AS OBJECT (
  ...
  MAP MEMBER FUNCTION ReturnID RETURN NUMBER
);

CREATE OR REPLACE TYPE BODY Room AS
  ...
 MAP MEMBER FUNCTION ReturnID RETURN NUMBER IS
  BEGIN
    RETURN SELF.ID;
  END ReturnID;
END;
```

A MAP method is identified by the keyword MAP in front of the declaration. This function must take no parameters, and return one of the following scalar types: DATE, NUMBER, VARCHAR2, CHAR, or REAL. The **ReturnID** function returns the room ID number, which is how **Room**s will be sorted. After this function has been created, we can compare two **Room**s, as the following example illustrates.

-- Available online as part of compare.sql

```
SQL> DECLARE
  2    v_Room1 Room :=
  3      Room(20000, 'Building 7', 201, 1000, 'Large Lecture Hall');
  4    v_Room2 Room :=
  5      Room(20001, 'Building 6', 101, 500, 'Small Lecture Hall');
  6  BEGIN
  7    IF v_Room1 < v_Room2 THEN
  8      DBMS_OUTPUT.PUT_LINE('Room 1 < Room 2');
  9    ELSIF v_Room1 = v_Room2 THEN
 10      DBMS_OUTPUT.PUT_LINE('Room 1 = Room 2');
 11    ELSE
 12      DBMS_OUTPUT.PUT_LINE('Room 1 > Room 2');
```

```
13    END IF;
14  END;
15  /
Room 1 < Room 2
PL/SQL procedure successfully completed.
```

ORDER METHODS   Alternatively, you can create an ORDER method. ORDER methods take one parameter (of the object type) and return a numeric result with one of the following values:

- ■ >1 if the parameter is greater than SELF

- ■ <1 if the parameter is less than SELF

- ■ 0 if the parameter is equal to SELF

An ORDER method is used similar to the MAP method. We can create an ORDER method for students which sorts by name with the following:

```
-- Available online as part of objTypes.sql
CREATE OR REPLACE TYPE Student AS OBJECT (
  ID                NUMBER(5),
  first_name        VARCHAR2(20),
  last_name         VARCHAR2(20),
  major             VARCHAR2(30),
  current_credits   NUMBER(3),
  ...
 -- ORDER function used to sort students.
  ORDER MEMBER FUNCTION CompareStudent(p_Student IN Student)
    RETURN NUMBER
);

CREATE OR REPLACE TYPE BODY Student AS
  ...
  ORDER MEMBER FUNCTION CompareStudent(p_Student IN Student)
    RETURN NUMBER IS
  BEGIN
    -- First compare by last names
    IF p_Student.last_name = SELF.last_name THEN
      -- If the last names are the same, then compare first names.
      IF p_Student.first_name < SELF.first_name THEN
        RETURN 1;
      ELSIF p_Student.first_name > SELF.first_name THEN
        RETURN -1;
```

```
      ELSE
        RETURN 0;
      END IF;
    ELSE
      IF p_Student.last_name < SELF.last_name THEN
        RETURN 1;
      ELSE
        RETURN -1;
      END IF;
    END IF;
  END CompareStudent;
END;
```

Once this is created, we can compare **Student**s, as the following example illustrates.

```
-- Available online as part of compare.sql
SQL> DECLARE
  2     v_Student1 Student :=
  3        Student(10002, 'Joanne', 'Junebug', 'Computer Science', 8);
  4     v_Student2 Student :=
  5        Student(10006, 'Barbara', 'Blues', 'Economics', 7);
  6  BEGIN
  7     IF v_Student1 < v_Student2 THEN
  8        DBMS_OUTPUT.PUT_LINE('Student 1 < Student 2');
  9     ELSIF v_Student1 = v_Student2 THEN
 10        DBMS_OUTPUT.PUT_LINE('Student 1 = Student 2');
 11     ELSE
 12        DBMS_OUTPUT.PUT_LINE('Student 1 > Student 2');
 13     END IF;
 14  END;
 15  /
Student 1 > Student 2
```

GUIDELINES   There are several things to keep in mind about MAP and ORDER methods:

- ■ A given object type can have either a MAP or an ORDER method, but it is an error to define both.

- ■ A MAP method will be more efficient when sorting large groups of objects, since it will convert the entire set of objects to a simpler type (operating as a hash function), which is then sorted directly. With the ORDER method, only two objects can be compared at a time, and thus the ORDER method must be called repeatedly.

■ Without either a MAP or ORDER method, objects can be compared only for equality or inequality, and only in SQL statements. The MAP or ORDER method allows the object to be sorted and also to be compared in procedural statements. If you try to compare two objects that don't define either method, Oracle will raise the PLS-526 error, as illustrated next.

```
-- Available online as part of compare.sql
SQL> DECLARE
  2    v_Point1 Point := Point(1, 1);
  3    v_Point2 Point := Point(0, 0);
  4  BEGIN
  5    IF v_Point1 = v_Point2 THEN
  6      DBMS_OUTPUT.PUT_LINE('Equal!');
  7    ELSE
  8      DBMS_OUTPUT.PUT_LINE('Not equal!');
  9    END IF;
 10  END;
 11  /
DECLARE
*
ERROR at line 1:
ORA-06550: line 5, column 15:
PLS-00526: A MAP or ORDER function is required for comparing
           objects in PL/SQL.
```

■ Objects without MAP or ORDER methods can be tested for equality in SQL, however. This simply compares all of the attributes. We will see this in Chapter 13.

Using %TYPE with Objects

The %TYPE attribute cannot be applied to an attribute of an object type directly. Rather, it must be applied to an attribute of an instantiation of an object type. This restriction also applies to records. This is illustrated in the following example:

```
-- Available online as percentType.sql
SQL> DECLARE
  2    -- First declare a record type, and a variable of the record
  3    -- and object type.
  4    TYPE t_Rec IS RECORD (
  5      f1 NUMBER,
  6      f2 VARCHAR2(10));
  7    v_Student Student;
  8    v_Rec     t_Rec;
  9
```

```
 9    -- This declaration is legal, since %TYPE is applied to a
10    -- variable.
11    v_ID v_Student.ID%TYPE;
12    -- This declaration raises PLS-206, since %TYPE is applied to
13    -- an object type.
14    v_ID2 Student.ID%TYPE;
15
15    -- This declaration is legal, since %TYPE is applied to a
16    -- variable.
17    v_F1 v_Rec.f1%TYPE;
18    -- This declaration raises PLS-206, since %TYPE is applied to
19    -- a record type.
20    v_F2 t_Rec.f2%TYPE;
21  BEGIN
22    NULL;
23  END;
24  /
DECLARE
*
ERROR at line 1:
ORA-06550: line 14, column 9:
PLS-00206: %TYPE must be applied to a variable, column, field or
           attribute, not to "STUDENT.ID"
ORA-06550: line 14, column 9:
PL/SQL: Item ignored
ORA-06550: line 20, column 8:
PLS-00206: %TYPE must be applied to a variable, column, field or
           attribute, not to "T_REC.F2"
ORA-06550: line 20, column 8:
PL/SQL: Item ignored
```

Exceptions and Object Type Attributes

As we discussed in Chapter 4, the values of OUT and IN OUT parameters are not assigned their values if a stored subprogram does not handle a raised exception. This is also true if an unhandled exception is raised inside a method. In addition, any attribute assignments that the method has done are not completed. Consider the **Error** object:

```
-- Available online as part of Error.sql
CREATE OR REPLACE TYPE Error AS OBJECT (
  attribute NUMBER,
  MEMBER PROCEDURE RaiseError(p_RaiseIt IN BOOLEAN,
                              p_OutParam IN OUT NUMBER),
  MEMBER PROCEDURE Print(p_Comment IN VARCHAR2 DEFAULT NULL)
);
```

```
CREATE OR REPLACE TYPE BODY Error AS
  MEMBER PROCEDURE RaiseError(p_RaiseIt IN BOOLEAN,
                              p_OutParam IN OUT NUMBER) IS
  BEGIN
    -- Assign the IN value to attribute, and increment it by 1
    -- for the OUT value.
    SELF.attribute := p_OutParam;
    p_OutParam := p_OutParam + 1;
    IF p_RaiseIt THEN
      RAISE NO_DATA_FOUND;
    END IF;
  END RaiseError;

  MEMBER PROCEDURE Print (p_Comment IN VARCHAR2 DEFAULT NULL) IS
  BEGIN
    -- Print the comment as well as the attribute value.
    IF p_Comment IS NOT NULL THEN
      DBMS_OUTPUT.PUT(p_Comment || ', ');
    END IF;
    DBMS_OUTPUT.PUT_LINE('attribute = ' || attribute);
  END Print;
END;
```

If we then execute the following block:

```
-- Available online as part of Error.sql
DECLARE
  v_Test Error := Error(1);
  v_NumVal NUMBER := 10;
BEGIN
  -- First print the attribute and v_NumVal
  v_Test.Print('After initialization, v_NumVal = ' || v_NumVal);
  -- Call RaiseError with FALSE, so the parameter and attribute
  -- are assigned.
  v_Test.RaiseError(FALSE, v_NumVal);
  v_Test.Print('After call with no exception, v_NumVal = ' ||
               v_NumVal);
  -- Call RaiseError with TRUE, so the parameter and attribute
  -- are not assigned.
  v_Test.RaiseError(TRUE, v_NumVal);
EXCEPTION
  WHEN NO_DATA_FOUND THEN
    v_Test.Print('After call with exception, v_NumVal = ' ||
                 v_NumVal);
END;
```

we get the following output:

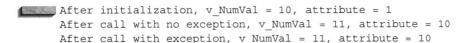
```
After initialization, v_NumVal = 10, attribute = 1
After call with no exception, v_NumVal = 11, attribute = 10
After call with exception, v_NumVal = 11, attribute = 10
```

Both the attribute and OUT value are assigned if the procedure completes successfully, but if NO_DATA_FOUND is raised, they keep their original values.

NOTE
The NOCOPY modifier can be used in Oracle8i for method parameters as well. Assignments to NOCOPY parameters will be kept if an exception is raised by the method. Likewise, assignments to attributes in SELF will be kept only if SELF is explicitly declared as a NOCOPY parameter. For more information on NOCOPY, see Chapter 4.

Altering and Dropping Types

Similar to other kinds of schema objects, you can modify an existing object type using the ALTER TYPE statement. ALTER TYPE can be used to compile the type specification or body, or to add methods to a type. Object types can be dropped using the DROP TYPE statement.

ALTER TYPE ... COMPILE

This format of the ALTER TYPE command has the following structure:

ALTER TYPE *type_name* COMPILE [SPECIFICATION | BODY];

where *type_name* is the type to be altered. This command will compile either the specification or body of the type, using the existing definition as stored in the data dictionary. If neither the SPECIFICATION nor the BODY keywords are present, both the specification and the body are recompiled. For example, the following command will recompile the body of **Student**:

```
ALTER TYPE Student COMPILE BODY;
```

ALTER TYPE ... REPLACE AS OBJECT

An alternate format of ALTER TYPE is used to add methods. The syntax is

ALTER TYPE *type_name* REPLACE AS OBJECT (
  object_type_specification);

where *type_name* is the name of the object type, and *object_type_specification* is a complete type definition as defined for CREATE TYPE. The new definition must be the same as the original definition, except for the addition of new methods. The original attributes and types must be included. If a type body exists, it is invalidated because it does not define the new methods. (The CREATE OR REPLACE TYPE BODY command can be used to add the new methods to the body.) The following SQL*Plus session illustrates the use of ALTER TYPE ... REPLACE AS OBJECT:

```
-- Available online as alterObj.sql
SQL> -- Create a simple object type with two attributes and two
SQL> -- methods.
SQL> CREATE OR REPLACE TYPE Dummy AS OBJECT (
  2    f1 NUMBER,
  3    f2 NUMBER,
  4    MEMBER PROCEDURE Method1(x IN VARCHAR2),
  5    MEMBER FUNCTION Method2 RETURN DATE
  6  );
  7  /
Type created.

SQL> -- Create the type body.
SQL> CREATE OR REPLACE TYPE BODY Dummy AS
  2    MEMBER PROCEDURE Method1(x IN VARCHAR2) IS
  3    BEGIN
  4      NULL;
  5    END Method1;
  6
  6    MEMBER FUNCTION Method2 RETURN DATE IS
  7    BEGIN
  8      RETURN SYSDATE;
  9    END Method2;
 10  END;
 11  /
Type body created.

SQL> SELECT object_name, object_type, status
  2    FROM user_objects
  3    WHERE object_name = 'DUMMY';
OBJECT_NAME          OBJECT_TYPE      STATUS
-------------------- ---------------- -------
DUMMYOBJ             TYPE             VALID
DUMMYOBJ             TYPE BODY        VALID

SQL> -- Alter the type to add a new method.  This invalidates
SQL> -- the type body.
SQL> ALTER TYPE Dummy REPLACE AS OBJECT (
```

```
 2    f1 NUMBER,
 3    f2 NUMBER,
 4    MEMBER PROCEDURE Method1(x IN VARCHAR2),
 5    MEMBER FUNCTION Method2 RETURN DATE,
 6    MEMBER PROCEDURE Method3
 7  );
Type altered.

SQL> SELECT object_name, object_type, status
 2    FROM user_objects
 3    WHERE object_name = 'DUMMY';


OBJECT_NAME           OBJECT_TYPE       STATUS
--------------------  ----------------  -------
DUMMYOBJ              TYPE              VALID
DUMMYOBJ              TYPE BODY         INVALID
```

DROP TYPE

The DROP TYPE command is used to drop an object type or type body. The syntax is

DROP TYPE [*schema.*]*type_name* [FORCE];

If the FORCE option is not specified, then the object type will be dropped only if there is no other schema object that depends on it. If FORCE is specified, then the object is dropped, possibly invalidating any dependent objects.

DROP TYPE BODY can be used to drop just the body of an object type, leaving the specification and any dependent objects intact. It is defined with

DROP TYPE BODY [*schema.*]*type_name;*

Object Dependencies

Similar to records, an object type can have another object type embedded within it. Consider the following declarations:

```
-- Available online as objDepend.sql
CREATE OR REPLACE TYPE Obj1 AS OBJECT (
  f1 NUMBER,
  f2 VARCHAR2(10),
  f3 DATE
);

CREATE OR REPLACE TYPE Obj2 AS OBJECT (
```

```
    f1 DATE,
    f2 CHAR(1)
);

CREATE OR REPLACE TYPE Obj3 AS OBJECT (
  a Obj1,
  b Obj2
);
```

Note that **Obj3** has attributes of type **Obj1** and **Obj2**. As a result of this, **Obj3** depends on both **Obj1** and **Obj2**, in the same way that a procedure can depend on a table. Because of this, it is illegal to drop or alter either **Obj1** or **Obj2** without first dropping **Obj3**. Consider the following SQL*Plus session:

```
-- Available online as part of objDepend.sql
SQL> -- This will fail, since Obj3 depends on Obj1 and Obj2
SQL> DROP TYPE Obj1;
DROP TYPE Obj1
*
ERROR at line 1:
ORA-02303: cannot drop or replace a type with type or table dependents

SQL> -- But if we drop Obj3 first:
SQL> DROP TYPE Obj3;
Type dropped.

SQL> -- Then it will succeed.
SQL> DROP TYPE Obj1;
Type dropped.
```

NOTE
If an object has an attribute that is a reference to a different object type, it also depends on that type. Likewise, if an object table is defined for a particular type, the object type depends on the table. Object references and object tables are discussed in the next chapter.

Summary

This chapter began with a general discussion of object-oriented design methodologies and how Oracle implements such a paradigm with object types. We discussed the syntax for defining object types and methods, including MAP and ORDER methods and STATIC methods, available in Oracle8*i*. In the next chapter, we will see how objects can be stored in the database, and manipulated using SQL.

CHAPTER 13

Objects in the Database

I n Chapter 12, we discussed how you can create and use object types and object instances in PL/SQL. However, that is only half of the story. The true benefit of Oracle8's object functionality comes from the ability to store objects in the database. In this chapter, we will discuss different ways of storing and referencing objects, as well as how to treat relational data using the object model.

Objects in Oracle8

Oracle **8**
and higher

The object features that we have examined in Chapter 12 are very similar to the features of any object-oriented design language. Issues such as declaring, creating, and initializing objects, and invoking methods are common to any object framework, as well as any object language such as C++ or Java. Oracle8 extends this framework by allowing objects to be stored in the database and accessed through SQL or PL/SQL. This capability adds persistence to objects.

Object Locations

Objects can be found in different places in an Oracle8 application: stored in a database table, declared locally in a PL/SQL block, or kept in a client-side cache. An object has different properties, and different operations are allowed on it, depending on where the object is located. An application will typically move objects between these locations as part of its execution. The following sections describe these locations, and Table 13-1 summarizes this discussion.

Transient Objects

All of the objects that we examined in the previous chapter are examples of transient objects. A *transient object* is local to a PL/SQL block, and is deallocated when the variable holding it is no longer visible. Transient objects are not stored in the database, and thus cannot last beyond the life of a database session. The following SQL*Plus session illustrates several transient objects:

```
-- Available online as transObjects.sql
SQL> DECLARE
  2    v_Point1 Point := Point(0, 0);
  3  BEGIN
  4    DBMS_OUTPUT.PUT_LINE('Point 1 is ' || v_Point1.toString);
  5    -- v_Point1 will no longer be visible after this block, and so
  6    -- will be deallocated.
  7  END;
  8  /
```

```
Point 1 is (0, 0)
PL/SQL procedure successfully completed.

SQL> CREATE OR REPLACE PACKAGE PointPkg AS
  2     v_Point2 Point := Point(-7, -8);
  3   END PointPkg;
  4   /
Package created.

SQL> -- Because v_Point2 is in a package header, it will last until
SQL> -- the end of the session.  For example, we can refer to it in
SQL> -- another anonymous block:
SQL> BEGIN
  2     DBMS_OUTPUT.PUT_LINE(
  3       'Point 2 is ' || PointPkg.v_Point2.toString);
  4   END;
  5   /
Point 2 is (-7, -8)
PL/SQL procedure successfully completed.
```

NOTE

*See Chapter 12 for the declaration of the **Point** object type. It can also be found in **Point.sql** online with the code for Chapter 12.*

Transient Objects	Persistent Objects	Client Objects
Contain instances that are local to a PL/SQL block or package	Contain instances that are stored in a database table	Contain instances that are stored in the client cache of an OCI or Pro*C program
Are manipulated using PL/SQL statements	Are manipulated using SQL statements	Are manipulated using OCI or Pro*C statements
Cannot have references to them	Can have references to them (row objects only)	Can have references to them
Exist as long as the PL/SQL variable referring to them is visible	Exist until they are explicitly deleted from the database	Exist until they are flushed from the cache

TABLE 13-1. *Object Locations*

Like a PL/SQL variable of a scalar type, transient objects are manipulated using PL/SQL statements. SQL statements are used to store transient objects in the database, and thus make them persistent.

Persistent Objects

A *persistent object* is an object that is stored in the database and is available until it is explicitly deleted. Persistent objects are stored in database tables, just like the predefined scalar types (NUMBER, VARCHAR2, DATE, and so on). Like scalar types, they are manipulated using DML commands. There are two different ways of storing an object in a table—as a column or row object.

COLUMN OBJECTS   A *column object* is stored as a database column, like the scalar types. To create a table with a column object, simply use the object type for the column type in the table CREATE statement. A table can have a combination of scalar and column object types. For example, given the **Polygon** type which we examined in Chapter 12, we can create a table that stores **Polygon**s as follows:

```
-- Available online as part of objTables.sql
CREATE TABLE shapes (
   key          NUMBER PRIMARY KEY,
   shape_type VARCHAR2(20),   -- square, triangle, etc.
   shape        Polygon);
```

NOTE
*The **objTables.sql** script (available as part of the online distribution) creates all of the tables described in the objects and LOB chapters. **objTables.sql** redefines many of the example tables in this book (including **students** and **classes**). The new tables are used in the objects (Chapters 12 and 13), collections (Chapter 14), and LOB chapters (Chapters 15 and 16 on the CD-ROM included with this book). **objTables.sql** requires that the object types that we examined in Chapter 12 be created first.*

The **shapes** table has three columns, two of which (**key** and **shape_type**) are scalar types, and one of which (**shape**) is an object type. We can therefore insert some rows into **shapes** as follows:

```
-- Available online as part of objTables.sql
INSERT INTO shapes VALUES
  (shapes_seq.NEXTVAL, 'square',
   Polygon('Square A', 4,
          PointList(Point(1, 1), Point(1, -1),
                   Point(-1, -1), Point(-1, 1))));
INSERT INTO shapes VALUES
  (shapes_seq.NEXTVAL, 'trapezoid',
   Polygon('Trapezoid A', 4,
          PointList(Point(1, 1), Point(1, 2),
                   Point(2, 3), Point(3, 3))));
INSERT INTO shapes VALUES
  (shapes_seq.NEXTVAL, 'trapezoid',
   Polygon('Trapezoid B', 4,
          PointList(Point(-4, -3), Point(-1, -1),
                   Point(2, -1), Point(-4, -3))));
INSERT INTO shapes VALUES
  (shapes_seq.NEXTVAL, 'star',
   Polygon('Star A', 5,
          PointList(Point(-1, -2), Point(0, 1), Point(1, -2),
                   Point(-1.5, 0), Point(1.5, 0))));
```

Note that the constructor is used to insert the object type. Tables with column objects cannot be viewed under the relational model.

TIP
Although tables with column objects cannot generally be viewed with the relational model, SQL*Plus will format column objects in a query in a readable form, as shown in the following:

```
SQL> SELECT *
  2      FROM shapes
  3      WHERE key = 100;
KEY SHAPE_TYPE SHAPE(NAME, NUM_POINTS, POINTS(X, Y))
---- ---------- --------------------------------------------------------
 100 square      POLYGON('Square A', 4, POINTLIST(POINT(1, 1), POINT(1,
                 -1), POINT(-1, -1), POINT(-1, 1)))
```

ROW OBJECTS   A *row object*, on the other hand, takes up an entire database row. The row contains only the object and no other columns. A table defined like this is known as an *object table*, and is created using the syntax

   CREATE TABLE *table_name* OF *object_type*;

where *table_name* is the name of the table to be created, and *object_type* is the type of the row object. For example, given the **Student**, **Class**, and **Room** objects that we examined in Chapter 12, we can create the **students**, **classes**, and **rooms** object tables with the following declarations:

```
-- Available online as part of objTables.sql
CREATE TABLE students OF Student;
CREATE TABLE rooms OF Room;
CREATE TABLE classes OF Class;
```

   Each row of an object table contains an instantiation of its object type. Thus, only objects of that type can be inserted into the table. The following example shows some sample INSERT statements into each of the three tables. Note the use of the constructors for the object types.

```
-- Available online as part of objTables.sql
-- Two inserts into the students table
INSERT INTO students
  VALUES (Student(student_sequence.NEXTVAL, 'Scott', 'Smith',
                  'Computer Science', 11));
INSERT INTO students
  VALUES (Student(student_sequence.NEXTVAL, 'Margaret', 'Mason',
                  'History', 4));

-- Two inserts into the rooms table
INSERT INTO rooms VALUES
  (Room(room_sequence.NEXTVAL, 'Building 7', 201, 1000,
   'Large Lecture Hall'));
INSERT INTO rooms VALUES
  (Room(room_sequence.NEXTVAL, 'Building 6', 101, 500,
   'Small Lecture Hall'));

-- And two inserts into the classes table
INSERT INTO classes VALUES
  (Class('HIS', 101, 'History 101', 30, 11, 4, NULL));
INSERT INTO classes VALUES
  (Class('HIS', 301, 'History 301', 30, 0, 4, NULL));
```

An object table is very similar to a standard relational table. In fact, all relational operations will work for an object table. For example, we can also insert into the **students** object table with the following statements:

```
-- Available online as part of objTables.sql
INSERT INTO students(id, first_name, last_name, major,
                     current_credits)
   VALUES (student_sequence.NEXTVAL, 'Timothy', 'Taller',
        'History', 4);
INSERT INTO students(id, first_name, last_name, major,
                     current_credits)
   VALUES (student_sequence.NEXTVAL, 'Barbara', 'Blues',
        'Economics', 7);
```

The column list is optional, just like an INSERT into a relational table. This feature makes it easier to migrate to Oracle8 from Oracle7. Many relational tables can be re-created as object tables, and existing applications can be used against them without change. New applications can be written to use the object constructor and any methods defined for the object. For more information on viewing relational data as object data, and vice versa, see the Oracle documentation.

Client Objects

The third location for object instances is inside a client cache, and these objects are known as *client objects*. The client cache is available inside Pro*C or OCI programs, and it allows you to manipulate objects using embedded commands or OCI calls. Client objects can be manipulated with SQL statements or by navigating between object references. For more information on the client cache and how to use it, see either the *Pro*C/C++ Precompiler Programmer's Guide* or the *Oracle Call Interface Programming Guide*.

Object Identifiers and Object References

An *object identifier* (OID) is a unique locator for certain types of persistent objects. Similar to a ROWID, which uniquely identifies a row, an object identifier uniquely identifies an object. There are two types of OIDs in Oracle8 and Oracle8*i*. For an object table, Oracle will generate an OID for each row object. These types of OIDs are guaranteed to be unique across the entire Oracle8 universe—it is impossible for two objects to have the same system-generated OID. Furthermore, once a system-generated OID is created it will not be used again, even if the object it identifies is deleted. An OID is an internally defined structure that has the capacity for 2^{128} different values. The second type of object identifier is one created for an object view, which allows you to view a relational table (or tables) as if it were an object table. In this case, the OID is created from the primary keys of the table(s) making up the view. For more information on object views, see the Oracle documentation.

Only row objects and rows in object views have OIDs. Neither column objects nor transient objects (those local to a PL/SQL block) have OIDs. If an object has an OID, then you can construct a *reference* to it. An object reference is a pointer to an object, and not the object itself. The syntax for declaring an object reference in a declarative section or table definition is

variable_or_column_name REF *object_type*;

where *variable_or_column_name* is the name of the object reference, and *object_type* is the object type. For example, the **Class** object type contains a reference to a **Room**:

```
-- Available online as part of objTypes.sql
CREATE OR REPLACE TYPE Class AS OBJECT (
   department       CHAR(3),
   course           NUMBER(3),
   description      VARCHAR2(2000),
   max_students     NUMBER(3),
   current_students NUMBER(3),
   num_credits      NUMBER(1),
   roomP            REF Room
);
```

Object references can be used in PL/SQL blocks and in SQL statements by using the VALUE and REF operators, defined later in this chapter. They can also be used to implement referential integrity constraints. For more information, see "REFs and Referential Integrity," later in this chapter.

Dependencies Between Object Types and Tables

Just like other types of database objects, object types and tables can have dependencies. Specifically, an object table will depend on the object type on which it is created, and a table with column objects will likewise depend on its object type. These types of dependencies are illustrated by the following SQL*Plus session:

```
-- Available online as dropObjects.sql
SQL> -- First create two object types.
SQL> CREATE OR REPLACE TYPE RowObject AS OBJECT (
  2    attributeA NUMBER
```

```
  3  );
  4  /
Type created.

SQL> CREATE OR REPLACE TYPE ColObject AS OBJECT (
  2    attributeB NUMBER
  3  );
  4  /

Type created.

SQL> -- Now create tables referencing the types.
SQL> CREATE TABLE RowTable OF RowObject;
Table created.

SQL> CREATE TABLE ColTable (
  2    theObject ColObject
  3  );
Table created.

SQL> -- Dropping the types will yield errors.
SQL> DROP TYPE RowObject;
DROP TYPE RowObject
*
ERROR at line 1:
ORA-02303: cannot drop or replace a type with type or table dependents

SQL> DROP TYPE ColObject;
DROP TYPE ColObject
*
ERROR at line 1:
ORA-02303: cannot drop or replace a type with type or table dependents

SQL> -- Forcing it will work, but invalidate the tables.
SQL> DROP TYPE RowObject FORCE;
Type dropped.

SQL> DROP TYPE ColObject FORCE;
Type dropped.

SQL> SELECT object_name, object_type, status
  2    FROM user_objects
  3    WHERE object_name IN ('COLTABLE', 'ROWTABLE');
OBJECT_NAME      OBJECT_TYPE      STATUS
---------------  ---------------  -------
ROWTABLE         TABLE            INVALID
COLTABLE         TABLE            INVALID
```

Objects and SQL

In many ways, objects behave the same as scalars with regard to DML statements. For example, you can select an object from a database table into a variable of the same type, or update an object table using an object in the WHERE clause. All DML operations on tables that contain either row or column objects operate the same as relational DML operations. They operate within a transaction and have the same read-consistency and rollback issues. In the following sections, we will discuss the specifics of using SQL to access different types of objects in various ways.

Accessing Column Objects

SQL statements that reference column objects behave just like SQL statements on purely relational tables. SELECT, INSERT, UPDATE, and DELETE statements can reference PL/SQL variables as well as newly created and initialized objects. The following example illustrates various DML operations on the **shapes** table:

```
-- Available online as part of colObjects.sql
DECLARE
    -- A cursor that will select shapes whose type matches the
    -- given pattern.
    CURSOR c_Shapes(p_ShapePattern IN VARCHAR2) IS
      SELECT *
      FROM shapes
      WHERE shape_type LIKE p_ShapePattern;

    v_Star1   Polygon;
    v_Star2   Polygon;
    v_Point   Point;
    v_Key     shapes.key%TYPE;
BEGIN
    -- Print out the circumference of all the trapezoids, using a
    -- cursor to query the rows.
    FOR v_Rec IN c_Shapes('trapezoid') LOOP
      -- v_Rec.shape is a Polygon.  Thus we can call the Circumference
      -- method on it.
      DBMS_OUTPUT.PUT_LINE('Circumference of ' ||
        v_Rec.shape.name || ' is ' || v_Rec.shape.Circumference);
    END LOOP;

    -- SELECT the star into v_Star1, and print it out.
    SELECT shape, key
      INTO v_Star1, v_Key
      FROM shapes
      WHERE shape_type = 'star';
    DBMS_OUTPUT.PUT('v_Star1 is ');
    v_Star1.Print;
```

```
-- Copy v_Star1 to v_Star2, and then get the point at the end of
-- v_Star1 and multiply it by 5.  Put the new point at the end of
-- v_Star2, rename it, and insert it into the table.
v_Star2 := v_Star1;
v_Point := v_Star1.returnPoint;
v_Point := v_Point.Times(5);
v_Star2.removePoint;
v_Star2.changeName('Star B');
v_Star2.insertPoint(v_Point);

-- Insert the new polygon into the table.
INSERT INTO shapes (key, shape_type, shape)
  VALUES (v_Key + 1, 'star', v_Star2);
DBMS_OUTPUT.PUT_LINE('After INSERT, stars are:');
FOR v_Rec IN c_Shapes('star%') LOOP
  v_Rec.shape.Print;
END LOOP;

-- Change the type of the newly inserted polygon.
UPDATE shapes
  SET shape_type = 'star 2'
  WHERE shape = v_Star2;
DBMS_OUTPUT.NEW_LINE;
DBMS_OUTPUT.PUT_LINE('After UPDATE, stars are:');
FOR v_Rec IN c_Shapes('star%') LOOP
  v_Rec.shape.Print;
END LOOP;

-- And finally delete the new row.
DELETE FROM shapes
  WHERE key = v_Key + 1;
DBMS_OUTPUT.NEW_LINE;
DBMS_OUTPUT.PUT_LINE('After DELETE, stars are:');
FOR v_Rec IN c_Shapes('star%') LOOP
  v_Rec.shape.Print;
END LOOP;
END;
```

This example selects a column object into a PL/SQL variable, manipulates it by calling methods on it, and then puts it back into the table with SQL commands. The output from this code is as follows:

```
Circumference of Trapezoid A is
  6.2426406871192851464050661726290942357l
Circumference of Trapezoid B is
  12.930106595800747957117008356335933013G9
```

```
v_Star1 is Polygon Star A: Total endpoints: 5
   1: (-1, -2)
   2: (1.5, 0)
   3: (-1.5, 0)
   4: (1, -2)
   5: (0, 1)
After INSERT, stars are:
Polygon Star A: Total endpoints: 5
   1: (-1, -2)
   2: (1.5, 0)
   3: (-1.5, 0)
   4: (1, -2)
   5: (0, 1)
Polygon Star B: Total endpoints: 5
   1: (-1, -2)
   2: (1.5, 0)
   3: (-1.5, 0)
   4: (1, -2)
   5: (0, 5)

After UPDATE, stars are:
Polygon Star A: Total endpoints: 5
   1: (-1, -2)
   2: (1.5, 0)
   3: (-1.5, 0)
   4: (1, -2)
   5: (0, 1)
Polygon Star B: Total endpoints: 5
   1: (-1, -2)
   2: (1.5, 0)
   3: (-1.5, 0)
   4: (1, -2)
   5: (0, 5)

After DELETE, stars are:
Polygon Star A: Total endpoints: 5
   1: (-1, -2)
   2: (1.5, 0)
   3: (-1.5, 0)
   4: (1, -2)
   5: (0, 1)

PL/SQL procedure successfully completed.
```

Column Object Attributes

All of the SQL statements in the example in the previous section manipulated the
column object in **shapes** in its entirety—they did not refer to the attributes of the

shape column directly. All of the attribute access was done through PL/SQL. In order to access an attribute of a column object from SQL, you must use a correlation identifier for the table. A *correlation identifier* (also known as an *alias*) for a table is an alternate name for a table in a statement, found directly after the table name.

For example, suppose we want to change the name of the shape with key 100 from "Square A" to "The Square." We could do this with the following PL/SQL block, which selects the object from the table, changes the **name** attribute, and updates the row again:

```
-- Available online as part of colObjects.sql
DECLARE
  v_Shape Polygon;
BEGIN
  SELECT shape
    INTO v_Shape
    FROM shapes
    WHERE key = 100;

  v_Shape.name := 'The Square';

  UPDATE shapes
    SET shape = v_Shape
    WHERE key = 100;
END;
```

If we want to use a single UPDATE statement to accomplish the same thing, we need a correlation identifier for the table, as follows:

```
-- Available online as part of colObjects.sql
SQL> UPDATE shapes s
  2    SET s.shape.name = 'The Square'
  3    WHERE key = 100;
1 row updated.
```

References to attributes of a column object must use the correlation identifier (**s** in the above example) rather than the column name directly. Using the column name results in an ORA-904 error:

```
-- Available online as part of colObjects.sql
SQL> UPDATE shapes
  2    SET shape.name = 'The Square'
  3    WHERE key = 100;
  SET shape.name = 'The Square'
           *
ERROR at line 2:
ORA-00904: invalid column name
```

Unlike other uses of correlation identifiers (such as joins), you cannot use the table name directly:

```
-- Available online as part of colObjects.sql
SQL> UPDATE shapes
  2     SET shapes.shape.name = 'The Square'
  3     WHERE key = 100;
   SET shapes.shape.name = 'The Square'
                    *
ERROR at line 2:
ORA-00904: invalid column name
```

Correlation identifiers must be used wherever the attribute is referenced inside a SQL statement. The following example illustrates the correlation identifier on a query that references two attributes as part of the select list:

```
-- Available online as part of colObjects.sql
SQL> SELECT s.shape.name, s.shape.points
  2     FROM shapes s
  3     WHERE shape_type = 'triangle';

SHAPE.NAME SHAPE.POINTS(X, Y)
---------- ------------------------------------------------------------
Triangle A POINTLIST(POINT(2, 2), POINT(5, 3), POINT(1, 7))
Triangle B POINTLIST(POINT(0, 0), POINT(0, -10), POINT(3, 1))
Triangle C POINTLIST(POINT(-2, -2), POINT(-5, -3), POINT(-1, -7))
```

Column Object Methods

A correlation identifier is also necessary to refer to a method of a column object within a SQL statement. For example, the following query will return the first point in each of the shapes stored in the **shapes** table:

```
-- Available online as part of colObjects.sql
SQL> SELECT shape_type, s.shape.name "Name",
  2              s.shape.ReturnPoint(1) "First Point"
  3     FROM shapes s;
SHAPE_TYPE           Name             First Point(X, Y)
-------------------- ---------------- --------------------
square               Square A         POINT(1, 1)
square               Square B         POINT(6, 6)
square               Square C         POINT(0, 0)
square               Square D         POINT(10, 10)
square               Square E         POINT(1, 1)
triangle             Triangle A       POINT(2, 2)
triangle             Triangle B       POINT(0, 0)
triangle             Triangle C       POINT(-2, -2)
```

```
trapezoid          Trapezoid A     POINT(1, 1)
trapezoid          Trapezoid B     POINT(-4, -3)
star               Star A          POINT(-1, -2)
11 rows selected.
```

NOTE
The method must have the necessary purity levels asserted (with pragma RESTRICT_REFERENCES) in Oracle8 to be called from SQL. Oracle8i relaxes this requirement, but the method must still meet certain restrictions. For more information, see Chapter 5.

METHODS WITH NO PARAMETERS   When you call a method with no parameters from PL/SQL, the parentheses for the call are optional. However, they are required when calling the method from SQL. Without them, Oracle will return the ORA-904 error, even if a correlation identifier is present:

 -- Available online as part of colObjects.sql
```
SQL> SELECT s.shape.name "Name", s.shape.Circumference
  2    FROM shapes s;
SELECT s.shape.name "Name", s.shape.Circumference
                                           *
ERROR at line 1:
ORA-00904: invalid column name
```

If we include parentheses, the query succeeds:

 -- Available online as part of colObjects.sql
```
SQL> SELECT s.shape.name "Name", s.shape.Circumference()
  2    FROM shapes s;

Name              S.SHAPE.CIRCUMFERENCE()
---------------   -----------------------
Square A                                8
Square B                                4
Square C                               28
Square D                               80
Square E                                8
Triangle A                      13.918151
Triangle B                      24.564032
Triangle C                      13.918151
Trapezoid A                     6.2426407
Trapezoid B                     12.930107
Star A                           15.72768
11 rows selected.
```

STATIC METHODS Static methods can be called from SQL statements as well. Since static methods are referenced using the object type itself rather than an instance of them, they are called similar to a packaged function, as the following example illustrates.

```
-- Available online as part of colObjects.sql
SQL> SELECT Polygon.CreateSquare('New Square', 1.5,
  2                                 Point(0.5, 0.5)) "A Square"
  3    FROM dual;
A Square(NAME, NUM_POINTS, POINTS(X, Y))
---------------------------------------------------------------
POLYGON('New Square', 4, POINTLIST(POINT(-0, 1), POINT(1, 1),
                            POINT(1, -0), POINT(-0, -0)))
```

Accessing Row Objects

As we saw in the previous section, column objects are accessed in SQL (in their entirety) simply by the column name (with a correlation identifier). This cannot be done for row objects, however, since the entire row is the object and there is no column name to use. Attributes of row objects can be accessed directly through relational statements, or a correlation identifier can be used to access their methods.

Relational Access

An object table can be accessed using standard DML statements on it, referencing the attributes of each row object as if they were columns in a standard relational table. This method works for all DML statements and queries and is illustrated by the following example.

```
-- Available online as part of rowObjects.sql
SQL> DECLARE
  2    v_FirstName students.first_name%TYPE;
  3    v_LastName students.last_name%TYPE;
  4    v_Major students.major%TYPE;
  5  BEGIN
  6    -- We can do all types of DML operations on the students object
  7    -- table, as if it were a relational table.
  8
  9    -- Insert a new student
 10    INSERT INTO students(ID, first_name, last_name)
 11      VALUES (20000, 'Yvonne', 'Yeller');
 12
 13    -- Update the new row to modify the major
 14    UPDATE students
 15      SET major = 'Nutrition'
 16      WHERE ID = 20000;
 17
```

```
18     -- Select the new row into PL/SQL variables, and print it out.
19     SELECT first_name, last_name, major
20       INTO v_FirstName, v_LastName, v_Major
21       FROM students
22       WHERE last_name = 'Yeller';
23     DBMS_OUTPUT.PUT_LINE(
24       'Name: ' || v_FirstName || ' ' || v_LastName);
25     DBMS_OUTPUT.PUT_LINE('Major: ' || v_Major);
26
27     -- And delete the row.
28     DELETE FROM students
29       WHERE first_name = 'Yvonne';
30  END;
31  /
Name: Yvonne Yeller
Major: Nutrition
PL/SQL procedure successfully completed.
```

%ROWTYPE AND OBJECT TABLES   Although %TYPE works the same for both relational and object tables (as the previous example illustrated), %ROWTYPE does not. For a relational table, %ROWTYPE will return a PL/SQL record with fields that match the table columns. For an object table, %ROWTYPE will return the object type, which will not match the same types of queries. For example, consider the following tables:

```
-- Available online as part of rowtype.sql
-- Create a relational table.
CREATE TABLE rel_tab (
  f1 NUMBER,
  f2 VARCHAR2(50)
);

-- Create an object table with the same attributes.
CREATE TYPE objType AS OBJECT (
  f1 NUMBER,
  f2 VARCHAR2(50)
);
CREATE TABLE obj_tab OF objType;

BEGIN
  -- Insert some rows into both tables.
  FOR v_Count IN 1..5 LOOP
    INSERT INTO rel_tab VALUES
      (v_Count, 'Relational row ' || v_Count);
    INSERT INTO obj_tab VALUES
      (v_Count, 'Object row ' || v_Count);
  END LOOP;
END;
```

Querying both tables from SQL*Plus yields the same result, as we would expect.

-- **Available online as part of rowtype.sql**

```
SQL> SELECT * FROM rel_tab;
       F1 F2
--------- --------------------
        1 Relational row 1
        2 Relational row 2
        3 Relational row 3
        4 Relational row 4
        5 Relational row 5

SQL> SELECT * FROM obj_tab;
       F1 F2
--------- --------------------
        1 Object row 1
        2 Object row 2
        3 Object row 3
        4 Object row 4
        5 Object row 5
```

If we select from both tables into a %ROWTYPE variable, we get the following:

-- **Available online as part of rowtype.sql**

```
SQL> -- Use %ROWTYPE to select from the relational table.
SQL> DECLARE
  2    v_Row rel_tab%ROWTYPE;
  3    CURSOR c_AllRows IS
  4      SELECT * FROM rel_tab;
  5  BEGIN
  6    OPEN c_AllRows;
  7    LOOP
  8      FETCH c_AllRows INTO v_Row;
  9      EXIT WHEN c_AllRows%NOTFOUND;
 10      DBMS_OUTPUT.PUT_LINE(v_Row.f1 || ' ' || v_Row.f2);
 11    END LOOP;
 12    CLOSE c_AllRows;
 13  END;
 14  /
1 Relational row 1
2 Relational row 2
3 Relational row 3
4 Relational row 4
5 Relational row 5
PL/SQL procedure successfully completed.

SQL> -- Use %ROWTYPE to select from the object table.  This fails with
SQL> -- a type mismatch error.
```

```
SQL> DECLARE
  2     v_Row obj_tab%ROWTYPE;
  3     CURSOR c_AllRows IS
  4       SELECT * FROM obj_tab;
  5   BEGIN
  6     OPEN c_AllRows;
  7     LOOP
  8       FETCH c_AllRows INTO v_Row;
  9       EXIT WHEN c_AllRows%NOTFOUND;
 10       DBMS_OUTPUT.PUT_LINE(v_Row.f1 || ' ' || v_Row.f2);
 11     END LOOP;
 12     CLOSE c_AllRows;
 13   END;
 14   /
DECLARE
*
ERROR at line 1:
ORA-06550: line 8, column 26:
PLS-00386: type mismatch found at 'V_ROW' between FETCH cursor and
           INTO variables
ORA-06550: line 8, column 5:
PL/SQL: SQL Statement ignored
```

The second example fails with a type mismatch error because **obj_tab%ROWTYPE** returns an **objType** object, rather than a PL/SQL record. We can resolve this error by changing the query to select the object type from the table, rather than the columns. This is done with the VALUE operator:

```
-- Available online as part of rowtype.sql
SQL> DECLARE
  2     v_Row obj_tab%ROWTYPE;
  3     CURSOR c_AllRows IS
  4       SELECT VALUE(o) FROM obj_tab o;
  5   BEGIN
  6     OPEN c_AllRows;
  7     LOOP
  8       FETCH c_AllRows INTO v_Row;
  9       EXIT WHEN c_AllRows%NOTFOUND;
 10       DBMS_OUTPUT.PUT_LINE(v_Row.f1 || ' ' || v_Row.f2);
 11     END LOOP;
 12     CLOSE c_AllRows;
 13   END;
 14   /
1 Object row 1
2 Object row 2
3 Object row 3
4 Object row 4
5 Object row 5
PL/SQL procedure successfully completed.
```

For more information on using the VALUE operator, see "Refs and Values," later in this chapter.

TIP
If you use a cursor FOR loop, which implicitly declares the loop counter into which the query will be fetched, PL/SQL will declare the loop counter as an object rather than a record, avoiding the error. This is illustrated by the following SQL*Plus session:

```
-- Available online as part of rowtype.sql
SQL> DECLARE
  2    CURSOR c_AllRows IS
  3      SELECT * FROM obj_tab;
  4  BEGIN
  5    FOR v_Row IN c_AllRows LOOP
  6      DBMS_OUTPUT.PUT_LINE(v_Row.f1 || ' ' || v_Row.f2);
  7    END LOOP;
  8  END;
  9  /
1 Object row 1
2 Object row 2
3 Object row 3
4 Object row 4
5 Object row 5
PL/SQL procedure successfully completed.
```

Object Access

Accessing the attributes of a row object can be done using relational statements, as we saw in the last section. If you want to get the object itself (to call a method, for example), you can use the correlation identifier for the table, just like a column object. The correlation ID can be used to reference both attributes and methods of the row object. The following example illustrates how to access the attributes.

```
-- Available online as part of rowObjects.sql
SQL> UPDATE students s
  2    SET s.major = 'Food and Diet'
  3    WHERE s.major = 'Nutrition';
2 rows updated.
```

A more useful application for correlation IDs, however, is to call a method on the row object. Again, like column objects, parentheses are required, even if the method takes no parameters:

```
-- Available online as part of rowObjects.sql
SQL> SELECT s.FormattedName()
  2      FROM students s;
S.FORMATTEDNAME()
----------------------------------
Scott Smith
Margaret Mason
Joanne Junebug
Manish Murgatroid
Patrick Poll
Timothy Taller
Barbara Blues
David Dinsmore
Ester Elegant
Rose Riznit
Rita Razmataz
Shay Shariatpanahy
12 rows selected.
```

Returning the entire object (or a reference to it) in a query, rather than the individual columns, can be done using the VALUE and REF operators. We will discuss these in the next section.

Refs and Values

One of the main differences between a row and column object is that a row object has an OID, and hence, you can construct a reference to it. Remember that an object reference is not the object itself—it is a pointer to the object, similar to a REF CURSOR. SQL provides several operators that allow you to construct and navigate object references, as well as to retrieve row objects themselves. PL/SQL provides similar functionality through the UTL_REF package.

SQL Operators and Predicates

SQL defines operators that can manipulate objects and object references. These are summarized in the following table and described in the following sections. All of these operators (VALUE, REF, DEREF, and IS DANGLING) can be used in SQL statements only. They cannot be used in procedural statements.

Operator	Valid In	Description
VALUE	Select lists of queries on object tables, WHERE clauses	Given a correlation ID, returns the row object for that table
REF	Select lists of queries on object tables, WHERE clauses	Given a correlation ID, returns a reference to the row object for that table
DEREF	Select lists of queries on object tables, WHERE clauses	Given a reference, returns the object to which it points
IS [NOT] DANGLING	WHERE clauses	Predicate that determines if an object reference does or does not point to a valid object

VALUE   The syntax for VALUE is

VALUE(*corr_ID*)

where *corr_ID* is a correlation identifier in a SQL statement. VALUE returns the row object for the table that *corr_ID* represents. The following example illustrates some uses of VALUE:

```
-- Available online as part of valueOp.sql
DECLARE
  v_Room Room;
  CURSOR c_Building7 IS
    SELECT VALUE(r)
      FROM rooms r
      WHERE building = 'Building 7'
      FOR UPDATE;
BEGIN
  -- Loop through all of the rooms in Building 7, and add
  -- 100 to the number of seats in each.
  OPEN c_Building7;
  LOOP
    FETCH c_Building7 INTO v_Room;
    EXIT WHEN c_Building7%NOTFOUND;

    v_Room.number_seats := v_Room.number_seats + 100;
    UPDATE rooms r
      SET r = v_Room
      WHERE CURRENT OF c_Building7;
  END LOOP;
  CLOSE c_Building7;
END;
```

As this example shows, the result set of a query returning VALUE is a set of objects, not a set of attributes. VALUE is used mainly in the select list of a query on an object table; it is an error to use it for a query on a relational table. You can generally use the correlation ID itself in other clauses, rather than VALUE.

VALUE can also be used in a WHERE clause when compared to the return value of a subquery or a PL/SQL variable, as the following illustrates.

```
SQL> SELECT * FROM rooms r1
  2    WHERE VALUE(r1) = (SELECT VALUE(r2)
  3                       FROM rooms r2
  4                       WHERE ID = 20007);
       ID BUILDING        ROOM_NUMBER NUMBER_SEATS DESCRIPTION
--------- --------------- ----------- ------------ -------------------
    20007 Building 7              300           75 Discussion Room D

SQL> DECLARE
  2      v_Room1 Room;
  3      v_Room2 Room;
  4   BEGIN
  5      -- Select into v_Room1
  6      SELECT VALUE(r)
  7        INTO v_Room1
  8        FROM rooms r
  9        WHERE ID = 20007;
 10
 10      -- And use VALUE in the where clause, compared to v_Room1.
 11      SELECT VALUE(r)
 12        INTO v_Room2
 13        FROM rooms r
 14        WHERE VALUE(r) = v_Room1;
 15
 15      v_Room2.Print;
 16   END;
 17   /
Room ID:20007 is located in Building 7, room 300, and has 75 seats.
PL/SQL procedure successfully completed.
```

REF   While VALUE returns a row object itself, REF returns a reference to the row object. The syntax is the same as VALUE, namely,

REF(*corr_ID*)

where *corr_ID* is the correlation identifier for an object table. REF is illustrated by the following example:

```
-- Available online as refOp.sql
SQL> DECLARE
  2    v_RoomRef    REF Room;
  3    v_Building   rooms.building%TYPE;
  4    v_RoomNumber rooms.room_number%TYPE;
  5  BEGIN
  6    -- Select a reference to the room, not the room itself.
  7    SELECT REF(r)
  8      INTO v_RoomRef
  9      FROM rooms r
 10     WHERE ID = 20000;
 11
 12    -- Use the reference in the WHERE clause of a query
 13    SELECT building, room_number
 14      INTO v_Building, v_RoomNumber
 15      FROM rooms r
 16     WHERE REF(r) = v_RoomRef;
 17
 18    DBMS_OUTPUT.PUT_LINE('Queried ' || v_Building || ', room ' ||
 19                         v_RoomNumber || ' using REF');
 20  END;
 21  /
Queried Building 7, room 201 using REF
PL/SQL procedure successfully completed.
```

DEREF   Given an object reference, the DEREF operator will return the object to which it points. The syntax is

DEREF(*object_ref*)

where *object_ref* is an object reference, either contained in a PL/SQL variable or selected from a table. DEREF is illustrated by the following example:

```
-- Available online as derefOp.sql
SQL> DECLARE
  2    v_StudentRef REF Student;
  3    CURSOR c_CSMajors IS
  4      SELECT REF(s)
  5        FROM students s
  6        WHERE s.major = 'Computer Science';
  7
```

```
  8     v_Student Student;
  9   BEGIN
 10     -- Query all of the Computer Science majors.
 11     OPEN c_CSMajors;
 12     LOOP
 13       FETCH c_CSMajors INTO v_StudentRef;
 14       EXIT WHEN c_CSMajors%NOTFOUND;
 15
 16       -- Get the row object itself using DEREF.
 17       SELECT DEREF(v_StudentRef)
 18         INTO v_Student
 19         FROM dual;
 20
 21       DBMS_OUTPUT.PUT_LINE(v_Student.FormattedName);
 22     END LOOP;
 23     CLOSE c_CSMajors;
 24
 25     -- DEREF(REF(corr_ID)) is the same as VALUE.
 26     SELECT DEREF(REF(s))
 27       INTO v_Student
 28       FROM students s
 29       WHERE ID = 10010;
 30     DBMS_OUTPUT.PUT_LINE('Selected ' || v_Student.FormattedName ||
 31                          ' using DEREF(REF)');
 32   END;
 33   /
Scott Smith
Joanne Junebug
Shay Shariatpanahy
Selected Rita Razmataz using DEREF(REF)
PL/SQL procedure successfully completed.
```

IS DANGLING   If the object to which a REF points is deleted, the REF is said to be *dangling*, since it now points to a nonexistent object. It is illegal to dereference a dangling REF. You can check for it, however, using the IS DANGLING predicate, as the following example illustrates.

```
-- Available online as dangling.sql
SQL> DECLARE
  2     v_Ref REF Class;
  3     v_Result VARCHAR2(20);
  4   BEGIN
  5     SELECT REF(c)
  6       INTO v_Ref
  7       FROM classes c
```

```
 8        WHERE c.department = 'ECN'
 9        AND c.course = 101;
10
10     -- Delete the row, which invalidates v_Ref.
11     DELETE FROM classes
12        WHERE department = 'ECN';
13
13     -- So, this query should return a row.
14     SELECT 'Dangling!'
15        INTO v_Result
16        FROM dual
17        WHERE v_Ref IS DANGLING;
18     DBMS_OUTPUT.PUT_LINE(v_Result);
19   END;
20   /
Dangling!
PL/SQL procedure successfully completed.
```

Navigating REFs in PL/SQL

The operators that we examined in the previous sections cannot be used in procedural statements, as the following example illustrates.

```
-- Available online as part of utl_ref.sql
SQL> DECLARE
  2     v_StudentRef REF STUDENT;
  3   BEGIN
  4     IF v_StudentRef IS DANGLING THEN
  5        NULL;
  6     END IF;
  7   END;
  8   /
DECLARE
*
ERROR at line 1:
ORA-06550: line 4, column 6:
PLS-00204: function or pseudo-column 'IS DANGLING' may be used inside
           a SQL statement only
ORA-06550: line 4, column 3:
PL/SQL: Statement ignored
```

The UTL_REF package allows you to perform operations on object references in PL/SQL. The package has four procedures, described in the following table and in more detail in the following sections. Each of the procedures takes an object reference, which can be of any object type. All of the procedures execute with the privilege set of the caller, not the definer (invoker's rights). We will see an example of UTL_REF following the descriptions.

Procedure	Description
SELECT_OBJECT	Retrieves an object from an object table, given a reference to it
LOCK_OBJECT	Locks and optionally retrieves an object from an object table, given a reference to it
UPDATE_OBJECT	Updates an object in an object table, given a reference to it
DELETE_OBJECT	Deletes an object from an object table, given a reference to it

SELECT_OBJECT   The SELECT_OBJECT procedure will return an object, given a reference to it. It is defined with

```
PROCEDURE SELECT_OBJECT(ref IN REF object_type,
                        object IN OUT object_type);
```

where *ref* is a reference to an object of *object_type*, and *object* is a variable of *object_type*. Both *ref* and *object* should be defined with the same object type. SELECT_OBJECT is similar to the following SQL statement:

```
SELECT VALUE(ot)
  INTO object
  FROM object_table ot
  WHERE REF(ot) = ref;
```

assuming that *object_table* is a table of *object_type*.

LOCK_OBJECT   LOCK_OBJECT will lock a row object (in the sense of SELECT FOR UPDATE) and optionally return it. It has two overloaded versions, defined with

```
PROCEDURE LOCK_OBJECT(ref IN REF object_type);

PROCEDURE LOCK_OBJECT(ref IN REF object_type,
                      object IN OUT object_type);
```

where *ref* is a reference to an object of *object_type*, and *object* is a variable of *object_type*. Both *ref* and *object* should be defined with the same object type. LOCK_OBJECT is similar to the following SQL statement:

```
SELECT VALUE(ot)
  INTO object
  FROM object_table ot
  WHERE REF(ot) = ref
  FOR UPDATE;
```

assuming that *object_table* is a table of *object_type*. The object pointed to by *ref* is locked regardless of the version of LOCK_OBJECT used, and the lock will persist until the transaction is committed. There is no equivalent of SELECT FOR UPDATE NOWAIT, so LOCK_OBJECT will block until the lock is available.

UPDATE_OBJECT   UPDATE_OBJECT will update an object, given a reference to it. It is defined with

```
PROCEDURE UPDATE_OBJECT(ref IN REF object_type,
                        object IN object_type);
```

where *ref* is a reference to an object of *object_type*, and *object* is a variable of *object_type*. Both *ref* and *object* should be defined with the same object type. UPDATE_OBJECT is similar to the following SQL statement:

```
UPDATE object_table ot
  SET VALUE(ot) = object
  WHERE REF(ot) = ref;
```

assuming that *object_table* is a table of *object_type*. The object does not have to be locked to perform the update.

DELETE_OBJECT   The final procedure in UTL_REF is DELETE_OBJECT. Given a reference to an object, it will delete it from the table. It is defined with

```
PROCEDURE DELETE_OBJECT(ref IN REF object_type);
```

where *ref* is a reference to an object of *object_type*. It is similar to a SQL statement like

```
DELETE FROM object_table ot
  WHERE REF(ot) = ref;
```

assuming that *object_table* is a table of *object_type*. The object does not have to be locked to perform the delete.

UTL_REF EXAMPLE   The following example illustrates some uses of UTL_REF. Note that the procedures can be called for objects and references of different types (as long as they are consistent within calls). All of the calls to UTL_REF are procedural.   .

```
-- Available online as part of utl_ref.sql
DECLARE
  CURSOR c_MajorRefs(p_Major IN VARCHAR2) IS
    SELECT REF(s)
      FROM students s
      WHERE major = p_Major;
  v_StudentRef REF Student;
  v_Student Student;
  v_Music100Ref REF Class;
  v_Music100 Class;
BEGIN
  -- Get a reference to Music 100, and then the object itself.
  SELECT REF(c)
    INTO v_Music100Ref
    FROM classes c
    WHERE department = 'MUS'
    AND course = 100;
  UTL_REF.SELECT_OBJECT(v_Music100Ref, v_Music100);

  -- Loop over all of the Music students, and update their
  -- credits for Music 100.
  OPEN c_MajorRefs('Music');
  LOOP
    FETCH c_MajorRefs INTO v_StudentRef;
    EXIT WHEN c_MajorRefs%NOTFOUND;

    -- Retrieve the student pointed to by the ref
    UTL_REF.SELECT_OBJECT(v_StudentRef, v_Student);

    -- Update their credits, and then update the row
    v_Student.UpdateCredits(v_Music100);
    UTL_REF.UPDATE_OBJECT(v_StudentRef, v_Student);
  END LOOP;
END;
```

REFs and Referential Integrity

The relational version of the **classes** table contains a column **room_id**, which specifies the room in which a class is to be held. The **Class** object (and hence the **classes** object table) has a **RoomP** attribute, which is a pointer to the room. In this way, object references can be used similar to a foreign key integrity constraint. For

example, we can update the classes to point to their correct rooms with the
following SQL:

```
-- Available online as part of classesRooms.sql
DECLARE
  -- Represents the room ID for a particular class.
  TYPE t_ClassRoom IS RECORD (
    department classes.department%TYPE,
    course classes.course%TYPE,
    ID rooms.ID%TYPE);

  -- Collection that will contain all of the mappings.
  TYPE t_ClassRoomList IS TABLE OF t_ClassRoom
    INDEX BY BINARY_INTEGER;
  v_ClassRoomList t_ClassRoomList;

  v_RoomRef REF Room;
  -- Assigns to the specified element of the list.
  PROCEDURE AssignRoom(p_Index IN BINARY_INTEGER,
                       p_Department IN classes.department%TYPE,
                       p_Course IN classes.course%TYPE,
                       p_RoomID IN rooms.ID%TYPE) IS
  BEGIN
    v_ClassRoomList(p_Index).department := p_Department;
    v_ClassRoomList(p_Index).course := p_Course;
    v_ClassRoomList(p_Index).ID := p_RoomID;
  END AssignRoom;

BEGIN
  -- Load the list.
  AssignRoom(1, 'HIS', 101, 20000);
  AssignRoom(2, 'HIS', 301, 20004);
  AssignRoom(3, 'CS', 101, 20001 );
  AssignRoom(4, 'ECN', 203, 20002);
  AssignRoom(5, 'CS', 102, 20003);
  AssignRoom(6, 'MUS', 410, 20005);
  AssignRoom(7, 'ECN', 101, 20007);
  AssignRoom(8, 'NUT', 307, 20008);

  -- For each room assignment,
  FOR v_Index IN 1..v_ClassRoomList.COUNT LOOP
    -- Update the class with a pointer to the room.
    SELECT REF(r)
      INTO v_RoomRef
      FROM rooms r
      WHERE ID = v_ClassRoomList(v_Index).ID;
```

```
   UPDATE classes
     SET roomP = v_RoomRef
     WHERE department = v_ClassRoomList(v_Index).department
     AND course = v_ClassRoomList(v_Index).course;
   END LOOP;
END;
```

After we run the above block, we can print out the rooms for each class with the following:

-- Available online as part of classesRooms.sql

```
SQL> DECLARE
  2     v_Room Room;
  3     v_Class Class;
  4     CURSOR c_AllClasses IS
  5       SELECT VALUE(c)
  6         FROM classes c
  7         WHERE roomP IS NOT NULL;
  8  BEGIN
  9     OPEN c_AllClasses;
 10     LOOP
 11       FETCH c_AllClasses INTO v_Class;
 12       EXIT WHEN c_AllClasses%NOTFOUND;
 13
 13       -- Get the room first
 14       UTL_REF.SELECT_OBJECT(v_Class.roomP, v_Room);
 15
 15       -- And print out the information.
 16       DBMS_OUTPUT.PUT(v_Class.description || ' will be held in ');
 17       DBMS_OUTPUT.PUT_LINE(v_Room.description);
 18     END LOOP;
 19  END;
 20  /
History 101 will be held in Large Lecture Hall
History 301 will be held in Discussion Room C
Computer Science 101 will be held in Small Lecture Hall
Economics 203 will be held in Discussion Room A
Computer Science 102 will be held in Discussion Room B
Music 410 will be held in Music Practice Room
Economics 101 will be held in Discussion Room D
Nutrition 307 will be held in Discussion Room E
PL/SQL procedure successfully completed.
```

For more information on using REFs for referential integrity, see *Oracle8 Concepts.*

Other Object Issues

In this section, we will discuss some remaining issues that arise when using SQL to manipulate persistent objects. These include the use of the RETURNING clause, and how MAP and ORDER methods allow you to sort and compare stored objects.

RETURNING Clause

Oracle8 provides a new clause for INSERT, UPDATE and DELETE statements. RETURNING can be used to retrieve information from the newly inserted or updated row, without requiring an additional query. The syntax of the RETURNING clause is

RETURNING *select_list* INTO *into_list*;

where *select_list* is similar to a select list of a query, and *into_list* is the same as the INTO clause of a query. For example, if you are inserting an object into an object table, you can get a reference to the newly inserted object with the following:

```
-- Available online as return.sql
DECLARE
  v_Class REF Class;
BEGIN
  INSERT INTO CLASSES c VALUES
(Class('HIS', 101, 'History 101', 30, 0, 4, NULL))
    RETURNING REF(c) INTO v_Class;
END;
```

MAP and ORDER Methods

As we saw in Chapter 12, objects by default can be compared only for equality. There is no ordering defined for objects. However, you can define one with either a MAP or ORDER method. Besides allowing objects to be compared with PL/SQL, a MAP or ORDER method allows objects to be compared in SQL. This means that they can be used in an ORDER BY clause, for example.

```
-- Available online as orderBy.sql
SQL> -- This is possible because Room has a MAP method.
SQL> SELECT VALUE(r)
  2    FROM rooms r
  3    ORDER BY 1;
```

```
VALUE(R)(ID, BUILDING, ROOM_NUMBER, NUMBER_SEATS, DESCRIPTION)
-------------------------------------------------------------
ROOM(20000, 'Building 7', 201, 1000, 'Large Lecture Hall')
ROOM(20001, 'Building 6', 101, 500, 'Small Lecture Hall')
ROOM(20002, 'Building 6', 150, 50, 'Discussion Room A')
ROOM(20003, 'Building 6', 160, 50, 'Discussion Room B')
ROOM(20004, 'Building 6', 170, 50, 'Discussion Room C')
ROOM(20005, 'Music Building', 100, 10, 'Music Practice Room')
ROOM(20006, 'Music Building', 200, 1000, 'Concert Room')
ROOM(20007, 'Building 7', 300, 75, 'Discussion Room D')
ROOM(20008, 'Building 7', 310, 50, 'Discussion Room E')

9 rows selected.

SQL>
SQL> -- And this succeeds because Student has an ORDER method.
SQL> SELECT s.FormattedName()
  2      FROM students s
  3      ORDER BY VALUE(s);

S.FORMATTEDNAME()
-------------------------------------------------------------
Barbara Blues
David Dinsmore
Ester Elegant
Joanne Junebug
Margaret Mason
Manish Murgatroid
Patrick Poll
Rita Razmataz
Rose Riznit
Shay Shariatpanahy
Scott Smith
Timothy Taller
12 rows selected.

SQL> -- However, Class does not have either a MAP nor an ORDER method,
SQL> -- so we can't sort by a Class.
SQL> SELECT VALUE(c)
  2      FROM classes c
  3      ORDER BY 1;
SELECT VALUE(c)
            *
ERROR at line 1:
ORA-22950: cannot ORDER objects without MAP or ORDER method
```

As this example illustrates, you will receive an error if a sort is required and there is no MAP or ORDER method defined for the object.

Summary

In the past two chapters, we have examined the syntax and semantics of object types available with Oracle8 and Oracle8*i*. Chapter 12 covered the basics of object types, including how to declare attributes and methods. In this chapter, we discussed the implications of storing objects in the database, including different types of persistent objects, and how to access them from both SQL and PL/SQL. We will continue our discussion of user-defined types with collections in Chapter 14.

CHAPTER
14

Collections

t is often convenient in a PL/SQL program to manipulate many variables at once, as one unit. Datatypes like this are known as *collections*. PL/SQL 2 (with Oracle7) provided one collection type—an index-by table. Oracle8 adds two more collection types—nested tables and varrays. Each of these collection types can be thought of as an object type, with attributes and methods. In this chapter, we will discuss the features of all the collection types, as well as the enhancements to them available with Oracle8*i*.

Declaring and Using Collection Types

Two of the Oracle8 collection types have very similar structure, and are known collectively as *PL/SQL tables*. *Index-by tables* were first introduced in PL/SQL 2.0 (with Oracle7 Release 7.0), and were significantly enhanced in PL/SQL 2.3 (with Oracle7 Release 7.3). *Nested tables*, introduced with Oracle8, extend the functionality of index-by tables by adding extra collection methods (known as *table attributes* for index-by tables). Nested tables can also be stored in database tables (which is why they are called nested) and can be manipulated directly using SQL. Index-by tables, on the other hand, exist entirely within PL/SQL and cannot be stored directly in a database table.

NOTE
In Oracle7, index-by tables were known as PL/SQL tables. Oracle8 PL/SQL tables include both index-by and nested tables.

The third collection type is the varray. Varrays were introduced in Oracle8 and are similar to PL/SQL tables in how they are accessed. However, varrays are declared with a fixed number of elements, whereas PL/SQL tables have no declared upper limit.

In this section, we will examine how to declare and use all three collection types. The differences and similarities between them are summarized at the end of the section.

Index-By Tables

Index-by tables are syntactically similar to C or Java arrays. In order to declare an index-by table, you first define the table type within a PL/SQL block, and then declare a variable of this type. The general syntax for defining an index-by table type is

   TYPE *tabletype* IS TABLE OF *type* INDEX BY BINARY_INTEGER;

where *tabletype* is the name of the new type being defined, and *type* is a predefined type or a reference to a type via %TYPE. The following declarative section illustrates several different PL/SQL table types and variable declarations:

 `-- Available online as part of indexBy.sql`
```
DECLARE
  TYPE NameTab IS TABLE OF students.first_name%TYPE
    INDEX BY BINARY_INTEGER;
  TYPE DateTab IS TABLE OF DATE
    INDEX BY BINARY_INTEGER;
  v_Names NameTab;
  v_Dates DateTab;
```

NOTE
*The **INDEX BY BINARY_INTEGER** clause is required as part of the table definition. This clause is not present for nested tables.*

Once the type and the variable are declared, we can refer to an individual element in the PL/SQL table by using the syntax

   tablename(*index*)

where *tablename* is the name of a table and *index* is either a variable of type BINARY_INTEGER or a variable or expression that can be converted to a BINARY_INTEGER. Given the declarations for the different table types, we could continue the previous PL/SQL block with

 `-- Available online as part of indexBy.sql`
```
BEGIN
  v_Names(1) := 'Scott';
  v_Dates(-4) := SYSDATE - 1;
END;
```

A table reference, like a record or variable reference, is an lvalue, since it points to storage that has been allocated by the PL/SQL engine.

Index-By Tables vs. C or Java Arrays

Consider the following PL/SQL block, which creates an index-by table and assigns to some of its elements:

 `-- Available online as part of indexBy.sql`
```
DECLARE
  TYPE CharacterTab IS TABLE OF VARCHAR2(10)
```

```
      INDEX BY BINARY_INTEGER;
  v_Characters CharacterTab;
BEGIN
  -- Assign to three elements of the table.  Note that the key
  -- values are not sequential.
  v_Characters(0)  := 'Harold';
  v_Characters(-7) := 'Susan';
  v_Characters(3)  := 'Steve';
END;
```

Although assignment to table elements is syntactically similar to assignment to a C or Java array, index-by tables are implemented differently. An index-by table is similar to a database table, with two columns—**key** and **value**. The type of **key** is BINARY_INTEGER, and the type of **value** is whatever datatype is specified in the definition (VARCHAR2(10) in the previous example).

After executing the assignments in the previous block, the data structure of **v_Characters** will look like Table 14-1. There are several things to note about index-by tables that are illustrated by this example:

- Index-by tables are unconstrained. The only limit (other than available memory) on the number of rows is that the key is a BINARY_INTEGER, and is therefore constrained to the values that can be represented by the BINARY_INTEGER type (–2147483647 .. +2147483647).

- The elements in an index-by table are not necessarily in any particular order. Since they are not stored contiguously in memory like an array, elements can be inserted under arbitrary keys. (If you pass an index-by table from PL/SQL to a host array in C or Java, the elements should be numbered sequentially starting from 1.)

- The keys used for an index-by table don't have to be sequential. Any BINARY_INTEGER value or expression can be used for a table index.

- The only type allowed for the key is BINARY_INTEGER.

Key	Value
0	Harold
–7	Susan
3	Steve

TABLE 14-1. *Contents of* **v_Characters**

Nonexistent Elements

An assignment to element *i* in an index-by table actually creates element *i* if it does not already exist, similar to an INSERT operation on a database table. References to element *i* are likewise similar to a SELECT operation. In fact, if element *i* is referenced before it has been created, the PL/SQL engine will return "ORA-1403: no data found" just like a database table. This is illustrated by the following SQL*Plus session:

```
-- Available online as part of indexBy.sql
SQL> DECLARE
  2    TYPE NumberTab IS TABLE OF NUMBER
  3      INDEX BY BINARY_INTEGER;
  4    v_Numbers NumberTab;
  5  BEGIN
  6    -- Assign to several of the elements.
  7    FOR v_Count IN 1..10 LOOP
  8      v_Numbers(v_Count) := v_Count * 10;
  9    END LOOP;
 10
 10    -- And print them out
 11    DBMS_OUTPUT.PUT_LINE('Table elements: ');
 12    FOR v_Count IN 1..10 LOOP
 13      DBMS_OUTPUT.PUT_LINE('  v_Numbers(' || v_Count || '): ' ||
 14                           v_Numbers(v_Count));
 15    END LOOP;
 16
 16    -- Read from v_Numbers(11).  Since it hasn't been assigned a
 17    -- value, this will raise NO_DATA_FOUND.
 18    BEGIN
 19      DBMS_OUTPUT.PUT_LINE('v_Numbers(11): ' || v_Numbers(11));
 20    EXCEPTION
 21      WHEN NO_DATA_FOUND THEN
 22        DBMS_OUTPUT.PUT_LINE(
 23          'No data found reading v_Numbers(11)!');
 24    END;
 25  END;
 26  /
Table elements:
  v_Numbers(1): 10
  v_Numbers(2): 20
  v_Numbers(3): 30
  v_Numbers(4): 40
  v_Numbers(5): 50
  v_Numbers(6): 60
  v_Numbers(7): 70
  v_Numbers(8): 80
  v_Numbers(9): 90
```

```
   v_Numbers(10): 100
No data found reading v_Numbers(11)!
PL/SQL procedure successfully completed.
```

Elements can be deleted from an index-by table using the DELETE method, described later in this chapter in "Collection Methods."

Index-By Tables of Nonscalar Types

From PL/SQL version 2.0 through version 2.2, index-by tables could only hold scalar types (NUMBER, VARCHAR2, BOOLEAN, and so on). PL/SQL 2.3 allowed index-by tables of records. Oracle8 allowed index-by tables of any type, including object types.

These enhancements significantly add to the functionality of index-by tables, since only one table definition is required to hold information about all the fields of a database table. Prior to version 2.3, a separate table definition is required for each database field.

PL/SQL 2.3 and higher

INDEX-BY TABLES OF RECORDS   The following example illustrates an index-by table of records:

```
-- Available online as tabRecord.sql
DECLARE
   TYPE StudentTab IS TABLE OF students%ROWTYPE
     INDEX BY BINARY_INTEGER;
   /* Each element of v_Students is a record */
   v_Students StudentTab;
BEGIN
   /* Retrieve the record with id = 10,001 and store it into
      v_Students(10001). */
   SELECT *
     INTO v_Students(10001)
     FROM students
     WHERE id = 10001;

   /* Directly assign to v_Students(1). */
   v_Students(1).first_name := 'Larry';
   v_Students(1).last_name := 'Lemon';
END;
```

NOTE
students *must be defined as a relational table (with **relTables.sql**), and not as an object table (with **objTables.sql**) for this example.*

Since each element of this table is a record, we can refer to fields within this record with the syntax

table(*index*).*field*

as this example illustrates.

 INDEX-BY TABLES OF OBJECT TYPES   Oracle8 allows index-by tables of object types as well, as the following example illustrates:

```
-- Available online as tabObject.sql
DECLARE
  TYPE StudentTab IS TABLE OF Student
    INDEX BY BINARY_INTEGER;
  /* Each element of v_Students is an instance of the Student object
   * type. */
  v_Students StudentTab;
BEGIN
  /* Retrieve the record with id = 10,001 and store it into
     v_Students(10001). */
  SELECT VALUE(s)
    INTO v_Students(10001)
    FROM students s
    WHERE id = 10001;

  /* Directly assign to v_Students(1).  First we have to initialize
   * the object type. */
  v_Students(1) := Student(NULL, NULL, NULL, NULL, NULL);
  v_Students(1).first_name := 'Larry';
  v_Students(1).last_name := 'Lemon';
END;
```

NOTE
students *must be defined as an object table (with* ***objTables.sql****), and not as a relational table (with* ***relTables.sql****) for this example. See Chapters 12 and 13 for more information on object types and how to create the* ***students*** *object table.*

Nested Tables

Oracle8 and higher   The basic functionality of a nested table is the same as an index-by table. A nested table can be thought of as a database table with two columns—**key** and **value**, as we saw in the previous section. Elements can be deleted from the middle of a nested table, leaving a sparse table with nonsequential keys, like index-by tables. However, nested tables must be created with sequential keys. Furthermore, nested tables can be stored in the database while index-by tables cannot. The maximum number of rows in a nested table is 2G.

The syntax for creating a nested table type is

TYPE *table_name* is TABLE OF *table_type* [NOT NULL];

where *table_name* is the name of the new type, and *table_type* is the type of each element in the nested table. *Table_type* can be a user-defined object type, or can be an expression using %TYPE, but cannot be BOOLEAN, NCHAR, NCLOB, NVARCHAR2, REF CURSOR, TABLE, or VARRAY. If NOT NULL is present, then elements of the nested table cannot be null.

NOTE
The only syntactic difference between index-by tables and nested tables is the presence or absence of the INDEX BY BINARY_INTEGER clause. If this clause is not present, then the type is a nested table type. If this clause is present, then the type is an index-by table type.

The following declarative section shows some valid nested table declarations:

```
-- Available online as part of nested.sql
DECLARE
    -- Define a nested table type based on an object type
    TYPE ClassesTab IS TABLE OF Class;

    -- A nested table type based on %ROWTYPE
    TYPE StudentsTab IS TABLE OF students%ROWTYPE;

    -- Variables of the above types
    v_ClassList ClassesTab;
    v_StudentList StudentsTab;
```

NOTE
*The **Class** object type is defined in Chapter 12 and is available online as part of **objTypes.sql**.*

Nested Table Initialization

When an index-by table is created, but does not yet have any elements, it is simply empty, rather than NULL. However, when a nested table is declared, but does not yet have any elements (as in the preceding block), it is initialized to be atomically NULL, like an object type. If you try to add an element to a NULL nested table, the error "ORA-6531: Reference to uninitialized collection," which corresponds to the predefined exception COLLECTION_IS_NULL, is raised. Continuing the previous example, the following execution section will raise this error:

```
-- Available online as part of nested.sql
BEGIN
  -- This assignment will raise COLLECTION_IS_NULL because
  -- v_ClassList is atomically NULL.
  v_ClassList(1) :=
    Class('HIS', 101, 'History 101', 30, 0, 4, NULL);
END;
```

So how do you initialize a nested table? This can be done by using the constructor. Like an object type constructor, the constructor for a nested table has the same name as the table type itself. However, it has a varying number of arguments, each of which should be type compatible with the table element type. The arguments become elements of the table, starting sequentially with index 1. The following example illustrates the use of nested table constructors:

```
-- Available online as tabConstruct.sql
SQL> DECLARE
  2    TYPE NumbersTab IS TABLE OF NUMBER;
  3
  4    -- Create a table with one element.
  5    v_Tab1 NumbersTab := NumbersTab(-1);
  6
  7    -- Create a table with five elements.
  8    v_Primes NumbersTab := NumbersTab(1, 2, 3, 5, 7);
  9
 10    -- Create a table with no elements.
 11    v_Tab2 NumbersTab := NumbersTab();
 12  BEGIN
 13    -- Assign to v_Tab1(1). This will replace the value already
 14    -- in v_Tab(1), which was initialized to -1.
 15    v_Tab1(1) := 12345;
 16
 17    -- Print out the contents of v_Primes.
 18    FOR v_Count IN 1..5 LOOP
 19      DBMS_OUTPUT.PUT(v_Primes(v_Count) || ' ');
 20    END LOOP;
```

```
21    DBMS_OUTPUT.NEW_LINE;
22  END;
23  /
1 2 3 5 7
PL/SQL procedure successfully completed.
```

EMPTY TABLES   Note the declaration of **v_Tab2** in the preceding block:

```
-- Create a table with no elements.
v_Tab2 t_NumbersTab := t_NumbersTab();
```

v_Tab2 is initialized by calling the constructor with no arguments. This creates a table that has no elements, but is not atomically NULL. The following SQL*Plus session illustrates this:

```
-- Available online as nullTable.sql
SQL> DECLARE
  2    TYPE WordsTab IS TABLE OF VARCHAR2(50);
  3
  3    -- Create a NULL table.
  4    v_Tab1 WordsTab;
  5
  5    -- Create a table with one element, which itself is NULL.
  6    v_Tab2 WordsTab := WordsTab();
  7  BEGIN
  8    IF v_Tab1 IS NULL THEN
  9      DBMS_OUTPUT.PUT_LINE('v_Tab1 is NULL');
 10    ELSE
 11      DBMS_OUTPUT.PUT_LINE('v_Tab1 is not NULL');
 12    END IF;
 13
 13    IF v_Tab2 IS NULL THEN
 14      DBMS_OUTPUT.PUT_LINE('v_Tab2 is NULL');
 15    ELSE
 16      DBMS_OUTPUT.PUT_LINE('v_Tab2 is not NULL');
 17    END IF;
 18  END;
 19  /
v_Tab1 is NULL
v_Tab2 is not NULL
PL/SQL procedure successfully completed.
```

Adding Elements to an Existing Table

Although a table is unconstrained, you cannot assign to an element that does not yet exist, and would thus cause the table to increase in size. If you attempt to do this, PL/SQL will raise the error "ORA-6533: Subscript beyond count," which is equivalent to the SUBSCRIPT_BEYOND_COUNT predefined exception. This is illustrated by the following SQL*Plus session:

```
-- Available online as tabAssign.sql
SQL> DECLARE
  2     TYPE NumbersTab IS TABLE OF NUMBER;
  3     v_Numbers NumbersTab := NumbersTab(1, 2, 3);
  4  BEGIN
  5     -- v_Numbers was initialized to have 3 elements. So the
  6     -- following assignments are all legal.
  7     v_Numbers(1) := 7;
  8     v_Numbers(2) := -1;
  9
 10     -- However, this assignment will raise ORA-6533.
 11     v_Numbers(4) := 4;
 12  END;
 13  /
DECLARE
*
ERROR at line 1:
ORA-06533: Subscript beyond count
ORA-06512: at line 11
```

TIP
You can increase the size of a nested table by using the EXTEND method, described later in this chapter.

Varrays

Oracle **8**
and higher

A *varray* (variable length array) is a datatype very similar to an array in C or Java. Syntactically, a varray is accessed similar to a nested or index-by table. However, a varray has a fixed upper bound on its size, specified as part of the type declaration. Rather than being a sparse data structure with no upper bound, elements are inserted into a varray starting at index 1, up to the maximum length declared in the varray type. The maximum size of a varray is 2G.

The storage for a varray is the same as a C or Java array; namely, the elements are stored contiguously in memory. This is different from the storage for a nested or index-by table, which are more like a database table.

Declaring a Varray
A varray type is declared using the syntax

TYPE *type_name* IS {VARRAY | VARYING ARRAY} (*maximum_size*)
OF *element_type* [NOT NULL];

where *type_name* is the name of the new varray type, *maximum_size* is an integer specifying the maximum number of elements in the varray, and *element_type* is a PL/SQL scalar, record, or object type. The *element_type* can be specified using %TYPE, but cannot be BOOLEAN, NCHAR, NCLOB, NVARCHAR2, REF CURSOR, TABLE, or another VARRAY type. The following declarative section shows some legal varray types:

-- Available online as part of varray.sql
```
DECLARE
    -- Some valid varray types.
    -- This is a list of numbers, each of which is constrained to
    -- be not null.
    TYPE NumberList IS VARRAY(10) OF NUMBER(3) NOT NULL;

    -- A list of PL/SQL records.
    TYPE StudentList IS VARRAY(100) OF students%ROWTYPE;

    -- A list of Class objects.
    TYPE ClassList IS VARRAY(20) OF Class;
```

Varray Initialization

Similar to tables, varrays are initialized using a constructor. The number of arguments passed to the constructor becomes the initial length of the varray, and must be less than or equal to the maximum length specified in the varray type. The following SQL*Plus session illustrates this:

-- Available online as varConstruct.sql
```
SQL> DECLARE
  2      -- Define a VARRAY type.
  3      TYPE Numbers IS VARRAY(20) OF NUMBER(3);
  4
  4      -- Declare a NULL varray.
  5      v_NullList Numbers;
  6
  6      -- This varray has 2 elements.
  7      v_List1 Numbers := Numbers(1, 2);
  8
  8      -- This varray has one element, which itself is NULL.
  9      v_List2 Numbers := Numbers(NULL);
 10  BEGIN
 11      IF v_NullList IS NULL THEN
 12          DBMS_OUTPUT.PUT_LINE('v_NullList is NULL');
 13      END IF;
 14
```

```
14    IF v_List2(1) IS NULL THEN
15      DBMS_OUTPUT.PUT_LINE('v_List2(1) is NULL');
16    END IF;
17  END;
18  /
v_NullList is NULL
v_List2(1) is NULL
PL/SQL procedure successfully completed.
```

Manipulating Varray Elements

Like nested tables, the initial size of a varray is set by the number of elements used in the constructor when it is declared. Assignments to elements outside this range will raise the error "ORA-6533: subscript beyond count," just like a nested table. The following SQL*Plus session illustrates this:

```
-- Available online as part of varAssign.sql
SQL> DECLARE
  2    TYPE Strings IS VARRAY(5) OF VARCHAR2(10);
  3
  4    -- Declare a varray with three elements.  The maximum size of
  5    -- this type is five elements.
  6    v_List Strings := Strings('Scott', 'David', 'Urman');
  7  BEGIN
  8    -- Subscript between 1 and 3, so this is a legal assignment.
  9    v_List(2) := 'DAVID';
 10
 11    -- Subscript out of range, raises ORA-6533.
 12    v_List(4) := '!!!';
 13  END;
 14  /
DECLARE
*
ERROR at line 1:
ORA-06533: Subscript beyond count
ORA-06512: at line 12
```

TIP

Like nested tables, the size of a varray can be increased using the EXTEND method, described later in this chapter. Unlike a nested table, which does not have a maximum size, a varray cannot be extended past the maximum size declared for the varray type.

Assignments to elements outside the maximum size of the varray, or attempts to extend the varray past the maximum size, will raise the error "ORA-6522: subscript beyond limit," which is equivalent to the predefined exception SUBSCRIPT_OUTSIDE_LIMIT. This is illustrated by the following:

```
-- Available online as part of varAssign.sql
SQL> DECLARE
  2     TYPE Strings IS VARRAY(5) OF VARCHAR2(10);
  3     -- Declare a varray with four elements,
  4     v_List Strings :=
  5        Strings('One', 'Two', 'Three', 'Four');
  6  BEGIN
  7     -- Subscript between 1 and 4, so this is legal.
  8     v_List(2) := 'TWO';
  9
 10     -- Extend the varray to 5 elements and set the value of
 11     -- the 5th element.
 12     v_List.EXTEND;
 13     v_List(5) := 'Five';
 14
 15     -- Attempt to extend the varray to 6 elements.  This will
 16     -- raise ORA-6532 .
 17     v_list.EXTEND;
 18  END;
 19  /
DECLARE
*
ERROR at line 1:
ORA-06532: Subscript outside of limit
ORA-06512: at line 17
```

Comparison Between Collection Types

This section describes some of the similarities and differences between the three collection types we have examined. Table 14-2 summarizes the behavior of the types, which are discussed in the following sections.

Index-By Tables	Nested Tables	Varrays
First available in Oracle7.0, enhanced in 7.3	First available in Oracle8	First available in Oracle8
Elements are accessed syntactically through parentheses	Elements are accessed syntactically through parentheses	Elements are accessed syntactically through parentheses

TABLE 14-2. *Collection Types*

Index-By Tables	Nested Tables	Varrays
Oracle 7.3 introduced table attributes for manipulation	Can use additional collection methods in addition to the 7.3 attributes	Can use additional collection methods in addition to the 7.3 attributes
Cannot be stored in database tables	Can be stored in database tables	Can be stored in database tables
Keys can be positive or negative	Keys must be positive	Keys must be positive
Can map to host arrays	Do not map to host arrays	Do not map to host arrays
Can be sparse with nonsequential key values	Can be sparse with nonsequential key values	Always have space allocated for each of the elements and have sequential key values
Cannot be atomically NULL	Can be atomically NULL	Can be atomically NULL
Referencing nonexistent elements raises NO_DATA_FOUND	Referencing nonexistent elements raises SUBSCRIPT_BEYOND_COUNT	Referencing nonexistent elements raises SUBSCRIPT_BEYOND_COUNT
Have no explicit maximum size	Have no explicit maximum size	Are constrained to a maximum size in the type definition— extending past this size raises SUBSCRIPT_OUTSIDE_LIMIT
Can be declared inside PL/SQL blocks only	Can be declared inside PL/SQL blocks, or outside with CREATE TYPE	Can be declared inside PL/SQL blocks, or outside with CREATE TYPE
Elements are assigned directly, without initialization	The table must be initialized before elements can be assigned	The varray must be initialized before elements can be assigned

TABLE 14-2. *Collection Types* (continued)

Varrays and Nested Tables
Varrays and nested tables have similarities:

■ Both types allow access to individual elements using subscript notation within PL/SQL.

■ Both types can be stored in database tables (when declared outside a PL/SQL block).

■ Collection methods can be applied to both.

However, there are also some differences:

- Varrays have a maximum size, while nested tables do not have an explicit maximum size.

- When used as a database column, varrays are stored inline with the containing table, while nested tables are stored in a separate table, which can have different storage characteristics. (In Oracle8*i*, varrays can be stored in LOBs, which can be separate from the containing table.)

- When stored in the database, varrays retain the ordering and subscript values for the elements, while nested tables do not.

Nested Tables and Index-by Tables

Nested tables are similar to the index-by tables found in Oracle7 in many ways, for example,

- Both table datatypes have the same structure.

- Individual elements in both are accessed using subscript notation.

- The methods available for nested tables include all of the 2.3 table attributes for index-by tables.

However, there are also several significant differences:

- Nested tables can be manipulated using SQL and can be stored in the database, while index-by tables cannot.

- Nested tables have a legal subscript range of 1..2147483647, while index-by tables have a range of –2147483647.. 2147483647. Thus, index-by tables can have negative subscripts, while nested tables cannot.

- Nested tables can be atomically NULL (testable with the IS NULL operator).

- Nested tables must be initialized and/or extended in order to add elements.

- Nested tables have additional methods available, such as EXTEND and TRIM (described in "Collection Methods," later in this chapter).

- PL/SQL will automatically convert between a host array and an index-by table, but cannot convert between a host array and a nested table. Conversion between a host array and a nested table must be done using the object interface.

Collection Methods

Nested tables and varrays are object types, and as such they have methods defined on them. By comparison, index-by tables have attributes (starting with PL/SQL 2.3). Both methods and attributes are invoked using the same syntax:

collection_instance.method_or_attribute

where *collection_instance* is a collection variable (not the type name), and *method_or_attribute* is one of the methods or attributes described in this section. These methods can be called only from procedural statements, and not from SQL statements.

All of the following examples assume the following declarations:

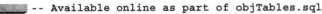

```
-- Available online as part of objTables.sql
CREATE OR REPLACE TYPE NumTab AS TABLE OF NUMBER;
CREATE OR REPLACE TYPE NumVar AS VARRAY(25) OF NUMBER;
CREATE OR REPLACE PACKAGE IndexBy AS
  TYPE NumTab IS TABLE OF NUMBER INDEX BY BINARY_INTEGER;
END IndexBy;
```

The methods are listed in Table 14-3, and are described in the following sections.

Method or Attribute	Return Type	Description	Valid for
EXISTS	BOOLEAN	Returns TRUE if the specified entry exists in the collection	Index-by tables, nested tables, varrays
COUNT	NUMBER	Returns the number of elements in a collection	Index-by tables, nested tables, varrays
LIMIT	NUMBER	Returns the maximum number of elements for a collection	Nested tables (always returns NULL), varrays

TABLE 14-3. *Collection Methods*

Method or Attribute	Return Type	Description	Valid for
FIRST & LAST	BINARY_INTEGER	Returns the index of the first (or last) element in a collection	Index-by tables, nested tables, varrays
NEXT & PRIOR	BINARY_INTEGER	Returns the index of the next (or prior) element, relative to a given element, in a collection	Index-by tables, nested tables, varrays
EXTEND	N/A	Adds elements to a collection	Nested tables, varrays (up to the maximum size for the type)
TRIM	N/A	Removes elements from the end of a collection	Nested tables, varrays
DELETE	N/A	Removes specified elements from a collection	Index-by tables, nested tables

Note: The methods that are valid for index-by tables require PL/SQL 2.3 or later.

TABLE 14-3. *Collection Methods* (continued)

EXISTS

EXISTS is used to determine whether the referenced element is present in the collection. The syntax is

EXISTS(*n*)

where *n* is an integer expression. It returns TRUE if the element specified by *n* exists, even if it is NULL. If *n* is out of range, EXISTS returns FALSE, rather than raising the SUBSCRIPT_OUTSIDE_LIMIT exception (for nested tables or varrays) or ORA-1403 (for index-by tables). EXISTS and DELETE can be used to maintain sparse nested tables. The following example illustrates the use of EXISTS:

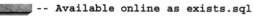

```
-- Available online as exists.sql
SQL> DECLARE
  2    v_NestedTable NumTab := NumTab(-7, 14.3, 3.14159, NULL, 0);
```

```
 3    v_Count BINARY_INTEGER := 1;
 4    v_IndexByTable IndexBy.NumTab;
 5  BEGIN
 6    -- Loop over v_NestedTable, and print out the elements, using
 7    -- EXISTS to indicate the end of the loop.
 8    LOOP
 9      IF v_NestedTable.EXISTS(v_Count) THEN
10        DBMS_OUTPUT.PUT_LINE(
11          'v_NestedTable(' || v_Count || '): ' ||
12          v_NestedTable(v_Count));
13        v_Count := v_Count + 1;
14      ELSE
15        EXIT;
16      END IF;
17    END LOOP;
18
18    -- Assign the same elements to the index-by table.
19    v_IndexByTable(1) := -7;
20    v_IndexByTable(2) := 14.3;
21    v_IndexByTable(3) := 3.14159;
22    v_IndexByTable(4) := NULL;
23    v_IndexByTable(5) := 0;
24
24    -- And do a similar loop.
25    v_Count := 1;
26    LOOP
27      IF v_IndexByTable.EXISTS(v_Count) THEN
28        DBMS_OUTPUT.PUT_LINE(
29          'v_IndexByTable(' || v_Count || '): ' ||
30          v_IndexByTable(v_Count));
31        v_Count := v_Count + 1;
32      ELSE
33        EXIT;
34      END IF;
35    END LOOP;
36  END;
37  /
v_NestedTable(1): -7
v_NestedTable(2): 14.3
v_NestedTable(3): 3.14159
v_NestedTable(4):
v_NestedTable(5): 0
v_IndexByTable(1): -7
v_IndexByTable(2): 14.3
v_IndexByTable(3): 3.14159
v_IndexByTable(4):
v_IndexByTable(5): 0
PL/SQL procedure successfully completed.
```

As this example shows, if element *n* of a collection contains NULL, EXISTS(*n*) will return TRUE. EXISTS can also be applied to an atomically NULL nested table or varray, in which case it will always return FALSE.

COUNT

COUNT returns the number of elements currently in a collection, as an integer. It takes no arguments and is valid wherever an integer expression is valid. The following SQL*Plus session illustrates the use of COUNT:

```
-- Available online as count.sql
SQL> DECLARE
  2    v_NestedTable NumTab := NumTab(1, 2, 3);
  3    v_Varray NumVar := NumVar(-1, -2, -3, -4);
  4    v_IndexByTable IndexBy.NumTab;
  5  BEGIN
  6    -- First add some elements to the index-by table.  Note that
  7    -- the index values are not sequential.
  8    v_IndexByTable(1) := 1;
  9    v_IndexByTable(8) := 8;
 10    v_IndexByTable(-1) := -1;
 11    v_IndexByTable(100) := 100;
 12
 13    -- And print out the counts.
 14    DBMS_OUTPUT.PUT_LINE(
 15      'Nested Table Count: ' || v_NestedTable.COUNT);
 16    DBMS_OUTPUT.PUT_LINE(
 17      'Varray Count: ' || v_Varray.COUNT);
 18    DBMS_OUTPUT.PUT_LINE(
 19      'Index-By Table Count: ' || v_IndexByTable.COUNT);
 20  END;
 21  /
Nested Table Count: 3
Varray Count: 4
Index-By Table Count: 4
PL/SQL procedure successfully completed.
```

For varrays, COUNT always equals LAST (described later in this section), since elements can't be deleted from a varray. However, elements can be deleted from the middle of a nested table, so COUNT could be different from LAST for a table. COUNT is useful when selecting a nested table from the database, since the number of elements is unknown at that point. Deleted elements are ignored by COUNT.

LIMIT

LIMIT returns the current maximum number of elements for a collection. Since nested tables have no maximum size, LIMIT always returns NULL when applied to a nested table. LIMIT is not valid for index-by tables. The following SQL*Plus session illustrates the use of LIMIT:

```
-- Available online as limit.sql
SQL> DECLARE
  2     v_Table NumTab := NumTab(1, 2, 3);
  3     v_Varray NumVar := NumVar(1234, 4321);
  4  BEGIN
  5     -- Output the limit and count for the collections.
  6     DBMS_OUTPUT.PUT_LINE('Varray limit: ' || v_Varray.LIMIT);
  7     DBMS_OUTPUT.PUT_LINE('Varray count: ' || v_Varray.COUNT);
  8     IF v_Table.LIMIT IS NULL THEN
  9       DBMS_OUTPUT.PUT_LINE('Table limit is NULL');
 10     ELSE
 11       DBMS_OUTPUT.PUT_LINE('Table limit: ' || v_Table.LIMIT);
 12     END IF;
 13     DBMS_OUTPUT.PUT_LINE('Table count: ' || v_Table.COUNT);
 14  END;
 15  /
Varray limit: 25
Varray count: 2
Table limit is NULL
Table count: 3
PL/SQL procedure successfully completed.
```

Note that the varray limit is 25, as defined in the CREATE TYPE statement, even though **v_Varray** currently contains only two elements. COUNT returns the current number of elements, as described in the previous section.

FIRST and LAST

FIRST returns the index of the first element of a collection, and LAST returns the index of the last element. For a varray, FIRST always returns 1 and LAST always returns the value of COUNT, since a varray is dense and elements cannot be deleted. FIRST and LAST can be used along with NEXT and PRIOR to loop through a collection, as illustrated by the example in the next section.

NEXT and PRIOR

NEXT and PRIOR are used to increment and decrement the key for a collection. The syntax is

NEXT(*n*)
PRIOR(*n*)

where *n* is an integer expression. NEXT(*n*) returns the key of the element immediately after the element at position *n*, and PRIOR(*n*) returns the key of the element immediately prior to the element at position *n*. If there is no next or prior element, NEXT and PRIOR will return NULL. The following SQL*Plus session illustrates how to use NEXT and PRIOR, along with FIRST and LAST, to loop through a nested table:

```
-- Available online as collectionLoops.sql
SQL> DECLARE
  2     TYPE CharTab IS TABLE OF CHAR(1);
  3     v_Characters CharTab :=
  4       CharTab('M', 'a', 'd', 'a', 'm', ',', ' ',
  5               'I', '''', 'm', ' ', 'A', 'd', 'a', 'm');
  6
  7     v_Index INTEGER;
  8  BEGIN
  9     -- Loop forwards over the table.
 10     v_Index := v_Characters.FIRST;
 11     WHILE v_Index <= v_Characters.LAST LOOP
 12       DBMS_OUTPUT.PUT(v_Characters(v_Index));
 13       v_Index := v_Characters.NEXT(v_Index);
 14     END LOOP;
 15     DBMS_OUTPUT.NEW_LINE;
 16
 17     -- Loop backwards over the table.
 18     v_Index := v_Characters.LAST;
 19     WHILE v_Index >= v_Characters.FIRST LOOP
 20       DBMS_OUTPUT.PUT(v_Characters(v_Index));
 21       v_Index := v_Characters.PRIOR(v_Index);
 22     END LOOP;
 23     DBMS_OUTPUT.NEW_LINE;
 24  END;
 25  /
Madam, I'm Adam
madA m'I ,madaM
PL/SQL procedure successfully completed.
```

FIRST, LAST, NEXT, and PRIOR work the same way for varrays and index-by tables as well.

EXTEND

EXTEND is used to add elements to the end of a nested table or varray. It is not valid for index-by tables. EXTEND has three forms:

EXTEND

EXTEND(*n*)

EXTEND(*n, i*)

EXTEND with no arguments simply adds a NULL element to the end of the collection, with index LAST+1. EXTEND(*n*) adds *n* NULL elements to the end of the table, while EXTEND(*n*, *i*) adds *n* copies of element *i* to the end of the table. If the collection has been created with a NOT NULL constraint, then only the last form can be used, since it does not add a null element.

Since a nested table does not have an explicit maximum size, you can call EXTEND with *n* as large as needed (the maximum size is 2G, subject to memory constraints). A varray, however, can be extended only up to its maximum declared size, so *n* can be (LIMIT – COUNT) at most. The following SQL*Plus session illustrates the use of EXTEND:

```
-- Available online as extend.sql
SQL> DECLARE
  2    v_NumbersTab NumTab := NumTab(1, 2, 3, 4, 5);
  3    v_NumbersList NumVar := NumVar(1, 2, 3, 4, 5);
  4  BEGIN
  5    BEGIN
  6      -- This assignment will raise SUBSCRIPT_BEYOND_COUNT, since
  7      -- v_NumbersTab has only 5 elements.
  8      v_NumbersTab(26) := -7;
  9    EXCEPTION
 10      WHEN SUBSCRIPT_BEYOND_COUNT THEN
 11        DBMS_OUTPUT.PUT_LINE(
 12          'ORA-6533 raised for assignment to v_NumbersTab(26)');
 13    END;
 14
 15    -- We can fix this by adding 30 additional elements to
 16    -- v_NumbersTab.
 17    v_NumbersTab.EXTEND(30);
 18
 19    -- And now do the assignment.
 20    v_NumbersTab(26) := -7;
 21
 22    -- For a varray, we can extend it only up to the maximum size
 23    -- (also given by LIMIT).  For example, the following will
 24    -- raise SUBSCRIPT_OUTSIDE_LIMIT:
 25    BEGIN
 26      v_NumbersList.EXTEND(30);
 27    EXCEPTION
 28      WHEN SUBSCRIPT_OUTSIDE_LIMIT THEN
 29        DBMS_OUTPUT.PUT_LINE(
 30          'ORA-6532 raised for v_NumbersList.EXTEND(30)');
 31    END;
 32
 33    -- But this is legal.
 34    v_NumbersList.EXTEND(20);
 35
 36    -- And we can now assign to the highest element in the varray.
```

```
37    v_NumbersList(25) := 25;
38  END;
39  /
ORA-6533 raised for assignment to v_NumbersTab(26)
ORA-6532 raised for v_NumbersList.EXTEND(30)
PL/SQL procedure successfully completed.
```

EXTEND operates on the internal size of a collection, which includes any deleted elements for a nested table. When an element is deleted (using the DELETE method, described later in this section), both the data and key are removed, leaving a gap in the keys. The following example illustrates the interaction between EXTEND and DELETE:

```
-- Available online as extendDelete.sql
DECLARE
  -- Initialize a nested table to 5 elements.
  v_Numbers NumTab := NumTab(-2, -1, 0, 1, 2);

  -- Local procedure to print out a table.
  -- Note the use of FIRST, LAST, and NEXT.
  PROCEDURE Print(p_Table IN NumTab) IS
    v_Index INTEGER;
  BEGIN
    v_Index := p_Table.FIRST;
    WHILE v_Index <= p_Table.LAST LOOP
      DBMS_OUTPUT.PUT('Element ' || v_Index || ': ');
      DBMS_OUTPUT.PUT_LINE(p_Table(v_Index));
      v_Index := p_Table.NEXT(v_Index);
    END LOOP;
  END Print;

BEGIN
  DBMS_OUTPUT.PUT_LINE('At initialization, v_Numbers contains');
  Print(v_Numbers);

  -- Delete element 3.  This removes the '0', but keeps a placeholder
  -- where it was.
  v_Numbers.DELETE(3);

  DBMS_OUTPUT.PUT_LINE('After delete, v_Numbers contains');
  Print(v_Numbers);

  -- Add 2 copies of element 1 onto the table.  This will add elements
  -- 6 and 7.
  v_Numbers.EXTEND(2, 1);
```

```
    DBMS_OUTPUT.PUT_LINE('After extend, v_Numbers contains');
    Print(v_Numbers);

    DBMS_OUTPUT.PUT_LINE('v_Numbers.COUNT = ' || v_Numbers.COUNT);
    DBMS_OUTPUT.PUT_LINE('v_Numbers.LAST = ' || v_Numbers.LAST);
END;
```

This example produces the following output. Note the value of COUNT and LAST after the DELETE and EXTEND operation.

```
At initialization, v_Numbers contains
Element 1: -2
Element 2: -1
Element 3: 0
Element 4: 1
Element 5: 2
After delete, v_Numbers contains
Element 1: -2
Element 2: -1
Element 4: 1
Element 5: 2
After extend, v_Numbers contains
Element 1: -2
Element 2: -1
Element 4: 1
Element 5: 2
Element 6: -2
Element 7: -2
v_Numbers.COUNT = 6
v_Numbers.LAST = 7
```

TRIM

TRIM is used to remove elements from the end of a nested table or varray. It has two forms, defined with

TRIM

TRIM(*n*)

With no arguments, TRIM removes one element from the end of the collection. Otherwise, *n* elements are removed. If *n* is greater than COUNT, the SUBSCRIPT_ BEYOND_COUNT exception is raised. After the TRIM, COUNT will be smaller, since the elements have been removed.

Similar to EXTEND, TRIM operates on the internal size of a collection, including any elements removed with DELETE. This is illustrated by the following example:

```
-- Available online as trim.sql
DECLARE
  -- Initialize a table to 7 elements.
  v_Numbers NumTab := NumTab(-3, -2, -1, 0, 1, 2, 3);

  -- Local procedure to print out a table.
  PROCEDURE Print(p_Table IN NumTab) IS
    v_Index INTEGER;
  BEGIN
    v_Index := p_Table.FIRST;
    WHILE v_Index <= p_Table.LAST LOOP
      DBMS_OUTPUT.PUT('Element ' || v_Index || ': ');
      DBMS_OUTPUT.PUT_LINE(p_Table(v_Index));
      v_Index := p_Table.NEXT(v_Index);
    END LOOP;
    DBMS_OUTPUT.PUT_LINE('COUNT = ' || p_Table.COUNT);
    DBMS_OUTPUT.PUT_LINE('LAST = ' || p_Table.LAST);
  END Print;

BEGIN
  DBMS_OUTPUT.PUT_LINE('At initialization, v_Numbers contains');
  Print(v_Numbers);

  -- Delete element 6.
  v_Numbers.DELETE(6);
  DBMS_OUTPUT.PUT_LINE('After delete , v_Numbers contains');
  Print(v_Numbers);

  -- Trim the last 3 elements.  This will remove the 2 and 3, but
  -- also remove the (now empty) spot where 1 was.
  v_Numbers.TRIM(3);
  DBMS_OUTPUT.PUT_LINE('After trim, v_Numbers contains');
  Print(v_Numbers);
END;
```

This example produces the following output:

```
At initialization, v_Numbers contains
Element 1: -3
Element 2: -2
Element 3: -1
Element 4: 0
Element 5: 1
Element 6: 2
```

```
Element 7: 3
COUNT = 7
LAST = 7
After delete , v_Numbers contains
Element 1: -3
Element 2: -2
Element 3: -1
Element 4: 0
Element 5: 1
Element 7: 3
COUNT = 6
LAST = 7
After trim, v_Numbers contains
Element 1: -3
Element 2: -2
Element 3: -1
Element 4: 0
COUNT = 4
LAST = 4
```

DELETE

DELETE will remove one or more elements from an index-by table or nested table. DELETE has no affect on a varray because of its fixed size (and in fact, it is illegal to call DELETE on a varray). DELETE has three forms:

DELETE

DELETE(*n*)

DELETE(*m*,*n*)

With no arguments, DELETE will remove the entire table. DELETE(*n*) will remove the element at index *n*, and DELETE(*m*,*n*) will remove all the elements between indexes *m* and *n*. After the DELETE, COUNT will be smaller, reflecting the new size of the table. If the element of the table to be deleted does not exist, DELETE will not raise an error, but will simply skip that element. The following example illustrates the use of DELETE:

```
-- Available online as delete.sql
DECLARE
  -- Initialize a table to 10 elements.
  v_Numbers NumTab := NumTab(10, 20, 30, 40, 50, 60, 70, 80, 90, 100);

  -- Local procedure to print out a table.
```

```
PROCEDURE Print(p_Table IN NumTab) IS
  v_Index INTEGER;
BEGIN
  v_Index := p_Table.FIRST;
  WHILE v_Index <= p_Table.LAST LOOP
    DBMS_OUTPUT.PUT('Element ' || v_Index || ': ');
    DBMS_OUTPUT.PUT_LINE(p_Table(v_Index));
    v_Index := p_Table.NEXT(v_Index);
  END LOOP;
  DBMS_OUTPUT.PUT_LINE('COUNT = ' || p_Table.COUNT);
  DBMS_OUTPUT.PUT_LINE('LAST = ' || p_Table.LAST);
END Print;

BEGIN
  DBMS_OUTPUT.PUT_LINE('At initialization, v_Numbers contains');
  Print(v_Numbers);

  -- Delete element 6.
  DBMS_OUTPUT.PUT_LINE('After delete(6), v_Numbers contains');
  v_Numbers.DELETE(6);
  Print(v_Numbers);

  -- Delete elements 7 through 9.
  DBMS_OUTPUT.PUT_LINE('After delete(7,9), v_Numbers contains');
  v_Numbers.DELETE(7,9);
  Print(v_Numbers);
END;
```

This example produces the following output:

```
At initialization, v_Numbers contains
Element 1: 10
Element 2: 20
Element 3: 30
Element 4: 40
Element 5: 50
Element 6: 60
Element 7: 70
Element 8: 80
Element 9: 90
Element 10: 100
COUNT = 10
LAST = 10
After delete(6), v_Numbers contains
Element 1: 10
Element 2: 20
Element 3: 30
```

```
Element 4: 40
Element 5: 50
Element 7: 70
Element 8: 80
Element 9: 90
Element 10: 100
COUNT = 9
LAST = 10
After delete(7,9), v_Numbers contains
Element 1: 10
Element 2: 20
Element 3: 30
Element 4: 40
Element 5: 50
Element 10: 100
COUNT = 6
LAST = 10
```

Collections in the Database

All of the examples we have examined so far involve the manipulation of collections in PL/SQL blocks. However, nested tables and varrays also can be stored in database tables. (Index-by tables cannot be stored in a database table.) In the following sections, we will discuss how to access and manipulate stored collections, as well as some of the implications.

Implications of Stored Collections

Storing collections in the database has implications with regard to the way that the table types need to be declared, and the syntax of creating tables with collection columns. We will examine these implications in this section.

Schema-Level Types

In order to store and retrieve a collection from a database table, the collection type must be known to both PL/SQL and SQL. This means that it cannot be local to a PL/SQL block, and instead should be declared using a CREATE TYPE statement, similar to an object type. The following example illustrates this:

```
-- Available online as typeLocation.sql
SQL> -- Create a stored type which is visible to SQL and PL/SQL.
SQL> CREATE OR REPLACE TYPE NameList AS
  2    VARRAY(20) OF VARCHAR2(30);
  3  /
Type created.
SQL> DECLARE
```

```
2     -- This type is local to this block.
3     TYPE DateList IS VARRAY(10) OF DATE;
4
4     -- We can create variables of both DateList and NameList here.
5     v_Dates DateList;
6     v_Names NameList;
7  BEGIN
8    NULL;
9  END;
10  /
PL/SQL procedure successfully completed.

SQL> DECLARE
2     -- Since NameList is global to PL/SQL, we can reference it in
3     -- another block as well.
4     v_Names2 NameList;
5  BEGIN
6    NULL;
7  END;
8  /
PL/SQL procedure successfully completed.
```

A type created at the schema level (with CREATE OR REPLACE TYPE) is considered global to PL/SQL, with scope and visibility rules similar to any other database object. A schema-level type can also be used as a database column, as we will see in the following sections.

A type declared local to a PL/SQL block, however, is visible only in that block and is not available for a database column. A type declared in a package header is visible throughout PL/SQL, but is still not available for a database column. Only schema-level types can be used for database columns.

THE books TABLE   In the following sections, we will create tables and types that will model the library used by the students. To facilitate this, we need the following table:

```
-- Available online as part of objTables.sql
CREATE TABLE books (
  catalog_number NUMBER(4)      PRIMARY KEY,
  title          VARCHAR2(40),
  author1        VARCHAR2(40),
  author2        VARCHAR2(40),
  author3        VARCHAR2(40),
  author4        VARCHAR2(40)
);
```

where the **catalog_number** uniquely identifies a given book, and **author1** through
author4 contain the book's authors, in "last_name, first_name" format. The
following rows are inserted into **books** by **objTables.sql**:

```
INSERT INTO books (catalog_number, title, author1)
   VALUES (1000, 'Oracle8i Advanced PL/SQL Programming',
                 'Urman, Scott');

INSERT INTO books (catalog_number, title, author1, author2, author3)
   VALUES (1001, 'Oracle8i: A Beginner''s Guide',
                 'Abbey, Michael', 'Corey, Michael J.',
                 'Abramson, Ian');

INSERT INTO books (catalog_number, title, author1, author2, author3,
                 author4)
   VALUES (1002, 'Oracle8 Tuning',
                 'Corey, Michael J.', 'Abbey, Michael',
                 'Dechichio, Daniel J.', 'Abramson, Ian');

INSERT INTO books (catalog_number, title, author1, author2)
   VALUES (2001, 'A History of the World',
                 'Arlington, Arlene', 'Verity, Victor');

INSERT INTO books (catalog_number, title, author1)
   VALUES (3001, 'Bach and the Modern World', 'Foo, Fred');

INSERT INTO books (catalog_number, title, author1)
   VALUES (3002, 'Introduction to the Piano',
                 'Morenson, Mary');
```

Structure of Stored Varrays

A varray can be used as the type for a database column. In this case, the entire
varray is stored within one database row, alongside the other columns. Different
rows contain different varrays. For example, consider the following declarations:

```
-- Available online as part of objTables.sql
CREATE OR REPLACE TYPE BookList AS VARRAY(10) OF NUMBER(4);

CREATE TABLE class_material (
  department      CHAR(3),
  course          NUMBER(3),
  required_reading BookList
);
```

The **class_material** table contains a list of the catalog numbers of the required books for a given class. This list is stored as a varray column. The type for any varray column must be known to the database and stored in the data dictionary, so the CREATE TYPE statement is necessary. The storage for **class_material** (with some sample data) is illustrated by Figure 14-1.

Oracle **8** *i* and higher Note that Oracle8*i* allows you to specify that the storage for varray data be stored in a LOB, rather than directly inline with the table. By default in Oracle8*i*, varrays larger than 4K will be stored in a LOB in the containing table. For information on how to specify the LOB storage clause, see the *Oracle8i SQL Reference*.

Structure of Stored Nested Tables

Like a varray, a nested table can be stored as a database column. Each row of the database table can contain a different nested table. For example, suppose we want to model the library catalog. We can do this with the following definitions:

```
-- Available online as part of objTables.sql
CREATE OR REPLACE TYPE StudentList AS TABLE OF NUMBER(5);

CREATE TABLE library_catalog (
  catalog_number NUMBER(4),
    FOREIGN KEY (catalog_number) REFERENCES books(catalog_number),
  num_copies     NUMBER,
  num_out        NUMBER,
  checked_out    StudentList)
NESTED TABLE checked_out STORE AS co_tab;
```

The **library_catalog** table contains four columns, including the catalog number of the books in the collection, and a nested table containing the IDs of the students

class_material				
Department	Course	Required_Reading		
MUS	100	3001		3002
CS	102	1000	1001	1002
HIS	101	2001		

FIGURE 14-1. *Varrays in the database*

who have checked out copies. There are a couple of things to note about storing nested tables:

- The table type is used in the table definition, just like a column object or built-in type. It must be a schema-level type created with the CREATE TYPE statement.

- For each nested table in a given database table, the NESTED TABLE clause is required. This clause indicates the name of the store table.

A *store table* is a system-generated table that is used to store the actual data in the nested table. Unlike a stored varray, the data for a nested table is never stored inline with the rest of the table columns; it is stored separately. The **checked_out** column will actually store a REF into the **co_tab** table, where the list of student IDs will be stored. The storage for **library_catalog** is illustrated by Figure 14-2. For each row of **library_catalog**, **checked_out** contains a REF to the corresponding rows in **co_tab**.

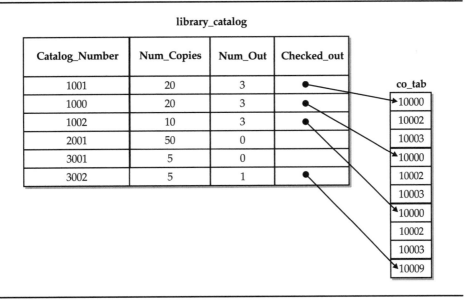

FIGURE 14-2. *Nested tables in the database*

NOTE
*The store table (**co_tab** in the previous example)
can have different storage parameters from the main
table. The store table can be described, and exists in
user_tables, but cannot be accessed directly. If you
attempt to query or modify the store table directly,
you will get the Oracle error "ORA-22812: cannot
reference nested table column's storage table." The
contents of the store table are manipulated through
SQL on the main table. For more information on the
STORE TABLE clause, see the Oracle8 SQL Reference.*

Manipulating Entire Collections

You can manipulate a stored collection in its entirety using SQL DML statements, as
we will see in the following sections. These types of operations affect the collection
as a whole, rather than the individual elements. Elements within a collection can
be manipulated using PL/SQL, or through the SQL operators that we will discuss in
"SQL Table Operators," later in this chapter.

INSERT

The INSERT statement is used to insert a collection into a database row. The
collection must first be created and initialized, and can also be a PL/SQL variable.
The following example will insert rows into **class_material** corresponding to
Figure 14-1.

```
-- Available online as part of collectionDML.sql
DECLARE
  v_CSBooks BookList := BookList(1000, 1001, 1002);
  v_HistoryBooks BookList := BookList(2001);
BEGIN
  -- INSERT using a newly constructed varray of 2 elements.
  INSERT INTO class_material
    VALUES ('MUS', 100, BookList(3001, 3002));

  -- INSERT using a previously initialized varray of 3 elements.
  INSERT INTO class_material VALUES ('CS', 102, v_CSBooks);

  -- INSERT using a previously initialized varray of 1 element.
  INSERT INTO class_material VALUES ('HIS', 101, v_HistoryBooks);
END;
```

UPDATE

Similarly, UPDATE is used to modify a stored collection. After completion of the
following example, **library_catalog** will look like Figure 14-2.

```
-- Available online as part of collectionDML.sql
DECLARE
   v_StudentList1 StudentList := StudentList(10000, 10002, 10003);
   v_StudentList2 StudentList := StudentList(10000, 10002, 10003);
   v_StudentList3 StudentList := StudentList(10000, 10002, 10003);
BEGIN
   -- First insert rows with NULL nested tables.
   INSERT INTO library_catalog (catalog_number, num_copies, num_out)
     VALUES (1000, 20, 3);
   INSERT INTO library_catalog (catalog_number, num_copies, num_out)
     VALUES (1001, 20, 3);
   INSERT INTO library_catalog (catalog_number, num_copies, num_out)
     VALUES (1002, 10, 3);
   INSERT INTO library_catalog (catalog_number, num_copies, num_out)
     VALUES (2001, 50, 0);
   INSERT INTO library_catalog (catalog_number, num_copies, num_out)
     VALUES (3001, 5, 0);
   INSERT INTO library_catalog (catalog_number, num_copies, num_out)
     VALUES (3002, 5, 1);

   -- Now update using the PL/SQL variables.
   UPDATE library_catalog
     SET checked_out = v_StudentList1
     WHERE catalog_number = 1000;
   UPDATE library_catalog
     SET checked_out = v_StudentList2
     WHERE catalog_number = 1001;
   UPDATE library_catalog
     SET checked_out = v_StudentList3
     WHERE catalog_number = 1002;

   -- And update the last row using a new nested table.
   UPDATE library_catalog
     SET checked_out = StudentList(10009)
     WHERE catalog_number = 3002;
END;
```

DELETE

DELETE can remove a row containing a collection, as the following example illustrates.

```
-- Available online as part of collectionDML.sql
DELETE FROM library_catalog
  WHERE catalog_number = 3001;
```

SELECT

Collections are retrieved from the database into PL/SQL variables using the SELECT statement, just like any other database type. Once the collection is in PL/SQL, it can be manipulated using procedural statements.

QUERYING VARRAYS   The **PrintRequired** procedure, which will print the required books for a given class, demonstrates how to SELECT a stored varray into a PL/SQL variable, where it can be manipulated.

```
-- Available online as part of PrintRequired.sql
CREATE OR REPLACE PROCEDURE PrintRequired(
  p_Department IN class_material.department%TYPE,
  p_Course IN class_material.course%TYPE) IS

  v_Books class_material.required_reading%TYPE;
  v_Title books.title%TYPE;
BEGIN
  -- Fetch the entire varray.
  SELECT required_reading
    INTO v_Books
    FROM class_material
    WHERE department = p_Department
    AND course = p_Course;

  DBMS_OUTPUT.PUT('Required reading for ' || RTRIM(p_Department));
  DBMS_OUTPUT.PUT_LINE(' ' || p_Course || ':');

  -- Loop over the table, printing out each row.
  FOR v_Index IN 1..v_Books.COUNT LOOP
    SELECT title
      INTO v_Title
      FROM books
      WHERE catalog_number = v_Books(v_Index);
    DBMS_OUTPUT.PUT_LINE(
      ' ' || v_Books(v_Index) || ': ' || v_Title);
  END LOOP;
END PrintRequired;
```

Assuming that **class_material** looks like Figure 14-1, we can call **PrintRequired** and receive the following output:

```
-- Available online as part of PrintRequired.sql
SQL> DECLARE
  2     CURSOR c_Courses IS
  3       SELECT department, course
  4         FROM class_material
  5         ORDER BY department;
  6  BEGIN
  7    FOR v_Rec IN c_Courses LOOP
  8      PrintRequired(v_Rec.department, v_Rec.course);
  9    END LOOP;
```

```
 10  END;
 11  /
Required reading for CS 102:
  1000: Oracle8i Advanced PL/SQL Programming
  1001: Oracle8i: A Beginner's Guide
  1002: Oracle8 Tuning
Required reading for HIS 101:
  2001: A History of the World
Required reading for MUS 100:
  3001: Bach and the Modern World
  3002: Introduction to the Piano
PL/SQL procedure successfully completed.
```

QUERYING NESTED TABLES   When a nested table is retrieved into a PL/SQL variable, it is assigned keys starting at 1, and ranging to the number of elements in the table. The latter can be determined with the COUNT method. The **Library.PrintCheckedOut** procedure, which will print the names of the students who have a particular book checked out, demonstrates this. See the online file **callLibrary.sql** for a call to **Library.PrintCheckedOut**.

```
-- Available online as part of Library.sql
CREATE OR REPLACE PACKAGE Library AS
  -- Prints out the students who have a particular book checked out.
  PROCEDURE PrintCheckedOut(
    p_CatalogNumber IN library_catalog.catalog_number%TYPE);
  ...
END Library;

CREATE OR REPLACE PACKAGE BODY Library AS
  PROCEDURE PrintCheckedOut(
    p_CatalogNumber IN library_catalog.catalog_number%TYPE) IS

    v_StudentList StudentList;
    v_Student Student;
    v_Book      books%ROWTYPE;
    v_FoundOne BOOLEAN := FALSE;
  BEGIN
    -- Select the entire nested table into a PL/SQL variable.
    SELECT checked_out
      INTO v_StudentList
      FROM library_catalog
      WHERE catalog_number = p_CatalogNumber;

    SELECT *
      INTO v_Book
      FROM books
```

```
        WHERE catalog_number = p_CatalogNumber;

    DBMS_OUTPUT.PUT_LINE(
      'Students who have ' || v_Book.catalog_number || ': ' ||
      v_Book.title || ' checked out: ');

    -- Loop over the nested table, and print out the student names.
    IF v_StudentList IS NOT NULL THEN
      FOR v_Index IN 1..v_StudentList.COUNT LOOP
        v_FoundOne := TRUE;

        SELECT VALUE(s)
          INTO v_Student
          FROM students s
          WHERE s.ID = v_StudentList(v_Index);

        DBMS_OUTPUT.PUT_LINE('  ' || v_Student.FormattedName);
      END LOOP;
    END IF;

    IF NOT v_FoundOne THEN
      DBMS_OUTPUT.PUT_LINE('  None');
    END IF;
  END PrintCheckedOut;
  ...
END Library;
```

NOTE
You may have noticed that none of the prior examples used a collection in a WHERE clause. This is a restriction on collections. Since there is no predefined MAP or ORDER method, collections cannot be compared for equality, which is required for the WHERE clause. This also means that collections cannot be used where an implicit comparison is necessary, such as in the ORDER BY, GROUP BY, or DISTINCT clauses.

STORED TABLES WITH NONSEQUENTIAL KEYS   Nested tables stored in the database cannot be manipulated directly with PL/SQL, only with SQL. As a result of this, the key values are not recorded. As we saw in the last example, when a nested table is SELECTed from the database, the keys are renumbered sequentially from 1. Consequently, if you INSERT a nested table with nonsequential keys into the database, the keys will change. This is illustrated by the following. First we declare a nested table type and database table that uses it:

```
-- Available online as part of nonSequential.sql
CREATE OR REPLACE TYPE PointTab AS
  TABLE OF Point;

CREATE TABLE points (
  key         NUMBER,
  point_list PointTab)
  NESTED TABLE point_list STORE AS points_tab;
```

The **Point** type here is the same as we examined in Chapters 12 and 13. Once we have the table and type created, we can run the following PL/SQL block:

```
-- Available online as part of nonSequential.sql
DECLARE
  -- Create a nested table with 5 Points.
  v_Points PointTab := PointTab(Point(1, 1),
                                Point(2, 2),
                                Point(3, 3),
                                Point(4, 4),
                                Point(5, 5));

  -- Local procedure to print out a PointTab.
  PROCEDURE Print(p_Points IN PointTab) IS
    v_Index BINARY_INTEGER := p_Points.FIRST;
  BEGIN
    WHILE v_Index <= p_Points.LAST LOOP
      DBMS_OUTPUT.PUT('  ' || v_Index || ': ');
      DBMS_OUTPUT.PUT_LINE(p_Points(v_Index).toString);
      v_Index := p_Points.NEXT(v_Index);
    END LOOP;
  END Print;

BEGIN
  -- Delete element 2 of the table.  This will result in a table of
  -- 4 elements.
  v_Points.DELETE(2);

  DBMS_OUTPUT.PUT_LINE('Initial value of the table:');
  Print(v_Points);

  -- INSERT the nested table into the database, and then SELECT it
  -- back out.
  INSERT INTO points VALUES (1, v_Points);
```

```
SELECT point_list
  INTO v_Points
  FROM points
  WHERE key = 1;

DBMS_OUTPUT.PUT_LINE('Table after INSERT and SELECT:');
Print(v_Points);
END;
```

This block first creates a nested table of five elements, then deletes the second element. The shortened table is then INSERTED into the database, and SELECTed back out. The output is as follows:

```
Initial value of the table:
  1: (1, 1)
  3: (3, 3)
  4: (4, 4)
  5: (5, 5)
Table after INSERT and SELECT:
  1: (1, 1)
  2: (3, 3)
  3: (4, 4)
  4: (5, 5)
```

The keys have been renumbered, although the data has remained the same.

Manipulating Individual Collection Elements

The examples we have seen so far have modified the entire stored collection. It is also possible, however, to manipulate individual collection elements using both PL/SQL and SQL operators.

PL/SQL Manipulations

The **Library** package also contains the **CheckOut** and **CheckIn** procedures, each of which selects the nested table into a PL/SQL variable, manipulates it, and then updates **library_catalog** again. We've already seen the **PrintCheckedOut** procedure, and the following listing completes the package:

```
-- Available online as part of Library.sql
CREATE OR REPLACE PACKAGE Library AS
  ...
  -- Checks out the book with p_CatalogNumber to the student with
  -- p_StudentID.
  PROCEDURE CheckOut(
    p_CatalogNumber IN library_catalog.catalog_number%TYPE,
    p_StudentID IN NUMBER);
```

```
  -- Checks in the book with p_CatalogNumber from the student with
  -- p_StudentID.
  PROCEDURE CheckIn(
    p_CatalogNumber IN library_catalog.catalog_number%TYPE,
    p_StudentID IN NUMBER);
END Library;

CREATE OR REPLACE PACKAGE BODY Library AS
  ...
  -- Checks out the book with p_CatalogNumber to the student with
  -- p_StudentID.
  PROCEDURE CheckOut(
    p_CatalogNumber IN library_catalog.catalog_number%TYPE,
    p_StudentID IN NUMBER) IS

    v_NumCopies library_catalog.num_copies%TYPE;
    v_NumOut library_catalog.num_out%TYPE;
    v_CheckedOut library_catalog.checked_out%TYPE;
  BEGIN
    -- First verify that the book exists, and that there is a copy
    -- available to be checked out.
    BEGIN
      SELECT num_copies, num_out, checked_out
        INTO v_NumCopies, v_NumOut, v_CheckedOut
        FROM library_catalog
        WHERE catalog_number = p_CatalogNumber
        FOR UPDATE;
    EXCEPTION
      WHEN NO_DATA_FOUND THEN
        RAISE_APPLICATION_ERROR(-20000,
          'There is no book with catalog number ' ||
          p_CatalogNumber || ' in the library');
    END;

    IF v_NumCopies = v_NumOut THEN
      RAISE_APPLICATION_ERROR(-20001,
        'All of the copies of book ' || p_CatalogNumber ||
        ' are checked out');
    END IF;

    -- Search the list to see if this student already has this book.
    IF v_CheckedOut IS NOT NULL THEN
      FOR v_Counter IN 1..v_CheckedOut.COUNT LOOP
        IF v_CheckedOut(v_Counter) = p_StudentID THEN
          RAISE_APPLICATION_ERROR(-20002,
            'Student ' || p_StudentID || ' already has book ' ||
            p_CatalogNumber || ' checked out');
        END IF;
```

```
      END LOOP;
    END IF;

    -- Make room in the list
    IF v_CheckedOut IS NULL THEN
      v_CheckedOut := StudentList(NULL);
    ELSE
      v_CheckedOut.EXTEND;
    END IF;

    -- Check out the book by adding it to the list.
    v_CheckedOut(v_CheckedOut.COUNT) := p_StudentID;

    -- And put it back in the database, adding 1 to num_out.
    UPDATE library_catalog
      SET checked_out = v_CheckedOut,
          num_out = num_out + 1
      WHERE catalog_number = p_CatalogNumber;

    COMMIT;
  END CheckOut;

  -- Checks in the book with p_CatalogNumber from the student with
  -- p_StudentID.
  PROCEDURE CheckIn(
    p_CatalogNumber IN library_catalog.catalog_number%TYPE,
    p_StudentID IN NUMBER) IS

    v_NumCopies library_catalog.num_copies%TYPE;
    v_NumOut library_catalog.num_out%TYPE;
    v_CheckedOut library_catalog.checked_out%TYPE;
    v_AlreadyCheckedOut BOOLEAN := FALSE;
  BEGIN
    -- First verify that the book exists
    BEGIN
      SELECT num_copies, num_out, checked_out
        INTO v_NumCopies, v_NumOut, v_CheckedOut
        FROM library_catalog
        WHERE catalog_number = p_CatalogNumber
        FOR UPDATE;
    EXCEPTION
      WHEN NO_DATA_FOUND THEN
        RAISE_APPLICATION_ERROR(-20000,
          'There is no book with catalog number ' ||
          p_CatalogNumber || ' in the library');
    END;

    -- Search the list to verify that this student has checked it
```

```
      -- out.
      IF v_CheckedOut IS NOT NULL THEN
        FOR v_Counter IN 1..v_CheckedOut.COUNT LOOP
          IF v_CheckedOut(v_Counter) = p_StudentID THEN
            v_AlreadyCheckedOut := TRUE;
            -- Delete it from the list.
            v_CheckedOut.DELETE(v_Counter);
          END IF;
        END LOOP;
      END IF;

      IF NOT v_AlreadyCheckedOut THEN
        RAISE_APPLICATION_ERROR(-20003,
          'Student ' || p_StudentID || ' does not have book ' ||
          p_CatalogNumber || ' checked out');
      END IF;

      -- And put it back in the database, subtracting from num_out.
      UPDATE library_catalog
        SET checked_out = v_CheckedOut,
            num_out = num_out - 1
        WHERE catalog_number = p_CatalogNumber;

      COMMIT;
    END CheckIn;
END Library;
```

Again assuming that **class_material** and **library_catalog** look like Figures 14-1 and 14-2, we can call **CheckOut** and **CheckIn** and receive the following output:

```
-- Available online as part of callLibrary.sql
SQL> DECLARE
  2    CURSOR c_History101Students IS
  3      SELECT student_ID
  4        FROM registered_students
  5        WHERE department = 'HIS'
  6        AND course = 101;
  7    v_RequiredReading class_material.required_reading%TYPE;
  8  BEGIN
  9    -- Check out the required books for all students in HIS 101:
 10
 11    -- Get the books required for HIS 101
 12    SELECT required_reading
 13      INTO v_RequiredReading
 14      FROM class_material
 15      WHERE department = 'HIS'
 16      AND course = 101;
 17
```

```
18      -- Loop over the History 101 students
19      FOR v_Rec IN c_History101Students LOOP
20        -- Loop over the required reading list
21        FOR v_Index IN 1..v_RequiredReading.COUNT LOOP
22          -- And check out the book!
23          Library.CheckOut(v_RequiredReading(v_Index),
                             v_Rec.student_ID);
24        END LOOP;
25      END LOOP;
26
27      -- Print out the students who have the book checked out now
28      Library.PrintCheckedOut(2001);
29
30      -- Check in the book for some of the students
31      Library.CheckIn(2001, 10001);
32      Library.CheckIn(2001, 10002);
33      Library.CheckIn(2001, 10003);
34
35      -- And print again.
36      Library.PrintCheckedOut(2001);
37    END;
38    /
Students who have 2001: A History of the World checked out:
  Scott Smith
  Margaret Mason
  Joanne Junebug
  Manish Murgatroid
  Patrick Poll
  Timothy Taller
  Barbara Blues
  David Dinsmore
  Ester Elegant
  Rose Riznit
  Rita Razmataz
Students who have 2001: A History of the World checked out:
  Scott Smith
  Patrick Poll
  Timothy Taller
  Barbara Blues
  David Dinsmore
  Ester Elegant
  Rose Riznit
  Rita Razmataz
PL/SQL procedure successfully completed.
```

SQL Table Operators

You can also manipulate the elements of a stored nested table directly using SQL, with either the THE (Oracle8) or TABLE (Oracle8*i*) operators. With these operators, you do not have to select the nested table into PL/SQL, manipulate it, and then update it back in the database. Elements of stored varrays cannot be manipulated directly with SQL, however—they must be manipulated in PL/SQL.

The operators are defined as follows:

THE(*subquery*)

TABLE(*subquery*)

where *subquery* is a query that returns a nested table column. Both THE and TABLE are available in all types of DML statements. THE has been replaced with TABLE in Oracle8*i*.

For example, we can change the **Library.PrintCheckedOut** procedure to use THE (or TABLE) as follows:

```
-- Available online as part of LibraryOperator.sql
PROCEDURE PrintCheckedOut(
  p_CatalogNumber IN library_catalog.catalog_number%TYPE) IS

  v_StudentList StudentList;
  v_Student Student;
  v_Book     books%ROWTYPE;
  v_FoundOne BOOLEAN := FALSE;

  CURSOR c_CheckedOut IS
    SELECT column_value ID
      FROM THE(SELECT checked_out
                 FROM library_catalog
                WHERE catalog_number = p_CatalogNumber);
BEGIN
  SELECT *
    INTO v_Book
    FROM books
    WHERE catalog_number = p_CatalogNumber;

  DBMS_OUTPUT.PUT_LINE(
    'Students who have ' || v_Book.catalog_number || ': ' ||
    v_Book.title || ' checked out: ');
```

```
  -- Loop over the nested table, and print out the student names.
  FOR v_Rec IN c_CheckedOut LOOP
    v_FoundOne := TRUE;

    SELECT VALUE(s)
      INTO v_Student
      FROM students s
      WHERE s.ID = v_Rec.ID;

      DBMS_OUTPUT.PUT_LINE('  ' || v_Student.FormattedName);
    END LOOP;

  IF NOT v_FoundOne THEN
    DBMS_OUTPUT.PUT_LINE('  None');
  END IF;
END PrintCheckedOut;
```

Summary

Collections are a useful construct for any programming language. In this chapter, we have examined index-by tables, nested tables, and varrays. We have discussed the differences between the collection types, including how to use collection methods and how to store and manipulate collections in the database. Depending on your needs, you can use whichever collection is most appropriate.

We have now completed the discussion of objects and collections. In the next few chapters, we will discuss large objects and how to manipulate them.

Index

NOTE: Page numbers in *italics* refer to illustrations or charts.

G

J

Get Your FREE Subscription to *Oracle Magazine*

Oracle Magazine is essential gear for today's information technology professionals. Stay informed and increase your productivity with every issue of *Oracle Magazine*. Inside each **FREE,** bimonthly issue you'll get:

- Up-to-date information on Oracle Database Server, Oracle Applications, Internet Computing, and tools
- Third-party news and announcements
- Technical articles on Oracle products and operating environments
- Development and administration tips
- Real-world customer stories

Three easy ways to subscribe:

1. Web   **Visit our Web site at www.oracle.com/oramag/. You'll find a subscription form there, plus much more!**

2. Fax   Complete the questionnaire on the back of this card and fax the questionnaire side only to **+1.847.647.9735.**

3. Mail   Complete the questionnaire on the back of this card and mail it to P.O. Box 1263, Skokie, IL 60076-8263.

If there are other Oracle users at your location who would like to receive their own subscription to *Oracle Magazine*, please photocopy this form and pass it along.

☐ YES! Please send me a FREE subscription to *Oracle Magazine*. ☐ NO

To receive a free bimonthly subscription to *Oracle Magazine*, you must fill out the entire card, sign it, and date it (incomplete cards cannot be processed or acknowledged). You can also fax your application to **+1.847.647.9735.** Or subscribe at our Web site at www.oracle.com/oramag/

SIGNATURE (REQUIRED)	X	DATE	

NAME		TITLE	
COMPANY		TELEPHONE	
ADDRESS		FAX NUMBER	
CITY		STATE	POSTAL CODE/ZIP CODE
COUNTRY		E-MAIL ADDRESS	

☐ From time to time, Oracle Publishing allows our partners exclusive access to our e-mail addresses for special promotions and announcements. To be included in this program, please check this box.

You must answer all eight questions below.

1 What is the primary business activity of your firm at this location? *(check only one)*
- ☐ 03 Communications
- ☐ 04 Consulting, Training
- ☐ 06 Data Processing
- ☐ 07 Education
- ☐ 08 Engineering
- ☐ 09 Financial Services
- ☐ 10 Government—Federal, Local, State, Other
- ☐ 11 Government—Military
- ☐ 12 Health Care
- ☐ 13 Manufacturing—Aerospace, Defense
- ☐ 14 Manufacturing—Computer Hardware
- ☐ 15 Manufacturing—Noncomputer Products
- ☐ 17 Research & Development
- ☐ 19 Retailing, Wholesaling, Distribution
- ☐ 20 Software Development
- ☐ 21 Systems Integration, VAR, VAD, OEM
- ☐ 22 Transportation
- ☐ 23 Utilities (Electric, Gas, Sanitation)
- ☐ 98 Other Business and Services
  _____

2 Which of the following best describes your job function? *(check only one)*
CORPORATE MANAGEMENT/STAFF
- ☐ 01 Executive Management (President, Chair, CEO, CFO, Owner, Partner, Principal)
- ☐ 02 Finance/Administrative Management (VP/Director/ Manager/Controller, Purchasing, Administration)
- ☐ 03 Sales/Marketing Management (VP/Director/Manager)
- ☐ 04 Computer Systems/Operations Management (CIO/VP/Director/ Manager MIS, Operations)
IS/IT STAFF
- ☐ 07 Systems Development/ Programming Management
- ☐ 08 Systems Development/ Programming Staff
- ☐ 09 Consulting
- ☐ 10 DBA/Systems Administrator
- ☐ 11 Education/Training
- ☐ 14 Technical Support Director/ Manager
- ☐ 16 Other Technical Management/Staff
- ☐ 98 Other _____

3 What is your current primary operating platform? *(check all that apply)*
- ☐ 01 DEC UNIX
- ☐ 02 DEC VAX VMS
- ☐ 03 Java
- ☐ 04 HP UNIX
- ☐ 05 IBM AIX
- ☐ 06 IBM UNIX
- ☐ 07 Macintosh
- ☐ 09 MS-DOS
- ☐ 10 MVS
- ☐ 11 NetWare
- ☐ 12 Network Computing
- ☐ 13 OpenVMS
- ☐ 14 SCO UNIX
- ☐ 24 Sequent DYNIX/ptx
- ☐ 15 Sun Solaris/SunOS
- ☐ 16 SVR4
- ☐ 18 UnixWare
- ☐ 20 Windows
- ☐ 21 Windows NT
- ☐ 23 Other UNIX _____
- ☐ 98 Other _____
- 99 ☐ **None of the above**

4 Do you evaluate, specify, recommend, or authorize the purchase of any of the following? *(check all that apply)*
- ☐ 01 Hardware
- ☐ 02 Software
- ☐ 03 Application Development Tools
- ☐ 04 Database Products
- ☐ 05 Internet or Intranet Products
- 99 ☐ **None of the above**

5 In your job, do you use or plan to purchase any of the following products or services? *(check all that apply)*
SOFTWARE
- ☐ 01 Business Graphics
- ☐ 02 CAD/CAE/CAM
- ☐ 03 CASE
- ☐ 05 Communications
- ☐ 06 Database Management
- ☐ 07 File Management
- ☐ 08 Finance
- ☐ 09 Java
- ☐ 10 Materials Resource Planning
- ☐ 11 Multimedia Authoring
- ☐ 12 Networking
- ☐ 13 Office Automation
- ☐ 14 Order Entry/Inventory Control
- ☐ 15 Programming
- ☐ 16 Project Management

- ☐ 17 Scientific and Engineering
- ☐ 18 Spreadsheets
- ☐ 19 Systems Management
- ☐ 20 Workflow
HARDWARE
- ☐ 21 Macintosh
- ☐ 22 Mainframe
- ☐ 23 Massively Parallel Processing
- ☐ 24 Minicomputer
- ☐ 25 PC
- ☐ 26 Network Computer
- ☐ 28 Symmetric Multiprocessing
- ☐ 29 Workstation
PERIPHERALS
- ☐ 30 Bridges/Routers/Hubs/Gateways
- ☐ 31 CD-ROM Drives
- ☐ 32 Disk Drives/Subsystems
- ☐ 33 Modems
- ☐ 34 Tape Drives/Subsystems
- ☐ 35 Video Boards/Multimedia
SERVICES
- ☐ 37 Consulting
- ☐ 38 Education/Training
- ☐ 39 Maintenance
- ☐ 40 Online Database Services
- ☐ 41 Support
- ☐ 36 Technology-Based Training
- ☐ 98 Other _____
- 99 ☐ **None of the above**

6 What Oracle products are in use at your site? *(check all that apply)*
SERVER/SOFTWARE
- ☐ 01 Oracle8
- ☐ 30 Oracle8*i*
- ☐ 31 Oracle8*i* Lite
- ☐ 02 Oracle7
- ☐ 03 Oracle Application Server
- ☐ 04 Oracle Data Mart Suites
- ☐ 05 Oracle Internet Commerce Server
- ☐ 32 Oracle *inter*Media
- ☐ 33 Oracle JServer
- ☐ 07 Oracle Lite
- ☐ 08 Oracle Payment Server
- ☐ 11 Oracle Video Server
TOOLS
- ☐ 13 Oracle Designer
- ☐ 14 Oracle Developer
- ☐ 54 Oracle Discoverer
- ☐ 53 Oracle Express
- ☐ 51 Oracle JDeveloper
- ☐ 52 Oracle Reports
- ☐ 50 Oracle WebDB
- ☐ 55 Oracle Workflow
ORACLE APPLICATIONS
- ☐ 17 Oracle Automotive

- ☐ 35 Oracle Business Intelligence System
- ☐ 19 Oracle Consumer Packaged Goods
- ☐ 39 Oracle E-Commerce
- ☐ 18 Oracle Energy
- ☐ 20 Oracle Financials
- ☐ 28 Oracle Front Office
- ☐ 21 Oracle Human Resources
- ☐ 37 Oracle Internet Procurement
- ☐ 22 Oracle Manufacturing
- ☐ 40 Oracle Process Manufacturing
- ☐ 23 Oracle Projects
- ☐ 34 Oracle Retail
- ☐ 29 Oracle Self-Service Web Applications
- ☐ 38 Oracle Strategic Enterprise Management
- ☐ 25 Oracle Supply Chain Management
- ☐ 36 Oracle Tutor
- ☐ 41 Oracle Travel Management
ORACLE SERVICES
- ☐ 61 Oracle Consulting
- ☐ 62 Oracle Education
- ☐ 60 Oracle Support
- ☐ 98 Other _____
- 99 ☐ **None of the above**

7 What other database products are in use at your site? *(check all that apply)*
- ☐ 01 Access
- ☐ 02 Baan
- ☐ 03 dbase
- ☐ 04 Gupta
- ☐ 05 IBM DB2
- ☐ 06 Informix
- ☐ 07 Ingres
- ☐ 08 Microsoft Access
- ☐ 09 Microsoft SQL Server
- ☐ 10 PeopleSoft
- ☐ 11 Progress
- ☐ 12 SAP
- ☐ 13 Sybase
- ☐ 14 VSAM
- ☐ 98 Other _____
- 99 ☐ **None of the above**

8 During the next 12 months, how much do you anticipate your organization will spend on computer hardware, software, peripherals, and services for your location? *(check only one)*
- ☐ 01 Less than $10,000
- ☐ 02 $10,000 to $49,999
- ☐ 03 $50,000 to $99,999
- ☐ 04 $100,000 to $499,999
- ☐ 05 $500,000 to $999,999
- ☐ 06 $1,000,000 and over

If there are other Oracle users at your location who would like to receive a free subscription to *Oracle Magazine*, please photocopy this form and pass it along, or contact Customer Service at +1.847.647.9630

Form 5

OPRESS

Think you're
smart?

Think you're ready to wear this badge?

The time is right to become an Oracle Certified Professional (OCP) and we're here to help you do it. Oracle's cutting edge Instructor-Led Training, Interactive Courseware, and this exam guide can prepare you for certification faster than ever. OCP status is one of the top honors in your profession. Now is the time to take credit for what you know. *Call 800.441.3541 (Outside the U.S. call +1.310.335.2403)* for an OCP training solution that meets your time, budget, and learning needs. Or visit us at *http://education.oracle.com/certification* for more information.

ORACLE®
E d u c a t i o n

About the CD-ROM

Inside the back cover you will find the CD-ROM that accompanies *Oracle8i Advanced PL/SQL Programming*, by Scott Urman. The CD-ROM contains three different types of information:

- Online versions of all of the examples used in the book. These can be found in the **code** directory.

- Electronic versions of Chapters 15 and 16, along with Appendixes A through C. Due to space constraints, these chapters are not in printed form and can be found only on the CD-ROM, in **Online Chapters** directory. Some of the screenshots from Chapter 2 can be found there as well. The chapters are in Adobe Acrobat PDF format. If you don't have the Acrobat reader installed, it can be installed (on Windows systems) by running **ar405eng.exe** on the root level of the CD.

- Demo versions of five complete PL/SQL development environments from four different vendors. All of these versions are complete, and are licensed for a limited number of days or executions. The tools can be found in the **Development Tools** directory, and are described here:

Tool	Version	Vendor
Rapid SQL	5.5	Embarcadero Technologies, **www.embarcadero.com**
SQL Navigator	3.1e5	Quest Software, **www.quest.com**
SQL Programmer	IX SP2b	Sylvain Faust International, **www.sfi-software.com**
TOAD (Tool for Oracle Application Developers)	6.3.2.16	Quest Software, **www.quest.com**
XPEDITER/SQL	3.1.1	Compuware Corporation, **www.compuware.com**

When you insert the CD-ROM on Windows systems, a small application will start automatically that contains more information about the CD-ROM, including details about how to install each of the tools. For more information, see **readme.html** in the root level of the CD-ROM.

WARNING: BEFORE OPENING THE DISC PACKAGE, CAREFULLY READ THE TERMS AND CONDITIONS OF THE FOLLOWING COPYRIGHT STATEMENT AND LIMITED CD-ROM WARRANTY.

Copyright Statement

This software is protected by both United States copyright law and international copyright treaty provision. Except as noted in the contents of the CD-ROM, you must treat this software just like a book. However, you may copy it into a computer to be used and you may make archival copies of the software for the sole purpose of backing up the software and protecting your investment from loss. By saying, "just like a book," The McGraw-Hill Companies, Inc. ("Osborne/McGraw-Hill") means, for example, that this software may be used by any number of people and may be freely moved from one computer location to another, so long as there is no possibility of its being used at one location or on one computer while it is being used at another. Just as a book cannot be read by two different people in two different places at the same time, neither can the software be used by two different people in two different places at the same time.

Limited Warranty

Osborne/McGraw-Hill warrants the physical compact disc enclosed herein to be free of defects in materials and workmanship for a period of sixty days from the purchase date. If the CD included in your book has defects in materials or workmanship, please call McGraw-Hill at 1-800-217-0059, 9am to 5pm, Monday through Friday, Eastern Standard Time, and McGraw-Hill will replace the defective disc.

The entire and exclusive liability and remedy for breach of this Limited Warranty shall be limited to replacement of the defective disc, and shall not include or extend to any claim for or right to cover any other damages, including but not limited to, loss of profit, data, or use of the software, or special incidental, or consequential damages or other similar claims, even if Osborne/McGraw-Hill has been specifically advised of the possibility of such damages. In no event will Osborne/McGraw-Hill's liability for any damages to you or any other person ever exceed the lower of the suggested list price or actual price paid for the license to use the software, regardless of any form of the claim.

OSBORNE/McGRAW-HILL SPECIFICALLY DISCLAIMS ALL OTHER WARRANTIES, EXPRESS OR IMPLIED, INCLUDING BUT NOT LIMITED TO, ANY IMPLIED WARRANTY OF MERCHANTABILITY OR FITNESS FOR A PARTICULAR PURPOSE. Specifically, Osborne/McGraw-Hill makes no representation or warranty that the software is fit for any particular purpose, and any implied warranty of merchantability is limited to the sixty-day duration of the Limited Warranty covering the physical disc only (and not the software), and is otherwise expressly and specifically disclaimed.

This limited warranty gives you specific legal rights; you may have others which may vary from state to state. Some states do not allow the exclusion of incidental or consequential damages, or the limitation on how long an implied warranty lasts, so some of the above may not apply to you.

This agreement constitutes the entire agreement between the parties relating to use of the Product. The terms of any purchase order shall have no effect on the terms of this Agreement. Failure of Osborne/McGraw-Hill to insist at any time on strict compliance with this Agreement shall not constitute a waiver of any rights under this Agreement. This Agreement shall be construed and governed in accordance with the laws of New York. If any provision of this Agreement is held to be contrary to law, that provision will be enforced to the maximum extent permissible, and the remaining provisions will remain in force and effect.

NO TECHNICAL SUPPORT IS PROVIDED WITH THIS CD-ROM.